Prai

This collection offers a thought-provoking opportunity to parse multiplicities and recent directions in global justice organizing. Sen's framing in this book sets us up to take stock of two decades of social and political movement in terms of dynamic motion: Not only as strategy and organization, but as kinaesthetic experience, embodied transformation through space and time. The nuanced, critical emphases on indigeneity, spirituality, gender, and ecology, rich with specificity and insight, locate us unmistakably in our present moment with its lessons gleaned of recent history and praxis, even while bringing us full circle to the themes introduced an unbelievable twenty years ago. We shall not be moved. We shall move. We shall keep moving.

   —Maia Ramnath, teacher, writer, activist, and dancer/aerialist;
      author of *Decolonizing Anarchism*

An important contribution to a developing internationalism that doesn't assume that the North Atlantic left has all the answers for the rest of the world and which recognizes that emancipatory ideas and practices are often forged from below. Refreshingly free of tired dogmas, non-sectarian, taking internationalism seriously, and reaching back to 1968, the book provides a bracing window into some of the central ideas to have emerged from within movements in the sequence of struggle that unfolded from 2006 to 2010. This book will be useful for activists and intellectuals in movement—be they in universities, parties, trade unions, social movements, or religious organisations—around the world.

   —Richard Pithouse, researcher and lecturer in politics, Rhodes
      University, Grahamstown, South Africa

Someone once suggested that movement cannot be thought, it has to be lived. In other words, social movements—the coming together in processes that build the power to bring about change—stem not from any kind of blueprint that can set out an ideal for the world we ought to live in, nor can there be a simple step-by-step guide on how to get there. At the same time, there can't be movement without a collective effort to understand the shared and embodied experiences that constitute it, along with the problems, concerns, and trajectories that arise in struggle. It's this kind of critical reflection that the authors assembled in this volume undertake, providing intelligent and engaged analyses that avoid any stifling dichotomies, whether between theory and practice, activism and academia, or indeed between thinking and feeling. Possible futures, right now in the making, become legible in how *The Movements of Movements* doesn't shy away from the complex and unsettling issues that shape our time, while thinking through struggles for social and ecological justice in the wider contexts of their past and present.

—Emma Dowling, Senior Researcher in Political Sociology at the Institute for Sociology, Friedrich-Schiller-University Jena, Germany

The Movements of Movements

Part 1

What Makes Us Move?

Jai Sen, editor

Volume 4 in OpenWord's
Challenging Empires series

The Movements of Movements, Part 1: What Makes Us Move?
© 2017 This collection as a whole, Jai Sen
© 2017 The individual essays, the respective authors
© 2017 This edition, OpenWord and PM Press

Volume 4 in the OpenWord's *Challenging Empires* series

ISBN: 978-1-62963-240-7
Library of Congress Control Number: 2016948146

Editor: Jai Sen
Contributing Editor: Peter Waterman
Associate Editor: Madhuresh
Content Editors: Parvati Sharma, Vipul Rikhi, and Jai Sen
Text Compilation: Jim Coflin
Cover: John Yates/stealworks.com
Layout: Jonathan Rowland
Wordle Illustrations: Christina Sanchez and Yih Lerh Huang

PM Press
P.O. Box 23912
Oakland, CA 94623, USA
www.pmpress.org

OpenWord
R-21 South Extension Part II - Ground floor
New Delhi 110 049, India
www.openword.net.in

10 9 8 7 6 5 4 3 2 1

Printed in the USA by the Employee Owners of Thomson-Shore in Dexter, Michigan
www.thomsonshore.com

This book is dedicated to

Peter Waterman

(January 26 1936–June 17 2017)

Friend, comrade, compañero, and fellow birthday bearer
for the past thirty-five years;
labour internationalist, cyberian, feminist,
and feisty and fearless, always.
And to his indomitable spirit and infectious
humour—and to the optimism of his will.
May those live on forever!

JS

Contents

Acknowledgements and Credits for *The Movements of Movements, Part 1: What Makes Us Move?*

Jai Sen

Content Editors

Beyond the features discussed in the Introduction, an important background feature of this book (and of all the books in the *Challenging Empires* series to which this book belongs) has again been the intensive and extensive background work that has gone into the preparation and finalisation of the essays we are publishing. The Content Editors for this book—and I as editor—have tried to work closely with our authors in helping them more fully develop and articulate their ideas, and I have therefore of course been very happy indeed that so many of our authors have appreciated this and said that they have rarely experienced this degree of attention. Most of the credit for this goes to our Content Editors, Parvati Sharma and Vipul Rikhi, and I warmly thank them for their contributions to making this book what it is.

Since this book is being published in two parts—see the Introduction—I here list acknowledgements and credits only for the material in Part 1. The chapters are listed here in alphabetical order by the author's surname:

Parvati Sharma, for:
James Toth—Local Islam Gone Global: The Roots of Religious Militancy in Egypt and its Transnational Transformation

Parvati Sharma and Jai Sen, for:
Daniel Bensaïd—The Return of Strategy
Cho Hee-Yeon—From Anti-Imperialist to Anti-Empire: The Crystallisation of the Anti-Globalisation Movement in South Korea
Lee Cormie—Re-Creating the World: Communities of Faith in the Struggles for Other Possible Worlds
Jeff Corntassel—Rethinking Self-Determination: Lessons from the Indigenous-Rights Discourse
Guillermo Delgado-P—Refounding Bolivia: Exploring the Possibility and Paradox of a Social Movements State
André C Drainville—Beyond *Altermondialisme*: Anti-Capitalist Dialectic of Presence
Emilie Hayes—Open Space in Movement: Reading Three Waves of Feminism
Roel Meijer—Fighting for Another World: Yusuf al-'Uyairi's Conceptualisation of Praxis and the Permanent Salafi Revolution
Peter North and David Featherstone—Localisation as Radical Praxis and the New Politics of Climate Change
Andrea Smith—Indigenous Feminism and the Heteropatriarchal State

Vipul Rikhi, for:

Taiaiake Alfred and Jeff Corntassel—Being Indigenous: Resurgences against Contemporary Colonialism

Tariq Ali—Storming Heaven: Where Has the Rage Gone?

François Houtart—Mahmoud Mohamed Taha: Islamic Witness in the Contemporary World

Fouad Kalouche and Eric Mielants—Antisystemic Movements and Transformations of the World-System, 1968–1989

Alex Khasnabish—Forward Dreaming: Zapatismo and the Radical Imagination

David McNally—From the Mountains of Chiapas to the Streets of Seattle: This is What Democracy Looks Like

Emir Sader—The Weakest Link? Neoliberalism in Latin America

Anand Teltumbde—Anti-Imperialism, Dalits, and the Annihilation of Caste

Peter Waterman—The Networked Internationalism of Labour's Others

Vipul Rikhi and Jai Sen, for:

Xochitl Leyva Solano—Geopolitics of Knowledge and the Neo-Zapatista Social Movement Networks

Jai Sen, for:

Laurence Cox—'Learning to be Loyal to Each Other': Conversations, Alliances, and Arguments in the Movements of Movements

Xochitl Leyva Solano and Christopher Gunderson—The Tapestry of Neo-Zapatismo: Origins and Development

Roma and Ashok Choudhary—Ecological Justice and Forest Right Movements in India: State and Militancy—New Challenges

Virginia Vargas—International Feminisms: New Syntheses, New Directions

Concept, Design, and Production

As discussed in the Introduction, working with OpenWord has been an integral part of the conceptualisation and reality of this book—as a book and in its first incarnation, as an ebook—and as in the case of the previous book (*World Social Forum: Critical Explorations*), much of the credit for this goes to *Nishant*, former Co-Coordinator at OpenWord. My warm thanks to him once again, in helping me down this road.

In the case of this book however, I have had the great privilege of also having the partnership of three new volunteers and fellow travellers: *Giulio Maffini*, an old friend I have had the privilege of rediscovering recently, for nudging me into the use of diagrams to unpack and open up the meanings of the sometimes dense content of this book (and of my writing!); *Yih Lerh Huang*, a new friend and colleague, for joining Giulio in nudging me into the use of diagrams in the book, and for infusing fresh energy and professionalism into our work at OpenWord; and *Christina Sanchez*, for helping me think through my Introduction to this book and also for generating the Wordle and other diagrams that we have used here in our books for the first time—and more generally for her enthusiasm and her creative and critical engagement with my work. My warm appreciation to all three, for their ideas and contributions, and for their critical engagement and encouragement.

And most recently, we have also received the generous help of another new friend, *Jim Coflin*, in compiling all the text into the one file required by our co-publishers, PM Press.

Rights and Permissions

In addition to the mentions that we have made in the first endnote of the respective essays, I am happy to also warmly acknowledge here the rights and permissions we have got from the following publishers for republishing the following essays in this book, which they had earlier published:

- Blackwell's (now Wiley-Blackwell's), for James Toth's 'Local Islam Gone Global: The Roots of Religious Militancy in Egypt and its Transnational Transformation'
- Duke University Press, for Virginia Vargas's 'International Feminisms: New Syntheses, New Directions'
- International Socialism, for the late Daniel Bensaïd's 'The Return of Strategy'
- Koninklijke Brill NV, for Roel Meijer's 'Fighting for Another World: Yusuf al-'Uyairi's Conceptualisation of Praxis and the Permanent Salafi Revolution'
- Lynne Rienner Publishers Inc, for Jeff Corntassel's 'Rethinking Self-Determination: Lessons from the Indigenous-Rights Discourse'
- New Left Review, for Emir Sader's 'The Weakest Link? Neoliberalism in Latin America'
- Paradigm Publishers, for Fouad Kalouche and Eric Mielants's 'Antisystemic Movements and Transformations of the World-System, 1968–1989'
- Taylor & Francis, for André C Drainville's 'Beyond *Altermondialisme*: Anti-Capitalist Dialectic of Presence'; and—
- Wiley's, for Taiaiake Alfred and Jeff Corntassel's 'Being Indigenous: Resurgences against Contemporary Colonialism'.

Equally, aside from giving credit in the appropriate footnote, I would also like to warmly acknowledge the following permission that the rights-holder so readily and generously gave us:

- Thinkmap Inc, for the image and text that we have used in the Introduction, from the Visual Thesaurus (http://www.visualthesaurus.com). Copyright ©1998–2014; all rights reserved; and—
- Jonathan Feinberg, the creator of Wordle diagrams (http://www.wordle.net/), both for creating this wonderful 'toy' and for making it freely available.

Material Resources

As in the case of our previous book, *World Social Forum: Critical Explorations*, I would like to acknowledge the support we at CACIM received back in 2007–9 from Oxfam-Novib, based in The Netherlands, for covering professional editorial expenses in the early stages of the preparation of what became this book, as a part of a grant that they made available to us titled 'The World Social Forum: A Critical Engagement' (Project No BORX-505275-4713). As discussed in the Introduction both in this book and in its predecessor, both these books have in many ways come out of our experience of working through that period.

I would equally like to also thank InterPares, Canada, for its supplementary support in 2009 for our work around the World Social Forum; even if its grant was small and not really support for our books as such, this act of solidarity when we needed support was very important for what we were then more generally trying to do with respect to the WSF, and in a more general way for our broader project of working with movement worldwide, and where its support therefore also helped this particular project move forward.

Networking as Resource: The CACIM Community as Cloud

Finally, as editor, I also want to note and acknowledge the fact that (as was also the case with its predecessor), this book is the product of an immense amount of almost global networking over several years, between several people and in different permutations and combinations over the years; indeed, that a book like this is perhaps only possible through such a cloud-like process. Aside from a certain amount of professional support for which we were initially able to raise funds for the bulk of the conceptualisation of this book (and also of the book project outlined in the Introduction), and its preparation has involved intense voluntary input from almost countless individuals, over these many years:

- *All the contributors*—whose names are given in the Table of Contents and in the document 'Notes on the Contributors'—and without whom, of course, this book would just not have been possible;
- *All members of the original OpenWord Working Group* and then subsequently, of an OpenWord Editorial Collective that took shape for a while, aside from myself as editor;
- *Adityan M*, of New Delhi, India, who was earlier associated to CACIM as our graphic designer, and with whom it has always been fun and thought-provoking to discuss ways to represent what we are trying to do and the ideas and worlds we are trying to engage with; and—
- *Matt Meyer*, of Brooklyn, in the US, who has more recently come on board this project and is now collaborating with us in our ongoing work at CACIM of conceiving and formulating a larger book project around the material in these books, and where he has also played the vital role in this project of introducing me, and our original publisher OpenWord, to PM Press, as a result of which the two are now co-publishing the two volumes of *The Movements of Movements*.

All of these people—all of whom were or have become members of the CACIM Community through this fact of association—have made key contributions to the crystallisation of this book and of this book project, in different ways and at different levels. I warmly thank them all!

0
INVOCATIONS

What Moves Us[1]
Shailja Patel

Some moments
history comes to us and says:
What do you truly want?

We tremble.
Often we run.
From the terrifying possibility
that we could choose
movement.
That we could begin
exactly where we are
in all our screwed-up
imperfection.

Some days we stand
before our world
and the question
vibrates the air around us:
What do you choose?

This day?
This moment?
This
heartstopping
glorious
adventure?

There's strong like patriarchy
strong like institutions
strong like two-billion dollars a day
military occupations
spiked with genocide
anchored in neoliberal greed
buttressed by terror

designed to deliver
200-volt shocks
on contact.

Then there's the strength
of what flows.
Tears, grief, memory.
Blood, energy, breath.
Collective action.

The strength of what moves us
opens our throats
ignites our hips
unleashes our voices
puts the move back into movement
distils the motion from emotion.

Movement
strong as a river,
current of joyful resilience
wave and curl
crash and swirl
patterns that constantly change.

Movers who channel each day
the courage of divers
to plunge again
into this churning water.

Thankful
for what yields results
curious
about what does not.
Building lung capacity
to finally embrace
the wholeness of our struggles
exactly as they are.

Some moments, life asks of us:
What do you hope?

There's hope like a battleground
hope that's all soundbites
hope that rehashes a thousand manifestos.
What we intend, believe, imagine
what we propose and plan and dream
what we say, expect, pretend, how we think
things should look.

Then there's the truth on the ground.

What we show up for
each day
with our fearful, angry,
tired, clumsy selves.
With our complex, precious,
wounded, brilliant selves.

We grapple with the chasms
of all that's gone before.
Negotiate the heartbreak
of decades of betrayal.
Stretch our brains and wills
until we feel it,
to hard analysis
until we get it
unpack systems, structures, models
mine the data, map
the stories
'til we know
what works and what does not.
What truly
moves
us.

Some years, life comes to us and says:
What do you know?
Why we kept at it, for forty, fifty years.
Why we have never regretted it.

That this movement
Still moves us

In our guts, our hips, our hearts

That this laughter
this trust
this earned and tried and tested respect
is a house we have built,
brick by brick
and it will hold.

Some mornings life wakes us up
sets our hearts beating
sets our nerves thrumming
warns us
we're about to leap
into our iciest fear
our largest growth
our most piercing joy.
Some mornings,
We take a huge breath, say
Yes
to it all.

Some evenings, life wraps us round
in the softness of twilight,
asks:
What are you waiting for?

Truth.
Justice.
Reparation.
Healing.
In our lifetimes. In our
lifetimes. In
Our
Lifetimes.

Each day, love comes to us and says:
What will you show up for?
What, in the end, is the truth of your heart?
We answer with our bodies.

We show up
for the struggle.
We show up
for each other.
We show up
just as we are.
Precious, flawed
limited, magnificent
Human.

We show up
for change.
We choose
the power of movement.
We love
by showing up.

Notes

1. This poem was first performed at the Cape Town Conference of the Association For
    Women's Rights In Development and then posted on the Women's United Nations
    Reporting Network (WURN). Copyright Shailja Patel 2010; all rights reserved.

    Ed: I warmly thank the author for generously making this poem available to us
    as a contribution to this book.

The Movements of Movements:
An Introduction and an Exploration[1]
Jai Sen

Another world is not only possible, she is on her way. On a quiet day, I can hear her breathing.
—Arundhati Roy

Movement, motion, is a fundamental facet, fact, of life; of all life processes. Indeed, in some ways it is life itself. It is the most fundamental characteristic of change.

Movement intrinsically involves the flow of energy; of power in the sense of *shakti*.[2]

Movement links points, in space and in time. Power radiates.

In a sense therefore, *all movement is about energy*—about energy harnessed, energy expressed, energy experienced, energy directed—and all movement is therefore about power, understood in a generic sense.[3]

I do not pretend to be a sage, but my sense is that at this moment in history, we are entering—or perhaps have already entered—a period of another great transformation, where almost despite ourselves, we as human beings are embarking on a profound search for truth and for meaning.[4]

This book and its companion volume *The Movements of Movements, Part 2: Rethinking Our Dance* are about what I suggest is a fundamental expression not only of this moment in history but also of the unfolding of human history and of life itself: Social (and political) movement.

Unfortunately, as in too many fields in the contemporary world, these terms and their meanings have come to be captured by particular and increasingly specialised disciplines and as a result have almost lost (or arguably, been made to lose) their generic meanings for us. At one level therefore, these two books are also an attempt to allow these more fundamental meanings to come out and to live, and to critically explore them.

This book, then, is about people in movement; it is about women and men who feel moved to do something about the world around them and about the social and political movements for justice and liberation that they form. But, in a way, it is more than this. It is an attempt to present (and to see and to hear and to feel) the extraordinary drama of the flow of social movement taking place across the world in our times, that we are so privileged to be a part of or to be witness to, perhaps more than ever before in history. It is also an attempt to take a look across the landscape of movement that is sweeping the world in our times, towards understanding it.

In this Introduction, I argue that what we see and understand as 'movement' is not merely what we now normally understand it to be—crowds of people around an issue, important as that is—but a fundamental expression of the human spirit, of life itself, and of the life of Mother Earth herself. Perceiving it in this way opens up many new doors.

Among other things, the fact that movement is so fundamental to our lives is reflected in the simple fact that the term 'movement' occurs in so many different spheres of life—the social, the scientific, the creative (an 'art movement' or a movement in music), and also the intensely personal and private (such as when we are moved by a poem or a song or a picture, or by a piece of music, and at a very different level, the experience of what in some contexts is called a 'bowel movement'). This is perhaps true in all languages and cultures. Even the word 'emotion'—which gives expression to such a basic part of what makes us human—is rooted in motion, in moving, and in being moved. Accordingly, I suggest that we need to try to see and comprehend what we otherwise understand as 'social and political movement' in this much wider and deeper sense and that we can gain new understandings both of movement and of the world around us if we can see them in this way.

In particular, and with this lens, I would like to invite readers to see this book not just as a space where we, as outsiders, can view and read the work of the contributors, and/or where we can then comparatively and critically present and discuss movements. Rather, I invite you to consider this book as a space where movements themselves are speaking to each other, and where they can perhaps grow through their interactions, learning from their exchanges. Through this we all—including those of us in movement—can perhaps move towards a more full understanding of the deeper meanings of movement and of their potentials and limitations, individually and collectively, and of the worlds of movement around us.

As a contribution to this, I have also tried in these two books to go one step further. By attempting to see the essays contained in them as the diverse and varying politico-cultural compositions that they are, and by attempting to compose the book with the essays as movements in themselves (using the terms 'composition' and 'movement' here in the sense they are commonly used in music), I have tried to see the two books themselves as compositions, and to consciously compose them (with the limited skills I have), and so to perhaps make manifest something of the dance and the music of movement, and of worlds in movement.[5]

As discussed later in this Introduction, these two books are the fourth and fifth in a series titled the *Challenging Empires* series.[6] Our aim—in this series and in these books—is to strengthen movement by critically exploring its transformative power, and to widen and deepen a critical understanding of movement by outsiders and by participants as not an auxiliary but core part of politics, governance, democracy, and social transformation, and of life and of hope. In the case of these books, we attempt to do this by presenting a range of analyses of and reflections on both the everyday praxis of a wide range of movement and insistently, and simultaneously, also the wider worlds within which movements take place—and of which they are an integral part.

This Introduction attempts both to sketch out this book and also contains some reflections on what we are attempting by a book of this kind. It has the following sections:

- About This Book
- Locating Myself
- Worlds in Movement
- Meanings of Movement, the Movements of Movements, and This Book
- Reading Across the Essays
- Closing Comments.

About This Book

I feel I must make clear at the outset that although this two-volume book contains a large number of essays (see the Table of Contents for details, and more on this below), it does not in any way attempt or pretend to be a comprehensive ency-clopaedia of movement today, or even an up-to-date reportage of all movement that has recently taken place or that is taking place today. It goes without saying that no one book can cover everything; nor, arguably, is it even preferable that any one book attempts this. Rather, this book is merely one attempt to bring together some outstanding essays that in my editorial judgement can, both individually and collectively, help us all to perceive the larger world of movement, and to begin to understand it; and to the extent possible in the format of a book, to make this book a space where conversations between movements begin to open up, at different levels.

In all, we have commissioned and/or collected some 50 essays for this book, as well as two major Afterwords, one in each book.[7] As already mentioned above, in order to present and make available as wide a range of movements as possible however, and to make these essays as accessible as we can, we are publishing this book in two volumes, or parts. This present book is *Part 1*, and has three Sections. It opens with a Section 0 titled 'Invocations', containing a Proem by Shailja Patel on 'What Moves Us' and this Introduction, and then goes on to sketch out, in Section 1, certain key features of the landscape of contemporary movement in the world from 1968 till about 2010. The sketches are by people from different parts of the world and intentionally include essays by both indigenous peoples and by settlers,[8] thereby offering fundamentally—and structurally—different views of the landscape they inhabit and see. It is the same world, but seen through different eyes and different experiences.

In Section 2, we present a wide range of sensitive and reflective portraits of movement, several of which are critical discussions of how different movements move (and/or have moved) in different contexts. The essays in this book and in its companion volume are by authors (both activists and researchers) from many parts of the world, North and South, and from many different persuasions;[9] and broadly speaking, though mostly written during and focussing on the period 2006–10, over the past fifty years. This book ends with a major, specially-commissioned Afterword by Laurence Cox, co-author of *We Make Our Own History: Marxism and Social Movements in the Twilight of Neoliberalism*,[10] that reads across all the essays in this book and critically engages with several.[11]

The Movements of Movements

Part 1: What Makes Us Move?	Part 2: Rethinking Our Dance
0: Invocations	0: Invocations
1: Movementscapes	3: Interrogating Movement
2: The Movements of Movements	4: Reflections on Possible Futures
Afterword	Afterword
References	References

Part 2 of this two-part book—titled *The Movements of Movements, Part 2: Rethinking Our Dance*—also has three sections, as above. Looking at movements as the dances of warriors—and here drawing on and inspired by the lives and cosmologies of aboriginal peoples across the world, and in particular on the magnificent body of work by Taiaiake Alfred, a contributor to the book[12]—the book asks the question: *How can, and should, we rethink our dance?*

Here too, and following another stunning Proem by the same author as in this book, Shailja Patel, and an introduction by myself as "Invocations", Section 3 brings together a wide range of essays—again, by both activists and researchers from different parts of the world—but in this case critically reflecting on movement and drawing out fundamental issues that those in movement are concerned with. Part 2 closes with Section 4, composed of several rich and provocative reflections on movement and on possible futures. A major Afterword by Lee Cormie (researcher / teacher / writer and sometime activist concerning social justice movements and coalitions, and a professor emeritus of theology and interdisciplinary studies, who has published many articles on liberation theologies and social movements and been involved in major church-based social justice initiatives over the entire span of movement covered by this book) follows this. This essay reads across both parts of this two-part book and reflects on the meanings of this collection as a whole.[13]

For an overview of the contents of each of the two parts that make up this book, see the Table of Contents in this book; for a discussion of some cross-readings of the essays in this Part, see the subsection further on in this Introduction titled 'Reading Across the Essays'.

Locating Myself

Writing an introduction—just as much as producing a book, or taking part in a movement—is an act of power (though where I use the term 'power' here not in its common sense of power-over, but of power-to).[14] For an introduction such as this then, and to a book (and book project) such as this, it is probably useful for me to introduce and situate myself in relation to the book, as compiler and lead editor.[15] In short, I am not a disinterested observer, nor a 'scholar' (understood in the sense of a well-informed person trained in academic skills who seeks to document, report on, and analyse what she sees and understands, in the somewhat detached manner that the conventions of scholarship demand). Rather, I have been deeply immersed in social movement as a participant, organiser, and strategist, and then more as researcher, commentator, convener of gatherings, and facilitator (and as a compiler and editor of books!) for the past forty years. I have for some time now, and as a part of my research and writing work and my work on the World Social Forum and world movement, been trying to nurture and build transnational and transcommunal exchange and reflection on it. I therefore come to this book with a very subjective and committed position on movement and the subject of this book.[16]

I have come to realise only recently that my first experiences of movement, and of resistance and struggle, happened almost without my being aware of it. In school, and then in college, I all but unconsciously got involved in raising issues with those who ran the institutions, organising resistance, and fighting my way through them. After a first career through the 1970s as an architect and urban planner (first in Montreal, in Canada, then in Kolkata [then still Calcutta] in India) I moved to working as a community organiser / activist, movement strategist, and campaignist based in Kolkata. As an architect, I came to be radically re-educated by this experience of working on the ground.

Although this was an enormously creative and productive period for me personally (and, I think, for all of us who worked and struggled together through this period, in different formations),[17] I also got burned out by continuously being a frontline activist—as well as being an outsider, because I was not born in Kolkata but had moved there (and to what I realise, in retrospect, was a quite closed political environment that was often suspicious of outsiders such as myself). It was in Kolkata that I became aware of 'politics' and cut my political teeth, such as they are (and perhaps lost some of them).

My burnout led me to consciously move in the early 1990s to research and to studying the dynamics of social and political movement. I did this in part as therapy, but also in the hope of making some contribution to movement as an activist doing reflective research. Flowing out of my work as an activist for a couple of decades, my research was on popular movements in India for a place to live in security and dignity, and took the form of depth studies of 3–4 major movements in India over the past fifty years. My work also took me into studying the globalisation of movement and campaigning that had started in the 1980s, and into comparative studies with the globalisation of movement around issues in Brazil and elsewhere in the world. These studies helped me realise the importance and potentials of cross-cultural, transcommunal conversations between movements, which was then still quite limited and just beginning to take place, and from this, I was inspired to create contexts and spaces where this could take place.

As I was writing up my research, I learned in the early 2000s of the World Social Forum, got interested in it (especially in relation to my studies into the globalisation of movement, to the spaces for critical discussion of this, and to the work we had by then started at CACIM, an organisation some of us started at around the same time), and began to write on it—based both on my research and on my prior experience as a movement strategist.[18] Because of what I wrote, I was invited to join the WSF process that was then beginning in India. After briefly co-representing the nascent process on the WSF's International Council, and then being a member of the WSF India Organising Committee, I dropped out of the formal organisational WSF India process, and therefore also from the formal global WSF process. I did this partly because of a tragedy that took place in my life but more because I realised that I was a misfit there and felt I might be able to contribute more to the WSF from outside than inside.[19]

I have since then written widely on the WSF and on emerging global movements, edited books on them, organised research and debate around them, moderated a listserv that was at one time specifically about the WSF (WSFDiscuss), and taught courses on movement, all as a member of CACIM. I have done and do all this therefore not as a 'scholar' but as a student of movement, as someone who is struggling to understand and communicate how movements move, what the nature and roots of their power are, and—so, perhaps—how to help them move 'better'.

What I say in this Introduction therefore, and also my contributions to conceptualising and editing this book, naturally draws on my work over the years in organising, listening, editing, and writing—and from what my friend and fellow traveller Lee Cormie has reminded me is also "a privileged vantage point, of having been located in the South, at the crossroads of several networked (and transcommunal, transnational) dialogues, burgeoning solidarity, and expanding collaboration, at an extraordinary moment in history".[20] As Cormie has helped me to glimpse and to begin to grasp, perhaps largely as a result of my location with respect to emerging movement, this book—and the book project of which it is a part (more on this, below)—is somewhat chaotic and emergent, just as the world of movement itself.[21]

Finally, my demographic coordinates have surely also come into play. I am now an older, middle-upper caste and class, relatively rootless cosmopolitan male from India, an important if sometimes overbearing part of the political 'South', where I was born and have spent the past forty years of my life. This has both given me great privilege—especially in India but perhaps also elsewhere—but has also sometimes been a handicap. My motivations for doing what I have done in and through movement have at times been questioned and sometimes challenged; in some cases justifiably, I think. But I think because of this privileged background, and perhaps also because of other background reasons, I have tended to remain 'independent', to the extent of sometimes being a loner, which has not been easy, in movement.

In all, my being immersed in movement for most of my adult life, growing up in the famous '1960s' in Britain and then in Canada, and spending most of my life in India but important, formative parts of it in the North—all this has surely also had its own strong influence on what I say here and on the books I have put together.

Worlds in Movement[22]

We live today in times of movement. We live in a world of movement; of surging movement, of churning movement; *of worlds in movement*. And because of the onset of climate change and of the new winds that are blowing across the globe as a consequence, we live also at a time when, perhaps as never before, we need to look at and face our future, individually, collectively, and as a species. I personally believe, and spell out in more detail below, that ordinary people everywhere are already grasping this—instinctively and biologically, as sentient living beings who are not yet totally alienated from Mother Earth, and that this internalisation is contributing in its own myriad ways to the movement/s that we are witnessing.

Our world continues to be wracked by war, greed, and violence. It is wracked not only by the effects of authoritarianisms, fundamentalisms, and communalisms, and by the social institutions of race, caste, class, patriarchy, heterosexuality, and ableism, but also by the rapacious impacts of so-called forced 'civilisation', 'development', and 'democracy'. All of these interweave in vicious ways.

By and large, and especially from the point of view of the victims of these processes, this has historically been as true under contemporary isms as under earlier ones from feudalism, theocracy, and monarchy through to capitalism, fascism, and authoritarian socialism, and all too sadly, also under social democracy.[23] Today, and I suggest increasingly, only further impelled by the impacts of the global warming that is a direct outcome of the massive over-'development' to which Mother Earth has been subjected, irruptions and movements are taking place all over the world—in the South (the so-called 'developing countries') and in the North (the 'advanced', 'developed' countries), in countries large and small, in societies new and old, almost like volcanoes and storms. As I see it, all these movements are organic surges that are seeking to break past this phase of history and to break out of the worlds and the dynamics they feel trapped in: Movements of resistance, movements of hope, movements of and for freedom, movements that are fundamentally challenging traditional leadership (and both the more traditional authoritarian but also including by those who consider themselves 'progressive'), and movements of other ways of seeing the world; movements also of retreat to fundamentalisms in the face of the onslaught that peoples all over the world are facing; and equally, movements everywhere to democratise democracy. In some contexts, movement leaders are even saying that the surge that is taking place today is much ahead of the leadership of 'the movement'.[24] To paraphrase the historian Eric Hobsbawm,[25] our world today could well be said to be going through an Age of Movement, including birthing new movement that is increasingly independent of traditional social and political institutions (such as unions and political parties) and/or that is forging new institutions, and that is daily taking new shapes and struggling to rebuild the world in new ways.

To be more specific and to name just a few (with the understanding that many of these movements of course overlap, intersect, and/or intertwine): Movements across the globe of refugees and migrants, impelled by war, economic devastation, and now also the impacts of climate change, many of which are challenging the "imperialism of national borders";[26] movements among indigenous peoples in so many parts of the world who seem to be once again achieving a critical consciousness and mass that challenge the historical oppression and savagery of the 'civilisational project' by outsiders (settlers) and seek to reclaim their identities, powers, and lands, and put forward alternative visions of change;[27] movements among peoples of varied sexualities towards gaining and defending their freedoms; movements challenging the arrogance and criminality of 'development' and of neoliberalism, and the massive hyper-concentration of wealth that they have created and continue to relentlessly create; movements challenging authoritarianism and the increasingly authoritarian and profoundly anti-democratic tendencies in supposedly democratic societies under neoliberalism, such as intensified surveillance; anti-capitalist and alter-globalisation movements; movements against war; movements among structurally oppressed peoples such as the Dalits of South Asia who have been scattered across the globe over the past two centuries by the rape of colonisation (these are people who are condemned by Hindu societal norms to live outside 'civilised' society and have historically been subjected to barbaric discrimination);[28] movements of faith, especially among peoples who believe that values integral to their beliefs are being corrupted and/or overwhelmed; and continuing movements among women fighting for equality, justice, and respect.

All these movements, and more, have been building up over the past 2–3 decades. In addition, a whole set of new movements have also irrupted in a series of spectacular and very visible explosions during 2011 and beyond, in several parts of the world. They include the movements that toppled dictatorial regimes in Tunisia and then Egypt (2011); the Occupy movement in North America and then across Europe (2011); the *indignados* movement in Spain (2011); the massive rebellion against EU-imposed austerity programmes in Greece and the anti-corruption movement in India (both also in 2011); the massive students' protest against fee hikes in Québec, Canada (2012); the growing assertion by indigenous peoples across Turtle Island ('North America') (2012), including the Defenders of the Land and the Idle No More movements; democratisation movements across Africa; movements that have rocked Turkey, Brazil, and Romania (2013) and Hong Kong (2014). All this, aside from the countless continuing, sustained, even if less publicised movements all over the world by social movements, student organisations, trade unions, and political formations, and locally among ordinary peoples everywhere.

These 'movements' are of course not only social, political, and cultural but often also fundamentally and massively *physical* in nature—such as the enormous migrations that are today taking place across the world, and which are movements that will only greatly intensify under intensifying conditions of climate change and what I argue will be accompanying conflict and war in the decades to come.[29]

In addition however, I suggest—as I have argued in an earlier essay[30]—that these movements are not only social, political, cultural, and/or physical *but fundamentally also biological in nature*, and an integral expression of the pulse and life of Mother Earth as a living being. On the one hand, they are organic manifestations and expressions of the agonies and ecstasies that she is experiencing and are therefore—literally—'natural' reactions, the organic reactions and expressions of nature, and where in a way therefore (though one also has to be cautious when cross-applying specialised terms), movements are angiogenic—life-giving—in nature. In a very fundamental way, they are assertions and manifestations of a natural, self-organising world, and indeed, by their very nature, they convey the immanent potential that is always there in the living world that (here echoing the slogan of the World Social Forum) 'another world is possible'. On the other hand, and just as angiogenesis plays a key role in the transition of tumours from a benign state to a malignant state, movements can also be 'regressive' in nature, however 'organic' they might be, and/but where 'regressive' and 'progressive' always depend on one's point of view.[31]

A crucial further aspect of this phenomenon is that many of these movements are not only exertions of 'power-over' (which is the default frame given to them not only by traditional movement leaders and strategists, but also by most academics and theorists) but also vehicles for vast numbers of people both to engage with and to learn about the times we live in, and so to gain control over their own lives. In short, they are critical spaces for the exercise of the power of 'power-to'. Through their very presence and occurrence and by their scale—which today is only further hugely amplified (and perhaps also influenced and given shape to through social technologies and the media)—these movements are enormous contexts for the exchange of life experiences among participants. The significance of this, as I have suggested elsewhere, is that this kind of exchange takes place not only in the more obvious sense, but also through the exchange of pheromones—trace chemicals—where whole databases of personal and social histories are exchanged.[32] In a larger picture, the occurrence and human experience of movement therefore literally changes the world, in countless subliminal and non-linear ways.

Movements also contribute to and manifest what biologist Rupert Sheldrake has termed 'morphic resonance' across time and space.[33] This happened so dramatically, for instance, across North Africa during 2011 (hugely amplified, again, by the new world of social technologies that we, and especially younger people, today not just 'use' but live, as these technologies have become an inseparable part of the web of the lives we lead). And through all this, movements seed, contaminate, electrify, and change the world, and give new meanings to it in many more ways than we commonly know. As I argue in my essays as referred to above and elsewhere, drawing heavily on the work of others, it is very much through all these processes that societies are today emerging and evolving through processes of emergence.[34]

Increasingly, as the crises we are living through intensify, these movements—these heavings, these swellings, in the body of Mother Earth—are also being fed and even impelled by changes and shifts that are taking place in the very structure and substructure of societies. These changes are also 'movements', but of a fundamental, structural, and tectonic nature: Movements of capital; movements of constantly evolving information and communication technologies (and of the historically new perception of the rise of a new commons, the web); movements of the rapidly rising emancipatory awareness on the part of the historically marginalised, across the world; and of the even more recent perception, planetary climate change. All these deep currents and movements are today also increasingly intertwining in virtuous and/or vicious spirals.

The consequence of all this is that the movements we see or hear are in fact quite profound and are leaving indelible marks on societies and on history; indeed, in many cases, they are scripting and rewriting history itself.

Given all this, I believe and suggest that it is important to stop and think about the meanings of movement in our lives. On the one hand, as political scientist and movement sociologist Sidney Tarrow and others have argued, movements act as the "carriers and transmitters" of cognitive meanings and understandings and, among other things, are "actively engaged in the production of [new] meaning for participants, antagonists, and observers".[35] In other words, and where this is of profound significance, movements render events and processes intelligible and meaningful not only for participants but also for much wider audiences.

On the other hand, it is also well worth our while to consider the simple but radical thesis put forward by transnational sociologist André Drainville that the world economy—and the world order that we are taught to perceive and to respect as permanently ordained—does not exist by itself, but only in relation to social forces; indeed, that "The world economy is [only] wherever social forces meet world ordering".[36] In other words, that the world we know is made and made real not only by world institutions or by the powerful, from above (as we are educated and socialised by them and by our teachers to understand), but as much and perhaps much more by the agency and actions of ordinary peoples everywhere, from 'below', at the countless points of local, place-based contact between these actions and the structures of world ordering erected by the powerful.

The meaning of this is that the movements that are taking place in our times—and as has always been the case—are therefore nothing short of fundamental in giving shape to the world that is emerging around us; they are literally, as Lee Cormie argues in his contribution to this book, "re-creating the world".[37] They are thus as important in giving meaning and order to the world we live in as all the structures and institutions of world order that we are so domesticated and trained to believe in.[38]

Meanings of Movement, the Movements of Movements, and This Book

If we can agree that even some of this is the case, then we need to perhaps push the boundary further and ask ourselves some questions about movement. For instance, if movements are in fact not merely superficial and passing phenomena but arising from far deeper causes and part of deeper dynamics, what then are the deeper *meanings* of the movements that we are seeing around us and of these apparent 'worlds of movement'? (What indeed, is the existential meaning of 'movement' itself?) What is all this movement saying to us? Crucially, what are movements saying to each other, not only in terms of detail or even strategy, but in existential terms? What does the existence of one movement 'do' for another movement?

To address these questions, I believe we need to do at least three things. First, we need to step back and come to terms with the fact that movement is not just a phenomenon 'out there'—of idealistic people waving flags and making demands, which is the common media-created image, only reinforced by all too much social science. Rather, it is a fundamental, commonplace, and everyday fact and expression of life forces on earth welling up and taking shape in the forms that are familiar to us; like waves, they are only surface expressions of much deeper currents in the rivers and oceans of our lives. Thus, I suggest that we try to see and recognise that these movements, just as much as oceans or rivers or the winds, are giving shape to the world that we know. In short, they are organic forces and an integral part of the web of life.

Second, I believe we need to also reflect on how and why the concept of movement—in one sense or another—exists in so many spheres of human life and endeavour. It is useful to reflect, for instance, on how and why in T'ai Chi philosophy, stillness and motion are seen as being fundamentally interrelated, where the action of being still is understood as a part of moving, of a journey. The counterpart of this in social and political movement (as in the martial arts and in war, and in dance), might be that restraint and stillness is as important as action:

> Stillness of motion is not true stillness, only when there is stillness within movement does the universal rhythm manifest itself.[39]

See also, for instance, the following diagram from the Visual Thesaurus,[40] and then below that, a standard dictionary definition of the word 'movement'.[41] Neither of these are complete definitions, limited as they are by the cultures within and by which they have been generated. Nevertheless, they are stunning insofar as they immediately give us a much wider and more holistic picture of movement than most of us normally have, and a far more organic one:

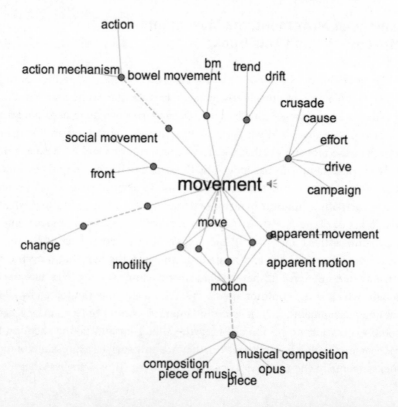

Movement

— n	
1.	a. The act, process, or result of moving
	b. An instance of moving
2.	The manner of moving
3.	a. A group of people with a common ideology, esp. a political or religious one
	b. The organized action of such a group
4.	A trend or tendency in a particular sphere
5.	The driving and regulating mechanism of a watch or clock
6.	(Often plural) a person's location and activities during a specific time
7.	a. The evacuation of the bowels
	b. The matter evacuated
8.	Music: A principal self-contained section of a symphony, sonata, etc, usually having its own structure
9.	Tempo or pace, as in music or literature
10.	Fine arts: The appearance of motion in painting, sculpture, etc
11.	Prosody: The rhythmic structure of verse
12.	A positional change by one or a number of military units
13.	A change in the market price of a security or commodity.

Third, I believe that we—individually and collectively—need to progressively build a larger picture, or 'map', of the much wider world of the movement and churning that is taking place in the world during our times (and that have taken place historically), in order to 'locate' the movements that we can see. But because such a picture or map, if done literally, would tend to reduce this extraordinary, pulsating planetary phenomenon—this live, worldwide web—to merely two dimensions, and because we as outsiders (rather than those in movement) would lead such a process and determine what is portrayed and how it portrayed, we need a three- and four-dimensional simulation in which movements themselves play the central roles.

To underline something I have already said, a simulation such as this must also of necessity not be one where outsiders present and discuss movement—social, cultural, political, physical, and socio-biological—but a space where movements themselves can speak to each other. It must be a space where people in movement can gain the possibility of growing through their interactions, learning from their exchanges, and where the possibility also exists of new actors entering and joining the discussions.

Many argue that the World Social Forum was (and to some extent still is) precisely such a space, and that in the decade and more since its formation in 2001 it has been an extraordinary lens through which to perceive a great deal—if not all—of contemporary and emerging social and political movement;[42] others argue that along with similar movements, the WSF has indeed been something of 'a movement of movements'.[43] These characterisations have been widely debated, and this is not the place to debate how accurate they are; I mention this only to go on to say that as a part of a wider process of our critical engagement with movement, my colleagues and I at CACIM, along with several members in the wider CACIM community, have accepted this potential of the WSF, and have collectively tried over the past decade to contribute to this deeper understanding of the WSF by taking a series of interrelated initiatives. These initiatives have included organising seminars and debates on the WSF during successive WSF events and outside over nearly a decade; initiating a series of fellowships for students and activists to reflect on the WSF; hosting a listserv for critical reflection and discussion on the WSF (WSFDiscuss); organising and hosting a website for material on the WSF and the alter-globalisation movement (and which also acts as an archive for all exchange taking place on WSFDiscuss), *OpenSpaceForum*; and producing edited collections on the World Social Forum and related matters, including the *Challenging Empires* series as already mentioned, and also the *Open Space* series of books.[44]

Aside from ongoing discussion on WSFDiscuss, our most recent contribution in this area was the book that has preceded the present one in the *Challenging Empires* series, titled *World Social Forum: Critical Explorations*.[45] This present book, along with its companion volume titled *The Movements of Movements, Part 2: Rethinking Our Dance*, is thus one more contribution in this direction, but now going far past the WSF alone and looking at some of the much larger and wider galaxies of 'global' and intergalactic movement, within which the WSF is just one star.

The Movements of Movements

There are of course many excellent books that have come out over the past decade or so on movement, and in particular many that have presented, celebrated, and in some cases critically engaged with the emergence of what has variously been called the 'anti-globalisation movement', the 'alter-globalisation movement', the 'global justice movement', or what writer Naomi Klein at one point famously referred to as "the movement of movements"[46]—and which, indeed, is a phrase that several authors in this book also use. This present collection, however, titled and focused on *the movements* (plural) *of movements*, takes a somewhat different approach. First, it focuses on the verb 'movement', and not the noun. This radical shift of focus opens up whole new worlds.[47]

Second, this collection does not focus on the so-called 'alter-globalisation movement' alone, which is often used as a synonym for the so-called 'movement of movements', but explores a much wider range of movement. And third, rather than suggesting that there is one single, larger, encompassing 'movement' taking place in our world, it accepts that there are many different movements taking place in our world today, and differing perceptions of justice, and many ways of moving, all of which we can learn from. By making visible at least a wide range of the many movements of movements, and their multiple praxes, it tries to enable us—readers, activists, and editors alike—to see movements comparatively and to draw our own lessons from this.[48]

Reaching back to the great sweeps and swells of movement that have taken place across the world since the 1960s (see, for instance, the essays by Fouad Kalouche and Eric Mielants, by David McNally, and by Lee Cormie),[49] and more specifically to some of the more iconic movements that have taken place during this period—the student-led revolt in France in 1968, the Zapatista movement in Mexico since 1994, the 'Battle of Seattle' in 1999, and also the emergence during this period of what some today call 'political Islam'[50]—and also reaching forward in time to look at, for instance, the Occupy movement from 2011 on, the essays in this book focus on the period 2006–10. They range from discussions and re-theorisations of struggles at and from the margins to essays on feminisms, queerdom, struggles of faith; from the struggles of workers and re-imagining the world and 'forward dreaming' to reflections on issues of division, marginalisation, and exclusion within progressive movement and more. By juxtaposing essays by a range of people that discuss how movements move, in different ways and from different points of view—each with its own cultural and political cadence and rhythm—this book seeks to make more visible and comprehensible the movements and praxis *of* movements, and also of the larger world of movement within which individual movements take place. It seeks to contribute to learnings and movements *between and across* movements, including in terms of the language, grammar, and syntax of movement.

Conscious of difference and multiplicity, and committed to engaging across standpoints, the two books together are an attempt at sketching out not 'a grand metanarrative of movement' but rather a landscape that begins to reveal the many intersectionalities of movements and their organic nature. Each of us, from our positions in relation to what we are seeing, will have our own perceptions. Through this, they hope to contribute to readers developing their own meta-analyses of movement, and in that sense, to becoming a part of movement and not only a spectator.

Along with other volumes in the series of which they are a part,[51] these books therefore aim to make contemporary movement/s more meaningful to the observer—and perhaps also, in some ways, to those who take part in movement.

They hope to be spaces where multidirectional and transcommunal conversations can open up, not only between and across movements but also between movements and readers; where movements and their ideas speak to each other, and perhaps even begin to move together; and where it also perhaps becomes possible for all to perceive and sense both the vastness of the universe of movement and also, at the same time, the extraordinary range of tactics and rhythms in movement—and just possibly, also some of the fundamental characteristics of movement as life force. And through this, in turn, and by building on the diverse politico-cultural compositions that the essays represent, they hope to make audible / visible / comprehensible the dance and the music of movement—and of a world in movement.

Reading Across the Essays

Each of the essays in this book is individually fascinating; the movement of the human spirit radiates from each one. And even though it would be difficult if not impossible to do full justice to them, I have been sorely tempted in the case of this book in particular to attempt a reading of each of them and also across essays.

But I have not attempted this, not least because, as I have already mentioned earlier on, a very welcome part of the emergence of this book has been the agreement of Laurence Cox, a fellow traveller and *compañero* in the worlds of movement, and a mover and teacher like few I know, to write an Afterword for this book, and of Lee Cormie—a good friend and fellow traveller, a valuable discussant and collaborator for these book as they have emerged, and also otherwise author of one of the essays contained in them—to write an Afterword for the companion book, *The Movements of Movements, Part 2: Rethinking Our Dance*, in which he has overviewed all the essays in both books. Their essays therefore, in their different ways, reflect on the meanings of this collection as a whole, offering independent, detailed, and critical perspectives on points of divergence and convergence among these movements and what they reveal about the dimensions, scales, and magnitude of changes that are today sweeping the world. They also address the collections as collections.

Given this—and which I believe is a marvellous privilege—I will therefore keep here to a few overall comments and explanations, and do just a partial reading of the text of this book as a whole, as it were.

Plurality, Diversity, Transcommunality
As will be evident from the Table of Contents of this book and from the Notes on the Contributors, we have tried to make the book truly international, intercultural, and transcommunal,[52] both in terms of the contributors as well as in terms of the essays included and in terms of how they have been arranged.

In particular, we have been able to include in this collection several differing essays by women and men who come from and work on the structural margins of society: Anand Teltumbde (on 'Anti-Imperialism, Dalits, and the Annihilation of Caste'); Andrea Smith (on 'Indigenous Feminism and the Heteropatriarchal State'); Taiaiake Alfred and Jeff Corntassel (on 'Being Indigenous: Resurgences against Contemporary Colonialism'); Jeff Corntassel alone (on 'Rethinking Self-Determination: Lessons from the Indigenous-Rights Discourse'); Xochitl Leyva Solano (on 'Geopolitics of Knowledge and the Neo-Zapatista Social Movement Networks') and with Christopher Gunderson (on 'The Tapestry of Neo-Zapatismo: Origins and Development'); and where in the companion book, among others, we have Anila Daulatzai (on 'Believing in Exclusion: The Problem of Secularism in Progressive Politics') and Josephine Ho (on 'Is Global Governance Good for East Asian Queers?').

In addition, and because of who they have written about, I also mention here the essays in this book by the late François Houtart ('Mahmoud Mohamed Taha: Islamic Witness in the Contemporary World') and by Roel Meijer ('Fighting for Another World: Yusuf al-'Uyairi's Conceptualisation of Praxis and the Permanent Salafi Revolution').

Each of these authors and/or actors bring to us substantially different points of view, and therefore different lenses through which to comprehend the worlds we live in; and different headphones—as it were—to hear the languages and the music of movement!

For me, it is—for instance—not a minor issue that in Taiaiake Alfred and Jeff Corntassel's essays, almost all their citations and references are to works by indigenous peoples, which only serves to make their essays that much more outstanding. In my limited experience, this fact itself is all too unusual and constitutes a loud reminder to all of us, indigenous or settler, 'marginal' or mainstream, that there is a lot of excellent work out there by indigenous peoples, by both women and men at the margins. Accordingly, reading, internalising, and citing this 'knowledge from below' is possible, if we are only willing to prioritise it. Depending on where one is located socially, this is a question of pride in ourselves and/or respect for such peoples and their knowledges. Though seemingly only a small step, this practice has profound epistemological and political meanings and is therefore a vital contribution to building other politics and other worlds, because it has the possibility of changing where one locates oneself and how one sees things, and because it demands that we make this shift consciously, as a political act.

As another aspect of the diversity and plurality in this collection, among the contributors to this book are six streetfighting activists and strategists: Tariq Ali, the late Daniel Bensaïd, Ashok Choudhary, Roma, the late Yusuf al-'Uyairi (whose life and struggles are presented and discussed by Roel Meijer), and also, at a different level, the late Mahmoud Mohamed Taha (whose life struggle is presented by the late François Houtart). I single these essays out for the obvious reason that the location of these individuals in movement is structurally different from those of scholars and observers, as are the perspectives that they offer us on movement and on the world in movement.

The essay by Tariq Ali, for instance, thinks back to 1968 and raises angry questions about contemporary movement. In some ways, this essay and the questions it puts forward are strongly complemented by the essay by the late Daniel Bensaïd (another veteran of 1968) who challenges contemporary approaches to movement strategy. I have found it provocative to read these essays in comparison with the ones in this book by, say, André Drainville and in Part 2 (the companion book) by David Graeber, John Holloway, Rodrigo Nunes, and Michal Osterweil, and to read all these essays on strategy against the essay by Roel Meijer on the late Yusuf al-'Uyairi as a strategist of a movement (al-Qaeda) who had a radically different understanding of modernity. These essays all challenge each other, but they also jam with each other and dance with each other. In a way, it becomes a fascinating display that reminds me of *capoeira*, "[the] Brazilian martial art and popular street dance that combines elements of dance, acrobatics, and music, and that is sometimes also referred to as a game".[53]

While the collection focuses on movement during the period 2006–10, to put this wave in perspective it also includes essays on movement at different time periods and—crucially—set in different cultural contexts. Mentioning here only those essays that deal with more specific places and time periods, we have essays ranging from the rise of an articulation of an alternative interpretation of Islam from the 1930s through to the 1980s in Sudan (by François Houtart), to '1968' and after in France and Britain (Tariq Ali), to a discussion of movement strategy in Europe and Latin America from the 1970s through to the 2000s (the late Daniel Bensaïd), to sweeps across the world from 1968 right through to 1989 (by Fouad Kalouche and Eric Mielants) and from 1994 through to the 2000s (David McNally). We also have essays ranging from the rise of the Muslim Brotherhood in Egypt during the 1970s through to the 2000s as an aspect of a renewed rise of a global Islam (James Toth), to the rise of the Zapatista movement in the jungles of Chiapas, Mexico, during the 1980s and 90s (Xochitl Leyva Solano and Christopher Gunderson), through to critical readings of—and reflections on—feminist movement/s during the 1980s through to the 2000s in Canada (Emilie Hayes) and in Latin America and globally (Virginia Vargas); from a discussion of the rise of indigenous peoples' social movements during the 1980s through to the 2000s in Bolivia (Guillermo Delgado-P), and to the 1990s and 2000s in the forests of India (Roma and Ashok Choudhary), in rural and urban South Korea (Cho Hee-Yeon), and in the 'clash of civilisations' emerging in West Asia (Roel Meijer), and the new movements against neoliberalism in Latin America during the 2000s

(Emir Sader); and through to the 2010s, looking at the politics and dialectics of anti-capitalist movements (André Drainville), the rise of new movements around labour (Peter Waterman), and—in the context of climate change—the emergence of new movements for radical localisation (Peter North and David Featherstone).

A glance at the Table of Contents will make clear we have a different but similarly dramatic spread of essays in the companion book.

Why 2006–10?

The start date 2006 emerged from very particular circumstances. As mentioned elsewhere, this book is a part of the *Challenging Empires* series, conceived in 2006–7 by contributing editor Peter Waterman and myself, along with my then colleague at OpenWord, Nishant.[54] During the years before this (2003–7), Peter and I had intensively collected and edited material for essays up to 2006–7 for our first two books in the series, the first two editions of *World Social Forum: Challenging Empires*.[55] At that point, at a political as well as a more personal and experiential level, it seemed natural to both of us to move on from that earlier period and to focus on the contemporary and the emerging.

The end date for the material in this book however came to be defined by two coincidental and conjunctural events. As lead editor, and after working and re-working the material we had collected through 2007–10 (during which time our book project burgeoned from one to two to three books), I finally took a call in late 2010 on how we would organise and bring out the material we had. Just at that moment however, '2011' irrupted on the world (and on us!), with the Tunisian revolution in December 2010[56] and Tahrir Square and the start of the Egyptian uprising in January 2011,[57] and following these, the amazing irruptions during 2011 in Spain, Greece, and the Occupy movement in North America, and then Europe and elsewhere.

Even as we—along with millions of others across the world—were swept up in the swirling spirals of tumult that progressively unfolded across so much of the world during that year and the next, and however tempted we were to try to also embrace in our books what was happening, it became clear to us that attempting to do this would further delay books that already taken a long time to put together. We therefore elected at that point to organise the material we already had in hand into three books: One as a direct sequel to our previous two books, focussing exclusively on the World Social Forum,[58] and the other two on movements in the world beyond the WSF (but also, at points, impinging on and including it). We subsequently and finally decided to put most of the non-WSF material we had collected into the second volume in the informal trilogy, which is this book; and to collect fresh material for the third book on the period 2011 on. We subsequently added two essays that look at and draw lessons from the Occupy movement. But in the belief that there is much to be learned by focussing on 2006–10 as a kind of crucible, we kept away from also trying to embrace and explore the almost entirely new landscape that subsequent and more contemporary movement has created.

Beyond this, it has all along been our approach to locate contemporary movement within a historical and cross-cultural perspective, and so we first decided to include four essays here that specifically took broad sweeps across movements over the past 40 to 50 years. The ones we decided to include are the ones here by David McNally, Fouad Kalouche and Eric Mielants, Tariq Ali, and Lee Cormie.

Aside from these four essays, however, we decided that we would also commission and/or harvest material that specifically related to major movements of the past whose resonance carried through to the period we were looking at, and including movements that had 'anniversaries' falling during the period we were focussing on, 2006–10. On this count, therefore, we have essays on '1968', with its fortieth anniversary in 2008 (the essays by Tariq Ali and Daniel Bensaïd); the Zapatista uprising in 1994, with its fifteenth anniversary in 2009 and twentieth anniversary in 2014 (in this Part, the essays by Xochitl Leyva Solano, by Xochitl Leyva Solano together with Christopher Gunderson, and by Alex Khasnabish; and in Part 2 / the companion book, by François Houtart and by Kolya Abramsky); and the Battle of Seattle in 1999 with its tenth anniversary in 2009 (by Rodrigo Nunes).

It is perhaps worth also mentioning here that there were some significant other movements from the past that we also tried to commission and/or collect material on, but where we weren't successful, in large part because of limited time and other resources. These included the great Naxalite uprising in India of 1967,[59] the resonances of which continue to reverberate widely in the country and region forty years and more later,[60] and PGA (People's Global Action), founded in 1998 as an outcome of the Zapatista encuentros in 1995–6, which had strong impacts on Seattle and on the anti-capitalist and alter-globalisation movements that subsequently emerged in the 2000s.

The Zapatistas

In particular, this book project includes four major essays on the Zapatistas in this collection—three in this book (by Xochitl Leyva Solano, by Leyva Solano together with Christopher Gunderson, and by Alex Khasnabish) and one in the companion book (by François Houtart, and another that draws inspiration from the Zapatistas, by Kolya Abramsky).

The first reason for this strong concentration is the strong resonance of this movement among activists and other young people in the North. (Though it is also interesting, and perhaps not unimportant, that the movement is perhaps much less known across the South—other than in Abya Yala [Latin America]—and does not seem to have had the same significance and resonance with activists there; I come back to this point below.)

Second, the range, depth, and sensitivity of writing that has emerged on the Zapatista movement is in my experience unsurpassed in relation to contemporary writing on movements, and that I believe speaks widely to all kinds of movement, and so needs to be made available more widely, and especially in the South.

And third, I have included these essays because each focuses brilliantly and radiantly on a different aspect of the Zapatista movement: Xochitl Leyva Solano and Christopher Gunderson on its genesis, cosmology, and meanings; Alex Khasnabish on the movement as it took place and on the imaginations it has fired transnationally (and where indeed, Kolya Abramsky's essay in the companion book is itself a case in point); François Houtart on its present form; and Xochitl Leyva Solano, writing alone, on how the movement provoked the empire to conceive of the concept of 'netwar' as countermovement and, it seems, to itself embark on such netwar.

'Global Resonance'?

Having said this, however, I must add some comments on the question of the 'global' nature and scale of what is called Zapatismo,[61] and more generally of what is called the 'alter-globalisation movement', the 'global justice and solidarity movement', etc. In some ways, I am also reflecting here on my own writing over this past decade.

On the one hand, there is no question that deep-rooted ferment has broken out across much of the world, in the North as well as the South. As mentioned above, from 2011 on there have been upsurges and irruptions in North Africa, Greece, Spain, across much of Western Europe, the US, Canada, India, Brazil, Turkey, and Hong Kong, and elsewhere on the globe. These are fairly well known because of media attention. Less known have been the irruptions that have been taking place across Africa throughout the 2000s,[62] and (perhaps because of the language divides that continue to colonise and divide us) the English-speaking world seems to know less of the movements that have also been taking place throughout South and Central America that have in many ways politically transformed that continent.[63] In Asia, aside from what is happening in India, irruptions have taken place and are continuing to take place in West Asia, Pakistan, Bangladesh, Burma, Thailand, and elsewhere.

But to my understanding at least, despite that fact that I, too, have argued (along with Nunes and others) that there is a new 'massification' taking place in movement worldwide;[64] that many, many movements in the North have been inspired by the Zapatistas; and that many activists and researchers use terms such as 'the alter-globalisation movement', I believe that there is good reason for not seeing or characterising what has emerged out of this as being *one* movement (which is what happens when it is called either *an* 'alter-globalisation movement' or 'anti-globalisation movement', or *a* 'global justice and solidarity movement', and especially as *the* 'movement of movements'). There is reason, too, for not too easily characterising such movements as 'global' or referring to their 'global resonance', simply because they are not, in reality, 'global'. (Here, as in so many places, it also makes so much more sense to refer to 'movement', generically, rather than to 'a movement' or 'the movement'.)

The reasons for this caution are fairly straightforward. One is simply the epistemological implication of asserting that Zapatismo and/or the 'global justice and solidarity movement' carry a similar worldwide resonance as 1968, or as Mao and the Chinese Revolution, or Che Guevara, or Mahatma Gandhi; this leads only to iconising them. In short, should we use the term 'global' for movements whose resonance is more limited to particular regions of the world?[65]

Second is that, to my knowledge at least, almost all the authors who use these terms are from or located in the North, whereas (again, within the limited range of my knowledge) these terms are hardly used in the South, or at least are used much less. If so, then we need to ask ourselves why this is the case. But if this is indeed the case, then writers in the North surely need to reflect on this, and on the consequences of using such terms. To take a leaf from Maia Ramnath's argument that there is a certain coloniality about formal (and Western, Northern) capital-A Anarchism,[66] there is equally reason I think to consider the possibility that something similar can happen if we overgeneralise the globality of particular strands of movement, and if we singularise 'the movement'.

None of this is to deny the reality of the resonance of the Zapatista movement or of the so-called 'global justice and solidarity movement'; it is only to suggest caution when describing movements or resonance as global and/or singular.

The Rise of Political Islam, and the Importance of Faith in Movement

The relevance in our times of including three essays in this book on political Islam, and an overview of faith in movement is perhaps already evident from what I have said above. (In addition, we also have in the companion book a directly related, powerful, and challenging essay that critiques the fundamentalism of progressive secularism and of [Western] feminism.[67])

For all the differences that the secular world may have with it and its underlying concepts, political Islam sees itself as being a contemporary, insurgent, and in its own terms, anti-systemic in nature. By its scale alone, it has perhaps an equal if not much greater claim to being global, in relation to other currents of contemporary 'global' movements for social justice. And as Lee Cormie demonstrates in his essay in this book[68] (and as most readers are perhaps already somewhat aware), movements of the faithful in all faiths continue to have huge followings throughout the world and continue to make and re-make the world.

Beyond this, while the rise of political Islam over the past 2–3 decades is perhaps a phenomenon that most young Muslims are today aware of, across the world, it is deeply unfortunate that until recently the subject (and to some extent that of faith in movement more generally) has seemed to be almost excluded from social movement scholarship and activism in the self-professedly 'secular' and advanced parts of the world. As a result, and because of the hegemonic power of the knowledge and publishing industries of the North, the subject has been all but invisibilised and/or demonised as being uncivil. This is in sharp contrast to the reality that the scale, breadth, depth, and sustained intensity of this movement is far wider than any other in recent history, and our lack of knowledge of this other world again speaks only for our insularity and of tendencies towards coloniality and hegemony.[69]

This simple reason of this absence (or more bluntly put, invisibilisation) is— along with the brilliance of the individual essays themselves—enough for their inclusion in this book. Of the three on Islam, two are on what are among the most powerful currents within the now well-known stream known as political Islam (by Roel Meijer on al-Qaeda and by James Toth on the Muslim Brotherhood). The third (by François Houtart), giving us perspective on the first two, is on an extraordinary but very different current of political Islam in Sudan.

Although I am all too aware of the poverty of my own understanding of the subject, I believe that together the three essays give us a rich understanding not only of political Islam but also of movement, generically. This is all the more the case because (aside from the differing subject matters) the style and rhythm of the essays is so different: One, a very material, ethnographic analysis of the development and growth of what in time has become a very major movement, the Muslim Brotherhood, that is at the epicentre of struggle over meaning and power in one of the major societies in the world, Egypt; another, a detailed ethnographic presentation and discussion of the life, beliefs, and actions of a key activist and strategist within a profoundly militant movement, al-Qaeda; and the third a tantalisingly brief account of the life, philosophy, and practice of someone who formulated a radical new interpretation of his religion, and who was martyred as a heretic precisely for this by others of his faith.[70]

This said, I am all too aware of the fact that all the three essays have been written by three men originating from places other than the areas in which these movements germinated and grew, however intimately they clearly know their respective subjects. In an ideal world, I would have liked to have included additional/complimentary essays by people—women as well as men—from the region. I however have to face the fact that their absence is not coincidence but a function of 3–4 factors. One, as already mentioned, has been the impact of the limited financial and human resources available to us in this ambitious book project. This has been only amplified by the reality that we at CACIM are outside the increasingly intellectual property–conscious academy and where, given the nature and structure of the knowledge and publishing industries, most of the knowledge that I as an English-speaking person could access was generated by people in the North and published in the North (and at increasingly unaffordable prices!); three, my very limited knowledge of the worlds of Islam; and four, in contrast to my relative ease of access to material from the North, I realised that I hardly knew or had easy access to individuals or institutions in the West Asian / North African regions, and my limited if fairly sustained attempts to get somewhat similar material from such people ultimately failed. Within these constraints, I succeeded in finding these marvellous essays and individuals whose work I have now included, and I finally went with what I had.

By saying the above, I do not mean to be apologetic for what we have been able to include here in order to open up this vital subject. Quite the opposite, I feel fortunate to have met and/or found these authors and deeply privileged to be associated with them and their essays. But this experience has once again reminded me of the uneven terrain on which we all move and of the relentless struggle to also make this terrain level.

Closing Comments

I want to close this Introduction by more personally acknowledging the contributions to this book of many people—and without whom, this book / these books could never have been what they are.

First, *Peter Waterman*, as co-founder and co-editor of the *Challenging Empires* series and contributing editor to this book. As summarised above, Peter and I, along with my colleague at OpenWord Nishant, conceived of the *Challenging Empires* series in 2006–7, and all three of us then worked together on the first book that came out of that project, *World Social Forum: Critical Explorations*, published in 2012 (Peter and I on the editorial side and Nishant on the production).[71] In the course of working on this present book however, and of conceptualising its subject and focus, we agreed that Peter would be more appropriately described here as contributing editor. Notwithstanding this small change however, Peter's contributions to this book, and to the evolution of my thinking through these books, has been huge, ranging from sourcing essays from his seemingly limitless networks to his always challenging comments on concepts. I deeply appreciate the generosity of his always-critical embrace and his friendship.

Second, I want to most warmly thank all the authors for all their many contributions to this book, not least their essays, but also their patience in staying with this long-emerging book project and its somewhat chaotic emergence. There are of course too many names to list out here, and where this is also a little unnecessary since they have pride of place in both the Table of Contents and in the List of Contributors!

A small footnote to this is that, as some readers might notice, I think I have in all cases taken the step of 'especially thanking' authors of the essays for which we had to get permission for republication—specifically, for their help in getting the permission, and in some cases where they managed to get their prior publishers to reduce or even to waive their fees. In short, my not doing this in the case of the authors who have written for us, or who we requested permission to publish something that they had written but not yet published, does not at all mean that I am not grateful to them. To the contrary, I am in fact even more deeply grateful to each one of them for writing for us and/or for bearing with the fairly intense content editing that we did on their writing, and also—and especially to them—for their patience in bearing with the long delay that has taken place in our publishing their original work.

I would also like to warmly thank *Ramsey Kanaan and Craig O'Hara of PM Press* for accepting the challenge of bringing out these two books in co-publication with OpenWord—and therefore also making them part of their own rich collection of powerful books on movement.

And finally, I also want to warmly acknowledge the contributions to this book of certain old and new colleagues: *Adityan M*, the conceptualiser and designer of a concept for the covers of the *Challenging Empires* series, including for the first, rough version of the cover for this book, and also for designing CACIM's forthcoming revised website; *Christina Sanchez*, for helping me think through this Introduction and for generating the Wordle and other diagrams that we have tried using in our books for the first time, and more generally for her enthusiasm and her creative and critical engagement with my work; *Giulio Maffini*, an old friend and college classmate I have had the privilege of rediscovering recently, for nudging me into the use of diagrams to unpack and open up the meanings of the sometimes dense content of such a book (and of my writing); *Lee Cormie*, fellow traveller and friend, for thinking through with me both this book and its likely sequel, and as already mentioned, for agreeing to write an Afterword for these books; *Madhuresh*, my colleague at CACIM, for his contributions to the conceptualisation of this book and its predecessor back in 2010, and for his constant fellowship over many years; *Nishant,* my colleague at OpenWord, for his companionship till the end of 2014 in helping me think out—and then bring out—this book; *Yih Lerh Huang*, a new friend and colleague, for joining Giulio Maffini in nudging me into the use of diagrams in the book and for infusing fresh energy and professionalism into our work at OpenWord; and *Matt Meyer*, someone I have come to know through the struggle for peace—and also a contributor to these books[72]—for introducing us to Ramsey and Craig at PM Press and for being the midwife for the birth of these two books. Thank you, all!

—Jai Sen
New Delhi and Ottawa, December 2013, revised December 2015

Postscript, June 2017: It is with the greatest sadness that I add this note, that my co-Series Editor for the Challenging Empires series, and the Contributing Editor to this set of two books, and my dear friend and comrade, Peter Waterman, has recently walked on, on June 17, 2017, just before publication of this volume. His contribution to the series, and to my thinking—for forty-five years now—has been profound; and my debt to him is incalculable. To this I should add that he had always wanted me to bring out this book and its companion much earlier than this, and if necessary as 'quick and dirty' books rather than the very careful editing that has gone into them. I resisted, and have now lost the game; because I would have loved him to have seen these books in their final shape and to have had his comments on them. Who knew that you would suddenly go, and as fast as this … Travel well, my friend.

References

Taiaiake Alfred, 1999—*Peace, Power, Righteousness: An Indigenous Manifesto*. Don Mills, ON: Oxford University Press

Taiaiake Alfred, 2005—*Wasáse: Indigenous Pathways of Action and Freedom*. Peterborough: Broadview Press

Taiaiake Alfred and Jeff Corntassel, 2017—'Being Indigenous: Resurgences against Contemporary Colonialism', in Jai Sen, ed, 2017a—*The Movements of Movements, Part 1: What Makes Us Move?*. Volume 4 in the *Challenging Empires* series. New Delhi: OpenWord, and Oakland, CA: PM Press

Karen Armstrong, 2006—*The Great Transformation: The Beginning of Our Religious Traditions*. New York: Anchor Books

John Berger, 1977 [1972]—*Ways of Seeing*. London: British Broadcasting Corporation

Giuseppe Caruso, 2012—*Cosmopolitan Futures—Global Activism for a Just World*. Helsinki: Into Books, at http://www.into-ebooks.com/book/cosmopolitan_futures/ (Accessed April 2017)

Giuseppe Caruso, November 2013—'Justice, Equality and Conviviality: The World Social Forum's Cosmopolitan Vision', in *Interface*, vol 5 no 2, pp 78–97, at http://www.interfacejournal.net/2013/11/interface-volume-5-issue-2-tenth-issue-celebration/ (Accessed April 2017)

John Brown Childs, 2003a—*Transcommunality: From the Politics of Conversion to the Ethics of Respect*. Philadelphia: Temple University Press

Janet Conway, 2012—*Edges of Global Justice: The World Social Forum and Its 'Others'*. London and New York: Routledge

Lee Cormie, 2017a—'Re-Creating the World: Communities of Faith in the Struggles for Other Possible Worlds', in Jai Sen, ed, 2017a—*The Movements of Movements, Part 1: What Makes Us Move?*. Volume 4 in the *Challenging Empires* series. New Delhi: OpenWord, and Oakland, CA: PM Press

Lee Cormie, 2017b—'Another World Is Inevitable … but Which Other World?'. Afterword for Jai Sen, ed, 2017b—*The Movements of Movements, Part 2: Rethinking Our Dance*. Volume 5 in the *Challenging Empires* series. New Delhi: OpenWord, and Oakland, CA: PM Press

Laurence Cox, 2017—'"Learning to Be Loyal to Each Other": Conversations, Alliances, and Arguments in the Movements of Movements'. Afterword for Jai Sen, ed, 2017a—*The Movements of Movements, Part 1: What Makes Us Move?*. Volume 4 in the *Challenging Empires* series. New Delhi: OpenWord, and Oakland, CA: PM Press

Laurence Cox and Alf Gunvald Nilsen, 2014—*We Make Our Own History: Marxism and Social Movements in the Twilight of Neoliberalism*. London: Pluto

Anila Daulatzai, 2017—'Believing in Exclusion: The Problem of Secularism in Progressive Politics', in Jai Sen, ed, 2017b—*The Movements of Movements, Part 2: Rethinking Our Dance*. Volume 5 in the *Challenging Empires* series. New Delhi: OpenWord, and Oakland, CA: PM Press

Paul Divakar Namala, 2011—'Making Caste a Global Issue', in Jai Sen, ed, 2011a—*Interrogating Empires*, Book 2 in the *Are Other Worlds Possible?* series (New Delhi: OpenWord and Daanish Books), pp 140–147

André C Drainville, 2012—*A History of World Order and Resistance: The Making and Unmaking of Global Subjects*. London and New York: Routledge

André C Drainville, 2017—'Beyond *Altermondialisme*: Anti-Capitalist Dialectic of Presence', in Jai Sen, ed, 2017a—*The Movements of Movements, Part 1: What Makes Us Move?*. Volume 4 in the *Challenging Empires* series. New Delhi: OpenWord, and Oakland, CA: PM Press

Susan George and Fabrizio Sabelli, 1994—*Faith and Credit: The World Bank's Secular Empire*. London: Penguin Books

Eric Hobsbawm, 1962—*The Age of Revolution, 1789–1848*. London: Penguin

John Holloway, May 2002—'Beyond Power?', Chapter 3 in *Change the World Without Taking Power*, as published in *The Commoner* No 4, May 2002, at http://www.thecommoner.org (Accessed April 2017)

John Holloway, 2005 [2002]—*Change the World Without Taking Power*. London: Pluto Press

Chloé Keraghel, 2005—'Forum as *raga*', Chapter 13 in Jai Sen and Mayuri Saini, eds, January 2005—*Are Other Worlds Possible? Talking New Politics*, (New Delhi: Zubaan), pp 168–173

Alex Khasnabish, 2017—'Forward Dreaming: Zapatismo and the Radical Imagination', in Jai Sen, ed, 2017a—*The Movements of Movements, Part 1: What Makes Us Move?*. Volume 4 in the *Challenging Empires* series. New Delhi: OpenWord, and Oakland, CA: PM Press

Naomi Klein, 2004—'Reclaiming the Commons', in Tom Mertes, ed, 2004—*A Movement of Movements: Is Another World Really Possible?* (London: Verso), pp 219–229

Naomi Klein interviewed by Michelle Chihara for AlterNet, September 2002—'Naomi Klein Gets Global', on *AlterNet*, September 24 2002, at http://www.alternet.org/story/14175/naomi_klein_gets_global (Accessed April 2017)

Xochitl Leyva Solano, 2017—'Geopolitics of Knowledge and the Neo-Zapatista Social Movement Networks', in Jai Sen, ed, 2017a—*The Movements of Movements, Part 1: What Makes Us Move?*. Volume 4 in the *Challenging Empires* series. New Delhi: OpenWord, and Oakland, CA: PM Press

Tomás Mac Sheoin and Nicola Yeates, 2017—'The Anti-Globalisation Movement: Coalition and Division', in Jai Sen, ed, 2017b—*The Movements of Movements, Part*

2: Rethinking Our Dance. Volume 5 in the *Challenging Empires* series. New Delhi: OpenWord, and Oakland, CA: PM Press

Firoze Manji and Sokari Ekine, 2011—*African Awakenings: The Emerging Revolutions*. Cape Town, Dakar, Nairobi, and Oxford: Pambazuka Press

Roel Meijer, 2017—'Fighting for Another World: Yusuf al-'Uyairi's Conceptualisation of Praxis and Permanent Revolution', in Jai Sen, ed, 2017a—*The Movements of Movements, Part 1: What Makes Us Move?*. Volume 4 in the *Challenging Empires* series. New Delhi: OpenWord, and Oakland, CA: PM Press

Tom Mertes, ed, 2004—*A Movement of Movements: Is another world really possible?*. London: Verso

Matt Meyer and Oussenia Alidou, 2017—'The Power of Words: Reclaiming and Re-Imagining Revolution and Nonviolence', in Jai Sen, ed, 2017b—*The Movements of Movements, Part 2: Rethinking Our Dance*. Volume 5 in the *Challenging Empires* series. New Delhi: OpenWord, and Oakland, CA: PM Press

Notes from Nowhere, eds, 2003—*We Are Everywhere: The Irresistible Rise of Global Anti-Capitalism*. London / New York: Verso, at http://artactivism.members.gn.apc.org/stories.htm (Accessed April 2017)

Rodrigo Nunes, 2005b—'Nothing Is What Democracy Looks Like: Openness, Horizontality and the Movement of Movements', in David Harvie, Keir Milburn, Ben Trott, and David Watts, eds, 2005—*Shut Them Down! The G8, Gleneagles 2005 and the Movement of Movements*, pp 299–319 (Leeds: Dissent, and Brooklyn: Autonomedia), pp. 299–319, at http://www.shutthemdown.org/contents.html (Accessed April 2017)

OpenWord, 2017—'A Note on the *Challenging Empires* Series', in Jai Sen, ed, 2017a—*The Movements of Movements, Part 1: What Makes Us Move?*. Volume 4 in the *Challenging Empires* series. New Delhi: OpenWord, and Oakland, CA: PM Press

Geoffrey Pleyers, 2010—*Alter-Globalization: Becoming Actors in the Global Age*. Foreword by Alain Touraine. London: Polity Press

Karl Polanyi, 2001 [1944]—*The Great Transformation: The Political and Economic Origins of Our Time*. Boston: Beacon Press

Maia Ramnath, 2012—*Decolonizing Anarchism: An Anti-Authoritarian History of India's Liberation Struggle*. Oakland, CA: AK Press, and Washington, DC: Institute for Anarchist Studies

Emir Sader, 2017—'The Weakest Link? Neoliberalism in Latin America', in Jai Sen, ed, 2017a—*The Movements of Movements, Part 1: What Makes Us Move?*. Volume 4 in the *Challenging Empires* series. New Delhi: OpenWord, and Oakland, CA: PM Press

Jai Sen, January 2002a—'The World Social Forum—Some Concerns and Considerations for a WSF Process in India', January 5 2002, at http://www.choike.org/PDFs/concerns.pdf (Accessed April 2017). Subsequently published in: Jai Sen with Madhuresh Kumar, compilers, August 2003—*Are Other Worlds Possible? The Open Space Reader on the World Social Forum and Its Engagement with Empire*, (New Delhi), pp 198–206

Jai Sen, January 2002b—'Thinking Strategy: Some Suggestions for the World Social Forum's Strategic Perspective', at http://www.choike.org/PDFs/thinking.pdf (Accessed April 2017)

Jai Sen, January 2003c—'The Long March to Another World: Porto Alegre—Hyderabad—Porto Alegre: Reflections on the World Social Forum Process in India and Internationally. A Paper for Discussion'. 65 pp, plus Annexures.

Jai Sen, 2004c—'The Long March to Another World: Reflections of a Member of the WSF India Committee in 2002 on the First Year of the World Social Forum Process in India', in Jai Sen, Anita Anand, Arturo Escobar, and Peter Waterman, eds, 2004— *World Social Forum: Challenging Empires* (New Delhi: Viveka), pp 293–311, at http://www.choike.org/documentos/wsf_s409_jai.pdf (Accessed April 2017)

Jai Sen, November 2005—'Strategies and Cultures of Movement: Some Preliminary Thoughts, for Discussion'. Prepared for the first CACIM Consultation, Sanskriti Kendra, New Delhi, India. First draft, November 9 2005, 4 pp

Jai Sen, March 2006—'Understanding the World Social Forum: The WSF as an Emergent Learning Process—Notes on the Dynamics of Change', in *Mainstream* (New Delhi), March 25 2006, pp 9–24, at http://www.openspaceforum.net/twiki/tiki-download_file.php?fileId=34 (Accessed April 2017)

Jai Sen, January 2007—'The World Social Forum as an Emergent Learning Process', in *Futures*, vol 39 (2007), pp 505–522. Available through subscription at http://dx.doi.org/10.1016/j.futures.2006.10.006

Jai Sen, 2010b—'On Open Space: Explorations towards a Vocabulary of a More Open Politics', in *Antipode*, vol 42 no 4, 2010 (ISSN 0066-4812), pp 994–1018. Full original unedited version available at http://cacim.net/twiki/tiki-index.php?page=Publications (Accessed April 2017)

Jai Sen, January 2011a—'Confronting the Consequences of Climate Change: Conflict, War, Resistance, and Movement in the Coming Half Century'. Event Outline for Workshop being organised on February 9 at the World Social Forum in Dakar, Senegal, February 6–11 2011, on behalf of CACIM—Critical Action: Centre in Movement, ABN—African Biodiversity Network, Climate SOS, GGJ—Grassroots Global Justice Alliance, IEN—Indigenous Environmental Network, and NFFPFW—National Forum of Forest People and Forest Workers, at http://cacim.net/twiki/tiki-index.php?page=CACIM+at+WSF+2011 (Accessed April 2017)

Jai Sen, January 2011c—'Towards Critical Explorations of Worlds in Movement'. An Introduction to Jai Sen and Peter Waterman, eds, February 2011— *World Social Forum: Critical Explorations—A Sampler* to Volume 3 in the *Challenging Empires* series. New Delhi: OpenWord

Jai Sen, 2011a—'Understanding the World: Interrogating Empire and Power'. Introduction to Jai Sen, ed, 2011a—*Interrogating Empires*, Book 2 in the *Are Other Worlds Possible?* series (New Delhi: OpenWord and Daanish Books), pp 12–33

Jai Sen, 2012b—'Another World Is Possible!': Critical Explorations of the World Social Forum and the Dreams it Has Inspired'. Introduction to Jai Sen and Peter Waterman, eds, 2012—*World Social Forum: Critical Explorations*. Volume 3 in the *Challenging Empires* series. New Delhi: OpenWord

Jai Sen, 2012c—'Towards Understanding the World Social Forum: Three Proposals', in Jai Sen and Peter Waterman, eds, 2011a—*World Social Forum: Critical Explorations*. Volume 3 in the *Challenging Empires* series. New Delhi: OpenWord

Jai Sen, 2012e—'Preface' to André C Drainville, 2012—*A History of World Order and Resistance: The making and unmaking of global subjects*. London and New York: Routledge

Jai Sen, Anita Anand, Arturo Escobar, and Peter Waterman, eds, 2004—*World Social Forum: Challenging Empires*. New Delhi: Viveka. Slightly reduced version available at http://www.openspaceforum.net/twiki/tiki-index.php?page=WSFChallengingEmpires2004 and at http://www.choike.org/nuevo_eng/informes/1557.html (Both accessed April 2017)

Jai Sen and Peter Waterman, eds, 2009—*World Social Forum: Challenging Empires*, updated second edition, Montréal: Black Rose Books.

Jai Sen and Peter Waterman, eds, February 2011—*World Social Forum: Critical Explorations—A Sampler* to Volume 3 in the *Challenging Empires* series. New Delhi: OpenWord

Jai Sen and Peter Waterman, eds, 2012—*World Social Forum: Critical Explorations.* Volume 3 in the *Challenging Empires* series. New Delhi: OpenWord

Rupert Sheldrake, February 2005—'Morphic Resonance and Morphic Fields: An Introduction', at http://www.sheldrake.org/Articles&Papers/papers/morphic/morphic_intro.html (Accessed April 2017)

David A Snow and Robert D Benford, 1988b—'Ideology, Frame Resonance, and Participant Mobilization', in Bert Klandermans, Hanspeter Kriesi, and Sidney Tarrow, eds, 1988—*From Structure to Action: Social Movement Participation across Cultures.* Greenwich, CT: JAI Press

Sidney Tarrow, 1992—'Mentalities, Political Cultures, and Collective Action Frames: Constructing Meaning through Action', Chapter 8 in Aldon D Morris and Carol McClurg Mueller, eds, 1992—*Frontiers in Social Movement Theory* (New Haven, CT: Yale University Press), pp 174–202

John F C Turner, 1970—'Housing as a Verb', in John F C Turner and Robert Fichter, eds, 1970—*Freedom to Build.* New York: Macmillan

Hilary Wainwright, 2004—'The Forum as Jazz', foreword to Jai Sen, Anita Anand, Arturo Escobar, and Peter Waterman, eds, 2004—*World Social Forum: Challenging Empires* (New Delhi: Viveka), pp xvii–xx

Harsha Walia, 2013—*Undoing Border Imperialism.* Oakland: AK Press and IAS (Institute for Anarchist Studies)

Chico Whitaker, 2004—'The WSF as Open Space', in Jai Sen, Anita Anand, Arturo Escobar, and Peter Waterman, eds, 2004—*World Social Forum: Challenging Empires* (New Delhi: Viveka), pp 111–121, at http://www.choike.org/nuevo_eng/informes/1557.html (Accessed April 2017)

Notes

1. I want to acknowledge, right from the outset of this essay, my profound debt to so many others for the conversations and exchanges we have had in the course of compiling these books, and that have in many ways inspired me and shaped the thoughts that I try and express here in this Introduction. In particular, I warmly thank Lee Cormie, Madhuresh, Matt Meyer, and Peter Waterman, and more recently, Laurence Cox. In addition, I also thank all the contributors to this book and its companion volume *The Movements of Movements, Part 2: Rethinking Our Dance* for the great privilege of working with them on their contributions to these books, for all that I have learned from their writings and their reflections, and for the role—the many

roles—that their work and their thoughts, individually and collectively, have played in pushing my own thoughts forward and for inspiring me in so many ways. It is not at all an overstatement to say that I cannot thank them enough.

2. *Shakti*, a term in Sanskrit, Hindi, and other Indian languages, means power or empowerment, but referring to primordial cosmic energy. See http://en.wikipedia.org/wiki/Shakti.

3. Sen, November 2005.

4. I should clarify that I am referring here not to the great work by Karl Polanyi of this name (*The Great Transformation: The Political and Economic Origins of Our Time*; Polanyi 2001 [1944]), but to another work with the same primary title, by Karen Armstrong, *The Great Transformation: The Beginning of Our Religious Traditions* (Armstrong 2006).

5. For the idea of using music as a metaphor to understand social movement—in this case, the World Social Forum—see Wainwright 2004 and Keraghel 2005. But here I try to take the next step of dancing with the essays that we collected for the book and of composing (or attempting to compose!) a larger composition, with its own harmonies, rhythms, and riffs.

6. For information on the *Challenging Empires* series, see the Note in this book from the original publisher, OpenWord, 'A Note on the *Challenging Empires* Series'.

7. I use the term 'we' variously to refer both to the initial team responsible for conceiving this book in its original form as a follow-up to the earlier volumes in the *Challenging Empires* series (see OpenWord's Note on the *Challenging Empires* series), Peter Waterman and myself, and also to the broader team that came together over time, in different combinations at different times, to think out this book: In particular, Madhuresh at CACIM and Nishant at OpenWord. But ultimately I have to take responsibility for what the books are now. Peter Waterman walked on on June 17, 2017. For more details, see the end of this Introduction, and his bio.

8. I use the term 'settler' here as it is used in certain but not all contexts of colonisation, as referring to those who come later to a land and 'settle' in and on it, usually the first waves displacing and sometimes decimating the indigenous populations that had lived there for hundreds and sometimes thousands of years prior. See http://en.wikipedia.org/wiki/Settler.

This historical situation has however become a lot more complicated over the past century or so in structural terms, and all the more during the post-colonial period from the 1950s onwards and then since the 1980s and the ravages of neoliberalism, where structurally oppressed and often internally colonised peoples from other parts of the world, such as refugees, have in certain contexts become the major immigrants. And where the second generation—the children—of such immigrants are today asking themselves, can and should they also be categorised—together with the original colonisers—as 'settlers'? Is that how they see themselves? And most importantly, how should they relate with the indigenous peoples of their new home? (For an example of such reflection, see 'South Asians in Solidarity with Idle No More', at https://www.facebook.com/nishant.upadhyay.18/posts/10100389033191971?notif_t=like).

9. For details on the contributors to this ebook, see 'Notes on the Contributors'.

10. Cox and Nilsen 2014.

11. Cox 2017.

12. Alfred and Corntassel 2017.

13. Cormie 2017.

14. For a very interesting discussion of this crucial question, see John Holloway's book *Change the World Without Taking Power* (Holloway 2005), and especially Chapter 3, 'Beyond Power' (Holloway, May 2002). Following Holloway, I also tried engaging with this question in an introduction to an earlier book, *Interrogating Empires* (Sen 2011a).

15. Since little has changed in my life since the time when I first wrote these words, this section of the Introduction is a somewhat revised version of a similar note in the Introduction to an earlier book I edited, *World Social Forum: Critical Explorations* (Sen and Waterman, eds, 2012).

16. For those interested, most of my more recent work—since about 2002—has been with and through CACIM, [the India Institute for] Critical Action: Centre in Movement.

17. Throughout this period, I was a member of Unnayan (meaning 'development' in Bengali, in the sense of 'unfolding, self-realisation'), a social action group in Calcutta-then-Kolkata that I helped form in 1977. And through Unnayan, I helped build, first the Chhinnamul Sramajibi Adhikar Samiti ('Organisation for the Rights of Uprooted Labouring People'), a mass organisation in Calcutta, and then the NCHR—the National Campaign for Housing Rights—an all-India platform for a wide range of social movements, trade unions, and political parties and entities for campaigning to make a place to live in security and dignity a Fundamental Right. In the course of this, and of the kind of organisation Unnayan was and the work it did, I also came to be closely associated with several other struggles and campaigns for social justice in different parts of India.

18. Sen, January 2002a and January 2002b.

19. Summarised briefly, most people on the WSF India organising body became—perhaps for understandable reasons—increasingly interested in getting the event done, whereas I was as (and even more) concerned with the social and political potentials of the organising process, and in particular with addressing the potentials—and contradictions—of organising something like the WSF in India. I had earlier written on this (Sen, January 2002a and 2002b), and agreement on this—addressing these concerns—was why I had agreed to join the organising body. Although there was some agreement with this approach among some members of the WSF India Organising Committee, the organising process came to be progressively dominated by one big organisation, and when the experience of the process became increasingly difficult, and the tragedy occurred in my life, I dropped out, and then came back to the WSF later but now working from outside. I reflected on this experience in Sen, January 2003c, which was published in edited form as Sen 2004c.

20. Personal communication.

21. Along with Lee Cormie, I am here using the terms 'chaotic' and 'chaos' not in its popular sense of randomness or with an apparent lack of intelligible pattern or combination, but in the way the term is used in emerging theory in mathematics and physics and now also social sciences that deals with the behaviour of nonlinear dynamical systems, as a particular open-ended form of order. Similarly, the term

'emergent' also comes from new theory in biology, which is now being applied by some to explain social behaviour; processes that learn from what they do, and through this progressively develop ('emerge') into new forms. For a breakthrough discussion of the World Social Forum in terms of emergence, see Escobar 2004; and for something that tries to build on Escobar's work, see Sen 2007 and Sen 2012c.

22.   Several paragraphs in this section are based on the Introduction to the Sampler to the earlier book that I co-edited, (as above, Sen and Waterman, eds, February 2011). Since the Sampler, in the form of a CD, was circulated only in limited numbers at the World Social Forum held in Dakar, Senegal, in 2011, and not in any other form, the Introduction there (Sen, January 2011c) remained all-but-unpublished. I am therefore taking the liberty here of drawing extensively from that essay. Just as a footnote, I also completely re-wrote the Introduction for the final version of that book, which was published in 2012 (Sen 2012b).

23.   Just as one example among many, at last count more than sixty million women, men, and children have been forcibly uprooted, 'displaced', and discarded—and devastated—in supposedly socialist and democratic India since the country gained independence in 1947, in the name of 'development' and 'democracy'. This number is greater than the populations of most countries in the world. Millions more continue to be displaced, today. See the essay by Roma and Ashok Choudhary in this book, for just one aspect of this disaster (Roma and Choudhary 2017).

24.   I am indebted to my comrade and fellow traveller Ashok Choudhary, of the NFFPFW (National Forum of Forest People and Forest Workers) and now the AIUFWP (All India Union of Forest Working People) in India, for helping me to begin to see this.

25.   Hobsbawm 1962, on 'The Age of Revolution'.

26.   Walia 2013. See also http://www.nooneisillegal.org/ and http://en.wikipedia.org/ wiki/No_one_is_illegal. At the time of writing (October 2015), the critical situation in and around Europe—which is challenging the very core of the modern European project, and with its waves of resonance across the North Atlantic North—is just one more indication of the enormous significance of this issue.

27.   See, for instance, the work of Taiaiake Alfred, a contributor to this book, such as in Alfred 1999; and also as discussed in one of his two contributions to this book, Alfred and Corntassel 2017.

28.   See, for instance, Divakar Namala 2011, on 'Making Caste a Global Issue'.

29.   Sen, January 2011a.

30.   Sen 2012c.

31.   I would like here to express my thanks to my daughter Jayita Sen for helping me think through this point and for introducing me to the biological terms and concepts 'angiogenic' and 'angiogenesis'—which I think express and address what I am trying to say here—and for explaining them to me.

32.   Sen, March 2006; Sen, January 2007; also in Sen 2012c.

33.   Sheldrake, February 2005.

34.   Sen, March 2006; Sen, January 2007.

35.   Tarrow 1992, quoting Snow and Benford 1988.

36.   Drainville 2012, and where I have also drawn in this paragraph from my preface to that book, Sen 2012e.

37.   Cormie 2017.

38. See, for instance, George and Sabelli 1994.
39. http://www.taichitoronto.ca/Lao%20Tzu%20Taoism%20and%20T%27ai%20Chi. htm. I have however also found an interesting and slightly different statement of this maxim: "The stillness in stillness is not real stillness. Only when there is stillness in movement does the Universal Rhythm manifest itself"; see http://www. knightflowermartialarts.com/Work/kijujutsu.html.
40. http://www.visualthesaurus.com/. Image from the *Visual Thesaurus* (http://www. visualthesaurus.com). Copyright ©1998–2014 Thinkmap, Inc. All rights reserved. Ed: I warmly thank Thinkmap Inc for their permission to reprint this image.
41. Source: *Collins World English Dictionary—Complete & Unabridged 10th Edition* 2009 © William Collins Sons & Co. Ltd. 1979, 1986 © HarperCollins Publishers 1998, 2000, 2003, 2005, 2006, 2007, 2009.
42. See, for instance, Whitaker 2004 (which is an edited version of an essay written in 2003), and then a decade later, Caruso 2012, and Caruso, November 2013.
43. Mertes, ed, 2004.
44. For more details on CACIM's engagement with the WSF, see http://www.cacim.net/ twiki/tiki-index.php?page=WSF and also http://www.cacim.net/twiki/tiki-index. php?page=Publications; and for our major publications, also OpenWord.
45. Sen and Waterman, eds, 2012.
46. Naomi Klein perhaps first used this term in 2002; see Naomi Klein interviewed by Michelle Chihara for AlterNet, September 2002. For more discussion of the movement as it emerged, see Klein 2004; Mertes, ed, 2004; Notes from Nowhere, eds, 2003; Pleyers 2010; and for a very different view on the phenomenon, Drainville 2012, and also André Drainville's essay in this book (Drainville 2017).
47. I would like to warmly acknowledge here my introduction to this conceptual shift, first by reading the seminal work of John Turner on housing back in the 1970s, and then by the great privilege of getting to know John and of working closely with him, through to the early 80s. In particular, see John F C Turner 1970—'Housing as a Verb'. This shift that I made in how to see things was also greatly liberated, and further inspired, by the equally seminal work of John Berger, for instance his book *Ways of Seeing* (Berger 1977 [1972]).
48. Indeed, if we for instance look at the essay in the companion volume to this book by Tomás Mac Sheoin and Nicola Yeates, they argue that "Overall, then, there is no one unitary AGM to be described, and diversity is the essence of the AGM. It is highly diverse in composition, organisational features, targets, and tactics; it expresses itself at local, national, regional, and global levels in very different ways"; and that even in the case of the 'AGM' itself, "the AGM has been able to maintain its unity through inclusiveness" and that "the development of what della Porta calls 'tolerant identities': "The self-definition as a 'movement of movements' … emphasises the positive aspects of heterogen[eity]" (Mac Sheoin and Yeates 2017).
49. Kalouche and Mielants 2016; McNally 2016; and Cormie 2016.
50. Though I use this phrase in this Introduction, I remain uncomfortable with it for obvious enough reasons; see the opening sections of the essay in this book by Roel Meijer for a rich discussion of this world of movement (Meijer 2017).

51. As above, for information on the *Challenging Empires* series see the Note in this book from the original publisher, OpenWord, 'A Note on the *Challenging Empires* Series'.

52. I use this term 'transcommunal' in the sense developed by John Brown Childs in his wonderful book *Transcommunality: From the Politics of Conversion to the Ethics of Respect* (Childs 2003). See also http://transcommunality.org/.

53. https://en.wikipedia.org/wiki/Capoeira.

54. I discuss our book project in more detail in my Introduction to the book before this in the *Challenging Empires* series, *World Social Forum: Critical Explorations*. See Sen 2012b.

55. Sen, Anand, Escobar, and Waterman, eds, 2004, and Sen and Waterman, eds, 2009.

56. "The Tunisian Revolution, also known as the Jasmine Revolution, was an intensive campaign of civil resistance, including a series of street demonstrations taking place in Tunisia. The events began on 18 December 2010 and led to the ousting of longtime President Zine El Abidine Ben Ali in January 2011". For one summary, see http://en.wikipedia.org/wiki/Tunisian_Revolution.

57. http://en.wikipedia.org/wiki/Egyptian_Revolution_of_2011.

58. As mentioned above, *World Social Forum: Critical Explorations* (Sen and Waterman, eds, 2012).

59. http://en.wikipedia.org/wiki/Naxalite.

60. Even though we didn't manage to include an essay specifically on this movement, we are privileged to have an essay within this book that gives some of that history and comments on its contemporary form. For a critical view on current resonance of the Naxalite movement, see the essay by Roma and Ashok Choudhary (Roma and Choudhary 2017).

61. See the essays in this book by Alex Khasnabish (Khasnabish 2017) and by Xochitl Leyva Solano (Leyva Solano 2017) for discussions of Zapatismo.

62. See the book by Firoze Manji and Sokari Ekine, *African Awakenings: The Emerging Revolutions* (Manji and Ekine, 2011).

63. For a summary discussion, see the essay by Emir Sader in this book (Sader 2017).

64. Sen 2010b, citing Nunes 2005b.

65. Again referring to the Mac Sheoin and Yeates essay in the accompanying volume to this book, it becomes quickly clear from the survey they do, and from the evidence they cite, that aside from the reality of the diversity and plurality that they stress the 'anti-globalisation movement' that they analyse largely took place only in the North (Mac Sheoin and Yeates 2017).

66. Ramnath 2012.

67. Daulatzai 2017.

68. Cormie 2017.

69. For critical discussions of such issues within the World Social Forum and the global justice movements, see the essay by Anila Daulatzai in the accompanying volume to this book (Daulatzai 2017), and the book by Janet Conway (Conway 2012).

70. I want to take the liberty of adding a footnote here. While two of the essays are edited versions of already published essays (by James Toth and Roel Meijer), and two were specially written for us (by François Houtart and Lee Cormie), it was perhaps precisely my own lack of knowledge of the subject that led me to demand

the most of these four authors in particular in terms of revising and editing their essays, in order to make their essays as comprehensible as possible to as wide an audience as possible. While this characterisation may not be literally true—because I have to confess to also being pretty demanding of several other authors!—I want to very specially thank each of them for their patience in putting up with me, and for what I believe is the resulting comprehensibility of their essays for those of who are reading about such movements in depth for the first time. As a consequence of this, these four essays—individually and collectively—read so richly in relation to so many other essays in this collection, and in different ways.

71.   Sen and Waterman, eds, 2012.
72.   Meyer and Alidou 2017.

1
MOVEMENTSCAPES

WORKERS

POPULAR
HOPE
SIX
YET
MILLIONS
NEOLIBERAL
ACTIVISTS
WOMEN
REVOLT
WTO
HALF
POLITICAL
BANK
CONTROL
STRUGGLE
FIRST
STUDENTS
SEATTLE
PROTESTS
EAST
EVEN
STUDENT
RIGHT
SOMETHING
VICTORY
EVERY
CAPITALISM
DEMOCRACY
NOVEMBER
UNIVERSITY
COCHABAMBA
OAXACA
DAY
WAR
STATE
BEGAN
POLITICS
DESPITE
SOLIDARITY
ACTION
ECONOMIC
RESISTANCE
IMF
GREAT
THOUSANDS
DECEMBER
MONTHS
RADICAL
LAUNCHED
OCCUPIED
AROUND
HELD
ELITES
JOINED
PEOPLES
LATER
MILITANT
MANY
POLICE
MOVEMENTS
ALSO
POWER
ORGANISATIONS
DELEGATES
COURSE
MARCH
YOUTH
OPPOSITION
PROTESTERS
POWERFUL
MILLION
THROUGHOUT
YOUNG
KOREA
EZLN
COUNTRIES
TURNED
GENERAL
YEAR
STRIKE
HIGH
ANOTHER
STREETS
MASS
TOOK
DEMOCRATIC
MEXICO
SOUTH
SOCIETY
CONTINUED
LABOUR
EARLY
TIME
PEOPLE
FREE
ZAPATISTA
FRENCH
ASIAN
CITY
CAMPAIGN
SCHOOL
CLASS
PRIVATISATION
HISTORY
REVOLUTION
BOLIVIA
OPPRESSED
MAY
BATTLE
POOR
MAJOR
PER
WORLD
GOVERNMENT
TWO
DEMONSTRATIONS
JANUARY
ASSEMBLIES
PROTEST
MOVEMENT
FRANCE
EVENTS
WATER
GAS
WITHOUT
NEW
JUSTICE
TRADE
YEARS
ONE
MUCH
GLOBAL
BILLION
UNION
PARIS
PUBLIC
STRUGGLES
ZAPATISTAS
LIKE
NORTH
INDIGENOUS
GLOBALISATION
SOCIAL
SOON
LEADERS
REPRESSION
STRIKES
CENTRE
POSSIBLE

From the Mountains of Chiapas to the Streets of Seattle:
This Is What Democracy Looks Like[1]
David McNally

A new lie is sold to us as history. The lie about the defeat of hope, the lie about the defeat of dignity, the lie about the defeat of humanity.
—From the 'First Declaration for Humanity and Against Neoliberalism', by the
Zapatista Army of National Liberation, January 1996

When History Moves

When history moves—really moves, that is—it does so in great convulsive jolts. Suddenly, the predictable pace of everyday life is disrupted and world-shaking events occur. At such moments, the downtrodden may rise from their knees to claim some control over their lives and history moves onto a stage where the powerful no longer write all the lines. With such shifts in the tectonic plates of political life, an era of protest, resistance, and change begins. At other times, the rich and powerful of the world gather their forces to clamp down on the oppressed of the world. Then begins an era of repression, empire, and war.

History also knows moments of great tension when both trends are simultaneously at work. We find ourselves at precisely such a moment. In the mid-1990s, when the Zapatista rebellion in southern Mexico kick-started a wave of global justice movements, we entered an era of protest and resistance—one that largely continues today in countries like Bolivia. Then, in September 2001, another great historic shift occurred as the US government cynically manipulated the terrible attacks on the Twin Towers in New York to launch war and occupation against Afghanistan and Iraq. We live at present at the complex intersection of these events—a growing revolt against global injustice, on the one hand, and an aggressive drive toward empire and war, on the other.

As a result, we also live amidst great hope and debilitating despair. Much of the time, particularly for those of us who live in the North, it is the latter sentiment that dominates public life. These are, after all, nasty and brutal times. War machines march across Iraq and Afghanistan. Haiti and Palestine are occupied by invading armies. Human rights are in retreat almost everywhere, most notably in Europe and North America, where governments systematically violate civil freedoms in the name of a 'war on terror'. Meanwhile, a variety of religious fundamentalisms—Christian, Hindu, Jewish, and Muslim—nourish themselves on bigotry and repression. Often it seems as if our entire world is governed by intolerance and oppression.

Yet, there is something radically incomplete about such a picture. Like so many interpretations of the world in which we live, it forgets and conceals the real movements of resistance, the heroic struggles for global justice, which take place every day across this planet. In the midst of poverty and violence, something else, something better and more hopeful, is also at work. The dream of a better world can regularly be found in the streets, marching, chanting, building blockades, and challenging oppression. These movements, as they always do, stir hope around the globe.

Hope rises up with each revolt of the downtrodden: The 40,000 indigenous peoples who revolted against the government in Quito, Ecuador (January 15–22 2000); the hundreds of thousands who joined the general strike against electricity privatisation in Puerto Rico during the same month; the workers and indigenous peoples whose revolt overturned water privatisation in Cochabamba, Bolivia (April 2000); the one million South African workers who held a one-day strike against poverty (May 11 2000); the Nigerian workers who have waged half a dozen mass strikes against fuel and transport hikes in the last five years; the millions of Indian workers who struck against 'globalisation, privatisation, and liberali-sation' (April 2001); the thousands of students and poor people in Papua New Guinea who revolted against their government's capitulation to the International Monetary Fund (IMF) in June 2001; the one million courageous workers who took strike action in Colombia during the same month to protest the 'neoliberal model' imposed by the IMF; the 200,000 who faced the riot police in Genoa, Italy (July 20–22 2001); the millions of workers in South Africa who launched a three-day general strike against privatisation (August–September 2001); the half million poor and indigenous people who seized control of the capitol city, La Paz, on two different occasions in 2005 and 2006 to demand public control of oil and natural gas; the million and a half students, workers, and unemployed youth who successfully shut down Paris and other French cities in early 2006 to force with-drawal of legislation that would have made it much easier for employers to fire young workers; and the one million South Koreans—responding to a campaign initiated by high school students—who marched with candles on June 10 2008 to protest a Free Trade Agreement with the United States.

All these events, and many others over recent history,[2] are stirring evidence that, in the face of violence and brutality, oppressed people around the world regularly re-emerge as conscious makers of history. For the elites in North America and Western Europe, the first great shock, the first recent recognition that they couldn't have everything their own way, came in late fall of 1999 when mass protests in Seattle shut down the Millennium Round meetings of the World Trade Organization (WTO). Having been lulled by the success of the neoliberal juggernaut and the claim, made triumphantly in 1989 by US State Department functionary Francis Fukuyama, that we had arrived at the permanent victory of capitalism and 'the end of history',[3] global elites were thrown into a state of 'shock and surprise' by the Seattle protests, to use the words of the Canadian Security Intelligence Service (CSIS).[4] Despite acts of brutality by riot police wielding tear gas and pepper spray, and despite mass arrests and the declaration of a state of emergency, protesters stared down the authorities. In the process they publicly humiliated the political leaders associated with the WTO and served notice that a militant new movement might be in the making.

At least until the terror attacks of September 11 2001, the global justice movement was winning key battles for public opinion, even in the North. And in parts of the South, it has continued to do so. *The Economist* magazine, one of Britain's major voices of ruling class opinion, suggested earlier that year that "the anti-globalisation movement is unlikely to fade quickly", and that "[t]he demonstrators are ... succeeding better than might have been expected in the court of public opinion".[5] Similarly, writing about the 1999–2001 wave of global justice protests, a columnist for *Fortune* magazine bluntly opined in 2000 that "the movement appears to have legs".[6] The CSIS report mentioned above—issued in 2000 with the intriguing title, 'Anti-Globalisation: A Spreading Phenomenon'—suggested the same.[7] And closer to the mainstream, a cover article in the Canadian weekly magazine *Maclean's* mused in June 2001 that we might be witnessing the emergence of a 'new New Left'.[8]

This is why the September 11 attacks in the US came as a godsend for ruling classes. Deliberately promoting fear and panic within the public, Western governments introduced draconian legislation authorising indefinite detention without charges, secret trials, random deportations, and gulag-style prisons. Dissent was criminalised, civil rights curtailed.

Without a doubt, these developments seriously damaged protest politics and ended talk of a new left, at least in the North, for the time being. But they did not stop struggles for global justice. Indeed, after something of a pause in many parts of the world, such struggles seem to be resurging today.

But before turning to the latest developments, it will be helpful to return to the moment when a new wave of global justice protests first announced itself in dramatic style.

The Mountains Roared and the Zapatistas Launched a Movement

Although few realised it at the time, a new left of sorts was in fact launched on January 1 1994 in the form of a global justice movement. That day saw two momentous events. First, the North American Free Trade Agreement (NAFTA) became law in Canada, Mexico, and the United States, inaugurating the globalisation regime throughout the region.[9] Second, and more important, a hitherto-unknown guerrilla movement called the Zapatista Army of National Liberation (EZLN) occupied the town of San Cristóbal de las Casas, the old colonial capital of the Mexican state of Chiapas, declaring that NAFTA was a 'death sentence' for indigenous peoples and peasants throughout Mexico.[10]

Central to the Zapatista uprising was opposition to the repeal of Article 27 of the Mexican constitution, which preserved rights of indigenous peoples to their communal lands, the *ejidos*. The Mexican government repealed this article in preparation for NAFTA. In so doing, they demonstrated the unrelenting hostility of neoliberalism to all things communal.[11] And in taking their stand on this issue, the EZLN signalled that its movement would defend the commons against commodification, a theme that has emerged repeatedly in the neoliberal era, perhaps nowhere more forcefully than in Bolivia, to which I turn later in this article.

From the start, the Zapatista insurgents denounced Mexico's elites for their commitment to policies that benefit only the rich:

> They don't care that we have nothing, absolutely nothing, not even a roof over our heads, no land, no work, no health care, no food or education, not the right to freely and democratically elect our political representatives, nor independence from foreigners. ... We declare that we will not stop fighting until the basic demands of our people have been met, by forming a government for our country that is free and democratic.[12]

On the face of it, these were not particularly new words—echoing, as they did, the rhetoric of the American Revolution of 1776 or the French Revolution of 1789. But in the context of the neoliberal offensive embodied in NAFTA, they were radical, and a virtual declaration of war. Rather than appeal to the elites to behave righteously, the Zapatistas called on all the oppressed—indigenous peoples, poor peasants, women, and rural and urban workers—to organise themselves for struggle. Proclaiming their solidarity with working-class movements, for instance, the EZLN explained, "[w]e, the insurgent combatants, use the colours of red and black in our uniform, symbols of the working people in their strike struggles".[13]

And the independent workers' movements of Mexico responded in kind. A week later, on January 7 1994, tens of thousands of urban workers demonstrated their opposition to the military siege against the EZLN in the Lacandon jungle. Five days later, workers and students marched in massive numbers to the centre of Mexico City to demand an end to the government's offensive against indigenous peoples. Electrical workers, teachers, autoworkers, healthcare, and transportation workers all held meetings to oppose the government's war in Chiapas and its privatisation policies. By early 1995, a new independent workers' movement, the *Intersindical,* had been formed, uniting democratic unions, rank-and-file caucuses of the corrupt 'official' unions, workers' cooperatives, parties of the left, and community organisations. Later, when 1,111 indigenous leaders arrived in

Mexico City as part of a Zapatista march in September 1997, they were greeted by half a million cheering people, the vast majority militant workers.[14]

The Zapatistas did more than just galvanise support in Mexico. Their inspiring communiqués resonated with activists around the world. They came to represent a renewal of hope. In the face of unbridled, triumphant, naked capitalism, the EZLN had raised up the banner of resistance. They had brazenly announced that it is the oppressed of the world that represent democracy—not the rich men (and a few women) shuttled to directors' meetings and global conferences in limousines.

At a time when capitalist globalisation was declared the salvation of humankind, the EZLN vividly challenged the orthodoxy promoted by the press and politicians everywhere. They reclaimed words like freedom, democracy, and prosperity from the globalisers, and replaced them with words like crime and misery:

> During the last years, the power of money has presented a new mask over its criminal face. ...

> A new world war is waged, but now against the entire humanity. As in all wars, what is being sought is a new distribution of the world.

> By the name of 'globalisation' they call this war which assassinates and forgets. The new distribution of the world consists in concentrating power in power and misery in misery. ...

> Instead of humanity, it offers us stock market indexes, instead of dignity it offers us globalisation of misery.[15]

Of course, not everyone who took to the streets to protest a globalising capitalism had encountered the Zapatistas. But their spirit—the spirit of protest, resistance, freedom, and democracy—spread from one corner of the world to another. And so too did the conviction that, despite their pious phrases, what our rulers are offering us is little more than 'globalization of misery'.[16]

Given the echoes of the French Revolution in Zapatista declarations, it is perhaps fitting that the next great explosion against globalisation came in France. That nation, after all, is the land of European revolution, having given birth to the continent's most profound revolutionary experience of the eighteenth century, to another revolution in 1830, to two great revolutionary uprisings in February and June of 1848, to the first (though short-lived) workers' government in history, the Paris Commune of 1871, and to the great modern revolt of students and workers in May of 1968.

France 1995: "Take to the streets, before they throw us into them!"

While the French newspaper *Le Monde* may have exaggerated in describing the events that took place in France in December 1995 as "the first revolt against globalisation",[17] it is probably fair to say that these were the first mass strikes against the globalisation agenda.

The wave of struggle that peaked in December 1995 had actually started with youth and student protests more than a year earlier. Only a matter of weeks after the Zapatistas occupied San Cristóbal de las Casas, tens of thousands of young people throughout France—high school and university students, young workers, and the unemployed—launched school strikes and mass demonstrations against the government's plans to lower the minimum wage for those under twenty-five. Banners at demonstrations urged students to "Take to the streets, before they throw us into them!". These militant youth mobilisations forced the government to backtrack. But the most impressive actions were yet to come.

The heat began to rise in early October 1995 with an enormous strike by five million public sector workers against legislation to freeze their wages. This was followed by a nation-wide strike by university students protesting overcrowded classrooms and libraries, deteriorating facilities, and poor job prospects for graduates. Unlike bureaucratic mass actions where students or workers protest for a day or two and then go back to work and school when instructed to do so, the student strikes were highly democratic, participatory, and sustained. More than 60 campuses were occupied by student protesters, some of whom took their university presidents hostage. Student strikers held regular general assemblies which democratically decided upon tactics; the assemblies also elected delegates to a national student strike coordinating committee. Street demonstrations were held every day, sometimes on a rotating round-the-clock basis, alongside occasional bouts of streetfighting with police.[18]

In late November, the students were joined by millions of workers protesting the government's introduction of a major neoliberal reform programme, known as the Juppé plan, after the prime minister who introduced it, Alain Juppé. This plan involved $12 billion in cuts to healthcare, family allowances, and pensions; privatisation of France Telecom and the public railway company, SNCF; closure of whole sections of the rail system (and layoffs of thousands of workers); and a 2 per cent hike in the regressive value-added sales tax.

To protest the programme, two major union federations called for twenty-four-hour strikes on November 24 and 28. When one million workers struck on the 24th itself, rail workers decided to stay out on indefinite strike action. They also persuaded other workers to join them. Postal and transit workers soon took up their call. And the movement kept growing. Nurses, teachers, sanitation workers, telephone operators, airport maintenance staff, autoworkers, and many others joined the action. Virtually the whole public sector was paralysed.

What is remarkable is that despite the disruption of public services, the strikers received huge support: A remarkable two-thirds of people polled in France favoured a general strike to defeat the Juppé plan. Soon, students and workers began to organise together, planning common marches and protest actions. Things peaked in early December with two-and-a-half million workers on strike and an estimated two million people marching in three hundred demonstrations across the country. In a wonderful display of solidarity, a rally of 100,000 in Marseilles was led by unemployed workers.

At the mass demonstrations, students mixed with workers, and street performers turned out to add a festive air to the events. Homeless people and immigrant workers played central roles in the burgeoning movement. The very character of the working class seemed to be getting transformed in the process. As one commentator put it:

> There were young and old workers, black workers, women workers, white and 'grey' collar workers, university and college-educated workers, and so on. There they all were in the streets of every city, town, and village of France, headed up by the railworkers, chanting, "tous ensemble, tous ensemble!" ("everyone together, everyone together!").[19]

As the movement grew and the radicalisation deepened, solidarity blossomed, transforming people's sense of themselves. At night, striking Paris bus drivers took out buses to drive homeless people to shelters, their vehicles adorned with banners exclaiming, "Bus drivers in solidarity with the most dispossessed layers of the population".

The women's movement too came back to life, mobilising 40,000 people—its largest action in years—on November 25 in an action dedicated, among other things, to the defence of abortion rights.

This amazing outpouring of solidarity took even the participants by surprise. They began to experience themselves as social beings, members of a real human community, and not as atomised, passive consumers of the products of capitalism. As one sociologist observed, "people are surprised to find themselves expressing a spontaneous solidarity in the streets and are reminded that they belong to a social entity whose only objective is not the production and consumption of merchandise".[20]

Faced with such formidable opposition, Juppé blinked, reversing cuts to the rail system and pledging more funds for universities. At that moment, rather than push for complete victory by toppling the government and the whole of its programme, the trade union officials and some student leaders agreed to a compromise and de-escalated the struggle. While much more could have been achieved, the December 1995 events in France nonetheless indicated the tremendous power of a grassroots working-class struggle involving women, students, immigrant workers, and homeless people. They also served notice that anti-globalisation protests would not be confined to countries of the South. Instead, resistance would henceforth also occur at the very centres of global capitalism—indeed, as we shall see, the struggles in France itself were far from over. And few guessed that the United States would soon get a taste of the action.

Before the Shock of Seattle: Meltdown and Revolt in East Asia

Before the surprise of the Battle in Seattle, another great shock was in the offing: A massive economic collapse in the pet capitalist economies, the East Asian 'tigers' and 'dragons'.[21] For years IMF and World Bank officials had been telling everyone who would listen that East Asia was living proof of their successful formula for economic growth: Low wages (ably assisted by restrictions on union freedoms); high levels of foreign investment; low taxes; and minimal spending on public services. So taken were the global elite by developments in countries like South Korea, Thailand, Indonesia, the Philippines, Malaysia, and Taiwan that the World Bank issued a report in 1993 with the title *The East Asian Miracle*. The economic model applied in East Asia was touted as a cure-all for the world's poor.[22]

The 'miracle' soon stood exposed as a fraud. With a calamitous economic collapse sweeping through one East Asian economy after another in the course of 1997–98, in 2001 the World Bank prepared a new report: *Rethinking the East Asian Miracle*.[23] And small wonder: The East Asian meltdown was one of the most devastating experienced anywhere since the Great Depression of the 1930s.

The crisis began in July 1997 when global investors—the very people the World Bank and IMF lauded as the keys to prosperity—pulled the plug on Thailand. Growing sour on the country's prospects, especially the foreign debt encouraged by the World Bank and IMF, banks and investment agencies began withdrawing their funds. Overnight the Thai currency, the baht, collapsed. Economists then rushed to reassure investors that Indonesia was not vulnerable to such a collapse. They should have saved their breath. So severe was the ensuing Indonesian meltdown that 260 of the 282 companies on the country's stock exchange disintegrated.

South Korea's collapse followed within weeks. At its peak, ten thousand Korean workers were laid off each day—300,000 per month. As the crisis reverberated throughout the region, US $600 billion were wiped off the balance sheets of East Asia's stock markets.

In a matter of months, miracle had turned to nightmare. Like any addict, countries hooked on foreign investment learned the pain of forced withdrawal. Whereas Indonesia, Korea, Malaysia, Thailand, and the Philippines received an inflow of $95 billion in 1996, a year later they experienced a capital outflow of $20 billion—a reversal of $115 billion in the space of twelve months. Suddenly, the globalisation model had been turned upside down. As easily as foreign capital flows could boost economies, so could they devastate them. And, as always in such situations, it was the poor who suffered the most.

In the course of five months, between August and December 1997, wages in South Korea were cut by half—for those still lucky enough to have jobs. In Thailand, the cost of rice and flour jumped by 47 per cent in a single month, signalling calamity for the poor. Meanwhile, Indonesia saw the annual per capita income collapse from US $1,200 to US $300. In Surabaya, the country's largest industrial city, the minimum wage fell from $2 a day to 30 cents. So severe was the ensuing poverty that many mothers, no longer able to buy milk, began feeding tea to their babies.

Alongside suffering and deprivation, however, grew anger and resistance. In Indonesia, it took fewer than six months for anger over economic hardship to push hatred for the dictatorship of Suharto to a point of no return. Six days after the dictatorship shot and killed six student protesters on May 12 1998, the student movement took to the streets of Jakarta. Seizing the parliament building, students danced on the roof chanting "Bring Suharto down!".

With food riots sweeping the islands that make up Indonesia and students in open revolt, Suharto gave up power on May 21. A pro-Western dictatorship that had come to power in 1965 by drowning half a million people in blood was knocked over like a bowling pin. The Asian crisis had brought global elites their first casualty. All eyes turned next to South Korea, the most industrialised of the East Asian economies, and one where workers had a decade-long experience of militant resistance.

In the late 1980s, a tremendous working-class upheaval had swept South Korea. Union membership doubled from one to two million in the course of a huge strike wave between 1986 and 1990. Sit-down strikes—where strikers occupy their places of work—became increasingly widespread. The industrial cities of Masan and Changwon witnessed a full-fledged workers' revolt in 1987–88, in the course of which thirty new independent unions joined together. So impressive was the solidarity and so powerful the militancy that radical workers at the time described Masan-Changwon as a 'liberated zone'. Following the formation of the Korean Confederation of Trade Unions (KCTU) in November 1995, the largest-ever strikes erupted in December 1996 and January 1997. In a mere decade, the South Korean working class had built one of the most combative union movements in the world.[24]

This new workers' movement faced its biggest challenge with the economic meltdown of 1997–98. As a condition of its $57 billion aid package to 'alleviate' the crisis, the IMF insisted on massive job cuts. Given that workers had recently fought a general strike against layoffs, the government had to tread softly, convening a tripartite commission of business, government, and labour leaders to negotiate an agreement. In early 1998, to the dismay of union activists, the leaders of the KCTU signed an accord which, in exchange for modest concessions, accepted mass layoffs and all the basic terms of the IMF bailout. Hundreds of angry KCTU delegates rebelled, voting down the agreement and removing the leaders who had signed the deal. Their call for a nationwide general strike, however, did not receive adequate support.

Nevertheless, resistance to the IMF conditions continued to mount. On May 27 and 28 1998, about 120,000 workers took strike action against layoffs. On the heels of that mass strike, workers at Kia Motors forced concessions from management after waging a three-week series of strikes against wage cuts. Throughout 1999, 2000, and 2001, militant resistance to layoffs, privatisation, and wage-cuts continued. Shipyard workers, bank clerks, subway workers, autoworkers at Daewoo Motors, and hotel workers, particularly the courageous employees of the luxurious Lotte Hotel in Seoul, fought employers, government, and often pitched battles with thousands of riot police personnel.

This trend has continued, despite significant setbacks. The year 2004 witnessed an inspiring campaign of organisation and resistance by migrant workers in Korea. In the spring of 2008 high school students launched a campaign of nightly candlelight rallies against free trade with the United States. This campaign had one million people pouring into the streets on June 10 in a powerful expression of popular protest.

All this, of course, lay well in the future during the crisis of 1997. Yet during those weeks, mourning the loss of a dictator and fretting about the workers' resistance in Korea, Western elites might have been having trouble sleeping. Then resistance exploded right in their faces—in the tear-gas filled streets of Seattle.

The Battle of Seattle: "The spirit that makes revolution possible"

To make history—to change the actual course of world events—is intoxicating, inspiring, and life-transforming. So it was for those in the streets of Seattle on Tuesday, November 30 and Wednesday, December 1 1999. Capturing a crucial dimension of the experience, activist Vicki Larson reported that "(t)he spirit that makes revolution possible was strong on the streets of Seattle".[25] Luis Hernandez Navarro even proclaimed that "[t]he new century was born on November 30 1999 with the revolt of the globalised in Seattle, Washington".[26]

Seattle transformed the political climate in the centres of capitalism. "The terms of the free trade debate have been forever changed", wrote a reporter for the *Seattle Times*. "For one day a ragtag army of nonviolent global citizens spoke— and the world listened". Indeed they did. In workplaces and schools, in *barrios* (neighbourhoods) and pubs, millions of conversations took place about what had transpired on Seattle's streets. People with only a foggy notion of the World Trade Organization (WTO) understood the elementary fact that presidents, prime ministers, and their entourages had been challenged and shut down by young people and their labour and community supporters.

In an important sense, the editors of *In These Times* were right when they opined that "the real story of Seattle was the youth".[27] Organised into small, democratic affinity groups coordinated through Direct Action Network, thousands of activists chose to put their bodies between the WTO delegates and their convention centre. They danced, sang, and chanted in the streets, locked themselves down and withstood tear gas, pepper spray, police truncheons, and over 500 arrests—all to make sure people throughout the world heard their message. And hear it they did.

In the predawn hours of Tuesday, November 30, around two thousand direct action protesters hit the streets, staking out all the main intersections that approached the Convention Centre where WTO delegates were due to converge. For the next five or six hours their numbers grew steadily. At 10 am, the police launched their first major attack with tear gas and rubber bullets, followed by baton bashes to heads and bodies. Demonstrators had their eyes washed out, and their wounds bandaged, but they would not be moved. Four hours later, all the intersections had been held. "By darkness on Tuesday," recorded one observer, "the 2,000 or so street warriors had won the day".[28]

It was a tremendous victory. But it was also a tainted one—tainted by the knowledge that 40,000 labour demonstrators had been led away from the protest zone by their leaders, a tactic that would be repeated a year and a half later in Québec City. A few thousand union activists did break away to join the young activists in the streets, but a glorious opportunity to put up to 50,000 people on the streets outside the convention centre was lost, as was the opportunity to build greater unity and solidarity between organised workers and a diverse group of environmentalists, students, anarchists, and socialists committed to direct action against corporate rule.

Not everything about the labour mobilisation was a lost cause, however. To begin with, getting more than 40,000 union activists out for the event was a major achievement. The union crowd was also highly diverse, with significant numbers of women and workers of colour. In addition, one labour leader's speech even went so far as to identify capitalism as the problem.

The labour rally also had an internationalist flavour, with guests and speakers from the Dominican Republic, Barbados, El Salvador, Brazil, Mexico, South Africa, India, Malaysia, and China. That's not to say nationalist protectionism of the 'save American jobs' variety was not in evidence. It was, as were some US flags. But, the atmosphere of the event was much more internationalist than any substantial US labour gathering in many years. Yet, the decision of the labour leaders to divert their demonstration from the protest zone was a terrible betrayal of those resisting in the streets.

More than one thousand activists took again to the streets the next day. As chants of "Whose streets? Our streets!" and "This is what democracy looks like!" echoed throughout downtown Seattle, it was clear that police repression had failed to break the movement.

Meanwhile, WTO delegates from the poorer countries of the South, perhaps sensing that activists in the street would not be bullied, became more assertive, denouncing the backroom manipulations of the richest nations. In particular, these delegates attacked the process by which they were denied access to the 'Green Room' meeting where the WTO Secretariat held informal discussion among the richest nations. As the protests in the streets became more defiant, so the attacks on the lack of transparency and accountability inside the conference grew louder. With their public relations exercise blowing up in their faces, the then-US president Bill Clinton and his advisers decided to cut their losses and send everyone home. As news leaked out that the WTO talks had been cancelled, euphoric celebrations began in the streets.

Despite a barrage of media condemnation denouncing the protesters and associating them with 'violence',[29] a majority of US Americans polled indicated that they sympathised with the rebels in Seattle. The effect of young people, students, and workers taking the streets, as well as the headlines, away from the rich and powerful was electrifying. The demonstrators had succeeded in dramatically redefining the 'free trade' debate by putting issues like the environment, jobs, and social programmes on the agenda. But they had done more than that. They had also established that resistance is possible. And not just token resistance—but effective, coordinated resistance that can upset the plans of the world's rulers.[30]

After Seattle, radical protest became a credible strategy even in the world's dominant nation. A whole new way of doing politics was now on the agenda, since the victory was undeniably achieved through militant direct action. A perceptive commentator summed it up nicely right after the events:

> In the annals of popular protest in America, these have been shining hours, achieved entirely outside the conventional arena of orderly protest and white-paper activism and the timid bleats of the professional leadership of big labour and environmentalism. This truly was an insurgency from below.[31]

And that is what unites the Seattle protesters, the Zapatistas, the French students and workers of December 1995, the Indonesian students who toppled Suharto, the South Korean workers waging mass strikes, and the workers and indigenous activists in Bolivia who blocked the privatisation of water and gas— they have all been insurgents from below. More than anything else, this is the key to the new radical movements that have emerged since the Zapatistas rode out of the hills of Chiapas. A new movement based on insurgency from below has emerged, and with it a new model of radical democracy is taking root. To be sure, the movement confronts all sorts of internal weaknesses and contradictions. But the fact that it has redefined the terrain of politics is a signal achievement.

As the Zapatistas' Subcomandante Marcos put it in his March 11 2001 speech in Mexico City:

> We are not those who, foolishly, hope that from above will come the justice that can only come from below, the freedom that can only be won with all, the democracy which is struggled for at all levels and all the time.

When History Moved, Again

After September 11 2001: Repression, War, Resistance

Exactly six months after Marcos's speech, the dynamics of world politics shifted once more, this time to the benefit of the ruling classes. The terror attacks on the World Trade Center and the Pentagon created a glorious opportunity for squelching political dissent. After several years during which public opinion was moving into closer synch with global justice protesters, governments were able to use fear, lies, and 'patriotism' to create a 'law and order' mentality that discredited protest movements and justified escalating levels of police repression. Unions and non-governmental organisations (NGOs) that had once been prepared to flirt with street protests quickly abandoned youth activists. In North America and most of Europe, demonstrations grew smaller and state repression intensified. The global justice movement in the North went into marked decline.

But the post-9/11 neoliberal offensive, led by the government of George W Bush in Washington DC, did not have everything its way. In fact, Bush's belligerent imperial agenda soon reignited opposition movements.

First, disgusted by the Bush administration's campaign of misinformation and deception about Saddam Hussein's alleged 'weapons of mass destruction' and links to al-Qaeda, and horrified by the impending destruction of Iraq, millions of people rallied to worldwide protests. On February 15 2003, in the build-up to the war, between 15 and 30 million people took to the streets in 800 cities around the world. February 15 represents the largest day of anti-war protests in world history. Indeed, the demonstration of three million people in Rome is listed in the *Guinness Book of World Records* as the biggest anti-war rally ever. These events clearly indicated that lies and repression had not stifled the spirit of resistance and that millions of people remained determined in their opposition to the globalisation of poverty and war.

The second great problem for global rulers has been the continuing havoc that globalisation wreaks on the lives of the world's poor. Unwilling to accept condemnation to lifetimes of hardship and suffering, millions of people across the world have continued to fight back. In Latin America, huge popular movements have periodically broken through the neoliberal agenda, toppling governments and rolling back privatisation policies. In countries like Venezuela and Bolivia, mass movements are rejecting neoliberal globalisation and searching for alternatives to capitalism. During the World Social Forum of the Americas in Caracas in early 2006, which I was fortunate to attend, thousands of participants engaged in spirited discussions over the idea of 'a socialism for the twenty-first century' that would provide an alternative to war and exploitation.

So, even though global justice movements have been affected in the North, political and street level opposition to globalisation, empire, and war have continued to grow in much of the rest of the world. Sooner or later, the winds of change blowing from the South may yet sweep another storm of protest into the North, as they have done in the past with Cuba, Vietnam, and South Africa.

From Bolivia to France to Mexico: The Unbroken Resistance That Will Not Die

The early months of 2006 saw two great victories for popular movements. In January of that year, the battle of the people of Cochabamba in Bolivia to de-privatise their water supply won a crucial legal victory, when Bechtel Corporation dropped its suit before the World Bank. After a popular uprising in 2000—known as the Water War, in which tens of thousands of protesters took over the centre of Cochabamba, drove out the police, and established an assembly-style democracy that governed their city for weeks at a time—forced Bolivia's government to tear up a water privatisation contract, Bechtel had sued, demanding $50 million in damages from the Bolivian people. But the workers, indigenous peoples, and urban poor of Bolivia would not yield. Mass protests continued year after year, expanding their demands to include public ownership of natural gas. Then, on December 18 2005, Evo Morales of the Movement toward Socialism was elected president, becoming one of the first indigenous persons elected as head of state anywhere in the Americas. Recognising that the whole political climate in the country had shifted against multinational capital, Bechtel dropped its legal suit, an extraordinary action from a $17 billion company with close ties to the Bush administration in Washington.

None of this, including Morales's election, would have been possible without absolutely heroic levels of self-mobilisation by the lower orders in Bolivia. Claudia Lopez, an organiser for the Cochabamba chapter of the Federation of Factory Workers of Bolivia, explains that here too, insurgency from below has been decisive:

> We have shut out and defeated the claims to perpetual power of those interests throughout these heroic past six years by means of: road blockages, closing off the city, uprisings and insurrections and marches, land occupations, closing the

valves of the gas pipelines, occupation of oil wells. It has been six years filled with struggles, bravery, and indignation turned into public protest.[32]

Three months after Bechtel dropped its case in the face of popular resistance, youth, students, and workers scored a major victory against neoliberalism in France. For more than a decade, the French government's efforts to implement an aggressive globalisation agenda had encountered powerful opposition. As we have seen, student protests and mass strikes defeated the Juppé plan in 1995. Nevertheless, in 2003 the French government overrode protests to cut social entitlements by raising the retirement age and inflicting major cuts to healthcare. Then, in early 2006, it introduced a Youth Labour Contract scheme (known as CPE by its French initials) which gave employers the power to fire workers under 26 year of age without having to give cause.

Not surprisingly, students launched a series of protests, beginning with a day of action on February 7 2006, which drew 400,000 into the streets. A month later, one million people filled the streets. A million and a half turned out on March 18. Then the numbers soared, as three million joined the demonstrations on March 28, while even more did so on April 4. Hundreds of thousands of workers began taking strike action in concert with the protests from end March, forging vital links with the students.

But it wasn't only the size of the demonstrations that shook the government. It was also the militant forms of self-organisation. More than three-quarters of the 88 universities in France were shut down by student strikes. Many were occupied, as student assemblies of thousands deliberated over the struggle, and students organised 'open university' programmes on everything from globalisation to sexual liberation and the conditions of women workers. In the middle of March, huge numbers of high school students joined the movement. Hundreds of schools were closed by student strikes, including half the high schools in Paris. Notable here were schools in communities with large concentrations of immigrants, and where the government had already been rocked by powerful protests against racism and unemployment in November 2005, as youth of colour in the suburbs of Paris established their presence as new political actors.

As in every genuine mass struggle, there was a great and exciting ferment of ideas and self-organisation. New structures of democratic discussion and action were created, among them a Student Coordination, to which students from every striking university elected delegates, and which met every weekend at a different school.

By early April, it was clear that the CPE would have to go. Once again, opinion polls revealed that 70 per cent of the French people—and 80 per cent of the youth—opposed the plan. The *Economist* magazine lamented that only 36 per cent of the French people thought the 'free market' was the best conceivable economic system.

With workers on strike, universities and high schools occupied, the streets overflowing with protesters, the French government gave way, withdrawing the CPE. Another crucial battle against globalisation had been won.

No sooner had the students and workers of France won their victory than the oppressed of the Mexican state of Oaxaca launched their own heroic and inspiring resistance to neoliberalism. It began with a May Day strike by teachers. When the state government refused to meet their demands, the teachers, supported by an array of community organisations, set up an encampment in the centre of Oaxaca. A month into their struggle, a mass demonstration drew out 80,000 people. Two weeks later, the police tried to evict the encampment from the city centre. Having successfully resisted the assault, teachers and their allies formed the Popular Assembly of the Peoples of Oaxaca (APPO). This new popular assembly brought together nearly 400 organisations—women's, environmental, labour, indigenous, student, and human rights groups, among others—into a common front that would soon develop into a forum for popular power in Oaxaca. Indeed, for several months APPO effectively operated as a popular municipal government, running Oaxaca as an assembly-style democracy of the oppressed in defiance of the police and state and national authorities.

Demonstrations of angry women seized radio and television stations and turned them into media of the mass movement. Popular organisations demanded the resignation of the state governor. Mass meetings debated crucial social and political issues affecting the poorest classes of Mexican society. A radical, participatory democracy was in the making.

In the following months, the government tacked and turned between trying to negotiate with and trying to repress the popular movement. By November 2006, APPO was convening assemblies across the state of Oaxaca and passing resolutions condemning capitalism and imperialism. Altogether, over one million Oaxacans participated in the struggle. [33]

But in late November 2006, a terrifying campaign of police repression finally set back the movement: Barricades were destroyed, hundreds arrested, two dozen killed. The government did retake control of the city. But even in retreat, APPO continued to declare its defiance, continuing to organise mass marches, notably on International Women's Day, March 8 2007. While it may have lost the battle, APPO proudly and courageously declared that the struggle of the oppressed classes of Oaxaca would continue.

Searching for a Political Model

Among the greatest strengths of the new movements is their reliance on the self-activity and self-mobilisation of thousands upon thousands of oppressed people. New notions of politics, new senses of the possible, are created in the heat of such struggles. The emphases on direct action, on participatory democracy (often organised through mass assemblies), and on the festive and celebratory side of political protest, distinguish these as a truly popular movements, upheavals that are reclaiming and improvising upon great traditions of mass insurgence. In the streets of Cochabamba, Oaxaca, Paris, Seoul, and elsewhere, one hears the irregular rhythms of popular revolt. Freed from the constraints of bureaucratically-dominated electoral politics, these movements are reinventing a language and a poetry of resistance. Utilising mass strikes and uprisings, land occupations, popular assemblies, and direct democracy, they are carving open the spaces of opposition to globalising capitalism.

And yet, these movements also confront strategic challenges and dilemmas. As much as they have been able to create new political hopes and aspirations—particularly the belief that another world is possible—and as much as they have been able to win real victories (such as the defeat of water privatisation in Cochabamba), they have thus far failed to build mass movements designed to displace the power of capitalist classes and create lasting forms of democratic popular power. And so they confront the dilemma of moving from a politics of resistance to a politics of liberation.

Whether it is by occupying lands in Brazil, or blocking roads leading to giant dam projects in India, or taking over a city square in Bolivia to break a water privatisation contract, or filling the streets of Paris with determined demonstrators, these movements have refused to accept that a tiny fraction of the world's population ought to control all decisions related to the use, distribution, and ownership of the world's economic wealth. Similarly, they have refused to accept that democracy ends where 'economics' begins, that the people have no right to affect the ownership, production, and distribution of society's wealth. Instead, these movements insist that there can be no just society without the right of people to control those relations that affect their livelihood and their survival. In so doing, they mobilise a radical democracy against capitalism.

And yet, thus far, these movements have been much more effective at resisting than at overturning; while capable of stopping something regressive, they only episodically venture toward the beginning of something entirely new. As the late Daniel Singer explained in a perceptive analysis of the French strikes and demonstrations of 1995, the great accomplishment of the movement was that it had shattered "the fatalistic acceptance" of neoliberal dogma by showing that people could stop a government in its tracks. Yet, as Singer warned, winning a single battle is not enough:

> The rulers give up individual proposals but not their strategy. The protesters win
> a battle and, then, lacking objectives, are unable to launch a counteroffensive. ...
> It is ... the idea that there can be no alternative that the French protesters have

now battered. ... They did not, however, ... offer an alternative project, the vision of a different society.[34]

Radical movements cannot change societies without such a vision. To be sure, it is possible to resist, to engage in the powerfully negative act of saying 'no', without a clear vision of an alternative. But that accomplishment, while immensely important in terms of building confidence and capacities for struggle, only postpones the next battle. For capitalism is unrelenting; give it a chance to try again and it will, often with devastating consequences. What Singer goes on to say about the French events, might be said about any of the struggles we've examined, even ones as powerful as the uprisings in Cochabamba or Oaxaca:

> After twenty years or so of total ideological domination, the very refusal, rejection, and resistance were vital. ... It is a crucial beginning. But it is only a beginning. On the basis of this negative achievement, the genuine search for a radically different society must begin.[35]

And this search for a radically different society has to mean clarifying concepts of anti-capitalism. It has to mean exploring the history of socialism for those visions of a self-emancipatory *socialism from below* that might offer resources to struggles for a new society based on radical, participatory democracy, communal property, and cooperative modes of economic life. It also has to mean building new forms of sustained (not merely episodic) mass movements that can provide frameworks for self-organisation, popular education, and new forms of popular power. There are no textbook formulae for how we begin these processes. But there is also no avoiding the challenges that have been thrown up by the emergence—and the limitations—of new movements against capitalist globalisation. Addressing them both theoretically and practically is indispensable if we are to move from resistance to liberation. And move we must, if we are to make another world possible.

References

Seth Ackerman, 2000—'Prattle in Seattle: Media Coverage Misrepresented Protests', in Kevin Danaher and Roger Burbach, eds, 2000—*Globalize This! The Battle Against the World Trade Organization and Corporate Rule*. Monroe, ME: Common Courage Press

Craig Araron, 2000—'The Kids Are All Right', in *In These Times*, January 10 2000

APPO (*Asamblea Popular de los Pueblos de Oaxaca*), November 2006—'Constitutive Congress of the Popular Assembly of the Peoples of Oaxaca: General Summary of the Results of the Work Groups', November 13 2006. at http://deletetheborder.org/node/1718 (Accessed April 2017)

Brett Cemer, 1996—'France: Students and Workers Fight Back', in *New Socialist*, no 1, January–February 1996

Cho Hee-Yeon, 2017—'From Anti-Imperialist to Anti-Empire: The Crystallisation of the Anti-Globalisation Movement in South Korea', in Jai Sen, ed, 2017a—*The Movements of Movements, Part 1: What Makes Us Move?*. Volume 4 in the *Challenging Empires* series. New Delhi: OpenWord, and Oakland, CA: PM Press

CSIS, 2000—Anti-Globalisation—A Spreading Phenomenon. CSIS, August 22 2000

The Economist, April 2001—'Mayhem in May', April 28 2001

EZLN (Zapatista Army of National Liberation), 1996a—'First Declaration of La Realidad for Humanity and Against Neoliberalism', in the archivi delle proteste globali / archives of global protests, at http://www.nadir.org/nadir/initiativ/agp/chiapas1996/en/first_declaration.htm (Accessed April 2017)

EZLN (Zapatista Army of National Liberation), 1998—*Zapatista Encuentro: Documents from the 1996 Encounter for Humanity and Against Neoliberalism.* New York: Seven Stories Press

Francis Fukuyama, Summer 1989—'The End of History?', in *The National Interest*, at http://www.wesjones.com/eoh.htm#source (Accessed April 2017)

Luis Hernandez Navarro, 2000—'The Revolt of the Globalised', in Kevin Danaher and Roger Burbach, eds, 2000—*Globalize This! The Battle Against the World Trade Organization and Corporate Rule.* Monroe, ME: Common Courage Press

Erik Izraelwicz, December 1995—'*La premiere revolte contre la mondialisation*' ['The first revolt against globalisation', in French], in *Le Monde*, December 7 1995

Brian D Johnson, 2001—'Naomi and the Brand-New Left', in *Maclean's*, March 12 2001

Alex Khasnabish, 2017—'Forward Dreaming: Zapatismo and the Radical Imagination', in Jai Sen, ed, 2017a—*The Movements of Movements, Part 1: What Makes Us Move?*. Volume 4 in the *Challenging Empires* series. New Delhi: OpenWord, and Oakland, CA: PM Press

Raghu Krishnan, 1996—'December 1995: "The First Revolt Against Globalisation"', in *Monthly Review*, vol 48, December 1996

Vicki Larson, January 2000—'Notes from the Editors', in *Monthly Review*, vol 51 no 8

Bertrans Leclair, December 1995—'*Roger Callois, la grève, et les totems*' ['Roger Callois, strikes, and totems', in French], in *Politis*, December 14 1995

Xochitl Leyva Solano and Christopher Gunderson, 2017—'The Tapestry of Neo-Zapatismo: Origins and Development', in Jai Sen, ed, 2017a—*The Movements of Movements, Part 1: What Makes Us Move?*. Volume 4 in the *Challenging Empires* series. New Delhi: OpenWord, and Oakland, CA: PM Press

Claudia Lopez, May 2006—'Cochabamba's Water War: The Start of Other Struggles', translated by Nancy Wallace, in *Upside Down World*, May 29 2006, at http://upsidedownworld.org/main/bolivia-archives-31/300-cochabambas-water-war-the-start-of-other-struggles (Accessed April 2017)

Firoze Manji and Sokari Ekine, 2011—*African Awakenings: The Emerging Revolutions.* Cape Town, Dakar, Nairobi, and Oxford: Pambazuka Press

Elizabeth (Betita) Martinez, January 2000—'Where Was the Color in Seattle? Looking for Reasons Why the Great Battle Was So White'. Extended version of article in *ColorLines*, February 2000, at http://www.nadir.org/nadir/initiativ/agp/free/seattle/color.htm

B Gloria Martínez González and Alejandro Valle Baeza, 2007—'Oaxaca: Rebellion Against Marginalisation, Extreme Poverty, and Abuse of Power', in *Monthly Review*, July–August 2007

David McNally, September 1998—'Globalisation on Trial: Crisis and Class Struggle in East Asia', in *Monthly Review*, vol 50 no 4 (September 1998)

David McNally, 2006—*Another World Is Possible: Globalisation and Anti-Capitalism*. Winnipeg: Arbeiter Ring Publishing, and London: Merlin Press

Rodrigo Nunes, 2017a—'Nothing Is What Democracy Looks Like: Openness, Horizontality, and the Movement of Movements', in Jai Sen, ed, 2017b—*The Movements of Movements, Part 2: Rethinking Our Dance*. Volume 5 in the *Challenging Empires* series. New Delhi: OpenWord, and Oakland, CA: PM Press

OECF (Overseas Economic Cooperation Fund), nd (c 1994)—*The East Asian Miracle*. Proceedings of a symposium jointly hosted by the World Bank and the OECF, in Tokyo, December 3 1993, 57 pp, bilingual, in Japanese and English

Richard Roman and Edur Velasco Arregui, 1998—'Worker Insurgency, Rural Revolt, and the Crisis of the Mexican Regime', in Ellen Meiksins Wood, Peter Meiksins, and Michael Yates, eds, 1998—*Rising from the Ashes? Labour in the Age of 'Global' Capitalism*. New York: Monthly Review Press

Richard Roman and Edur Velasco Arregui, 2008—'Mexico's Oaxaca Commune', in Leo Panitch and Colin Leys, eds, 2008—*Socialist Register* 2008. Black Point, Nova Scotia: Fernwood Publishing

Daniel Singer, 1999—*Whose Millennium? Theirs or Ours?*. New York: Monthly Review Press

Jeffrey St Clair, November–December 1999—'Seattle Diary', in *New Left Review* no 238

Joseph E Stiglitz and Shahid Yusuf, eds, 2001—*Rethinking the East Asian Miracle*. Washington, DC: World Bank

Jerry Useem, 2000—'There's Something Happening Here', in *Fortune*, May 15 2000

Notes

1.   Ed: This is a revised and edited version of the author's chapter of the same title, in his 2006 book *Another World Is Possible: Globalisation and Anti-Capitalism* (Winnipeg: Arbeiter Ring Publishing, and London: Merlin Press). We warmly thank David McNally for specially preparing this version for us and for getting us permission from his publisher to republish this version in this book, and his publisher for their generous agreement. For further reproduction permission, contact the author at dmcnally@yorku.ca.

For those unfamiliar with this phrase, the second part of the title riffs a much quoted statement about the Seattle demonstrations cited also in Elizabeth (Betita) Martinez, January 2000:

> *"I was at the jail where a lot of protesters were being held and a big crowd of people was chanting 'This Is What Democracy Looks Like!'. At first it sounded kind of nice. But then I thought: Is this really what democracy looks like? Nobody here looks like me."* —Jinee Kim, Bay Area youth organizer

And / but for a comparative and contrary discussion of the issue of what democracy is like, see also in the accompanying volume (Sen, ed, 2017) the essay by

Rodrigo Nunes 'Nothing is what democracy looks like: Openness, horizontality, and the movement of movements' (Nunes 2017a).

2. As presented and discussed throughout my book *Another World Is Possible: Globalisation and Anti-Capitalism* (McNally 2006). Ed: This essay was finalised for this book in 2009. As is widely known, the period since then has witnessed a series of renewed waves of revolt, all of which only reinforces this discussion: The beginning of a much wider Arab intifada, the *indignados* movement in Spain, the resistance against externally-imposed austerity and conditionality in Greece, the Occupy movement on Turtle Island and some of Europe, and then more recently, in Turkey and Brazil; and as is less known, also widely across Africa (see Manji and Ekine 2011).

3. Ed: Fukuyama, Summer 1989.

4. CSIS, August 2000.

5. *The Economist*, April 2001.

6. Useem, May 2000.

7. CSIS, August 22 2000, as above.

8. Johnson, March 2001.

9. Of course, globalisation did not begin with NAFTA. In using the term 'globalisation regime', I refer to a set of legally enforceable agreements designed to 'lock in' the neoliberal policies associated with 'globalisation'.

10. Ed: For a detailed discussion of the genesis of the Zapatista movement, see Leyva Solano and Gunderson 2017, in this volume.

11. Ed: 'Communal' here is used in the sense of 'of the community', and not in the sectarian sense usually implied in the use of the word in India.

12. EZLN 1998.

13. ibid.

14. Much of the information in this paragraph is drawn from the excellent article by Roman and Arregui, 1998. My discussion of the 2006 rebellion in Oaxaca later in this chapter draws from another piece by Roman and Arregui, 'Mexico's Oaxaca Commune' (2008), and by Martinez Gonzalez and Valle Baeza 2007.

15. EZLN 1998, pp 11–13.

16. Ed: For a discussion of the resonance of the Zapatista movement in other parts of the world, see the essay by Alex Khasnabish in this volume (Khasnabish 2017).

17. Izraelwicz, December 1995.

18. My account of the student protests and the mass strikes is indebted particularly to two accounts: Raghu Krishnan, December 1996, and Brett Cemer, January–February 1996.

19. Krishnan 1996, p 6.

20. Leclair, December 1995.

21. Much of the analysis I offer here draws on my article 'Globalisation on Trial: Crisis and Class Struggle in East Asia' (1998), reprinted in *Rising from the Ashes?*.

22. Ed, OECF nd, c 1994.

23. Stiglitz and Yusuf, eds, 2001.

24. Ed: For a detailed discussion of the dynamics of the struggle in South Korea, see the essay by Cho Hee-Yeon in this volume (Cho 2017).

25. Larson, January 2000, p 64.

26. Hernandez Navarro 2000, p 41.

27. Araron, January 2000.

28. St Clair, November/December 1999, p 89.

29. For a good overview of the cynical mainstream media coverage see Ackerman 2000.

30. That the ruling elites were seriously shaken was obvious from the response they created in the mainstream media. The *Wall Street Journal* denounced the Seattle demonstrators as "global village idiots". Thomas Friedman of the *New York Times* disparaged them as "a Noah's ark of flat-earth advocates, protectionist trade unions, and yuppies looking for their 1960s fix". *Newsweek* rushed to condemn the Seattle protesters as losers who "have virtually no grasp of the issues". British Prime Minister Tony Blair exclaimed that the protesters threaten "nothing less than civilisation", while Canada's Trade Minister called them "dinosaurs".

31. St Clair 1999, p 96.

32. Lopez, May 2006.

33. See: APPO (*Asamblea Popular de los Pueblos de Oaxaca*), November 2006.

34. Singer 1999.

35. ibid.

Anti-Systemic Movements and Transformations of the World-System, 1968–1989[1]

Fouad Kalouche and Eric Mielants

Introduction: World-System, 'Anti-systemic', and Social Imaginaries

The indeterminate totality that surrounds us is a World-System where the interplay between the domains—arbitrarily referred to as 'economic', 'cultural', 'political', and 'social'—reflects a constant interaction between and within forces.

One could distinguish, for analytical purposes, between 'internal' and 'external' forces—those that are englobed within certain social-historical conditions or historical systems (ie, those that are actively or passively affecting and being affected at varying levels), and those that are not englobed. A powerful military intervention that destroys an existing system and its centres of organisational and political infrastructure, and which transforms social relations in such a way that a different system emerges, is the best example of *external* 'anti-systemic' forces at work. While such an external intervention may have been possible in the past, as in the case of the Dorian invasion and destruction of the Mycenaean system (c 1400 BC),[2] such a form of anti-systemic intervention is no longer possible mainly for two reasons: First, the geographical extension of the existing system has expanded to engulf the whole globe; and second, those benefiting from and upholding the Modern World-System control the major military powers and are in charge of maintaining law and order on the world scene.

As for 'internal' forces—these encompass most of what we would nowadays describe as 'anti-systemic'—they could consist of forces of opposition and resistance to the consolidation, expansion, and stability of the existing system. Opposition and resistance may take on different forms, whereby forces varying in intensity and effectiveness could transform the existing system through their intercourse with dominant systemic forces. Because the world-system is in a constant state of transformation, anti-systemic forces may transform and shape the system in ways that are deemed oppositional at a particular social-historical intersection but that may not be oppositional in the long run. This can make 'anti-systemic' an elusive description over long periods of time.

It is against this observation that we would like to examine in this essay the interplay of systemic and anti-systemic forces in relation to the contemporary world-system from 1968 to 1989. This period and the one following it[3] have been marked by the permeation of the world-system's multiple cultural systems by

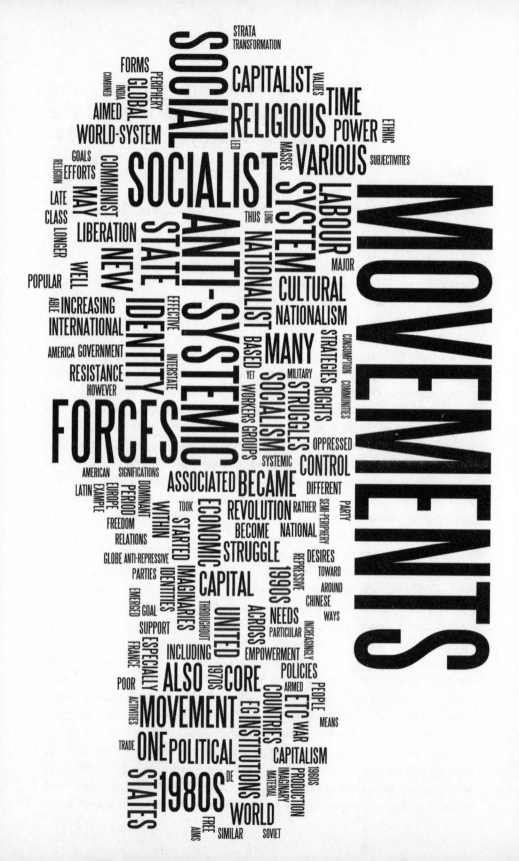

dominant capitalist social imaginaries, provoking reactions and adaptations that have become inherent to the world-system itself. Social imaginaries encompass sites of both intangible and material forces pertaining to psyche (affects, desires, intentions, representations, etc); social institutions underlying ethics and norms; political institutions underlying power relations; economic interactions encompassing production, consumption, distribution, and exchange; and other social and environmental relations enveloping varied ways of living.[4]

Anti-Systemic Movements

Within historical systems, forces of resistance do not necessarily have to be 'conscious' or 'self-reflective' and are not exclusively based on various associations of human beings. As a matter of fact, most forms of resistance that delayed development towards incorporation and most forces that opposed compounded systemic forces, have been related to social imaginaries.

We have not yet used the word 'movement' since it entails conscious and self-reflective teleology. Movements are new historical constructs dating back to the era of 'revolutions': They are associated with the will of the masses, the voice of the people, or the needs of 'humanity'. Movements have rarely been expressions of the lower strata of the oppressed classes since they are usually intertwined with aesthetic ('bourgeois') values. Movements are motivated and directed, as conscious or self-reflective action, towards specific goals or aims that are provided through social imaginaries at particular social-historical intersections. It is always through emerging social imaginary significations (in the name of something that becomes historically accessible to others within a social imaginary) that movements may undermine dominant economic, social, political, or cultural aspects of social-historical institutions.

Many movements, it should be remembered, are not anti-systemic per se but can be described as 'anti-repressive', aimed at the repressive state apparatus. They may contribute to the well-being of the oppressed without being anti-systemic, as in 'liberal reform' movements. As Wallerstein has suggested, most anti-repressive and liberal reformist movements are clearly motivated by systemic forces permeated through a "capitalist civilisation" that demands "more" for "us".[5]

Throughout history, social and political institutions have managed to effectively control, and to eventually produce, the needs and desires of the populace by relying on the manipulation of various social imaginary significations—especially those transcendent and extra-social projections associated with religion and universal laws, as well as with (cultural or national) identity and difference (based on a construct of the 'other'). Social movements in general, and anti-systemic movements in particular, were constantly thwarted through the provision, creation, or fulfilment of needs that tended to become less and less material or 'tangible'—but that nonetheless played increasing roles in the material life of populations across the globe: From 'immortality' and the 'afterlife' to 'freedom, equality, fraternity', or 'human rights'. It is only of late that the 'economic' has been able to shed its religious or political façade and to claim its place as the 'centre' of control of social needs and desires: The nation-state slowly emerged as the contested site of such a centre, and with it capitalism was able to consolidate its powers.

Most anti-systemic movements after 1800—including labour, socialist, and communist movements—situated themselves in relation to the 'state', with the purpose of evading, abolishing, or controlling it.[6] But while anti-systemic movements were actively looking to control the state, systemic forces were developing into polished and perfected ways of producing desires and needs and of shaping subjectivities—mainly through the intercourse (*Verkehr*, in German) of systemic and anti-systemic tendencies. Such a trajectory could be traced through various methods including, but not limited to, historical analyses studying institutions (education, prisons, etc), social relations and interactions (manners, sexuality, etc), and other interconnected domains. What Gilles Deleuze (in the name of Michel Foucault) described as the transition from "disciplinary" regimes to the "societies of control" would best exemplify how systemic forces were engaged— for a long period culminating in 1968 and beyond—in moving away from a centre (the state) to permeate all aspects of "material life", thus dominating social imaginaries and inhabiting the "cultural worlds" at the basis of a less stable "interstate system".[7] By the time of our epoch, both systemic and anti-systemic forces have undergone significant transformation.

Anti-systemic Movements 1968–1989

If 1968 was a period of disillusionment with the historic anti-systemic movements (nationalist, socialist, labour, and social democratic),[8] it was also a time of transformation for anti-systemic struggles across the globe. While it is impossible to present a comprehensive overview of all major anti-systemic events and processes that took place at this juncture, we consider a pool of significant representative events. We proceed chronologically to point to possible effects, links, and transformations.

World-Historical Events circa 1968
Three major world-historical events were influential in determining forms of popular struggle throughout the 1968 period: The Chinese Cultural Revolution, the Cuban Revolution, and the Vietnam War. The 'Cultural Revolution' emerged in 1966–1967 as the Red Guards conducted destructive attacks against the People's Liberation Army (especially high-ranking officers) and the Communist Party bureaucracy. Only in 1968 did it change to a struggle supposedly carried out by peasants and workers rather than armed militants. The Cultural Revolution was

meant to reshuffle the cards of class struggle and to enhance the self-importance of certain strata of the population that were oppressed by other strata. But the violence of the destruction that was meant to destabilise an entrenched system resonated around the globe. Armed struggle now came to be deemed necessary in continuous class warfare, where the masses could take on the task of shaping their future rather than trusting specialised bureaucrats or party apparatchiks. The anti-bureaucratic struggle was thus a way of ensuring that the masses, voiceless and shapeless, could take an active role in self-government.[9]

This orientation was echoed in Cuba where Ernesto Che Guevara, a member of the Castro government from 1959 until 1965, decided to disseminate the practice of guerrilla warfare. Around the same time that the Red Guards and other revolutionary groups were actively engaged in armed struggle in China, Guevara was engaged with Latin American peasants in rebellions aimed at regaining control of their future. Like the Red Guards, this engagement was halted in 1967 when Guevara was killed in Bolivia. Interestingly, as early as February 1963, Guevara wrote a piece entitled 'Against Bureaucracy' in which he presented a form of re-education, invigorated with nationalism, as the median between what he called "guerillarism" and "central planning" (*Junta Central de Planificación*).[10]

Nationalism, of course, was behind the Vietnamese successes in opposing their French and US American aggressors. But this nationalism was characterised by a socialist ideology and was related to a struggle against imperialism that used any means necessary to achieve liberation. In the Tet offensive of 1968, for example, the romantic construction of a David versus Goliath scenario permeated the imagination of an entire generation that felt empowered to struggle against all authoritative and dominant powers and to liberate itself not only from imperialism but also from other forms of oppression.

These three processes were combined with numerous other struggles that inspired 'popular' movements around the globe, and a variety of movements would flourish throughout this period. While nationalist struggles often took on ideologies of socialism, the popular imaginary in core countries[11] started veering toward what we will call 'identity' movements—paralleled in later periods, particularly in the periphery, by orientations toward 'ethnic' and 'religious' identities.

The Decline of Traditional Anti-systemic Movements and Rise of Identity Movements

Reshuffling the cards of class struggle enhanced the self-importance of certain oppressed strata of society. In Cambodia, this process led to taking class struggle to its logical limits. The Khmer Rouge took literally the (Chinese) Cultural Revolution's aims of transforming education, literature, art, and all other parts of the superstructure which do not correspond to the socialist economic base, and decided that the only logical attainment of such aims would be through a single class system. This led to the systematic elimination of the intelligentsia, the class thought to carry within it the ingrained bourgeois values that sustained the capitalist superstructure.[12] Most core-based imaginaries, however, interpreted this aspect of the Cultural Revolution as a new crisis of legitimacy of authority, accompanied by a prevailing anti-bureaucratic tendency. In the core, similar struggles aimed at the superstructure occurred with the proliferation of various identity movements combating sexism, racism, as well as authority, assimilation, and integration—which in turn came to compete with nationalist or socialist identities.

A new *student consciousness* emerged in many parts of the world during the 1960s amid a crisis of education and a growing dissatisfaction with the economic and political conditions that were dominated by the repressive 'old' parties and an ominous Cold War. To this was added a desire for autonomy that reflected the proliferation of revolutionary and anti-authoritarian imaginaries. From 1967 to May 1968 and continuing until 1973, student unrest exploded across France, West Germany, Spain, Italy, Poland, the United States, Brazil, Mexico, the United Kingdom, Argentina, Algeria, and Senegal. Similar unrest occurred in Canada, Japan, South Korea, Greece, India, Zambia, Pakistan, Colombia, Costa Rica, Ecuador, and Venezuela.[13] However, as an identity group aimed at empowering itself, the 'students' as an independent movement did not last beyond the 1980s,[14] although some elements became part of other movements or causes.

By this time the Soviet Union could no longer be counted on to offer an alternative system, much less a replacement for the capitalist world-economy. This resulted in reforms and reassessment of the roles and functions of the communist and socialist parties worldwide. Communist parties split into factions, with many individuals marginalised and persecuted in the semi-periphery by socialist or social democratic parties. Maoism inspired a few communist parties in power (eg, Albania, Cambodia) but mostly left its mark in the periphery. It inspired peasant-based and localised, cultural, socialist approaches to government. Combined with Che Guevara's guerrilla *focos* (centres) strategy, Maoism inspired guerrilla warfare and armed propaganda struggles across the globe. During the late 1960s and 1970s, guerrilla warfare became a socialist as well as nationalist instrument of armed struggle aimed at taking control of the state. But by this time it was no longer as effective. While it may have worked earlier in Cuba (and elsewhere in decolonisation struggles), few socialist armed struggles successfully took over a state.

One successful example was the Sandinista National Liberation Front (*Frente Sandinista de Liberación Nacional*) of Nicaragua in 1979. The front relied on a complicated "practice of social transformation" that involved combining socialist goals with nationalist, anti-repressive, indigenous, and other aspirations.[15] A monolithic socialistic strategy would probably not have been as successful in defeating both President Somoza's forces and in holding back the US-supported Contras. As elsewhere, when social self-identification or 'identities' proliferated (women, men, peasants, urban dwellers, students, workers, unemployed, international socialists), social movements were transformed. Socialist or nationalist movements that could not cater to, and combine the interests of, numerous strata of the population were not able to sustain their struggles effectively. In El Salvador, for example, the Popular Liberation Forces (*Fuerzas Populares de Liberación*) aimed at a "prolonged popular war" by building on strong peasant support. While at times militarily effective, they were however not able to engage the "masses".[16] One result of these trends was that more guerrilla warfare–style armed struggles started turning toward desperate terrorism.

The 1980s prepared the way for the 1990s, as finance and speculative capital advanced wildly and state socialism was tossed out the window. While Reagan and Thatcher were unleashing the fury of conservative forces against the 'evil empire', socialism was collapsing and new forces came to motivate the masses. US American direct and indirect interventions—as in Nicaragua, Honduras, El Salvador, Grenada, Colombia, Afghanistan, and Panama—showed that capitalist forces were ready to save hundreds of thousands from the clutches of socialism, even if it took killing most of them. Militarily, capital was able to create soldiers for itself everywhere through the production and support of 'right-wing' identities built on pure ideologies of the free market (eg, Colombia, Nicaragua, El Salvador) or through 'Muslim' defenders of a pure faith fighting infidels (Afghanistan).

By the 1990s, states and corporations increasingly used mercenary armies (such as Executive Outcomes or DynCorp), led mostly by US American ex-military personnel. The economic policies implemented by the Washington Consensus throughout the 1980s, along with those of the US-dominated international financial institutions, had a lasting impact, ranging from US pressures exerted on Japan, to extensive international regulation and manipulation of trade, foreign currencies, tariffs, and the widespread use of the dollar, to the imposition of 'liberalisation' schemes (and 'structural adjustment') on Third World countries.[17] State socialist policies everywhere (including France in the early 1980s) could not last in this global environment, and the Soviet Union and its satellite states were led to collapse through compounded causes including the ever-accelerating arms race. As state socialism was expiring, new religious and ethnic identities developed.

The 1979 Iranian Revolution reflected what was happening across various geocultural spaces in the world-system. In the 1980s, identity, religious, and ethnic movements flourished as forms of resistance to an internationalisation or regionalisation that grew more and more capitalistic. Afghanistan reinforced Vietnam as yet another David fighting another Goliath and joined the Iranian Revolution in inspiring anti-systemic religious ways of relating to a world repressed through modernist, socialist, and liberal discourses.[18] Religion became an effective component of various social movements in the Middle East, North and West Africa, as well as in India, Europe, and the United States, where Muslims, Hindus, Jews, and Christians organised themselves politically and economically in order to confront the changing face of their societies. Nationalist and socialist struggles were greatly affected by these transformations. In 1989, the Soviet withdrawal from Afghanistan contrasted with the Vietnamese withdrawal from Cambodia; the first was leaving behind a 'spectre' while the second was abandoning a cadaver.

In this climate the fall of the Berlin Wall was widely proclaimed to be the success of liberal dreams in fostering the imaginaries of 'freedom' and 'equality of rights', surpassing all dreams of 'justice' and 'economic equity'. Reaganism and Thatcherism provided for a counter-resistance that not only undermined communism worldwide, but also changed the meaning of socialism itself. The reign of Mitterand in France and the sweeping victory for socialists throughout Europe ironically marked a reformation and liberalisation of socialism. Meanwhile struggles against European unification revealed a growing opposition to centralisation and an imaginary that demanded less centralised control and more localised interests. 'Freedom' became the catchword of this era, and with it the expansion of markets and elimination of restrictions on capital.

Under these pressures 'internationalism' was transformed into an empty discourse of rights that overrode discourses of equity and distribution. Freedom brought with it the proliferation of global investments, the formalisation of international intellectual property rights, and the increasing role of international institutions promoting privatisation and deregulation. These capitalistic forces also revived, however, oppositional forces that drew on a left-oriented ideology: Anarchism, anti-authoritarianism, squatters' movements, and anti-racist and pro-immigrant groups started to multiply in the core, especially in Western Europe.

Following the Chinese model of reorganisation into collectives and cooperatives, pockets within countries such as France or Italy reacted to the growing social crisis by calling for workers' autonomy and self-management.[19] Although they fell short of generating autonomy, various cooperatives, collectives, and communes flourished throughout the West and the Third World, advocating self-management and non-hierarchical relations; sometimes these reactions were combined with other communal, religious, or identity movements. Throughout the 1980s and into the 1990s, local communities interested in cooperative efforts and communal autonomy flourished everywhere, out of necessity in the periphery and semi-periphery, and as a political engagement in the core. Neo-Luddite or anti-consumer sentiments emerged as alternatives to capitalism, as did many identity-based communities, with their anti-systemic drive made more effective through collaborative efforts and active resistance to capitalist values.

Some of these communities built their identity on an oppositional ideology that was neither ethnically nor religiously based; cults proliferated (from Guyana to Switzerland, to Waco in the US) as did military or semi-military associations or hate groups (anti-state militias, white supremacists, anti-immigrant groups). Some communities were also built on anarchist principles (especially in Italy, the Netherlands, France, Greece, Spain, Mexico, Argentina, and the East Coast and Midwest of the United States), while others flourished as squatters (especially in Germany, Italy, France, Mexico, and the United States).

At the height of the 1980s, homeless individuals, impoverished people, immigrants, destitute families, and young migrants found refuge in parks and abandoned buildings in core countries. Millions of the impoverished and desti-tute of the periphery and the semi-periphery, in addition to increasing numbers of refugees fleeing a variety of wars and conflicts, started building shantytowns or *bidonvilles*, mostly in urban areas—from Rio de Janeiro to Cape Town. Inevitably, confrontations between these poor populations and the state followed and move-ments were formed. In Europe, the height of confrontations with the state and supporting demonstrations emerged in the 1980s (especially 1975–1977 in Italy; 1980 in the Netherlands; 1980–1981 and 1985–1987 in Germany and France; and 1989–1990 in Germany, France, and the United States).[20]

The global nature of these movements was also extended through a new 'internationalism' associated with new identities. The struggle against the war in Vietnam and against the Cold War and the possibility of a nuclear holocaust brought people together in peace movements, which reached their peak in Europe during the mid-1980s. Meanwhile environmental movements aiming at the pro-tection of human, animal, and earth rights came to the fore. Coalitions among these movements and their cooperation on transnational issues also reflected the internationalisation of the period, and the proliferation of similar problems across national boundaries. These kinds of coalitions initially emerged as alliances of na-tion-states under the banners of such internationalist tendencies and sometimes against dominant ideologies. The nonaligned movement (NAM), for example, in-spired various movement-based coalitions to evolve into cartels of power politics based on regional economic and political interests. Although most regional state coalitions emerged in the 1950s–1960s—eg, the Organisation of American States (OAS), Organisation for Economic Cooperation and Development (OECD), Southeast Asia Treaty Organisation (SEATO), the Arab League, the Economic Community of West African States), in the 1980s international institutions that were either independent (the Bretton Woods institutions, the General Agreement on Tariffs and Trade (GATTS), the World Trade Organization (WTO)—or as part of the United Nations system (World Health Organisation, UN Development Programme, UN Children's Fund), and that flourished on the basis of post-1945 internationalism, also started to become effective global forces.

The freedom and human rights campaigns of the 1980s also had numerous unexpected consequences, as new internationalist and egalitarian orientations started inhabiting international institutions and creating hundreds of international nongovernmental organisations (NGOs) with anti-systemic orientations. The United Nations started investigating the importance of 'economic' and 'social' rights. In the late 1980s and early 1990s, mass movements of solidarity for the humane and / or equal treatment of immigrants, minorities, and the poor started to spread in the core and formed a constellation of new movements calling for policies opposing traditional mechanisms of upholding the interstate system and the capitalist world-economy. These ranged from pro-immigration rights movements, anti-racist movements, and movements calling for the elimination of debt and redistribution of wealth. These movements of the 1980s would become the backbone of today's global egalitarian and anti-globalisation movements.

The Decline of Anti-Systemic Labour Movements

While these new movements based on new identities were emerging, older movements died. Most prominent were labour movements in the core and in a few countries of the 'rising' semi-periphery—including 'communist' countries such as Poland or Czechoslovakia—which became more preoccupied with their self-interest associated with the professionalisation of workers. Indeed, in the core, the labour movement was predominantly guided by liberal-reformist tendencies interested in reforming the system institutionally in order to guarantee certain rights and privileges for those already legally residing within the core, rather than transforming the system as a whole.[21] In the 1980s and 1990s, labour movements in the core ceased to generate any anti-systemic activities and many of their constituents felt as if they belonged to a 'professional class', that is an amalgamation of 'white-collar' with 'blue-collar' workers, all working toward higher levels of credit and purchasing power.

During the same period, labour movements in the periphery and other 'rising' semi-peripheral countries, especially in Southeast Asia and Latin America, were mushrooming into anti-repressive struggles. The 'outsourcing' policies of core countries, which benefitted semi-peripheral nations first, initially led to a growth of unionisation that was in many cases anti-systemic in orientation. Only in the 1990s, with 'subcontracting' to smaller and non-unionised factories, and with yet another wave of 'outsourcing' from the semi-periphery to the periphery, did the piecework system replace assembly lines in the semi-peripheral countries. This led to the decimation of labour unions and to more repressive work conditions encouraged and allowed by the 'savage' capitalism of the 1990s, which reintegrated in the world-system the extraction of absolute surplus value or 'new slavery' (eg, sweatshops, sexual slavery, indentured labour).[22] The majority of the peasants or farmers living in the periphery and the semi-periphery were hit hard in the 1990s after the dismantlement of Fordist policies and the implementation of structural adjustment programmes or neoliberal trade policies that undermined farm subsidies and, in some cases, food subsidies. Some may become 'professionals' but most will become 'casual labourers'. The worst off and their families may end up trapped in 'migrant-importing' or 'slave-exporting' schemes, thus swelling the ranks of the 'new slavery'.[23]

Our aim is not to map the anti-systemic labour movements across our period; a good start for such an endeavour would be the excellent survey of labour unrest across the world-system conducted by a research working group a decade ago.[24] Representative cases to support our observations are now many. In Latin America, the state-controlled trade unions in Argentina, Mexico, and Brazil gave way to new forms of labour alliances with various anti-repressive movements. In Brazil, for instance, a new Brazilian Workers' Party (PT or *Partido dos Trabalhadores*) was formed in 1979, through an alliance of rural unions, radical Catholics, left-wing intellectuals, and shantytown movements.[25] Invigorated by the metalworkers' strikes in 1978–1980 in São Paolo, and in 1980 in São Bernardo, the PT became an important movement precisely because it reached out to other popular movements not representing workers but a variety of oppressed people (landless peasants, the homeless and unemployed, women's groups, indigenous movements, etc). Unlike other labour union–based parties, the PT increased in popularity and power in the 1980s and 1990s, culminating in the election of PT leader Luiz Inácio 'Lula' da Silva as president in 2002.

Peru's trade unionists also combined their efforts with popular neighbourhood movements (*barrios populares*) in their nationwide strikes between 1977 and 1979.[26] The factors that made Latin America a hotbed of anti-systemic activities in the 1970s and 1980s included: Repressive military regimes; radical Catholic 'liberation theology' and 'Base Christian Communities' established after the 1968 Medellin Conference of Latin American Bishops; and the increasing pauperisation of mass urban populations and the disruption and destruction of peasants' livelihoods. When labour combined its forces with other movements, it was able to grow as a movement as happened in Brazil. However, Latin America was also a popular site for socialist guerrilla movements backed by labour and / or the peasantry. While 1979 was the year of the founding of the Brazilian PT, it was also the year of the successful Nicaraguan Revolution. Grenada and Iran were other sites of change in 1979, and like Nicaragua, they revealed that 'labour' could no longer function independently of other movements, be they socialist-based (Nicaragua), religious-based (Iran), or identity-based (eg the women's movement in Grenada).

These lessons spread. A reinvigorated internationalist orientation of labour, with special links between the core, the periphery, and the semi-periphery, was re-established in the late 1990s, but its mobilisation power remained negligible.

Massive efforts of international institutions (not limited to the International Labour Organisation) and NGOs were undertaken to support workers' rights in various outsourcing sites in the (semi-)periphery. In the core, a reinvigorated but dwindling labour force in industrial production opted for joining the ranks of those dissatisfied with regionalisation and deregulation efforts, and would, by the late 90s, play a major role in the emerging 'anti-globalisation' movement.[27]

The Transformation of Nationalism and Socialism and the Rise of Terrorism

Nationalist movements were only anti-systemic in the anti-colonial stage, as they tended to undermine the resources and threaten the economic—as well as the political and socio-cultural—stability of core capitalist countries. They were considered anti-systemic when the outcome of their liberation struggle was to create a socialist space, or to provide an egalitarian, distributive, and communitarian form of government that countered capitalist exploitative conditions (based on class and / or race and gender). Most nationalist movements that achieved control of the state ultimately participated in the consolidation of the interstate system.[28] Throughout their anti-colonisation strategies and tactics of liberation, some adopted socialist orientations while others carried on their nationalist struggle under the banner of capitalistic 'freedom', and many such opposing movements within contested national boundaries ended up being the playground for US American and Soviet *realpolitik* and fell victim to the so-called 'Cold War'.

Socialism was greatly affected by the USSR's withdrawal of support for 'world socialism' and its becoming an entrenched bureaucratic system engaged in a 'Cold War' with capitalist centres. This meant limited support provided for state socialism and for socialist liberation struggles (although Cuba did fill that gap in many parts of Africa). But it also meant a reassessment of socialist doctrines and an attempt to realise socialist goals in a capitalist-dominated world (an impossibility, as socialism was supposed to succeed and flourish as a historical system in its own right). The second set of forces that undermined socialism was associated with the aggressive neoliberal policies implemented in the 1980s as well as by the increasing effects of US hegemony.

Nationalist movements that did not have adequate resources (or the patience) needed to take over the state carried over the necessary mix of 'direct action' and 'counter-violence' to become 'terrorists', along with socialist and communist forces that rejected statist and bureaucratic communism and were disillusioned by the state. Immersed in desperate situations, dwindling members of these movements resorted to desperate means: Terrorised by capitalism and / or by the state, they returned the package 'back to sender'. But instead of smashing the state machine, as recommended by the Marx of the *18th Brumaire*, they strengthened it—through the fabricated need of security. It was instead the interstate system, under US hegemony, that smashed most anti-systemic terrorists (those terrorists who targeted capitalist institutions or centres of power and who were motivated by a socialist or communist ideologies), one after the other, using its new found tool of controlling imaginary significations—along with the military and economic muscle necessary for any hegemon to control the means of terror and mass genocide.

'Terrorism' is a charged word with a long history of use and abuse.[29] We use it here to designate "a strategy that generates fear and anxiety, through violent methods, in order to achieve political aims". In most cases then, terrorism is proper to state institutions and to the state's ideological or repressive state apparatuses. The terror of random violence, when it is not applied through dominant state powers, becomes the "weapon of the weak".[30] Such a form of desperate resistance that proliferated in the 1960s and 1970s, and reached unprecedented heights in the mid-1980s (reported 'terrorist' incidents increased from 572 in 1975 to 3,525 in 1984)[31] seems to have been born again as socialist, communist, and nationalist promises started to wane.

When faced with desperate situations and devoid of hope for the success of their movements (eg, in taking over the state), some individuals or groups have taken it upon themselves to appropriate this strategy, as in Czarist Russia, in Nazi-occupied Europe, in China's liberation wars, and in Algeria's decolonisation struggle. The strategy was also appropriated by desperate national liberation movements, such as the Palestinian liberation movements, the Irish Republican Army (IRA), and yet other groups desiring a separate nation-state based on a shared religion, ethnicity, language, or another identity trait. Socialist strategies also started appropriating terrorism in an attempt to counter the violence of capitalism, as was the case with Baader-Meinhof, Action Directe, Brigate Rossa, the Black Panthers, Tupac Amaru, the Japanese Red Army, Sendero Luminoso, etc. Socialist activists also appropriated various dimensions of 'terrorism' and spread them across the globe in the 1970s and 1980s, as in the targeting of chief executive officers and rich politicians for kidnappings or assassinations, and the targeting of symbolic locations, meetings, companies, and brand names for destruction or disruption. These strategies were soon reappropriated in different contexts and performed in the name of a different set of meanings and goals; some became associated with religious and ethnic movements—which replaced socialism and nationalism as dominant movements—while others became associated with 'anti-globalisation' tendencies.

Rise of Religious Nationalism

In the aftermath of 1968, 'liberation theology' merged with many socialist and nationalist anti-repressive struggles across Latin America and in Mexico where leading Catholic figures, as well as common practitioners of the faith, reaffirmed a social commitment to helping the poor and to assisting the oppressed. This commitment materialised itself in a large-scale organisational attempt at offering assistance, education, and in building communities. In South America and Mexico, countless people hoped to liberate themselves from military regimes and repressive governments. In Central America, liberation did not come easily; priests, bishops, nuns, and scores of believers and lay people were massacred by right-wing militias and armies trained, financed, and supported by the US government. In El Salvador, Guatemala, and Honduras, armies and militias trained by the US Army and its School of the Americas helped to defeat the liberation theology of those clergy within the Catholic Church who made the mistake of choosing "the preferential option for the poor".[32] As archbishop Dom Helder Camara of Recife, Brazil, famously put it: "When I give bread to the poor, they call me a saint; but when I ask why people are poor, they call me a communist".[33] During the same period, in the 1970s and 1980s, a different set of religious beliefs took hold of oppressed populations in the Middle East, India, and elsewhere. The face of nationalism was changing, especially as it reflected the plight of the impoverished by increasing neoliberalism; it was no longer socialist in orientation, but often religious or ethnic.

In the Middle East, postcolonial governments cracked down on communist parties and highlighted socialist versions of nationalism that soon evolved into a form of Arab pan-nationalism. Every government was eliminating radical egalitarians, even if those governments declared allegiance to socialism and allied themselves with the Soviet Union or were nonaligned. In Iraq, the socialist Baath government started an extensive purge from government and systematic elimination of members of the Iraqi Communist Party (from 1978 to 1986). Similarly, Gamal Abdel Nasser's regime in Egypt was working on land reform and creating an 'Arab socialism' while exterminating communists.

At the same time religious movements—such as the Islamic Brotherhood—were also persecuted, as Arabism was defined in secular terms. The pan-Arab movement reached its peak in the late 1950s and continued through the 1960s as Egypt, Syria, Yemen, Libya, and the Sudan attempted—unsuccessfully—different combinations of unitary or cooperative schemes. These failed attempts at federation continued until the early 1970s when Nasserism and pan-Arabism started to wither; by 1973, after the last major Arab-Israeli military confrontation and the OPEC attempt at empowerment, they declined rapidly. Nationalist and socialist movements in the Arab world were held together during the 1980s primarily for two reasons: One, a shared commitment to the Palestinian cause (which was used by most Arab dictators as a political tool); and two, a shared opposition to the imperialism manifested in the region by the United States and its allies through direct US interventions, as in Iran in 1953, Lebanon in 1958 and 1982, Iraq in 1991, and through the staunch US support of repressive and criminal governments (eg, Israel from the 1960s to the present, Iran under the Shah in the 1970s and 1980s, and Iraq under Saddam in the 1980s). The imaginary significations of an entire generation, produced through a pan-Arabism that was supposed to provide equality and common goals, collapsed. Revivalist Islam not only filled the meaning gap but also offered the only viable form of cultural resistance to neoliberalism and the cultural hegemony experienced by the growing masses of impoverished and oppressed men and women.[34]

At the same time, most Islamist movements, be they Shi'a or Sunni, were offering communist or socialist ideals as part of their goal of social justice. Starting in the 1980s and extending into the 1990s, Islamist movements went into the business of welfare and took over the responsibilities of Arab states by building hospitals and schools, assisting the poor and the homeless, and providing cooperative stores with subsidised prices. The Islamic Brotherhood communities in Egypt own their own financial institutions and businesses, along with hospitals, cooperative stores, religious schools, etc. , in Lebanon, also has hospitals and schools and is engaged in helping the poor and needy (especially the Shi'a community in south Beirut and southern Lebanon). Algeria's current Islamic revolution, led by the FIS (Islamic Salvation Front), has massive popular support and has generated cooperative efforts and quasi-socialist practices (eg, resource sharing, social assistance, etc), notwithstanding the occasional brutality in reaction to a repressive and terrorist government. All this is to show that religious movements and religious nationalism replaced socialist movements and socialist nationalism across the Middle East and North Africa.[35]

Similar reactions occurred in India and Pakistan, often in association with the creation of an 'other' upon whom one could transfer the discontent with savage capitalism's effects on local communities. After the socialist policies of Nehru and Indira Gandhi, resistance to neoliberalism in India collapsed. The Congress Party had till then resisted playing the divisive religious and ethnic card. However, a few old and new groupings, organisations, and parties started in the 1980s and the 1990s to make 'Hindu nationalism' the backbone of their goal or platform; they aimed at re-creating an identity based on the demonisation of the 'Muslim' (as the 'other') upon whom the ill effects of neoliberalism and 'globalisation' could be projected: The RSS (Rashtriya Swayamsevak Sangh—'National Association of Volunteers', in Hindi), the VHP (Vishva Hindu Parishad—'the Global Council for Hindus'), and lately, the BJP (Bharatiya Janata Party—'Indian People's Party').[36]

While the BJP was at the forefront of consolidating this enormous and powerful 'religious nationalist' movement, the RSS nonetheless expressed a desire to build an 'identity' opposed to global forces that it associated with multinational corporations. As an RSS pamphlet stated, "[e]very morning we begin the job of cleansing our body with the help of products manufactured by these filthy companies which have a history of exploiting poor countries of the world".[37] Hindu radicalism thus creates an internal threat as it reacts to an external threat; its helplessness at reversing or affecting global forces associated with savage capitalism can only be repressed or compensated for through a campaign to create a strong and cohesive identity built on a tradition that is constantly threatened (and that does not adequately address the content of the tradition, be it in reformist or revivalist mode). This development is quite similar to that of Islamic radicalism, particularly in South Asia.

In Pakistan, Kashmir, Serbia, Bosnia, and Afghanistan, a similar desire for religious or ethnic independence has reacted to global conditions that have created the impoverished masses and brings these masses together under the banner of identity. In the core, such a transformation was reflected in the extreme right and in the popular opposition to immigration and migrants—the transference of local government's failures on an 'other'. Anti-immigration policies have become an 'occupation' of the jobless and resource-less masses who are offered the 'other' as a bone: The Vietnamese to the unemployed Australians; the Turks to the discontented Germans; the North Africans to the disenchanted French workers, etc.

It is important, however, to point out that while we are trying to describe the emerging sets of forces we are associating with 'religious nationalism', these forces were not always dominant, nor were they unique to particular religions or regions. These forces coexist and interact with numerous other forces, including old nationalist or socialist forces, or ideological or religious forces. What we are pointing to is that many social movements, potentially anti-systemic or not, were increasingly driven by a combination of religious and nationalist forces, especially in places where socialist or liberal nationalisms are on the decline. This includes the various political brands of religious nationalism, be they Christian (eg, the United States), Muslim (eg, Pakistan, Algeria), Hindu (eg, India), or Jewish (eg, Israel).

Some have argued that this applies to China as well, where an official revival of 'Confucianism' was to lend legitimacy to a nationalist identity in transition from socialism to 'market socialism'. In the 1990s, the Chinese Communist Party leadership formally proclaimed Confucianism as another "guiding principle" besides Marxism-Leninism-Mao Zedong thought.[38] China is indeed a contested site; for while many in the middle class or the nouveau riche may be driven by determinable beliefs or ideologies, it is difficult if not impossible, as Robert Weil points out, to assess what drives the majority of the Chinese peasantry.[39] The Tiananmen movement of 1989 revealed the increasing range of different and contradictory tendencies within the urban strata of Chinese society, from anti-statist and socialist orientations to staunch beliefs in the 'democracy' myth and the 'free market' gospel. With various countries moving from socialist orientations to neoliberal experiments legitimised by free trade propaganda, it is difficult to project whether China will follow Eastern Europe and the former Soviet Union in succumbing to the so-called 'American dream' of freedom and democracy or whether a new religious nationalism built on traditional Confucian ethics (or on racial superiority) may emerge there.

Identity Movements

As the foregoing survey of the demise of socialist and nationalist movements and the emergence of new movements demonstrates, new forms of identity have increasingly come to define anti-systemic movements. The term 'identity' may be initially associated with those strata of populations whose empowerment accords with the effects of the early stages of the Chinese Cultural Revolution—whereby an 'oppressed stratum' gains privilege over a general class, be it the proletariat, the bourgeoisie, or capital. There have, of course, been numerous 'identity' movements that preceded the Chinese Revolution or that were not influenced by it: The Civil Rights Movements in the United States (especially from the 1963 March on Washington until the declaration of 'Black Power' in 1965–66),[40] the feminist movement (initially predominantly radical and socialist), as well as new radical environmental movements (from Greenpeace to Earth First!). Many of these are representative of a strand of movements whose anti-repressive struggles became inextricably linked to anti-systemic activity aimed at undermining the world-system's established hierarchies and exploitative mechanisms.

Along with these anti-systemic forces should be listed anti-colonialist movements that could be called 'nationalist' (notably Algeria, Northern Ireland, South Africa, Palestine, etc). Some of these anti-colonialist movements were also combating social hierarchies based on identity (race, religion, ethnicity, caste, etc). The late 1960s witnessed the proliferation of 'identities' built around common interests, aims, occupations, ways of living, as well as around common histories and backgrounds not limited to ethnic, religious, or linguistic groups. These differences served to define one's being and goals and provided the means of empowerment and liberation as well as a basis of cooperation. Ethnic or religious movements emerged initially as 'identity' movements, from the late 1960s until the late 1970s (in Malaysia, Indonesia, India, Sri Lanka, Thailand, Philippines, Spain, Lebanon, Turkey, Iraq, Nigeria, Morocco, China, Australia, and the United States). Many were soon transformed, especially after 1979, into movements that posed serious threats to the stability of the interstate system and, by rejecting the basic tenets of modernist capitalist values, acquired an anti-systemic label.[41]

While the peace movement that was linked to the anti-nuclear movement of the 1970s and 1980s is not based on an ethnicity or religion, it is an example of a phenomenon that redefines the identity of its participants: Pacifists can be religious or laypeople, but what links them together is their belief in peace and their opposition to war, and that is a 'part' of who they are and what they believe in. So while the peace movement may have been—in the 1970s in the United States, or in the 1980s in Europe, or elsewhere—an organised mass movement opposed to the policies of the United States and / or that of the Soviet Union during the Cold War, and while it may have included committed individuals united in one goal (peace or elimination of nuclear threats), over time it has become a manifestation of the fragmented identities of many in the core. The solidarity movement of the 1980s reflects a similar pattern: 'SOS Racisme' in France, or the variety of German coalitions and movements opposing anti-immigrant policies and / or practices, express an opposition while presenting an aspect of the participants' 'identity'—aspects that do not define that identity but may be reflective of 'parts' of one's declared or assumed identity.

The Relevance of 1968 and the Primacy of Consumption

While identity movements blossomed, ruling elites forged ahead with their own projects as well. In this respect the period 1945–1989 was a decisive one, with 1968 falling at the midpoint. Through the interaction of various forces, a major transformation of the system became manifest as ruling elites sought to address the social needs of their peoples. At the centre of this effort were the increasing primacy of consumption as *the* domain of capitalist expansion and consolidation, and the projection of 'consumerism' as a basic societal need and a motivation for peoples everywhere. Through a very long process, extending as far back as the preliminary individuation forces carried through Modernity and Enlightenment, a major shift in economic, political, social, and cultural forces was slowly able to establish *purchasing power as a universal human value*, making it the motivation equated with *the* social needs of populations around the globe.

This long and complex process allowed capitalism to establish its centre within the production of subjectivities by producing global 'consumer subjects', rather than by relying on the state as its epicentre of power. That does not mean that the interstate system and the particular states forming it lost their ability to control the populace's desires and needs but that the primordial forces controlling those desires and needs became 'global' by permeating the 'cultural worlds' at the basis of the interstate system and were thus able to directly influence the meanings and values embedded in the 'material life' of various populations. This shift occurred with the help of the expanding networks of communication and information that were disseminating 'consumerism' (associated with the ideological banners of 'freedom', 'rights', and 'choice') as *the* way of living and relating to the world.[42]

The years following 1968 also emboldened capitalism, after vigorous and long-term mechanisms were implemented to circumvent the possibility of a takeover of states across the world. Those anti-systemic movements that posed a serious threat were put in check in the United States, Europe, Latin America, Africa, and in many parts of Asia, through targeted assassinations, covert actions, infiltrations, or the purchase of loyalties. These efforts ranged widely, from Iran (1953–1954), Guatemala (1955), Cuba (1960s), Chile (1973), and the COINTELPRO ('Counter Intelligence Program') projects in the United States, to many other similar efforts.

At the same time capitalist powers launched a juridical effort to take over the international order and to depict it as 'free', associated with a discourse of 'human rights' that intensified after 1968. While the various explosions of 1968 momentarily perturbed the order necessary for the functioning of some states, capitalism flourished as new markets were opened when targeted by 'brands' and lifestyles that catered to the revolutionary demands of various groups. The revolution of 1968 suddenly became 'hip'. Thus the media and integrated marketing strategies depicted their brands and products as directly associated with the life experiences of the sexual revolution, the hippie movement, the feminist movement, the peacenik movement, etc. It was soon the 'product' that expressed one's identity, and one's individuality was expressed through the things that one consumed. This opened a vast array of possibilities for change and an incredible potential for an intensive proliferation of consumer goods without the actual need for geographic expansion.[43] 'War by other means' became a war of words and of control of interpretation and meaning.

While the global media and its control of the flow of information has always reflected the moneyed elite in core countries,[44] 'advertising' became the weapon of choice for capitalist infiltration first within the core, and later globally, undermining the European communist dictatorships in the process. The 'advertising' we are referring to is not merely about selling goods, but about selling images, lifestyles, attitudes, ways of living, hopes, dreams, and other significations associated with capitalist imaginaries. It is precisely the period around 1968 that marked the initial expansion of this kind of advertising power in the United States, a power that has since reached unimaginable proportions, due to the expansion of informational and communicational flows that became global in reach via various media conglomerates—including the film and music industries, cable and television networks, news, radio stations, print and internet media, etc—and marketing and advertising campaigns for products and services, international institutions and organisations, etc).

Meanwhile the anti-Taylorist and anti-Fordist practices that became the norm in the 1980s and 1990s were transforming the face of 'work' everywhere. Marx did predict that, "[as] the number of co-operating workers increases, so does their resistance to the domination of capital, and necessarily, the pressure put on by capital to overcome their resistance",[45] but he could never have imagined how capital would overcome such resistance. He dreamed of a "real subsumption" that, with increasing relativisation of surplus value extracted from labour, would create some "free time" for the development of the individual. As he wrote in *Grundrisse*:

The saving of labour time [is] equal to an increase of free time, ie time for the full development of the individual, which in turn reacts back upon the productive power of labour as itself the greatest productive power. From the standpoint of the direct production process it can be regarded as the production of fixed capital, this fixed capital being man himself.[46]

The transition from "formal" to "real subsumption", as elaborated by Marx in *Capital*, volume one (including the discarded draft of its sixth section), combined with Marx's writings on "consumption" and "fixed capital", have allowed a few scholars to discover in Marx an analysis of capital's "production of subjectivities" (related to capital's investment in the aforementioned 'free time') that is linked to the increasing importance of "immaterial labour"—that takes on the task of shaping and producing "fixed capital".[47]

Subjectivities are still produced through the web of social relations, but these relations are increasingly situated within the 'immaterial' or 'intangible' field that inhabits one's 'free time'. 'Free time' is constantly expanding to encompass all other time, including 'production time', due to the decreasing relevance of assembly lines in factories, so-called cooperative efforts in the workplace and in the household, the increasing relevance of 'individuation' in the workplace, schools, and households. Consumption and the desires and needs for consumption—of tangibles (eg, consumer goods or material possessions) and of intangibles (eg, representational or ideological constructs, including styles, identities, and illusions of proximity, of belonging, or of possibilities)—became productive of social subjectivities, as a major productive activity (physical and mental)—in the same way factory labour was one of the major productive activities in the nineteenth century.

At the same time, and through this production of needs and desires, capitalist imaginaries are inhabiting, permeating, and transforming other social imaginaries and various aspects of the 'cultural worlds' of the interstate system, through various direct (but mostly 'indirect') means including the media, multiple information and communication networks, and global entertainment and marketing industries (that are producing and shaping people's activities, desires, needs, etc). Consumption became a primary player in the transformed system of the late twentieth century.

Conclusion: Twentieth-Century Transformations of Movements and the System

Our claim is that anti-systemic activity has been radically recast as capitalism in the last half of the twentieth century has increasingly penetrated and permeated every aspect of the economy and of material life. Consumption everywhere is increasingly regulated through capitalist forces, rather than by daily necessities and cultural spheres of influence; everywhere capitalism effectively manipulates local socio-cultural values and epistemologies. These developments have in turn reawakened identities and localised groups based on common interest, religion, ethnicity, or 'tribe',[48] while the ideological forces inherent in socialism, nationalism, and communism have been weakened. The challenges of migration have, moreover, served to intensify the trend toward 'identity formation' through the vilification and demonisation of an 'other'.

While national education curricula and the national state are still effective mechanisms of producing political subjects, they are no longer as effective in counterbalancing the 'global' forces of production and reproduction of meanings and values associated with dominant capitalist imaginaries. It is therefore no surprise that after 1968 protests and demonstrations have no longer exclusively targeted capital or specific national governments, but rather institutions such as the United Nations, WTO, IMF, World Bank, international NGOs, and multinational companies.[49] These have all become effective sites of control, as well as sites of struggles for hegemony and increasing competitiveness between various forms of capital still centred in core—and some semi-peripheral—countries.

As for the movements, they, too, have been transformed along with the nature of social relations and social consciousness. After the 1970s, and increasingly in the 1980s and 1990s, committed individuals with ideals that stood for moral values have participated in many demonstrations and occasional actions. Yet these actions cannot usually be described as a 'movement'. The peace marches of 2003, for example, as in many demonstrations in support of specific issues, have offered only a limited opportunity for more individuated selves to express shared goals with others. Unlike past movements aimed at the capture of the state, these new movement manifestations are most often aimed at lobbying policymakers or affecting public opinion. Movements that are organised toward a specific goal with anti-systemic aims have thus become the exception to the rule.

Identity movements are in this respect easily contrasted with traditional 'unidirectional' movements that worked toward the achievement of a general (rather than a particular) goal through generalised means. The takeover of the state that was the explicit goal of socialist movements, for example, stands in stark contrast with the movements of the 1980s and after that rarely entertained the possibility of the overhaul of the political and economic system through collective action.

The transformations at work in the structures of knowledge across the world-system, and the new technological advances and informational and communicational possibilities, provided for imaginary significations that undermined linear and determinate 'realities' for more complex and multiple ones. In other words, from a purely Marxist perspective, the more complex the social experiences, the productive activities, and the mechanisms of production of subjectivities (no longer limited to simple forms of acculturation, socialisation, and individuation), the more complicated and diverse the 'social consciousness' of social actors. In a world where one is bombarded by constantly changing significations, meanings, images, and where one is involved in diverse forms of activities, one's 'social consciousness' could no longer be that of a 'worker'—in any circumscribed sense, be it produced in the factory, in the village, or in the city. If the world 'globalisation' is to mean anything at all, it should designate these conditions that produce today's subjectivities that lend themselves easily to multiple aims, numerous goals, and various strategies.

Thus, with the withering away of the state as the 'promised land' of traditional movements, social movements aimed at gaining power wherever they could locate it and 'empowerment' became the aim of most movements in the 1990s. Agents were no longer participating in 'one' movement; instead they were participating in as many commitments as their social consciousness called for. While we could talk of different strategies and tactics of empowerment, it would be impossible to outline contemporary movements based on their 'identity', 'adversary', or 'societal goal' (as Castells and Touraine suggest),[50] for such criteria could not elucidate the nature of movements but would rather 'construct' it.

At the forefront of strategies of empowerment were concerted efforts at influencing and shaping public opinion (via information and communication), catering to the media and to a culture of numbers (polls, surveys, and votes) proper to certain so-called democratic processes (by organising demonstrations, massively attended marches or events, etc), and demanding transparency and more open participation (so that more diverse 'interest' groups could lobby and influence policy setting). Other strategies included escaping the overall political (and sometimes economic) processes, by choice or by necessity, to pursue particular forms of empowerment (through a lifestyle, a belief system, etc). Many other empowerment strategies could be listed, from the basic construction of a shared 'identity' (ethnicity, religion, ideology, cult, etc) to engagement in coalition and cooperative activities aimed at achieving a specific goal (anti-war demonstrations, boycott of certain brands, voting for a candidate, pushing for a project, etc).

What has interested us here is to illuminate those that could be called 'anti-systemic' or have displayed strategies of empowerment that could have anti-systemic tendencies. Such strategies may pose an increasing threat to the equilibrium of the capitalist world-system. They do not yet, however, constitute an 'anti-systemic movement' with an organisational infrastructure that sustains the effective power of consistent, recurring, and threatening actions. Many contemporary movements, as we have pointed out, are disempowered either through the capitalist control of the same processes of communication they aim to influence, or by the ways through which capitalism has learned to flourish and ignore 'pockets' of resistance or delinked sites. It remains to be seen how the worldwide interaction between these different—indeed often divergent—forces will have specific impact on the system in the decades to come. We can only hope that this analysis may contribute to rethinking current paradigms and traditional strategies for political action.

References

Theodor Adorno and Max Horkheimer, 1989—*Dialectic of Enlightenment*. Translated by John Cumming. London: Verso

Tariq Ali, 2017—'Storming Heaven: Where Has the Rage Gone?', in Jai Sen, ed, 2017a— *The Movements of Movements, Part 1: What Makes Us Move?*. Volume 4 in the *Challenging Empires* series. New Delhi: OpenWord, and Oakland, CA: PM Press

Philip G Altbach, 1970—'Student Movements in Historical Perspective: The Asian Case', in *Journal of Southeast Asian Studies*, vol 1 no 1, pp 74–84

Samir Amin, 1997—*Capitalism in the Age of Globalization: The Management of Contemporary Society*. London: Zed Books

Samir Amin, Giovanni Arrighi, Andre Gunder Frank, and Immanuel Wallerstein, 1990— *Transforming the Revolution: Social Movements and the World System*. New York: Monthly Review

Giovanni Arrighi, 1994—*The Long 20th Century*. New York: Verso

Giovanni Arrighi, Terrence K Hopkins, and Immanuel Wallerstein, 1989—*Antisystemic Movements*. New York: Verso

Jean Baudrillard, 1970—*La Société de Consommation* ['The Consumption Society', in French]. Paris: Editions Denoêl

Daniel Bensaïd, 2017—'The Return of Strategy', in Jai Sen, ed, 2017a—*The Movements of Movements, Part 1: What Makes Us Move?*. Volume 4 in the *Challenging Empires* series. New Delhi: OpenWord, and Oakland, CA: PM Press

Cheton Bhatt, 2001—*Hindu Nationalism*. New York: Berg

Fabrizio Calvi, ed, 1977—*Italie 77: Le 'mouvement', les intellectuals* ['Italy 77: "The movement", the intellectuals', in French]. Paris: Seuil

Manuel Castells, 1997—*The Power of Identity*. Cambridge, MA: Blackwell

Cornelius Castoriadis, 1984 [1957]—*Workers' Councils and the Economics of a Self-Managed Society*. Philadelphia: Wooden Shoe pamphlet, Philadelphia Solidarity

Cornelius Castoriadis, 1987 [1975]—*The Imaginary Institution of Society*. Cambridge, MA: MIT Press

Adrian Chan, 1997—'In Search of a Civil Society in China', in *Journal of Contemporary Asia*, vol 27 no 2, pp 242–251

Noam Chomsky, 1986—*Pirates and Emperors, Old and New: International Terrorism in the Real World*. Cambridge, MA: South End Press

Noam Chomsky, 1991—*Media Control: The Spectacular Achievements of Propaganda*. Westfield, NJ: Open Media

Noam Chomsky, 2000—*Rogue States: The Rule of Force in World Affairs*. Cambridge, MA: South End Press

Noam Chomsky, 2001—*Propaganda and the Public Mind*. Cambridge, MA: South End Press

Noam Chomsky, 2003—*Power and Terror*. New York: Seven Stories

Youssef M Choueiri, 1997—*Islamic Fundamentalism*. London: Pinter

José Luis Coraggio, 1985—'Social Movements and Revolution: The Case of Nicaragua', in David Slater, ed, 1985—*New Social Movements and the State in Latin America* (Amsterdam: CEDLA), pp 203–231

Gilles Deleuze, May 1990—'Postscript on the Societies of Control', in *L'Autre Journal* ['The Other Journal', in French], no 1 (May 1)

Gilles Deleuze, 1995—*Negotiations: 1972–1990*. Translated by Martin Joughan. New York: Columbia University Press

Wilma A Dunaway, ed, 2003—*Emerging Issues in the 21st Century World-System*. Westport, CT: Praeger

Mike Featherstone, 1991—*Consumer Culture and Postmodernism*. London: Sage

Michel Foucault, 1982—'The Subject and Power', Appendix in Hubert A Dreyfus and Paul Rabinow, eds, 1982—*Michel Foucault: Beyond Structuralism and Hermeneutics*. Chicago: University of Chicago Press

Michel Foucault, 2000—*Power: Essential Works of Foucault 1954–1984*, vol 3. Edited by James D Faubion. Translated by Robert Hurley et al. New York: New York Press

Thomas Carr Frank, 1995—*Commercialization of Dissent: Counterculture and Consumer Culture in the American 1960s*, vols 1 and 2. Ann Arbor: University of Michigan

Thomas Carr Frank, 1997—*The Conquest of Cool: Business Culture, Counterculture, and the Rise of Hip Consumerism*. Chicago: University of Chicago Press

Duncan Green, 1997 [1991]—*Faces of Latin America*. London: Latin American Bureau

Ernesto Che Guevara, 1968—*Oeuvres III: Textes Politiques* ['Works Vol III: Political Texts', in French]. Paris: François Maspero

Thomas Blom Hansen, 1999—*The Saffron Wave: Democracy and Hindu Nationalism in Modern India*. Princeton, NJ: Princeton University Press

David Harvey, 1989—*The Condition of Postmodernity: An Enquiry into the Origins of Cultural Change*. Oxford: Blackwell

David Harvey, 2003b—*The New Imperialism*. New York: Oxford University Press

Etienne Henry, 1985—'Urban Social Movements in Latin America: Towards a Critical Understanding', in David Slater, ed, 1985—*New Social Movements and the State in Latin America* (Amsterdam: CEDLA), pp 127–146

Edward Herman, 1983—*The Real Terror Network: Terrorism in Fact and Propaganda*. Boston: South End Press

Edward Herman and Noam Chomsky, 1988—*Manufacturing Consent: The Political Economy of the Mass Media*. New York: Pantheon

François Houtart, 2017—'Mahmoud Mohamed Taha: Islamic Witness in the Contemporary World', in Jai Sen, ed, 2017a—*The Movements of Movements, Part 1: What Makes Us Move?*. Volume 4 in the *Challenging Empires* series. New Delhi: OpenWord, and Oakland, CA: PM Press

Fouad Kalouche, 2007—'"New Slavery" within the Context of the Contemporary Transformations of Capitalism', in *International Studies in Philosophy*, vol 39 no 2, 2007, pp 73–96

Fouad Kalouche and Eric Mielants, 2008a—'Transformations of the World-System and Antisystemic Movements: 1968–2005', Chapter 4 in William G Martin et al, eds,

2008—*Making Waves: Worldwide Social Movements, 1750–2005* (Boulder, Colorado, and London: Paradigm Press), pp 128–167

Fouad Kalouche and Eric Mielants, 2008b—'The Significance of Religious or Ethnic Movements in the 21st Century World-System: From South Asia to the Low Countries', in Khaldoun Samman and Mazhar Al-Zoby, eds, 2008—*Islam and the Modern Orientalist World-System* (Boulder, Colorado: Paradigm Press Publishers), pp 129–153

George Katsiaficas, 1987—*The Imagination of the New Left: A Global Analysis of 1968*. Boston: South End Press

Alex Khasnabish, 2017—'Forward Dreaming: Zapatismo and the Radical Imagination', in Jai Sen, ed, 2017a—*The Movements of Movements, Part 1: What Makes Us Move?*. Volume 4 in the *Challenging Empires* series. New Delhi: OpenWord, and Oakland, CA: PM Press

Ben Kiernan, 1996—*The Pol Pot Regime: Race, Power, and Genocide in Cambodia under the Khmer Rouge*. New Haven, CT: Yale University Press

Hanspeter Kriesi, Ruud Koopmans, Jan Willem Duyvendak, and Marco Giugni, 1995—*New Social Movements in Western Europe: A Comparative Analysis*. Minneapolis: University of Minnesota Press

Xochitl Leyva Solano, 2017—'Geopolitics of Knowledge and the Neo-Zapatista Social Movement Networks', in Jai Sen, ed, 2017a—*The Movements of Movements, Part 1: What Makes Us Move?*. Volume 4 in the *Challenging Empires* series. New Delhi: OpenWord, and Oakland, CA: PM Press

Michel Maffesoli, 1996 [1998]—*The Time of the Tribes*. London: Sage

Manning Marable, 1991—*Race, Reform, and Rebellion: The Second Reconstruction in Black America, 1945–1990*. Jackson: University of Mississippi Press

Herbert Marcuse, 1966—*One-Dimensional Man: Studies in the Ideology of Advanced Industrial Society*. Boston: Beacon

William G Martin et al, eds, 2008—*Making Waves: Worldwide Social Movements, 1750–2005*. Boulder, Colorado, and London: Paradigm Press

Karl Marx, 1973—*Grundrisse: Foundations of the Critique of Political Economy*. New York: Vintage

Karl Marx, 1977—*Capital: A Critique of Political Economy*, vol 1. New York: Penguin

David McNally, 2017—'From the Mountains of Chiapas to the Streets of Seattle: This Is What Democracy Looks Like', in Jai Sen, ed, 2017a—*The Movements of Movements, Part 1: What Makes Us Move?*. Volume 4 in the *Challenging Empires* series. New Delhi: OpenWord, and Oakland, CA: PM Press

Aníbal Quijano and Immanuel Wallerstein 1992—'Americanity as a Concept of the Americas and the Modern World-System', in *International Journal of the Social Sciences*, vol 134 (November 1992), pp 549–557

Jason Read, 2003—*The Micro-Politics of Capital: Marx and the Prehistory of the Present*. Albany: State University of New York Press

Beverly J Silver, Giovanni Arrighi, and Melvyn Dubofsky, eds, 1995—'Labor Unrest in the World Economy, 1870–1990', special issue of *Review*, vol 18 no 1

James Toth, 2017—'Local Islam Gone Global: The Roots of Religious Militancy in Egypt and its Transnational Transformation', in Jai Sen, ed, 2017a—*The Movements of Movements, Part 1: What Makes Us Move?*. Volume 4 in the *Challenging Empires* series. New Delhi: OpenWord, and Oakland, CA: PM Press

Peter Van Der Veer, 1994—*Religious Nationalism: Hindus and Muslims in India*. Berkeley: University of California Press

Jean-Pierre Vernant, 1982—*The Origins of Greek Thought*. Ithaca, NY: Cornell University Press

Immanuel Wallerstein, 1978—'Civilizations and Modes of Production', in *Theory and Society*, vol 5 no 1, pp 1–10

Immanuel Wallerstein, 1991a—'The French Revolution as World Historical Event', in Immanuel Wallerstein, 1991—*Unthinking Social Science: The Limits of Nineteenth-Century Paradigms* (Cambridge, UK: Polity), pp 7–22

Immanuel Wallerstein, 1999b—'Islam, the West, and the World', in *Journal of Islamic Studies*, vol 10 no 2, pp 109–125

Immanuel Wallerstein, August 2004—*World System Analysis: An Introduction*. Durham, NC: Duke University Press

Robert Weil, 1996—*Red Cat, White Cat: China and the Contradictions of 'Market Socialism'*. New York: Monthly Review Press

Notes

1. Ed: This essay is a substantially revised extract from a chapter titled 'Transformations of the World-System and Anti-systemic Movements: 1968–2005' that appeared in William G Martin et al, eds, 2008—*Making Waves: Worldwide Social Movements, 1750–2005* (Boulder, CO: Paradigm Publishers), pp 128–167; Kalouche and Mielants 2008a. I am very grateful indeed to the authors and to the publishers for their respective generous permissions allowing us to prepare and publish this extract. For further reproduction permission, contact sharond@paradigmpublishers.com.

2. See Vernant 1982.

3. As above in Note 1, the more comprehensive original essay on which this one is based covered the longer period 1968–2005, including 'Part Two: Anti-systemic Movements after 1989'; Kalouche and Mielants 2008a. Although it is true that the full essay brought the authors' analysis more closely to our 'present', quite aside from considerations of length we chose to ask them to focus on the period 1968–1989 because of the iconic nature of the two dates—1968 being the year of the great "disillusionment" and "transformation" for what the authors refer to as "anti-systemic movements" (see Section II), and 1989 marking the collapse of the Soviet Union, and with that, a lot else, in social, political, and artistic terms.

4. The term 'social imaginary' as used throughout this chapter is meant to go beyond the limited significations associated with such concepts as 'social consciousness' or 'ideology'. The term accentuates forces or powers associated with imagination rather than images and representations, and is intricately connected to discourses across time, space, and disciplinary boundaries. The concept of 'social imaginary' has been used specifically by political philosophers and social scientists to indicate the signifying social forces that drive the beliefs and practices of populations beyond the theory-practice distinction as reflected, for example, in the Marxist dichotomy of 'base-superstructure' or 'productive forces-ideology'. Our use of the term 'social imaginary' is closest to that of the late political philosopher Cornelius Castoriadis. Castoriadis 1987 (1975).

5. Wallerstein 1978, pp 1–10.

6. See Martin 2008.

7. Cf Foucault 1982, 2000; Deleuze 1990, 1995.

8. See Amin, Arrighi, Frank, and Wallerstein 1990; Arrighi, Hopkins, and Wallerstein 1992, pp 221–242; Wallerstein 1991a, pp 65–83; and Wallerstein 1999b, pp 109–125. Ed: See also the chapters in this book on '1968' by Tariq Ali and the late Daniel Bensaïd, respectively Ali 2017 and Bensaïd 2017.

9. Ed: While the authors do also refer to the Zapatista movement in the latter part of their original essay on which this chapter is based (Kalouche and Mielants 2008a), for a discussion of the global resonance of a very different movement, see the essays by Alex Khasnabish and by Xochitl Leyva Solano in this book (Khasnabish 2017 and Levya Solano 2017); and also the essay by David McNally (McNally 2017).

10. Guevara 1968, pp 121–127.

11. In Wallerstein's main thesis, capitalism is a specific socioeconomic system characterised by a global division of labour resulting from intense yet unequal bulk trade linkages between different zones, which he labelled the 'core', 'periphery', and 'semi periphery'. This 'capitalist world-system' emerged in sixteenth-century Europe and subsequently expanded to incorporate more areas. In the context of the colonialism and imperialism that unfolded from 1492 until the early twentieth century, the entire world became interlinked through these trade patterns constitutive of unequal exchange. By stressing the importance of economic cycles and commodity chains of leading sectors, Wallerstein espoused the idea that the upward and downward social mobility of specific polities was possible. The crucial Wallersteinian concept of semi-periphery was introduced to clarify this idea theoretically: The three zones in which different political entities (nation-states, principalities, etc) are located contain divergent practices (in terms of life expectancy, standard of living, labour control, production of items for sale on the world market, and political regimes) precisely because of their hierarchical location within the capitalist world-economy. Though anti-systemic movements such as labour unions and anti-colonial activists opposed the logic of ceaseless accumulation of capital in the system as well as its racial hierarchy (Quijano and Wallerstein 1992), they only obtained limited successes.

12. Kiernan 1996.

13. Katsiaficas 1987, pp 37–57. Ed: As above, see also the chapters on '1968' by Tariq Ali and Daniel Bensaïd in this book (Ali 2017 and Bensaïd 2017).

14. Altbach 1981.

15. Coraggio 1985, pp 203–231.

16. Green 1997 (1991), pp 150–154.

17. Arrighi 1994, pp 323; Harvey 2003b.

18. Various manifestations of Islamist movements that can be described as anti-systemic are also reflected in other religious traditions, from Christianity to Hinduism. Varied reactions to neoliberalisation can be described as: 'fundamentalist' (going back to the fundamentals of a religious teaching through overreliance on recognised texts), 'revivalist' (rekindling interest in a religion as the basis for a renewed identity and as a guide for how to live within a community of shared beliefs), and 'radical' (rejection of the dominant social, political, and economic environment as incompatible with

religious beliefs *and* commitment to radically alter these dominant conditions in a variety of ways). See Choueri 1997.

19. Calvi 1977; Castoriadis 1984 (1957).

20. Katsiaficas 1998; Hamel, Lustiger-Thaler, and Mayer 2000; Kriesi et al 1995.

21. The majority of strikes in the United States (around 2,560 in 1968) were short-term and concerned mainly with the improvement of workers' conditions. The *Confédération Général du Travail* (CGT) in France stopped its major strike in 1968 after concessions by Pompidou. The days when workers controlled the means of production expired with the last breath of the self-management movements that flourished in factories throughout Europe c 1968–1971. Self-management and *'autonomia'* movements were predominant in countries like Italy, inspired by anarchists and radical groups on the extreme left, while the less numerous factory-based experiments in self-management in England, France, and West Germany were led by Trotskyist and Maoist groups, with some influenced by student movements. This trend, however, was quite limited and soon expired as the communist or socialist party line, or the major labour unions, decided to limit their free ride on the wave of popular discontent and social upheavals. Eastern European reactions, especially the thwarted reformist efforts in Czechoslovakia, Poland, and Hungary, left their mark in new forms of labour organising reaching their peak in Poland's 'Solidarity' movement in the next decade.

22. Ed: For a discussion of the "savage capitalism" in the 1990s outlined by the authors here, see the second part of their original essay, on which this essay is based; as in Note 1 above.

23. See the section '1989 and Beyond: "Savage" Capitalism and US Hegemony' in the original essay, Kalouche and Mielants 2008. See also Kalouche 2007.

24. See Silver, Arrighi, and Dubovsky 1995.

25. Green 1997 (1991), p 155.

26. Henry 1985, pp 127–146.

27. Ed: Again, see Part 2 of the authors' original essay, among other authors; Kalouche and Mielants 2008a.

28. The approach to historical development as linear has been an impediment to understanding the transformative processes of the world-system. Take for example the case of decolonisation: It is not sufficient, for an adequate historical understanding, to look at the struggles in the colonies as mere anti-systemic movements aiming at taking control of the resources and escaping colonial oppression. It is equally important to look at the systemic forces within such movements in tandem with the anti-systemic ones: The possibility of becoming a full-fledged partner of the camaraderie of the interstate system and of becoming an independent producer along with other systemic tendencies of creating new spaces for consumption, new identities, new ethnicities, and new 'free' markets. Needless to say, one should also acknowledge the role of imperialism and colonialism in initiating the process of production of subjectivities necessary for both anti-systemic and systemic orientations. Hence the need to look at transformative processes as the complex intercourse of multiple forces, some of which will be more effective than others in shaping short-term outcomes, while others will determine long-term outcomes—without undermining the complexity of the process as a whole.

29. Onwudiwe 2001, pp 28–49.
30. See Onwudiwe 2001; Chomsky 1986, 2000; Herman 1983.
31. Katsiaficas 198, p 182.
32. Chomsky 2003, pp 48–51.
33. ibid.
34. Ed: See the essay in this book by James Toth (Toth 2017).
35. Ed: For a discussion of a significant movement against these tendencies, and arguing for a synthesis of Islam and socialism in Sudan, see the essay by François Houtart in the companion volume to this book (Houtart 2017).
36. Van Der Veer 1994; Hansen 1999; Bhatt 2001. For an elaboration of the argument we make here, see Kalouche and Mielants 2008b.
37. Hansen 1999, pp 170–172.
38. Chan 1997, p 244.
39. Weil 1996, p 17.
40. Marable 1991.
41. See Kalouche and Mielants 2008b.
42. See Adorno and Horkheimer 1989; Marcuse 1966; Baudrillard 1970. This development may mark one of the most important transformations in twentieth-century capitalism. It consists of the change of modes of control of needs and desires that effectively contributed to the deep infusion of capitalistic values into the various cultural worlds and the different manifestations of 'material life' at the basis of the world-system. This was achieved through various means, not least of which were the proliferation of immaterial labour, the commodification of 'free time', the increasing dominance of capitalistic forces in 'global' processes of production of human desires and needs—through images, significations, communicational and informational flows, etc—and of transforming localised socio-cultural values and epistemologies.
43. See Frank 1995, 1997; Featherstone 1991; Harvey 1990.
44. See Chomsky and Herman 1988; Chomsky 1991, 2001.
45. Marx 1977, p 449.
46. Marx 1973, pp 711–712.
47. Read 2003. Cf also the work of Antonio Negri and Maurizio Lazzarato.
48. Dunaway, ed, 2003; Amin 1997; Maffesoli 1996 (1988); Castells 1997.
49. See Part 2 of the original chapter on which this essay is based ('Anti-systemic Movements after 1989'; Kalouche and Mielants 2008a), for our discussion of this period and phase.
50. For instance, Castells 1997, p 71.

Beyond *Altermondialisme*:
Anti-Capitalist Dialectic of Presence[1]
André C Drainville

Action, the only activity that goes on directly between men without the intermediary of things or matter, corresponds to the human condition of plurality, to the fact that men, not Man, live on the earth and inhabit the world. While all aspects of the human condition are somewhat related to politics, this plurality is specifically the condition—not only the conditio sine qua non, but the conditio per quam—of all political life.
—Hannah Arendt[2]

Introduction

Four years after its spectacular coming out in Seattle, the political riddle that is the anti-globalisation movement is already in the process of being resolved by being wrapped up into alternative agendas for world order, as what *The Economist* had labelled the "fight for globalisation"[3] is settling into programmatic chicanery: "Another world ...", the new slogan goes (borne of unquestioned common sense, validated by 27,600 hits on Google), "... is possible".[4] Do, the settling discourse instructs, forget about Emma Goldman's woolly radicalism; to be reasonable is no longer to demand the impossible, another world is now possible, and what is possible can be circumscribed, realistic objectives defined, the path to a new order plotted, do follow the guide.

For lack of having been thought through and for want to take it all in, the new reasonableness has given itself a hollow name with a ring to it: *Altermondialisme*. Notwithstanding fashionable certainties, everything about it needs to be problematised, both because, in carrying on the century-old internationalist drive for programmatic coherence, *altermondialisme* stands more at the rearguard of the movement than at its forefront, and because in its relationship to it, it reproduces rather than challenges attempts by the World Bank et al to contain contemporary anti-capitalism and empty it of political possibilities.

Between the First (1864–1876) and Second International (1889–1914), during what Frits van Hoolthon and Marcel van der Linden called the "classical age" of left internationalism, programmatic *a priorism* came to overdetermine the building of transnational social coalitions.[5] Rather than actually participate in what Marx called the creation of "fraternal concurrences", left internationalism came to be about the drawing of ever more coherent programmes on behalf of increasingly abstract subjects, which grew in political rightness as they became more and more removed from bounded interventions into quotidian life. The last and perhaps most synthetic expression of this drive for programmatic coherence was the G77's plan for a New International Economic Order, which brought about a medley of UN resolutions detailing the common interest of a wholly principled humanity.

In the thirty years since the end of that, a 'new internationalism' has begun to take shape, which, in many ways, signals a return to the social movement internationalism of the early nineteenth century. As I have argued elsewhere,[6] what defines this 'new internationalism' is its radical ordinariness: Where classical left internationalism was shaped by programmatic fights fought on behalf of abstract subjects, the 'new internationalism' drags actually-existing human beings, in all their bounded plurality, into the terrain of the world economy.[7] Located within the realm of civil rather than strictly political society, unfixed by referents to unitary subjects, as tactically focused as it is organisationally diverse, prone to direct action, and shaped by concerns over what Melucci or Touraine would have called 'life' issues,[8] the 'new internationalism' stands in relationship to classical internationalism much like new social movements vis-à-vis old ones.

From the point of view of political neatness, the radical indeterminacy of the new internationalism seems a problem to be solved. This is the impulse that *altermondialisme* answers to, with unquestioned precipitation and a political immodesty that risk stifling what is most radical about it. This risk is even greater in the present moment, when global regulatory agencies are labouring to assemble exactly the kind of abstract subject on whose behalf the World Social Forum (WSF) and attendant regional fora want to draw political programmes. At this juncture, it is absolutely critical that we take a step back from *altermondialiste* revelries and try not to resolve the new internationalism, but to understand it. This has to be done both with respect for its specificity as a social movement and with a sense of the workings of two intimately related orders of dialectics: i) That between the dynamics of order and counter-order in the world economy, and ii) that between what goes on in the world economy and in national social formations. Only by taking those into account can we situate contemporary anti-globalisation in relation to actually-existing anti-capitalism.

Both as a discourse and, increasingly, as an ideology, *altermondialisme* rests on foundationalist assumptions. *Altermondialisme* wants to begin *ad novo*, as if the world economy really was virgin territory, by drawing programmes for a new subject in a new world. To problematise what it takes for granted, we must work more dialectically and question the newness and the separateness of the global anti-capitalist movement and of what it might be up against. Concretely, this means that we have to think not only from the most spectacular and explicitly global moment of appearance of the 'anti-globalisation' movement (anti-WTO demonstrations in Seattle or Québec City, anti-IMF riots in Washington, Caracas, and elsewhere), but also from more situated and quotidian practices of resistance being born in the present context, whether in global cities, export zones, tourist destinations, or other sites of the world economy. If, as Raymond Williams might have said, "we are serious ... about political life, we have to enter that world in which people live as they can themselves".[9] To understand the significance of anti-capitalism as a way of life and struggle, we have to look at the situated practices of knowable communities, where the action is; to think, then, not *of* politics, but *into* it.

This text is divided into three parts. In the first, I identify what I take to be an essential political dynamic of contemporary world order, about which I have written before:[10] The attempt by regulatory agencies of global capitalism to invent a functional, civil, and perfectly apolitical global subject that could serve as an ideal social companion to global neoliberalism. In the second part, I work from concepts that originated with the *Internationale Situationniste* ('Situationist International') to begin making political sense of contemporary anti-capitalist praxis. In the third, I extract from the first two principles of articulation that may allow us to understand contemporary anti-capitalism for what it is, without containing or reifying it.

Birth and Death of Global Subjects

In what was the West, the paradigmatic subject of Cold War exterminism was a nuclear family buried for its own good, cowering comfortably in a basement bunker, absolutely reduced to survival. Less dramatic but also stuck in place, and as bound and reduced, were variously constituted groups, from schoolchildren minding Turtle Burt's advice to "duck and cover",[11] to mothers in the kitchen, to 'old' social movements bound to officines of the Keynesian state. In the East, state socialism made the twinned processes of confinement and reduction more thorough, direct, and sometimes brutal, involving as it did "... the organisation of grass-roots frameworks capable of reaching, mobilising and controlling all citizens":[12] house committees, comrade's courts, asylums, Gulags, and *kolkhozes* ('collective farms'). In allied peripheries, 'overdeveloped' states and regimes ('bloody Taylorism', 'peripheral Fordism', popular democracies, dictatorships) created and contained political subjects that belonged less to themselves, or to national social formations, than they did to the world economy as a whole.[13]

When the Cold War's official nightmare lost its capacity to overdetermine and contain political subjects, global capital—isolated, as it were, in a *nébuleuse* ('nebula') of private and semi-private boards and agencies[14]—imagined a '*no society*' neoliberalism and sought to apply new concepts of control unsocially. It did however fine-tune the concepts to the limits and possibilities of different national social formations, applying monetarism in the old West, shock therapy in the old East—to "clean up the shambles of communist mismanagement"[15]—and harsh conditionality everywhere else that it could, especially in countries at the epicentre of the debt crisis, in Latin America and, increasingly, in Sub-Saharan Africa.

Almost as soon as they began to be put into operation however, neoliberal concepts of control proved unworkable and unsustainable. Monetarism, the first neoliberal conditioning framework applied to Keynesian countries, was useless both at controlling the growth of monetary aggregates and at disciplining social relations.[16] In countries in transition from state-planned economies, the insufficient autonomy of central banks, the weakness of market mechanisms, and the absence of a market-based civil society made shock therapy difficult and inefficient at "sustaining the human capital base for economic growth".[17] In some debtor countries where elements of civil societies had already assembled themselves with a measure of autonomy from state institutions (in Bolivia, Ecuador, Panama, Nicaragua, Mexico, Costa Rica, Indonesia, Venezuela, the Dominican Republic, Brazil, Peru, etc), harsh conditionality provoked riots and general strikes.[18] In others, where authoritarian rule had kept societies from developing means to protect themselves, corrupt administrations and rulers siphoned money earmarked for adjustment, increasing what the World Bank called "friction costs".[19]

This was the context in which ideas of 'global governance' began to move global neoliberalism beyond *no society* utopianism toward social constructivism. Central to 'global governance' as a hegemonical strategy is a broad attempt to assemble a global civil society in which to embed neoliberal concepts of control. Key here are twinned processes of severance and recomposition. In its essence, the making of global civil society involves: i) Cutting off social forces and organisations willing to work within a global market framework from other social contexts, and ii) Re-assembling the lot into a functional and efficient whole that will work to solve global problems and, in the process, fix the terms of social and political interaction in the world economy. In governance's schemes, then, global civil society is to be anything but an autonomous realm, or a theatre of history (in Marx's sense of civil society), but a collection of atomised organisations with little or no autonomous sense of itself, unable to develop what Foucault in his *Herméneutique du Sujet* ('Hermeneutics of the Subject') would have called *le souci de soi* ('care of the self').[20]

Notwithstanding foundationalist discourses carried by both the World Bank et al and *altermondialistes* fora (whose politics, in that respect, are two sides of the same coin), 'global governance' does not just aim to supplant or transcend existing structures of power, but dialectically seeks to integrate and transform them when and where it can, by consensus and coercion, only excluding or by-passing them when and where it must. Building from existing structures of inter-state and class power, governance works in relative connivance with imperialist strategies and projects of transnational capital, and gets applied with relative autonomy to countries, classes, and fractions of classes standing at the periphery of world order.

At the centre of governance's picture there is 'correspondence' (in Marx's sense of the term) between, on the one hand, attempts to create a functional global subject while circumscribing its realm by consent and coercion, and, on the other, the domestic forms and international policies of imperialist states. As "embedded liberalism"[21] in the post-Cold War period came out of Keynesian / Fordist regulation in advanced capitalist countries, governance's attempt to assemble a functional, problem-solving, global civil society bound by problem-solving ethics and "stakeholders' participation"[22] is a general expression of a post-Keynesian regime of 'shareholders' democracy'. Where Hanna Arendt could write of the "alliance between mob and capital" in the period when imperialist exploitation was growing into a colonial world-order,[23] we can now write of an alliance at the centre of the world economy, between shareholders-citizens and transnational capital, that gives social moorings to what David Harvey called the "new imperialism", characterised by a process of "accumulation by dispossession". In shareholder democracies, where neoliberalism is redefining the terms of social consensus on models of corporate governance, "the commodification of cultural forms, histories and intellectual creativity [and] the corporatisation and privatisation of hitherto public assets",[24] the privatisation of intellectual property rights (from the WTO's TRIPs agreements to national patent legislations), as well as the surveillance and disciplining of outsiders, dissidents, and non-compliers find their strongest social bases. Thus, we see convergence and connivance between what Stephen Gill called the "Global Panopticon"[25]—new national security regimes in Bush's US and Putin's Russia—and the definition and punishment of incivilities in France under Sarkozy and Chirac. As free-trade imperialism dealt with deviants and dissidents by sending them off to penal colonies, the new regime sends aliens back home under now anodyne processes of mandatory sentencing,[26] and exiles young offenders to extraterritorial 'boot camps'[27] and concentration camps (in Baghdad's airport or Cuba's Guantanamo Bay). For those, like middle-class students, who are too close to the social centre of the new imperialism for outright exclusion, it reserves such free-speech enclaves as are becoming the fashion on US campuses.

To describe the relationship between the centre of the new order and its periphery, we can speak of a kind of 'governance imperialism', enforced with as much autonomy, impunity, and coercion as nineteenth-century colonialism or, indeed, the Bretton Woods world order in peripheral countries.[28] In this respect as well there is complicity between, for instance, UN interventionism in Kosovo, the World Bank's sovereign war on corruption, and the US-led wars on drugs and terrorism; as between the World Bank's strategies for dealing with 'Highly Indebted Poor Countries' (which requires them to draw up 'Poverty Reduction Strategies' whereby they abdicate power to 'civil society and other stakeholders'), and US attempts to reconstruct 'failed states' though what Susanne Soederberg labelled "pre-emptive development",[29] which export rules of governance, with dramatic, disarticulating consequences, to the periphery—which, in turn, has given neo-colonialist critics of governance occasion to argue that some parts of the world are just not ready for democracy.

There are, then, force-lines running through governance's world picture. As we follow them from the centre outwards, the impunity of the new order, and the violence of its enforcement, increases. At the centre is governance's "global neighbourhood",[30] newly opened up by global regulatory agencies and imperialist countries for paradigmatic subjects of the new order; what may be called 'problem-solving' NGOs, organisations that "... run the refugee camps, provide disaster relief, design and carry-out development projects, monitor and attempt to contain the international spread of disease, and try to clean up an ever more polluted environment",[31] all the while remaining—confined, yes, but in comfortable quarters—within the limits of the new world order, and only linked to one another by the machinery of 'governance'—that obligatory intermediary between all things and matters. At the margins of the new order are critical sites of de-contextualisation: Export zones, detention camps, peripheral social formations, free-speech zones. These are the barrios of governance, where are confined its non-subjects.

Where exterminism buried national societies for their own protection from nuclear annihilation, 'global governance' builds from problems, emergencies, and crises of all sorts (poverty, development, habitat, credit, service delivery, corruption, health, human and food insecurities) to foster a state of permanent preparedness that creates a new global civil society as it reduces it to mere functionalities. What gets severed in the process is the space between distinct men and women in action; the site of what Arendt called the *vita active*, the birthplace of politics.[32]

Dérives and Hubs: How and Where New Subjects might be Making Themselves in the World Economy

Before they began concerning themselves with matters related to *La société du spectacle* ('The society of spectacle'), the principal theoreticians of the *Internationale Situationniste* (1957–1972) worked primarily with reference to the conditions of life in contemporary cities, where the modern regulation of existence had reached its most explicit form.[33] The functional grid of cities, *Situationnistes* argued, provided revolutionary artists with the clearest *maquette* ('model') of modern life, and, dialectically, with a privileged site for experimenting with non-alienating practices.

To fight off the alienating grid, *Situationnistes* invented *dérives*, an experimental technique borrowed from surrealist *déambulations*[34] and adapted to the exigencies of life in cities.[35] Wilfully abandoning their usual, grid-regimented reasons for moving about the city, teams of two of three *Situs* rather followed scattered hints and solicitation from topography and ambient architecture, as well as chance encounters, moving about in a manner they considered closer to being in tune with the creative unity of the city.[36]

What *dérive* teams specifically aimed to unearth in interstices between functionally-designated areas was what they called *plaques psychogéographiques* ('psychographic hubs'): Contingent, polysemic, and radically whole sites of unreduced life that were both sovereign places unto themselves—oases in the desert as Heidegger or Arendt might have put it, as well as connecting points—much in the same manner that, for E P Thompson, corresponding societies were "junction points" where London's working men could assemble outside sites of production.[37]

From the manner by which *Situs* sought to unearth psychographic hubs, we can derive means to discover in the world economy subjects that might be, if not truer, than at least more self-directed—and possibly more capable of self-invention—than the paradigmatic constructs of global governance. Who, then, *dérives* across the terrain of the world economy that might lead us to where junction points may be found? Who are the men and women who have foregone, by choice or obligation, both the political ways of classical left internationalism and the grids of governance, to follow more immediate hints and solicitations, moving not by politics or programmes but by tactical and strategic necessities?

Two decades ago, finding men and women who were moving across the terrain of the world economy following tactical and strategic solicitations rather than political highways would have meant either falling back on examples predating classical left internationalism (the anti-slavery campaign for instance, or attempts during the 1868 strike movement in Europe to organise what Marx called "guerrilla battles" against capital and get workers of different countries "not only [to] *feel* but [to] *act* as brethren and comrades in the army of emancipation,"[38] or making too much of a few exceptional twentieth-century occurrences (the Sacco and Vanzetti, Rosenberg, or Mandela campaigns, or the global 'anti-systemic' occupation movement of May 1968).[39]

In the last twenty years, however, there has been a veritable explosion of transnational movements that have followed the fluid paths of tactical and strategic opportunities across the whole of the world economy, hopping and skipping from issue to issue, creating strategic alliances from chance encounters, opening and defending positions and institutions. This is the movement that was beginning to be known a generation ago as the 'new left internationalism', which then got associated with—and sometimes reduced to—the 'anti-globalisation movement' after the WTO demonstrations in Seattle, and is now in danger of being wrapped up in the settling politics of *altermondialiste* reformism. To centre questioning on its praxis rather than its assumed politics, to look *into* it rather than *at* it, we will forego these problematical handles and rather consider the movement as a collection of *dérives*, made necessary by the globalisation of production, finance, and, more generally, of everyday life in contemporary capitalism.

Tactical *dérives* have already transformed institutions born of previous internationalist efforts, and they have created others. The most spectacular, most often cited, example of new global institutions is the Indymedia network, born of anti-summit protests in Seattle and elsewhere, that has had some success in short-circuiting the highways of commercial network and state-sponsored media.[40] In the world of labour, transnational campaigns have, to an extent, transformed International Trade Secretaries, World Industry Councils, and International Confederations. Also worthy of note are what are beginning to be known as 'strategic organising alliances' linking otherwise unrelated union locals. A model here is the alliance between the United Electrical Workers' Union (UE) and the Mexican *Frente Auténtico del Trabajo* ('Authentic Workers' Front', FAT), which led to the creation in 1992 of the North American Workers to Workers Network (NAWWN), which has had considerable impact in shaping individual organisers and coordinating unionising drives, especially in maquila industries.[41] Following supply, production, or commodity chains, informed by what Andrew Herod in his analysis of the 1998 strike at General Motors called "guerrilla cartography",[42] workers have also created such links as the International Coordinating Committee of Solidarity Amongst Sugar Workers (ICCSASW) or Banana Action Net, which has organised a worldwide campaign for respect for labour rights on banana plantations, in solidarity with the *Coordinadora Latinoamericano de Sindicatos Bananeros* ('Banana Workers' Union'), the European Banana Action Network, and the US / Labor Education in the Americas Project (US / LEAP). This latter organisation, founded in 1987 as the US / Guatemala Labour Education Project (US / GLEP) by trade unionists and human rights advocates concerned about the basic rights of Guatemalan workers[43] now links trade unionists in Central America, Asia (Korean House of International Solidarity, Focus on Globalisation in Taiwan, etc) with a broad range of religious, human rights, student, and US trade union organisations such as Campaign for Labour Rights, United Students Against Sweatshops, Network in Solidarity with the People of Guatemala (NISGUA), Interfaith Centre on Corporate Responsibility, Global Exchange, STITCH, the Maquila Solidarity Network, Witness for Peace, the AFL-CIO Solidarity Centre, etc.[44] In turn, these links have made possible campaigns on behalf of workers directly or indirectly employed by such US companies as Starbucks, Dole, and Phillips-Van Heusen.[45] Similarly, transnational women's campaigns have led to the creation of such linkage points as the Women's International Information and Communication Service (WIICS), the Feminist International Networks of Resistance to Reproductive Technologies and Genetic Engineering (FINR-Rage), and Women Living Under Muslim Laws (WLUML).[46]

The list of transnational *dérives* and of the new links they have created could, of course, be lengthened, perhaps *ad infinitum*. Indeed, analyses of transnational doings often do little more than assemble such a list, putting side by side everything in sight and labelling the lot 'anti-globalisation', or 'globalisation from below'—the title of a groundbreaking book,[47] and a particularly popular moniker: 5,270 hits on Google. We live in a moment of such profound restructuring that we do not lack for examples of people organising in any way they can to resist their impoverishment, the destruction of their communities, or the degradation of their living and working conditions. But listing is not theorising. More needs to be done to make sense of the political meanings and possibilities of what gets created when people forego set ways.

Again, anti-summit happenings offer us a good starting point for thinking this through. In Québec City, where this article was written, mobilisation against the Summit of the Americas in April 2001 brought about a few days of direct actions and anti-capitalist carnivaling, as did anti-summit mobilisations elsewhere.[48] It also led, in what was already routine fashion, to the creation of an Indymedia outlet: The *Centre des Médias Alternatif du Québec* (Québec's Indymedia outfit, the 'Centre for Alternative Media of Québec'). In the year after the Summit of the Americas, social forces that had been mobilised in Québec City, which quickly fell below the radar of anti-globalisation watchers, resituated their actions on more local issues, most notably the housing shortage (in 2002, Québec City became the Canadian city with the lowest rate of apartment vacancy). The same people and organisations that, a year previously, had organised demonstrations against the US-led drive for a Free Trade Area of the Americas (FTAA) organised the city's first political squat in more than a generation, on Rue de la Chevrotière, within sight of where the Summit of the Americas' security perimeter had been breached a year previously. When the war in Iraq began, the movement resurfaced as a part of a global movement, organising what were, proportionately, the largest anti-war gatherings in the world. Again, the movement disappeared from view when the conjunctural sense of urgency abated. As the time of writing, it is in the process of reorganising itself against social re-engineering programmes of the liberal government, elected in April 2003. The same movement, then, animated by a global sense of place, has repositioned and reformed itself once more.

No Logo campaigning offers us other telling examples of the dialectical linking between transnational *dérives* and the socialisation of more localised and positional struggles. For instance, campaigns launched in the US by the United Students Against Sweatshops (USAS), that at times has brought USAS reps in contacts with anti-sweatshop campaigns elsewhere in the world (in Indonesia in support of the struggle of workers at the Kahatex Sweater Factory in Bandung; in Colombia against Coke-sponsored death squads, etc), have also led them to socialise and politicise struggles on some of the most commodified US campuses, both privileged marketing points for Nike et al and critical sites of decontextualisation.[49] This, in turn, has activated the struggle against efforts to contain political protests within free-speech zones, perhaps the most important point of convergence of the US student movement since the days of the Vietnam war.

In the world of labour, the experience of the Coalition of Immokalee Workers (CIW) offers us another telling experience. Founded in 1992 by migrants working as tomato pickers for Taco Bell subcontractors in Florida, the CIW first organised for wage increases (of one cent a pound). Drawing on experiences of workers schooled in social struggles in Mexico, Guatemala, Central and South America, and the Caribbean, the workers organised community-wide general strikes in 1995, 1997, and 1999.[50] In 2001, the CIW organised its first Taco Bell Truth Tour, an 8,000-miles-long crisscrossing of the US that brought workers from Florida to Taco Bell headquarters in Orange County, California. In the process, they linked with workers in countries of origins, who organised support events in the context of continent-wide struggles against the US project for a FTAA. Rather than political organising in the classical left international sense of the term, it is this shared context of struggle that prompted support actions outside the US, and gave them resonance and meaning.

In the most immediate terms, the CIW strikes and campaigns have succeeded in strengthening local bonds of solidarity between workers, and thus in diminishing field bosses' ability to pit workers of different national origins, about 90 per cent of whom are new each season, against one another.[51] Beyond this, the CIW was key to defeating the so-called Guestworker's Bill, which would have allowed agribusiness to bring in seasonal workers under a visa contract specific to individual employers and thus created a class of indentured workers the likes of which has not been seen, or rather validated by legislation, since the days of slavery. Defining their struggle as a civil and human rights issues,[52] and their movement as a modern "underground railroad",[53] the CIW has not only been able to give enough resonance to its struggle to win considerable recognition (and the 2003 Robert F Kennedy Human Rights Award), but also to link with such organisations as the United States Student Association, the Student Labour Action Project, Jobs with Justice, the Student / Farmworker Alliance, etc.[54]

Here as well, there would be countless fragments—from the campaign of workers from Bibong Apparel Corporation in the Dominican Republic,[55] to the campaign of the Movement for the Survival of the Ogoni People, from the *Confédération Paysanne* ('Peasants' Federation') to the transnational doings of the *Confederación de Nacionalidades Indígenas de Ecuador* ('Confederation of Indigenous Nations of Ecuador')—that could tell us of the dialectical linking between transnational struggles and the socialisation of positional struggles. All suggest the possibility that transnational *dérives* might usher in a context in which particular, locally-bound struggles shaped by tactical necessities 'over-leap' the bounds of parochial or corporatist tussles—to borrow from Rosa Luxemburg's theorising on the dynamics of mass strikes. Against *altermondialiste* will-to-programme, we might then profitably invoke her critique of Lenin's "ultra-centralism":[56]

> Instead of the rigid and hollow scheme of an arid political action carried out by the decision of the highest committees ... we see a bit of pulsating life of flesh and blood.[57]

At the very least, we can begin thinking of something besides governance's processes of severance and recomposition. While regulatory agencies of the world economy wish to provoke a controlled rupture that would give appointed representatives of 'global civil society' the full weight of political authority, transnational praxis re-establishes the continuum of experience between global and local contexts of struggle, in a manner that may radicalise and socialise both.

About Articulation

Seeing the global neighbourhood not as an all-inclusive new world built on empty land but as a new development in a historic city, we can break with the developers' mentality shared by the World Bank et al and *altermondialiste* fora, and look elsewhere for distinct, perhaps revolutionary, ways of life and struggle.

To move towards a theoretical understanding of the present moment, what we have to do is think about terms of articulation between practices born of specific actions without reifying them. I am thinking here not of a post-materialist sense of articulation between signified events brought together into a discursive whole,[58] but of a political articulation between the bounded actions invented by men and women in the process of their struggles.

Looking into where the action is, we can find the beginnings of a dialectics of presence that contrasts sharply with governance's processes of depoliticisation by severance and recomposition. The poles of this dialectics are obvious: Tactical *dérives* in the world economy and positional struggles within national social formations. In Gramscian terms these strategies, which have not been invented by the decisions of committees but have grown almost organically, are perfectly appropriate to their respective contexts: A war of movement has emerged in the world economy—a relatively new social formation where the earthworks of social hegemony have not yet been dug—and a war of position is continuing in national social formations—where earthworks have been dug and adventurism would amount to recklessness. What looking into transnational actions suggests to us is that movements and positions should not be thought of as episodes to be put into a chronological sequence (as they were for Gramsci), but as coincidental, and intimately related, moments of a dialectical process. *A contrario* to *altermondialisme*, we do not have to choose between them, celebrate one rather than the other, or reduce one to the other. What we have to do is follow hints from what is being done in praxis and think the dialectic through.

Transnational *dérives* need strong positions to begin with and draw from. The anti-FTAA campaign, the US / GLEP, or the NAWWN would not have been born but for the support unions provided, nor would transnational campaigns, whether of anti-Logo organisations, the Banana Action Net, or WLUML, amount to much without support from institutions that have fought to secure positions and build institutions inside national social formations. More generally, the fragile positions opened up by transnational *dérives* could not be held without support from other, stronger positions that have been held in more mature social formations. That much is obvious, and it corresponds to what intuitive knowledge would suggest.

But transnational *dérives* and positions are not just fragile outposts in need of supplies, they also broaden possibilities for the struggle of positioned social forces.

A century and a half ago Marx and Engels argued, in the founding manifesto of classical left internationalism, that even though the proletariat was a universal subject, workers first had to settle matters with their own bourgeoisies. Twenty years ago, when global governance was only beginning to take shape, and before transnational *dérives* had made anything of themselves, Robert Cox restated this position when he advocated a patient war of position that would begin with "the long, laborious effort to build new historic blocs within national boundaries".[59] Since then, the context for struggles that take place at the level of national social formations has clearly shrunk, both in advanced capitalist countries (where even social democracy cannot shrivel fast enough) and in countries at the periphery of the world economy, which are disciplined with increasing impunity by governance's, and the US's, imperialisms. In this period, transnational *dérives* have also begun to activate a dialectic of presence that may have very few precedents in the history of capitalism organised on a world scale. If *pratique* ('practice') is understood as a process whereby a given situation is transformed by human agency, and if *political praxis* is the transformation of a given material situation by political subjects who are making themselves in specific junctures,[60] it is not its carnivalesque aesthetics, its tactics (*dérives*, direct actions, No Logo campaigns, etc), or its targets (OMC, IMF, World Bank, or Davos gatherings) that have defined contemporary anti-capitalism. Nor is it the "global-network" form of it all.[61] What has defined it is its putting into dialectical relation transnational movements and positional struggles.[62]

For this dialectic to be most effective—that is, for it to broaden as much as possible possibilities for transformative politics—its terms have to be separated as much as possible without their relationship being threatened. What Henri Lefebvre would have called the *logique de différence* ('logic of difference') has to gain as much amplitude as possible while still remaining disciplined by the exigencies of the *logique dialectique* ('dialectical logic').[63] To put it as clearly as possible: Transnational movements and positional struggles have to be as separate and specific as possible without the link between them being severed—at which point moments of a dialectic become mere objects separated from one another and weaker because of it.

In a way, this theoretical position seems to echo the 'diversity of tactics' call often heard in anti-summit manifestations. But this position, like *altermondialisme*'s, is grounded on only half of the emerging dialectic of presence in the world economy, and therefore it entirely misses what is most radical about present anti-capitalist struggles. In its petty-bourgeois ways, *altermondialisme* aspires to return to the old capitalist means of controlling social relations by foregoing some forms of struggle and bringing global financial capital under national, neo-Keynesian discipline. To give a social basis to this project, it tries to fast-freeze the transnational movement of the multitude and pin it to what is essentially a national form. By advocating indiscriminate variability, the diversity-of-tactics argument unfolds as if the anti-capitalist movement was little more than global agitation with no political integrity whatsoever. The battle against capitalist globalisation, of course, will be fought on many fronts and take many forms, but not all forms of struggle are equivalent and not all can be brought into equal relations with anti-capitalist politics.

But coherence and discipline cannot come, as they do for *altermondialisme*, from the *ex officio* expurgation of some or other means of struggle. Nor can it be overdetermined, as governance agencies would have it, by some fabricated sense of responsibility toward humanity construed as an abstract, and thus malleable, bearer of rights. This false universality, what Adorno would have called a "cult of Being",[64] stands at the heart of "humanitarian ideology",[65] a privileged vehicle of governance's interpellation. Rather, what should discipline anti-capitalist politics is the necessity to activate and sustain the dialectical relationship between the war of movement taking shape in the world economy and the war of position in national social formations.

Borrowing avant-garde techniques has given us the means to discover a field of practice that had been hidden from view by governance's gridding grids, and it has given us tools to think about the workings of a dialectic that may have few precedents in the five-centuries-old history of global capitalism. It has also allowed us to carry on a kind of experimental mapping of the new terrain and let us imagine an anti-capitalist world-picture that would have its own, distinct force-lines running through it. At the centre would be sites of action where the terms of anti-capitalist dialectic are most separated, and where the transformative possibilities of anti-capitalist politics might be strongest; at the periphery would be struggles where this dialectic is most reduced, or where its terms are so autonomous from one another that they cannot be thought of as being part of a dialectic at all.

That being said, everything needs to be done to operationalise and specify concepts of resistance. To move beyond experimental mapping to operational cartography, we need to discover what the exigencies of the new dialectic are within the context of specific struggles, what possibilities exist for variability within it, and where points of rupture at given moments in given junctures are. These, of course, are all matters for empirical investigation and for the kind of strategic thinking that cannot be synthesised with any intelligence or brought into political form, lest we fall into the trap of programmatic reasoning and resolve what we should be trying to understand.

Conclusion

That "Another World is Possible" has become the ensign of the left's common sense. For all its engaging cheerfulness, and for all the hope and energy that can be drawn from it,[66] this slogan advertises the wrong kind of anti-capitalist politics. Aping the ways of the ruling class is a sure way to fall into ambushes.[67] This is no less true now that governance is trying to humanise neoliberal concepts of control than it was when Gramsci wrote. Rather than abide by the immense condescension of drawers of programmes wishing to order and stabilise the global movement of multitudes, we need to think from concepts of resistance drawn from what men and women acting against capitalist restructuring have already invented; rather than consider these inventions too small or not political enough for the task of world restructuring at hand, we need to think with enough imagination to see the relative coherence—and thus the depth and the strength—of what is being born of present circumstances.

References

Theodore Adorno, 1973—*Negative Dialectics*. New York: Seabury Press

Louis Althusser, 1985—*Pour Marx* ['For Marx', in French]. Paris: Le Découverte

Hannah Arendt, 1976—*The Origins of Totalitarianism*. A Harvest Book. New York: Harcourt, Inc

Hannah Arendt, 1985—*Essai sur la revolution* ['Essay on Revolution', in French]. Paris: Fayard

Hannah Arendt, 1998—*The Human Condition*, second edition. Chicago: University of Chicago Press

Giovanni Arrighi, Terrence K Hopkins, and Immanuel Wallerstein, 1989—*Antisystemic Movements*. London: Verso

Antonin Artaud, 1979—'*Surréalisme et révolution*' ['Surrealism and Revolution', in French], in Antonin Artaud, ed, 1979—*Messages révolutionnaires* ['Revolutionary Messages']. (Paris: Gallimard)

Banque Mondiale, 1993—*Obtenir des Résultats: Ce que la Banque Mondiale veut faire pour mieux agir sur le développement* ['Obtaining Results: What the World Bank wants to do to act better for development', in French]. Washington, DC: World Bank

David Beacon, April 2002—'Florida Farmworkers Take On Taco Bell: Interview with Lucas Benitez of the Coalition of Immokalee Workers', in *Labor Notes* April 16

Didier Bigo, 1992—'*Contestations populaires et émeutes urbaines; les jeux du politique et de la transnationalité*' ['Popular protests and urban riots: The games of politics and transnationality', in French], in *Cultures et contacts*, Special issue on urban riots, 1992, pp 3–22

Juan Pablo Bohorquez-Montoya, September 2003—'*Entrevista a Lucas Benitez*' ['Interview with Lucas Benitez' in Spanish], September 25–26 2003

John Bowe, 2003—'Nobodies: Does Slavery Exist in America?', in *The New Yorker*, April 21

Jeremy Brecher, Tim Costello, and Brendan Smith, 2000—*Globalization from Below*. Boston: South End Press

André Breton, 1952—*Entretiens 1913–1952, nrf* ['Interviews 1913–1952', in French]. Paris: Gallimard

Robin Broad, ed, 2002—*Global Backlash: Citizen Initiatives for a Just World Economy*. Lanham, MD: Rowman & Littlefield Publishers

Manuel Castells, 1996—*The Rise of the Network Society—The Information Age: Economy, Society and Culture*. Oxford: Basil Blackwell

Commission on Global Governance, 1995—*Our Global Neighbourhood*. Oxford: Oxford University Press

Maria Lorena Cook, 2002—'Cross-Border Labor Solidarity', in Robin Broad, ed, 2002—*Global Backlash: Citizen Initiatives for a Just World Economy*. Lanham, MD: Rowman & Littlefield Publishers

Robert W Cox, 1983—'Gramsci, Hegemony, and International Relations: An Essay in Methods', in *Millennium: Journal of International Studies*, vol 12 no 2 (Summer 1983), pp 162–175

Robert W Cox, 1992—'Global Perestroika', in Ralph Miliband and Leo Panitch, eds, 1992—*The Socialist Register: New World Order*. London: Merlin

Guy Debord, 1958—'*Théorie de la dérive*' ['Theory of drift', in French], in *Internationale Situationniste*, edited by G E Debord. Paris: IS (*Internationale Situationniste*)

Guy Debord, 1992 [1967]—*La société du spectacle* ['The Society of Spectacle', in French], Paris: Gallimard

Guy Debord and Jacques Fillion, August 1954—'Résumé 1954', in *Potlatch*, August 17–30 1954, p 63

André C Drainville, 1994—'International Political Economy in the Age of Open Marxism', in *Review of International Political Economy*, vol 1 no 1, pp 105–132

André C Drainville, 1995a—'Left Internationalism and the Politics of Resistance in the New World Order', in David Smith and József Böröcz, eds, 1995—*A New World Order: Global Transformations in the Late Twentieth Century*. Westport, CT: Praeger

André C Drainville, 1995b—'Monetarism in Canada and the World Economy', in *Studies in Political Economy*, vol 46, pp 7–42

André C Drainville, 1997—'The Fetishism of Global Civil Society: Global Governance, Transnational Urbanism and Sustainable Capitalism in the World Economy', in *Comparative Urban and Community Research*, 6, pp 35–63. Also translated and published as: André Drainville, 1999—'*El fetichismo de una sociedad civil global: gobernancia global, urbanismo transnacional y capitalismo sostenible en la economía mundial*', in *Anuario de Espacios Urbanos*, 5, UNAM (National Autonomous University of Mexico) Mexico, pp 219–245

André C Drainville, 1999 [1997]—'The Fetishism of Global Civil Society: Global Governance, Transnational Urbanism and Sustainable Capitalism in the World Economy', in *Comparative Urban and Community Research*, vol 6, pp 35–63

André C Drainville, 2001—'Québec City 2001 and the Making of Transnational Subjects', in Leo Panitch and Colin Leys, eds, 2001—*Socialist Register 2001*, London and New York: Merlin Press

André C Drainville, 2004—*Contesting Globalization: Space and Place in the World Economy*. London: Routledge

André C Drainville, 2012—*A History of World Order and Resistance: The Making and Unmaking of Global Subjects*. London and New York: Routledge

The Economist, 1999a—'The Battle in Seattle', November 27 1999, pp 21–23

The Economist, 1999b—'Storm Over Globalisation', November 27 1999, pp 15, 17

Michel Foucault, 1994—'*L'herméneutique du sujet*' ['The hermeneutics of the subject', in French], in F E Daniel Defert and Jacques Lagrange, eds, 1994—*Dits et écrits (1976–1988)* ['Sayings and Writings']. Paris: Gallimard

Theodore H Friedgut, 1979—*Political Participation in the USSR*. Princeton, NJ: Princeton University Press

John Gallagher and Ronald Robinson, 1953—'The Imperialism of Free Trade', in *The Economic History Review*, vol 6 no 1

Susan George, 2001—'Another World Is Possible', in *Dissent* (Winter 2001), pp 5–8

Stephen Gill, 1995—'The Global Panopticon? The Neoliberal State, Economic Life, and Democratic Surveillance', in *Alternatives* 1995 no 2, pp 1–49

David Harvey, 2003a—'The "New" Imperialism: Accumulation by Dispossession', in *Socialist Register*, vol 40, pp 63–88

Andrew Herod, 2001—*Labor Geographies: Workers and the Landscapes of Capitalism*. New York: The Guilford Press

Quintin Hoare and Geoffrey Nowell-Smith, eds, 1998—*Selections from the Prison Notebooks of Antonio Gramsci*. London: Lawrence and Wishart

Peter Hogness, 1989—'One More Hole in the Wall; the Lunafil Strikers on Guatemala', in *Solidarity Across Borders*. Chicago: Midwest Center for Labor Research

Stewart Home, 1996—'Basic Banalities', in Stewart Home, ed, 1996—*What Is Situationism? A Reader*. San Francisco: AK Press

Bernard Hours, 1998—'*L'idéologie humanitaire ou la globalisation morale*' ['Humanitarian ideology or moral globalisation', in French], in *L'homme et la société* ['Man and Society'], vol 129 no 3, pp 47–56

Allen Hunter, 1995—'Globalization from Below? Promises and Perils of the New Internationalism', in *Social Policy*, Summer 1995, pp 6–13

IDB (Inter-American Development Bank), 1997—'Echoes of Forging Links with NGOs'. Washington, DC: Inter-American Development Bank

Gilles Ivain, June 1958—'*Formulaire pour un urbanisme nouveau*' ['Formulation for a New Urbanism', in French], in *Internationale Situationniste*, vol 1 (June 1958), pp 15–20

David Jessup and Michael E Gordon, 2000—'Organizing in Export Processing Zones: The Bibong Experience in the Dominican Republic', in M E Gordon and Lowell Turner, eds, 2000—*Transnational Cooperation Among Labor Unions*. Ithaca, NY: ILR Press / Cornell University Press

Rebecca A Johns, 1998—'Bridging the Gap between Class and Space: US Worker Solidarity with Guatemala', in *Economic Geography*, vol 74 no 3, pp 252–271

Naomi Klein, 2000—*No Logo: Taking Aim at the Brand Bullies*. Toronto: Alfred A Knopf

Naomi Klein, July 2000b—'The Vision Thing', in *The Nation*, July 10 2000, pp 18–21

Koch Crime Institute, 2000—'Juvenile Boot Camps and Military Structured Youth Programs', KCI

Ernesto Laclau and Chantal Mouffe, 1985—*Hegemony and Socialist Strategy: Towards a Radical Democratic Politics*. London: Verso

Henri Lefebvre, 1969—*Logique formelle, logique dialectique* ['Formal logic, dialectical logic', in French]. Paris: Anthropos

Rosa Luxemburg, 1971—*The Mass Strike*. New York: Harper Torchbooks, Harper & Row

Gilberto Mathias and Pierre Salama, 1983—*L'État surdéveloppé: des métropoles au tiers-monde* ['The overdeveloped state: From the core to the periphery of the world economy', in French]. Paris: La Découverte/Maspero

Alberto Melucci, 1989—*Nomads of the Present: Social Movements and Individual Needs in Contemporary Society*. Edited by John Keane and Paul Mier. Translated from the original Italian. Philadelphia: Temple University Press

Valentine M Moghadam, 2001—'Transnational Feminist Networks: Collective Action in an Era of Globalization', in Pierre Hamel et al, eds, 2001—*Globalization and Social Movements*. Houndmills, UK: Palgrave

Craig N Murphy, 2002—'Why Pay Attention to Global Governance?', in Yazar-Rorden Wilkinson and Stephen Hughes, 2002—*Global Governance: Critical Perspectives*. London: Routledge

Muto Ichiyo, 1988—'Possibilities of New Internationalism: A View from Japan', in *AMPO: Japan-Asia Quarterly Review*, pp 60–71

Leo Panitch and Sam Gindin, 2003—'Global Capitalism and American Empire', in *Socialist Register*, pp 1–42

V Spike Peterson and Anne Sisson Runyan, 1993—'Global Gender Issues', in G A Lopez, ed, 1993—*Dilemmas in World Politics*. Boulder, CO: Westview Press

Robert Redeker, 1998—'*Inhumain humanitaire: essai sur une écologie de l'humain*' ['Inhuman humanitarian: essay on an ecology of the human', in French], in *L'homme et la société* ['Man and Society', in French] 129 (March 1998), pp 57–66

Candace Rondeaux, December 2002—'Fear and Knowing in Immokale', in *St Petersburg Times*, December 1 2002

John Gerard Ruggie, 1982—'International Regimes, Transactions, and Change: Embedded Liberalism in the Post-War Economic Order', in *International Organization*, Spring 1982, pp 195–231

Jeffrey Sachs, 1990—'Eastern Europe's Economies: What is to be done?', in *The Economist*, January 13 1990, pp 21–26

Shirin Sinnar, 2003—'Patriotic or Unconstitutional? The Mandatory Detention of Aliens under the USA Patriot Act', in *Stanford Law Review*, vol 55 no 4, p 1419

Susanne Soederberg, 2003—'American Empire and "Excluded States": The Millennium Challenge Account and the Shift to Pre-Emptive Development'. Edmonton: University of Alberta, Department of Political Science

E P Thompson, 1980 [1963]—*The Making of the English Working Class*. London: Penguin

Alain Touraine, 1988—*Return of the Actor: Social Theory and Postindustrial Society*. Minneapolis: University of Minnesota Press

Carol R Van Cleef, 2003—'The USA Patriot Act: Statutory Analysis and Regulatory Implementation', in *Journal of Financial Crime*, vol 11 no 1, p 73

Frits van Hoolthon and Marcel van der Linden, 1988—*Internationalism in the Labour Movement 1830–1940*, Vol II. Leiden, Netherlands: E J Brill

Raoul Vaneigem, 1967—*Traité de savoir-vivre à l'usage des jeunes générations* ['Treatise on know-how for the use of younger generations', in French]. Paris: Gallimard

Lynn Waddell, February 2001—'Florida Farmworkers Take On Fast-Food Giant', in *Christian Science Monitor*. February 1 2001, http://www.csmonitor.com/2001/0201/p2s1.html (Accessed April 2017)

John Walton, 1987—'Urban Protests and the Global Political Economy: The IMF Riots', in Michael Peter Smith and Joe R Feagin, eds, 1987—*The Capitalist City: Global Restructuring and Community Politics*. Oxford: Basil Blackwell

Peter Waterman, 1988—'The New Internationalism: A More Real Thing Than a Big, Big Coke?', in *Fernand Braudel Center* vol XI no 3 (Summer 1998), pp 289–332

Eric Williams, 1961—*Capitalism and Slavery*. New York: Russell & Russell

World Bank, 1992—'Governance and Development'. Washington, DC: World Bank

World Bank, 1994—'Partners in Reform: The Special Program of Assistance for Africa (SPA)', in *Findings*, October 1994

World Bank, 1996a—'West Central Africa: Building Ownership for Environmentally Sustainable Development', in *Findings (Africa Region, World Bank)*, June 1996, at: http://www.worldbank.org/aftdr/findings/english/find76.htm (Accessed April 2017)

World Bank, 1996b—'World Bank Development Report 1996: From Plan to Market'. Washington, DC: World Bank

Notes

1. Ed: This is an edited version of the author's essay with the same title, 'Beyond *Altermondialisme*: Anti-Capitalist Dialectic of Presence', published in the *Review of International Political Economy*, no 5 (December 2005), pp 884–908. I thank the author for preparing this condensed version for us, and most sincerely thank the publishers, Taylor & Francis (UK) Journals, for giving us the rights to reprint the essay without charge. (This is the way it should be, between people interested in a subject!) For further reproduction permission, contact michelle.whittaker@informa.com.

2. Arendt 1998.

3. *The Economist* 1999a, 1999b.

4. 'Exact phrase match' search carried out on January 21 2004.

5. Drainville 1995; van Hoolthon and van der Linden 1988.

6. Drainville 1999 [1998]; Drainville 2001; Drainville 2004.

7. Hunter 1995; Ichiyo 1988; Waterman 1988.

8. Touraine 1988; Melucci 1989.

9. Williams 1961.
10. Drainville 2004.
11. Turtle Burt was the star of the 1961 'civil defence' documentary 'Duck and Cover', shown in school to keep US American children in a state of permanent readiness for nuclear war (and in permanent fear of life). The Wikipedia entry is quite comprehensive and contains a link to the film: http://en.wikipedia.org/wiki/Duck_and_Cover_(film).
12. Friedgut 1979
13. Mathias and Salama 1983.
14. Cox 1992; Drainville 1994.
15. Sachs 1990.
16. Drainville 1995b.
17. World Bank 1996a.
18. Bigo 1992; Walton 1987.
19. Banque Mondiale 1993.
20. Foucault 1994.
21. Ruggie 1982.
22. IDB 1997; World Bank 1992, 1994, 1996a.
23. Arendt 1976.
24. Harvey 2003a.
25. Gill 1995.
26. Van Cleef 2003; Sinnar 2003.
27. Koch Crime Institute 2000.
28. Gallagher and Robinson 1953, cited in (Panitch and Gindin 2003)
29. Soederberg 2003.
30. Commission on Global Governance 1995.
31. Murphy 2002.
32. Arendt 1995.
33. *La société du spectacle* (Debord 1992) is one of two defining texts of the *Internationale Situationniste*. The other is Raoul Vaneigem's *Traité de savoir-vivre à l'usage des jeunes générations* (Vaneigem 1967).
34. Artaud 1979; Breton 1952.
35. *Dérive* ('drift') is most succinctly defined (Debord 1958) as a technique of rapid passage through varied ambiences. It is more deliberate, and more tightly constructed as an experimental technique than surrealist *déambulations* ('walkabouts'). The 'Bureau of Public Secrets' has a good introduction of *Situationniste* terminology for English readers, as well as a point of entry into the world of the *Internationale Situationniste*, at: http://www.bopsecrets.org/SI/2.derive.htm. Wikipedia also provides a useful beginning point: http://en.wikipedia.org/wiki/D%C3%A9rive.
36. Debord and Fillion 1954; Debord 1958; Home 1996; Ivain 1958.
37. Thompson 1980 (1963).
38. The citation is from Marx's instructions to delegates at the Geneva congress of the First International in 1866, cited in van Hoolthon and van der Linden 1988.
39. Arrighi, Hopkins, and Wallerstein 1989.
40. The first Independent Media Center was created in November 1999 to cover protests against the World Trade Organization in Seattle. The Seattle IMC website was

said to have 'received almost 1.5 million hits during the WTO protests'. See: http://docs.indymedia.org/view/Global/FrequentlyAskedQuestionEn#how. At last count, there were more than one hundred members of the Indymedia family.

41. Cook 2002.
42. Herod 2001.
43. Johns 1998; Hogness 1989.
44. Information on the Chiquita campaign can be found at: http://bananas.xs4all.be (Inactive April 2017).
45. See http://www.usleap.org.
46. Peterson and Runyan 1993; Moghadam 2001.
47. Brecher 2000.
48. Drainville 2001.
49. Broad 2002.
50. Beacon 202
51. Bohorquez-Montoya, September 25–26 2003; Bowe 2003.
52. Waddell 2001.
53. Rondeaux 2002.
54. Since this article was first published, the CIW has won its campaign against Taco Bell and has moved to McDonalds and broader political issues. News of CIW struggles can be had at their website: http://www.ciw-online.org.
55. Jessup and Gordon 2000.
56. Melograni 1989.
57. Luxemburg 1971.
58. Laclau and Mouffe 1985.
59. Cox 1983, p 174.
60. Althusser 1985.
61. Castells 1996; Klein 2000, July 2000b.
62. This article is part of a broader theoretical project informed by historical research on a wide variety of movements of resistance against world ordering—from slave and coolie revolts at the beginning of the nineteenth century, to IMF riots and gas and water wars at the end of the twentieth. In this project, I have come to distinguish between two *modes of relation to the world economy*. In *creative severance* this gets resolved before being taken to the world economy and a docile global subject gets made that carries a false, reified sense of itself. In the *dialectics of presence,* the whole of everyday life gets taken unresolved to the world economy; in critical junctures, a global subject sometimes appears that is conscious not only of itself but of the whole world. Over two centuries of (liberal and neoliberal) globalisation—so the argument goes—these *modes* have become increasingly coherent, increasingly distinct from one another, and they have increasingly taken a political form. A book-length presentation of this argument was published in 2012 under the title *A History of World Order and Resistance: The making and unmaking of global subjects* (Drainville 2012).
63. Lefebvre 1969.
64. Adorno 1973.
65. Redeker 1998; Hours 1998.
66. George 2001.
67. Hoare and Smith 1998.

Storming Heaven:
Where Has the Rage Gone?[1]
Tariq Ali

A storm swept the world in 1968. It arose in Vietnam, blew across Asia, and crossed the sea and the mountains to Europe and beyond. The signs and portents had been there for some years, but the speed with which it spread was not foreseen. A brutal war waged by the United States against a poor Southeast Asian country was seen every night on television. The cumulative impact of watching the bombs drop, villages on fire, and a country being doused with napalm and Agent Orange triggered a wave of global revolts never seen on this scale before or since. Solidarity with the communist-led Vietnamese resistance intermingled with numerous local contradictions. If the Vietnamese were defeating the world's most powerful state, surely we, too, could defeat our own rulers. That was the dominant mood amongst the more radicalised segments of the Sixties generation.

An invigorating political, cultural, and intellectual fever dazzled the world. It was as if contemplating the heavens at night one saw the sky occupied by comets and shooting stars. The tale has been told many times and in many languages. When a revolution is defeated all its attributes, good and bad, go down with it—but 1968 refuses to die.

In 2003 the situation was very different. People came out again in Europe and America, and in much larger numbers than ever before, to try and stop the Iraq war. But the pre-emptive strike against the warmongers failed. The movement lacked the stamina of its predecessors. Within forty-eight hours it had virtually disappeared, highlighting the changed times.

How Can One Forget?
In 1966–67 I spent six weeks in Indochina on behalf of the Bertrand Russell War Crimes Tribunal. My diary for January 29 1967 records:

> A new bombing raid has begun and our visit to the town [Than Hoa], scheduled for 2.30, that afternoon is off. I argue strongly that we should go, but suddenly the bombs seem very close. We can hear them. I plead again that we should move since this is our task: To report on what is being bombed and why. Major Van Bang refuses to permit us to leave. The Mayor of Than Hoa looks worried. He's convinced they're bombing the heart of the town. Two hours later, after the raid, we visit the city. We were supposed to have been at the hospital at

2.30. At 3 pm it was bombed. Several patients were killed by the first bombs. While they were being removed from the hospital and taken to the first-aid station there was another attack and the first-aid station was totally obliterated ... we saw houses still smouldering. Mrs Nguyen Thi Dinh had rushed out of her house just in time to see it burn to the ground. She was weeping silently when I spoke to her. "Do you think I will ever forgive them for what they are doing to us? Never, never. They must be punished for this". Two hundred dwellings have been destroyed. Dang Batao, the local Red Cross organiser, was burnt to death. Ms Ho Thi Oanh is also dead, a few weeks before her wedding. Her trousseau lies scattered, half-burnt and scarred ... impossible to visualise this agony in the West.

The devastation and daily deaths of civilians, mainly women and children, remain etched in the memory. How can one forget? Agitating for a different world that would outlaw all wars and for solidarity with the Vietnamese was the logical outcome for many from our generation. It was a ten-year struggle.

The eruptions of '68 challenged the power structures north and south, east and west. Countries in each continent were infected with the desire for change. Hope reigned supreme.

In February that year the Vietnamese communists launched their famous Tet (spring) offensive attacking US troops in every major South Vietnamese city. The grand finale was the sight of Vietnamese guerrillas occupying the US embassy in Saigon (Ho Chi Minh City) and raising their flag from its roof. It was undoubtedly a suicide mission, but incredibly courageous. The impact was immediate. For the first time a majority of US citizens realised that the war was unwinnable. The poorer amongst them brought Vietnam home that same summer in a revolt against poverty and discrimination as black ghettoes exploded in every major US city, with returned black GIs playing a prominent part as snipers.

This single spark set the world alight. In March 1968 the students at Nanterre came out on to the streets and the 22 March Movement was born with two Daniels (Cohn-Bendit and Bensaïd) challenging the French lion—Charles de Gaulle, the aloof, monarchical President of the Fifth Republic—who, in a puerile outburst, would later describe the events as "shit in the bed".[2] From demanding university reforms the students soon moved on to revolution. That same month a Vietnam Solidarity Campaign demonstration outside the US Embassy in Grosvenor Square in London turned violent.

Like the Vietnamese, we wanted to occupy the Embassy, but mounted police was deployed to protect the citadel. Clashes occurred, and the US Senator Eugene McCarthy, watching the images, demanded an end to a war that he said had led among other things to "our embassy in Europe's friendliest capital being constantly besieged". As Mick Jagger sang in 'Street Fighting Man', compared to elsewhere not all that much happened in Britain that year—university occupations and riots in Grosvenor Square did not pose a real threat to the Labour Government, which backed the US but refused to send troops to Vietnam:

> Ev'rywhere I hear the sound of marching, charging feet, boy
> 'Cause summer's here and the time is right for fighting in the street, boy
> Well then what can a poor boy do
> Except to sing for a rock 'n' roll band
> 'Cause in sleepy London town
> There's just no place for a street fighting man
> No!
>
> Hey! Think the time is right for a palace revolution
> 'Cause where I live the game to play is compromise solution
> …
>
> Hey! Said my name is called disturbance
> I'll shout and scream, I'll kill the king, I'll rail at all his servants
> Well, what can a poor boy do
> Except to sing for a rock 'n' roll band
> 'Cause in sleepy London town
> There's no place for a street fighting man
> No
> Get down.[3]

In Vietnam, the war entered its third and final phase. Occupied by France, later Japan, briefly Britain, and then France again, the Vietnamese had honed the skills of popular resistance to an art form that wasn't pretty or decorative. Despite half a million soldiers and the most advanced military technology ever known, the US could not defeat the Vietnamese. It was this that triggered an anti-war movement inside the US and infected the military. 'GIs Against The War' became a familiar banner, with tens of thousands of ex-GIs demonstrating outside the Pentagon and hurling their medals at the building.

Politics, Renewal, Utopia

The glorious decade (1965–75), of which the year 1968 was only the high point, consisted of three concurrent narratives. The uncontested primacy of politics was the dominant feature, but there were two others—sexual liberation and a hedonistic entrepreneurship from below—that left a deeper imprint. The first two would be considered impious by many who have sought refuge in religion. The third is now happily integrated.

We were constantly appealing for funds from readers when I edited *The Black Dwarf* in 1968–69. One day a guy in overalls walked in to our Soho office and counted out twenty-five grubby five pound notes, thanked us for producing the paper, and left. He would do this regularly every fortnight. Finally, I asked who he was and if there was a particular reason for his generosity. He had a stall on the Portobello Road and as to why he wanted to help, it was simple. "Capitalism is so non-groovy, man." It's only too groovy now, and far more vicious.

The Sixties were a response to the shallow, fading Cold War decades that characterised the middle period of the last century. In the United States in the Fifties, the McCarthyite witch-hunts had created havoc before the Senator went too far and had to be unceremoniously dumped. Blacklisted writers could work again, though the executed Rosenbergs could not be brought back to life. In Russia, hundreds of political prisoners were released, the Gulags were closed down, and the crimes of Stalin were denounced by Khrushchev as Eastern Europe trembled with excitement and hopes of rapid reform. They hoped in vain.

The spirit of renewal infected the realm of culture as well: Solzhenitsyn's first novel was serialised in the USSR, in the official literary magazine *Novy Mir*, and a new cinema took over most of Europe. Differences in content and style could not disguise a common cinematic language. Censorship persisted nonetheless and not just in Spain and Portugal ruled at the time by NATO's favourite fascists, Franco and Salazar. D H Lawrence's *Lady Chatterley's Lover*, written in 1928, was first published in Britain only in 1960. The publishers (Penguin) were tried for obscenity in a British court and after a dramatic trial lasting weeks were acquitted. The book was then published in its complete form and sold two million copies. Homosexuality in Britain was decriminalised in 1967.

In France, the existentialist philosopher Jean-Paul Sartre was at the peak of his influence. His views were now beginning to disturb the sterile counter-position of ends and means so loved by Stalinist apologists. Sartre argued that there was no reason to prepare for happiness tomorrow at the price of injustice, oppression, or misery today. What was required were improvements now that would prepare the path to the future. Socialism must be defined in terms of freedom and creation. His criticisms of Hegelians and Marxists for constructing a dialectic of history that ignored China, Japan, and India, regions that had fifty centuries of history behind them, now seem incredibly prescient. For him the first contingency of history was demography, the number of human beings who set it in motion. Nor was he alone.

The desire to re-inscribe Utopia on the map of a globalised world remained strong. France finally exploded in 1968, making it an uncommonly memorable and beautiful summer. We were preparing the first issue of *The Black Dwarf* as Paris erupted on May 10. Jean-Jacques Lebel, our tear-gassed Paris correspondent, was ringing in reports every few hours. He told us:

A well-known French football commentator is sent to the Latin Quarter to cover the night's events and reported: "Now the CRS [riot police] are charging, they're storming the barricade—oh my God! There's a battle raging. The students are counter-attacking, you can hear the noise—the CRS are retreating. Now they're regrouping, getting ready to charge again. The inhabitants are throwing things from their windows at the CRS—Oh! The police are retaliating, shooting grenades into the windows of apartments ..."

The producer interrupts: "This can't be true, the CRS don't do things like that!".

"I'm telling you what I'm seeing ..." His voice goes dead. They have cut him off.

The police failed to take back the Latin Quarter, which was renamed the Heroic Vietnam Quarter. Three days later a million people occupied the streets of Paris demanding an end to rottenness, plastering the walls with slogans: 'Defend the Collective Imagination', 'Beneath the Cobblestones the Beach', 'When the finger points at the moon the IDIOT looks at the finger', 'Commodities are the Opium of the People', 'Revolution is the Ecstasy of History'.

Eric Hobsbawm wrote in *The Black Dwarf*:

They [the people] know that the official mechanisms for representing them—elections, parties, etc—have tended to become a set of ceremonial institutions going through empty rituals. They do not like it—but until recently they did not know what to do about it ... What France proves is that when someone demonstrates that people are *not* powerless, they may begin to act again.

The revolution did not happen, but France was shaken by the events. The debate on 1968 was recently revived by Nicolas Sarkozy, the French President, who boasted that his victory in the 2007 presidential elections was the final nail in the '68 coffin:

May 1968 imposed intellectual and moral relativism on us all. The heirs of May '68 imposed the idea that there was no longer any difference between good and evil, truth and falsehood, beauty and ugliness. The heritage of May 1968 introduced cynicism into society and politics.[4]

He even blamed the legacy of May '68 for immoral business practices: The cult of money, short-term profit, speculation, and the abuses of finance capitalism.

The French philosopher Alain Badiou's tart response to Sarkozy was to compare the new President of the Republic to the Bourbons of 1815 and to Philippe Petain during the second world war. They, too, had talked about nails and coffins.

Other Places, Other Ruptures, Other Nails

The events of 1968 were, apart from everything else, an elegy for the print revolution. A libertarian bulletin published by French students in 1968 was a hymn to the written word:

> Leaflets, posters, bulletins, street words or infinite words: They are not imposed for the sake of effectiveness ... They belong to the decision of the present moment. They appear, they disappear. They do not say everything; on the contrary, they ruin everything: They are outside everything. They act, they think in fragments. They do not leave a trace ... as speech on walls, they are written in insecurity, communicated under threat, carry danger in them, then they pass by along with the passers-by, who pass them on, lose them or even forget.

In Prague, too, a lot of leaflets and documents were being produced. Communist reformers—many of them heroes of the anti-fascist resistance during World War II—had earlier that spring proclaimed 'socialism with a human face'. The country was bathed by the lava of the resulting debates and discussions in the state press and on television. The aim of Alexander Dubček and his supporters was to democratise political life in the country. It was the first step towards a socialist democracy and seen as such in Moscow and Washington. On August 21 1968, the Russians sent in the tanks and crushed the reform movement.

In every West European capital there were protests. The tabloid press in Britain was constantly attacking us as 'agents of Moscow' and were genuinely taken aback when we marched to the Soviet Embassy denouncing the invasion of Czechoslovakia in strong language and burning effigies of the bloated Soviet leader, Leonid Brezhnev. Aleksandr Solzhenitsyn later remarked that the Soviet invasion had been the last straw for him. Now he realised that the system could never be reformed from within but would have to be overthrown. He was not alone. The Moscow bureaucrats had sealed their own fate.

In October 1968, Mexican students took over their universities demanding an end to oppression and one-party rule. The army was sent in to occupy the universities and did so for many months, making it the best-educated army in the world. When the students poured out on to the streets they were massacred just before the arrival of the Olympic flame. Afro-American gold and silver-medallists raised their fists in a Black Power salute to express their solidarity.

And then in November 1968, Pakistan erupted. The students took on the state apparatus of a corrupt and decaying military dictatorship backed by the US (sounds familiar?). They were joined by workers, lawyers, white-collar employees, prostitutes, and other social layers. Despite the severe repression (hundreds were killed) the struggle increased in intensity and toppled Field Marshal Ayub Khan.

When I arrived in Pakistan in February 1969, the country was in a state of total excitement. The mood was joyous. Speaking at rallies all over the country with the poet Habib Jalib, I encountered a very different atmosphere to Europe. Here power did not seem so remote. The victory led to the first general election in the country's history. The Bengali nationalists in East Pakistan won a majority that the elite and key politicians refused to accept. Bloody civil war led to Indian military intervention and ended the old Pakistan. Bangladesh was the result of a bloody caesarean.

Much of this seems utopian now and some for whom '68 wasn't radical enough at the time have embraced the present and, like members of ancient sects who moved easily from ritual debauchery to chastity, they now regard any form of socialism as the serpent that tempted Eve in paradise.

The daughters of Eve were also on the march at that time. In 1949, Simone de Beauvoir's pioneering work, *The Second Sex*, was published in France and became the inspiration for a new generation of women. In December 1966, Juliet Mitchell fired off a new salvo. Her lengthy essay, 'Women: The Longest Revolution', appeared in the *New Left Review* and became an immediate point of reference, its opening paragraph summarising the problems faced by women:

> The situation of women is different from that of any other social group. This is because they are not one of a number of isolable units, but half a totality: The human species. Women are essential and irreplaceable; they cannot therefore be exploited in the same way as other social groups can. They are fundamental to the human condition, yet in their economic, social, and political roles, they are marginal. It is precisely this combination—fundamental and marginal at one and the same time—that has been fatal to them. Within the world of men their position is comparable to that of an oppressed minority: But they also exist outside the world of men. The one state justifies the other and precludes protest. In advanced industrial society, women's work is only marginal to the total economy. Yet it is through work that man changes natural conditions and thereby produces society. ... But women are offered a universe of their own: The family. Like woman herself, the family appears as a natural object, but it is actually a cultural creation. There is nothing inevitable about the form or role of the family any more than there is about the character or role of women. ... Both can be exalted paradoxically, as ideals. The 'true' woman and the 'true' family are images of peace and plenty: In actuality they may both be sites of violence and despair.

In September 1968, US feminists disrupted the Miss World competition in Atlantic City, the first shots of a women's liberation movement that would change women's lives by demanding recognition, independence, and an equal voice in a male-dominated world. Macho socialists in parts of South America who locked up their wives to prevent them from joining women's protests on International Women's Day became a rarity. The compulsory fulfilment of three functions—providing sex on demand to their partners, giving birth to children, and rearing them while the man worked—was no longer acceptable.

The Black Dwarf cover on its January 1969 issue dedicated the year to women. Inside we published Sheila Rowbotham's spirited feminist call to arms whose message escaped our hippie designer. He had put Sheila's carefully crafted words on a pair of luscious breasts. We parted company with the designer and the breasts.[5]

And yes, there was the pleasure-principle. That the Sixties were hedonistic is indisputable, but it was different from the recuperated and corporatised version of today. At the time it marked a break with the hypocritical Puritanism of the Forties and Fifties when film censors prohibited married couples being shown on screen sharing a bed and pyjamas were compulsory. Radical upheavals challenge all social restrictions.

Gay liberation movements erupted as well, with activists demanding an end to all homophobic legislation and taking out Gay Pride marches, inspired by the Afro-American struggles for equal rights and black pride. All the movements learnt from each other. The advances of the civil rights, women, and gay movements, now taken for granted, had to be fought for on the streets against enemies who were the fighting the 'war on horror'.

Echoes and Refrains

History rarely repeats itself, but its echoes linger. Take, for instance, the North American poet Thomas McGrath, who in the middle of the last century defended the radicalism of the 20s and 30s against the cynics and the worshippers of accomplished facts, who presided over the conformist and cold-war dominated 50s. His poem 'Letter To an Imaginary Friend' remains apposite in relation to the 60s:

> Wild talk, and easy enough to laugh.
> That's not the point and never was the point.
> What was real was the generosity, expectant hope,
> The open and true desire to create the good.
> Now, in another autumn, in our new dispensation
> Of an ancient, man-chilling dark, the frost drops over
> My garden's starry wreckage.
> Over my hope.
> Over
> The generous dead of my years.
> Now, in the chill streets

I hear the hunting and the long thunder of money ... [6]

The epochal shift that took place in 1989 relegated most things radical to the museum of horrors. All revolutions and all revolutionaries became monsters, mass murderers, and, of course, terrorists. How can the lyrical sharpness of politics in 1968 be anything but alien to the spirit of this age that has followed? The radical politics and culture of 1968 do not cater to the needs of the current rulers any more than they did to the needs of the rulers of that time. The autonomy of the past has to be defended.

The collapse of 'communism' (how will that anniversary be marked next year?)[7] created the basis for a new social agreement, the Washington Consensus, whereby deregulation and the entry of private capital into hitherto hallowed domains of public provision would become the norm everywhere, making traditional social democracy redundant and threatening the democratic process itself.

Some, who once dreamt of a better future, have simply given up. Others espouse a bitter maxim: Unless you relearn you won't earn. The French intelligentsia, that had from the Enlightenment onwards made Paris the political workshop of the world, today leads the way with retreats on every front. Renegades occupy posts in every West European government, defending exploitation, wars, state terror, and neo-colonial occupations; others now retired from the academy specialise in producing reactionary dross on the blogosphere, displaying the same zeal with which they once excoriated factional rivals on the far-left. This, too, is nothing new. Shelley's rebuke to Wordsworth—who, after welcoming the French Revolution, retreated to a pastoral conservatism—expressed it well:

In honoured poverty thy voice did weave
Songs consecrate to truth and liberty,
Deserting these, thou leavest me to grieve,
Thus having been, that thou shouldst cease to be.[8]

Were the dreams and hopes of 1968 all idle fantasies? Or did cruel history abort something new that was about to be born? Revolutionaries—utopian anarchists, Fidelistas, Trotskyist allsorts, Maoists of every stripe, etc—wanted the whole forest. Liberals and social democrats were fixated on individual trees. The forest, they warned us, was a distraction, far too vast and impossible to define, whereas a tree was a piece of wood that could be identified, nurtured, improved, and crafted into a chair or a table or a bed.

Now the tree, too, has gone.

References

Aidan Crawley, 1969—*De Gaulle*. London: The Literary Guild

Mick Jagger and Keith Richards, 1968—'Street Fighting Man', at http://www.keno.org/stones_lyrics/street_fighting_man.htm (Accessed April 2017)

Thomas McGrath, 1997—*Letter to an Imaginary Friend*. Port Townsend, WA: Copper Canyon Press

Percy Bysshe Shelley, 2002—'To Wordsworth', in Percy Bysshe Shelley, 2002—*The Selected Poetry and Prose of Shelley*. Introduction and notes by Bruce Woodcock. The Wordsworth Poetry Library, at https://books.google.co.in/books?id=1fHVdkB-fmXMC&pg=PA120&source=gbs_toc_r&hl=en#v=onepage&q&f=false

Notes

1. Ed: This is a longer, reworked, and edited version of an article that appeared in 2008 (Tariq Ali, March 2008—'Where Has All the Rage Gone?', in *The Guardian*, Saturday, March 22 2008, at http://www.guardian.co.uk/politics/2008/mar/22/vietnamwar accessed js 030408). I warmly thank the author for offering us this version for publication.

2. See Crawley 1969, p 454.

3. Jagger and Richards 1968.

4. Ed: See, for instance, http://timescorrespondents.typepad.com/charles_bremner/2008/02/france-feuds-ov.html for a report (Inactive April 2017).

5. As I write this in 2008, Professor Rowbotham, now a distinguished scholar, is under threat from the ghastly, grey accountants who run Manchester University. They have no idea who she is and are desperate to get rid of her. Student support for her confirms their corporate prejudices. We are now in an epoch of production-line universities with celebrities paid fortunes to teach eight hours a week and genuine scholars dumped in the bin.

6. McGrath 1997.

7. Ed: This essay was finalised in 2008, and so the author is referring to the twentieth anniversary of the collapse of the Soviet Union in 1989 that was coming up in 2009.

8. Shelley 2002.

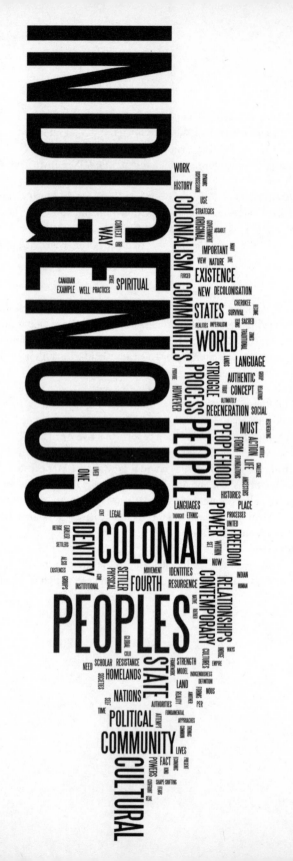

Being Indigenous:
Resurgences Against Contemporary Colonialism[1]
Taiaiake Alfred and Jeff Corntassel

On Indigenousness

Indigenousness is an identity constructed, shaped, and lived in the politicised context of contemporary colonialism. The communities, clans, nations, and tribes we call *Indigenous peoples* are just that: Indigenous to the lands they inhabit, in contrast to and in contention with the colonial societies and states that have spread out from Europe and other centres of empire. It is this oppositional, place-based existence, along with the consciousness of being in struggle against the dispossessing and demeaning fact of colonisation by foreign peoples, that fundamentally distinguishes Indigenous peoples from other peoples of the world.[2]

There are, of course, vast differences among the world's Indigenous peoples in their cultures, political-economic situations, and their relationships with colonising Settler societies. But the struggle to survive as distinct peoples on foundations constituted in their unique heritages, attachments to their homelands, and natural ways of life is what is shared by all Indigenous peoples, as well as the fact that their existence is in large part lived out as determined acts of survival against colonising states' efforts to eradicate them culturally, politically, and physically. The challenge of 'being Indigenous', in a psychic and cultural sense, forms the crucial question facing Indigenous peoples today in the era of contemporary colonialism—a form of post-modern imperialism in which domination is still the Settler imperative but where colonisers have designed and practise more subtle means (in contrast to the earlier forms of missionary and militaristic colonial enterprises) of accomplishing their objectives.

Contemporary Settlers follow the mandate provided for them by their imperial forefathers' colonial legacy, not by attempting to eradicate the physical signs of Indigenous peoples as human *bodies* but by trying to eradicate their existence as *peoples* through the erasure of the histories and geographies that provide the foundation for Indigenous cultural identities and sense of self. The geographer Bernard Nietschmann has demonstrated the need for critical translations of the artificial, state-created identities (such as 'ethnic group') that are imposed on original peoples in this colonising process of redefinition from autonomous to derivative existence and cultural and political identities. State-imposed conceptions of supposedly Indigenous identity are seen by Indigenous peoples, from perspectives rooted in their own cultures and languages, not as moves towards 'justice' and 'positive integration' (as the strategy is framed in colonial discourses) but as indicators of an on-going colonial assault on their existence, and signs of the fact that they remain, as in earlier colonial eras, occupied peoples who have been dispossessed and disempowered in their own homelands.[3]

For example, in Canada today, many Indigenous people have embraced the Canadian government's label of 'aboriginal', along with the concomitant and limited notion of postcolonial justice framed within the institutional construct of the state. In fact, this identity is purely a state construction that is instrumental to the state's attempt to gradually subsume Indigenous existences into its own constitutional system and body politic since Canadian independence from Great Britain—a process that started in the mid-twentieth century and culminated with the emergence of a Canadian constitution in 1982. Far from reflecting any true history or honest reconciliation with the past or present agreements and treaties that form an authentic basis for Indigenous-state relations in the Canadian context, 'aboriginalism' is a legal, political, and cultural discourse designed to serve an agenda of silent surrender to an inherently unjust relation at the root of the colonial state itself.

The acceptance of being 'aboriginal' (or its equivalent term in other countries, such as 'ethnic groups') is a powerful assault on Indigenous identities. It must be understood that this assault takes place in a politico-economic context of historic and ongoing dispossession and of contemporary deprivation and poverty; this is a context in which Indigenous peoples are forced by the compelling needs of physical survival to cooperate individually and collectively with the state authorities to ensure their physical survival. Consequently, there are many 'aboriginals' (in Canada) or 'Native Americans' (in the United States) who identify themselves solely by their political-legal relationship to the state rather than by any cultural or social ties to their Indigenous community or culture or homeland. This continuing colonial process pulls Indigenous peoples away from cultural practices and community aspects of 'being Indigenous' towards a political-legal construction as 'aboriginal' or 'Native American', both of which are representative of what we refer to as being 'incidentally Indigenous'.

There are approximately 350 million Indigenous peoples situated in some 70 countries around the world.[4] All of these people confront the daily realities of having their lands, cultures, and governmental authorities simultaneously attacked, denied, and reconstructed by colonial societies and states. This has been the case for generations. But there are new faces of empire that are attempting to strip Indigenous peoples of their very spirit as nations and of all that is held sacred, threatening their sources of connection to their distinct existences and the sources of their spiritual power: Relationships to each other, communities, homelands, ceremonial life, languages, histories. ... These connections are crucial to living a meaningful life for any human being.

In this essay, we discuss strategies for resisting further encroachment on Indigenous existence by Settler societies and states—as well as by multinational corporations and other elite organisations controlled by state powers and elements of the imperial institutional network—and we focus on how Indigenous communities can regenerate themselves to resist the effects of the contemporary colonial assault and renew politically and culturally. We ask the fundamental question: How can we resist further dispossession and disconnection when the effects of colonial assaults on our own existence are so pronounced and still so present in the lives of all Indigenous peoples?

Colonial legacies and contemporary practices of disconnection, dependency, and dispossession have effectively confined Indigenous identities to state-sanctioned legal and political definitional approaches. This political-legal compartmentalisation of community values often leads Indigenous nations to mimic the practices of dominant non-Indigenous legal-political institutions and adhere to state-sanctioned definitions of Indigenous identity. Such compartmentalisation results in a "politics of distraction"[5] that diverts energies away from decolonising and regenerating communities, and frames community relationships in state-centric terms, such as the aforementioned 'aboriginality'.

Given that Indigenous identities are (re)constructed at multiple levels—global, state, community, individual—it is important to recognise these multiple sites of resistance to encroachment by states and other Settler colonial entities. The quest for definitional authority goes well beyond state borders; the United Nations, the World Bank group, the International Labour Organisation, as well as other global actors, also attempt to determine who is Indigenous.[6] However, as Taiaiake Alfred has pointed out, "demands for precision and certainty disregard the reality of the situation: that group identity varies with time and place".[7] How effectively have researchers and theorists accounted for the dynamic nature of being Indigenous?

Theories rooted in Indigenous cultural and spiritual principles, such as the 'Fourth World' and 'Peoplehood' schools of thought, seem to offer promise. Yet it is ultimately our lived collective and individual experiences as Indigenous peoples that yield the clearest and most useful insights for establishing culturally sound strategies to resist colonialism and regenerate our communities.

Ground Realities

Colonial Powers as Shape Shifters

It is important to identify all of the old and new faces of colonialism that continue to distort and dehumanise Indigenous peoples—often pitting us against each other in battles over authentic histories. "Colonisation" is the word most often used to describe the experience of Indigenous encounters with Settler societies, and it is the framework we are employing here. However, there is a danger in allowing colonisation to be the only story of Indigenous lives. It must be recognised that colonialism is a narrative in which the Settler's power is the fundamental reference and assumption, inherently limiting Indigenous freedom and imposing a view of the world that is but an outcome or perspective on that power. As stated earlier, we live in an era of postmodern imperialism and manipulations by shape-shifting colonial powers; the instruments of domination are evolving and inventing new methods to erase Indigenous histories and senses of place. Therefore, 'globalisation' in Indigenous eyes reflects a deepening, hastening, and stretching of an already-existing empire. Living within such political and cultural contexts, it is remembering ceremony, returning to homelands, and liberation from the myths of colonialism that are the decolonising imperatives. In their seminal treatise, *The Fourth World*, Manuel and Posluns explained the effects of contemporary colonial processes:

> The colonial system is always a way of gaining control over another people for the sake of what the colonial power has determined to be 'the common good.' People can only become convinced of the common good when their own capacity to imagine ways in which they can govern themselves has been destroyed.[8]

From such a Fourth World viewpoint, the 'common good' becomes whatever it is defined as by shape-shifting colonial elites. Nietschmann documents a number of shape-shifting strategies imposed by Settler states that confront Indigenous peoples on a daily basis, such as creating a bogus 'we are you' agenda, calling for a vote to legitimise the occupation, referring to state camps as 'economic development' and 'new communities', and offering amnesty to resistant military leaders and their forces in order to co-opt their movements.[9] While some of these shape-shifting tactics may appear to be mild or subtle, they, like other brutal forms of oppression, threaten the very survival of Indigenous communities.

For instance, consider the government of Bangladesh's official position that all of the country's inhabitants are 'Indigenous' and 'Bengalee', despite the existence of sixteen different Indigenous communities (collectively referred to as Jumma) in the area of the country known as the Chittagong Hill Tracts (CHT) alone. In order to implement this 'we are you' mythology, the Bangladesh government, with the assistance of international aid agencies, has engaged in a tactic of 'swamping' by initiating a massive ethnic Bengalee settlement of the CHT region since 1971. Consequently, the area has been purposely overloaded with over 400,000 Bengalee Settlers who have dislocated the much smaller local indigenous populations from their homelands. (The Jumma population of the region, for instance, adds up to approximately 50,000 people.) From comprising just three per cent of the population of the CHT in 1947, Bengalee Settlers now constitute roughly half the total population of the area.[10]

Such new faces of colonialism encroach on Indigenous sacred histories, homelands, and cultural practices in somewhat familiar ways, but use diplomatic language and the veneer of 'economic development' to mask ugly truths. The great North African anti-colonial writer Frantz Fanon described this process as an ongoing dialectic:

> Colonialism is not satisfied merely with holding a people in its grip and emptying the native's brain of all form and content. By a kind of perverted logic, it turns to the past of the oppressed people, and distorts, disfigures, and destroys it. This work of devaluing pre-colonial history takes on a dialectical significance today.[11]

It is these perverted logics and lies that must be confronted now, just as troops were fought courageously with guns and bombs in previous eras of the struggle for Indigenous freedom. When lies become accepted and normal, the imperative of the warrior is to awaken and enliven the truth and to get people to invest belief and energy into that truth. The battle is a spiritual and physical one fought against the political manipulation of the people's own innate fears and the embedding of complacency, that metastasising weakness, into their psyches. Fanon pointed out that the most important strength of Indigenous resistance, unity, is also constantly under attack as colonial powers erase community histories and senses of place to replace them with doctrines of individualism and predatory capitalism:

> In the colonial context ... the natives fight among themselves. They tend to use each other as a screen, and each hides from his neighbour the national enemy.[12]

As Fanon illustrates, these battles occurring amongst ourselves distract us from the bigger picture of decolonisation and sap the crucial energy and solidarity that are essential to effective confrontation of imperial power in whatever form it presents itself. Large-scale Indigenous efforts to confront state power by mimicking state institutions (via land claims and self-government processes) only deepen these divisions. For a long time now, Indigenous peoples have been on a quest for governmental power and money. Contemporary forms of postmodern imperialism attempt to confine the expression of Indigenous peoples' right of self-determination to a set of domestic authorities operating within the constitutional framework of the state (as opposed to the right of having an autonomous and global standing) and actively seek to sever Indigenous links to their ancestral homelands.

In Canada, for example, the so-called British Columbia Treaty Process (ongoing for over a decade) has been structured to achieve the legalisation of the Settler society's occupation of unceded and non-treaty lands that make up 90 per cent of the territory in that province, to have the Indigenous peoples "surrender their Aboriginal title to the Crown, whereupon it becomes vested in the province".[13]

The secondary goal of the process is to achieve a set of binding agreements that accord the federal and provincial government legal supremacy over First Nations' governments. In fact, the Nisga'a Nation's agreement, implemented in 2000—which was the culmination of a negotiation that began much earlier than the current treaty process but which was conducted under the same mandate and objectives—was voted on by only 40 per cent of the Nisga'a people and makes no mention of the word 'treaty' anywhere in the text of the document.[14]

A similar process of 'domestication' of Indigenous issues is taking place in the United States, during this era of widespread institutionalisation of the Indigenous–state compacts to legalise gaming enterprises on tribal lands, a process Corntassel refers to as 'Forced Federalism'.[15] As pre-constitutional and treaty-holding nations, Indigenous peoples in what is now called the United States have historically been considered to transcend all local non-Indigenous government jurisdictional claims in matters of their homeland's autonomy. However, since the passage of the 1988 Indian Gaming and Regulatory Act (IGRA) and the further integration of Indigenous governments into the state system through the forced federalism process, non-Indigenous governments and officials have increasingly asserted their jurisdictional authority over Indigenous people and the territories of Indigenous nations that exist within arbitrary boundaries established by the colonial state.

Refocusing on Autonomy

How can we refocus and restore the original objective of Indigenous autonomy and nation-to-nation relations between original and immigrant peoples to its orienting primacy? In advocating a break from the colonial path, Nez Perce / Chicana scholar Inés Hernández-Ávila speaks of the power of Indigenous languages in articulating a transformative agenda in Mexico that is "dignifying, validating and ensuring the continuance of their peoples' languages and cultures".[16]

Hernández-Ávila's interview with Feliciano Sanchez Chan, a Maya / Yucateco, highlights the need for 'zones of refuge' that are immune to the reaches of imperialism and globalisation. These zones of refuge are places where

> knowledge has been historically guarded, exercised and sustained. These zones of refuge represent safe (physical and psychological) spaces where Mesoamerican cultural matrices continue to find expression, even as the advocates of the imaginary Mexico persist in their obstinate project of erasure and substitution.[17]

This is a powerful conceptualisation of a strategic and cultural objective that remains consistent with traditional goals yet stands against the integrative goals of the contemporary colonial agenda. In addition to creating zones of refuge and other breaks from colonial rule that create spaces of freedom, we will begin to realise decolonisation in a real way when we begin to achieve the re-strengthening of our people as individuals so that these spaces can be occupied by decolonised people living authentic lives. This is a recognition that our true power as Indigenous people ultimately lies in our relationships with our land, relatives, language, and ceremonial life. As the eminent Lakota scholar Vine Deloria, Jr, asserts, "[w]hat we need is a cultural leave-us-alone agreement, in spirit and in fact".[18]

Refractions and Reflections

Universalised Definitions, Compartmentalised Communities
The scholarly literature on being Indigenous predominantly focuses on identity constructions that reflect the colonised political and legal contexts in which Indigenous peoples are forced to live and operate. Academics tend to examine wider phenomena of what is known as pan-Indigenism or focus on theories of individual self-identification; very few are themselves grounded in real Indigenous community life or perspectives. For example, Joane Nagel's work describes 'Red Power activism' as the "progenitor of an American Indian ethnic rebirth"[19] during the 1970s, and finds that so-called 'Indian' resurgence through the American Indian Movement had its roots in urban areas as a direct response to federal assimilation policies of the 1950s and 1960s.[20] However, her work (though making an important contribution) falls short when discussing relationships between urban and reservation communities and overemphasises the role of urban people in this cultural renaissance. Anthropologist Ronald Niezen attempts to overcome this kind of shortcoming in his study of what he calls 'Indigenism',[21] as he documents the widespread mobilisation and unity of Indigenous peoples in global forums as they resist encroachment by the state and other Settler colonial entities. However, his work neglects the grassroots dimensions of Indigenous mobilisation and emphasises colonial narratives of 'victimisation' and 'grievance' as the cornerstones of Indigenous identity.

Other researchers have examined the identity choices made by individuals as they respond to social, economic, and political influences around them. For example, Devon Mihesuah adapted a 'life stages' model, based on the work of African-American scholars William Cross and Thomas Parham, to the identity choices of Indigenous people. In this four-stage, linear process, one strives to reach the 'internalisation' stage eventually, where "inner security about their identity" is attained.[22] However, this approach emphasises interactions with non-Indigenous people in precipitating identity awareness and personal change, and de-emphasises relationships with communities and family. As Jace Weaver points out, Indigenous identity can only be confirmed by others "who share that identity."[23] Cherokee sociologist Matthew Snipp also notes that the "boundaries of [Indigenous] populations are best defined in social terms" and where "human beings are born into a closely linked and integrated network of family, kinship, social and political relations".[24]

In their attempts to establish universal definitions of Indigenous peoples, scholars have rewritten Indigenous histories and imposed political and cultural limits on the freedom of Indigenous people to live lives of their own choosing. For example, Ted Gurr, a prominent scholar in the field of international relations, established the comprehensive Minorities at Risk (MAR) project in 1988, and tracked the activities of 275 ethno-political groups from 1980 to 1999. Upon closer examination, the utility of Gurr's conceptual scheme, which divides Indigenous and ethnonationalist phenomena into mutually exclusive categories, is highly questionable. For Gurr, Indigenous peoples are defined as:

> Conquered descendants of earlier inhabitants of a region who live mainly in conformity with traditional social, economic, and cultural customs that are sharply distinct from those of dominant groups. ... Indigenous peoples who had durable states of their own prior to conquest, such as Tibetans, or who have given sustained support to modern movements aimed at establishing their own state, such as the Kurds, are classified as ethnonationalists, not Indigenous peoples.[25]

According to Gurr's definition, being conquered and being dominated by another group are preconditions for being considered Indigenous. However, not all Indigenous peoples were 'conquered' militarily by the colonial powers that now dominate them. Treaty-making, rather than outright military conquest, took place in North America on a wide scale between Holland, France, or Great Britain and the original peoples of what is now called Canada and the United States. Nor are all Indigenous peoples non-dominant, whether one looks at the large populations of Indigenous peoples within certain states, such as Bolivia (66 per cent), or in terms of Indigenous peoples mobilising to pose a credible political threat to the survival of the state. As Niezen concludes, "[a] rigorous definition [of Indigenous peoples] ... would be premature and, ultimately, futile. Debates over the problem of definition are actually more interesting than any definition in and of itself".[26]

Indigenous Foundations for Being Indigenous

What, then, does it mean to be Indigenous, given the colonial legacies of blood quantum measurements,[27] state assimilation policies, self-identification as a challenge to community citizenship standards, acceptance of colonial labels of 'aboriginalism', and gendered identity constructions?[28] Postmodern imperialists attempt to partition Indigenous bodies and communities by imposing political / legal fictions on cultural peoples. How can we promote balance between political and cultural notions of being Indigenous? Cree / Métis writer Kim Anderson outlines several "foundations of resistance" for being Indigenous, which include:

Strong families, grounding in community, connection to land, language, story-telling, and spirituality.[29] For Anderson, these form a basis for action. However, we believe that the interrelationships between these fundamental principles must be examined further in order to generate a foundation for effective resistance to contemporary colonialism.

Peoplehood models, which discuss the interconnected factors of community, language, and cultural practices, appear to have some promise for discussing the adaptability and resurgence of Indigenous communities. Indigenous peoples them-selves have long understood their existence as peoples or nations (expressed not in these terms but in their own languages, of course) as formed around axes of land, culture, and community. Scholars have investigated these traditional understand-ings and derived theories based on such Indigenous philosophies. The concept of 'peoplehood' has its roots in anthropologist Edward H Spicer's work on 'enduring peoples.'[30] Spicer's discussion of an 'Indian sense of identity' (as distinct from 'ethnic groups') centred on three key factors: Their relationship to the land, common spir-itual bond, and language use.[31] The peoplehood concept was further developed by Cherokee anthropologist Robert K Thomas, who added 'sacred history' as a fourth factor in community relationships.[32] Thomas also described the four components of peoplehood as being interwoven and dependent on one another.

Current work by the Cherokee / Creek scholar Tom Holm, along with Diane Pearson and Ben Chavis, revives the original peoplehood concept and devel-ops it as the foundational concept framing their view of the ideal direction for Indigenous research and teaching.[33] Holm and his colleagues view peoplehood as four interlocking concepts: Sacred history, ceremonial cycles, language, and an-cestral homelands. Unlike the multipart, ahistorical definitions of Indigenousness proffered by most academics and practitioners, the Holm model is predicated on a view of identity that is both dynamic and interconnected: "No single element of the model is more or less important than the others".[34] Apache scholar Bernadette Adley-Santa Maria illustrates this concept of peoplehood with her grandmother's words: "If you do not sing the songs—if you do not tell the stories and if you do not speak the language—you will cease to exist as 'Ndee' (Apache)".[35]

Building on this notion of a dynamic and interconnected concept of Indigenous identity constituted in history, ceremony, language, and land, we consider relationships (or kinship networks) to be at the core of an authentic Indigenous identity. Clearly, it is the need to maintain and renew respectful re-lationships that guides all interactions and experiences with community, clans, families, individuals, homelands, plants, animals, etc in the Indigenous cultural ideal. If any one of these elements of identity, such as sacred history, is in danger of being lost, unified action can be taken to revitalise and restore that part of the community by utilising relationships, which are the spiritual and cultural foundations of Indigenous peoples. Tewa scholar Gregory Cajete contrasts this

Indigenous sense of kinship and "ensoulment of nature" with the (relatively) one-dimensional Newtonian-Cartesian perspectives characteristic of European and colonial worldviews: "[Indigenous] people understood that all entities of nature—plants, animals, stones, trees, mountains, rivers, lakes and a host of other living entities—embodied relationships that must be honoured".[36]

It follows that for many Indigenous communities, peoplehood, as we are describing it, is seen as an aspiration rather than a recognised present reality. As Thomas states, "[a]mong some enduring peoples the very absence of, or the losing of, one of these important four symbols can, in itself, become a strong symbol of peoplehood".[37] This somewhat counter-intuitive response to cultural loss further illustrates the adaptive nature and contextual relevance of peoplehood to particular Indigenous communities. This also reinforces our view that the peoplehood concept is a flexible and dynamic alternative to static political and legal definitional approaches to Indigenous identities.

There are obvious strengths of the peoplehood model as a foundation for developing Indigenous cultures of resistance. But where should strategies to generate a resurgence of Indigenous nationhood be focused? Manuel and Posluns's theory of the Fourth World is again instructive, revealing the unifying nature of Indigenous *action* in the struggle against colonialism throughout the world:

> My belief in the Fourth World is an act of faith. But it is no illusion. I have told you of the strength of my ancestors. My faith is simply that the strength of the present generation and those who are still coming toward us is no less than the strength of our forebears. The Fourth World is far more of a Long March than an Eternal Resting Place. My faith is that we, and our children's children, are willing and able to take up the burden of our history and set out on our journey. Were there no more to it than that I should ask no more of other men than to let us pass freely.[38]

For Manuel and Posluns, the Fourth World is founded on active relationships with the spiritual and cultural heritage embedded in the words and patterns of thought and behaviour left to us by our ancestors. The legacies of their struggles to be Indigenous form the imperatives of our contemporary struggles to regenerate authentic Indigenous existences.

A Fourth World theory asserting Indigenous laws on Indigenous lands highlights the sites of ongoing state-nation conflicts while reaffirming the spiritual and cultural nature of the struggle. This is not simply another taxonomy relating Indigenous realities in a theoretical way to the so-called First, Second, and Third Worlds, but a recognition of a spiritual "struggle to enter the Fourth World" and to decode state motivations as they invade under the "mantle of liberation and development".[39] The Canadian historian Anthony Hall describes this as a battle against the "empire of possessive individualism" and the "militarisation of space":

"[T]he idea of the Fourth World provides a kind of broad ideological umbrella to cover the changing coalitions of pluralistic resistance aimed at preventing the monocultural transformation of the entire planet".[40]

Recovery, Regeneration, Resurgence

Corruption, Regeneration, and the Self

While the concepts of peoplehood and the Fourth World undoubtedly provide solid bases for thinking about strategies of resurgence, the question remains: How can these be put into practice? In *Real Indians: Identity and the Survival of Native America*, the Cherokee sociologist Eva Marie Garroutte discusses the concept of 'Radical Indigenism' as a process of pursuing scholarship that is grounded in Indigenous community goals and which "follows the path laid down in the models of inquiry traditional to their tribal community".[41] This intellectual strategy entails utilising all of the talents of the people inside and within a community to begin a process of regeneration.

The larger process of regeneration, as well as the outwardly focused process of decolonisation, begins with the self. It is a self-conscious kind of traditionalism that is the central process in the "reconstruction of traditional communities" based on the original teachings and orienting values of Indigenous peoples.[42] Colonialism corrupted the relationship between original peoples and the Settlers, and it eventually led to the corruption of Indigenous cultures and communities, too. But our discussion thus far has, we hope, illustrated the fact that decolonisation and regeneration are not at root collective and institutional processes. They are shifts in thinking and action that emanate from recommitments and reorientations at the level of the self that, over time and through proper organisation, manifest as broad social and political movements to challenge state agendas and authorities. To a large extent, institutional approaches to making meaningful change in the lives of Indigenous people have not led to what we understand as decolonisation and regeneration; rather they have further embedded Indigenous people in the colonial institutions they set out to challenge. This paradoxical outcome of struggle is because of the logical inconsistencies at the core of the institutional approaches.

Current approaches to confronting the problem of contemporary colonialism ignore the wisdom of the teachings of our ancestors reflected in such concepts as peoplehood and the Fourth World. They are, in a basic way, building not on a spiritual and cultural foundation provided to us as the heritage of our nations, but on the weakened and severely damaged cultural and spiritual and social results of colonialism. Purported decolonisation and watered-down cultural restoration processes that accept the premises and realities of our colonised existences as their starting point are inherently flawed and doomed to fail. They attempt to reconstitute strong nations on the foundations of enervated, dispirited, and decultured people. That is the honest and brutal reality; and that is the fundamental illogic of our contemporary struggle.

Indigenous Pathways of Action and Freedom

Indigenous pathways of authentic action and freedom struggle start with people transcending colonialism on an individual basis—a strength that soon reverberates outward from the self to family, clan, community, and into all of the broader relationships that form an Indigenous existence. Regenerating inter-Indigenous alliances might be one outcome of this process, which might include revitalising Indigenous trade networks throughout the Americas as well as enacting new forms of inter-Indigenous treaty-making, further illustrating the wide spectrum of Indigenous powers of self-determination. In this way, Indigenousness can be reconstructed, reshaped, and actively lived as resurgence against the dispossessing and demeaning processes of annihilation that are inherent to colonialism.

There is no concise, neat model of resurgence in this way of approaching decolonisation and the regeneration of our peoples. Nor are there clear and definite steps that we can list for people to check off as milestones on their march to freedom. But there are identifiable directions of movement, patterns of thought and action that reflect a shift to an Indigenous reality from the colonised places we inhabit today in our minds and in our souls. Derived from experience of Indigenous warriors old and new who have generated an authentic existence out of the mess left by colonial dispossession and disruption, these pathways can be thought of as the general direction of freedom, whether we have in mind the struggle of a single person or conceptualising an eventual global Indigenous struggle founded on the regeneration of ourselves and our communities.

The following are the *mantras* of a resurgent Indigenous movement:

- *Land is life*. Our people must reconnect with the terrain and geography of their Indigenous heritage if they are to comprehend the teachings and values of the ancestors, and if they are to draw strength and sustenance that is independent of colonial power, and which is regenerative of an authentic, autonomous, Indigenous existence.
- *Language is power*. Our people must recover ways of knowing and relating from outside the mental and ideational framework of colonialism by regenerating themselves in a conceptual universe formed through Indigenous languages.
- *Freedom is the other side of fear*. Our people must transcend the controlling power of the many and varied fears that colonial powers use to dominate and manipulate us into complacency and cooperation with its authorities. The way to do this is to confront our fears head-on through spiritually grounded action; contention and direct movement at the very source of our fears is the only way to break the chains that bind us to our colonial existences.

- *Decolonise your diet.* Our people must regain the self-sufficient capacity to provide our own food, clothing, shelter, and medicines. Ultimately important to the struggle for freedom is the reconstitution of our own sick and weakened physical bodies and community relationships accomplished through a return to the natural sources of food and the active, hard-working, physical lives lived by our ancestors.
- *Change happens one warrior at a time.* Our people must reconstitute the mentoring and learning-teaching relationships that foster real and meaningful human development and community solidarity. The movement toward decolonisation and regeneration will emanate from transformations achieved by direct-guided experience in small, personal, groups and one-on-one mentoring towards a new path.

These *mantras* and the pathways they represent will be put into practice by every person in their own way, in response to the particular context and set of challenges that form each person's and community's colonial reality.

Bringing it all together, *being Indigenous* means thinking, speaking, and acting with the conscious intent of regenerating one's indigeneity. Each Indigenous nation has its own way of articulating and asserting self-determination and freedom. For example, in Kanien'keha, the word is *Onkwehonweneha*, which translates as the 'way of the original people'. Tsalagi (Cherokee) have the tradition of *Wigaduwaga*, which translates into 'I will always be up above in all things that influence me in life; in the uppermost; for us to follow or emulate'. The Lyackson people have the term *Snuw'uw'ul*, Hopis say *Hopit Pötskwani'at*, and Maori say *Tino rangatiratanga*.[43] As Indigenous peoples, the way to recovering freedom and power and happiness is clear: It is time for each one of us to make the commitment to transcend colonialism as *people*, and for us to work together as *peoples* to become forces of Indigenous truth against the lie of colonialism.

We do not need to wait for the coloniser to provide us with money or to validate our vision of a free future; we only need to start to use *our* Indigenous languages to frame *our* thoughts, the ethical framework of *our* philosophies to make decisions, and to use *our* laws and institutions to govern ourselves.

References

Taiaiake Alfred, 1995—*Heeding the Voices of Our Ancestors: Kahnawake Mohawk Politics and the Rise of Native Nationalism.* Oxford: Oxford University Press

Taiaiake Alfred, 1999—*Peace, Power, Righteousness: An Indigenous Manifesto.* Oxford: Oxford University Press

Taiaiake Alfred, 2001—'Deconstructing the British Columbia Treaty Process', in *Balayi: Culture, Law and Colonialism,* vol 3 (2001)

Taiaiake Alfred, 2005—*Wasáse: Indigenous Pathways of Action and Freedom*. Peterborough, ON: Broadview Press

Kim Anderson, 2000—*A Recognition of Being: Reconstructing Native Womanhood*. Toronto: Sumach Press

Gregory Cajete, 2000—*Native Science: Natural Laws of Interdependence*. Santa Fe, NM: Clear Light Publishers

Jeff Corntassel, 2003a—'Who Is Indigenous? "Peoplehood" and Ethnonationalist Approaches to Rearticulating Indigenous Identity', in *Nationalism & Ethnic Politics*, vol 9 (2003), pp 75–100

Jeff Corntassel, 2003b—'"Deadliest Enemies" or Partners in the "Utmost Good Faith": Conflict Resolution Strategies for Indian nation/state Disputes in an Era of Forced Federalism', in *Ayaangwaamizin: International Journal of Indigenous Philosophy*, vol 3 (Summer 2003), pp 141–167

Jeff Corntassel and Richard C Witmer II, 2008—*Forced Federalism: Contemporary Challenges to Indigenous Nationhood*. Norman: University of Oklahoma Press

Vine Deloria, Jr, 1988—*Custer Died for Your Sins*. Norman: University of Oklahoma Press

Frantz Fanon, 1963—*The Wretched of the Earth*. New York: Grove Press

Eva Marie Garroutte, 2003—*Real Indians: Identity and the Survival of Native America*. Berkeley: University of California Press

Ted Robert Gurr, 2000—*Peoples versus States: Minorities at Risk in the New Century*. Washington, DC: United States Institute of Peace Press

William T Hagan, 1985— 'Full Blood, Mixed Blood, Generic and Ersatz: The Problem of Indian Identity', in *Arizona and the West*, vol 27 (1985), pp 309–326

Anthony J Hall, 2003—*The American Empire and the Fourth World*. Montreal: McGill-Queen's University Press

Inés Hernández-Ávila, 2003—'The Power of Native Languages and the Performance of Indigenous Autonomy: The Case of Mexico', in Richard Grounds, George E Tinker, and David E Wilkins, eds, 2003—*Native Voices: American Indian Identity and Resistance*. Lawrence: University Press of Kansas

Graham Hingangaroa Smith, 2000—'Protecting and Respecting Indigenous Knowledge', in Marie Battiste, ed, 2000—*Reclaiming Indigenous Voice and Vision*. Vancouver, BC: UBC Press

Tom J Holm, Diane Pearson, and Ben Chavis, 2003—'Peoplehood: A Model for American Indian Sovereignty in Education', in *Wicazo Sa Review*, vol 18 no 1 (Spring 2003), pp 7–24

Will Kimlycka, ed, 1995—*The Rights of Minority Cultures*. Oxford: Oxford University Press

Roger Maaka and Augie Fleras, 2000—'Engaging with Indigeneity: Tino Rangatiratanga in Aotearoa', in Duncan Ivison, Paul Patton, and Will Sanders, eds, 2000—*Political Theory and the Rights of Indigenous Peoples* (Cambridge: Cambridge University Press), pp 89–109

Patrick Macklem, 2001—*Indigenous Difference and the Constitution of Canada*. Toronto: University of Toronto Press

George Manuel and Michael Posluns, 1974—*The Fourth World: An Indian Reality*. New York: Collier Macmillan Canada

Devon A Mihesuah, 1998—'American Indian Identities: Issues of Individual Choices and Development', in *American Indian Culture and Research Journal*, vol 22 (1998), pp 193–226

Devon A Mihesuah, 2003—*Indigenous American Women: Decolonization, Empowerment, Activism*. Lincoln: University of Nebraska Press

James Minahan, 2002—*Encyclopedia of the Stateless Nations, Volume II*. Oxford: Greenwood Press

Joane Nagel, 1996—*American Indian Ethnic Renewal: Red Power and the Resurgence of Identity and Culture*. Oxford: Oxford University Press

Bernard Nietschmann, 1995—'The Fourth World: Nations Versus States', in George J Demko and William B Wood, eds, 1995—*Reordering the World: Geopolitical Perspectives on the 21st Century*. Philadelphia: Westview Press

Ronal Niezen, 2003—*The Origins of Indigenism: Human Rights and the Politics of Identity*. Berkeley: University of California Press

Rajkumari Chandra Roy, 2000—*Land Rights of the Indigenous Peoples of the Chittagong Hill Tracts, Bangladesh*. Copenhagen: IWGIA

C Matthew Snipp, 1989—*American Indians: The First of This Land*. New York: Russell Save Foundation

Edward H Spicer, 1962—*Cycles of Conquest: The Impact of Spain, Mexico and the United States on the Indians of the Southwest, 1533–1960*. Phoenix: University of Arizona Press

Charles Taylor, 1992—*Multiculturalism and 'The Politics of Recognition'*. Princeton, NJ: Princeton University Press

Robert K Thomas, 1990—'The Tap-Roots of Peoplehood', in Daphne J Anderson, ed, 1990—*Getting to the Heart of the Matter: Collected Letters and Papers* (Vancouver: Native Ministries Consortium), pp 25–32

Hilary N Weaver, 2001—'Indigenous Identity: What Is It and Who Really Has It?', in *American Indian Quarterly*, vol 25 (2001)

Notes

1. Ed: The original version of this essay appeared as: Taiaiake Alfred and Jeff Corntassel, 2005—'Being Indigenous: Resurgences against Contemporary Colonialism', in *Government and Opposition* (Oxford and Malden, MA: Blackwell Publishing), pp 597–614. Reproduced with permission of Blackwell Publishing Ltd. I very warmly thank the authors for reviewing and revising their essay in the light of comments we sent them. For further reproduction permission, contact JournalsRights@oxon.blackwellpublishing.com.

2. The essay draws on analyses and concepts developed in Alfred 2005.

3. Nietschmann 1995, pp 228–231.

4. See, for instance, http://www.un.org/esa/socdev/unpfii/en/history.html.

5. Hingangaroa Smith 2000, p 211. For examples of classic colonial-liberal discourse with liberatory pretences, see Macklem 2001; Taylor 1992; and Kimlycka 1995.

6. For more on the global nature of Indigenous identity construction, see Corntassel 2003a.

7. Alfred 1999, p 85. For the explanation of his concept of Indigenous identity, one that is often characterised as a sort of strategic essentialism—meaning that it is multifaceted and flexible, yet rooted in Indigenous cultural ground—see also Alfred 1995.

8. Manuel and Posluns 1974, p 60.

9. Nietschmann 1995, pp 236–237.
10. Minahan 2002, pp 845–850; Roy 2000.
11. Fanon 1963, p 210.
12. Fanon 1963, pp 306–307.
13. Alfred 2001, p 49.
14. Alfred 2001, p 41.
15. Corntassel 2003b. For a further elaboration of this argument, see Jeff Corntassel, forthcoming—*Forced Federalism: Contemporary Challenges to Indigenous Nationhood*. Norman, Oklahoma: University of Oklahoma Press.
16. Hernández-Ávila 2003, p 56.
17. Hernández-Ávila 2003, p 38.
18. Deloria, Jr 1988, p 27.
19. Nagel 1996, p 113.
20. The fish-ins of the 1960s along with the occupation of Alcatraz Island by Indians of All Tribes from 1969 to 1971 marked the beginning of the Indigenous activist movement in the US, known as 'Red Power', and heralded the rise to prominence of the American Indian Movement during the 1970s. This inter-Indigenous movement, which occurred in cities and on reservations, entailed a reassertion of Indigenous identity, treaty rights, and self-determination through direct action, such as protests, and the reoccupation of Indigenous territories.
21. Niezen 2003.
22. Mihesuah 1998.
23. Weaver 2001, p 245.
24. Snipp 1989, p 27.
25. Gurr 2000, p 17.
26. Niezen 2003, p 19.
27. Snipp 1989; Hagan 1985.
28. Anderson 2000; Mihesuah 2003.
29. Anderson 2000, pp 116–136.
30. Spicer 1962.
31. Spicer 1962, pp 576–578.
32. Thomas 1990.
33. Holm 2003, pp 7–24.
34. Holm 2003, p 15.
35. Quoted from Hernández-Ávila 2003, p 62.
36. Cajete 2000, p 178.
37. Thomas 1990, p 29.
38. Manuel and Posluns 1974, p 261.
39. Nietschmann 1995, pp 235–236.
40. Hall 2003, pp 523, 530.
41. Garoutte 2003, p 144.
42. Alfred 1999, p 81.
43. See, for example, Maaka and Fleras 2000.

OpenWord

Indigenous Feminism and the Heteropatriarchal State[1]
Andrea Smith

'Native Women Aren't Feminists'

In Native communities we often hear the mantra that Native women aren't feminists. Supposedly, feminism is not needed in Native communities because before
colonisation, these communities treated women with respect. Thus, any Native
woman who calls herself a feminist is often condemned as being really 'white'.
However, when I started interviewing Native women organisers as part of my
book project,[2] I was surprised by how many community-based activists described
themselves as "feminists without apology". They were arguing that feminism is
actually an indigenous concept co-opted by white women. They further argued
that the fact that Native societies were egalitarian 500 years ago was not stopping
women from being hit or abused now. And in my years of anti-violence organising, I would often hear "We can't worry about domestic violence; we must worry
about *survival* issues first". But, since Native women are the ones most likely to be
killed by domestic violence, they are clearly *not* surviving. So when we talk about
the survival of our nations, who are we including in these nations?

Native feminists are not only challenging patriarchy within Native communities, but also white supremacy and colonialism within mainstream feminism.
That is, they are questioning why it is that white women get to define feminism.
For instance, the feminist movement is generally broken up into the so-called
first, second, and third waves of feminism. The first wave is characterised by the
suffragette movement; the second by the formation of the National Organisation
for Women (NOW), abortion rights politics, and the fight for the Equal Rights
Amendment. Suddenly, during the third wave, women of colour appear to transform feminism into a multicultural movement. This periodisation thus centres
the histories of white middle-class women, to which women of colour attach
themselves.

If however, we re-centre[3] Native women in an account of feminist history, we
might begin with 1492, when Native women collectively resisted colonisation. In
this new history, the importance of anti-colonial struggle would be central in our
articulation of feminism. We might then understand that there are multiple feminist histories emerging from multiple communities of colour, which intersect at
points and diverge at others. Such an alternative periodisation would not dismiss
the contributions made by white feminists, but would de-centre them from our his-
toricising and analyses. This re-centring is critical today when you have mainstream

feminist groups supporting the US bombing of Afghanistan with the claim that this will free women from the Taliban (apparently bombing women somehow liberates them), because indigenous feminism centres anti-colonial practice within its organising. Such re-centring is also particularly important in World Social Fora, where I have noticed that speakers who address the politics of revolution are generally male, whereas feminist speakers usually espouse more liberal political frameworks. This form of representation obscures revolutionary feminist analyses.

In addition, an indigenous feminist analysis goes beyond a politics of inclusion—that is, of merely including the voices of Native women in social movements. In the US or World Social Forums (USSF and WSF), discussions on gender and sexuality are often reduced to discussions on the status of women or LGBT communities. We pay less attention to how the logic of heteropatriarchy fundamentally structures colonialism, white supremacy, and capitalism. The question that gets asked is: How are women and queer communities being oppressed? By contrast, we do not examine how gender is an analytic of power complicit in all forms of oppression. My experience at various WSF and USSF events is that we unfortunately see gender as an add-on to the 'real' issues of global domination and thus fail to see how heteropatriarchy structures global domination.

Indigenous feminists challenge how we conceptualise indigenous sovereignty—it is not an add-on to the heteropatriarchal nation-state. Rather it challenges the nation-state system itself. To see the relationship between heteronormativity and the nation-state, we can turn to Charles Colson, prominent Christian Right activist and founder of Prison Fellowship, who explains why same-sex marriage leads to terrorism:

> Marriage is the traditional building block of human society, intended both to unite couples and bring children into the world. ... There is a natural moral order for the family. ... The family, led by a married mother and father, is the best available structure for both child-rearing and cultural health. Marriage is not a private institution designed solely for the individual gratification of its participants. If we fail to enact a Federal Marriage Amendment, we can expect not just more family breakdown, but also more criminals behind bars and more chaos in our streets. It's like handing moral weapons of mass destruction to those who would use America's depravity to recruit more snipers, more hijackers, and more suicide bombers.
>
> When radical Islamists see American women abusing Muslim men, as they did in the Abu Ghraib prison, and when they see news coverage of same-sex couples being 'married' in US towns, we make our kind of freedom abhorrent—the kind they see as a blot on Allah's creation. [We must preserve traditional marriage in order to] protect the United States from those who would use our depravity to destroy us.[4]

Other articles in Christian Right magazines have opined that in addition to homosexuality, feminism also contributed to the Abu Ghraib scandal by promoting women in the military. When women do not know their assigned role in the gender hierarchy, they become disoriented and abuse prisoners.[5] The implicit assumption in such analyses is that heteropatriarchy is the building block of empire. Colson is linking the well-being of the US empire to the well-being of the heteropatriarchal family. Heteropatriarchy is the logic that makes social hierarchy seem natural. Just as the patriarchs rule the family, the elites of the nation-state rule their citizens. Consequently, when colonists first came to this land they saw the necessity of instilling patriarchy in Native communities because they realised that indigenous peoples would not accept colonial domination if their own indigenous societies were not structured on the basis of social hierarchy. Patriarchy, in turn, rests on a gender-binary system; hence, it is not a coincidence that colonisers also targeted indigenous peoples who did not fit within this binary model, in Native communities that had more than two genders.

In addition, gender violence is a primary tool of colonialism and white supremacy. Colonisers did not just kill off indigenous peoples in this land—Native massacres were always accompanied by sexual mutilation and rape. The goal of colonialism is not just to kill colonised peoples, but also to destroy their sense of being people. It is through sexual violence that a colonising group attempts to render a colonised people inherently rapeable, their lands inherently invadeable, and their resources inherently extractable.

Unfortunately, it is not only the Christian Right, but also our own progressive movements that often fail to critique heteropatriarchy. The issue is not simply how women are treated in the movement; rather, that heteropatriarchy fundamentally shapes, in countless ways, how we think about resistance and organising.

The Internalisation of Social Hierarchy and Its Effects

First, because we have not challenged heteropatriarchy, we have deeply internalised the notion that social hierarchy is natural and inevitable. This internalisation limits our revolutionary imagination. For instance, the theme slogan of the 2007 USSF is "Another World is Possible: Another US is Necessary". But the critical question we must ask ourselves is, if another world is possible, then is the US itself necessary? If we put all our revolutionary imaginations together, is the best thing we can come up with a kindler, gentler, settler colonial nation-state based on slavery and genocide? This is where we should be informed by the work of indigenous peoples (particularly indigenous women) in exposing the liberal myth that the US was founded on democratic principles that have been eroded through the practices of slavery and genocide, rather than as a state that is fundamentally constituted by capitalism, colonialism, and white supremacy.[6] The US could not have existed without the genocide of Native peoples—genocide is not a mistake or aberration of US democracy, it is foundational to it.[7]

As Sandy Grande states:

The United States is a nation defined by its original sin: the genocide of American Indians. ... American Indian tribes are viewed as an inherent threat to the nation, poised to expose the great lies of US democracy: that we are a nation of laws and not random power; that we are guided by reason and not faith; that we are governed by representation and not executive order; and finally, that we stand as a self-determined citizenry and not a kingdom of blood or aristocracy. ... From the perspective of American Indians, 'democracy' has been wielded with impunity as the first and most virulent weapon of mass destruction.[8]

Native feminist analyses question the idea that what we need is basically a 'kinder, gentler' US. By extension, they question whether nation-states in general are either necessary or beneficial forms of government. Such a political project is particularly important for colonised peoples seeking national liberation because it allows us to differentiate 'nation' from 'nation-state'. Helpful in this project of imagination is the work of Native women activists who have begun articulating notions of nation and sovereignty that are distinct from nation-states. Whereas nation-states are governed through domination and coercion, indigenous sovereignty and nationhood is predicated on interrelatedness and responsibility. In Crystal Ecohawk's words:

Sovereignty is an active, living process within this knot of human, material and spiritual relationships bound together by mutual responsibilities and obligations. From that knot of relationships is born our histories, our identity, the traditional ways in which we govern ourselves, our beliefs, our relationship to the land, and how we feed, clothe, house and take care of our families, communities and Nations.[9]

This interconnectedness exists not only among the nation's members but among all creation—human and non-human. As Ingrid Washinawatok writes:

Our spirituality and our responsibilities define our duties. We understand the concept of sovereignty as woven through a fabric that encompasses our spirituality and responsibility. This is a cyclical view of sovereignty, incorporating it into our traditional philosophy and view of our responsibilities. There it differs greatly from the concept of western sovereignty, which is based upon absolute power. For us absolute power is in the Creator and the natural order of all living things; not only in human beings. ... Our sovereignty is related to our connections to the earth and is inherent.

The idea of a nation did not simply apply to human beings. We call the buffalo or the wolves, the fish, the trees, and all are nations. Each is sovereign, and equal part of the creation, interdependent, interwoven, and all related.[10]

These models of sovereignty are not based on a narrow definition of 'nation' as equivalent to nation-state, which would entail a closely bounded community and ethnic cleansing. For example, one activist distinguishes between a chauvinistic notion of 'nationalism' versus a flexible notion of 'sovereignty':

> Nationalism is saying, our way is the only right way. ... I think a real, true sovereignty is a real, true acceptance of who and what's around you. And the nationalist doesn't accept all that. ... Sovereignty is what you do and what you are to your own people within your own confines, but there is a realisation and acceptance that there are others who are around you. And that happened even before the Europeans came, we knew about the Indians. We had alliances with some, and fights with some. Part of that sovereignty was that acceptance that they were there.[11]

It is interesting to me, for instance, how often I have found in personal experience that non-Indians presume that if Native people regained their land-bases, they would necessarily call for the expulsion of non-Indians from those land-bases. Yet, it is striking that a much more inclusive vision of sovereignty is articulated by many Native women activists. For instance, this activist describes how indigenous sovereignty is based on freedom for all peoples:

> If it doesn't work for one of us, it doesn't work for any of us. The definition of sovereignty [means that] ... none of us are free unless all of our free. We can't, we won't turn anyone away. We've been there. I would hear stories about the Japanese internment camps ... and I could relate to it because it happened to us. Or with Africans with the violence and rape, we've been there too. So how could we ever leave anyone behind?[12]

This analysis also reconfigures what can be meant by an 'indigenous land-based struggle'. The issue is not primarily about 'giving land back', but actually questioning the presumed normative relationship between peoples and lands: Of land as property to be controlled. As Mishuana Goeman and Patricia Monture-Angus argue, indigenous nationhood is not based on control of territory or land, but is based on relationships and on the responsibility for land:

> Although Aboriginal Peoples maintain a close relationship with the land ... it is not about control of the land. ... Earth is mother and she nurtures us all ... it is the human race that is dependent on the earth and not vice versa. ...

> Sovereignty, when defined as my right to be responsible ... requires a re-
> lationship with territory (and not a relationship based on control of that ter-
> ritory). ... What must be understood then is that Aboriginal request to have
> our sovereignty respected is really a request to be responsible. I do not know of
> anywhere else in history where a group of people have had to fight so hard just
> to be responsible.[13]

It is within the realm of recognition in both legal and cultural battles that
Native peoples are forced to argue for their right to control to be recognised by
the settler colonial state. While such short-term strategies may be necessary at
times, it would be a mistake to presume that this is the most beneficial long-
term political goal for Native peoples. As described by Glen Coulthard, this battle
for recognition can even make Native peoples forget that they have alternative
genealogies for their relationship with land, relationships based on respect for
land rather than control over territory, genealogies that fundamentally question
nation-state forms of governance premised on control, exclusivity, domination,
and violence. As he puts it,

> [the] key problem with the politics of recognition when applied to the colonial
> context. ... [is that it] rests on the problematic assumption that the flourishing
> of Indigenous Peoples as distinct and self-determining agents is somehow de-
> pendent on their being granted recognition and institutional accommodation
> from the surrounding settler-state and society. ... Not only will the terms of
> recognition tend to remain the property of those in power to grant to their
> inferiors in ways that they deem appropriate, but also under these conditions,
> the Indigenous population will often come to see their limited and structurally
> constrained terms of recognition granted to them as their own. In effect, the
> colonised come to identify with 'white liberty and white justice'.[14]

Thus, we can say that not questioning heteropatriarchy and the sense of
inevitable social hierarchy that it produces causes even radical social justice organisers to identify with colonial justice.

Second, our sense of social hierarchy as natural undermines our ability to create movements for social change that do not replicate the structures of domination we seek to eradicate. Unfortunately, in our efforts to organise against white,
Christian America, racial justice struggles often articulate an equally heteropatriarchal racial nationalism. Jennifer Denetdale, in her critique of the Navajo tribal
council's passage of a ban on same-sex marriage, argues that Native nations are
furthering a Christian Right agenda in the name of "Indian tradition".[15] This trend
is also equally apparent within racial justice struggles in other communities of
colour. As Cathy Cohen contends, heteronormative sovereignty or racial justice

struggles will maintain rather than challenge colonialism and white supremacy because they are premised on a politics of secondary marginalisation, where the most elite class of these groups will further their aspiration on the backs of those most marginalised within the community.[16] Through this process of secondary marginalisation, the national or racial justice struggle takes on, implicitly or explicitly, a nation-state model as the ultimate goal of its struggle—a model of governance in which elites govern the rest through violence and domination, while excluding those not members of 'the nation'.

This model of organising either hopes to assimilate into White America or to replicate it within an equally hierarchical and oppressive racial nationalism. Such struggles often emphasise the importance of preserving the 'Black family' or the 'Native family' as the bulwark of this nationalist project, the family being conceived of in capitalist and heteropatriarchal terms. The result is often increased homophobia, whereby lesbian and gay community members are construed as a 'threat' to the family. Of course, not all responses are uniformly disapproving. But, perhaps we should move the debate forward to challenge the 'concept' of the family itself. Perhaps we can reconstitute alternative ways of living together in which 'families' are not seen as isolated islands. Certainly, indigenous communities were not ordered on the basis of a nuclear family structure—this is the result of colonialism, not the antidote to it. Whether it is the neo-colonial middle managers of the non-profit industrial complex,[17] or the revolutionary vanguard elite, the assumption is that patriarchs of any gender are required to manage and police the revolutionary family. Any liberation struggle that does not challenge heteronormativity cannot substantially challenge colonialism or white supremacy.

Third, our organising often follows a gendered model based on a split between private and public spheres. That is, in the public sphere of social protest we are supposed to be completely united people who have no internal problems. However, when it turns out we do have problems, we are supposed to address those problems in the private sphere—at home, or through social services. Because we cannot bring our whole selves to the movement, we end up undermining our work through personal dysfunctionality that cannot be publicly addressed. In addition, when we think to work collectively, our collective action is confined to the public spheres of protests and other actions. But our movements do not think to collectivise the work that is seen as part of the private sphere, such as day care, cooking, and tending to basic needs. Consequently, we build movements that are accessible to very few people and are particularly burdensome for women, who are often responsible for caretaking in the private sphere.

Finally, because we lack an intersectional analysis of how heteropatriarchy structures white supremacy and colonialism we end up developing organising strategies that are problematic, to say the least. To give a few examples based on my personal organising experiences: We have anti-violence groups supporting the bombing of Afghanistan in order save women from the Taliban, while also supporting the build-up of the prison industrial complex by relying on criminalisation as the primary strategy against domestic and sexual violence. These groups fail to see how the state itself is the primary perpetrator of violence against women, particularly women of colour, and that state violence in the form of either the military or prison industrial complexes is not going to liberate anyone. We have racial and anti-war groups organising against state violence in Iraq and elsewhere, but they do not seem to do anything about ending violence against women in their own organisations. These groups fail to see that it is primarily through sexual violence that colonialism and white supremacy work. And then we have mainstream reproductive rights and environmental groups supporting population control policies in order to save the world from poverty and environmental destruction, implicitly blaming women of colour for the policies wrought by corporate and government elites, and thus letting these elites off the hook. In all these cases and many more, activists fail to recognise that if we do not address heteropatriarchy, we do not just undermine the status of women but we fundamentally undermine our struggles for social justice for everyone.

Operationalising Non-Heteronormative Politics

Today, indigenous and non-indigenous peoples are striving to operationalise non-heteronormative visions of organising through the process of revolution by 'trial and error'. That is, rather than presuming a vanguardist perspective on revolution, the philosophy behind this work is that we all need to be part of the collective process of determining how to create a more sustainable and just world by sharing our struggles, our successes, *and* our failures. We must be committed to our long-term vision, but we must also be flexible with our strategies, understanding that these will change constantly as we strive together for a more just world. Below are descriptions of experimental methods used by two kinds of groups, both working towards what could be seen as a different politic. These are not definitive accounts of their work but some reflections on the work they are trying to do, the difficulties they face, and some of the lessons that can be gleaned from their struggles. These sites also do not hold 'the answer' for us, but they can be conversation partners within the global struggle for social justice.

Making Power, Taking Power

Adjoa Jones de Almeida and Paula Rojas's contributions to *The Revolution Will Not Be Funded* detail the organising philosophy of "Taking Power, Making Power" that is influential in indigenous-led social movements in Latin America and is spreading among many women of colour organising in the US and Canada.[18] According to this philosophy, it is, on the one hand, necessary to engage in oppositional politics to corporate and state power (in this framework, taking power). However, if we only engage in the politics of taking power, we will have a tendency to replicate the hierarchical structures in our movements. Consequently, it is also important to 'make power' by creating those structures within our organisations, movements, and communities that model the world we are trying to create.

These 'autonomous zones' can be differentiated from the projects of many groups in the US that often try to create separatist communities based on egalitarian ideals, in that these 'making power' movements do not just create autonomous zones, but *proliferate* them. These movements developed in reaction to what they saw as the revolutionary vanguard model of organising in Latin America that was criticised as 'machismo-leninismo'. These models were so hierarchical that in the effort to combat systems of oppression, they inadvertently re-created the systems they were trying to replace. In addition, this model of organising was inherently exclusivist because not everyone can take up guns and go to the mountains to become revolutionaries. Women, who have to care for families, were particularly excluded from such movements. So movements began to develop organising models based on integrating the organising into one's everyday life so that all people could participate. For instance, a group might organise through communal cooking, but during the cooking process—which everyone must do to eat—they might educate themselves on the nature of agribusiness.

At the 2005 WSF in Brazil, activists from Chiapas reported that their movement began to realise that one cannot combat militarism with militarism because the state always has more guns. However, if movements began to build their own autonomous zones and proliferated them until they reached a mass scale, eventually there would be nothing the state's military could do. If the mass-based peoples' movements began to live life using alternative governmentality structures and stopped relying on the state, then the power of the military would become obsolete. Of course, during the process of making power, there may be skirmishes with the state, but conflict is not the primary work of these movements. And as we see these movements literally take over entire countries in Latin America, it is clear that it is possible to do revolutionary work on a mass-scale in a manner based on radical participatory rather than representational democracy, or through a revolutionary vanguard model.

Many leftists will argue that nation-states are necessary to check the power of multinational corporations or that nation-states are no longer important units of analysis.[19] These groups, by contrast, recognise the importance of creating alternative governmentalities outside of a nation-state model based on principles of horizontalism. In addition, these groups are taking on multinational corporations directly. An example would be the factory movement in Argentina, where workers have appropriated factories and seized the means of production. They have also developed cooperative relationships with other appropriated factories. In addition, in many factories all the work is collectivised. For instance, a participant from a group I work with, who recently had a child and was breastfeeding, went to visit a factory, in 2007. She tried to sign up for one of the collectively organised tasks and was told that breastfeeding was her task. The factory recognised breast-feeding as on par with all the other work in the factory.

Building a Fun Revolution: Incite!

The practice of making power also speaks to the need for building a fun revolution. I was a co-founder of Incite! Women of Color Against Violence, a national organisation of feminists of colour who organise around the intersections of interpersonal gender and state violence through direct action, grassroots organising, and critical dialogue. Organised in 2000, it currently has approximately fifteen chapters and affiliates in the US. When we began to develop our structure, we looked to a variety of organising models for inspiration—not only to groups on the left, but also to Christian Right groups to see why they seemed so effective. An Incite! member attended a Promise Keepers rally with me as part of my academic research, and one thing we concluded was that Christian Right events were much more fun (scary politics aside) than the leftist events we attended. At the Promise Keepers rally there was singing, comedy, sharing, and joy, whereas on the left, we had long, boring meetings with bad food at which everyone yells at each other for being counter-revolutionary—and then we wonder why no one wants to join!

In that spirit, one year, instead of holding a conference, we organised a multi-media tour throughout the US which featured performance artists, singers, dancers, film-makers, etc, who not only gave performances but helped community groups use arts and media as tools for organising. The events featured not only education, but massage therapists, day care, good food, etc, to make this work an act of celebration. The thought behind this work is: How do we build movements that engage our whole selves, and from which we get back as much as we give? What this theorising of Native feminist activists suggests is that by starting to build the world we want to live in, we create a revolutionary movement that is sustainable over the long-term.

Conclusion

In this unsystematic account of practices emerging from grassroots organising practices that dialogue at World Social Fora, it is clear that there are no clear pathways to liberation. As the saying goes, there is no way; we make the way as we walk. Yet, at the same time, while some post-structural accounts call for the end of liberation as a metanarrative, these groups challenge heteropatriarchal logics to unleash their political imaginaries as they struggle for a liberation without guarantees. In large part, these political imaginaries are based on indigenous feminist critiques of the nation-state and articulations of alternative governmentalities based on mutual respect, consensus decision-making, and inclusivity. They provide an alternative vision of globalisation that is not structured through empire but through principles of mutual cooperation and social justice. The strategies for this kind of revolution are contextual, flexible, ever-changing, and open to all possible alliances. To be flexible, however, we must dislodge those heteropatriarchal logics that are unable to imagine another world not structured on hierarchy and domination. If we are not serious about dismantling heteropatriarchy, then we are not serious about ending colonialism or white supremacy. We might as well go home and tell the Christian Right activists to retire because we will be doing their job for them.

References

Joel Belz, 2004—'No Preservatives', in *World*, no 19, p 8

Cathy Cohen, 1999—*The Boundaries of Blackness*. Chicago: University of Chicago Press

Charles Colson, 2004—'Societal Suicide', in *Christianity Today*, no 48, p 72

Glen Coulthard, 2007a—'Indigenous Peoples and the "Politics of Recognition" in Colonial Contexts'. Paper presented at the Cultural Studies Now Conference, University of East London, London, UK, July 22 2007

Jennifer Denetdale, June 2008—'Carving Navajo National Boundaries: Patriotism, Tradition, and the Dine Marriage Act of 2005', in *American Quarterly*, no 60, pp 289–294

Crystal Echohawk, 1999—'Reflections on Sovereignty', in *Indigenous Woman*, vol 3 no 1, pp 21–22

Sandy Grande, 2004—*Red Pedagogy*. Lanham, MD: Rowman & Littlefield

Michael Hardt and Antonio Negri, 2000—*Empire*. Cambridge, MA: Harvard University Press

Incite!, 2007—*The Revolution Will Not Be Funded: Beyond the Non-Profit Industrial Complex*. Boston: South End Press

David Kazanjian, 2003—*The Colonizing Trick*. Minneapolis: University of Minnesota Press

Chandra Mohanty, 2003—*Feminism Without Borders*. Durham, NC: Duke University Press

Patricia Monture-Angus, 1999—*Journeying Forward*. Halifax: Fernwood Publishing

Ted Olsen, 2004—'Grave Images', in *Christianity Today*, no 48, p 60

Andrea Smith, 2002—*Bible, Gender and Nationalism in American Indian and Christian Right Activism*. Santa Cruz: University of California–Santa Cruz

Andrea Smith, 2005—*Conquest: Sexual Violence and American Indian Genocide*. Cambridge, MA: South End Press

Andrea Smith, 2008—*Native Americans and the Christian Right: The Gendered Politics of Unlikely Alliances*. Durham, NC: Duke University Press

Gene Edward Veith, 2004—'The Image War', in *World*, no 19, pp 30–35

Ingrid Washinawatok, 1995—'Sovereignty as a Birthright', in Indigenous Women's Network, 1995—*Indigenous Women Address the World* (Austin, TX: Indigenous Women's Network), pp 12–13

Notes

1. 'Heteropatriarchy' is defined as the combination of male supremacy and heterosexual supremacy.
2. Smith 2008.
3. By re-centring, however, I do not imply that there should be a stable centre—but that this re-centring is a continual process.
4. Colson 2004, p 72.
5. Belz 2004, p 8; Olsen 2004, p 60; Veith 2004, pp 30–35.
6. Kazanjian 2003.
7. Smith 2005.
8. Grande 2004.
9. Echohawk 1999.
10. Washinawatok 1995.
11. Smith 2002.
12. ibid.
13. Monture-Angus 1999.
14. Coulthard 2007a.
15. Denetdale, June 2008, pp 289–294.
16. Cohen 1999.
17. See Incite! 2007.
18. ibid.
19. Hardt and Negri 2000; Mohanty 2003.

OpenWord

Geopolitics of Knowledge and the Neo-Zapatista Social Movement Networks[1]
Xochitl Leyva Solano[2]

This essay attempts a departure from common approaches to Zapatismo in order to obtain a different view; not necessarily a better one, but a distinct one. My focus is on some of the alliances and convergences that the Zapatista Army of National Liberation (*Ejército Zapatista de Liberación Nacional*—EZLN) has developed since January 1 1994, the date on which it declared war against the Mexican government—and, implicitly, on the geopolitics of knowledge. These alliances and convergences are not fixed or permanent, but rather contingent, fluid, and multifaceted. They occur in different ways at different moments and with different objectives. They have highs and lows, and within them we can identify tensions, ruptures, and continuities. These alliances and convergences allow the construction of neo-Zapatism as *social movement networks*.[3] The metaphor of a 'network in movement' gives us a vivid image of "multi-layered entanglements of movement actors with the natural-environmental, political-institutional, and cultural-discursive terrains in which they are embedded".[4] Alvarez, Ribeiro, Slater, and Yúdice[5] show how many movement networks in Latin America are increasingly regional and transnational in scope. Alvarez et al argue that social movements should be understood "not only to rely and draw upon networks of everyday life but also to construct or configure new interpersonal, interorganisational, and politico-cultural linkages with other movements as well as with a multiplicity of cultural and institutional actors and spaces".[6]

I have not found a more adequate conceptualisation of social movement networks than this one for capturing what the EZLN and neo-Zapatism have generated around themselves. As we will see below, the neo-Zapatista networks have local roots while they are at the same time the product of transnational political convergences that generate adherents who define themselves as Zapatistas, no matter whether in Las Cañadas in the Lacandon forest of Chiapas or in the cities of Venice, Berlin, London, or Barcelona, to mention but a few.

It should be noted that the Zapatista political identity, originally forged in the context of the Mexican Revolution in the early 20th century,[7] has been re-created and filled with new contents at the end of the same century to make room for a political-ideological diversity that can include both an anarchist unionist from the General Workers' Confederation (CGT) in Madrid and a German human rights defender; both an Italian member of the Social Centres and an exiled Chilean in London; as well as a woman from former Sandinista brigades and a Catalan businesswoman. All of them are interwoven in neo-Zapatista networks that go beyond transnational defence networks, and also beyond mere cybernetic networks.[8]

These neo-Zapatista networks cannot be understood outside of the 'Information Age' and of the rise of the 'Network Society' that Manuel Castells invites us to ponder as part of a new societal, cultural, and economic model;[9] a new model that suffers fractures in the current phase of rupture being experienced by the capitalist world-system.[10] These networks should also not be considered outside of an important debate on the knowledge production that goes on within the movements themselves and that finds itself at a crossroads with academia and politically committed social sciences. Indeed, this is the other central theme the essay develops as we focus on such questions as: From where or from which sites are we producing our knowledge(s)? And more particularly we ask: What has been the history of this production in the case of the neo-Zapatista networks? How have the wider system and the war contributed to outlining the contents of these networks? And what about the people who reflect, write, and act within and from them, as some of us do?

Situated Knowledge in the Capitalist World-System

To begin, let me point out my basic premise: Knowledge is not abstract and unlocated. On the contrary, any knowledge production is geo-historically marked and has a specific value that is due to its place of origin.[11] In this sense I here inscribe myself in a long tradition that seeks to produce knowledge which is useful not only for academics but that, above all, supports the strengthening of the processes of transformation, liberation, and emancipation put in motion by the collectives, organisations, and movements of which I am an active part. For instance, many of those present at different national and international gatherings share the characteristic of being academics and activists at the same time, and of being committed to, and active in, the struggles of indigenous peoples and the *altermundista* (alterglobalist) networks.[12] It is from this position that we speak and from which we build our discourses, practices, and reflections.[13] This position distances itself from those of analysts who see the movements purely as 'objects of study' or as 'raw material' out there awaiting 'expert' study and interpretation.

In light of the above, the present text is conceived and attempts to be written in both codes and for both publics—committed academics and activists—while at the same time aiming to contribute to the *de-coloniality* of power, of knowledge, and of being. In other words, with this text I modestly aim to contribute to the development of the de-colonial option which, as Walter Mignolo points out, already does occur in various semiotic forms parallel and complementary to social movements that exist on the margins of the political (states, political parties) and economic (exploitation, accumulation, oppression) structures.[14] We aim to build a critical thinking and practice that sets itself against the image of a totality that makes us believe that there is literally no way out, that other worlds are not possible. To the contrary, many of these other worlds are already in the process of planetary construction. The challenge—Mignolo adds—is to be capable of thinking and imagining (and, I would add, of acting) beyond the imperial categories of modernity / coloniality. The incapacity to think beyond these categories is not due to an individual limitation but due to the imperial success in handling the coloniality of knowledge that leads us to "accept that other forms of thinking, of political theory, of political economics, of ontology, of Being do not exist".[15]

In the same direction, Wallerstein's *world-system analysis* allows us to achieve a holistic and historic vision that highlights in detail the linkage between the rise of the capitalist world-system and the development of science and technology.[16] Modern science (and therefore the social sciences) are the offspring of capitalism and have always depended on it. Without denying this connection, it is important to add that today, at the beginning of the twenty-first century, new social relations are emerging in the interstices between committed academics, flexible activisms, and indigenous as well as anti-systemic movements. This allows us to affirm that new forms of knowledge production are in process.[17] This new knowledge can no longer be labelled as exclusively activist or academic. Such labels serve as boxes that weigh us down, as they classify and objectify us and fail to express the richness of these new processes. The de-colonial option should lead us to demonstrate that the movements (networks, organisations, collectives, etcetera) are also places where 'knowledge-practices' are produced. As Casas-Cortés, Osterweil, and Powell point out, the recognition of such knowledge-practices leads us to challenge established scientific borders and promote a more relational and symmetrical approach among us and within the movements in which we take part.[18]

It is in these new interstices that knowledge-practices are being produced, and also collective epistemic reflections on the processes of knowledge production itself with the purpose of constructing another kind of power and politics (and of course another kind of social sciences). Such epistemic reflection is put forward by university students, committed academics, activists, and members of grassroots organisations and civil society committed to social struggles (in particular indigenous, feminist, anti-neoliberal, and anti-capitalist struggles). This reminds us that it is from particular universities, academies, and social sciences that hardened activists and severe critics of the capitalist world-system have emerged. One can look at the case of Immanuel Wallerstein himself or of many of the Latin American critical thinkers whose intellectual contributions have been key for the development of our social struggles, movements, and political networks. As Walter Mignolo writes:

> Not only capitalism expanded gradually across the planet. With it and alongside
> capital came thought forms of both analysis and justification and of critique.[19]

Mignolo points to Wallerstein's demonstration of how the social sciences were companions of the empire. It is also Wallerstein who suggests that "their transformation can purge them of the guilts of birth … and guarantee that they be critical of the empire (today of globalization) and that they not be at their service supplying knowledge of 'how things are' without asking for 'the what and the why'".[20]

Since the late 1990s, Immanuel Wallerstein has emphasised that the current systemic crisis we find ourselves in is present not only in the economic scenario but also in the political scenario of the anti-systemic movements and in the cultural scenario of the metaphysical presuppositions of knowledge. Concerning these last two levels, that of the movements and the epistemic, Wallerstein predicted that reformulations and reconsiderations of strategies and concepts would take place; and indeed, that is what we are already seeing and experiencing today. For that reason we must continue to act and contribute on these two levels. This is my basic motivation as well as direction as I put forward my present reflections.

Geopolitics and the 'Zapatista Social Netwar'

It was neither coincidence nor innocent curiosity that made researchers working at the core of Empire and the capitalist system among the first to worry and write about the EZLN. They did so within a framework of war and, in particular, pointed to new forms of making war beyond a bipolar Cold War dynamic. The economic relations and the border between Mexico and the United States of America made the Zapatista uprising of January 1 1994, an (inter)national security issue. For this reason, David Ronfeldt, John Arquilla, Graham Fuller, and Melissa Fuller, researchers in the service of the United States government and its army, were the first to publish a book about 'social netwar' and Zapatism. Their emphasis was on military rather than political aspects, and for a particular and very practical reason: Orienting the military and political strategy of Empire. This orientation would in time also influence the actions of the Mexican government and its army. Let us then look then at the postulates of these authors embedded in Empire.

For Ronfeldt et al, the Zapatista uprising created a model that contributed both to understanding the new social movements and actors in the 1990s and to building new concepts for the development of perspectives on contemporary and emerging military organisation, doctrine, strategy, and technology.[21] This innovative model came to be paradigmatic given the characterisation of social conflicts in a New World Order in which network-based conflicts and crimes are continuously increasing. One example given by Ronfeldt et al is the way in which groups such as the Irish Revolutionary Army (IRA), Hamas, or the Shining Path have used the Internet to broaden their battles. Another example they give is the way in which the effects of the information revolution have opened spaces of communication with the world in relatively closed contexts such as China, Iran, Iraq, and Cuba, contributing to the 'advance of democracy'. Ronfeldt et al added the cases of Saudi Arabia and Burma in which social netwars have eroded authoritarian regimes.

From Ronfeldt et al's perspective, the post-1994 instability and conflict in Mexico presented the challenge of the existence of social netwars such as the Zapatista network coexisting with armed guerrilla networks or criminal drug-trafficking networks. As these authors pointed out in 1998, the stability needed to govern Mexico would depend in large part on the control and destruction of all these networks. Ten years on, we know that the criminal and drug-trafficking networks control almost three-quarters of the country and are in open and declared war against the federal government.

The Zapatista social netwar was characterised by Ronfeldt et al as having emerged from an early solidarity between the EZLN and Mexican, US, and Canadian NGOs. By 1994 these NGOs had already consolidated social networks that were being reactivated and updated with new contents. After the Ocosingo massacre in 1994, autonomous groups created new alliances with rhizomatic connections in which the key principles were mutual consultation, collaboration, information-sharing, planning of joint actions, decentralisation, and the rejection of hierarchies. From this perspective, netwar means dense and constant information, and permanent and multilateral flows of communication. In netwars, each of the existing nodes may represent an individual, an organisation, or the state itself. Social netwars are segmented, polycentric, and ideologically integrated, thanks to shared objectives and despite the fact that not every participant thinks alike.[22]

In post-1994 Chiapas, according to Ronfeldt et al, the Zapatista "social netwar" was activated both on land (with the arrival of NGO activists in Chiapas and in Mexico) and in cyberspace. In the latter domain, the Zapatistas and the cybernauts aimed to shape people's beliefs and attitudes. The NGO activists released both "information operatives" and public relations "battles" to legitimise the EZLN and to delegitimise its enemy, the government. The former were very effective, enabling the dissemination of information on Chiapas that came back to the Mexican government in the form of pressure. Ronfeldt et al concluded that had it not been for that pressure, the Zapatista demands would not have had the effect they did have both on the government and on public opinion. These tactics were combined with the dissemination of faxes, face-to-face interviews with diplomats, marches, protests, organisation of conferences, and with the use of "old mechanisms of war".

In Ronfeldt et al's formulation, social netwars do not aim to destroy the enemy but to disrupt it with flexible, adaptable, and versatile "offensives". The tactic is "pulsing" or "swarming" the target, that is, the nodes converge from multiple directions, coalesce rapidly and stealthily, and then dissever and disperse, immediately ready to recombine for a new pulse.[23] Under this logic, the effects of the Zapatista social netwar were multiple. For the EZLN, the network gave it legitimacy and the possibility to resist the Mexican government.[24] In a broader framework, the idea of a 'Zapatista social netwar' contributed to sharpening international perceptions of crisis and instability in Mexico, at the same time that it was affecting the predominance of the Mexican national state in key areas.

Ronfeldt et al pointed out that this netwar was something alien and new for the Mexican government. The government therefore had to learn how to combat it, despite the fact that it considered the Zapatista network only a "threat" and not a real "challenge".[25] The new governmental actions involved the army and the NGOs, the latter being perceived as "the bracketing forces" of the network. In that perspective, the army was part of centralised state power, while the NGOs were part of the emerging anti-hierarchical power. From that logic, the actions of persecution or repression against national and international NGO activists formed part of a well-studied and well-planned governmental counterattack against the Zapatista social netwar. Such an outlook also justified the "constitutionally sustained" deportation of foreigners with tourist visas (that do not permit any form of political participation) who came for the Zapatista Intergalactic Encounter of 1996 and participated in the installation of Zapatista autonomous municipalities. Ronfeldt et al mention the creation of "special visas" for international observers as a loophole to allow foreign participation in human rights and electoral certification issues.[26] These visa politics implied a total control by the government of all foreigners who entered the country and allowed it to effectively restrict their observation to certain processes, at a time when human rights violations occurred in many more areas than the government's legal observation permits allowed to be monitored. In Ronfeldt et al's political-military vision that was precisely what the Mexican government should have done. Of course, in the interpretation of these authors there is no room for consideration of the human rights abuses that were denounced by several local NGOs, relating to the way in which many of the "deportations" (of those sympathising with Zapatismo) were carried out. In many cases these were arbitrary expulsions and human rights violations.[27]

The Mexican army realised that it needed to remake its public image and its relationship with the mass media. The army undertook psychological warfare, sky shooting, and leafleting out of helicopters, while also tightening its relations with the United States army in terms of weapons exchange, training, and advisory services.[28] The most exemplary case of this exchange was Mexico's Airborne Special Forces Groups (GAFEs), trained in the United States to carry out counternarcotics operations. These forces then "also gained counterinsurgency, antiterrorist and other internal security roles" in accordance with the counter-netwar policies.[29]

Two years later these new tasks were denounced in an investigation undertaken by Global Exchange, CIEPAC, and CENCOS.[30] According to their report, between 1996 and 1999 Chiapas had the highest concentration of GAFEs and was host to the "first Rapid Intervention Force (FIR) formed in the country". As indicated by their data, by late 1999 30 per cent of the Mexican armed forces were stationed in Chiapas.[31] Just a few months prior to the publication of their report, 45 indigenous persons, primarily women and children from the *Las Abejas* civil society organisation, were gunned down by paramilitary forces in the Acteal massacre.

Ronfeldt et al emphasised that the Mexican army "eagerly wanted to crush the rebellion forcefully" but had to readjust itself to the new situation and respond to the network with a counter-netwar policy. They even asserted that the Mexican government was advised to abandon heavy-handed counterinsurgency methods. However, they conceded that in the case of the Chiapas conflict zone, the Mexican army used an exhaustive covering or "blanketing" strategy to prevent the outbreak of additional fighting and to impede the movement of EZLN forces. This strategy confined the EZLN to limited areas of action.[32] Such an account of events does not, of course, explain how the militarisation and paramilitarisation of Chiapas later expanded beyond the so-called conflict zone.

A final observation by Ronfeldt et al in 1998 was that the United States army was also readjusting to the new circumstances, by using a new language, developing new strategies, and founding new military schools. This was due, in part, to the fact that the impact of this netwar was greater in the United States because this country was leading in Internet use in the world. But it was not really until after the terrorist attacks of September 11 2001 that the notion of social netwars was popularised in the US through the media. This was after the revelation that the terrorist cells that perpetrated the attacks on the Twin Towers in New York City had operated through transnational networks crisscrossing both the Muslim and the Christian world. Then, for the first time, we heard the United States Secretary of Defense publicly declare on the CNN television network that "we cannot predict the end of this war because we are not confronting, as before, a state or a nation, but instead terrorist networks".[33]

Ronfeldt et al's book presented itself as an academic study, when it was in fact based on research carried out in order to orient the political-military strategy of the Empire. Despite the references cited in what appears to be a kind of theoretical framework, the book cannot conceal its true intention: A war logic that aimed to identify an enemy in order to isolate, destroy, and immobilise this enemy. Therein lies the danger for those labelled 'enemies' (the EZLN, activists, NGOs, and those of us who form part of the pro-Zapatista networks). It is also important to point out that many of Ronfeldt et al's interpretations were evolutionist, romanticising the indigenous world and simplifying the entanglement of the networks. The authors went so far as to affirm that the Council of Indigenous and *Campesino* Organisations of the State of Chiapas (CEOIC) was an "NGO",[34] when those of us who participated in this council know that it was a political convergence of *campesino*, social, and civil organisations formed in the heat of the war. None of this would be relevant if it were not for the lives of real people who in many cases have been persecuted, attacked, or repressed due to the interpretations derived from this type of study.

It is clear from subsequent events that Ronfeldt et al's book has not remained hidden in the library of some obscure university, but has served both the United States and Mexican governments to encourage and justify the persecution and, very often, the political, physical, psychological, or cybernetic annihilation of individuals and groups labelled as being part of the Zapatista social networks. The study has served to sustain xenophobic policies that pretend to "protect the nation and Mexicans from pernicious foreigners". But even more, the term 'social netwars' itself from the outset criminalises social movements, organisations, networks, collectives, individuals, and politicised groups. This criminalisation is evident when social movement networks are placed on a par with drug trafficking or organised crime networks. They are said to fit the same bill because they share a network structure. But it is obviously not the same to struggle for justice, dignity, and equality as to break the laws of the state for personal benefit and profit. In the end, perhaps the only point on which we can concur with these authors is that, without any doubt, the Zapatista networks were born, live, and reproduce in a war context. The following section presents a very different way of understanding the articulations between war, networks, and social movements—that is, the neo-Zapatista networks.

My approach is from within social movement networks and is therefore clearly very different to that of these authors. It corresponds to another logic, that of anti-imperialist and anti-capitalist struggles. Unlike the approach of these authors, reviewed extensively in this section, ours does not pretend to reflect upon the networks from the outside, aiming at controlling, dominating, or destroying them. On the contrary, I propose to rethink them from the inside in order to strengthen our shared political work that thrives on an anti-systemic orientation, rhythm, and meaning. This fundamental difference reminds us of our starting point, the importance of bearing witness to the positionality of every actor and taking it into account in order to understand what he or she says and which practices are backing up his or her words, ideas, or arguments.

From Guerrilla Warfare to neo-Zapatista Networks

Before entering the topic of the Zapatista networks, it is important to clarify that it is one thing to speak of the EZLN before 1994 and another to refer to it after January 1 of that same year. Its pre-1994 history has been the centre of heated polemics, but to date there is a certain consensus regarding the existence of a past that is rooted in the ideas of revolutionary change so typical of Latin American leftists in the 1960s, 70s, and 80s.[35] For example, it is well known that the political origin of the EZLN, the National Liberation Forces (*Fuerzas de Liberación Nacional*—FLN), had among their objectives "to organise, direct, and lead the revolutionary struggle of the people in order to seize power from the bourgeoisie", and to "liberate our *patria* from foreign domination and instate the dictatorship of the proletariat ... as a [new] government of workers that will impede the counterrevolution and begin to build socialism in Mexico".[36] It is also documented that up to 1992, those who enlisted in the ranks of the EZLN confirmed their adherence to the "international proletariat" and swore to defend "the revolutionary principles of Marxism-Leninism and their application to national reality".[37] The oath concluded with the statement: "I swear that I will combat the enemies of my *patria*, until death if necessary ... and [I will do so] for socialism. Let us live for the *patria* or die for freedom".[38]

On this point, Subcomandante Marcos explained in an interview with Yvon Le Bot that the movement's tradition was that of Guevara and not Marxism-Leninism, and that during its years of clandestine existence it had received no assistance from any Latin American guerrilla group.[39] Carlos Tello and the journalists La Grange and Rico wrote books to demonstrate the contrary; in other words, that Subcomandante Marcos had been trained in Nicaragua with the *Sandinistas* and that Fidel Castro's Cuba had made an exception with the FLN by supporting them unconditionally.[40] But neither Cuba nor the *Sandinistas* confirmed these statements.

Much has been written about the revolutionary and guerrilla origins of the EZLN. Subcomandante Marcos himself has indicated that the political ideology that he and his companions from the FLN brought to the forest was transformed "from a square one to a round one" in light of the indigenous reality they were faced with.[41] The historic reconstruction of the guerrilla or revolutionary origins of the EZLN have been undertaken by many, and often with negative intentions, for instance, to point a finger at its supposed incongruities. Carlos Tello attempted to discredit the Zapatistas by accusing them of a double discourse, a socialist one within their own ranks and a democratic one for the rest of the world.[42] Pedro Pitarch, on the other hand, tried to show how the Zapatistas went from using a "revolutionary-socialist" discourse in 1992 to a "national-populist" one in 1995, by which time the indigenous people had become the centre of the discourse and the good guys of the picture.[43]

Tello and Pitarch coincide in highlighting the transformations of the discourse and the identity of the Zapatistas over time. For any active member of a social movement or one of its scholars, this is not an issue of congruence or a lack of it. As we all know, any movement is in movement and constantly makes and re-makes practices, identities, and ideologies in the development and evolution of the movement itself. Only by starting from that perspective can we see beyond the governmental discourse that after 1994 invented, used, and broadly disseminated the term 'Zapatista guerrilla' in order to discredit and minimise the impact and importance of Zapatism. The governmental discourse, however, should neither blind us nor keep us from recognising and understanding the guerrilla origins of the movement, since the Zapatista grassroots themselves permanently refer to them.

At the same time we should emphasise that, in the course of its development and evolution, the EZLN has distanced itself from that guerrilla tradition which had as its declared goal the taking over of power. We also have to highlight the weight that the EZLN has accorded to political solutions. This and the way the EZLN perceives politics clearly differentiates the Zapatistas from their anteced-ents. As Subcomandante Marcos indicates:

> We have been pondering that if we were able to conceive a change of premise on the view of power, that is, the problem of power, proposing that we don't want to take it, this might produce another form of doing politics and another type of politician, other human beings that would do politics in a different way, unlike those people that we have to put up with today all across the political spectrum.[44]

At the risk of being schematic, one could propose the following equation: While the neo-Zapatista networks are part of what Manuel Castells calls the *network so-ciety* and the *Information Age*,[45] the guerrilla war flourished in the old framework of the Cold War. The FLN, and to a certain degree the EZLN itself, at least prior to 1994, belong to this latter framework;[46] but the neo-Zapatista networks have moved way beyond these origins. At this moment in time (2009), they are nevertheless im-portant referential nodes that have been contributing since the end of the twentieth century to the construction of what Boaventura de Sousa Santos has called 'count-er-hegemonic globalisation' and François Houtart the 'globalisation of resistances'. We have to see the internationalist pro-Zapatista networks within this framework and, in order to do that, we shall attempt to rethink them in the next section.

Internationalist Neo-Zapatista Networks and an Encounter in Europe [47]

The different socio-political networks that made up neo-Zapatism after 1994 have been constituted by members of NGOs and collectives, as well as neighbourhood, urban, and university movements, not to mention *campesino* (peasant), indige-nous, teachers', and women's organisations. Other members of these networks were individuals without a history of prior political affiliation or militancy, and still others have had a long-, medium-, or short-term history of political experiences. All of them organised and expressed themselves through coordinating committees, conventions, workshops, fora, assemblies, congresses, meetings, collectives, and consultations. All these organisational forms have backed the Zapatista political de-mands at different moments, but they have also contributed to transforming them. For purely analytical purposes, we have therefore come to speak of neo-Zapatista agrarian networks, democratic-electoral networks, indigenous-autonomist networks, revolutionary-alternative networks, and internationalist networks.[48]

I will not go into the details concerning each of the different kinds of networks that we can identify.[49] But to provide a clearer idea of the nature of the internationalist neo-Zapatista networks, I would like to share some of my personal experiences and exchanges with European Zapatistas. In 1999, in a small city near Barcelona, the Second European Encounter of Zapatista Collectives was held. I attended the meeting along with members of 21 Zapatista collectives from eight central European countries.[50] At this level, international neo-Zapatism is prismatic and multifaceted, with the translation of EZLN ideals into many languages, ideologies, and political cultures. Many of these European Zapatistas were able to construct from their local realities and everyday problems a shared agenda with the EZLN. Undoubtedly, this is possible because the anti-neoliberal and anti-capitalist struggles have fostered the construction of a 'moral grammar' that sustains transnational political agendas.[51] I found that among the most relevant grammars shared by the members of different neo-Zapatista networks are those that are based on the struggles for recognition and advocacy of rights, be they human, indigenous, ethnic, or women's rights, as well as those based on autonomy and resistance.

At the European Zapatista Encounter, the Zapatistas of the Lugano collective in Switzerland were labourers, students, and farmers who struggle against transnationals like the Coca-Cola Company and the advance of neoliberalism. Those of the Sicily collective in Italy worked on confronting problems of immigration, exclusion, and poverty in the southern regions of their country. Those from Copenhagen, Denmark, described themselves as part of the Danish resistance movement, and of a much broader resistance organisation stretching from Chiapas to Kurdistan. In Granada, Spain, the neo-Zapatista experience was embedded in a spiritual commune that ran an autonomous cultural centre in a squatted house. In Paris, the MAR defined itself as part of the anti-neoliberal struggle within the most radical wing of the Parisian left.[52] Another Parisian neo-Zapatista was a colourist in a fashion company and the daughter of a Colombian immigrant working as a cleaner.

In Bristol, England, the residents of an alternative community centre, part of the autonomous movement, made Zapatism a meeting ground for individuals who had participated in solidarity actions with Central America, and members of a soccer club that had become politicised while facing problems of immigration and racism. In Madrid, the anarchist unionists of the General Workers' Confederation (CGT), libertarians *par excellence*, saw in Zapatism the possibility to advance the idea of forming a broader international front while revitalising their own organisation.

In Geneva, Switzerland, a member of a Zapatista collective defined himself as a rebel, craftsman, and squatter, in rejection of the advance of capitalism in general and of the bourgeois form of life of his wealthy family in particular. In an industrial town of the eastern valleys of Cataluña, a solidarity group working in support of indigenous peoples in Chiapas was headed by a prosperous businesswoman from the furniture industry who found similarities between the autonomous Zapatista communities and the Catalan resistance against the occupation of the Spanish state. In a nearby town, the neo-Zapatistas emerged from an experience of solidarity with Nicaragua that they now extended to Kosovo and Chiapas. And in Tuscany, Italy, the neo-Zapatistas were anarchists, grassroots Catholics, and local industrialists.

In the European capitals of Barcelona, London, and Berlin, I found that the neo-Zapatistas had all been members of old solidarity networks with the Central American guerrilla movements that had been founded in the 1980s, or with leftist militants, victims of South American dictatorships and *coups d'état* dating back to the 1970s. The United States and Canadian neo-Zapatistas also came from Central American support networks, as well as anti-NAFTA networks organised prior to 1994. Members of either an Evangelical or the Catholic Church, working within the liberation theology paradigm or following the Theology of the Poor, often constructed the pro-Central America networks. Support received by Nicaragua from Barcelona and London was particularly relevant. Latin American Houses (*Casas Latinoamericanas*) existed in Barcelona, London, and Berlin—each with its particular name—and played a central role in the formation of the cultural and political movement of the old solidarity movements with Central America. More than anything, these were the loci of socio-political networks that were being reactivated after 1994 in response to war like those fought in Chiapas and Kosovo.

In London and Berlin, the neo-Zapatistas were also part of the local socio-political networks created around Chilean political refugees who had left their country after the military takeover in 1973 led by Augusto Pinochet. In Berlin, these refugees promoted the foundation of a centre for Latin American information and analysis. In recent years this centre has sheltered pro-indigenous groups from Chiapas. Other Chileans residing in London circulated information on Zapatism in local Spanish-language newspapers and through the distribution of flyers in salsa clubs and dance schools owned by Colombian immigrants, thus giving Zapatism a new international dimension.

The internationalist neo-Zapatista networks addressed in this section are not only cybernetic. They were, and are still, constructed from the organisational lives of the participants in movements, networks, and collectives. Not all of their dimensions, nodes, ruptures, and reaches have been developed here. A detailed study of the historical formation and transformation of the neo-Zapatista networks exceeds the range of this essay.[53] Here we have only begun to address some of the issues that will allow us to understand how the EZLN and we, its followers, have formed the neo-Zapatista networks. In these networks, the transnationalisation of Zapatista demands has been made possible thanks to the construction of knowledge-practices developed around cognitive frameworks, moral grammars, and concrete practices that are based on the defence of rights and autonomy, and on anti-neoliberal, anti-capitalist, and anti-systemic resistances.[54] These knowledge-practices have many local meanings and nuances, but as we saw in the case of the 1999 European Zapatista Encounter, they have in common a global resonance in the current crisis of the capitalist world-system.

When I first published my ideas on the neo-Zapatista networks in 1998 and 1999,[55] the reactions were varied. On the one hand, several colleagues, students, and activists showed interest in the perspective I proposed. On the other hand, some activists verbally criticised that first article because I did not include in it the political-military aspects of the conflict, that is, the context of the war in Chiapas in which the EZLN and the neo-Zapatista networks had to act. The criticism of these activists was not a minor issue, considering that in December 1997 the Acteal massacre had been perpetrated, and since 1994 the government had embarked on a low-intensity warfare that was aimed at destroying the EZLN and its allies. This counterinsurgency campaign continued despite the fact that the government had formally declared a unilateral ceasefire on January 12 1994, and that in February 1996 the first peace agreements between the federal government and the EZLN had been signed. The original idea behind these peace accords was that they would lead to profound constitutional reforms. On the contrary, the paramilitary attacks, the suspension of peace negotiations and dialogue, and the descent of the peace process into the government's counterinsurgency operations demonstrated that the EZLN and the extended neo-Zapatista networks had to act in a war context that was identified by some political actors as an "unresolved political and military conflict".[56]

For all these reasons, we should stress that the neo-Zapatista networks are without a doubt a very important actor, particularly in terms of denouncing the abuses committed by the government and the Mexican state in the context of a war aimed at making the EZLN disappear, as well as its autonomous municipalities and Good Government Committees (*Juntas de Buen Gobierno,* JBG).[57] Indeed, these Good Government Committees continue operating to this very day (October 2009) as they give shape to real Zapatista autonomy and inform a concrete anti-neoliberal and anti-capitalist struggle.

Final Comments: Knowledge Is Always Situated

As a final comment, I would like to add part of my own story in order to return to the point of departure of this essay, which was the knowledge production developed from and within neo-Zapatista networks. As a child, I went to a so-called 'active primary school', the teaching method of which was inspired by the philosophy of Freinet,[58] based on the principles of respect, commitment, dignity, love, freedom of expression, and a co-responsibility shared by pupils, teachers, and parents alike. The school encouraged the free writing of texts, presentations, and collective and horizontal discussions around the central issues concerning our school and its educational policies, and provided a printing workshop to foment a cooperative but critical spirit that we exercised verbally in assemblies and through in-school writing communications. I grew up in tune with all these vital collective forms that would later allow me to identify with the ways of life in Zapatista communities, which are also based on collective work, consensual decision-making in assemblies, and autonomous processes.

This education also shaped my vocation as a politically committed anthropologist. That became clear when I started working before 1994 with *campesino* communities and independent indigenous organisations in the Lacandon forest as it was turning into the political-military centre of the EZLN. My identification with the political demands of the EZLN emerged almost naturally, and in the first days of January 1994 I joined in the wide range of civil society activities that were aimed at breaking the military siege, implementing the peace belts, and forming the local political fronts that would give body to the Zapatista demands and struggle. In 1996, I became a member of the international pro-Zapatista networks from where we started to construct what we would later come to call 'activist research' in search of the de-coloniality of power, knowledge, and being.[59]

I enter into this personal story only in order to return to the two central arguments that formed the starting block of this essay. Knowledge is always situated.[60] And, reflection upon the positionality of knowledge production comes out of a radical critique of patriarchal objectivity and invites us to recognise from where we are speaking and producing knowledge, and how this process is intricately bound up with our class membership, race, gender, ethnic affiliation, etcetera. According to this epistemic premise, there cannot exist only one single truth waiting to be uncovered by an impartial observer; rather all knowledge is partial and contingent. A number of feminists,[61] pioneers of this debate, have asserted and demonstrated through their own practices that our representations are the product of our own position(ing). As we have seen, the case of Ronfeldt et al and my own are no exception.

Finally, as I have already mentioned, the importance of the neo-Zapatista networks is evident in many instances and in a variety of forms. Suffice it to mention only the arrival on Zapatista territory of the 'National and International Caravan of Observation and Solidarity with the Zapatista Communities in Chiapas',[62] to express its solidarity with the *Caracoles* and to celebrate the fifth anniversary of the creation of the Good Government Committees. The significance of such a mobilisation cannot be underestimated. It occurs at a time when dialogue between the EZLN and the government remains suspended, and the policy of the Mexican state continues to be one of repression and criminalisation of the EZLN and the country's social movements. Under these circumstances, the importance of the existence and mobilisation of these networks is more than palpable as they denounce, both in the national and international arena, the abuses committed by the powers of the state, police, military, and paramilitary groups that operate in Chiapas.

References

Sonia E. Alvarez, 1998—'Latin American Feminisms "Go Global": Trends of the 1990s and Challenges for the New Millennium', in Sonia E. Alvarez, Evelina Dagnino, and Arturo Escobar, eds, 1998—*Cultures of Politics/Politics of Cultures: Re-Visioning Latin American Social Movements* (Boulder, CO: Westview Press), pp 293–324

Sonia E. Alvarez, Evelina Dagnino, and Arturo Escobar, eds, 1998—*Cultures of Politics/Politics of Cultures: Re-Visioning Latin American Social Movements*. Boulder, CO: Westview Press

Felipe Arturo Ávila Espinosa, 2001—*Los orígenes del zapatismo* ['The Origins of Zapatismo', in Spanish]. Mexico City: El Colegio de México & UNAM

María Isabel Casas-Cortés, Michal Osterweil, and Dana E Powell, 2008—'Blurring Boundaries: Recognizing Knowledge-Practices in the Study of Social Movements', in *Anthropological Quarterly*, vol 81, no 1 (Winter 2008), pp 17–58

Manuel Castells, 1998—*End of Millennium: The Information Age: Economy, Society and Culture*, vol 3. Oxford: Blackwell Publishers

EZLN, 1996b—*Crónicas intergalácticas EZLN. Primer Encuentro Intercontinental por la Humanidad y contra el Neoliberalismo* [The EZLN Intergalactic Chronicle: The First Intercontinental Encounter for Humanity and Against Neoliberalism', in Spanish]. Chiapas, Mexico: Tierra Montañas del Sureste

Francis Fukuyama, 1992—*The End of History and the Last Man*. New York: Free Press

Global Exchange, CIEPAC, and CENCOS, 2000—*Siempre Cerca, Siempre Lejos. Las fuerzas armadas en México* ['Always Near, Always Far: The armed forces in Mexico', in Spanish]. Mexico City: Global Exchange, CIEPAC, and CENCOS

Charles Hale, 2008 [2004]—'*Reflexiones sobre la práctica de una investigación descolonizada* ['Reflections on the practice of decolonising research', in Spanish]', in Axel Köhler, coord, 2008 [2004]—*Anuario 2007. Centro de Estudios Superiores de México y Centroamérica* ['2007 Yearbook of the Centre for Higher Studies of Mexico and Central America']. *New Era* (Tuxtla Gutiérrez [Chiapas, México]: CESMECA-Universidad de Ciencias y Artes de Chiapas), pp 299–315

Donna Haraway, 1988—'Situated knowledges: The science question in feminism and the privilege of partial perspective', in *Feminist Studies*, vol 14, pp 575–599

Rosalva Aída Hernández Castillo, 2010—'*Hacia una antropología socialmente comprometida desde una perspectiva dialógica y feminista*' ['Towards a socially engaged anthropology from a feminist and dialogic perspective', in Spanish], in Xochitl Leyva

Solano et al, 2010—*Conocimientos, poder y prácticas políticas. Reflexiones desde nuestras experiencias de trabajo* ['Knowledge, Power, and Political Practices: Reflections from our experiences of working']. Mexico, Lima, and Guatemala: CIESAS, Programa de Democracia y Transformación Global

Axel Honneth, 1996—*The Struggle for Recognition: The Moral Grammar of Social Conflicts.* Cambridge, MA: MIT Press

bell hooks, 1995—'The Oppositional Gaze: Black Female Spectators', in Peggy Zeglin Brand and Carolyn Korsmeyer, eds, 1995—*Feminism and Tradition in Aesthetics* (University Park, PA: Pennsylvania State University Press), pp 142–159

Alex Khasnabish, 2017—'Forward Dreaming: Zapatismo and the Radical Imagination', in Jai Sen, ed, 2017a—*The Movements of Movements, Part 1: What Makes Us Move?.* Volume 4 in the *Challenging Empires* series. New Delhi: OpenWord, and Oakland, CA: PM Press

Axel Köhler, Xochitl Leyva Solano, Juan López Intzin, Damián Martínez Martínez, Rie Watanabe, Juan Chawuk, José Alfredo Jiménez Pérez, Floriano Henríquez Hernández Cruz, Pedro Agripino Icó Bautista, and Mariano Estrada Aguilar, forthcoming—*Sjalel Kibeltik: Tejiendo nuestras raíces* ['*Sjalel Kibeltik:* Weaving our roots', in Spanish]. San Cristóbal de las Casas: Mexico: Red de Artistas, Comunicadores Comunitarios y Antropólogos de Chiapas (RACCACH), UNAM, UNICACH, CIESAS, XENIX Filmdistribution, and IWGIA

Bertrand La Grange and Maite Rico, 1997—*Marcos, la genial impostura* ['Marcos, the genial imposter', in Spanish]. Mexico City: Aguilar, Nuevo Siglo

Yvon Le Bot, 1997—*Subcomandante Marcos: El sueño Zapatista* ['*Subcomandante Marcos*: Zapatista Dream', in Spanish]. Mexico City: Plaza y Janés

Xochitl Leyva Solano, 1995—'*Militancia político-religiosa e identidad en la Lacandona*' ['Politico-religious militancy and identity in the Lacandona', in Spanish], in *Revista Espiral: Estudios sobre Estado y Sociedad*, vol 1 no 2 (January–April), pp 59–88

Xochitl Leyva Solano, 1998—'The New Zapatista Movement: Political Levels, Actors and Political Discourse in Contemporary Mexico', in Valentina Napolitano and Xochitl Leyva Solano, eds, 1998—*Encuentros antropológicos: Power, Identity and Mobility in Mexican Society* (London: Institute of Latin American Studies), pp 35–55

Xochitl Leyva Solano, 1999—'*De Las Cañadas a Europa: niveles, actores y discursos del Nuevo Movimiento Zapatista (NMZ) (1994–1997)*'. ['From Las Cañadas to Europe: Levels, actors, and discourses of the New Zapatista Movement (1994–1997), in Spanish'], in *Desacato: Revista de antropología social*, no 1 (Spring 1999), pp 56–87

Xochitl Leyva Solano, 2001—*Neo-Zapatismo: Networks of Power and War.* Thesis submitted to obtain the degree of Doctor of Philosophy in the Faculty of Social Sciences and Law, Department of Social Anthropology, The University of Manchester

Xochitl Leyva Solano, 2006—'Zapatista Movement Networks Respond to Globalization', in *LASA Forum*, vol XXXVII, no I (Winter 2006), pp 37–39

Xochitl Leyva Solano, 2008—'*Investigación Social y Pueblos Indígenas: ¿En dónde estamos, de dónde venimos y hacia dónde parece que vamos?*' ['Social Research and Indigenous Peoples: Where are we, where have we come from, and where does it seem that we are going?', in Spanish], in Santiago Bastos, compilador, 2008—*Multiculturalismo y futuro en Guatemala* ['Multiculturalism and the Future in Guatemala'] (Guatemala City: FLACSO-Guatemala and Oxfam), pp 175–215

Xochitl Leyva Solano, 2009—'*Nuevos procesos sociales y políticos en América Latina: las redes neozapatistas*' ['New social and political processes in Latin America: The Zapatistas networks', in Spanish], in Raphael Hoetmer, coord, 2009—*Repensar la Política desde América Latina: Cultura, Estado y Movimientos Sociale* ['Rethinking politics in Latin America: Culture, State, and social movements', in Spanish]. (Lima: Programa Democracia y Transformación Global & Fondo Editorial de la Facultad de Ciencias Sociales de la UNMSM), pp 109–130

Xochitl Leyva Solano, 2010—'¿Academia versus activismo? Repensarnos desde y para la práctica-teórico-política' ['Academy versus activism? Rethinking practice-theory-politics', in Spanish], in Leyva Solano et al, 2010—*Conocimientos, poder y prácticas políticas. Reflexiones desde nuestras experiencias de trabajo* ['Knowledge, Power, and Political Practices: Reflections from our experiences of working']. Chiapas, Mexico City, Lima, and Ciudad de Guatemala: CIESAS, Programa de Democracia y Transformación Global, and UNICACH

Xochitl Leyva Solano and Gabriel Ascencio, 1996—*Lacandonia al filo del agua* ['Lacandonia—the edge of water', in Spanish]. Mexico: CIESAS, UNAM, and FCE

Xochitl Leyva Solano and Christopher Gunderson, 2017—'The Tapestry of Neo-Zapatismo: Origins and Development', in Jai Sen, ed, 2017a—*The Movements of Movements, Part 1: What Makes Us Move?*. Volume 4 in the *Challenging Empires* series. New Delhi: OpenWord, and Oakland, CA: PM Press

Xochitl Leyva Solano and Willibald Sonnleitner, 2000—'¿Qué es el neo-zapatismo?' ['What is neo-Zapatismo?', in Spanish], in *Revista Espira: Estudios sobre Estado y Sociedad*, vol 6, no 17 (January–April), pp 163–202. Guadalajara, Jalisco, Mexico

Xochitl Leyva Solano and Shannon Speed, 2008—'*Hacia la investigación descolonizada: nuestra experiencia de co-labor*' ['To research decolonised: Our experience of co-work', in Spanish], in Xochitl Leyva Solano, Araceli Burguete, and Shannon Speed, coords, 2008—*Gobernar (en) la diversidad: experiencias indígenas desde América Latina. Hacia la investigación de co-labor* ['Governing (in) diversity: Indigenous experiences from Latin America—Research as co-work'] (Mexico City: CIESAS, FLACSO-Ecuador, and FLACSO-Guatemala), pp 65–109

Sylvia Marcos and Margarite Waller, 2008—*Diálogo y Diferencia. Retos feministas a la globalización* ['Dialogue and Difference: Feminist Challenges to Globalization', in Spanish]. Mexico City: CEIIH-UNAM and Instituto de la Mujer of the State of Morelos

Walter Mignolo, 2001—'*Introducción*' ['Introduction', in Spanish], in Walter Mignolo, compiler, 2001—*Capitalismo y geopolítica del conocimiento. El eurocentrismo y la filosofía de la liberación en el debate intelectual contemporáneo* ['Capitalism and the Geopolitics of Knowledge: Eurocentrism and the philosophy of liberation in contemporary intellectual debate'] (Buenos Aires: Ediciones del Signo and Duke University), pp 9–53

Walter Mignolo, 2006—'*El desprendimiento: pensamiento crítico y giro descolonial*' ['Detachment: Critical thinking and decolonial spin', in Spanish], in Walter Mignolo, Freya Schiwy, and Nelson Maldonado, 2006—*(Des)colonialidad del ser y del saber (videos indígenas y los límites coloniales de la izquierda) en Bolivia* ['(De)coloniality of being and knowing (Indigenous visions and colonial boundaries on the left) in Bolivia']. Notebook no 1. Ediciones del Signo, and Globalization and the Humanities Project. (Durham, NC: Duke University Press), pp 11–26

Trinh T Minh-ha, 1989—*Woman, Native, Other: Writing Postcoloniality and Feminism*. Indianapolis: Indiana University Press

Chandra Mohanty, 2003—*Feminism without Borders: Decolonizing Theory, Practicing Solidarity*. Durham, NC: Duke University Press

Cherríe Moraga and Gloria Anzaldúa, 2002—*This Bridge Called My Back: Writings by Radical Women of Color*. San Francisco: Third Woman Press

Pedro Pitarch, 2001—'Los zapatistas y la política' ['The Zapatistas and politics', in Spanish] in *Letras Libres*, October 2001, at http://www.letraslibres.com/index.php?art=7023 (Accessed April 2017)

Eduardo Restrepo and Arturo Escobar, 2004—'*Antropologías en el mundo*' [Anthropology in the world', in Spanish], in *Jangua Pana*, vol 3 pp 110–131. Santa Marta: Anthropology Program, Universidad de Magdalena

Gustavo Lins Ribeiro, 1998—'Cybercultural Politics: Political Activism at a Distance in a Transnational World', in Sonia E. Alvarez, Evelina Dagnino, and Arturo Escobar, eds, 1998—*Cultures of Politics/Politics of Cultures: Re-Visioning Latin American Social Movements* (Boulder, CO: Westview Press), pp 325–352

David Ronfeldt, John Arquilla, Graham E Fuller, and Melissa Fuller, 1998—*The Zapatista 'Social Netwar' in Mexico*. Santa Monica, CA: RAND Arroyo Centre, at http://www.rand.org/pubs/monograph_reports/MR994/ (Accessed April 2017)

Jai Sen, Anita Anand, Arturo Escobar, and Peter Waterman, 2004—*World Social Forum: Challenging Empires*. New Delhi: Viveka Foundation

David Slater, 1998—'Rethinking the Spatialities of Social Movements: Questions of (B)orders, Culture, and Politics in Global Times', in Sonia E. Alvarez, Evelina Dagnino, and Arturo Escobar, eds, 1998—*Cultures of Politics/Politics of Cultures. Re-Visioning Latin American Social Movements* (Boulder, CO: Westview Press), pp 380–401

Jesús Sotelo Inclán, 1970—*Raíz y razón de Zapata* ['Zapata's Roots and Rationale', in Spanish], second edition. Mexico City: Fondo de Cultura Económica

Shannon Speed, 2006—'*Entre la antropología y los derechos humanos: hacia una investigación activista y críticamente comprometida*' ['Between anthropology and human rights: Towards a critically engaged activist research', in Spanish], in *Alteridades*, year 16, no 31, January–June 2006, pp 73–85

Liliana Suárez and Rosalva Aída Hernández, eds, 2008—*Descolonizando el feminismo. Teorías y prácticas desde los márgenes* ['Decolonizing Feminism: Theories and practices from the margins', in Spanish]. Madrid: Ediciones Cátedra, Universitat de Valencia and Instituto de la Mujer

Carlos Tello, 1995—*La rebelión de Las Cañadas* ['The Rebellion in *Las Cañadas*', in Spanish]. Mexico City: Cal y Arena

Gilberto Valdés, 2010—'*Reflexiones ético-político desde los talleres de paradigmas emancipatorios*' [Ethical-Political Reflections from Workshops on Emancipatory Paradigms', in Spanish], in Xochitl Leyva Solano et al, 2010—*Conocimientos, poder y prácticas políticas. Reflexiones desde nuestras experiencias de trabajo* ['Knowledge, Power, and Political Practices: Reflections from our experiences of working']. Mexico, Lima, and Guatemala: CIESAS, Programa de Democracia y Transformación Global

José Ramón Vidal, 2007—'*Comunicación y luchas contrahegemónicas*' ['Communication and counter-hegemonic struggle', in Spanish], in *Caminos: Revista Cubana de Pensamiento Socioteológico*, no 43, January–March, pp 2–8

Immanuel Wallerstein, 1998—*Impensar las ciencias sociales. Límites de los paradigmas decimonónicos* ['Unthinking Social Science: Limits of nineteenth-century paradigms', in Spanish]. Mexico City: Siglo XXI Editores

Immanuel Wallerstein, 2006—*Análisis del sistemas-mundo. Una introducción* [World-System Analysis: An Introduction', in Spanish]. Mexico City: Siglo XXI Editores

John Womack, Jr, 1999a [1969]—*Zapata y la revolución Mexicana* [Zapata and the Revolution', in Spanish] 23rd edition. Mexico City: Siglo XXI Editores

George Yúdice, 1998—'The Globalization of Culture and the New Civil Society', in Sonia E. Alvarez, Evelina Dagnino, and Arturo Escobar, eds, 1998—*Cultures of Politics/ Politics of Cultures: Re-Visioning Latin American Social Movements* (Boulder, CO: Westview Press), pp 353–379

Notes

1. A previous version of this text has been published in Peru, in Spanish (Levya Solano 2009). Ed: I warmly thank the author for her permission to publish this English translation of her essay here, and for revising it for this publication.

2. I wish to express my sincere gratitude to the EZLN and to all the members of neo-Zapatista networks in different places around the world, as well as to the members of the CIDECI Wallerstein Seminar and to the *compañeros* of the UNITIERRA-Chiapas that I belong to. All of them have allowed me to participate, learn, and construct collectively *knowledge-practices* and other epistemes, and to encourage the *de-colonial option* and neo-Zapatista critical thinking.

3. The prefix 'neo' in the concept of neo-Zapatism is used here not only to point out that the EZLN, which rose up in arms on January 1 1994, is different from the revolutionary Zapatism of 1910, but also to indicate, as already argued in previous publications, that neo-Zapatism goes beyond the EZLN. The latter is a social, political, and military organisation, while neo-Zapatism is understood to include the EZLN, as well as all the networks, movements, organisations, collectives, and individuals who link, align, co-align, and converge around the EZLN demands (Leyva Solano 1999).

4. Alvarez et al 1998, pp 15–16.

5. Alvarez 1998; Ribeiro 1998; Slater 1998; and Yúdice 1998.

6. Alvarez et al 1998, pp 15.

7. Cf Ávila 2001; Womack 1999a [1969]; and Sotelo 1970.

8. Cf Leyva Solano 1999, 2006; Leyva Solano and Sonnleitner 2000.

9. What I consider particularly important in the analysis of Manuel Castells (1998) is his argument that now, during the Information Age, we are confronting the rise of new societal forms that remind us of the ways in which industrialisation wrought changes. But I also agree with José Ramón Vidal (2007) that at the end of the twentieth century, the ideas of the *Information Society* and of the *End of History* (Fukuyama 1992) formed part of a "hegemonic discourse that was spreading ... all over the planet and proclaimed one single world, subject to the 'blind' forces of the market".

10. Wallerstein 2006.

11. Mignolo 2001.

12. Examples of these spaces where activists and committed academics converge in their social struggles and movements are the World Social Fora (Sen et al 2004), the Emancipatory Paradigm Workshops (*Talleres de Paradigmas Emancipatorios*) organised in Cuba since 1995 (Valdés 2010, and http://ecaminos.org/leer.php/5738), festivals like that of the Honourable Rage (*Digna Rabia*) that the EZLN convened for in 2008 (http://dignarabia.ezln.org.mx), or the First International Colloquium in Memoriam Andrés Aubry (www.coloquiointernacionalandresaubry.org) also convened by the EZLN, together with the journal *Rebeldía* (Rebellion) and the CIDECI/UNITIERRA-Chiapas in 2007.

13. For a detailed account of the challenges in assuming a *situated knowledge position*, see Haraway 1988; Hale 2008 [2004]; Restrepo and Escobar 2004; Hernández Castillo 2010, Speed 2006; Leyva Solano and Speed 2008; Leyva Solano 2008; Marcos and Waller 2008; and Suárez and Hernández 2008. These texts provide an overview of authors and debates that have aimed at decolonising and *unthinking social sciences* since the 1970s.

14. Mignolo 2006.

15. ibid, pp 12–13.

16. Wallerstein 1998.

17. Examples that come to mind include the World Social Fora, the Universidad de la Tierra in Chiapas and Oaxaca, the Center for Integration of Research and Action (CIRA) in North Carolina, the Democracy and Global Transformation Program in Peru and the Chiapas Network of Artists, Community Communicators and Anthropologists (*Red de Artistas, Comunicadores Comunitarios y Antropólogos de Chiapas*, RACCACH, see Köhler et al, forthcoming).

18. Casas-Cortés, Osterweil, and Powell 2008.

19. Mignolo 2001, pp 16–17.

20. Mignolo 2001, pp 38.

21. Ronfeldt et al 1998.

22. ibid., pp 9–16, 40–43, 52, 149.

23. ibid., p 15.

24. ibid., pp 53, 102.

25. ibid., pp 70, 106, 120.

26. ibid., p 83.

27. Cf Archives of the 'Fray Bartolomé de Las Casas' Human Rights Centre.

28. Ronfeldt et al 1998, p 78.

29. ibid., p 79.

30. Global Exchange, CIEPAC, and CENCOS 2000, p 112.

31. ibid., p 132.

32. Ronfeldt et al 1998, pp 74–77, 79, 107, 110.

33. BBC World News, October 5 2001.

34. Ronfeldt et al 1998, pp 54 and 59.

35. Cf Leyva Solano and Ascencio 1996; Leyva Solano 1995, 2001; and Le Bot 1997. See also the essay in this book by Xochitl Leyva Solano and Christopher Gunderson (Leyva Solano and Gunderson 2017).

36. 1992 Declaration of Principles by the National Liberation Forces Party, cited in La Grange and Rico 1997, p 226.

37. ibid, p 228.
38. ibid.
39. Le Bot 1997.
40. Tello 1995; La Grange and Rico 1997.
41. Cited in Le Bot 1997.
42. Tello 1995, pp 206–208.
43. Pitarch 2001.
44. Cited in EZLN 1996b, p 69.
45. According to Castells (1998, p 336) a new world was taking shape towards the end of the twentieth century: "It originated in the historical coincidence, around the late 1960s and mid-1970s, of three *independent* processes: the information technology revolution; the economic crisis of both capitalism and statism, and their subsequent restructuring; and the blooming of cultural social movements, such as libertarianism, human rights, feminism and environmentalism. The interaction between these processes, and the reactions they triggered, brought into being a new dominant social structure, the network society; a new economy, the informational / global economy; and a new culture, the culture of real virtuality. The logic embedded in this economy, this society, and this culture underlies social action and institutions throughout an interdependent world".
46. Those interested in the evolution of the National Liberation Forces (*Fuerzas de Liberación Nacional*, FLN) and how they became the EZLN, may consult the interview that Subcomandante Marcos gave to Yvon Le Bot in 1997, as well as the multiple communiqués that the EZLN issued through the General Command of the Clandestine Revolutionary Insurgent Committee (*Comité Clandestino Revolucionario Insurgente-Comandancia General*, CCRI-CG) and its spokesperson, Subcomandante Marcos. Many of these communiqués have been published by the journals *Rebeldía* (Rebellion), *Contrahistorias* (Counter-histories), and *Chiapas*. There is also a collection of five volumes with EZLN documents and communiqués published by ERA.
47. A more detailed account of this encounter can be found in Leyva Solano 2001 and 2006.
48. For a more detailed reflection on these different kinds of networks, see Leyva Solano 2001.
49. Those interested in the different kinds of networks can consult Leyva Solano 1999, and Leyva Solano and Sonnleitner 2000.
50. I personally attended this event not as an external researcher but as an active member of the neo-Zapatista networks. I presented myself as such when I requested permission in the plenary to work on our shared experiences. In particular, I would like to thank the members of the Solidarity Collective for the Zapatista Rebellion (*Colectivo de Solidaridad con la Rebelión Zapatista*) living in Barcelona. They received me warmly both in their offices and their homes.
51. Honneth 1996.
52. Ed: In the context of the Zapatista movement in Chiapas, 'MAR' stands for '*Municipios Autonomos Rebeldes Zapatistas*' ['Zapatista Autonomous Rebel Communities', in Spanish]; see http://www.sipaz.org/en/chiapas/facts-about-chiapas/397-zapatista-autonomous-municipalities-and-regions.html (Inactive April

2017). What MAR stands for in Paris though is less clear, though it's entirely possible that some activists there were inspired by and—as it were—fashioned and named themselves this, in solidarity. Unfortunately, I haven't been able to get clarification from the author on this point as we finalised her text and went to press, so this is the only expansion and explanation I can offer here, based on suggestions and advice from Christopher Gunderson and Jeffrey Juris. My thanks to them.

53. A detailed study of the historical formation and transformation of the neo-Zapatista networks can be found in Leyva Solano 2001. Ed: And for a discussion of the widespread resonance of these networks, see the essay in this book by Alex Khasnabish (Khasnabish 2017).

54. Casas-Cortés, Osterweil, and Powell (2008, pp 50–51) point out that "there is yet to be a common recognition leading to a coherent theoretical framework of knowledge-practices. Such a framework would understand knowledge-practice as an important part of the collective, crucial work movements do". They add that "we can understand many movement related activities as knowledge-practices, which not only critically engage and redraw the map of what comprises the political, but also produce practices and subjects according to different logics. As such, knowledge-practices are part of the investigative and creative work necessary for (re)making politics, both from the micro-political inscribed on our bodies and lived in the everyday, to broader institutional and systemic change. It is in this sense that movements can be understood in and of themselves as spaces for the production of situated knowledges of the political".

55. Cf Leyva Solano 1998, 1999.

56. Global Exchange et al 2000. Cf also the web pages of CIEPAC, SIPAZ, CAPISE, and the 'Fray Bartolomé de Las Casas' Human Rights Centre.

57. The JBG are the *de facto* autonomous spaces in which the Zapatista political theory of 'leading by obeying' is being put into practice.

58. In the 1920s, Elise and Célestin Freinet were pioneers of an educational philosophy in France that led them to found the Cooperative for Secular Education and to challenge the principles of traditional education. In its place they proposed as a starting point an experimental process of trial and error, the functionality of work, and the principle of cooperation.

59. Cf Leyva Solano 2010.

60. Haraway 1988.

61. Cf Haraway 1998; hooks 1995; Mohanty 2003; Minh-ha 1989; Moraga and Anzaldúa 2002; Suárez and Hernández 2008; Leyva Solano and Speed 2008.

62. Participants in this Caravan in support of the Zapatista communities in resistance have included organisations and individual sympathisers from Chiapas, Baja California, Colima, Chihuahua, Mexico City, Mexico State, Jalisco, Michoacán, Morelos, Oaxaca, Puebla, and Veracruz; from other parts of the continent, including Argentina, Uruguay, Canada, and the United States; and from Europe: Aragón, Euskal Herria, Madrid, Catalunya, Valencia, Murcia, Galicia, Castilla, and Leon in Spain, as well as parts of Italy, Greece, Belgium, Germany, Switzerland, and Denmark.

2
THE MOVEMENTS OF MOVEMENTS: STRUGGLES FOR OTHER WORLDS

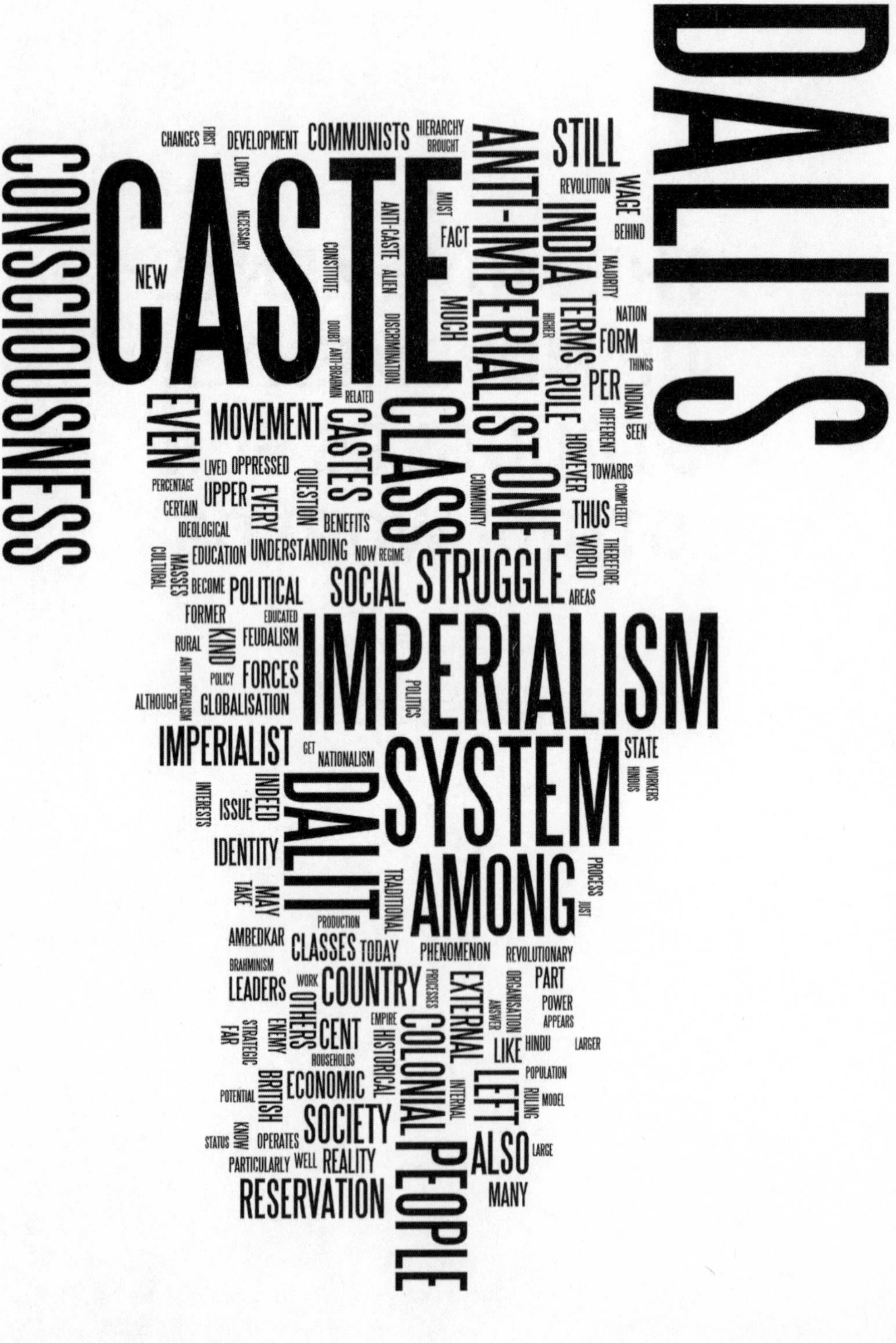
DALITS
CASTE
CONSCIOUSNESS
ANTI-IMPERIALIST
IMPERIALISM
SYSTEM
DALIT
CLASS
ONE
STRUGGLE
AMONG
PEOPLE
COLONIAL
STILL
INDIA
CASTES
MOVEMENT
EVEN
SOCIAL
IMPERIALIST
COMMUNISTS
DEVELOPMENT
CHANGES
FIRST
HIERARCHY
BROUGHT
LOWER
NECESSARY
NEW
ANTI-CASTE
CONSTITUTE
ALIEN
MUST
FACT
MUCH
TERMS
REVOLUTION
WAGE
BEHIND
MAJORITY
NATION
FORM
THINGS
PER
RULE
INDIAN
DIFFERENT
SEEN
HOWEVER
TOWARDS
DOUBT
ANTI-BRAHMIN
DISCRIMINATION
RELATED
LIVED
OPPRESSED
QUESTION
PERCENTAGE
UPPER
EVERY
CERTAIN
BENEFITS
COMMUNITY
THUS
COMPLETELY
IDEOLOGICAL
WORLD
THEREFORE
CULTURAL
EDUCATION
UNDERSTANDING
NOW
REGIME
MASSES
BECOME
POLITICAL
AREAS
FORMER
EDUCATED
RURAL
KIND
FEUDALISM
ANTI-IMPERIALISM
POLICY
FORCES
POLITICS
ALTHOUGH
GLOBALISATION
GET
NATIONALISM
STATE
HINDUS
WORKERS
INTERESTS
ISSUE
INDEED
IDENTITY
TAKE
MAY
TRADITIONAL
PROCESS
JUST
PRODUCTION
AMBEDKAR
CLASSES
TODAY
PHENOMENON
REVOLUTIONARY
BRAHMINISM
PART
LEADERS
WORK
COUNTRY
PROCESSES
EXTERNAL
ORGANISATION
POWER
ANSWER
APPEARS
OTHERS
EMPIRE
FAR
STRATEGIC
ENEMY
CENT
HISTORICAL
LIKE
HINDU
LARGER
HOUSEHOLDS
LEFT
POPULATION
BRITISH
ECONOMIC
INTERNAL
POTENTIAL
RULING
MODEL
SOCIETY
STATUS
KNOW
OPERATES
ALSO
LARGE
PARTICULARLY
WELL
REALITY
RESERVATION
MANY

OpenWord

Dalits, Anti-Imperialist Consciousness, and the Annihilation of Caste[1]
Anand Teltumbde

The British have an Empire. So have the Hindus. For is not Hinduism a form of imperialism and are not the Untouchables a subject race, owing their allegiance and their servitude to their Hindu Master? If Churchill must be asked to declare his war aims, how could anybody avoid asking Mr Gandhi and the Hindus to declare their war aims?

—Dr BR Ambedkar, in *Mr Gandhi and the Emancipation of the Untouchables*

Caste Is Also an Empire

One of the weaknesses of the anti-imperialist movement led by the left in India has been its inability to identify and assimilate all people potentially in contradiction with imperialism and infuse in them requisite anti-imperialist consciousness. A large number of people who could rank high in their anti-imperialist potential are as such excluded, denting the movement in terms of quality as well as quantity. Dalits, who constitute one sixth of the total population, are a significant part of these excluded people. As a social group they could have been rightly reckoned the organic proletariat, that otherwise comprises in significant part of peasants and workers, the classes universally recognised as antagonistic to imperialism. Dalit exclusion apart, there appears to be a general lack of anti-imperialist consciousness even among other sections of people in India. Whether this lack is a cause or a consequence of the weakness of anti-imperialist forces needs to be examined. Generally, the tribals living in and around forests, despite their spatial distance from civilisation (so-called), are seen to be keen in anti-imperialist struggles. The same however is not true of Dalits and people from other castes in the plains.

There is no doubt that imperialism is the biggest enemy of the people world over. Its vice-like grip on every individual and every aspect of his / her life has become so integral with our life processes that we hardly feel its presence. It is as pervasive as the air we breathe. It has entered our vitals through the cultural poison it spews, and with which it has virtually taken control of our lives. The way we live, the things we consume, the manner in which we relate, the language we speak, and the way we react—everything is moulded by imperialism. Unlike olden days, when it had to subjugate nations with visible force, it has become completely invisible today. It operates through the network of transnational and multinational companies, which while pretending to oblige poor countries by their entry—taken as synonymous to 'development'—and serving them their wares, create a web of incessant exploitation. Imperialism also operates through multilateral institutions which, donning the garb of global governor, and with seeming independent professionalism, serve its interests. It operates through a cobweb of financial, educational, religious, and philanthropic institutions, not to speak of thousands of NGOs which, while mimicking peoples' movements, have completely emasculated them. They represent the new stratagem of imperialism to subsume peoples' movements under the imperialist umbrella. Imperialism operates through its *comprador* (intermediary, colonial agent) network of politicians, bureaucrats, academicians, etc, who, while swearing by patriotism, professionalism, and intellectualism, keep serving their imperialist masters. Indeed, imperialism has infiltrated so deeply into our lives that it is difficult to discern its existence, let alone target it.

Imperialism is far stronger than ever before. The term is no longer used in plural. The rivalry among imperialists that grew from the late nineteenth century culminating in two World Wars during the early half of the twentieth century—and where exploiting this rivalry which was an integral part of the anti-imperialist strategy—appears to be a thing of past. After the collapse of the Berlin Wall and the dismantling of the Soviet regime, the unipolarity of the world has become an established fact. Imperialism has reconfigured itself as a unitary system with the USA at the apex and other regional powers at the second and third levels to act as its gendarme under the ultimate threat of the unrivalled missile power of the US war machine.

It is by no means simple for the centre at Washington to manage this gendarme network but the model has its self-regulating features, quite like the caste system of India. Indeed, the model of imperialist organisation today has striking similarity with the caste system. It is not necessary to consciously emulate the caste model; anyone seeking to make exploitation systemic—in the sense of being self-organising and self-regulating—will independently arrive at a model similar to that of the caste system. The caste system is the most potent system of exploitation of imperialist nature ever devised anywhere. Interestingly, these two imperialist systems, one driven from Washington (external), and the other, the homegrown caste system (internal), are closely related, providing certain strategic clues for anti-imperialist forces in India to conduct their struggle. I return to this point later in this essay.

There is no doubt about the necessity to fight against both feudalism and imperialism for a comprehensive democratic revolution—the present phase of revolution in most countries like India. The anti-imperialist struggle is related with nationalism, whereas the anti-feudal struggle is related with democracy. In the present era, with imperialism and feudalism being closely tied to each other, semi-feudal and semi-colonial countries like ours—which are thus doubly exploited and oppressed by this coalition—have to wage both a national struggle for democracy and a democratic struggle for nationalism. While this analysis is broadly accurate, it does not prevent the practice being stereotypical. Why, for instance, is the anti-feudal struggle—oriented towards the peasants' cause—so apathetic about combating caste? While external imperialism is identified as an enemy, imperialism in the form of home-grown institutions that more visibly oppress people is conveniently ignored. Should the anti-imperialist struggle take cognisance of imperialism only of the outsiders? If so, why should people who perceive themselves being more oppressed by insiders than outsiders join in such struggles?

The struggle against external imperialism is based on nationalism. Relative to the physically segregated collectivities of the outcastes, this is only an abstraction. If the anti-imperialist struggle is a nationalism-based struggle, it must essentially assume that India is a nation. However, the analyses of the left would not support this assumption. As a matter of fact, India is not one nation, but a country with many nationalities. The weakness of the anti-imperialist consciousness among Indians provides proof of this postulation. There is another reason that is perhaps far more damaging than even this one: Having lived with the system of *internal* imperialism for millennia, Indians have internalised the imperialist ideology and absorbed the imperialist ethos to such an extent that they do not now sense nor feel any type of imperialism engulfing them.

At the ideological level, imperialism and Brahminism are the same. Indeed, Brahminism is imperialism in every sense of the term. Not only does it satisfy the broad social criterion for imperialism, as the enduring oppression of one section of a society by another, but it also works well in relation to the considerations of a more particularly defined nationalism.

Nationalism is not a necessary correlate of a state-boundary, neither is it essentially based on a geographical attribute. One has only to recall Babasaheb Ambedkar's statement that in India every caste is a nation! Dalits, with their segregated living conditions and dehumanised status for millennia, can well be taken as an oppressed nation. For them, Brahminism—the source ideology behind their oppression—is the worst exploitative system and represents the imperialist nation. Ask them to choose between foreign rule and the rule of Manu, mythical lawgiver and progenitor of the caste system, and they might answer in favour of the former. The anti-imperialists may dismiss this as an indication of 'backwardness', but they cannot impose their forwardness on others' lived realities and expect them to follow their agenda. By calling caste a mere vestige of feudalism, the left forces have underrated its menacing power as a self-regulating imperialist system that has been able to survive even after the formal demise of feudalism. Caste represents the dreaded unity of feudalism and imperialism, and should logically constitute the target of any revolutionary struggle.

The anti-imperialist movement needs to take cognizance of this internal imperialism of the so-called upper castes from even its own strategic viewpoint—because its victims are the very same people who could constitute its core constituency. Dalits are the worst victims of imperialism—internal as well as external—and they are therefore inherently against *any* kind of imperialism. In class terms, they should be considered as the organic proletariat of this country. Although afflicted by caste divisions, the history of suffering has forged a workable identity for them. Nowhere in the world would such a large mass of have-nots be so readily available for radical change! The anti-caste struggle of Dalits is truly an expression of anti-imperialism. The anti-imperialist forces could see in it a rebellion of the meek against their oppressors, a big leap in the democratisation of the country, and rush to express their support. Instead, they ignore it almost in disdain and focus on external imperialism, something that is—relatively speaking—abstract. Dalits are naturally perplexed to find that the people who swear by anti-imperialism are apathetic to their struggle. It is in reaction to this attitude that Dalits have not been enthusiastic about the anti-imperialist movement. The persistent neglect of the caste oppression suffered by them has made them suspicious of it.

However, it is not the case either that Dalits would automatically rally against outsiders as imperialists. Ostensibly, imperialism, in the form of rule of outsiders, whether they settled here like the Muslims did or sent the colonial loot to the imperialist centres as the British did, has helped Dalits in terms of opening up new avenues for them and loosening the grip of those they know as their oppressors. Although Dalits knew that external imperialism was not there to help them and that whatever benefits accrued to them were incidental, a kind of by-product of the external imperialist process, they still felt beholden to it because for them the internal imperialism that deprived them of their human identity was a far more fundamental evil than the other exploitations they suffered on account of external imperialism. They did not give so much importance to the incremental burden that came to their share on account of the imperialist impoverishment of the country, as to their awakening to human identity, which was attributed to the rule of foreigners. In absence of these alien rulers, they could not have been exposed to the horizons of their emancipation. This historical dynamic has created a consciousness among Dalits that does not see much wrong with external rule.

Beyond this, when there is a general hue and cry raised by the upper castes against any issue, Dalits instinctively take the issue as being possibly favourable to them, on the lines of the dictum that one's enemy's enemy is one's friend. As a persecuted minority, Dalits have developed a particular identity that is suspicious of, if not outrightly opposed to, the general identity of Hindus, which is automatically associated with the *savarna* (upper caste) mass. Dalit consciousness thus treats others, particularly the upper castes, as the enemy. Unless there is a conscious initiative by progressive forces to take up the issue of annihilation of caste in thought and deed, it will be difficult to efface this kind of inimical consciousness and win the confidence of Dalits.

The Dalit movement today is hopelessly fragmented among self-seeking leaders. These leaders are a kind of *comprador* to the community, brokering the interests of Dalit masses to the enemy camp. This realisation is slowly dawning on Dalits but in the absence of any alternative, they still passively throng to these leaders and lend them legitimacy. These leaders are wise enough to keep parroting the issues that still appeal to Dalits. It reflects a sort of umbilical cord that is extant even now. Their anti-caste, anti-Brahmin rhetoric, the issues of dignity and self-respect, the articulation of caste-specific demands, and above all fidelity to that great icon of Dalit movement, Dr Ambedkar—all this still appeals to Dalits, as compared to the abstract slogans and apathetic attitude of the left towards their problems. If the left mends its ways and takes steps to gain Dalit confidence, one could hope to see a much-desired democratic revolution round the corner in a reasonable period.

I examine now in detail two of my propositions: Caste is *the* issue that the left must address; and the question of building anti-imperialist consciousness among Dalits.

Caste Is *the* Issue

In leftist circles, the understanding of caste has evolved from 'caste as a non-issue' to the recognition of 'caste as also an issue' along with many others such as gender, nationality, minorities, communalism, and so on. Bracketing caste with the issues that exist in every country and every society, albeit with some variation, smacks of belittling the uniqueness and importance of caste in the Indian context. Every society has several contradictions but they cannot and need not all be resolved without consideration of their stage of development. Dialectics teaches us that contradictions can be successfully resolved only when they reach their irreconcilable peak. At any stage of development thus, there is a single principal contradiction that craves for resolution through a revolution. In contrast, the current left understanding treats caste as just one of the contradictions in society, not the primary or principal one, and also as one which may either get resolved in the course of the class struggle or may be dealt with in the post-revolution society.

In the context of the left's demonstrated historical refusal to acknowledge the caste question as *the* problem, the slight shift in understanding of caste over eight decades—from non-issue to 'also an issue'—becomes utterly inconsequential for the victims of the caste system. The left has already exhausted all kinds of arguments, such as the stand that there was nothing special about caste since it existed in other societies as well, or that caste is a feudal vestige that would automatically disappear with the spread of capitalism. Indeed, way back in 1920s some even saw

India as a capitalist country, meaning thereby that the fact of Indian feudalism was irrelevant in the ensuing struggle.[2]

The folly of these arguments stands exposed today. The caste system is now incontrovertibly acknowledged as the unique institution of the Indian subcontinent, which in view of its ubiquitous menace, warrants specific efforts from those engaged in bringing about revolutionary change to understand its character. Communist efforts have swung from understanding India through borrowed learning from the West to the indigenous interpretation of history through Brahminical spectacles that sees no evil in it. Both these types of understanding negate the Dalit viewpoint and undermine Dalits' emancipatory aspirations.

The caste system is a comprehensive organisation of Indian society, with its specific structural and superstructural aspects; it has also always been an indisputable part of the organisation of production. Caste has ordained the entire process of social production and reproduction. Even today, caste in rural areas is an integral part of the production system. Even beyond rural areas, the economic organisation of the society still reflects caste alignment; all the sweeping and scavenging jobs are still being done by the castes that were meant to do it in a classical caste society, while all the elite and high-paying jobs are being virtually monopolised by the traditional upper castes. If the Brahmins and other upper caste people have rushed into some professions that were the traditional preserve of certain Dalit castes (for instance, the footwear business),[3] they have done this not with a motive of defying caste but of making money from the economic potential of these professions under the capitalist paradigm; and the reverse has not happened. On the contrary, this transformation has rendered jobless many hapless Dalits engaged in these professions.

Dalits still face a huge amount of economic discrimination and exclusion, as reflected in statistics on the state of Dalits on certain salient parameters. To summarise, about two-thirds of Dalit households are landless or near landless, compared to one-third in the case of others. Less than one-third of households have acquired access to capital assets, compared to 60 per cent among others. About 60 per cent of Dalit households have to depend on wage labour, much higher than the one-fourth among others. The employment rate and wage earnings also tend to be low. Disparities of similar magnitude are observed in literacy, educational levels, and health status. The cumulative impact of these disparities is reflected in high levels of poverty among Dalits: About 36 per cent as compared to only 21 per cent among others. In the case of wage labour households, it reaches as high as 60 per cent in rural and 70 per cent in urban areas.[4]

In rural areas for instance, over the last five decades, there has not been a significant change in the occupational pattern among the Dalit and non-Dalit population. A majority of Dalits (more than 50 per cent) still work as agricultural wage labourers; besides, the 19 per cent classified as self-employed in agriculture are really small and marginal farmers with inferior land, who necessarily have to supplement their income by working on others' farms. In secular terms, this vast army of an utterly dependent rural proletariat keeps agricultural wage rates depressed. Caste domination is thus not social alone; it helps in many extra-economic forms of exploitation and ensures the security of the system.

The System of Caste-Based Reservations

Although the caste-based reservation system that has been place in India since it gained independence in 1947 ensures that Dalits are today represented in every profession and across all the organisational hierarchies, caste still acts as a veritable drag in their progress. In terms of numbers they may not be insignificant but in terms of power they are still nowhere. After all, the reservation system, devoid of any punitive provisions, does not govern the organisational dynamics that determine the distribution of power. There has not been any dent in the cultural segregation of Dalits, notwithstanding their economic upliftment. While it is a fact that most of those Dalits who occupy the senior echelons of bureaucracy do constitute a different class from that of the ordinary Dalits, even they are not completely free of humiliation on account of their caste. The class transformation of these people renders them useless to the Dalit masses, who are on the contrary adversely affected by the former's monopoly over the reservation benefits.

While this kind of broad-brush observation on the beneficiaries of reservation appears in order, the phenomenon is complex enough to warrant a deeper look. If one takes a look at the statistics about reservation, one finds that it is only in the class D posts in government institutions that the representation of Dalits fulfils the mandated percentage, while in all other higher classes it continues to diminish.[5] In fact, the class D percentage of Dalits, including sweepers, far exceeds the mandated percentage, and with the sweeper category being 100 per cent occupied by Dalits. Therefore, while the total number of beneficiaries of the reservation system appears significant, class D and C employees, who do manual labour in some form, constitute more than 90 per cent of it. Thus, and even if the reservation system had not been there, one may imagine which caste would have found its way to these jobs.

Where the system has made an impact is in the classes B and A which, left to the sweet will of society, would not otherwise have allowed Dalits in. The profile of people coming under these classes ranges from the high-grade clericals to the most senior bureaucrats. The greater percentage of Dalits' already paltry number in these classes is understandably constituted of the lower category of officials, leaving thus a very small number in positions of authority. On an economic scale, however, these people do represent a different class in reality, even if they also suffer caste discrimination at a different plane.

Typically, by virtue of their location in society, educated Dalit employees imbibe middle-class (petty-bourgeois) characteristics. Those who reach the relatively higher echelons of hierarchy correspondingly imbibe higher-class characteristics, and knowingly or unknowingly toe the line of the ruling classes. All of these people however, are not uniformly raised in their economic status; indeed many of them have not come out of their economic malaise, and so their relative status, vis-à-vis Dalit masses, places them in a different class. A typical first generation Dalit (first generation beneficiary of the reservation system) is torn between the pull of his people whose investment he represents and the push of the circumstances of his placement away from the former into an alien world. Typically, he fails in both; neither can he do anything for his people who are left behind, nor can he be accepted by the other world that he is impelled to and may even unconsciously aspire for. His marriage creates another drag (not to speak of 'her', who does not even get as much education as him), both financial and psychological, as the differential development in the community rarely makes for good matches in marriages. His relationship with his siblings marks a practical disconnect with his people who are left behind. The phenomenon of the development of Dalits through reservation has thus created an alienated mass that is typically torn between its obligations and its aspirations. Except for catalysing the spread of education among Dalits and being of some financial help to their kith and kin, the reservation system has not been of much use to the Dalit community.

The consciousness that bound these Dalits to their setting gets thinner with advancing generations. Now that the class of reservation-beneficiaries has come of age, the probability of someone not belonging to them getting into their fold has reached its nadir. The second generation of Dalits, so called in terms of getting education and other benefits from reservations, are on the one hand monopolising most benefits and on the other are lost to the community. This phenomenon, more strikingly observed as one rises up the class scale, is a painful paradox, albeit with valuable lessons. The question therefore arises: Should one declare the policy of reservation, which has been the main instrument of development of Dalits, as dysfunctional?

To answer in the affirmative to this is equivalent to throwing the baby out with the bathwater. There may be a need to mend the policy suitably to ensure that benefits flow to the needy; but to discard the policy of reservation, particularly in the context of its truncated application and pathetic implementation, would be disastrous. Fundamentally, such an observation is based on the false premise that the reservation policy is meant to uplift the Dalits economically. That it does so is incidental; the primary purpose of reservations is to serve as a countervailing measure against the societal inability to treat all of its members equally. Unless the state specifically mandates that their nominal share is guaranteed, the caste-ridden society that still exists will never let it happen. In this light, a proper question to ask is whether the Dalits scaled up in class terms are also uplifted in caste terms. The answer to this question is surely in the negative. There is no doubt that the economic standing of a Dalit person lowers the chance of him being subject to caste discrimination and humiliation; nevertheless the caste stigma does not stop haunting him. The form of discrimination and humiliation rather is transformed to a certain degree of sophistication commensurate with the class to which he belongs.

Social and Political Tenacity of Caste

The caste system has belied the fond hopes of post-colonial liberals that the spread of education would dampen the caste culture. One just needs to take a perfunctory glance at matrimonial advertisements in any newspaper anywhere in India to realise how, almost without exception, people—not only those who are highly educated but even people who have stayed abroad for years—specifically advertise their caste identity and solicit specified caste responses. This phenomenon is seen increasing year by year amongst the highly educated neo-rich globalised class. The incidence of religious fundamentalism, ritual-observation, temple-going, and following of godmen that is associated with the rise of Hindutva in recent years should be seen as contributing to caste consciousness too. Interestingly, the educated class has been the main prop of these neo-religious upsurges. Although the outward manifestation of this caste consciousness may not materialise because of political expediency and the potential resistors in the form of Dalit consciousness and legal provisions, there is no doubt that caste consciousness induces an increasing cultural segregation of Dalits.

The particular form of parliamentary politics that we adopted has also created its own paradoxes. The proliferation of political parties and quasi-political outfits of Dalits would normally have signified the political maturity of Dalits, but in reality it highlights their weakness and vulnerability. The abolition of the two-stage election system for Dalit representatives and its replacement by reserved seats—as agreed to in the Poona Pact between Gandhi and Ambedkar—opened up vast strategic spaces for the ruling class politics to create stooges from among the political class of Dalits. The two-stage system reasonably ensured that the ultimate elected representative of Dalits would have the approval of the majority of Dalits, as they would have actually voted for him or her. But the contestant for the reserved seat need not bother about the Dalit votes and can still get elected as 'their' representative. The first-past-the-post electoral system already gives scope to the ruling clan parties to engineer fragmentation of votes to ensure arithmetical majority. Caste and community identities play a big role in these electoral strategies. It is through these strategic processes that the ruling classes have effectively pulverised Dalit politics into numerous factions, all engaged in internecine battles for their survival. The one time rock-solid political bloc of

Dalits that emerged under the charismatic leadership of Dr Ambedkar has been completely brokered away to the ruling class parties by the self-appointed leaders who claimed his legacy. These political processes have been a predominant factor in keeping the system of caste alive.

Caste thus continues to control much of the social dynamics in the country and has become an important instrument in politics. It still ordains much of the production organisation and also controls the cultural paradigm. Caste has proved its resilience not only by adapting but by assuming a crucial role in the new formation. Caste consciousness has refused to die; neither education nor migration out of the country has been able to efface it. Its divisive potential continues to thwart the emergence of classes and thus blocks any possibility of radical transformation.

Building Anti-Imperialist Consciousness among Dalits

Anti-imperialism is particularly associated with communists and therefore its usage in the non-communist world, to which the majority of Dalits belong, is not in vogue. While there is considerable discontent among Dalits against neoliberal globalisation, they never refer to it as imperialism. It is not because they do not know what globalisation is, but fundamentally because they do not know what 'imperialism' is. They are rightly concerned about the ill-impacts of globalisation on their livelihood; other things are just outside their purview.

For Dalits, most of whom still grapple with the most mundane matters of life, anti-imperialism stands as a strange abstraction. Indeed, most communist terminology for them is an abstraction: When they are oppressed by the upper castes, the communists say they should wage class struggle; when they tried understanding class struggle, the communists were confused about their class; when they became workers and suffered discrimination at the hands of their fellow class members from other castes, or when as casual hands they came in conflict with the well-off organised workers, the communists condoned or ignored it in the name of working-class unity; when they adored their leaders as their emancipators, the communists abused them as stooges of imperialism; when the well-to-do workers in the organised sector bargained in air-conditioned rooms with the bourgeoisie for higher wages and fat perquisites, the communists hailed it as revolutionary work, but when Dalits struggled to recover their basic human identity, the same communists denigrated it as petty reform; and when they are harassed by the local elites, the communists expect them to wage struggle against the imperialist Bush. Whether it is a question of the political maturity of Dalits or the incapability of the communists to comprehend the reality of this land, the fact remains that there is this fundamental gap between the Dalit and communist camps.

This gap has unfortunately characterised the history of radical movement in this country. The most unfortunate part is that both camps are blissfully unaware of it. The gap is so wide that there is even a kind of ostracism of revolutionary language in the Dalit taxonomy. In such a situation there is no question of any anti-imperialist consciousness germinating in Dalits, though they bear the brunt of globalisation most severely. They are certainly opposed to it, not from any ideological standpoint but purely because it is devastating their lives. What they do not know is its genesis (where this monster comes from), its contents (what it precisely is), its dynamics (how it operates), and its props (which are the factors and forces behind it). In absence of this understanding, they are susceptible to being misled by vested interests towards pseudo targets. Indeed, some organisations like BAMCEF (All India Backward and Minority Communities Employees' Federation) have promoted the populist interpretation that this phenomenon (globalisation) is another conspiracy of the Brahmins against the Dalits. Because of the historical hatred for Brahmins that a section of Dalits bears, such interpretations enjoy considerable acceptability.

Stemming from historical reasons and their own life experiences, Dalits have a strong anti-Brahmin consciousness. Anything contrary to their interests therefore easily tends to get attributed to Brahmin intrigue. But what is the nature of this anti-Brahmin consciousness? Is it complementary to or against the anti-imperialist consciousness? And how can this be instilled in Dalits? These are the kind of questions that the anti-imperialist should grapple with.

Consciousness of any kind germinates from a lived reality in a congenial ideological soil. For a majority of the Dalit population, the lived reality of India has been caste bondage for ages—but even this could not engender the requisite anti-caste consciousness, simply because the ideological soil was not congenial. No sooner, however, than this soil became congenial with the infusion of external nutrients, as it were, in the form of a Western liberal ethos, some amount of modernity, and an institutional framework during the British colonial rule, that one finds anti-caste consciousness suddenly sprouting all over the country among the lower castes and Dalits, the worst victims of the caste system.

With the spread of education among Dalits, the opening of avenues to make money in urban and industrial areas, the growth of money economy itself, and growing job opportunities, a class among Dalits emerged during the colonial period for whom caste became a major hurdle in the path of further progress. The Dalit movement is to be seen as a product of this process. If one observes the consciousness beneath this movement (and for that matter, beneath the anti-Brahmin movement among the Shudras that preceded it), it could be described as anti-Brahminical and pro-British. The former attribute is fundamentally owed to the latter. Dalits were acutely aware that if the British had not ruled India, they would not have been freed from their caste bondage. Even though all the leaders of anti-caste movements (like Mahatma Phule and Babasaheb Ambedkar) were keenly aware of the colonial strategy of the British to exploit divisions among people, they nevertheless used it as an opportunity to leverage their emancipatory struggles. Here lies the historical paradox embedded in Dalit consciousness, that what is detrimental to the hegemony of Hindus (articulated as 'national interest') is beneficial to Dalits.

There is no denying the fact the British colonial state had an intricate strategy at work behind its benign intervention in Indian social issues. As D L Sheth explains:

> The colonial state assumed a dual role: Of a super brahmin who located and relocated disputed statuses of castes in the traditional hierarchy and of a just and modern ruler who wished to 'recognise' rights and aspirations of his weak and poor subjects. This helped the state to protect its colonial political economy from incursions of the emerging nationalist movement. Among other things, it also induced people to organise and represent their interests in politics in terms of caste identities and participate in the economy on the terms and through mechanisms set by the colonial regime.[6]

Notwithstanding these strategic motives there were many changes effected by the colonial state—many of them clearly unintended—which came as boons for Dalits. To quote DL Sheth again:

> On the whole, the colonial regime not only introduced new terms of discourse on caste, but brought about some changes in the caste system itself. A large part of these changes, however, were unintended consequences of the colonial policies; they were related to the larger historical forces of modernisation, secularisation, and urbanisation which had begun to make some impact on the Indian society by the end of 19th and the beginning of the 20th century. But some specific policies of the colonial regime, aimed at delegitimising the power of the traditional social elites and creating support for its own rule, had direct consequences for the caste system. Towards the end of the colonial rule such policies alongside the larger historical forces, had produced some profound and far-reaching changes in the caste system.
>
> The most important among the changes was the formation of a new, trans-local identity among 'lower castes', collectively as a people with the consciousness of being 'oppressed' by the traditional system of hierarchy. The discourse of rights, until then quite alien to the concepts governing ritual hierarchy, made its first appearance in the context of the caste system. New ideological categories like 'social justice' began to interrogate the idea of ritual purity and impurity according to which the traditional stratificatory system endowed

entitlements and disprivileges to hereditary statuses. The established categories of ritual hierarchy began to be confronted with new categories like 'depressed castes' and 'oppressed classes'.

Second, several castes occupying more or less similar locations in different local hierarchies began to organise themselves horizontally into regional and national level associations and federations, as it became increasingly necessary for them to negotiate with the state and in the process project their larger social identity and numerical strength.[7]

Indeed, foreign reigns in India have been consistently beneficial to Dalits. These reigns have symbolised refutation of the presumptuous superiority of Brahminism and exposed it as fake god. They brought new civilisation to the country, which people confined in a fossilised caste framework could not have imagined. They brought opportunities for Dalits, who had the lowest valency in the Hindu social structure, to escape their bondage by entering employment of the alien rulers or convert to the latter's religion. History testifies that a huge population of Dalits had converted to Islam during the early years of the Muslim rule. This exodus was only thwarted by the upper caste converts to Islam who imported their hierarchical notions and Hinduised the Muslim society.

The same thing is seen repeated with the arrival of the Europeans. Coming from relatively distant lands, the Europeans did not have as large numbers as the Muslim hordes from Central Asia, and hence had to rely primarily on local recruitment for their army and services. They found that the most enthusiastic response came from the lower castes, particularly the Dalits. It is the lower caste armies that helped them firmly establish their empire in India. The Koregaon pillar (near Pune), erected in memory of soldiers who died in the decisive battle with the Marathas that marked the establishment of British Empire in India, is a testimony to this phenomenon. European rule also brought with it the Christian missionaries who, among other things, started missionary schools that admitted Dalits along with others. Although fundamentally driven by a colonial logic, the building of infrastructure undertaken by the British, and the capitalist industrialisation that followed in its wake, benefitted Dalits tremendously. The cumulative benefits of these developments threw up a class of Dalits with the consciousness that alien rule was good for Dalits and native Hindu rule was bad. In their fight against native imperialism, they saw external imperialism as an ally!

That is the lived reality of Dalits—a reality that conditions a very particular kind of anti-imperialist consciousness among Dalits. It reveals a contradiction between the native socio-cultural imperialism and the global political-economic imperialism. Historically, they owe their consciousness against the former to the latter. The former is concrete, something they suffer at every step whereas the latter seems abstract, a learnt reality. It is not that they are incapable of seeing the larger picture; rather, they cannot comprehend the relationship of the exploitative processes at work at the global level with their oppression within the Hindu social order.[8] Why should they be against something that has historically benefitted them? If it has an adverse impact on them economically, they would take notice of it, but it would not change their priority. They are caught in the heuristic that what is bad for the *savarnas* must be good for them. This, precisely, is the confusion among Dalits about globalisation. They would rather believe their leaders speaking anti-caste rhetoric over their own experience of the effects of globalisation.

Why is this so? The answer is not far to seek. Dalits still find themselves essentially as they were for centuries; friendless and without empathy in this land. The rightists in this country are the Hindu fundamentalists whose creed it is to revive their Brahminic 'past glory', which is a natural anathema for Dalits. The leftists in this country still do not know what to do with caste. Though they seem to have come out of their confusion symbolised by the 'base-superstructure' syndrome, and are keen to acknowledge the economic aspects of the caste problem, there is not much appreciation of its social, religious, and cultural aspects. Dalit consciousness, laden with the influence of an upwardly mobile middle class during the last several decades, expectedly finds it inadequate. While it is necessary to cleanse the Dalit consciousness of the middle-class influence and orient it towards emancipation of the common masses, the process of achieving it cannot be sublimation as the left would have it. The left will have to build confidence among the Dalits by outcompeting other forces in waging and supporting the genuine struggles of Dalit masses.

If today many youth are found attracted to certain left formations, it is not so much because they are ideologically propelled to do so but because of the hopelessness of the Dalit movement. While there is nothing wrong with this negative propulsion at this stage, it needs to gather a more positive momentum. These Dalit youth must become conscious torchbearers of the revolutionary ideology, as Gramscian organic intellectuals, and be educators of the Dalit masses without detaching them, or themselves, from their settings, as has so far been the case.

References

M N Roy, 1917—*India In Transition*. Bombay: Nachiketa Publications Limited

D L Sheth, August 1999—'Secularisation of Caste and Making of New Middle Class', in *Economic & Political Weekly*, August 21–28 1999, at http://jan.ucc.nau.edu/~sj6/epwshethmclass1.htm (Accessed April 2017)

Anand Teltumbde, 2005—*Anti-Imperialism and Annihilation of Castes*. Thane: Ramai Prakashan

Sukhadeo Thorat, 2005—'Current Status of Dalits', in IIDS, 2005—*Occasional Papers*. New Delhi: IIDS (Indian Institute of Dalit Studies)

Notes

1. Ed: This essay is an edited combination of the Introduction, Chapter 2 ('Caste is "the" issue'), and Chapter 6 ('Anti-imperialist Consciousness among Dalits') from the author's 2005 book *Anti-Imperialism and Annihilation of Castes*. I am grateful to the author for his permission to prepare this combination and to publish the resulting essay.

2. M N Roy, 'Memoirs', pp 551–552, cited by G D Parikh, Foreword, in Roy 1917, pp 6–7.

3. Ed: This industry because footwear was traditionally made of leather and under the Brahminical caste system, handling carcasses of dead animals—required for making leather—was work it reserved for its 'untouchables', the Dalits.

4. All statistics from Thorat, 2005.

5. See Tables III, IV, and V in the author's 2005 book *Anti-Imperialism and Annihilation of Castes*.

6. Sheth, August 1999.

7. ibid.

8. Ed: For a more complete discussion of this important issue, see the author's 2005 book (Teltumbde 2005).

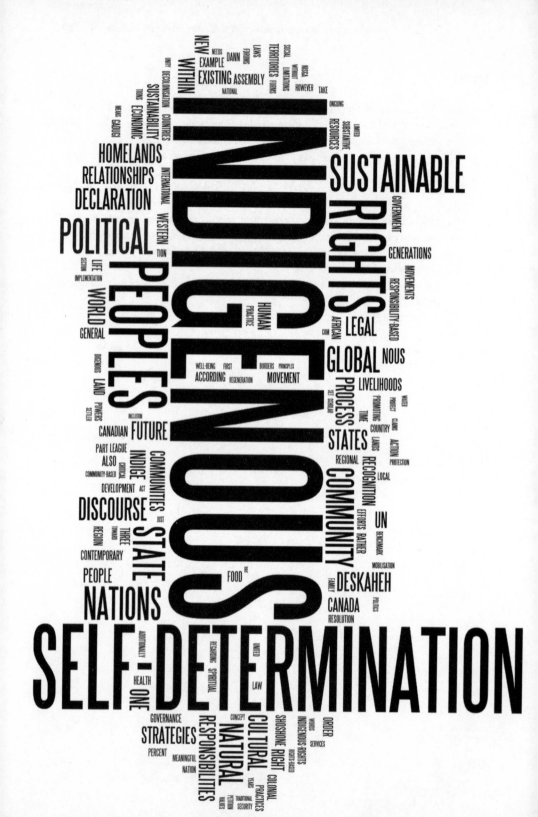

Rethinking Self-Determination:
Lessons from the Indigenous-Rights Discourse[1]
Jeff Corntassel

It is still true that the first part of self-determination is the self. In our minds and in our souls, we need to reject the colonists' control and authority, their definition of who we are and what our rights are, their definition of what is worthwhile and how one should live, their hypocritical and pacifying moralities. We need to rebel against what they want us to become, start remembering the qualities of our ancestors and act on those remembrances. This is the kind of spiritual revolution that will ensure our survival.

—Taiaiake Alfred[2]

What Is Self-Determination? Moving Past the Limitations of Existing Rights-Discourse

How is self-determination being framed in the contemporary indigenous-rights discourse? To what degree are indigenous peoples asserting visions of self-determination on their own terms in order to "start remembering the qualities of our ancestors and act on those remembrances"?[3] And what lessons can be drawn from the indigenous rights discourse that might be relevant both to indigenous peoples' movements and to other movements for peace and justice that are taking place in the world?

The '1999 Nisga'a Final Agreement', which resulted from the British Columbia Treaty Process (BCTP) and represents federal and provincial governmental efforts to permanently resolve indigenous land claims in Canada, provides some important insights into the current realities of indigenous self-determination movements in Canada and around the world.[4] According to the comprehensive analysis of the BCTC made by Kanien'kehaka (Mohawk) scholar Taiaiake Alfred, whose words provide the epigraph to this article, the $190 million paid to the Nisga'a tribal council, coupled with surrender of their tax exemption status under the Indian Act and the dire prospects for future economic growth in the Nass Valley, makes it "difficult to see how the Nisga'a people will find the money to survive as a nation".[5]

As Alfred points out, "Most likely, Nisga'a people will find themselves having to sell off land, mineral, fish and timber rights to fund their government and social programmes".[6] Political scientist Jim Tully provides a similar assessment:

As far as I am aware, this is the first time in the history of Great Turtle Island that an indigenous people, or at least 61 percent of its eligible voters, has voluntarily surrendered their rights as indigenous peoples, not to mention surrendering over 90 percent of their territory, and accepted their status as a distinctive minority with group rights within Canada. This appears to be the first success of strategies of extinguishment (release) and incorporation by agreement.[7]

Unfortunately, the land-settlement strategies employed by Canada extinguish original indigenous title to their territories and force community members to accept monetary payouts for their unrecovered land. In this case, the Nisga'a final agreement left 92 per cent of their original homelands to Canada and put the community at risk by leading them into an unsustainable future under the banner of "self-government". As with the Nisga'a Agreement, states tend to narrowly frame self-determination by focusing on state political / legal recognition of indigenous peoples as self-governing entities while diverting energies from more substantive discussions regarding the reclamation of indigenous territories, livelihoods, and natural resources, and the regeneration of community languages and culturally-based practices.

As the above example demonstrates, the rights discourse can take indigenous peoples only so far. Over the past 30–40 years, indigenous self-determination claims have been framed by states and global organisations in four distinct ways that jeopardise the futures of indigenous communities. First, the rights-based discourse has resulted in the compartmentalisation of indigenous powers of self-determination by separating questions of homelands and natural resources from those of political / legal recognition of a limited indigenous autonomy within the existing framework of the host state(s).[8] This was evident from the above-referenced Nisga'a Final Agreement, which provided a political / legal basis for limited autonomy but neglected to address interrelated issues of regenerating sustainable livelihoods, food security, and renewal of community relationships with the natural world.

Second, in several cases, the rights discourse has led states to deny the identities or very existence of indigenous peoples residing within their borders (or to reframe them as minority populations or other designations that carry less weight or accountability under international law).[9] For example, Botswana refuses to acknowledge peoples residing within its borders as indigenous (that is, San, Nama / Khoe), instead referring to them in its constitution as a "race", "community", or "tribe". Botswana staunchly opposed ratification of the nonbinding United Nations Declaration on the Rights of Indigenous Peoples (hereafter referred to as the Declaration), claiming that the Declaration "raised issues with serious economic, political, and constitutional ramifications, which in Botswana's view, could only contribute to ethnic conflicts within nations, of which Africans had had more than a fair share".[10]

Third, the framing of rights as political / legal entitlements has deemphasised the cultural responsibilities and relationships that indigenous peoples have with their families and the natural world (homelands, plant life, animal life, etc) that are critical for their well-being and the well-being of future generations. In contrast with the dominant Western and settler perspective on self-determination and sustainability premised on possessive individualism, indigenous peoples tend to "concern themselves with (and have based their whole worldview on) the idea of learning how to give back to Creation, rather than taking away".[11]

Finally, the rights discourse has limited the applicability of decolonisation and restoration frameworks for indigenous peoples by establishing ad hoc restrictions. This was clear with the ratification of UN General Assembly Resolution 1514 (1960), which set limits on decolonisation through the implementation of a so-called 'Salt Water Thesis', stipulating that only territories separated by water or those that were geographically separate from the colonising power could invoke self-determination.[12] There have been some promising initiatives undertaken recently for setting new global standards for restorative justice, such as UN General Assembly Resolution 60/147 (2006) to implement "Basic Principles and Guidelines on the Right to a Remedy and Reparation for Victims of Gross Violations of International Human Rights Law and Serious Violations of International Humanitarian Law".[13] However, the applicability of resolution 60/147 becomes limited when attempting to restore territories and natural resources to indigenous peoples as a result of ongoing colonial encroachment by their host states.

In order to move beyond the limitations of the existing rights discourse, I propose that indigenous powers and views of self-determination be rethought and reframed to meet contemporary challenges to indigenous nationhood. Strategies that invoke existing human rights norms and that seek solely political and legal recognition of indigenous self-determination will not lead to a sustainable self-determination process for the survival of future generations of indigenous peoples. Additionally, indigenous mobilisation strategies of *surveillance* and *shame* have not been effective for generating substantive changes in existing human-rights norms and customary international law.[14] In order for indigenous self-determination to be meaningful, it should be economically, environmentally, and culturally viable, and inextricably linked to indigenous relationships with the natural world. These relationships are discussed specifically in Special Rapporteur Erica-Irene Daes's comprehensive UN report entitled *Indigenous Peoples' Permanent Sovereignty over Natural Resources*.

In this report, Daes asserts that "the right of permanent self-determination *over natural resources* was recognised because it was understood early on that without it, the right of self-determination would be meaningless".[15] In other words, self-determination has to be *sustainable in practice* or it merely becomes another venerated paper right. Unfortunately, what is considered 'sustainable practice' by states comes at a high price for indigenous communities, often leading to further degradation of their homelands and natural resources.[16] It is time for indigenous peoples to reassert sustainability on their own terms. Therefore, I propose the concept of *sustainable self-determination* as a benchmark for the restoration of indigenous livelihoods and territories and for future indigenous political mobilisation.

In the next section of this essay, I examine some limitations of the existing rights discourse and how these limitations have been expressed by states and global institutions since Cayuga Chief Deskaheh's visit to the League of Nations in 1923–1924 (which I outline at the beginning of the section). The third section, "Towards Sustainable Self-Determination", elaborates the concept of sustainable self-determination, a concept that can become a credible benchmark for future indigenous political mobilisation. The fourth section, "Moving from Rights to Responsibilities", links theory to praxis by focusing on specific strategies that can move the discourse from rights to responsibilities. I conclude with certain findings and proposals from this study that I believe can yield significant theoretical and practical understandings regarding the effectiveness of indigenous transnational activist networks and for promoting a holistic, sustainable model of self-determination for future generations.

Illusions of Inclusion in the Contemporary Indigenous-Rights Discourse

Deskaheh, who lived from 1872 to 1925, and was Cayuga chief and Speaker of the Six Nations Council on Turtle Island,[17] set the tone in 1921–23 for the contemporary global indigenous-rights movement, and also exposed limitations in the rights discourse that persist to this day.[18] Deskaheh worked tirelessly during the eighteen months he lived in Geneva promoting Haudenosaunee self-determination. His strategies included seeking League of Nations recognition for Six Nations as a state, and attempting to take Canada before the World Court.[19] While he did not gain formal recognition at the League of Nations, Deskaheh's historic efforts inspired future indigenous activists.

In 1921, Deskaheh travelled to England to protest Canadian treaty violations and encroachment onto Iroquois homelands. Asserting that "they would not deal with a Canadian domestic problem", British authorities refused to even consider Deskaheh's request for assistance.[20] In September 1923, Deskaheh shifted tactics and left for Geneva, Switzerland, carrying a Haudenosaunee Confederacy passport. Deskaheh's Haudenosaunee passport was recognised by the Swiss government, and, once in Geneva, he sought to stave off Canadian attempts to "bring our lands under administration of Canadian laws and policy".[21] On August 7 1923, Deskaheh submitted a petition to the League of Nations via the government of the Netherlands to challenge Canadian encroachment into Iroquois territory:

> We have exhausted every other recourse for gaining protection of our sovereignty by peaceful means before making this appeal to secure protection through the League of Nations. If this effort on our part shall fail we shall be compelled to resist by defensive action upon our part this British invasion of our Home-land for we are determined to live the free people that we were born.[22]

The governments of the United Kingdom and Canada made great efforts to prevent a debate on Deskaheh's petition.[23] To stop his intervention at the League of Nations, the Canadian government formally protested "the Netherlands' Government's action in bringing a controversy between the Canadian government and individuals owing it allegiance, which is entirely of domestic concern".[24] Consequently, Deskaheh was never able to bring his petition before the League of Nations Assembly.

In 1924, while Deskaheh was still in Geneva, the Canadian government retaliated by dissolving the Six Nations Council and imposing an elected system under the rules of the Canadian Indian Act.[25] The Canadian authorities also broke into the records of the Six Nations Council and "took from there a number of wampum belts, revered as sacred by the Iroquois, refusing, on demand, to return them".[26] After being exiled from his homeland, Deskaheh passed away on June 27 1925, in Rochester, New York. Despite his unsuccessful effort to secure support from the League of Nations, Deskaheh's words and strategies are just as farsighted today.

Based on an analysis of Deskaheh's strategic interventions in Geneva, it is apparent that five major tactics were used by settler governments to obstruct Deskaheh's pursuit of self-determination:

1. The United Kingdom used major-power intervention and procedural appeals to block the Haudenosaunee claim from reaching the League of Nations General Assembly;

2. Canada claimed that this was not a global issue but "entirely of domestic concern";[27]

3. Canada asserted that this was not a matter of group / collective rights but a matter between "the Canadian Government and *individuals* owing it allegiance";[28]

4. Canada claimed that Haudenosaunee claims were not legitimate but were merely "calculated to embarrass this Government";[29]

5. Finally, Canada contended that Six Nations were not "an organised and self-governing people so as to form a political unit apart from Canada" but that they were integrated into the Canadian state as citizens.[30]

Over eighty years after Deskaheh's intervention, there is a broad recognition of indigenous rights in name only, accompanied by little movement in state discursive positions regarding the enactment of fundamental human rights within indigenous nations. Unfortunately, some of the above tactics of exclusion, domestication, and assimilation are still part of standard state practices towards indigenous peoples. While indigenous peoples now share a conference room with UN member states in the Permanent Forum on Indigenous Issues (PFII), this does not necessarily signal that indigenous / state relations have been significantly restructured, nor that indigenous voices are truly being heard. In this case, there is a danger of co-optation and an *illusion of inclusion* regarding indigenous participation within global and regional forums.[31]

This was especially evident in November 2006, when UN General Assembly member states voted to delay ratification of the Declaration on the Rights of Indigenous Peoples. This legally non-binding UN declaration, which had been approved by the UN Human Rights Council in June 2006 after twenty-two years of consultation and development with indigenous peoples and state governments, was initially blocked by a Namibian-led coalition of thirty African countries plus Western settler countries such as Australia, Canada, and New Zealand. Citing concerns over how to define indigenous, conflicts with existing state constitutions, and official government policies over land claims and natural resources, eighty-two countries then voted to delay action on the declaration until after widespread "consultations" had been held.

One year later, after some relatively minor modifications, the UN General Assembly voted to ratify the declaration on September 13 2007. The final General Assembly vote found 143 countries in favour of the declaration, with four voting against it: Australia, Canada, New Zealand, and the United States.[32] Amendments to the declaration included one section in the preamble that recognised "that the situation of indigenous peoples varies from region to region and from country to country". Another addition advocated the protection of "the territorial integrity or political unity of sovereign and independent States" (article 46).[33]

While this vote represents a step forward for the global indigenous-rights discourse, it is important to understand continued state resistance to indigenous self-determination and the failure to provide legally binding human-rights standards for indigenous peoples.

Some African countries initially opposed the Declaration on the Rights of Indigenous Peoples based on their understanding of UN General Assembly resolution 1514 (1960), which was entitled the "Declaration on the Granting of Independence to Colonial Countries and Peoples". Resolution 1514 set limits on decolonisation through the implementation of the Salt Water Thesis mentioned above.[34] In 1964, the Organisation of African Unity (known today as the African Union) passed a resolution concerning 'Border Disputes Among African States', which reaffirmed their commitment to the Salt Water Thesis by pledging "to respect the frontiers existing on their achievement of national independence".[35]

Ironically, this denial of 'internal' decolonisation only served to legitimate the arbitrary state boundaries drawn by colonial powers from the sixteenth century up to the Berlin Africa Conference of 1884–1885.[36] While indigenous peoples do not generally seek secession from host state(s), countries responding to indigenous self-determination claims often cite fears of a "domino effect" in which countless separatist movements would emerge within their borders and fragment the state while promoting instability in the region.[37]

Invoking similar themes of fears of secession and preservation of state borders, African states and Western countries (Australia, Canada, New Zealand, the United States) have actively opposed the ratification of the Declaration. For example, in January 2007 the African Union passed a resolution deferring a vote until key questions regarding how to define indigenous peoples, the scope of indigenous self-determination and land and resource ownership, and the maintenance of state territorial unity were addressed.[38]

In addition to promoting "national and territorial unity" at the expense of indigenous rights to self-determination, African states are also challenging the very identities of indigenous peoples. On May 17 2007, African states provided the UN General Assembly president with thirty proposed amendments to the Declaration. One of these focused on defining indigenous peoples within regional and state contexts:

> Recognising that the situation of indigenous peoples varies from region to region, country to country and from community to community, every country or region shall have the prerogative to define who constitutes indigenous people in their respective countries or regions taking into account its national or regional peculiarities.[39]

In order to counter frequent state denials of indigenous identities, "two of the most active global organisations promoting indigenous rights, the United Nations Working Group on Indigenous Populations (WGIP) and the International Labour Organisation (ILO), have advocated an unlimited right to self-identification."[40] Yet some of the changes proposed by the African states found their way into the amended declaration, indicating that conflicts over indigenous self-identification and identity remain:

> Recognising also that the situation of indigenous peoples varies from region to region and from country to country and that the significance of national and regional particularities and various historical and cultural backgrounds should be taken into consideration.[41]

Allowing for national and regional particularities appears reasonable on the surface, but is often a façade for denying indigenous self-determination. Even when particular country constitutions, whether in Kenya or Colombia, outline clear guidelines for the protection of indigenous knowledge, intellectual property, and community lands, and protection from the exploitation of natural resources within indigenous territories, these rights are compartmentalised to the point of detaching the issue of promoting sustainable livelihoods from questions of protecting indigenous knowledge. Additionally, despite the multilevel strategies indigenous peoples employ to change existing human rights norms, in many instances energy is being diverted from community regeneration efforts and channelled into the global indigenous-rights discourse without any noticeable local impact.

According to a recent survey of indigenous organisations conducted by the UN Office of the High Commissioner on Human Rights, 68 per cent of respondents indicated that, globally, the Indigenous Decade resulted in positive changes, including "better access to international activities, and exchange of experience and contacts with other Indigenous organisations and representatives".[42] However, it was telling that only 36 per cent saw positive changes at the community level, while 44 per cent said there had been "no improvements locally".[43] As these survey results suggest, meaningful strategies for self-determination and community regeneration have not been attained through active participation in state and global forums.

The contemporary activism of (US) Western Shoshone leaders Carrie and Mary Dann illustrates how paper rights do not always correspond with community realities.[44] For example, in what ways can a ratified, nonbinding Declaration on the Rights of Indigenous Peoples impact indigenous nations' struggles toward sustainable self-determination? In 1993, the Dann sisters filed a petition for redress with the Inter-American Commission on Human Rights (OAS). Like Deskaheh, the Dann sisters had exhausted all other physical and political options to protect their ancestral homelands. Responding to their petition, the US government argued that the treaty rights of the Western Shoshone to their territory had been extinguished in 1872 due to gradual encroachment by non-natives.[45] In 2003, the Inter-American Commission disagreed with the US assessment and concluded that the government had violated the Dann's ancestral homeland rights as well as due process and equality under the law.[46] Consequently, the OAS recommended that all US law and policy regarding indigenous peoples (especially property rights) be reviewed. Despite the symbolic victory, the case could not be referred to the Inter-American Court because the US had not ratified the Inter-American Convention or accepted the court's jurisdiction.

Carrie Dann has continued to seek the return of Western Shoshone ancestral lands. In August 2005, Shoshone elders filed a petition with the UN Committee on the Elimination of Racial Discrimination (CERD) calling for immediate action against the US for fraudulently claiming ownership of 90 per cent of Shoshone homelands. On March 10 2006, the committee responded to the petition by urging the US to "'freeze', 'desist' and 'stop' actions being taken or threatened to be taken against the Western Shoshone Peoples of the Western Shoshone Nation".[47] The CERD called for immediate US action to "respect and protect the human rights of the Western Shoshone peoples" and "freeze all efforts to privatise Western Shoshone ancestral lands for transfer to multinational extractive industries and energy developers".[48]

Finally, the committee gave the US a deadline—July 15 2006—"to provide it with information on the action it had taken".[49] While the US still refuses to comply with the rulings of the CERD and other global forums, Carrie Dann asks a key question: "Where else do we go?".[50] In a 2006 interview, Dann said, "I can't believe that this is happening supposedly in America where everybody talks about democracy, and how good democracy is. As far as the indigenous people go, we have not seen that democracy".[51] After fighting for their homelands for more than thirty years, the struggle of Carrie Dann and other Shoshone elders continues through the Western Shoshone Defence Project. It is clear from their struggles, and other examples of indigenous struggles throughout the world, that the rights discourse has not led to the realisation of sustainable self-determination for indigenous nations at the local level. As Dann suggests, now is the time to rethink existing strategies grounded in the global indigenous rights discourse.

Unfortunately, in the contemporary rights discourse, "Indigeneity is legitimised and negotiated only as a set of state-derived individual rights aggregated into a community social context—a very different concept than that of collective rights pre-existing and independent of the state".[52] Framing of indigenous rights by states and global institutions persists as indigenous peoples confront the *illusion of inclusion* in global forums such as the PFII. In his comprehensive examination of state positions regarding the Declaration on the Rights of Indigenous Peoples, legal scholar Patrick Thornberry found that several countries, led by the US, Australia, and New Zealand, consistently voiced five main objections to the UN Declaration during the last twenty-two years of deliberations:

1. Indigenous groups are not peoples entitled to self-determination;
2. The content of self-determination is too vague for inscription in the declaration;
3. Self-determination means secession;
4. Autonomy is enough—right of self-determination is superfluous;
5. Self-determination of indigenous peoples divides the state.[53]

When one compares these objections to the objections voiced during Deskaheh's time, it is clear that while the indigenous-rights terrain has changed, fundamental challenges to indigenous self-determination claims persist, nearly a century later. Yet while the global indigenous-rights movement has directed most of its energies toward responding to these objections in an effort to ratify the Declaration, a more subtle danger exists. The pursuit of a political / legal rights-based discourse leads indigenous peoples to frame their goals / issues in a state-centred (rather than a community-centred) way. According to Dene political theorist Glen Coulthard, "the politics of recognition in its contemporary form promises to reproduce the very configurations of colonial power that Indigenous peoples' demands for recognition have historically sought to transcend".[54] When they mimic the state-centric rights discourse, indigenous nations run the risk of seeking political and / or economic solutions to contemporary challenges that require sustainable, spiritual foundations. Rather than asserting community-based *powers* of sustainable self-determination, the quest for state recognition of political / legal rights has only entrenched some indigenous peoples within the colonial status quo:

> The dominance of the legal approach to self-determination has, over time, helped produce a class of Aboriginal 'citizens' whose rights and identities have become defined solely in relation to the colonial state and its apparatus. Similarly, strategies that have sought self-determination via mainstream economic development have facilitated the creation of a new elite of Aboriginal capitalists whose thirst for profit has come to outweigh their ancestral obligations to the land and to others.[55]

In order to overcome the limitations of the rights discourse, new strategies are needed to shift indigenous political mobilisation efforts from rights to responsibilities. Additionally, indigenous self-determination needs to be rearticulated on indigenous terms as part of a sustainable, community-based process rather than as narrowly constructed political / legal entitlements.

Towards Sustainable Self-Determination

Previous research on the self-determination of peoples tends to focus on political / legal recognition of this right, while giving little consideration to the environment, community health / well-being, natural resources, sustainability, and the transmission of cultural practices to future generations as critical, interlocking features of an indigenous *self-determination process*.[56] As indigenous legal scholar S James Anaya asserts, "Any conception of self-determination that does not take into account the multiple patterns of human association and interdependency is at best incomplete or more likely distorted".[57] Even when culture or land are mentioned as essential parts of indigenous self-determination, these linkages are often expressed within a narrow rights framework that diminishes the full scope of these ongoing relationships to the natural world and / or fails to describe sustainability as a critical benchmark for an indigenous self-determination process.[58]

While Anaya differentiates between *remedial* and *substantive* forms of self-determination however, he does not account for *sustainable self-determination* as a critical benchmark in the ongoing self-determination process. When differentiating substantive forms of self-determination from remedial ones, Anaya concedes that remedial forms of self-determination, such as decolonisation, tend to be limited by practices of state sovereignty, which "influence the degree to which remedies may be subject to international scrutiny".[59] Given the existing barriers to indigenous decolonisation through the enforcement of the Salt Water Thesis and other global norms designed to protect existing state borders, indigenous peoples have also found substantive forms of self-determination, which are described as "a standard of governmental legitimacy within the modern human rights frame", to be limited.[60] It remains to be seen whether UN General Assembly Resolution 60/147 (2006) on rights to remedies and reparations, as referred to above, will be widely applied to indigenous peoples and their decolonisation efforts. While there are existing political / legal foundations for substantive and remedial forms of self-determination, the attainment of these standards or global norms is meaningless in a discussion of ongoing self-determination without considering a third factor—the sustainability of self-determination in praxis.

It follows that a process of indigenous self-determination is more than a political / legal struggle; at its core are spiritual and relational responsibilities that are continuously renewed. Unfortunately, as Alfred and Corntassel point out, "there are new faces of empire that are attempting to strip indigenous peoples of their very spirit as nations and of all that is held sacred, threatening their sources of connection to their distinct existences and the sources of their spiritual power: Relationships to each other, communities, homelands, ceremonial life, languages, histories. ... These connections are crucial to living a meaningful life for any human being".[61] While previous studies have treated indigenous political autonomy, governance, the environment, and community health as separate concepts, in actuality they are intrinsically linked. For example, health has much deeper meaning than just the absence of disease or injury, as Arquette et al point out in their study of Mohawks of Akwesasne:

> Health, then, has many definitions for the Mohawk people of Akwesasne. Health is spiritual. Health is rooted in the heart of the culture. Health is based on peaceful, sustainable relationships with other peoples including family, community, Nation, the natural world, and spiritual beings.[62]

After considering this conceptualisation of community health / well-being, it becomes apparent that indigenous struggles to "make meaningful choices in matters touching upon all spheres of life on a continuous basis" warrant further exploration in terms of "What is sustainability?" and "What is being transmitted to future generations?".[63] Deskaheh's articulation of self-determination gets at the heart of indigenous struggles today: "We are determined to live the free people that we were born".[64]

Moreover, the process of living as the "free people that we were born" entails having the freedom to practice indigenous livelihoods, maintain food security, and apply natural laws on indigenous homelands in a sustainable manner.[65] Critical to this process is the long-term sustainability of indigenous livelihoods, which includes the transmission of these cultural practices to future generations. Tully elaborates: "The right of self-determination is, on any plausible account of its contested criteria, the right of a people to govern themselves by their own laws and exercise jurisdiction over their territories".[66] Embedded in this broader conceptualisation of self-determination is a set of interlocking and reciprocal responsibilities to one's community, family, clans / societies (an aspect of some, not all, indigenous nations), homelands, and the natural world.

While the Brundtland Commission defined sustainability in 1987 as "meeting the needs of the present without compromising the ability of future generations to meet their own needs", this definition does not go far enough as a benchmark for indigenous political, cultural, economic, and environmental *restorative* justice—both in theory and in practice.[67] For indigenous peoples, sustainability is intrinsically linked to the transmission of traditional knowledge and cultural practices to future generations.[68] Without the ability of community members to continuously renew their relationships with the natural world (gathering medicines, hunting and fishing, basket-making, etc), indigenous languages, traditional teachings, family structures, and livelihoods are all jeopardised.

Indigenous connections between well-being and food security / livelihoods are critical to the realisation and practice of *sustainable self-determination*. When such relationships are severed, "the knowledge, worldviews, values and practices about these relationships and about other aspects of their food and agro-ecological systems, commonly erode over time as well".[69] In other words, disruptions to indigenous livelihoods, governance, and natural-world relationships can jeopardise the overall health, well-being, identity, and continuity of indigenous communities.

Just as contemporary research on self-determination tends to exclude sustainability and environmental factors from the process, research on integrated ecosystem assessment tends to exclude culture as a key criterion for sustainability. However, according to one comprehensive ecosystem assessment framework, "cultural services" are important benefits that people obtain from ecosystems through "spiritual enrichment, cognitive development, reflection, recreation and aesthetic experiences".[70] Examples of cultural services include cultural diversity, knowledge systems, educational values, social relations, sense of place, and cultural heritage values.[71] Just as with the three other components that comprise a viable environmental ecosystem, such as "supporting services" (production of atmospheric oxygen, soil formation, etc), "provisioning services" (food, fibre, natural medicines, fresh water, etc), and "regulating services" (air-quality maintenance, climate regulation, regulation of human disease, and so on), cultural services are thus an integral part of an indigenous ecosystem.[72]

Sustainable self-determination as a process is premised on the notion that evolving indigenous livelihoods, food security, community governance, relationships with homelands and the natural world, and ceremonial life can be practiced today locally and regionally, thus enabling the transmission of these traditions and practices to future generations. Operating at multiple levels, sustainable self-determination seeks to regenerate the implementation of indigenous natural laws on indigenous homelands and expand the scope of an indigenous self-determination process.

First, it refutes global and state political / legal recognition and colonial strategies founded on economic dependency as the main avenues to meaningful self-determination. Second, this approach rejects the compartmentalisation of standard political / legal definitions of self-determination by considering social, economic, cultural, and political factors of shared governance and relational accountability for a broader view of self-determination that can be sustained over future generations. Third, rather than engaging solely in the global indigenous-rights discourse, sustainable self-determination operates at and focuses on the community level as a process to perpetuate indigenous livelihoods locally via the regeneration of family, clan, and individual roles and responsibilities to their homelands. Finally, indigenous peoples begin to significantly influence the global political economy, and contribute to global sustainability, by rebuilding and re-strengthening "their *local* and *regional* indigenous economies, which are by definition inherently sustainable".[73] By starting with the regeneration of individual and family responsibilities in the self-determination process, indigenous communities hold the potential to re-establish larger regional trading networks with each other to promote formidable alliances and sustainable futures.

What, then, does sustainable self-determination look like in practice? While applications vary according to indigenous and state contexts, one example is the Native Federation of Madre de Dios (FENAMAD), which is a coalition of twenty-seven indigenous groups who have created a three-thousand-square-mile territory in Peru for indigenous nations to live as free people, as they were born.[74] The three main indigenous nations of FENAMAD sustain their communities mainly through fishing from one of the three main waterways in the region. In order to protect their livelihoods, these nations have set up sentry posts along the Las Piedra and Hahumanu rivers to monitor traffic and report illegal loggers to

Peruvian authorities. Additionally, community members have fought to protect their homelands from encroachment. Over the past three years, two indigenous peoples and two loggers have died in direct confrontations.[75]

Another example of sustainable self-determination in principle and practice is the White Earth Land Recovery Project (WELRP), which was created in 1989 to restore the Gaawaabaabanikaag land base, increase ecological relationships to the land, facilitate language fluency, and strengthen cultural practices for the Anishnaabe peoples on Turtle Island. One of the major components of the WELRP is Mino Mijim ('good food programme'), which provides traditional foods such as wild rice, bison meat, and hominy corn to diabetic elderly Anishnaabes.[76] Additionally, while the White Earth Anishnaabe hold only 9 per cent of their original homelands, they seek to reclaim more of their territory so that a sustainable land base exists for future generations.[77] In an effort to fight the genetic modification of their traditional foods, such as corn and wild rice, WELRP has sought to regenerate traditional agricultural systems on the White Earth Reservation. As a testament to its local and global success, in 2003 WELRP received the International Slow Food Award for its work to protect wild rice from genetic modification, and for its efforts to restore community-based food security.[78]

Besides FENAMAD and WELRP, indigenous movements in Juchitan, Chiapas, and other parts of Mexico, as well as CONIAE in Ecuador, also demonstrate commitments to practices of sustainable self-determination. The above examples mark a stark contrast to state-sanctioned forms of legally oriented indigenous self-determination that are inherently unsustainable, such as indigenous nations' economies and livelihoods that are conditioned by state budgets / neoliberal reforms rather than community governance grounded in natural laws and relationships to homelands and natural resources. The UN Declaration offers additional insights into the implementation of sustainable self-determination in Article 20, including restitution for the deprivation of such a right:

1. Indigenous peoples have the right to maintain and develop their political, economic, and social systems or institutions, to be secure in the enjoyment of their own means of subsistence and development, and to engage freely in all their traditional and other economic activities;
2. Indigenous peoples deprived of their means of subsistence and development are entitled to just and fair redress.[79]

While the Declaration promotes a broader vision of indigenous self-determination, it ultimately does not go far enough in advocating global benchmarks for a sustainable self-determination process. Despite potential limitations, however, "a ratified Declaration could be a useful strategic platform for deeper Indigenous challenges to the state-centric system".[80] However, indigenous peoples would need to overcome the risks of co-optation and the politics of distraction, which are endemic to working within a rights-based discourse, in order to pose a credible threat to the state-centric system. After demonstrating the necessity for a sustainable self-determination discourse, what are some specific strategies for reshaping the indigenous political discourse from rights to responsibilities?

Moving from Rights to Responsibilities

By advocating a shift in focus from rights to responsibilities, I am urging that communities act to assert their powers and responsibilities as nations in order to promote an indigenous-centred discourse on sustainable self-determination. In order to reposition indigenous peoples philosophically and politically in a movement for community, family, and individual regeneration, it is critical to begin with indigenous community-based *responsibilities* in order to open new pathways for sustainable self-determination. For substantive decolonisation and community regeneration to take place on a wider scale, the identification and implementation of non-state, community-based solutions should take precedence. For substantive changes to occur in the state system, indigenous responsibility-based movements must supplant rights-based movements.

In the words of the late Lakota scholar Vine Deloria, Jr, "The basic problem is that American society is a rights society, not a responsibility society".[81] Oren Lyons, the faithkeeper of the Onon-daga nation, goes on to describe some of our responsibilities as indigenous peoples: "You choose your own leaders. You put 'em up, and you take 'em down. But you, the people, are responsible. You're responsible for your life; you're responsible for everything".[82] Ultimately, as Lyons and Deloria point out, it is one's individual and shared responsibilities to the natural world that form the basis for indigenous governance and relationships to family, community, and homelands. These are the foundational natural laws and powers of indigenous communities since time immemorial.

As Ani-yun-wiya,[83] our responsibilities to natural laws and communities govern us. Drawing on our indigenous languages can help identify our shared Ani-yun-wiya responsibilities and viable community self-determination strategies. Invoking our indigenous languages also exposes some of the incompatibilities between settler and indigenous values. In this regard, the Ani-yun-wiya concept of *Gadugi* provides some direction toward a new conceptualisation of responsibilities, which are relational or family-driven:

> Built in community camaraderie; whatever issues / concerns arising in collective living have to be addressed in a unity way; No one is left alone to climb out of a life endeavor; it is a collective community base.[84]

According to Tsalagi elder Benny Smith, Gadugi should be part of a continuous process rather than compartmentalised in everyday life. Commitment to the principles of Gadugi also demonstrates the interrelationships between spirituality and politics in indigenous communities. As with other indigenous nations on Turtle Island, Ani-yun-wiya viewed political actions of reciprocity and representation as going hand-in-hand with spiritual integrity.[85] Indigenous political actions emanate from our spiritual commitments; political or economic actions were not complete unless they were grounded in natural laws. According to Lyons, "Spirituality is the highest form of politics, and our spirituality is directly involved in Government".[86]

Rather than seeking recognition of our 'human rights' from colonial institutions, our focus can be redirected towards local, indigenous-centred, responsibility-based movements. A responsibility-based movement enacts powers (versus rights) of sustainable self-determination and emphasises diplomatic and trade relationships with other indigenous nations. To a large degree, the challenge is to make indigenous communities the central focus and take state recognition / involvement away from our everyday struggles as much as possible. Tsalagi scholar Andrea Smith addresses the question of how states should be excluded or de-emphasised from the futures of indigenous peoples:

> If we acknowledge the state as a perpetrator of violence against women (particularly indigenous women and women of colour) and as a perpetrator of genocide against indigenous peoples, we are challenged to imagine alternative forms of governance that do not presume the continuing existence of the US in particular and the nation-state in general.[87]

Our challenge in promoting responsibility-based movements is to de-centre the state from discussions of indigenous political, social, economic, and cultural mobilisation. What do responsibility-based movements look like? One example is the "deprofessionalisation" movement initiated by three indigenous scholars in Peru. Each of these three men believed that being professors at a university was the best way to help their communities, and each of them came to the slow and painful realisation that the development projects they were promoting were utter failures and "profoundly alien to the native peasantry".[88] So, in 1987, all three left their secure jobs and founded PRATEC, a nongovernmental organisation— in other words, "they deprofessionalised themselves".[89] They now assist Andean indigenous peoples in reappropriating their lands by forming *ayllus*, which is a local community of related persons (similar to the Tsalagi concept of Gadugi). Within these reconstituted *ayllus*, "they cultivate the land in their own manner, evidence of the vibrancy of native practices and culture".[90] PRATEC members work only through such direct action and avoid participation in formal politics, which they see as a "world committed to development and modernisation".[91] Their deprofessionalisation movement continues to gather new members in Peru as they see "the need to decolonise their minds in order to clearly see and participate in the Andean world".[92]

In another contemporary example of a responsibility-based action, Kanaka Maoli (Native Hawaiian) activists challenged the patenting of three varieties of taro (Palehua, Paakala, and Pauakea) by the University of Hawaii (UH) in January 2006. Kalo (taro) is a sacred plant and is considered an elder brother to the Kanaka Maoli people. After much pressure from students and kalo (taro) farmers, the University of Hawai'i relinquished their patents for the three varieties of kalo on June 20, 2006. At a news conference, the UH interim chancellor, Denise Konan, handed copies of the three patents to a kalo farmer, Chris Kobayashi; the director of the Centre for Hawaiian Studies, Jon Osorio; and Kanaka Maoli activist Walter Ritte. "In unison, the three tore them in half".[93]

A responsibility-based movement ultimately requires action to enact community-based powers of sustainable self-determination, which usually conflicts with the political / legal rights laid out by the state. According to Robert Odawi Porter:

> The most significant benefit of tribal disobedience is that it allows for the generation and affirmation of uniquely Indigenous interpretations of inherent and treaty-recognised rights. A hallmark attribute of the right of self-determination possessed by any people is their ability to interpret the scope of their own authority. This attribute may seem benign but it is essential to engaging in meaningful self-determination.[94]

Conclusions: Drawing Together the Web of Life

I began with a quotation from Taiaiake Alfred urging indigenous peoples to "start remembering the qualities of our ancestors and act on those remembrances". A responsibility-based process entails sparking a spiritual revolution rather than seeking state-based solutions that are disconnected from indigenous community relationships and the natural world. The pursuit of self-determination should be repositioned away from a narrowly constructed, state-driven rights discourse toward a responsibility-based movement centred on a sustainable self-determination process. As I have argued in my analysis of the global indigenous-rights discourse, states as well as global and regional forums are currently framing the right of self-determination for indigenous peoples through the compartmentalisation of political / legal rights from questions of sustainability, the denial of indigenous identities, engagement in the politics of recognition, and illusions of inclusion. Sustainable self-determination offers a new global benchmark for the praxis of indigenous livelihoods, food security, community governance, and relationships to the natural world and ceremonial life that enables the transmission of these cultural practices to future generations.

Utilising a more holistic, flexible, and dynamic model for the implementation of sustainable self-determination also allows for the creation of observable benchmarks for restoring indigenous cultural and ecological ecosystems. This model overcomes some of the Western epistemological biases often present in scientific assessments of ecosystems and / or political / legal assessments of indigenous rights, which ultimately discount cultural values and the needs of local communities. The inclusion of ecological, medicinal, food, and other cultural factors in this model assists indigenous communities in setting their own standards for restoring sustainable relationships.

Given the ongoing colonial legacies that impact indigenous futures, one also needs strategies to decolonise and restore indigenous relationships that have been long severed. To address questions of restorative justice, the UN General Assembly adopted a resolution in 2006 to implement "Basic Principles and Guidelines on the Right to a Remedy and Reparation for Victims of Gross Violations of International Human Rights Law and Serious Violations of International Humanitarian Law" (UN GA resolution 60/147). According to this, reparation is only effective if it involves remediation in the following five areas: Restitution, compensation, rehabilitation, satisfaction, and guarantees of non-repetition. Drawing on a benchmark of sustainable self-determination, indigenous peoples can frame these remedial strategies according to their own immediate and long-term community needs when mobilising to restore sustainable relationships on their homelands.

What, then, are some additional future strategies that indigenous peoples can engage in to promote a responsibility-based discourse and movement? One way to promote indigenous unity and regeneration is to encourage renewed treaty making between indigenous families and communities. Such a revitalised treaty process would follow the protocols of pipe ceremonies, not the paper diplomacy of states / global forums. Since states have not honoured indigenous treaties for the most part, it is time for indigenous peoples to lead by example and demonstrate once again their communities' approaches to principles of respect and diplomacy. Treaties of peace and friendship entail making sacred compacts that should be renewed ceremonially on an annual basis with all participating indigenous peoples. New inter-indigenous treaties might include those that affirm alliances, promote protection for crossing borders, and trade arrangements, further illustrating the wide spectrum of indigenous powers of Gadugi.

It may be useful to note here that there are some parallels between the Tsalagi practice of Gadugi—and where other indigenous nations around the world have their own concepts of governance expressed in their own languages—and the development of socially horizontal spaces such as within the World Social Forum (WSF). However, one should first consider the cultural, political, and geographic locations of these horizontal 'open spaces' if one is to truly honour and respect the relationships indigenous peoples of these places have with their homelands. In this sense, maintaining the premise of a 'neutral' or 'open' space can unintentionally mimic the colonial mentality of the state, which attempts to separate questions of indigenous self-determination from their territories. The responsibility to these 'open spaces' goes much deeper than merely a shared commitment to the opposition of neoliberalism.[95] As a potential starting point for building longer-term settler-indigenous alliances, there should be some acknowledgement on the part of settler participants regarding whose homelands they are meeting on. Additionally, in the spirit of reciprocity and accountability, gatherings being held on indigenous territories should follow the protocols of the land-based Indigenous cultures of that region.

One cannot have free exchanges of ideas without elements of trust and accountability just as one cannot separate the political aims of the WSF from the cultural and political contexts of the meeting place. As Juris points out, "Horizontal networks should not be romanticized. ... Horizontal relations do not suggest the complete absence of hierarchy, but rather the lack of formal hierarchical design".[96] In that same light, concepts of Gadugi and horizontal networking can be seen as guiding principles that can lead to meaningful cross-cultural dialogues and education for change.

Additionally, future indigenous mobilisation efforts should be directed toward engagement and activism in indigenous forums—not United Nations or regional institutional structures. Tsalagi legal scholar Valerie Phillips describes how we can re-establish alternative local economies that are premised on indigenous values:

> Existing indigenous sustainable economies in the South, combined with newly-resurging ones in North America, can together engender a more serious attitude within settler populations about indigenous peoples in general and sustainable development in particular as indigenous peoples progressively remove themselves from being under the economic thumb of the nation-state and finally thrive on their own terms.[97]

Capitalist / neoliberal projects and rights-based discourses can distract us from the real priorities to our homelands, families, clans, and communities. According to Deloria, "Having religious places and revolving your religion around that means you are always in contact with the earth—responsible for it and to it".[98] This is what it means to have a responsibility-based ethos and commitment to renewing our ongoing relationships. From this perspective, citizenship within indigenous nations should not be regarded as an entitlement but as a *responsibility* to be renewed annually, either through involvement in ceremony or some other cultural, educational, or leadership 'contribution' to one's own community that demonstrates respect for the principle of Gadugi.

We also have to remember that change happens in small increments: "One warrior at a time"—"The movement toward decolonisation and regeneration will emanate from transformations achieved by direct-guided experience in small, personal, groups and one-on-one mentoring towards a new path".[99]

As ancient nations, we have proven to be persistent because of our shared commitment to responsibility—we are nations that predate the rights-based state and will outlast it. Ani-yun-wiya power arises from Gadugi and *responsibilities* to our territories, families, and communities.

References

Pekka Aikio and Martin Scheinin, eds, 2000—*Operationalizing the Right of Indigenous Peoples to Self-Determination*. Turku, Finland: Institute for Human Rights

Akwesasne Notes, 1978—*Basic Call to Consciousness*. Summertown, TN: Native Voices

Taiaiake Alfred, 1999—*Peace, Power, Righteousness: An Indigenous Manifesto*. Oxford: Oxford University Press

Taiaiake Alfred, 2001—'Deconstructing the British Columbia Treaty Process', in *Balayi: Culture, Law, Colonialism* vol 3 (2001)

Taiaiake Alfred, 2005—*Wasáse: Indigenous Pathways of Action and Freedom*. Peterborough, ON: Broadview Press

Taiaiake Alfred and Jeff Corntassel, 2005—'Being Indigenous: Resurgences Against Contemporary Colonialism', in *Government & Opposition*, vol 40 no 4

Frédérique Apffel-Marglin, 2002—'From Fieldwork to Mutual Learning: Working with PRATEC', in *Environmental Values*, vol 11 (2002)

Frédérique Apffel-Marglin and PRATEC, eds, 1998—*The Spirit of Regeneration: Andean Culture Confronting Western Notions of Development*. London: Zed Books

S James Anaya, 2000—'Self-Determination as a Collective Human Right Under Contemporary International Law', in Pekka Aikio and Martin Scheinin, eds, 2000—Operationalizing the Right of Indigenous Peoples to Self-Determination. Turku, Finland: Institute for Human Rights

S James Anaya, 2004—*Indigenous Peoples in International Law*, second edition. Oxford: Oxford University Press

Mary Arquette, Maxine Cole, and the Akwesasne Task Force on the Environment, 2004—'Restoring Our Relationships with the Future', in Mario Blaser, Harvey A Feit, and Glenn McRae, eds, 2004—*In the Way of Development: Indigenous Peoples, Life Projects, and Globalization*. London: Zed Books

Mary Arquette, Maxine Cole, Katsi Cook, Brenda LaFrance, Margaret Peters, James Ransom, Elvera Sargent, Vivian Smoke, and Arlene Stairs, 2002—'Holistic Risk-Based Environmental Decision Making: A Native Perspective', in *Environmental Health Perspectives*, vol 110 (2002)

Botswana Press Agency, 2006—'UN Declaration Likely to Heighten Ethnic Conflicts',
December 1 2006, at: http://www.gov.bw/cgi-bin/news.cgi?d=20061201&i=UN_
declaration_likely_to_heighten_ethnic_conflicts (Inactive April 2017)

Ian Brownlie, 1971—*Basic Documents on African Affairs.* Oxford: Clarendon Press

Allen Buchanan, 1991—*Secession: The Morality of Political Divorce from Fort Sumter to
Lithuania and Québec.* Boulder, CO: Westview Press

Lee C Buchheit, 1978—*Secession: The Legitimacy of Self-Determination.* New Haven, CT:
Yale University Press

Government of Canada, Undersecretary of State for External Affairs, May
1923—'Letter to the Secretary-General, League of Nations', May 25 1923, on
the Petition to the League of Nations from the Six Nations of the Grand River
(C.500.1923.VII)

Jeff Corntassel, 2003a—'Who Is Indigenous? "Peoplehood" and Ethnonationalist
Approaches to Rearticulating Indigenous Identity', in *Nationalism and Ethnic
Politics*, vol 9 (2003)

Jeff Corntassel, 2007—'Partnership in Action? Indigenous Political Mobilization and
Co-optation During the First UN Indigenous Decade, 1995–2004', in *Human Rights
Quarterly*, vol 29 (2007)

Glen S Coulthard, 2007b—'Subjects of Empire: Indigenous Peoples and the "Politics of
Recognition" in Canada', in *Contemporary Political Theory*, vol 6 no 4, pp 437–460

Erica-Irene A Daes, 2004—*Indigenous Peoples' Permanent Sovereignty over Natural
Resources: Final Report of the Special Rapporteur, Erica-Irene A. Daes*, Commission
on Human Rights (E/CN.4/Sub.2/2004/30, July 13 2004)

Chief Deskaheh, 1923—*Petition to the League of Nations from the Six Nations of the
Grand River*, communicated by the Government of the Netherlands (C.500.1923.
VII, August 7 1923)

Susan Essoyan, 2006—'Activists Tear up 3 UH Patents for Taro', in *Honolulu Star
Bulletin*, June 21 2006, at http://starbulletin.com/2006/06/21/news/story03.html
(Accessed April 2017)

Ghida Fakhry, 2006—'Native Americans Fight Corporations', in *Al Jazeera International*, November 23 2006, at: http://www.wsdp.org/whatsnew.htm#carrie112306
(Accessed April 2017)

Ann Garibaldi and Nancy Turner, 2004—'Cultural Keystone Species: Implications for
Ecological Conservation and Restoration', in *Ecology and Society*, vol 9 (2004);
Arquette, Cole, and the Akwesasne Task Force on the Environment 2004, note 8

Lawrence Hauptman, 2007—'The Idealist and the Realist: Chief Deskaheh, Attorney
George Kecker, and the Six Nations' Struggle to Get to the World Court, 1921–
1925', paper presented at the International Indigenous Citizenship Conference, Center for Indigenous Law, Governance, and Citizenship, Syracuse University College
of Law, New York, April 28 2007

Emilie Hayes, 2017—'Open Space in Movement: Reading Three Waves of Feminism', in
Jai Sen, ed, 2017a—*The Movements of Movements, Part 1: What Makes Us Move?*.
Volume 4 in the *Challenging Empires* series. New Delhi: OpenWord and Oakland,
CA: PM Press

Indigenous Peoples of Africa Co-ordinating Committee, 2007—'Response Note to the
Draft Aide Memoire of the African Group on the UN Declaration on the Rights of

Indigenous Peoples', March 21 2007, at https://www.ipacc.org.za/images/reports/
human-rights/Response_to_Aide_Memoire_2007.pdf (Accessed April 2017)

Jeffrey S Juris, 2012a—'Social Forums and Their Margins: Networking Logics and the
Cultural Politics of Autonomous Space', in Jai Sen and Peter Waterman, eds, 2012—
World Social Forum: Critical Explorations. Volume 3 in the *Challenging Empires*
series. New Delhi: OpenWord

Onyeonoro S Kamanu, 1974—'Secession and the Right of Self-Determination: An OAU
Dilemma', in *Journal of Modern African Studies*, vol 12 (1974)

Paul Keal, 2003—*European Conquest and the Rights of Indigenous Peoples.* Cambridge:
Cambridge University Press

Benedict Kingsbury, 2000—'Reconstructing Self-Determination: A Relational Approach', in
Pekka Aikio and Martin Scheinin, eds, 2000—*Operationalizing the Right of Indigenous
Peoples to Self-Determination* (Turku, Finland: Institute for Human Rights), pp 19–38

David Knight, 1994—'People Together, Yet Apart: Rethinking Territory, Sovereignty, and
Identities', in George Demko and William Wood, eds, 1994—*Reordering the World:
Geopolitical Perspectives on the 21st Century.* Boulder, CO: Westview Press

Winona LaDuke, 2005—*Recovering the Sacred: The Power of Naming and Claiming.*
Cambridge, MA: South End Press. For more details on community initiatives, visit
the WELRP website, at http://www.nativeharvest.com (Accessed April 2017)

Matthew Russell Lee, 2007—'At UN, Indigenous Rights Are Threatened with Amendments, by Global Warming, and Agency Hot Air', in *Inner City Press*, May 22 2007,
at http://www.innercitypress.com/indigenous052207.html (Accessed April 2017)

Marty Logan, 2004—'Indigenous Peoples: Paper Trail Grows at UN Indigenous Forum',
in *IPS—Inter Press Service News Agency*, May 8 2004, at http://www.ipsnews.
net/2004/05/indigenous-peoples-paper-trail-grows-at-un-forum/ (Accessed
April 2017), cited in Jeff Corntassel, 2007—'Partnership in Action? Indigenous
Political Mobilization and Co-optation During the First UN Indigenous Decade
(1995–2004)', in *Human Rights Quarterly*, vol 29 pp 137–166, note 11, p 160

Barry Lopez, 2007—'The Leadership Imperative: An Interview with Oren Lyons', in
Orion, January–February 2007, at http://www.orionmagazine.org/index.php/
articles/article/94 (Accessed April 2017)

Oren Lyons, 1984—'Spirituality, Equality, and Natural Law', in Leroy Little Bear, Menno
Boldt, and J Anthony Long, eds, 1984—*Pathways to Self-Determination: Canadian
Indians and the Canadian State.* Toronto: University of Toronto Press

Roger Maaka and Augie Fleras, 2005—*The Politics of Indigeneity: Challenging the State in
Canada and Aotearoa New Zealand.* Dunedin: University of Otago Press

Deborah McGregor, 2004—'Traditional Ecological Knowledge and Sustainable Development: Towards Coexistence', in Mario Blaser, Harvey A Feit, and Glenn McRae, eds,
2004—*In the Way of Development: Indigenous Peoples, Life Projects, and Globalization.* London: Zed Books, at http://www.idrc.ca/en/ev-64525-201-1-DO_TOPIC.
html (Accessed April 2017)

Christopher McLeod and Malinda Maynor, 2001—'Vine Deloria Jr Extended Interview',
in *In the Light of Reverence.* Independent Television Service in association with
Native American Public Telecommunications

Millennium Ecosystem Assessment 2003—*Ecosystems and Human Well-Being: A Framework for Assessment.* Washington, DC: Island Press

Ted Moses, 2001—'The Right of Self-Determination and Its Significance to the Survival of Indigenous Peoples', in Pekka Aikio and Martin Scheinin, eds, 2001—*Operationalizing the Right of Indigenous Peoples to Self-Determination* (Turku: Institute for Human Rights), pp 155–178

Bernard Nietschmann, 1995—'The Fourth World: Nations Versus States', in George J Demko and William B Wood, eds, 1995—*Reordering the World* (Boulder, CO: Westview Press), pp 225–242

Ronald Niezen, 2003—*The Origins of Indigenism: Human Rights and the Politics of Identity.* Los Angeles: University of California Press

Nisga'a Nation (Joseph Gosnell Sr, Nelson Leeson, and Edmond Wright) and Her Majesty Queen in Right of Canada (Jane Stewart), 1999—'Nisga'a Final Agreement', at http://www.nnkn.ca/files/u28/nis-eng.pdf (Accessed April 2017)

Laura Parisi and Jeff Corntassel, 2007—'In Pursuit of Self-Determination: Indigenous Women's Challenges to Traditional Diplomatic Spaces', in *Canadian Foreign Policy*, vol 13 (2007)

Jo M Pasqualucci, 2006—'The Evolution of International Indigenous Rights in the Inter-American Human Rights System', in *Human Rights Law Review*, vol 6 (2006)

Valerie J Phillips, 2005—'Parallel Worlds: A Sideways Approach to Promoting Indigenous-Non-Indigenous Trade and Sustainable Development', in *Michigan State Journal of International Law*, vol 14 (2005)

Robert Odawi Porter, 2006—'Tribal Disobedience', in *Texas Journal of Civil Liberties and Civil Rights*, vol 11 (2006)

Haider Rizvi, 2006—'Native Group Takes Land Dispute to UN', in *Inter Press Service News Agency*, January 26 2006, at http://www.ipsnews.net/headlines.asp (Accessed April 2017)

Douglas Sanders, 1998—'The Legacy of Deskaheh: Indigenous Peoples as International Actors', in Cynthia Price Cohen, ed, 1998—*The Human Rights of Indigenous Peoples.* New York: Transnational Publishers

C J Schexnayder, April 2007—'The Mahogany Wars of Peru's Rain Forests', in *San Francisco Chronicle*, April 22 2007, at http://www.sfgate.com/cgi-bin/article.cgi?f=/c/a/2007/04/22/ING7VPBAH71.DTL (Accessed April 2017)

Andrea Smith, 2005—*Conquest: Sexual Violence and American Indian Genocide.* Cambridge, MA: South End Press

Victoria Tauli-Corpuz and Parshuram Tamang, 2007—*Oil Palms and Other Commercial Tree Plantations, Monocropping: Impacts on Indigenous Peoples' Land Tenure and Resource Management Systems and Livelihoods,* (E/C.19/2007/CRP.6, May 7 2007), at http://www.un.org/esa/socdev/unpfii/documents/6session_crp6.doc (Accessed April 2017)

Patrick Thornberry, 2000—'Self-Determination and Indigenous Peoples: Objections and Responses', in Pekka Aikio and Martin Scheinin, eds, 2000—*Operationalizing the Right of Indigenous Peoples to Self-Determination.* Turku, Finland: Institute for Human Rights

James Tully, 2000—'The Struggles of Indigenous Peoples for and of Freedom', in Duncan Ivison, Paul Patton, and Will Sanders, eds, 2000—*Political Theory and the Rights of Indigenous Peoples.* Cambridge: Cambridge University Press

Thomas R Van Dervort, 1998—*International Law and Organization*. Thousand Oaks, CA: Sage

Ellen Woodley, 2006—'Cultural Indicators of Indigenous Peoples' Food and Agro-ecological systems', paper at the Second Global Consultation on the Right to Food and Food Sovereignty for Indigenous Peoples, Puerto Cabezas, Nicaragua, at http://www.un.org/esa/socdev/unpfii/documents/E_%20C_19_2009_CRP3_en.pdf (Accessed April 2017)

World Commission on Environment and Development, 1987—*Report of the World Commission on Environment and Development*, A/RES/42/187, posted by UN Department of Economic and Social Affairs (DESA), December 11 1987, at http://www.un.org/documents/ga/res/42/ares42–187.htm (Accessed April 2017)

Notes

1. Ed: This is an edited and revised version of an essay with the same title, 'Toward Sustainable Self-Determination: Rethinking the Contemporary Indigenous-Rights Discourse', that was published in *Alternatives: Global, Local, Political*, vol 33, no 2, April–June 2008, by Lynne Rienner Publishers, Inc. It is published here with the kind permission of the author and the publisher. For further reproduction permission, contact permissions@rienner.com.
2. Alfred 2005, p 32.
3. ibid.
4. Nisga'a Nation and Her Majesty Queen in Right of Canada, 1999.
5. Alfred 2001, pp 37–65.
6. ibid, p 57.
7. Tully 2000, pp 36–59.
8. The term 'host state' is the most grammatically precise and widely used phrase describing those countries containing indigenous peoples within their borders. However, this term should not be construed to imply a sense of undue state cordiality, especially given the severe treatment that several indigenous populations have received at the hands of their host states.
9. Corntassel 2003, pp 75–100.
10. Botswana Press Agency 2006.
11. McGregor 2004.
12. Knight 1994, pp 71–86. As early as 1949, states began drafting a *Special Report of the United Nations Commission for Indonesia* in order to establish a clear distinction between "internal" and "external" self-determination. According to this logic, one could differentiate between "historical subjugation of an alien population living in a different part of the globe and the historical subjugation of an alien population living on a piece of land abutting that of its oppressors" (Buchheit 1978, p 18).
13. At http://www.ohchr.org/EN/ProfessionalInterest/Pages/RemedyAndReparation.aspx (Accessed April 2017)
14. Surveillance involves holding state institutions accountable for their actions through constant monitoring and reporting via indigenous communities, human rights organisations, and so forth. Shame entails motivating states to honour their

existing human rights obligations by publicising poor state practices. For more on these strategies, see Corntassel 2007, pp 137–166.

15. Daes 2004, p 7. Emphasis added.

16. For more on the state militarisation of indigenous homelands and natural resources, see Nietschmann, 1995 note 9, pp 225–242. For a current examination of how state production of biofuels impacts indigenous peoples worldwide, see Tauli-Corpuz and Tamang 2007.

17. 'Turtle Island' is a common term among First Nation peoples in North America for the North American continent.

18. Deskaheh means 'more than eleven'. Chief Deskaheh was also known as Levi General.

19. For more on the dialogue between Deskaheh and attorney George Kecker regarding strategies to bring the Six Nations' case before the World Court, see Hauptman 2007.

20. Notes 1978, p 19.

21. Deskaheh 1923, p 3.

22. ibid.

23. While the governments of the United Kingdom and Canada went to great efforts to prevent a debate on Deskaheh's petition, several states—Estonia, the Netherlands, Ireland, Panama, Japan, and Persia—expressed support for it. Maori leader TW Ratana also unsuccessfully petitioned the League of Nations and Britain in 1924 regarding land confiscations and recognition of the Treaty of Waitangi. His petitions were strongly opposed by the British government and New Zealand (Sanders 1998, pp 73–74).

24. Government of Canada, Undersecretary of State for External Affairs, May 1923, on the Petition to the League of Nations from the Six Nations of the Grand River (C.500.1923.VII).

25. Sanders 1998, note 19, pp 73–74.

26. Notes 1978, note 16, pp 21–22.

27. 'Letter to the Secretary-General', note 22.

28. ibid emphasis added.

29. ibid.

30. ibid.

31. Corntassel 2007, note 11, p 161.

32. 'General Assembly Adopts Declaration on the Rights of Indigenous Peoples', September 13 2007, at: http://www.un.org/News/Press/docs/2007/ga10612.doc. htm (Accessed April 2017).

33. The deleted sections of the Declaration were just as telling, relating to freely determining relationships with states and impositions by legislative, administrative, or other measures on indigenous nations (article 8), military activities on indigenous lands (article 30), and deletion of indigenous ownership of "mineral, water or other resources" (article 32). For a full text of the Declaration highlighting the amendments, see http://www.un.org/esa/socdev/unpfii/documents/Declaration_IPs_31August.pdf.

34. Knight 1994, note 9, p 79.

35. Brownlie 1971, pp 360–361.

36. Kamanu 1974, pp 355–376.

37. The 1970 UN 'Friendly Relations' declaration, which is essentially a handbook for statecraft, describes a standard state perspective on self-determination: "Nothing in the foregoing paragraphs shall be construed as authorising or encouraging any action which would dismember or impair, totally or in part, the territorial integrity or political unity of sovereign and independent States conducting themselves in compliance with the principle of equal rights and self-determination of peoples as described above and thus possessed of a government represent the whole people belonging to the territory without distinction as to race, creed or colour" (Dervort 1998, p 610).

38. Decision on the UN Declaration on the Rights of Indigenous Peoples (January 30 2007), at http://www.ohchr.org/EN/ProfessionalInterest/Pages/RemedyAndReparation.aspx (Accessed April 2017).

39. These proposals were never formally introduced at the UN General Assembly, and the UN General Assembly president described them as "so way off they should be ignored" (Lee 2007). For a full text of the African proposals, see http://www.converge.org.nz/pma/AGDraft0507.pdf.

40. The UN Permanent Forum on Indigenous Issues has not adopted an official definition of indigenous peoples, but working definitions, such as the one developed by the UN Working Group on Indigenous Peoples in 1986, offer some generally accepted guidelines for self-identifying indigenous peoples and nations:

    Self-identification as indigenous peoples at the individual level and accepted by the community as their member;

    Historical continuity with pre-colonial and / or pre-settler societies;

    Strong link to territories and surrounding natural resources;

    Distinct social, economic, or political systems;

    Distinct language, culture, and beliefs;

    Form non-dominant groups of society;

    Resolve to maintain and reproduce their ancestral environments and systems as distinctive peoples and communities

    Resource Kit on Indigenous Peoples' Issues, 2008, Department of Economic and Social Affairs, New York: United Nations, at http://www.un.org/esa/socdev/unpfii/documents/resource_kit_indigenous_2008.pdf (Accessed April 2017).

    While there is a great deal of discussion over the complexities of defining more than 350 million indigenous peoples around the world, ultimately the question, "Who is indigenous?" is best answered by indigenous communities themselves. For more on this definitional discourse, see Corntassel 2003, note 6, pp. 75–100.

41. See the amended declaration at: http://www.un.org/esa/socdev/unpfii/documents/Declaration_IPs_31August.pdf.

42. Logan 2004.

43. ibid.

44. Mary Dann passed away on April 22 2005, after an accident on an all-terrain vehicle while she was repairing fences on the family's Crescent Valley ranch in Nevada.

45. Pasqualucci 2006, pp 281–322.

46. ibid.

47. 'Western Shoshone Victorious at the United Nations', March 10 2006, at https://www.oxfamamerica.org/press/western-shoshone-victorious-at-united-nations/ (Accessed April 2017).

48. ibid.
49. ibid.
50. Rizvi 2006.
51. Fakhry 2006.
52. Alfred 2005, note 1, p 112.
53. Thornberry 2000, pp 47–57.
54. Coulthard 2007, pp 1–29.
55. ibid, p 22.
56. Even where cultural and economic factors are acknowledged as part of an overall indigenous right to self-determination, they are overly general or not adequately developed. See, for example, Buchanan 1991; Kingsbury 2003, note 51, pp 19–37; Keal 2003; and Niezen 2003.
57. Anaya 2004, p 103.
58. See, for example, Moses 2000, note 51, pp 155–178; Daes 2004; and Maaka and Fleras 2005.
59. Anaya 2004, note 55, p 109.
60. ibid, p 104.
61. Alfred and Corntassel 2005, pp 597–614.
62. Arquette et al 2002, pp 259–264.
63. Anaya 2000, note 51, pp 3–18.
64. Deskaheh 1923, note 17.
65. In this example, "food security is a situation that exists when all people, at all times, have physical, social and economic access to sufficient, safe and nutritious food that meets their dietary needs and food preferences for an active and healthy life. ... For Indigenous peoples, this definition also includes respect for their own cultures and their own systems of managing natural resources and rural areas" (Woodley 2006).

In this article, natural law takes on a much different meaning from Western legal traditions founded in Stoic and later Roman philosophies, which are premised on the notion that there are normative principles emanating from the 'rational' nature of human beings, discoverable by 'reason', and existing independently of their codification or enforcement. While there is no single definition of indigenous natural law, as it varies in practice from community to community, it entails collective and individual experiential knowledge "reflecting a spiritual connection with the land established by the Creator, gives human beings special responsibilities within the areas they occupy as indigenous peoples, linking them in a 'natural' way to their territories" (Alfred 1999, p 61).
66. Tully 2000, note 4, p 57.
67. The original definition reads: "sustainable development, which implies meeting the needs of the present without compromising the ability of future generations to meet their own needs" (from World Commission on Environment and Development 1987).
68. Woodley 2006, note 63, p 5; Garibaldi and Nancy Turner 2004, pp 1–18; and Arquette, Cole, and the Akwesasne Task Force on the Environment 2004, note 8.
69. Woodley 2006, note 63, p 3.
70. Millennium Ecosystem Assessment 2003, p 58.
71. ibid, pp 58–59.

72.   ibid, pp 57–60.

73.   Phillips 2005, pp 521–540.

74.   Schexnayder 2007.

75.   ibid.

76.   LaDuke 2005, p 205. For more details on community initiatives, visit the WELRP website, at, http://www.nativeharvest.com (Accessed April 2017).

77.   Thus far, the project has reclaimed 1,700 acres of their traditional homelands. See LaDuke 2005, note 74, pp 206–207.

78.   ibid.

79.   United Nations Declaration on the Rights of Indigenous Peoples, 2006, at http://www.un.org/esa/socdev/unpfii/documents/ResA_RES_61_178.doc (Accessed April 2017).

80.   Corntassel 2007, note 11, p. 162.

81.   McLeod and Maynor 2001.

82.   Lopez 2007.

83.   Traditional term used to describe Tsalagi (Cherokee nation), which means real or principal people.

84.   Telephone conversation, September 12 2006, with Benny Smith of the Cherokee nation, elder and director of counselling services at Haskell Indian Nations University, Kansas.

85.   Parisi and Corntassel 2007, p 84.

86.   Lyons 1984, p 5.

87.   Smith 2005, p 5.

88.   Apffel-Marglin 2002, pp 345–367. See also Apffel-Marglin and PRATEC 1998.

89.   Apffel-Marglin 2002, note 86, p 347.

90.   ibid, p 348.

91.   ibid, p 349.

92.   ibid.

93.   Essoyan 2006.

94.   Porter 2006, p 170.

95.   Ed: See the essay by Emilie Hayes in this book (Hayes 2017), also in Section II. (NB: In his finalised mss of this essay, the author in fact referred to an earlier version of this essay, titled 'Open Space and Dissent in Movement: Understandings and Lessons from the Canadian Feminist Movement', which was to be a chapter in a somewhat different book that was finally dropped and reformulated into this book (then titled: Jai Sen and Peter Waterman, eds, forthcoming (2009)—*Facing the Future: The World Social Forum and Beyond*). But since that draft of the essay—and with that title—has not been published, I have taken the liberty of instead giving the reference here to the finally published version of the essay in question.

96.   Juris 2012a, p 3.

97.   Phillips 2005, note 71, p 525.

98.   McLeod and Maynor 2001, note 79.

99.   Alfred and Corntassel 2005, note 59, p 613.

The Tapestry of Neo-Zapatismo:
Origins and Development
Xochitl Leyva Solano and Christopher Gunderson[1]

On January 1 1994, the previously unknown *Ejército Zapatista de Liberación Nacional* (EZLN, or Zapatista National Liberation Army) captured seven cities and towns in the state of Chiapas, Mexico—and with them the imaginations of progressive activists around the world. In the sixteen years since the Zapatista uprising, the Zapatistas' distinctive political discourse and practice, known as 'neo-Zapatismo', has had an enormous influence on the generation of activists identified with the counter-globalisation movement, perhaps especially in the North. Despite this influence however, in our experience the understanding of the actual origins and development of the EZLN and of neo-Zapatismo prior to the 1994 uprising remains limited among both scholars and activists outside of Mexico.

As noted by the neo-Zapatistas as well as by researchers, neo-Zapatismo is the product of a rich and complex convergence and interweaving of several radical political currents or threads with a process of profound social transformation within the indigenous communities of Chiapas.[2] In this paper we identify the major threads and give an account of how they came to be woven together to make the tapestry that is neo-Zapatismo. What allowed the EZLN's emergence and expansion? What factors converged to give life to the EZLN and to make it different from previous indigenous social and political movements? These questions cannot be properly answered in a single paper. What we do here is to present some elements of their story that we hope will invite readers to hear the voices that are to be found in the extensive body of materials documenting the neo-Zapatistas' own words and work[3]—as well as the web pages and blog spots cited below.

Situated and Committed Knowledge

We are two scholar-activists who have been inspired by the Zapatista experience who hope that this presentation on the roots of that experience might be a small contribution to the debates and discussions that our South Asian colleagues and *compañeros* have been pursuing around emerging global movements. We dedicate it to the Zapatista *compañeros* and *compañeras* who are the reason and inspiration for the international Zapatista solidarity networks of which we are part.

Xochitl is a scholar and activist who first came to work in the Lacandon Jungle in 1987, seven years before the 1994 uprising, unaware that one of the

most important movements in Chiapas, Mexico, Abya Yala (the Americas) and the world was being built there clandestinely at the very same time. The year 1987 was not just any year in the history of the EZLN. It was rather the beginning of the period that lasted until 1990 when the EZLN grew very rapidly taking in most of the communities in *Las Cañadas* region of the Lacandon Jungle. Since 1994 Xochitl has not only written about the neo-Zapatista networks but also contributed to building them.

Christopher is an activist turned scholar who threw himself into Zapatista solidarity work within days of the Zapatista uprising. He travelled to Chiapas first in 1996 for the First Intercontinental Encounter Against Neoliberalism and for Humanity organised by the EZLN, then spent two years from 1997 to 1999 working on the construction of a clinic in a Zapatista community, after a year of research under Xochitl's supervision, he completed his dissertation on the intellectual origins and development of Zapatismo prior to the 1994 uprising and is currently an assistant professor in sociology at Howard University in Washington, DC.[4]

The Beginning, in the Zapatistas' Own Words

Neo-Zapatismo can be divided into two parts: The military neo-Zapatismo of the EZLN proper and the civil neo-Zapatismo of the several hundred indigenous villages that are the EZLN's support bases.[5] The villages are in turn organised into 38 'autonomous municipalities', which in turn are organised into five regional *Juntas de Buen Gobierno* (Good Government Councils, or JBGs). If you want to know the civil neo-Zapatismo of the indigenous neo-Zapatista communities, the place to start is in the five neo-Zapatista *Caracoles*, the seats of the JBGs, composed of rotating delegates from the autonomous municipalities that govern on the basis of the principle of *mandar obedeciendo* ('to lead, obeying'). The JBGs operate year round administering justice, coordinating the work of various autonomous councils and committees of the region, and acting as the point of contact between the neo-Zapatista communities and the world, receiving those who wish to learn the history and demands of the movement or who want to aid the movement.

The JBGs and the *Caracoles* took shape in 2003 and made the neo-Zapatistas' regional autonomy real in the wake of the failure of the national government in 2001 to carry out the reforms promised in the San Andres Accords that the EZLN and the Mexican government signed in 1996.[6] They reflect a privileging of the non-violent civil and political dimensions of the neo-Zapatistas' struggle over the military dimension. While the military dimension has not disappeared, and the EZLN has retained their weapons and political-military organisation, the emphasis on the development of the communities' capacities for political self-governance has, for the present, pushed it into the background.

The term 'caracol', which refers to the spiral shape of a conch or snail shell, has several significances. First, it is a symbol with pre-Columbian Mayan-Mesoamerican roots. Conch shells are used in many communities to call people to village assemblies and spiral shaped processions are used ritualistically to symbolise the coming together of the whole community. The spiral image also stands in contrast with more linear categories of space and time rooted in the West and in modernity. Neo-Zapatismo is a movement that seems to move in a spiral fashion weaving together processes that occur in different times and spaces. And like a snail, from the perspective of non-indigenous observers, it often moves very slowly.

If the neo-Zapatistas captured the world's attention in 1994 and have since inspired many counter-globalisation activists with their experiments in autonomy, the question still remains, where did this movement come from?

It is well known that the EZLN is composed mainly of indigenous people and was founded on November 17 1983, in the Lacandon Jungle in Chiapas, the southernmost state in Mexico.[7] A neo-Zapatista *corrido* or ballad, titled 'Anniversary of November 17th' tells how:

> ... History has forgotten our step forward ...
> how the forces were organized ...
> to live for our country or to all die for freedom ...
> We fight for an end to exploitation,
> and to be done forever with the moneybags and the boss ...
> We want good food and housing for all,
> work, health, and peace,
> independence and education.
> We want to live liberation ...

The members of the Revolutionary Indigenous Clandestine Committee (CCRI) tell us of the EZLN's origins:

> First we decided to take possession of the land, and then on the path to get there. That is how the organization of campesinos began. The moment came when we had to strike, protesting and shouting out our demands. We were tired of being turned back, of putting so much in but never seeing a solution to anything. We had to make them respect us. Then the moment came in which we had to take up arms so that we would be heard. We came to this in secret while we struggled publicly, marching side by side with the legal organizations.[8]

Subcomandante Insurgente Marcos, the spokesman of the EZLN, tells how a small group of indigenous and non-indigenous members of the FLN arrived in one of the most inhospitable parts of the Lacandon Jungle to establish a guerrilla encampment and how gradually they began to make contact with the leaders of the indigenous communities in the region.[9] Members of the CCRI emphasise how the EZLN was transformed from a peasant self-defence organisation into a regular army as members of the communities began to join in large numbers. They tell how the communities themselves passed through times of great stress and division as some wondered if preparing for armed struggle was right or wrong,[10] but as Captain Elisa, a Tseltal officer in the EZLN, said in 1994:

> Nobody wants to become an insurgent, but with this situation we have to make the effort and endure it so that the people can have what they need. We have seen many times how people organized themselves for marches, for sit-ins, without anything ever being solved. That is why we thought it better to take up arms. And this is why we have to be in the mountains, suffering and enduring all the shit we go through, if the officer says you need to march through the night, withstand the cold sleet, rain.[11]

The decisions, first to go into the mountains and to build an army, and then to launch the uprising that captured the attention of the world, were each the product of long and complex processes of political development on the part of the indigenous communities of Chiapas. When the EZLN was founded in 1983 it was done in secrecy because the broader indigenous-*campesino* movement was then both facing murderous repression and also grappling with the exhaustion of dealing with reformist strategies. Given this, the communities were initially attracted by the EZLN's offers to train and organise them for armed self-defence. By the early 1990s however, the organisation had grown dramatically and a series of events (the collapse of coffee prices, the reversal of land reform guarantees in the Constitution, the quincentenary in 1992 of Columbus's initiation of the conquest of the Americas, and the signing of the North American Free Trade Agreement, NAFTA, in 1993, with its profound consequences for the peoples of Mexico) convinced most of its members that the time had come to go to war. In 1992 the communities began to vote in assemblies on whether or not to declare war. By early 1993 the decision was made and the preparations begun. By the end of the year roughly five thousand well-armed guerrilla *insurgents* and less well-armed members of village militias were in position and the uprising was launched on January 1 1994.

Neo-Zapatista Threads

As suggested above, neo-Zapatismo is the product of the weaving together of several distinct threads. In our view the seven main threads are as follows:

1. The indigenous philosophy of the *komon* and the *lekil kuxlejal* (or 'the full life') as a horizon of life, expressed in the efforts to build what the Zapatistas call 'good governance' and the commitment to *mandar obedeciendo* ('to lead, obeying').
2. The traditions of indigenous rebellions dating back to the colonial era.
3. The Zapatismo of the Mexican Revolution of the early twentieth century.
4. Liberation Theology, the 'preferential option for the poor', and Indigenous Theology, as developed within the Diocese of San Cristóbal de Las Casas.
5. The distinctly Mexican brand of Maoism that played a critical role in the development of independent *campesino* organisations in Chiapas.
6. The independent *campesino* movement that arose in Chiapas and Mexico in the 1970s and 80s, and in particular the fight against government policies aimed at evicting communities in *Las Cañadas* region of the Lacandon Jungle.
7. The broad national liberation movement that arose in Mexico in the 1960s and specifically the National Liberation Forces (FLN), an originally urban clandestine political-military organisation that formally initiated the EZLN in 1983.

These seven threads were mainly woven together in *Las Cañadas*, the canyons region of the Lacandon Jungle, a remote area settled in recent decades mainly by Mayan Indians fleeing intense competition for scarce lands, the repressive regime of the *fincas*,[12] and religious conflicts in other regions of Chiapas. It was in this micro-region that the guerrilla nucleus established by the FLN in 1983 germinated and became the core of the peoples' army that rose up in 1994. As it grew in secret, the EZLN also expanded into the Highlands and Northern Zone, areas characterised by their own particular dynamics. It was in *Las Cañadas*, however, that the EZLN won the broadest support, and this paper will concentrate its attentions on the process there, not least of all because it is the one we know best.

The paper is organised as follows: First, we look at each of the seven threads identified above, one by one. Second, as the paper progresses we chart their interweaving in order to more fully comprehend the EZLN and to understand its local, national, and global resonance.

The First Thread: From the Komon to 'Good Governance'

The heartland of the EZLN is the Lacandon Jungle. In pre-Hispanic times, its inhabitants were the original Lacandon Indians, who were ultimately exterminated by the Spanish colonisers in retaliation for their fierce resistance. The Province of Chiapas then became a part of the Audiencia of Guatemala "directly subject to the King of Spain and not to the Viceroy of New Spain".[13] In 1821 the *ladino*[14] elites of the Guatemalan province of Chiapas declared independence from Spain and Guatemala and joined the newly formed Mexican Empire. In the nineteenth century, and mainly under the dictatorship of Porfirio Díaz, different logging companies based in Tabasco, Guatemala, Mexico City, the United States, England, Spain, and France laid claim to large tracts of jungle in order to extract mahogany and other precious woods for shipment from ports located in the Gulf of Mexico to London, Liverpool, and New York. This situation prevailed until 1949.[15]

When Xochitl came to work in the Lacandon Jungle in 1987, the large timber companies of the Porfirian era were long gone. What remained were the names of the old logging camps taken for the new villages that had been established by settlers colonising the jungle. The settlers—in this case, indigenous and mestizo peoples, and not referring to the colonists—who had occupied *Las Cañadas* over the course of the nineteenth and twentieth centuries had moved from the colonial haciendas established by Dominican friars that ringed the jungle to the privately owned *fincas* of the *ladino* elite, and finally to the *ejidos*, a form of communal property re-established by the 1910 Mexican Revolution. These settlers had come in waves, occupying different subregions of the Lacandon Jungle each of which had its own history of occupation.[16]

But if we look only at *Las Cañadas*, which between 1987 and 1990 was almost entirely affiliated with the EZLN, we know from a census organised by *ARIC Union de Uniones*, the main legal *campesino* organisation, that 80 per cent of the inhabitants of that subregion came from neighbouring *ladino*-owned *fincas*.[17] We also know from other sources that, between 1910 and 1950, the fraction of people in the region living on the *fincas* fell from 84 per cent to 53 per cent.[18] Based on oral history, in 1996 Xochitl Leyva and Gabriel Ascencio identified several "cycles of colonization in *Las Cañadas*" in which, starting in the 1930s, new indigenous and mestizo settlers cleared lands to found a community and raise their families, and then saw their children settle another piece of virgin forest.[19] The resulting dense web of family connections between the communities would later serve to facilitate the clandestine growth of what the communities simply called "the organization" (or the EZLN).

The *finca* was an immediate historical and political reference point for the people in *Las Cañadas*. For many of the founders of the *ejidos*, their parents and grandparents had been peons exploited by large landowners on *fincas* dedicated to agricultural production based on cheap labour and the monopolisation of land. Today, when speaking of their liberation, both young and old in the EZLN begin with the time of the *fincas*. In testimonies collected by neo-Zapatista videographers, for example, one says:

> When I was with my patron I could not work my milpa (corn field). If someone wanted corn they had to get it from the big house, the company store, the same

went for beans, salt, and sugar. With every celebration of All Saints Day we also got a set of clothes, a pair of pants and a shirt, and women's clothing, depending on what you wore. Which was why you could never pay the debt, and why at the end of each year your debt increased and you could not pay and you had to stay. … But the amount of corn didn't change. 'It's very little', we would tell the patron, and he would say to us 'Don't bitch that you don't get more, it's a zonte between two, even though they ate much more.'

(Fragment taken from the video *Chul stes bil [The Sacred Earth]*, 2000).

In 1990, in a village in *Las Cañadas*, one community agreed to reconstruct with Xochitl Leyva and Gabriel Ascencio the history of their arrival in the jungle. The four elders appointed by the community assembly to tell the story made a strong emphasis on heavy labours from dawn until dusk, on eternal debts that tied them forever to the *finca*, on never having had the opportunity to learn to read and write, and on the suffering endured to leave the *finca* and to find a piece of land in the inhospitable jungle.[20] This kind of collective memory of grievances became one of the strongholds of the neo-Zapatista claims after 1994.

The communities established by the settlers fleeing the *fincas* organised themselves in accordance with the indigenous culture and values that they had kept alive and resignified over the course of centuries. Sometimes the process of resignification happened even inside the *fincas*. *Lekil kuxlejal* and the *komon* are the specific forms that were developed in the Lacandon Jungle, which are similar to the concepts respectively of *sumak kawsay* among the Quechuas and Aymaras of Bolivia and of *comunalidad* among the Mixes of Oaxaca, in Mexico. The Zapatistas of today are thus not the only ones to have this worldview, but what is their own is the way in which they have elaborated it into the political philosophy of *mandar obedeciendo* ('to lead, obeying').

One of the most relevant local and cultural institutions was the *komon*. Perhaps the most remote antecedent of the *komon* is the *común de tierras* or common lands granted to the Indians by the Spanish crown; or it may also come from a pre-Columbian form of social organisation. We do not know precisely, but what we do know is that the *komon* was reinforced by the Mexican government's post-revolutionary agrarian reform insofar as the reform promoted the formation of *ejidos*, which in turn encouraged collective forms of organisation and use of lands.

By the end of the 1980s, the Mayan Indians[21] used the term *komon* to refer both to the Council of Authorities that governed each village in a spirit of community service and to the collective way of life in which religious rituals were celebrated together, and where land, cattle, and sugar cane were worked in common. As well, decisions concerning almost every aspect of daily life were made by consensus in village assemblies.[22] After the neo-Zapatista uprising the principles of the *komon*, understood as participatory and radical democracy, would become one of the bases of the Zapatistas' practice of 'good governance'.[23]

Legacy of Indigenous Rebellions

The neo-Zapatista uprising in January 1994 was not the first indigenous rebellion in Chiapas. Indeed, its distinctive features cannot be understood without reference to the long legacy of indigenous resistance and rebellions against established powers (ie the Spanish Crown, the *criollo* elite, the *finqueros*, and the *ladinos*).

During colonial times, the first major sign of indigenous discontent occurred in 1693 when a revolt broke out in the Zoque town of Tuxtla in the Grijalva Valley, resulting in the deaths of two Spanish officials and the town's highest Indian authority before troops were sent into crush it. Twenty-one Indians were executed for their involvement in the rebellion and their dismembered bodies were displayed around the town and allowed to rot on the grounds that this "would serve as preventive medicine, such that neither present nor future Indians would lose their way".[24]

In 1712, starting in the Tzeltal town of San Juan Cancuc and spreading to other towns, a religious movement arose among the Indians of Highland Chiapas with the appearance of the Virgin of Rosario to a fourteen year old girl named María de la Candelaria. The movement took on the character of a rebellion with the appearance in Cancuc of Sebastián Gómez de la Gloria, a native of Chenalhó, who "transformed the cult of the virgin into a real church".[25] In early August 1712 leaders of all the Indian towns of Chiapas were called by Sebastián Gómez to come to Cancuc and to bring with them "all the silver of your churches, and the ornaments and bells, with all the coffers and drums and all the *cofradía*[26] books and funds".[27] The response to the call was overwhelming. With the exception of four towns, the entire Province of the Zendales responded to the call, as did many towns in the Tzotzil districts of Las Coronas y Chinampas in the Central Highlands.

Sebastián Gómez was putting in place a kind of indigenous theocratic dual power. He promoted a rapid break with Spanish colonial authority by replacing every significant office of Spanish power—civil, religious, or military—with a new indigenous authority. Under Gómez's leadership an *indigenista* theology was constructed that appropriated the narrative and symbolism of the Catholic Church but transformed them into instruments of indigenous power. Not only were religious vestments appropriated, but the very geography of the region was reconceived. Ciudad Real (the colonial capital) was renamed 'Jerusalem' and Cancuc was renamed 'Ciudad Real', presumably establishing the basis for a crusade to retake the city from the Spaniards who were declared to be "Jews" and therefore "barred from salvation".

The indigenous army was organised along Spanish lines.[28] In less than a week after a call to rise up in arms the indigenous peoples had "secured control of all the villages of the Province of the Zendales and the Gaurdianía of Huitiupán, with the solitary exceptions of Simojovel and Los Plátanos", and "by August 25 an Indian army of four to five thousand men had reached San Miguel Huixtán, a Tzotzil town within striking distance (six leagues) of Ciudad Real, and were preparing to attack it".[29] The attack was never made however, and eventually the Spanish authorities regained the offensive and reconquered Cancuc in late November 1712, though 'mopping up' operations continued for another seven months.[30]

Between 1867 and 1869 the Highlands of Chiapas were shaken again, this time by a series of events that became popularly known as the 'Caste War'[31] of Chamula.[32] In December 1867, a girl from the Tzotzil village of Tzajalhemel in the municipality of Chamula claimed to have found three stones that fell from the sky. The stones became the objects of a cult that obtained the approval of Pedro Díaz Cuscat, a high-ranking indigenous official from Chamula who performed religious functions when the *ladino* priest was absent. Cuscat interpreted the sounds of the stones as they banged against the inside of a box in which they had been placed. The stones were later replaced with clay figurines, the girl was declared 'the Mother of God', and by April 1868 "Tzajalhemel was transformed from an insignificant place to a regional socioreligious and commercial centre".[33] The transformation of the village into a major market struck at one of the main mechanisms by which the *ladino* elite extracted wealth from the indigenous peoples of the Highlands.

By the end of 1868, the authorities of San Cristóbal de Las Casas assembled 50 troops who marched on Tzajalhemel, trashed the temple, seized the figurines, and took the girl prisoner. Cuscat and several of his followers were arrested a little later after the soldiers opened fire on an unarmed crowd that was attempting to defend them. In June 1869, Miguel Martínez, the Catholic priest serving Chamula, and three others were killed in the course of an attempt to seize a new set of the figurines which had replaced the old ones. The killings were followed by several others of *ladino* ranchers and merchants and were attributed to Ignacio Fernández Galindo, a *ladino* anarchist schoolteacher who was accused of organising an indigenous army to attack San Cristóbal.

At this point, interpretations of events diverge. Several thousand Chamulans marched on San Cristóbal, but instead of launching an attack, Galindo, his wife, and a student offered themselves as hostages in exchange for Cuscat. The exchange was accepted, but the authorities in San Cristóbal then broke the deal by arresting the three hostages and charging them with treason. According to Jan Rus (1998) the Chamulans posted six hundred men armed with digging sticks and machetes on the road from San Cristóbal in anticipation of reprisals while other accounts describe this as a larger offensive force gathered with the intent to lay siege and then attack the city. What is clear is that the liberal governor mobilised lowland militias which marched on San Cristóbal and attacked the Chamulans, killing 300. According to Rus, the 43 *ladinos* killed were largely the victims of 'friendly' artillery fire.[34]

The *ladinos* waited several days to gather more forces before attacking Chamula directly, where there is little doubt that what then occurred was a massacre. Over the next several months the militia continued to carry out operations against people variously described as rebels or refugees. Rus correctly challenges the *ladino* justifications of these massacres as a response to a supposed 'caste war' waged by the Chamulans against the *ladino* population. However, in organising their own church, their own market, and ultimately their own security forces, the Chamulans had struck at three pillars of *ladino* power over them.

These indigenous Mayan rebellions (and others that happened nearly at the same time in others parts of the Mayan region[35]) left marks in the collective memories of both the *ladino* and the indigenous peoples of Chiapas. On one side, it created fear and resentment. For instance, on January 1 1994 it was very common to hear in the streets of San Cristóbal "The indigenous people are coming again!". On the other, in the collective indigenous memory resentment was mixed up with a new hope for justice, autonomy, and liberation. These elements played an important role in the development of the EZLN's national and international struggles.

The Third Thread: The Mexican Revolution and the Zapatistas

Neo-Zapatismo is influenced by the 1910 Mexican Revolution in several distinct ways, and not only in the name. The figure of the *Ejército Zapatista de Liberación Nacional*'s namesake, Emiliano Zapata, represents both a vision of agrarian reform and a practice of rural guerrilla warfare to secure it that remain important elements in the politics of the current neo-Zapatistas. The revolution that exploded in the centre and north of the country in opposition to the dictatorship of Porfirio Díaz, came late to Chiapas, but when it came it followed a course distinct from the rest of the country.

In Chiapas, the landowners attempted to put themselves at the head of the movement and to maintain control over their workers whom they promised some of their lands if they would fight at their side. Thus the revolution fought under the slogan of 'Land and Freedom' was limited in much of Chiapas. It was only as a result of the land reform set in motion in the 1940s by the followers of President Lázaro Cárdenas that the agrarian and political panorama of the state really came to be modified with the formation of *ejidos*, unions, and *campesino* organisations. Most of these, however, would become part of the apparatus of the official party, the Party of the Institutionalised Revolution (PRI) that governed the country for more than 70 years until it was ousted in the presidential elections of 2000. Rather than displacing the old landed oligarchy, the revolution had armed them with a new mechanism of control over the indigenous communities that—until the 1990s—was able to exercise absolute control over the electoral process in Chiapas through the corporatist cooptation of leaders, organisations, and movements. At the same time the revolution had legally enshrined principles of agrarian reform that even when they were ignored by the state, served to legitimise the land struggles of the communities.

The term "Zapatista" is central to the EZLN because the EZLN disputes the appropriation of the values, the imaginary, and the agrarian revolutionary guerrilla heroes by those in power—the government and the post-revolutionary nation state—and reclaims the heritage of this popular struggle. As part and parcel of its declaration of war against the 'bad government' in Mexico and its struggle against neoliberalism embodied in the Free Trade Agreement (NAFTA), the EZLN has recovered the Zapatista slogan 'Land and Freedom' and with it the struggle for land that

> acquires the value of a symbol of resistance against the dispossession of the communities' capacity for self-determination. At the same time, it constitutes the medium for a community spirit, that is, for what binds people together.[36]

The neo-Zapatistas have a history of community construction that we have already briefly examined here with the example of the *komon*. But they also have a history of struggle against *finqueros*, understood and experienced as big *ladino* landowners. These two elements were already present in the Zapatismo of the early twentieth century, and they also shaped the symbolic construction of neo-Zapatismo on a national level, not only in the Lacandon Jungle but across Mexico. These historic references are widely known by all Mexicans, and through them the neo-Zapatistas are understood to be

> reaffirming their membership in the group of the historically defeated, *los de abajo* (the ones from the bottom) of Mexican history, and not another group. ... [But] history [say the neo-Zapatistas] can be inverted ... [and transform itself] in an initiative whose meaning is hope ... so that dignity and rebellion turn into liberty and dignity.[37]

But beyond the mythical popular hero Emiliano Zapata, there are also other elements of the Mexican Revolution that are present in neo-Zapatismo, for example, the production of *corridos* (folk songs) and mural painting. But let us close this section with the words of the neo-Zapatistas themselves who outlined in the *Primera Declaración de la Selva Lacandona* (The First Declaration of the

Lacandon Jungle) the historic continuities that provide them with their symbolic, civil, and political strength:

> We are the product of 500 years of struggle: First against slavery, in the War of Independence against Spain headed by the Insurgents; then in order to avoid being absorbed by US expansionism; after that to enact our Constitution and expel the French Empire from our soil. Then Porfirio Díaz's dictatorship denied us the just application of the Reform Laws and so the people rebelled and formed their own leaders. That is how Villa and Zapata arose, both of them poor people like ourselves.[38]

Another aspect of the Mexican revolution was its anti-clericalism, which took on a particularly sharp form in Chiapas where the Catholic Church, already greatly weakened by the dispossession of its lands and the expulsion of the Dominicans and other religious orders in the nineteenth century, was made the object of intense persecution, culminating in attacks on churches, the burning of icons and the expulsion of the Bishop and remaining priests to Guatemala until 1944. This had two important consequences. The first was that responsibility for the maintenance of the faith was left entirely to laity, whether indigenous or ladino, reinforcing already strong tendencies towards autonomy in religious practice vis-à-vis the Church hierarchy. The second was to establish a pattern of profound distrust between the State and the Church. This distrust would later encourage the Diocese in its embrace of more radical and oppositional politics that would allow, at the end of the twentieth century, the growth of radical left-wing movements in Chiapas and the Lacandon Jungle.

The Word of God

Between the early 1950s and 1994 the indigenous communities of Chiapas underwent a profound and complex collective process of religious awakening, radicalisation, and political organisation. From the early 1950s to 1968, the Diocese of San Cristóbal undertook a process of training indigenous catechists—religious instructors—within a larger framework of missionary activity in the indigenous communities of the Diocese. This process became progressively more systematic and intensive over time, under two successive bishops.

While the methods and content of earlier catechist instruction had been very traditional, the renewed missionary orientation broke with prior parish practice by encouraging the missionaries to travel out of the cities and large towns and to establish closer contact with the villages.[39] In spite of the crude methods and meagre resources, the catechist movement took on a life of its own and soon spread from Tenejapa to the municipalities of Oxchuc, Huixtán, and Chanal.

The catechist movement had a very basic structure. Catechists, mainly in their teens and early twenties, were trained by and met regularly with the pastoral staff and then returned to their communities where they led small circles of the faithful. The movement spread as much by the initiative of the catechists themselves as by the efforts of the scanty pastoral staff of the Diocese. Catechists would identify promising candidates for training in their own or in neighbouring villages and then propose them to the pastoral staff. The greatest obstacle to the growth of the movement in this early period was the lack of pastoral staff able to meet the demand for continuous training.

In 1960 Bishop Lucio Torreblanca was replaced by the young new Bishop Samuel Ruiz García. Under Ruiz's leadership, the training and organisation of indigenous catechists would become the cornerstone of the pastoral practice of the Diocese for the next forty years. In the first eight years of Ruiz's tenure he methodically transformed the Diocese he had inherited, reducing its size, enlarging its staff, and decentralising its governance, all with an eye towards deepening its missionary work in the often remote indigenous communities.[40]

During this period the training of catechists was conducted largely as it had been under Torreblanca. While the training of catechists was expanded and systematised, the content of the courses remained highly traditional as did the methods of instruction.[41] The attitude of the pastoral staff towards the indigenous communities and their culture was generally patronising. The traditional religious practices of the communities were regarded as largely heretical and an obstacle to their economic improvement which was to be achieved, in Ruiz's words, by "teaching them Spanish, putting shoes on their feet, and improving their diets".[42] In spite of the appearance of continuity in practice, however, the thinking of the Bishop and of the pastoral staff of the Diocese was undergoing an important evolution under the simultaneous influence of its increasingly close contact with the lives of the indigenous communities and the upheavals within the larger Church associated with the Second Vatican Council.[43]

As Iribarren argues:

> The motor of the evolution of the Diocese ... was the contact with the indigenous and campesino communities, the contemplation of their situation of permanent conflict, the humiliation and poverty of their lives, and the unanticipated events that demanded rapid discernment. This was creating within the environment of our Diocese the basic principles of Liberation Theology.[44]

Another important aspect of the currents of change during this period was that the pastoral staff was also greatly enlarged under Ruiz, with the invitation of various orders of the Church to take up responsibility for missionary work in several parishes responsible for large portions of the Diocese. In 1962, the Diocese established two schools for indigenous catechists in San Cristóbal, one for men, to be run by the Marists, and the other for women, to be run by the Sisters of the Divine Shepherd.[45] The Marists would establish another centre shortly thereafter in the city of Comitán, and in 1963 the Dominicans were invited to establish the Mission of Ocosingo-Altamirano. Building on the missions already established in Tenejapa and Bachajón, Ruiz was putting in place the organisational means to extend the catechist movement to the whole of the Diocese.[46] Ruiz enjoyed the support of the larger Church in all of this because he was, in effect, rebuilding the Diocese that had been dismantled in the 1930s.

By 1968 the process of building up and reorganising the Diocese, the intellectual ferment generated by Vatican II, and the accumulated experience of contact with the conditions of life in the indigenous communities had set the stage for a radical rupture in the form and content of the training of indigenous catechists by the Diocese.[47] Importantly, by 1968 the Diocese had trained 700 indigenous catechists in Chiapas on whom the Church now depended to carry out its pastoral work.[48] In that year the Diocese undertook a review of their work during which indigenous elders expressed their frustration with the Church's concern for their souls when their bodies were suffering.

This process of transformation in which the catechists and their communities emerged decisively as subjects of their own history characterises the whole period from 1968 through 1974.[49] It begins with critical comments by some catechists in the course of an evaluation of the Diocese's pastoral practice in 1968 and culminates in the organisation of the Indigenous Congress in 1974 in which over a thousand delegates representing virtually all of the indigenous communities in the Diocese came together for the first time to articulate a common set of grievances and a program for their resolution.[50]

In a meeting called by the Ocosingo-Altamirano Mission's pastoral team in November 1971, the catechists challenged the traditional hierarchical methods of instruction associated with the idea of an instructor, or *nopteswanejetic* in Tzeltal, and advanced in its place the idea of a *tiwanej*, or facilitator. Leyva describes this conversion from

> nopteswanej in which everybody listens without further participation, to tiwanej, in which the catechist, on the presumption that the members of the community had 'the word in their hearts,' possessed the inherited wisdom of their elders and needed to communicate it, and further that the wisdom was not only to be found within the elders, but also within the children and the youth.[51]

The role of the *nopteswanejetic* was also criticised as an external imposition of the *ladino* world and a violation of the communities' own traditions of teaching and learning. This produced a lively discussion leading to the identification of four principles that were to inform the future activity of the team:

1. To respect the cultural identity and social reality of the subjects of the catechesis, or religious instruction;
2. To recognise the presence and value of pre-existing Christian tradition;
3. To encourage the participation of the whole community in the reflection on the Word of God; and–
4. To convert the catechists and pastoral agents from *nopteswanejetic* into *tiwanej*.[52]

This shift in pedagogical practice would eventually also have profound implications for the social structure of the communities themselves, calling into question traditional patterns of authority and promoting a democratisation of communal life.[53] Under its influence the catechists and the pastoral team set out to collectively produce a new catechesis based on discussions in the communities of selected biblical passages and their relevance to the experiences and situation of the communities. The story of Exodus became a central organising metaphor in this process as the majority of communities ministered to by the Mission were themselves the product of recent flight from what they saw as the slavery of the *fincas* and then the settlement in *Las Cañadas* region of the Lacandon Jungle which they viewed as their own 'promised land'. This new catechesis, published in 1974 as *Estamos buscando la libertad: Los tzeltales de la selva anuncian la Buena nueva* ('We Are Seeking Freedom: The Tzeltales of the Jungle Announce the Good News')[54] and the collective and communal process of its production, came to have an enormous impact not just on the pastoral practice of the Ocosingo-Altamirano Mission but also on the Diocese and the indigenous communities as a whole. The concept of a 'promised land' and the 'chosen people' allowed the hope of liberation to grow hand in hand with the clandestine armed movement of the EZLN, which we come to in the next section.

A culminating moment in this process of transformation was the 1974 Indigenous Congress, which began as an initiative of the state government of Chiapas to commemorate the quincentenary of the birth of Bartolomé de Las Casas but passed into the effective control of the Diocese by virtue of its privileged access to the indigenous communities. Bishop Ruiz insisted that if the Diocese was to participate that the Congress must enable the indigenous peoples themselves to have a voice and not simply to provide folkloric colour for an otherwise purely commemorative event.[55] The Congress brought together 1,230 delegates from the indigenous communities across the eastern half of Chiapas to discuss their common problems and would represent the most important historical reference for the broader *campesino* movement in Chiapas, which would burst forth immediately following the Congress.[56]

The Fifth Thread: Maoism's Long March in Chiapas

After the celebration of the 1974 Indigenous Congress, several Maoist groups—in particular, *Unión del Pueblo, Linea Proletaria,* and the *Organización Revolucionaria Compañero*—would play a significant if highly contradictory role in assisting the communities to organise themselves politically through political education courses and training in organisational methods that would powerfully inform the distinctive political culture of the EZLN long after many of the Maoists themselves were expelled from many of the communities.

The deadly repression of the Mexican student movement in 1968[57] produced a generalised turn in the country towards more revolutionary politics and forms of action. Inspired by the Cuban Revolution as well as by the rural guerrilla groups led by Lucio Cabañas and Genaro Vázquez in the state of Guerrero, small groups of students across the country formed urban guerrilla groups that captured headlines and became the target of a dirty war. At the same time, a larger fraction of the student movement turned towards Maoism, which in the Mexican context meant, for the most part, an orientation towards the building up of mass formations among *campesinos*, the urban poor, and industrial workers and not, as in South Asia and elsewhere, the launching of a 'peoples war'.

For the Mexican Maoists the most important element of what its adherents called 'Mao Zedong Thought' was the theory of the 'mass line' method of leadership. A concise statement of this theory can be found in Mao's *Some Questions Concerning Methods of Leadership*:

> In all the practical work of our Party, all correct leadership is necessarily from the masses, to the masses. This means: Take the ideas of the masses (scattered and unsystematic ideas) and concentrate them (through study turn them into concentrated and systematic ideas), then go to the masses and propagate and explain these ideas until the masses embrace them as their own, hold fast to them and translate them into action, and test the correctness of these ideas in such action. Then once again concentrate ideas from the masses and once again go to the masses so that the ideas are persevered in and carried through. And so on, over and over again in an endless spiral, with the ideas becoming more correct, more vital and richer each time.[58]

The mass line, in other words, is a recognition of the role of the experiences of 'the masses' themselves in the development of the ideas that are to guide the revolutionary movement. It is a rejection of the notion that the revolutionary leadership already has the answers and needs only figure out how to convey them to the masses. The mass line method does not reject the need for revolutionary leadership, but it does radically reconceive it. The role of leadership is thus to assist the masses in clarifying their own understanding of their conditions and the means by which they might be transformed through a continuous process of distilling the most 'advanced' elements out of the contradictory tangle of their ideas about their experiences in the course of their struggles, and then making those the basis for the next round of reflection.

Mexican Maoism had its roots in a series of expulsions and splits from the Mexican Communist Party in the late 1950s that gave rise to several small organisations that aligned themselves with the Chinese Communist Party in the latter's disputes with the Soviet Union, in particular in opposition to the Soviet policy of 'peaceful coexistence' with the West. In the wake of the 1968 student movement, the Mexico City based 'Ho Chi Minh Section' (or simply 'the Ho') of the largest of these groups, the *Liga Comunista Espartacist* (LCE, or Spartacist Communist League), began to develop and articulate an application of Maoist ideas to the Mexican political context that would enable them to play an important role in urban and rural popular movements in the 1970s and 80s.

Breaking with the sect-like character of its milieu, the Ho had been able to establish some links with and engage in some mass organising work with "militant workers in small factories in Mexico City, *campesino* groups in Morelos and Guerrero, and militant teachers in Hidalgo, Tlaxcala, Oaxaca, Guerrero and the valley of Mexico".[59] The Chinese Cultural Revolution that had begun in 1966 had led the members of the Ho to undertake a new and closer reading of the works of Mao more centred on the practice of the 'mass line' that seemed to point a way out of their previous inability to find a mass base.[60]

The members of the Ho were also affected by the support that had been shown by the urban poor for the student movement in 1968, support that stood in notable contrast with the often hostile stance of industrial workers concentrated in pro-government unions. The combined impact of the ideas emerging from the Cultural Revolution, the sympathy for the students among the urban poor, and critical reflection on their own marginal role in the student movement led the Ho (and others who had undergone similar experiences) to radically reorient their political activity.

It is in this context that we see the emergence of several self-proclaimed Maoist organisations that would play important roles in the burgeoning urban popular movements, in several labour unions, and, in Chiapas, in the indigenous *campesino* movement. The largest of these groups was *Política Popular* (PP). Led by Adolfo Orive, the son of an important leader of the ruling PRI and a student of Charles Bettelheim, the student cadres of PP were especially successful in building organisations among the urban poor in their struggles for land, housing, and basic services.

The first Maoist group to arrive in Chiapas however, was *Unión del Pueblo* (UP—Union of the People), which unlike most of the other Maoist groups did not have its roots in the LCE. Rather, UP had originally been organised as a clandestine urban guerrilla organisation in 1968 that gained notoriety for carrying out bombings. By the early 1970s, however, UP was internally divided with one faction won over to an orientation of patiently building up mass organisations similar to the approach of *Política Popular*. UP cadres from this faction entered into contact with the indigenous communities of Chiapas in 1973 when a trained linguist working with the Diocese and a secret member of UP himself brought in young UP members from the University of Chapingo to train multilingual members of the communities as translators for the 1974 Indigenous Congress.[61] The UP cadres included several students originally from Chiapas who proved adept at navigating the state's complex social and political terrain. Whether their decision to work in Chiapas was fortuitous or the result of a coherent strategic plan based in a countrywide analysis is unclear. What is clear is that the Maoists saw in the radicalisation of the Diocese under the influence of liberation theology an opening to build radical mass organisations.

Reflecting their understanding of the Maoist theory of the mass line the cadres of UP, working with the pastoral staff of the Diocese and the catechists, promoted the use of village level and regional popular assemblies to carry out discussions and develop collective analyses of the themes of the Congress. These in turn ensured that the Congress was regarded widely in the communities as a legitimate expression of their collective will.

In the early 1970s, as part of a populist turn intended to restore the damaged legitimacy of the PRI, Mexican President Luis Echeverría called for the creation of unions of *ejidos*. These were intended to serve as vehicles for reintegrating discontented *campesinos* back into the apparatus of the PRI, but the call created an opening to build the first such *ejidal* union in the Lacandon Jungle, *La Union de Ejidos Quiptic Ta Lekubtesel* (the last three words being Tseltal for 'Our force for progress'). Not surprisingly the village based leadership of *Quiptic* included many of the catechists who had been trained by the diocese, but who had also now been trained as political organisers by UP.

In 1976, another Maoist organisation the *Linea Proletaria* (LP), a split from *Política Popular*, was invited by the Diocese to send cadres to work in the communities of eastern Chiapas. Until then LP had been active mainly in the urban popular movement and in the labour movement in several cities in northern Mexico.[62] This invitation was undoubtedly facilitated by members of UP already working with the Diocese who were eager to develop a closer working relationship with LP. Indeed, within a few months of the arrival of LP cadres in Chiapas, the two organisations had fused.

The thoughts and tactics that Maoists brought with them, interweaving with the local ideology of the *komon* and with the ideas of liberation theology, had a profound impact on the communities of the Lacandon Jungle and beyond.

The Maoists trained leaders in at least 200 indigenous communities as political thinkers and organisers, many of whom would go on to play important roles in the development of the EZLN. While the Maoists had much in common with the political orientation of the Diocese, they also came into competition with the Church for influence within the communities. Importantly, while many villages would only see a priest once or twice a year, the Maoists immersed themselves in the daily lives of the communities in which they lived. Their visible commitment to the poor coupled with their often explicit atheism undermined the authority of the Church hierarchy. The growth of the *ejidal* unions and the concomitant growth in the influence of the Maoists however ultimately precipitated a breakdown in the working relationship between the diocese and the Maoist advisors living in the communities.

The problem came to a head in 1978 when the advisors associated with UP with the deepest roots in the communities participated in an 'exchange of experiences' with LP by moving to Monterrey (in northern Mexico) to participate in LP's work among the urban poor while LP *brigadistas* arrived in the communities to take their places. The newly arrived LP *brigadistas* began to articulate a critique of the ways in which the training of indigenous leaders was supposedly reinforcing inequalities and authoritarianism within the communities. Their answer to this problem was an ideological campaign they named "the struggle to the death against social democracy" in which they challenged the authority exercised in the communities by the catechists and *tuhuneles* (deacons). Not surprisingly, this campaign backfired on the LP *brigadistas* since, authoritarian or not, the indigenous catechists and *tuhuneles* enjoyed considerable prestige in their own communities whereas the *brigadistas* were recent arrivals and seen as *ladinos*.

The actual balance of power revealed itself when the villages sided with the catechists and the Diocese and expelled the Maoists who were compelled to walk out of the jungle and prohibited from even visiting communities along the way. The expulsion marked the end of a phase of formal collaboration between the pastoral staff of the Diocese and the Maoists. The two groups, nonetheless, continued to work together, with many ups and downs, until 1994. Meanwhile, the *campesinos* faced common enemies: Governors, *finqueros*, Lacandones, and the governmental functionaries promoting the *Brecha*.

The *Campesino* Movement Gets Organised

As already noted, the 1974 Indigenous Congress acted as a major impetus for the building of independent *campesino* organisations on the part of the indigenous communities of eastern Chiapas. At the same time that the government continued to pursue its practices of clientelism, cooptation, and corporatism, more and more independent *campesino* organisations began to openly fight for access to land, for greater government support for the production and marketing of agricultural products, and for election to political office. Thus, *campesino* organisations waged a series of intense struggles in the very areas in which the EZLN would later establish itself, acting independently of the PRI, in some cases affiliated with or advised by members of the Communist Party or Maoist organisations, in others more closely tied to the Diocese, sometimes acting alone and sometimes as part of larger national convergences or alliance. In municipalities like Venustiano Carranza, Simojovel, Palenque, Las Margaritas, and elsewhere, an independent *campesino* movement emerged. In the 1980s members of these organisations would suffer intense political repression at the hands of the state's landed oligarchy and the state government they controlled. This experience of repression encouraged the communities to see the value in developing their own capacity for military self-defence. Ocosingo was not the exception, nor were the indigenous *campesinos* who later founded the EZLN.

While the Diocese and the Maoists gave the communities greater access to political resources that greatly facilitated this process it was the vision and energies of the communities themselves that drove the growth of the new organisations and fuelled the explosion in militant land and related struggles in the late 1970s and 80s.

Initial efforts to constitute a single unitary organisation proved impossible, undoubtedly reflecting the considerable variation in political conditions between different regions. The efficient cooptation of village leadership that the PRI had been able to achieve in some parts of Chiapas, for example in San Juan Chamula or other Highland communities, was not so easily accomplished in some of the subregions of the Lacandon Jungle. This was not only because of the physically inhospitable nature of the jungle itself, but also because of the deliberate lack of state attention to these areas and especially the frustrations involved in obtaining recognition of land titles from the Department of Agrarian Reform.

It was probably, however, the efforts of the government from 1972 onwards to 'restore' land titles to 614,315 hectares in the Lacandon Jungle to 66 Lacandon Maya families, that most effectively promoted the radicalisation of the Tseltal, Tsotsil, Chol, and Tojolabal settlers who lived and worked on much of that land. The Lacandones of the twentieth century were commonly misrepresented as the descendants of the original inhabitants who had occupied much of the Jungle prior to their extermination in the late seventeenth and early eighteenth centuries. This gave the government's actions the appearance, especially at a distance, of restoring the lands of a conquered people. The truth however, was that by giving the Lacandones title to such extensive lands, the government sought to circumvent altogether the claims of more recently arrived but also more numerous settlers and thereby to facilitate the concession of valuable lumber extraction rights to a *parastatal* logging company known as COFOLASA.

The conflict between settlers, the Lacandones, and the government soon exploded when the government sent surveyors in order to establish the boundaries of the *Brecha*, as the lands intended for the Lacandones were known. The *Brecha* took in lands already occupied, under cultivation, and in various stages of legalisation before the Department of Agrarian Reform. The government's policy provoked demonstrations, marches, and often sharp confrontations, which were in turn met with often violent repression, including the burning of settlers' homes. All this contributed to a radicalisation of the communities that were pursuing a legal resolution of the conflict by means of *ejidal* unions.

Most of the *ejidos* that were among the first to join *La Union de Ejidos Quiptic Ta Lekubtesel* (or '*Quiptic*') were among those targeted for eviction from their lands in the *Brecha*. In 1976, the federal Secretariat for Agrarian Reform carried out the relocation of eight Chol and fifteen Tzeltal communities in compliance with the decree establishing the Lacandon Zone and in order to prevent them from cutting down any more trees intended for extraction by the *parastatal* logging company. The eviction of these communities however, also had the unintended effect of driving many communities not yet affiliated with *Quiptic* to join the organisation.

The arrival of Maoist cadres of *Línea Proletaria* (LP) in 1976, as discussed above, enabled an acceleration of the process of organising already taking place. An incident involving a more localised land dispute would further consolidate the position of *Quiptic*. On July 8 1977, an incident involving a struggle for control over La Nueva Providencia (legally organised as an *ejido* but in reality essentially a *finca*) precipitated a clash between state police sent in to protect the corrupt leaders of the *ejido* and members of a *Quiptic* meeting in a nearby community. When the smoke cleared, six police were dead and their weapons were in the possession of *Quiptic* (who would however use them only for ceremonial purposes thereafter). The state authorities were compelled by these events to meet the demands of the *ejidatarios* of La Nueva Providencia, and the reputation of *Quiptic* as an organisation willing and able to fight and win was established. In this context, *Quiptic* grew to 75 *ejidos* and 20 ranches, and another *Unión de Ejidos* called *Lucha Campesina* grew to 22 communities. A third *ejidal* union, the *Unión de Ejidos Tierra y Liberta* consisting of 31 Ch'ol communities, and three more *ejidal* unions were also established, drawing in another 44 more communities. The culmination of this process was the merger of the various *ejidal* unions in 1979 under the umbrella of the *Unión de Uniones*, an organisation from which the EZLN has subsequently recruited most of its militants since 1983.

The wave of governmental repression in the 1980s would leave many of the political leaders of the independent *campesino* movement in Chiapas dead or disappeared as the result of the actions of the state and federal police, and of the military as well as the 'white guards' or private security forces paid for by large landowners or rural bosses. At the same time an ethnocidal scorched earth policy on the part of the Guatemalan military against Mayan communities just across the border forced many of them to flee into the Lacandon Jungle.

While Subcomandante Insurgente Marcos notes that the leadership of the unified Guatemalan guerrilla forces (the *Unidad Revolucionaria Nacional Guatemalteca* or URNG) viewed the EZLN "with great suspicion, criticism and frank animosity",[63] the presence of hundreds of university educated middle and upper-class Guatemalan exiles in the cities of Chiapas and of tens of thousands of Mayan *campesinos* in refugee camps scattered through the Lacandon Jungle would have profound implications for both the organisational form and thinking of the indigenous settlers living in the jungle, many of whom would later joined the clandestine work of the EZLN.

The founding of the EZLN in the Jungle on 17 November 1983 occurred, then, in a very difficult moment: The Guatemalan state was pursuing a genocidal response to its own guerrilla insurgencies while the government of Chiapas was actively repressing the independent *campesino* movement in the state. In the face of the guerrilla wars being fought across its southern border in Central America the Mexican government decided to militarise the border, a decision reflected in the selection of Army General Absalón Castellanos Domínguez as governor of Chiapas. At the very same moment, the communities and political organisations operating in *Las Cañadas* had just emerged from an internal crisis that saw a second expulsion of Maoist advisors who had encouraged the organisations to pursue a strategy of improving production rather than fighting for land—a strategy that many communities felt had divided and weakened the *ejidal* unions that were the main independent *campesino* organisations in the region. The tension between the Maoists and the indigenous communities in the Lacandon Jungle remained alive until the EZLN openly declared war against the Mexican government on January 1 1994. And finally, as we shall see in the next section, the guerrilla groups that emerged in Mexico in the late 1960s and early 1970s were either destroyed or brought above ground with promises of amnesty.

The Seventh Thread: The Path of Fire

While the EZLN was formally established in 1983, the efforts to plant a guerrilla force in the Lacandon Jungle began fifteen years earlier. The EZLN was initiated by the National Liberation Forces (FLN) that was itself founded in 1969 in the northern city of Monterrey by a remnant of a very short-lived and poorly conceived attempt to establish a guerrilla group in the Lacandon Jungle under the banner of the Insurgent Mexican Army (*Ejército Insurgente Mexicano*, EIM).

Motivated by outrage at the massacre of students in 1968 and an egregious electoral fraud in the state of Yucatán, the EIM was inspired by the triumph of the strategy of guerrilla warfare in the Cuban Revolution and sought to reproduce that experience in Mexico. While the initiative came from the Yucatán, the EIM brought together young people from various parts of Mexico, including Monterrey. The EIM undertook the installation of the first guerrilla *foco* in the Lacandon Jungle, poorly disguised as a group of 'bearded researchers'.

While the EIM quickly collapsed as a result of internal organisational problems, the experience facilitated the subsequent formation of the FLN and taught the founders of the latter the value of a much more patient and deliberate approach to building a clandestine political-military organisation.[64] It also gave them an appreciation of the strategic potential of Chiapas. State institutions were weak there compared to other areas in Mexico. Furthermore, its proximity to Tabasco where the country is narrowest meant that an insurgency could potentially sever land communications between the Yucatán Peninsula and the rest of Mexico, creating a sizable rear area for guerrilla operations.

The students and professionals who founded the FLN were themselves radicalised through their participation in early and mid-1960s in the broad National Liberation Movement (MLN) inspired by the Cuban Revolution and led by former president of Mexico, Lázaro Cárdenas. While the MLN did not promote a strategy of armed struggle, many of the young activists who would later become guerrilla leaders participated in this formation and shared its perception of the need for a struggle against imperialism and for national sovereignty as a condition for realising a socialist transformation of Mexico.[65] The founders of the FLN were students of philosophy, law, and medicine. They proposed to "liberate the country from foreign exploitation and its local representatives" by overthrowing the government, seizing power, and installing a socialist government. As they declared in an internal communiqué on October 8 1971:

> When the FLN are large they will constitute an army of the people to satisfy the peoples hunger for democracy and dignity, and to provide to all those who today are despised and exploited, land, work, and shelter, and make us at last the owners and beneficiaries of our resources, our work, and our destiny.[66]

These were years of effervescent enthusiasm for guerrilla warfare inspired by the triumph of the Cuban Revolution in 1959, the apparent advances of armed national liberation struggles across Latin America in Peru, Venezuela, Brazil, and elsewhere, but also by the wave of anti-colonial independence struggles and wars of national liberation in Africa and Asia. In Mexico, those drawn to guerrilla activity were also inspired by their own country's long history of heroic guerrilla struggles. As Alonso Vargas notes:

> As a way of fighting [guerrilla warfare comes] from the Indians' resistance to the barbarity of the conquistadors. In the successful campaign in Morelos against the

Spanish Crown; in the armed resistance of the Mexican people against the U.S. invasion in 1847; in the fierce support for the Republican Government of Juárez in the face of the French invasion; and in the first offensives of Villa and Zapata against federal forces [in the 1910 Revolution]; up to the armed campesino struggle of Rubén Jaramillo. During the 1960s, the workers and peasants movement was controlled, subordinated and suppressed by governments ... carrying out a policy of complicity with the interests of U.S. power ... against this new form of domination and subjugation of the people arose new guerrilla fighters led by Arturo Gámiz and Pablo Gómez, on 23 September 1965 ... [who] proposed the construction of socialism in Mexico. Thus was born the contemporary armed socialist movement.[67]

In Mexico, members not just of guerrilla movements but of movements of electricians, telegraph operators, oil workers, doctors and nurses, teachers, and railroad workers that began to emerge in the mid-1950s, would become prime targets of the 'dirty war' of counter-insurgent violence by the state apparatus which disappeared, tortured, and killed with violence and impunity both leaders and rank and file members of such movements. The 'dirty war' was in certain respects a by-product of the cold war that offered a justification for the use of repressive violence for 'security reasons' and the strengthening of the authoritarian regime with a view to the 'threat of communism'.[68]

More than two dozen urban guerrilla groups emerged in the wake of the repression of the student movement in Mexico in 1968. In Monterrey in the northern state of Nuevo León, a struggle against the efforts of the state government and local manufacturers to impose a conservative regime on the university prompted students of the National Polytechnic Institute in Mexico City to protest in support of the demands of students in Monterrey. The ensuing massacre of students by elite Mexican Army troops further radicalised students in Nuevo Leon, driving a fraction to turn to armed struggle. Several other armed groups operated in Monterrey at the same time as the FLN.[69]

By 1972 the FLN had established a presence and was conducting clandestine work in the states of Nuevo León, Puebla, Mexico City, Tabasco, Chihuahua, and Chiapas. In Chiapas they established the Emiliano Zapata Guerrilla Nucleus on a small piece of purchased land in the Lacandon Jungle. In 1974 the police discovered an FLN safe house in Monterrey which led them to the FLN's headquarters in the town of Nepantla outside Mexico City, which in turn led them to the encampment in the Lacandon Jungle and a two-month-long hunt as the guerrilla nucleus fled into the jungle.[70] The operation was conducted in the brutal manner of the dirty war. Captured FLN members were variously tortured, disappeared, held secretly on military installations, and summarily executed. Conducted with impunity, the operation left a handful of survivors.[71] In spite of this blow, the FLN was able to reconstitute itself. Eventually new militants returned to Chiapas and by 1979 had recruited a small group of indigenous activists from the northern part of the state. By 1983 they were able to plant themselves in the jungle and begin the process of building the people's army they had spoken of in 1971.

With respect to the process of rooting themselves in the jungle and recruiting members of the indigenous communities, Comandante Tacho tells us that he was approached because he already had some political and organisational experience. He tells us that he was first chosen by comrades in the organisation in his region as a representative to go speak with presidents, governors, and military officials to explain the logging, agrarian, and economic problems of his region. With all this experience, the militants of the EZLN sought him out and befriended him. "Then they contacted me, immediately sending somebody from very far away to meet with me".[72] After this, and convinced of the cause, he began little by little to invite others and to work with the women of the communities, training them as a kind of 'political commissariat' charged with convincing their husbands and other members of the community until whole communities could be integrated into the clandestine structure of the EZLN.

Major Moisés describes how, at an early age, he left his *ejido* to go to the city to find work and there began to become politically conscious. When he returned to his community he found them waging a strike for land and struggling to obtain a truck to take the agricultural produce of their community from the jungle to the market. Little by little, Major Moisés realised that there were outsiders in the jungle whom at first he thought were tourists. Shortly later, however, a young man came to talk with him:

> We began to speak of the poverty, the injustice, the misery ... and that the people needed to organize themselves. I had already thought about this, and so I told him: "Well, there isn't really a good solution to this struggle we are in". But we didn't know any better and that is when the guy inquired: "But would you be ready?". So I told him: "I need you to tell me more, so that I know what it is about". And then he told me clearly that he was talking about a guerrilla group called the Zapatista Army and that they were clandestine. And then he explained to me the questions of security.[73]

Convinced of the cause, Major Moisés says he met with a group of seven men in the community in order that they might all join, and then took on the work of supplying provisions for the clandestine organisation from the city while at the same time learning to read and write. Later the organisation sent him to conduct recruitment work in factories and, finally in 1985, he went up into the mountains to become a guerrilla.

Concluding Remarks: Weaving the Word

We started with two basic ideas: That of a *caracol* (snail) and of a tapestry. We conceive of both as metaphors of the grammar and symbolisms of the neo-Zapatistas. The *caracol* can be understood as the structuring foundation of life in the communities, as the collective voice of a politically constructed 'us' with a Mayan Mesoamerican root.[74] The *caracol* can also be understood as a structuring foundation of neo-Zapatista text, above all of its written communiqués that are "elaborated via circumvolution" in which the speaker (speaking subject) selects the space of the detour in which both reality as well as an imaginary trip are captured. That means a constant return to the origin, indeed a multiple origin, that functions both as the site of an anchorage for the struggle, as well as its legitimisation. It is also a mythological, literary, and political origin of an unfinished history.[75]

By way of these two metaphors (of the *caracol* and of the tapestry) we have attempted to weave a kind of interwoven text with the genealogical threads of neo-Zapatismo. Unfortunately, these threads are not known in depth, not even by many of the followers of neo-Zapatismo.[76] We believe that without an understanding of the historical roots of this stance in traditions of indigenous self-governance in the Mexican political experience of the 1970s and in the particular conditions confronting the indigenous-*campesino* movement in Chiapas and Mexico, it is impossible to seriously discuss what neo-Zapatismo is about.

We do not pretend however, to have been able to identify here what is of universal significance for counter-systemic movements in neo-Zapatismo, or even what is particular to Chiapas or Mexico. In any case, most likely such claims would be sharply contested anyway. Instead, what we have chosen to do is to present an account of the genealogy of neo-Zapatismo the meanings and implications of which can perhaps both continue to unfold and to interweave, over time, in the hope that this can contribute both in helping other activists and scholars to answer such questions for themselves, and for the sake of the movement.

The neo-Zapatistas are indeed, as they declared in their first public statement on January 1 1994, "the product of 500 years of resistance". However, this long history of resistance is not composed of a single thread, but rather of many, which allow the neo-Zapatistas to draw on a rich body of symbolisms and political cultures that stretch from local traditions of indigenous revolt to the national revolutionary agrarian figure of Emiliano Zapata, as well as Che Guevara, the international symbol of guerrilla warfare. It is the interweaving of all these elements that has given neo-Zapatismo its distinctive character and local, national, as well as global resonance, making the EZLN one of the most influential anti-capitalist movements in the world today.

References

José Luis Alonso Vargas, 2008—'*La guerrilla socialista contemporánea en México*' ['The contemporary socialist guerrilla in Mexico', in Spanish], in Verónica Oikión Solano and Marta Eugenia García Ugarte, eds, 2008—*Movimientos armados en México, siglo XX* ['Armed movements in Mexico, 20th Century', in Spanish], vol 1 (Zamora, Michoacán: El Colegio de Michoacán, CIESAS), pp 129–143

Anon, 2000—*Chul stes bil* ['The Sacred Land', in Tzeltal and Spanish with English subtitles]. Video. San Cristóbal de Las Casas, Chiapas: PROMEDIOS-Chiapas

Fabio Barbosa, 1984—'*La izquierda radical en México*' ['The radical left in Mexico', in Spanish], in *Revista Mexicana de Sociología*, vol 46, pp 111–138

Vivienne Bennett and Julio Bracho, 1993—'*Orígenes del Movimiento Urbano Popular Mexicano: pensamiento político y organizaciones políticas clandestinas 1960–1980*' ['Origins of Mexican urban popular movements: Political thought and clandestine political organisations', in Spanish], in *Revista Mexicana de Sociología*, vol 55, pp 89–102

Victoria Reifler Bricker, 1981—*The Indian Christ, the Indian King: The Historical Substrate of Maya Myth and Ritual*. Austin: University of Texas Press

CCRI-EZLN, 1994—'El Comité Clandestino Revolucionario Indígena cuenta sus orígenes' ['The Clandestine Revolutionary Indigenous Committee recounts its origins', in Spanish], in Rovira Guiomar, ed, 1994—*Zapata Vive! La rebelión indígena de Chiapas contada por sus protagonistas* ['Zapata Lives! The Indian rebellion in Chiapas, told by its protagonists', in Spanish] (Barcelona: Editorial Virus), pp 37–45

Adela Cedillo, 2008—*El Fuego y el Silencio* ['The Fire and the Silence', in Spanish]. Mexico City: Comité 68

Community Document, 2004—*Historia de la colonización. Selva Lacandona* ['History of the Colonisation. Lacandon Forest', in Spanish]. San Cristóbal de Las Casas: Impresos Jovel

Jan de Vos, 1994—*Oro Verde. La conquista de la Selva Lacandona por los madereros tabasqueños 1822–1949* ['Green Gold: The conquest of the Lacandon Jungle by Tabascan Loggers', in Spanish]. Mexico City: Gobierno del estado de Tabasco, Fondo de Cultura Económica

Jan de Vos, 1995—'*Las rebeliones de los indios de Chiapas en la memoria de sus descendientes*' ['The rebellions of the Indians of Chiapas in memory of their descendants', in Spanish], in Jane-Dale Lloyd and Laura Pérez Rosales, 1995—*Paisajes rebeldes, Una larga noche de rebelión indígena* ['Rebel landscapes: A long night of indigenous rebellion', in Spanish] (Mexico City: Universidad Iberoamericana) pp 239–270

Jan de Vos, 2002—*Una tierra para sembrar sueños, Historia reciente de la Selva Lacandona, 1950–2000* ['A land for sowing dreams. A dream land for planting: A recent history of the Lacandon Jungle, 1950–2000', in Spanish]. Mexico City: Fondo de Cultura Económica

Ejército Zapatista de Liberación Nacional (EZLN), 1993—'*El Despertador Mexicano*' ['The Mexican Alarm', in Spanish], in *Órgano Informativo del EZLN*, no 1, Mexico City

Ejército Zapatista de Liberación Nacional (EZLN), 1994a—*Documentos y Comunicados* ['Documents and Communiqués', in Spanish], vol 1. Mexico City: Colección Problemas de México, Editorial ERA

Ejército Zapatista de Liberación Nacional (EZLN), 1994b—'*Declaración de la selva Lacandona. Hoy decimos ¡Basta!*' ['Declaration of the Lacandon Jungle—Today we say: Enough is Enough!', in Spanish], in *La palabra de los armados de verdad y fuego. Entrevistas, cartas y comunicados del EZLN* ['The word of the armed people of the truth and the fire: Interviews, letters, and communiqués of the EZLN', in Spanish]. Mexico City: Fuenteovejuna

Ejército Zapatista de Liberación Nacional (EZLN), 1995—*Documentos y Comunicados* ['Documents and Communiqués', in Spanish], vol 2. Mexico City: Colección Problemas de México, Editorial ERA

Ejército Zapatista de Liberación Nacional (EZLN), 1997a—*Documentos y Comunicados* ['Documents and Communiqués', in Spanish], vol 3. Mexico City: Colección Problemas de México, Editorial ERA

Ejército Zapatista de Liberación Nacional (EZLN), 1997b—*Crónicas Intergalácticas. Primer Encuentro Intercontinental por la Humanidad y contra el Neoliberalismo* ['Intergalactic Chronicles: First Intercontinental Encounter for Humanity and Against Neoliberalism', in Spanish]. Mexico City: Planeta Tierra, Montañas del Sureste Mexicano

Ejército Zapatista de Liberación Nacional (EZLN), 2003a—*Documentos y Comunicados* ['Documents and Communiqués', in Spanish], vol 4. Mexico City: Colección Problemas de México, Editorial ERA

Ejército Zapatista de Liberación Nacional (EZLN), 2003b—*Documentos y Comunicados* ['Documents and Communiqués', in Spanish], vol 5. Mexico City: Colección Problemas de México, Editorial ERA

Captain Elisa, 1994—'*Capitana Elisa, tseltal, 22 años*' ['Captain Elisa, Tseltal, 22 years old', in Spanish], in Rovira Guiomar, ed, 1994—*Zapata Vive! La rebelión indígena de Chiapas contada por sus protagonistas* ['Zapata Lives! The Indian rebellion in Chiapas, told by its protagonists', in Spanish] (Barcelona: Editorial Virus), pp 61–62

Carlos Fazio, 1994—*Samuel Ruiz, el caminante* ['Samuel Ruiz, the Sojourner', in Spanish]. Mexico City: Espasa Calpe

Óscar Flores, 2008—'*Del movimiento universitario a la guerrilla. El caso de Monterrey (1968–1973)*' ['From the campus movement to the guerrilla: The case of Monterrey (1968–1973)', in Spanish], in edited by Verónica Oikión Solano and Marta Eugenia García Ugarte, 2008—*Movimientos armados en México, siglo XX* ['Armed movements in Mexico, 20th Century'], vol 1 (Zamora, Michoacán: El Colegio de Michoacán, CIESAS), pp 129–143

Nathalie Galland, 2007—'*El sueño líquido. Metáfora y recorrido semántico por tierras rebeldes*' ['The liquid dream: Metaphor and semantic reconnaissance in rebellious lands', in Spanish], in Ana Lorena Carrillo and Nathalie Galland, eds, 2007—*Metáforas rebeldes* ['Rebellious Metaphors', in Spanish] (Puebla City: Benemérita Universidad Autónoma de Puebla), pp 93–183

Antonio García de León, 2002—*Fronteras Interiores, Chiapas: una modernidad particular* ['Internal Frontiers: Chiapas, A Modernity of Its Own', in Spanish]. Mexico City: Editorial Océano

Octavio Gordillo y Ortiz, 2006—*EZLN. Una aproximación bibliográfica* ['EZLN: A bibliographical approximation', in Spanish]. Mexico City: Editorial Praxis

Rovira Guiomar, ed, 1994—*Zapata Vive! La rebelión indígena de Chiapas contada por sus protagonistas* ['Zapata Lives! The Indian rebellion in Chiapas, told by its protagonists', in Spanish]. Barcelona: Editorial Virus

Christopher Gunderson, 2006—'The Provocative Cocktail: Origins of the Zapatista Revolt'. Paper presented at the Annual Meeting of the American Sociological Association held at the Montreal Convention Center, Montréal, Québec, Canada

Christopher Gunderson, 2007—'The Persistent Return of the Wretched of the Earth: Neo-Zapatismo and Revolutionary Theory'. Paper presented at the Social Theory Forum, University of Massachusetts, Boston, March 28 2007

Christopher Gunderson, November 2009—'Before the Storm: The Ideological Origins and Development of Zapatismo, 1960–1994'. Paper presented at Conference on Zapatismo and Globalization, Bildner Center for Western Hemisphere Studies, CUNY Graduate Center, November 20 2009

Christopher Gunderson, 2013—'The Provocative Cocktail: Intellectual Origins of the Zapatista Uprising, 1960–1994'. Doctoral Dissertation in Sociology, CUNY Graduate Center

Pablo Iribarren, 2003—'*Experiencia: Proceso de la Diócesis de San Cristóbal de Las Casas. Chiapas. México. 29 de Abril de 1985*' ['Experience: Process of the Diocese of San Cristóbal de Las Casas, Chiapas, Mexico, April 29 1985', in Spanish]. San Cristóbal de Las Casas: Ediciones Pirata

Yvon Le Bot, ed, 1997—*El sueño zapatista: entrevistas con el subcomandante Marcos, el mayor Moisés y el comandante Tacho del Ejército Zapatista de Liberación Nacional* ['The Zapatista dream: Interviews with Subcomandante Marcos, Major Moisés, and Comandante Tacho of the Zapatista National Liberation Army', in Spanish]. Barcelona: Plaza y Janés

María del Carmen Legorreta, 2008—*Desafíos de la emancipación indígena. Organización señorial y modernización en Ocosingo, Chiapas 1930–1994* ['Challenges of Indian emancipation: Manorial organisation and modernisation in Ocosingo, Chiapas 1930–1994', in Spanish]. Mexico City: Colección Alternativas, CIICH-UNAM

Gudrun Lenkersdorf, 2001—*República de Indios. Pueblos mayas en Chiapas. Siglo XVI* ['Indian Republic: Mayan peoples in Chiapas, 16th Century', in Spanish]. Mexico City: UNAM

Xochitl Leyva Solano, 1995a—'*Militancia político-religiosa e identidad en la Lacandona*' ['Politico-religious militancy and identity in the Lacandona', in Spanish], in *Revista Espiral: Estudios sobre Estado y Sociedad*, vol 1 no 2 (January–April), pp 59–88

Xochitl Leyva Solano, 1995b—'*Del Comon al Leviatán. Síntesis de un proceso político en un medio rural mexicano*' ['From the *Comon* to the Leviathan: Synthesis of a political process in a rural Mexican context', in Spanish], in *América Indígena*, nos 1–2, pp 201–234

Xochitl Leyva Solano, 1995c—'*Catequistas, misioneros y tradiciones en Las Cañadas*' ['Catechists, missionaries, and traditions in Las Cañadas', in Spanish], in Juan Pedro Viqueira and Mario Ruz, eds, 1995—*Chiapas, Los rumbos de otra historia* ['Chiapas: Paths to Another History', in Spanish] (Mexico City: UNAM, CIESAS, CEMCA, Universidad de Guadalajara), pp 375–405

Xochitl Leyva Solano, 1998—'The New Zapatista Movement: Political Levels, Actors and Political Discourse in Contemporary Mexico', in Valentina Napolitano and Xochitl

Leyva Solano, eds, 1998—*Encuentros antropológicos: Power, Identity and Mobility in Mexican Society* (London: Institute of Latin American Studies [ILAS]), pp 35–55

Xochitl Leyva Solano, March 2001—'*Las "autoridades-concejo" en Las Cañadas de la selva Lacandona: la excepción que cumple la regla*' ['The "authorities-council" in Las Cañadas in the Lacandon jungle: The exception that proves the rule', in Spanish], in *Cuadernos del Sur*, year 7, no 16, pp 49–64

Xochitl Leyva Solano, January–April 2008—'*El cosmoser y el comon prácticas de los mayas en movimiento*' ['The cosmos and the *comon*: Practices of the Mayas in movement', in Spanish], in *Revista Cultura de Guatemala. Los mayas: historia, discursos y sujetos*, Third Period, year 29, vol 1, pp 127–134

Xochitl Leyva Solano and Gabriel Ascencio Franco, 1996—*Lacandonia al filo del agua* ['Lacandonia at the water's edge', in Spanish]. Mexico City: Fondo de Cultura Económica, UNAM, CIESAS

Murdo J MacLeod, 1973—*Spanish Central America, A Socioeconomic History, 1520–1720*. Los Angeles, CA: University of California Press

SCI (Subcomandante Insurgente) Marcos, 1997—'*El mundo que queremos es uno donde quepan muchos mundos*' ['The world we want is one where many worlds fit', in Spanish], in Yvon Le Bot, 1997—*El sueño zapatista: entrevistas con el subcomandante Marcos, el mayor Moisés y el comandante Tacho, del Ejército Zapatista de Liberación Nacional* ['The Zapatista Dream: Interviews with Subcomandante Marcos, Major Moisés, and Comandante Tacho, of the Zapatista National Liberation Army', in Spanish] (Barcelona: Plaza y Janés), pp 123–357

Mao Tse-tung, 1967—'Some Questions Concerning Methods of Leadership', in *Selected Works of Mao Tse-tung*, vol III (Peking Press), pp 117–122. See also http://www.marx2mao.com/Mao/QCML43.html

Major Moisés, 1997—'*Encuentros con unos "turistas"*' ['Encounters with some "tourists"', in Spanish], pp 165–175; '*La elección de las armas*' ['The choice of weapons'], pp 220–230; '*La vida en las comunidades en tiempos "ni de guerra ni de paz"*' ['Life in the communities in times "neither of war nor peace"'], pp 289–293; and '*Marcos debe desaparecer*' ['Marcos should disappear'], pp 358–363, in Yvon Le Bot, ed, 1997—*El sueño zapatista: entrevistas con el subcomandante Marcos, el mayor Moisés y el comandante Tacho, del Ejército Zapatista de Liberación Nacional* ['The Zapatista Dream: Interviews with Subcomandante Marcos, Major Moisés, and Comandante Tacho of the Zapatista National Liberation Army', in Spanish]. Barcelona: Plaza y Janés

Jesús Morales Bermúdez, 1992—'*El Congreso Indígena de Chiapas: un testimonio*' ['The Indigenous Congress of Chiapas: Testimony', in Spanish] in *Anuario 1991* (Tuxtla Gutiérrez, Chiapas: Gobierno del estado de Chiapas, ICHC), pp 242–370

Luis Hernández Navarro and Ramon Vera Herrera, eds, 1996—*Acuerdos de San Andres* ['San Andres Accords', in English]. Mexico City: Ediciones Era

Nepantla, 2009—*La insurrección de la memoria. Un testimonio de las FLN* ['The insurrection of memory: A testimony of the FLN', in Spanish]. Video 36 minutes. Mexico City: AMY Videoproduction

Vicente Pineda, 1986—*Sublevaciones indigenas en Chiapas. Gramática y diccionario tzeltal* ['Indigenous uprisings in Chiapas: Tzeltal grammar and dictionary', in Spanish]. Mexico City: Instituto Nacional Indigenista

Enrique S Rajchenberg and Catherine Héau-Lambert, 2005—*'Historia y simbolismo en el movimiento zapatista'* ['History and Symbolism in the Zapatista Movement', in Spanish], in Gilberto Giménez, 2005—*Teoría y análisis de la cultura* ['Theory and Analysis of Culture',] (Mexico City: CONACULTA, Ic@cult), pp 168–185

Samuel Ruíz García, 1993—*En esta hora de gracia, carta pastoral con motivo del saludo de S.S. el Papa Juan Pablo II a los indígenas del continente* ['In this hour of grace: Pastoral letter on the occasion of SS Pope John Paul II's greeting to the indigenous peoples of the continent', in Spanish]. Mexico City: Ediciones Dabar

Samuel Ruiz García and Jorge Santiago, 1999—*La búsqueda de la libertad. Entrevista realizada en septiembre de 1996 de Monseñor Samuel Ruiz por Jorge Santiago* ['The quest for freedom: Interview conducted in September 1996 with Bishop Samuel Ruiz by Jorge Santiago', in Spanish]. San Cristóbal de Las Casas: Editorial Fray Bartolomé de Las Casas

Jan Rus, 1998—*'¿Guerra de castas según quién?: Indios y ladinos en los sucesos de 1869'* ['Caste war according to whom? Indians and whites in the events of 1869', in Spanish], in Juan Pedro Viqueira and Mario Humberto Ruz, eds, 1998—*Chiapas: Los rumbos de otra historia* ['Chiapas: Signposts of another history', in Spanish] (Mexico City: UNAM, CIESAS, CEMCA, Universidad de Guadalajara), pp 145–174

Jorge Santiago, January 2009—Interview done by Christopher Gunderson, January 22 2009. Teopisca, Chiapas, Mexico

Diana Spenser, 2008—*'La nueva historia de la guerra fría y sus implicaciones para México'* ['The new history of the Cold War and its implications for Mexico', in Spanish], in Verónica Oikión Solano and Marta Eugenia García Ugarte, 2008—*Movimientos armados en México, siglo XX* ['Armed movements in Mexico, 20th Century', in Spanish], vol 1 (Zamora, Michoacán: El Colegio de Michoacán, CIESAS), pp 99–109

Comandante Tacho, 1997—*'Cómo me hice Zapatista'* ['How I became a Zapatista', in Spanish], pp 163–165; *'Nos sublevamos para tener una vida digna'* ['We are rising up to lead a dignified life'], pp 230–238; *'Sobre la "democracia comunitaria"'* ['On "community democracy"'], pp 293–298, all in Yvon Le Bot, 1997—*El sueño zapatista: entrevistas con el subcomandante Marcos, el mayor Moisés y el comandante Tacho, del Ejército Zapatista de Liberación Nacional* ['The Zapatista Dream: Interviews with Subcomandante Marcos, Major Moisés, and Comandante Tacho of the Zapatista National Liberation Army', in Spanish]. Barcelona: Plaza y Janés

Juan Pedro Viqueira, 1995—*'Las causas de una rebelión india: Chiapas, 1712'* ['The causes of an Indian rebellion: Chiapas, 1712', in Spanish], in Juan Pedro Viqueira and Mario Humberto Ruz, 1995—*Chiapas: Los rumbos de otra historia* ['Chiapas: Paths to Another History', in Spanish] (Mexico City: UNAM, CIESAS, CEMCA, Universidad de Guadalajara), pp 103–143

Recommended Websites and Blogs

http://barrikadazapatista.wordpress.com/

http://contralarepresion.wordpress.com/2010/06/

http://detodos-paratodos.blogspot.com/2009/03/concluye-el-encuentro-de-mujeres-mama.html

http://dignarabia.ezln.org.mx/

http://enlacezapatista.ezln.org.mx/
http://lahorasexta.podomatic.com/
http://mujeresylasextaorg.wordpress.com/
http://revistarebeldia.org/
http://rinconzapatistazac.blogspot.com/
http://union-rebelde.blogspot.com/
http://zapateando.wordpress.com/
http://zeztainternazional.ezln.org.mx/
http://www.capise.org.mx/
http://www.cedoz.org/site/
http://www.chiapasmediaproject.org/
http://www.coloquiointernacionalandresaubry.org/
http://www.europazapatista.org/
http://www.nodo50.org/pchiapas/chiapas/documentos/caracol/caracol.htm
http://www.radioinsurgente.org/
http://www.radiozapatista.org/IIEncuentro.htm
http://radiozapatista.org/
http://www.serazln-altos.org/index.html

Notes

1. Xochitl Leyva Solano (1995a, b, and c, 1998, 2001, 2008) and Christopher Gunderson (2006, 2007, 2009) are scholar-activists who have been inspired by the neo-Zapatista experience and who hope that this presentation on the roots of that experience might be a small contribution to the debates and discussions that our South Asian colleagues and *compañeros* have been pursuing around emerging global movements. We dedicate it to the neo-Zapatista *compañeros* and *compañeras* who are the reason and inspiration for the international neo-Zapatista solidarity networks of which we are part.
2. CCRI 1994; Major Moisés 1997; Comandante Tacho 1997; SCI Marcos 1997; Leyva 1995a, 1998; Le Bot 1997.
3. See EZLN 1993, 1994a, 1994b, 1995, 1997a, 1997b, 2003a, 2003b, and journals such as *Rebeldía*, *Revista Chiapas*, and *Contrahistoria*.
4. Gunderson 2006, 2007, 2009, and 2013.
5. SCI Marcos 1997; Leyva 1998.
6. Hernández Navarro and Vera Herrera 1996.
7. With the exception of their spokesman Subcomandante Insurgente Marcos, the EZLN is composed mainly of indigenous people.
8. CCRI 1994, p 38.
9. Cited in Le Bot 1997a, p 137.
10. CCRI 1994, p 38.
11. Cited in Rovira 1996, p 62.
12. A *finca* in Chiapas is a large piece of land for agricultural use that has been expropriated by non-indigenous people for their private benefit.
13. Lenkersdorf 2001, p 27.
14. *Ladino* in Chiapas and Guatemala means a non-indigenous person. Sometimes this term refers to a white person, at other times to a *mestizo* or to a foreigner. *Mestizo*

is a term traditionally used in Spain and Spanish-speaking Latin America to mean any person of mixed-race descent (broadly), a person of combined European and Amerindian descent.

15. De Vos 1994.

16. Leyva and Ascencio 1996.

17. ibid, p 21.

18. Legorreta 2008, p 250.

19. Leyva and Ascencio 1996.

20. Community Document 2004.

21. Ed: As is well known, English and other European colonisers mistakenly used the term 'Indians' (and the equivalents in other European languages) to refer to the indigenous peoples they 'discovered' in what they then called 'the Americas'; thinking that they had arrived in the land called India. This term and its equivalents have subsequently become both widely internationalised—because of European colonialisms—and also relatively internalised, and even though it has come to be rejected by indigenous peoples in some contexts such as Turtle Island (North America, where the terms First Nations or Aboriginal Peoples are now used), it also continues to be used quite widely, especially in Abya Yala (Central and South America). In this book therefore, because it has been edited by Indians from India, and also published by OpenWord based in India, and in order to intervene in this history (rather than for nationalist reasons!) we have—with the agreement of the authors—used the term 'indigenous peoples' in place of 'Indians' wherever it appeared by itself, but have left the term as it is wherever it is qualified (and clarified) by another term, such as here.

22. Leyva 1995b, 2001.

23. Leyva 2008.

24. MacLeod 1973, pp 87–102.

25. De Vos 1995, p 248.

26. *Cofradía* is an institution of social and religious character and based in the principle of fraternity. It was introduced into the New World by the Spanish conquerors and resignified by the indigenous population, principally for the celebrations of the village Saints.

27. Bricker 1981, p 60.

28. ibid, pp 61–63.

29. Viqueira 1995, p 126.

30. De Vos 1995, pp 249–252.

31. In Latin America, the term *casta* was often used by the colonisers to describe the various racial categories and to divide the population.

   Ed: The term 'caste', to denote the structuring of society in South Asia (and now also among the South Asian diaspora globally), comes from the word *casta* but from the Portuguese, as a result of the Portuguese also establishing colonies in India. Given how strongly the middle and upper castes in India today resist any suggestion that the discrimination that Dalits experience and racial discrimination are related, which Dalits strongly assert, it is revealing for me as an Indian to see that the authors say that the term *casta* was used in Latin America to describe racial categories. For more details, see the Wikipedia entry at https://en.wikipedia.org/wiki/Caste#In_South_Asia.

32. Bricker 1981; Pineda 1986; De Vos 1995; Rus 1998.
33. De Vos 1995, pp 250–252.
34. Rus 1998.
35. The historic Maya region covered the south of Mexico (the states of Campeche, Quintana Roo, Tabasco, Yucatán, and Chiapas), Guatemala, Belize, and western Honduras.
36. Rajchenberg and Héau-Lambert 2005, p 174.
37. ibid, p 179.
38. EZLN 1994b, p 5.
39. Leyva 1995c; De Vos 2002.
40. Iribarren 2003, pp 4–5; Fazio 1994, pp 55–82.
41. Leyva 1995c.
42. Fazio 1994, p 57.
43. Bringing together cardinals, bishops, leaders of the various orders, as well as observers from other churches and advisors trained in the social sciences, the Second Vatican Council met every autumn between 1962 and 1965 and revisited questions of church doctrine on a wide range of questions. The Council set the stage for the 1968 Conference of Latin American Bishops from which the current known as liberation theology emerged. Liberation Theology fused elements of a Marxist critique of capitalism with the Catholic Church's tradition of social action and became a major influence on the radical left in Latin America in the 1970s and after.
44. Irribaren 2003, p 5; see also Santiago 2009.
45. De Vos 2002.
46. Irribaren 2003.
47. ibid.
48. Ruiz 1993, p 29; see also Ruiz and Santiago 1999.
49. Ruiz and Santiago 1999; Santiago 2009.
50. Morales 1992.
51. Leyva 1995c, p 394.
52. De Vos 2002, p 223.
53. Leyva 1995c.
54. Cited in Leyva 1995c.
55. Morales 1992.
56. Morales 1992, García de León 2002.
57. A major student movement, critical of the rule of the PRI, emerged in Mexico in 1968. A general student strike began in August and on October 2 1968 hundreds of student protesters were massacred in the Plaza de las Tres Culturas in Mexico City. Thousands of students were arrested and imprisoned; others were disappeared.
58. Mao 1967.
59. Bennett and Bracho 1993, pp 91–92.
60. Barbosa 1984, p 128.
61. García de León 2002, pp 166–170.
62. Barbosa 1984; Bennett and Bracho 1993.
63. Marcos 1997, p 135.
64. Cedillo 2008.

65. Cedillo 2008, pp 68–69.
66. Cedillo 2008, p 185.
67. Vargas 2008, p 129.
68. Spenser 2008, p 109.
69. Flores 2008.
70. Cedillo 2008.
71. Nepantla 2009.
72. In Le Bot 1997, p 164.
73. Moisés 1997, pp 171–172.
74. Leyva 2008.
75. Galland 2007, pp 97, 102.
76. We have three reasons for our argument that the historical roots of neo-Zapatismo are not known in all their depth. The first is that in the wake of the 1994 uprising, the air of mystery around the EZLN's origins proved to be a valuable political asset for the movement. It allowed the neo-Zapatistas to exercise greater power over their public image, encouraged continual interest in the group, and enabled a broad range of sympathisers to project their own vision onto the rebels. Second, since this is an unfinished war, information on neo-Zapatista origins can easily turn into booty for the enemy. Third, although there was a somehow erratic but nevertheless important local production before 1994 (academic articles, documents of *campesino* organizations, newspapers, governmental information, etc), a lot of this information has not been included in the work on neo-Zapatismo in a conscientious fashion. On the contrary, many have opted to focus on what took place (the events) after 1994. References to this pioneering material can be consulted in Leyva and Ascencio 1996. A first systematic listing of a wide-ranging bibliography on neo-Zapatismo produced after 1994 can be found in Gordillo 2006.

Ecological Justice and Forest Rights Movements in India:
State and Militancy—New Challenges
Roma and Ashok Choudhary[1]

An Introduction

Forest rights movements in India are today passing through a very critical period. They are engaged in a hard battle against the direct aggression from the Indian State, primarily in the context of governance over 75 million hectares of forest, forest land, and minerals—an area that constitutes nearly a quarter (23 per cent) of the total land area of this very large country.[2] At the same time, they are having to struggle to maintain their independent identity from the armed political groups, called 'Maoists', that are also active in the forest regions for their own strategic reasons.[3] There has however been a consistent effort from the ruling elites, and supported by the dominant groups, to prove that all forest rights struggles are essentially linked with the Maoist groups,[4] so that they do not need to confront the real and very material underlying issues of confrontation between the forest peoples[5] and the Indian nation-state. Regrettably, most civil society actors in India (barring a very few), which exist in the middle space, have preferred to be misled by this propaganda and knowingly or unknowingly have taken sides in the 'drama' of searching for a 'peaceful solution'.

But even if civil society ignores these struggles, people's voices are today rising from almost every corner of the country and from all over the entire subcontinent[6]—from inside the forest areas by the forest peoples, from all the struggles against forced land acquisition, eviction from livelihood resources, corporate projects, Special Economic Zones, and slavery in agricultural and unorganised labour, and in general from the desire and struggles of all such peoples to live with dignity and to work for prosperity and peace. So, it is necessary to focus on the real issues as raised by these voices and with a perspective gained from a history of people's movements in modern India.

This is all the more necessary in these days since, in addition to having been falsely labelled 'Maoist', such movements have faced criticism from a prominent and credible mainstream left intellectual for not being able to suggest any socialist alternative to the present globalised capitalism and for thus becoming a tool of capitalist reform.[7] Given this twin assault, a critical understanding of people's movements in contemporary India needs to be very seriously developed, especially in the context of the historical reality that all mainstream socialist alternatives have not only failed to address the very basic conflict that exists between the

Indian State and the disempowered marginal sections of the country, the *Adivasis* and the *Moolnivasis*, and its democratic resolution, but where these 'alternatives' have in fact basically also collaborated with the elitist perception of building a modern Indian state that is responsible for displacing more than seventy million people from their livelihood resources since independence and has made them 'development refugees'. About 70 per cent of these disempowered people are from Adivasi, Dalit,[8] and other marginalised sections. As activists directly involved in the movement, we feel it is important for us to articulate the views of the struggling people very clearly that the struggles are not just for a piece of land or some trees but to understand the wider context of this historic process of resisting the neoliberal regime and of struggling to achieve ecological justice.

We started writing this essay as activists and organisers in the NFFPFW (National Forum of Forest People and Forest Workers), a forum that was founded in 1998. The NFFPFW was transformed during 2013 into a union, the All India Union of Forest Working People (AIUFWP). One of us (Ashok Choudhary) was one of the founders of the NFFPFW and now has the designation of General Secretary in the AIUFWP; the other (Roma) was also a co-founder and is now Deputy General Secretary of the AIUFWP.[9] Both of us are long-time, middle-class activists coming from outside who have joined the struggles of the forest peoples and forest workers. Ashok earlier worked as a trade unionist among unorganised labour in small towns in northern India, such as rickshaw-pullers, and who in fact brought him to their communities in the forests—and which led to the formation of the NFFPFW. What we discuss in this essay is based on our experiences as activists and on our interactions with other organisers in the NFFPFW and with other sections of struggling peoples in India and elsewhere. The views we express here, however, are our personal views.

Struggles for Environmental Justice in India and Globally

The forest-dependent peoples of India regard what dominant society calls 'natural resources' as their habitat and heritage. The difference is that they do not see nature as a commodity. They have been strongly raising their voices against the loot of such 'natural resources' that has been going on in the country in the name of 'development' from colonial days and then on from when it attained independence in 1947, and more recently also for saving the environment and for facing the climate crisis that we are today all experiencing. In doing so, they are bringing forward fundamental issues of people's political economies of the protection of natural resources and of livelihoods vis-à-vis the interests of the elite and of capitalists in these 'natural resources'. According to Adivasis, Dalits, and other marginalised peoples, there can be no solution to the present climate crisis without ensuring the rights of the communities dependent on these resources.[10]

The connotation of these rights also means social equality and social justice that have been denied to them for centuries.

In other words, the devastation of environment is directly linked with increasing poverty across the world. Without proposing solutions to end poverty in the larger debate of climate change, the debate of saving the environment is futile. In the ongoing debates among the G8 and G20 nation-state governments, this crucial social and political aspect is completely missing. The dominant political class has only one yardstick, that of so-called 'growth'.

As in other parts of the world, in India too these voices of indigenous and forest peoples have forced the climate debate to move from being a technical debate in closed-door discussions to coming onto the streets, and to it becoming *a fundamental issue of governance and of environmental and ecological justice*—of protecting both Mother Earth and also the livelihoods and cultural resources of indigenous and other related subaltern communities all over the world. This emerging consciousness has raised serious questions about the negotiations on climate change that took place during the UN Copenhagen Climate meet in December 2009, and the failure of which led the government of the plurinational state of Bolivia, led by indigenous peoples, to then call a 'Peoples' World Conference on Climate Change and Mother Earth's Rights in April 2010'[11]—and also in the subsequent UN meetings in Cancún (in Mexico) and in Durban (South Africa). Governments everywhere are today facing large-scale opposition from indigenous communities and forest peoples to the climate change solutions that are being proposed by developed nations and big multinational companies, that are more like trade treaties between the rich nations and the rich, arrogant, dominating upper-class ruling classes of the developing countries.

The protection of 'natural resources' and of Mother Earth in general—and of forests in particular—is a political and social question as much as about ecology, science, and the environment. Unless those dependent on such resources are full partners with rights under the law, it is not possible to protect these resources from the onslaught of capital. The Cochabamba Conference in April 2010 was a very important initiative in this regard, where efforts were made to bring about 30,000 representatives from movement groups and Southern governments from around the world to discuss and come to agreement on these fundamental issues.[12]

It is not as if the political economy of climate has not been discussed at the international forums earlier. In 1972, the Declaration of the UN Conference on Environment in Sweden declared that there is a direct correlation between the degradation of the environment and increasing poverty across the world.[13] Global capitalist forces have their own interpretation of what is happening however, and in the garb of eradicating poverty across the world, they have instead pushed policies of promoting trade treaties between developed and developing countries. This policy has further accelerated the process of alienation of people from their livelihood resources, especially in the Global South. From that time on—from the 1980s on—and with the expansion of capitalist interests in these areas, people's struggles in India have only intensified around forest, land, and water issues. Social and environment activists also started joining these struggles, helping those in struggle to have a wider reach among other sections of society. In earlier movements, these linkages were missing. These struggles are now not only in the form of resisting these giant companies who have the backing of state power but also of asserting their political rights to re-occupy the democratic and political space that has been snatched away from them during a historical process.

Present Challenges for People's Movements

Today, the democratic struggles led by tribal, indigenous communities, other deprived communities, and women in the forest areas are posing a big challenge to the rulers of the modern Indian state. In Indian forests,[14] hundreds of militant mass struggles are going on against the hegemony of the state. All these popular struggles however, which are essentially democratic and militant and led by lo-cal people's organisations, are today being branded by the government as being 'Maoist' struggles. As mentioned above, according to the government the number of districts showing some Maoist influence has greatly increased: From 56 in 2003 to 200 in 2011, out of a total of 640 districts in the country—in other words, in nearly one-third of the country. Even if these figures have been inflated, in order to serve the government's own purposes, they are certainly active quite widely. But whereas the Maoists have entered these areas only in the 1970s, independent, democratic struggle within forest areas has a much longer history of around 250 years, and this has been and continues to be waged by the forest peoples today without any vanguards. Moreover, this tradition is constantly getting stronger, and is today far more extensive and powerful than the much-publicised activities of militant 'Maoist' groups. These democratic movements are present in almost all the forest regions of the country today.

Unfortunately, this history—and story—of democratic struggle and move-ment doesn't catch the attention of the media, researchers, or academics, and so is not generally known. And generally speaking, the mainstream national and regional political parties and their affiliated bodies are also not interested in addressing these democratic struggles because they feel threatened by the possi-bility that supporting these struggles might reduce their own ability to function in the autocratic and centralised manner they are used to. But the reality is that these independent democratic struggles are spreading like fire in many forest areas, and in some areas are becoming a major challenge to the eminent domain of the Indian state. In these areas, popular struggles are becoming the main op-position to the neoliberal policies adopted by the state to usurp natural resources and hand them over to industrialists and IFIs (international finance institutions). The struggles—carried out in a democratic framework and whose leaders are ordinary Adivasis, women, and youth—are challenging the state with their raised mass political consciousness. The state is also aware of this, and so, on the excuse that they are also Maoists, the Indian state is today trying to also crush all the democratic movements in the forests and backward areas.

Today, forest rights movements in India therefore have two fundamental challenges: Their direct contradiction with the Indian state and the resolution of this contradiction within a democratic framework, and secondly, maintaining their identity independent from the Maoist movements. The critical question is the state of the forest rights movements and how they are facing these challenges and will face them in the future. At the same time, we need to recognise that forest rights movements, throughout their history of the last 250 years, have faced many such challenges—and that they therefore have behind them a deep heritage of strong resistance against such aggression.

Forest Movements and Historical Injustice

The history of forest struggles in India is around 250 years old, in the first instances fought by tribal peoples to resist the imperial interests of the British when they invaded India in the eighteenth century.[15] We can say that the torchbearers of the forest rights movements in the country today have historically been poor, simple tribals and other forest dwelling peoples. Not only did they lead the movements but over time they also brought forward the vital political questions of anti-colonial struggle, community governance, land reforms in the forest region based on community rights, and environmental governance based on social and ecological justice. These glorious struggles were fought under the leadership of legendary revolutionary leaders such as Tilka Majhi (Jabra Pahadia), Sidhu Kanhu, Birsa Munda, and Kana Bhagat.[16] Their movements, that took place at different times in history, not only forced the British to keep away from the forests in struggling areas but also forced them to enact legislation that ensured community governance without the interference of the state. The Chhota Nagpur Tenancy Act (1908) and the Santhal Parganas Tenancy Act (1912) are just two examples of such legislation brought in after historic struggles in what is now the state of Jharkhand.

But these laws were implemented only in a piecemeal way, and they were further weakened after independence as the independent Indian state—instead of implementing the laws—kept on expanding its monopoly over these resources and adopted a policy of nationalising these resources. On the one hand, and in spite of such revolutionary activities earlier on, the movements in the 1920s and 30s were not able to enforce this legislation. On the other hand, and despite great changes that started taking place in the country after independence, these historic movements remained isolated and were not able to establish linkage with each other, and were therefore weakened. Along with this, subsequent laws like the Indian Forest Act in 1927 (IFA)[17] came to empower the Forest Department (FD) to become the biggest landlord in independent India and were fundamentally anti-people and anti-environment. Without any legislation in place to protect the rights of the forest peoples, and with a period of relative inactivity by the forest peoples, the FD increased its control very successfully over the six decades after India gained independence in 1947 and converted all the rights that the local people had gained into mere concessions—and later on, after the enactment of the Forest Conservation Act in 1980, it even terminated these concessions.

In the 1990s, and due to the adoption of neoliberal policies by the government of India, the forests were further thrown open to IFIs, multinational companies, and other megaprojects, and the Ministry of Environment and Forests gave many illegal environmental clearances to these companies. These clearances are now becoming a major bone of contention between the local communities and the Central and State governments. To name a few, the controversial projects include the Posco project in Orissa (now Odisha)[18] and the Jaypee industry in Himachal Pradesh.[19] Because these projects led to the mass evictions of forest peoples, this has resulted in direct conflict between the people and the FD.

A Brief History of the Fraud Committed by the Indian State on Forest Peoples

The process of historical injustice for forest peoples started from colonial rule, when the colonial state initiated an economic process in the nineteenth century for the accumulation of capital by encroaching upon the so-called 'natural resources' of the country—forests, land, and water; and which, as already mentioned, the forest peoples regard not as commodities but as their habitat and their heritage. Although the annexation of the forests had started in the eighteenth century, at the same time as the colonial power started to gain political power over various princely states in the Indian subcontinent, the process intensified in the following century. A section of the Indian merchant class also joined with the British colonial power in accumulating capital, and thus became a major partner in the exploitation of natural resources and in the use of Adivasis and Moolnivasis as cheap labour to strengthen the colonial power.

The emergence and concept of the modern Indian nation-state is in fact strongly linked with this exploitative economic process, and grew strongly through this exploitative system during the period of the national movement in the late nineteenth century. The native merchant class that collaborated with—and exploited, for their own interests—the colonial power also then joined the 'national movement', again in their own interests. This fundamental relationship between the exploitive colonial system and the development of the concept and practice of an Indian nation-state has however been rarely questioned. And whenever such questions were raised, even in embryonic form, they were brutally crushed.

As a result of this underlying nexus, the Congress Party, which was founded as far back as 1885 and which spearheaded the mainstream national movement, was able to take a resolution on political freedom only as late as in 1928. Till then, it only demanded economic freedom. This shows how mainstream national politics did not include or want fundamental change in the colonial administrative system, and more importantly that it was rooted in the socio-economic structure of the country that was based on a reactionary feudal and Brahminical[20] ideology.

For thousands of years, the dominantly Hindu mainstream society in India has remained divided as a function of the hierarchical caste system, which broadly speaking has two distinct classes, the privileged and the underprivileged. Historically, while the privileged—the elites—owned the resources and other institutions as a function of their control over kingdoms, the underprivileged in mainstream society had virtually no resources of their own and thus always remained dependent on the elites for survival. Indigenous societies (Adivasis) however—living within the forests and sustained by them—remained outside the hierarchical Hindu social structure, and as mainstream Indian society developed along with British colonialism and then as a part of the freedom movement, this history and culture of the independence of indigenous peoples became one of the main reasons for the conflict that developed between them and mainstream society. To address the continuing historical injustice that forest peoples face, we therefore need to go to and challenge its very root—which is this deep and longstanding social and material contradiction.

The Enactment of the Forest Rights Act in 2006:
A Historical Injustice Undone

It took almost sixty years for the Indian state to recognise the fact that the participation of local forest-based communities in managing the forests is essential to protect and manage both the forest and biodiversity. Sixty years after the Forest Act of 1927, and as a result of the growing movements among forest peoples from the 1970s onwards—along with many other related movements, such as over rivers—the government's Forest Policy of 1988 for the first time talked about the involvement of the forest peoples in the management of the forests; but that policy had no backing through proper legislation. It took another eighteen years for Parliament to pass legislation that protected the rights of the forest peoples, through the enactment of the Forest Right Act (FRA) in 2006.

The enactment of the FRA was however not just the wish of the government then in power in New Delhi (the United Progressive Alliance government, led by the Congress). The intensifying resistance and struggle by forest peoples themselves, and the new factor of growing actions in forested areas by the 'Maoists' by that time—which the government, supported by left parties, came to proclaim as 'the biggest threat to Indian democracy'—were first recognised by the Chief Ministers of three states in particular, Andhra Pradesh, Madhya Pradesh, and Tripura, who realised that they could neither manage the forests nor govern their states unless something was done. In addition, there was growing pressure from the European Union (and—very interestingly—even by the World Bank) for greater democratisation in forest governance. It was the combination of all these voices that finally forced the central government to bring in this legislation, in order both to try to isolate the Maoists in these areas and also to convince its own constituencies that it was being responsive. The new legislation, formally titled 'The Scheduled Tribe and Other Forest Dwellers (Recognition of Forest Rights) Act 2006 but popularly known as the Forest Rights Act (FRA),[21] admitted in its Preamble the need for mitigating the "historical injustices" committed on forest peoples since colonial times—but was silent, however, on giving any account of these historical injustices.

Why Is There Continuing Conflict between the Indian State and the *Adivasis and* Moolnivasis? *Some Examples*

Though in the wording of the new Forest Rights Act the Indian Parliament recognised that historical injustices have been done on forest people, the Central and the State governments have been and remain hesitant in showing their political will to implement this Act at the ground level, even six years after enactment. This is the case even though a very positive aspect of the Act is that it has created a political and democratic space for the forest dwelling communities to spell out these historical injustices—which did not exist before the Act came into existence.

According to Munnilal for instance, a prominent community leader of the *Taungiya* forest village settlements of Uttarakhand,[22] "We the forest people attained independence only on December 15 2006 when the FRA was enacted in Parliament and not on August 15 1947 when India attained freedom. We got independence from the tyrant rule of the Forest Department (FD) who is the carrier of the colonial legacy". The late Noor Alam, leader of the nomadic *Van Gujjar* tribal community of the Rajaji National Park in the state of Uttarakhand, took this even further: "Why there is so much hue and cry about 'saving the environment'? ... No climate can be protected without ensuring the rights of the people living in the forests, nobody talks about that. Even the animals are talked about, but we the human beings who have a symbiotic relationship with the forest are not consulted in any of the conservation programmes. Everyone talks about this, and about us, but without talking with us and as if we don't exist".

The enactment of the new legislation has both opened up a debate and also intensified struggles in various forest areas on the issue of land reform inside the forest areas—an issue that remained unaddressed over the previous six decades.

The forest area that remains in the eminent domain of the state of India through its FD, which is as much as 23 per cent of the total land area of this huge country, awaits effective agrarian reforms. The question that remains, however, is whether this question can be successfully addressed by the FRA or not. It is well known that the Congress government formed in India after independence brushed the issue of agrarian reforms under the carpet. Along with doing this however, and before any effective land reform legislation could be introduced and enacted in the country, the government was diligent enough to transfer vast tracts of forest land vested with the erstwhile princely estates, *zamindars*, and *talukdars*[23] to the FD without doing what is called 'the settlement of rights' of the peoples living in the forests. These included the forest and the forest land[24] within the boundaries of the *Gram Sabhas* (village bodies).

To give an example from the states of Bihar and Uttar Pradesh, where the pre-independence movement against the feudal landlord system was very strong, the forests of both these states were vested with the FD by bringing in a new legis-lation, the 'Bihar and UP Private Forests Act 1948', that was hurriedly passed in the respective Legislative Assemblies. This however was strategically done just before the enactment of important land reforms legislation, the 'Landlord Abolition and Land Reform Act' in 1952. In 1955 these lands were again notified as protected forests according to the Indian Forest Act 1927. The Land Reform Act came into existence in 1952, but the enforcement of this law took another eight to ten years in these states, and so before the land reform legislation could come into force, the Indian state strengthened the FD to become the biggest landlord in the country, in a manner that was against the spirit of the country's Constitution. All of these were moreover illegal transfers of land, as none of the State revenue laws had any provision to transfer lands that were under the jurisdiction of village councils.

Another glaring example took place in Khunti district, in what is now the state of Jharkhand, which is known as the '*Khuttkatti*' area and is governed under the Chhota Nagpur Tenancy (CNT) Act[25] that came into force in 1908. According to this Act, around 450 villages had the control of forest land and forests at that time. The land records locally known as *khatiyan* are with the tribal Munda, but in 1955 the FD demarcated its own boundaries in this very area without doing any verification of rights and demarcation. The Revenue Department notification dated July 1 1955 read as follows:

> The forest and the waste lands comprised in this notification shall be called Protected Forests. The nature of extent of rights and government and of private person in and over the forest and waste lands comprised in this notification has not been enquired and recorded as laid down in sec 29 of the IFA 1927, but as the State Government thinks that such enquiry and recording will occupy such length of time as in the mean time to endanger the rights of the Government,

and as the enquiry and record-of-rights will hereafter be made, this notification is issued subject to all existing rights of individuals or communities.[26]

This happened in an area where communities were already in possession, and where the legislation as powerful as the CNT Act existed, but despite this, by applying the IFA 1927 the Indian state acquired the land without settling claims. The Indian Government committed this fraud in all the states throughout the country, and illegally transferred millions of hectares of community, village council, and other common purpose lands to the FD.

To cite an example from another state, Himachel Pradesh (HP), the people of the state enjoyed traditional rights from these forests that were well recorded in a document that dated from Mughal Empire called *Wajib-ul-urz*. This was a record of rights in Urdu that existed from before British period. The rights granted to people under this regime were timber for house construction, grazing rights, timber for making agricultural implements, grass for thatched roofs, fodder, fuel wood, lopping trees for cattle, Chirgoza and Kail dry leaves for the bedding of cattle, wood for ceremonies, dry wood for cremating corpses, etc. In the local language these rights were known as *bartandari* rights. In 1927, the settlement of twenty-four rights was recorded according to the then new Indian Forest Act. But over the years the FD again transformed these rights into concessions, not rights. And at the onset of the twenty-first century, it eliminated all these concessions as well. From now on, and in independent and democratic India, the landless and the other poor communities of the area who depended on forest and commons came to be termed 'encroachers'. The FD also took over the Timber Distribution rights (TD) that the people customarily enjoyed from the commons. And today, several years after the passing of the FRA in 2006, the state of HP has not yet started enforcing the process of implementing this Act.[27]

Instead, and as part of an attempt to attract international capital, the state government is handing over these very resources to big multinational companies and hydro megaprojects without doing or giving any forest or environmental clearance. This despite the fact that various governmental committee reports have concluded that major projects in the state, such as the cement factory in Majathanl sanctuary in District Mandi, the Renuka Dam in District Sirmour, and the several hydropower projects in District Kinnaur—to name a few—should be halted because of their non-viability. In such a context, there is bound to be direct conflict between the people and the state.

The experience has been similar in the neighbouring state of Uttarakhand. Here, 65 per cent of the total land area is forest land, and after historic struggles, two types of forest management came to be practiced there since the time of the British regime. In what used to be called 'British Garhwal',[28] *van panchayats* (*van* means forest; local forest bodies) used to manage the forests adjacent to the villages. These forests provided the villagers with fuel, fodder, and other 'Non Timber Forest Produce' (NTFP) for their daily use. The *van panchayats* came under the Revenue Department and not under the FD, but over the years, and under the influence of the FD, various amendments were made in *van panchayat* rules, and gradually they were taken over by the FD. They virtually became non-functional except in some areas where women took initiatives to save the forests.

Secondly, in the interior forests there used to be Village Reserve Forests (VRF) that were managed by the communities and that would provide their daily requirements. But in 1962 the FD took control of these VRFs through a government order and without any consultation with the communities. The FD now started large-scale commercialisation of forest produce and commercial plantation, which had a very adverse impact on the communities, and they rose in resistance. One example was the famous Chipko movement to stop commercialisation of the forests that started in the 1970s in the tribal areas of Nanda Devi Forest Division in the upper Himalayas, in district Joshimath, bordering China. But in spite of strong movements by the forest peoples, the *van panchayat* rules were never converted into legislation, and now, after the FRA has been enacted, the Uttarakhand Government and the FD have both been opposing this Act since it will re-establish the rights of the communities in the hilly regions.

In short, in the name of scientific forestry—a fraudulent term given by the British—the FD has appropriated massive community forest land in the name of managing them, and over time has become its owner. These lands are today incorporated in the FD's ten-year plan document known as a 'working plan', where these lands are treated as 'forest land'. This loot of the community forest land is the very real historical and material injustice that has been done to the forest peoples, and that has continued and intensified after independence.

Beyond this, the FD gets revenue from these lands, but does not compensate the villagers.[29] Private lands were also not spared and were notified without any land acquisition process and without paying any compensation to the tribals in forest areas. This issue of forest land is thus the most critical issue of dispute in India between the people and the Indian state.

The Struggle

Ramchander Rana, a member of the Tharu tribe, who lives in and around Dudhwa National Park situated in the northeastern region of the state of Uttar Pradesh on the Indo-Nepal border, says very clearly that "There is a direct conflict inside the forest areas between the forest people and the Indian state". This tribal residing inside the forest is clear that this conflict is over the control of natural resources including minerals, and that the conflict is a question of community governance vs corporate interests of profit.

The period 2002–2006 is very important in the struggles of forest peoples in India, and in fact their struggles—along with other pressures, as discussed above—resulted in the enactment of the FRA in 2006. In 2002, and following an interim order by the FD and supported by the Supreme Court of India, large-scale evictions took place inside forest areas across the country, These evictions however resulted in strong resistance movements that started in almost all forest areas. To name a few, struggles erupted in Rewa, in the state of Madhya Pradesh; in Assam, Orissa, Jharkhand, Bihar, UP, and Uttarakhand—in other words, in a belt right across central India. By 2006—the year the FRA was passed—forest people had started forcefully reclaiming their lands that had been robbed from them during both the colonial and the post-colonial periods. This took place in many areas, such as in the Kaimur area that straddles the states of UP, Jharkhand, and Bihar, and where forest land conflicts are very complicated. By 2007, movements under the leadership of the Dalit and Adivasi women of Kaimur had reclaimed around 10,000 hectares of forest land. This movement only intensified during the following years, and especially after 2006 when the FRA was implemented. This vibrant struggle of the tribals of Kaimur was fought under the strong leadership of women, who even taught officials lessons about forest rights in their region and confidently argued that the land and forest belongs to them and that the Indian Parliament has given power to their village council. If any forest official came to evict them, they would show them a copy of the Act, which made their rights clear.[30]

In the present situation, this assertion by the oppressed communities—and especially by the women—is the most significant development in the ongoing movements. Women are taking the main initiative in organising and mobilising entire communities, not only to resist the neoliberal attack and onslaught but also to create alternative economic and political methodologies for holistic development. There are some remarkable case studies that merit special mention.

In the protected area within the 'core zone' of the Dudhwa National Park, on the Indo-Nepal border, by resisting and in time reversing the High Court order to evict them women forced the state to recognise the tribal village Surma. The villagers lost a case in the High Court that they fought for 23 years with the FD, because it provided false information to the Court. But they resisted the eviction order of HC and continued to stay there. The passing of the FRA helped them because in the light of the new Act the government referred the case of Surma village to the Law and Justice Department, which recommended recognising the rights of the village. Surma became the first forest village in any protected area in India whose rights were recognised under this Act, which enabled them to start the process of transformation of the status of their village to 'revenue village'.[31]

The leadership of women in such struggles in the various forest areas has given a new dimension to the entire forest peoples' movement. In September 2011, women of many forest areas came together to form a Women Forest Rights

Action Committee. The women deliberately called it an 'action committee' because they felt that the governments were not showing any political will to implement the FRA in its true spirit. So they declared that if government was not going to be sensitive to their rights, they would forcibly take over possession of their forest and land and implement the Act in their own way.

Through the formation of this Action Committee, women are taking many new initiatives, especially in the Kaimur area where they have taken over thousands of hectares of land that are now under their collective possession. With the land in hand, they have moved on to trying to form cooperatives in new forms to strengthen their community organisation. The NTUI (New Trade Union Initiative), an independent trade union for organised and unorganised working people, has been helping the local organisation in this initiative.

A New Phase

It is perhaps evident from this essay that mass political movements in India are today moving into a new phase, one that is beyond the stage of resistance and is focused on creating alternative models to the present neoliberal regime. But this emergence is also intersecting with the rising curve of climate change.

At present, the crisis that the forest peoples are facing is about how a few—the rich and powerful, and through corporations—usurp the rights and access of the vast majority of the disempowered over the commons: Air, water, land, minerals, and forests. Unsustainable economic development and inequitable growth based on an economy dependent on the use of fossil fuels and extractive industries—which has greatly intensified in the last 60 years—have led to a sharp rise in carbon emissions, way beyond what the Earth can absorb. There is an extremely urgent need to make sharp and immediate cuts in the emission of greenhouse gases across the globe. This urgency has not been reflected either in the Indian government's position and policy interventions or in the positions of governments worldwide. Climate change has become a serious threat to the poor. In India, widespread and significant impacts of climate change have been noticed in many regions. These impacts adversely affect the urban working poor, the lives and livelihoods of the Himalayan and other hill people, fishing communities and other coastal and island communities, small and marginal farmers and agricultural workers, Dalits, women, Adivasis, forest dwellers, and other disadvantaged and marginalised communities in different regions.

Neoliberalism has faced its toughest resistance across the globe from communities protecting their rights over the commons. While the thirst of capital for minerals and fossil fuels magnifies, so does the resistance to protect these vast tracts of land that are under forest cover and inhabited traditionally by Adivasis and other forest dwellers who are largely dependent on forest produce. Our forest peoples' struggles are today at this historic juncture, where, on the one hand, they have the affirmative and challenging FRA on their side, and on the other, where there are innumerable traps set for them in the form of JFMs,[32] REDDs,[33] and other programmes, all formulated in the name of addressing global climate change. The land grab that is taking place under this cover, particularly agricultural land being acquired by the state for the infrastructure project and industry, has greatly increased conflict between state authorities and developers and the local communities. Backed by the eminent domain that the State claims is its right, under neoliberalism government—and corporates backed by government—are free to violate the law of the land. Rampant displacement is taking place as a result of the projects they are undertaking, and there is no proper resettlement and rehabilitation at ground level. This intensified assault is however being met by intensifying resistance.

The period between 1980 and 2005 witnessed a series of social movements all over the country on fundamental issues such as these that questioned the government's developmental paradigm. The intensity and passion of protest against the neoliberal regime was strongly demonstrated during the WSF (World Social Forum), held in Mumbai in January 2004, within and also outside the event. More than 5,000 people participated in WSF Mumbai from forest struggle areas under the banner of the National Forum of Forest People and Forest Workers. Together with various international organisations from Latin America, the NFFPFW formulated a joint programme and declaration titled 'Mumbai Initiative' during the WSF towards resisting the onslaught of neoliberal policies in forest areas.[34] The next year, 2005, this initiative was taken forward and strengthened at the next WSF gathering in Porto Alegre, Brazil, when the 'Mumbai-Porto Alegre Initiative' was agreed on and signed by various international organisations and individuals.[35]

In India, the struggle to reclaim forest land intensified after tribal and other indigenous communities participated in the WSF in such a large scale in Mumbai. The forest peoples came back with a new understanding that poverty and dispossession is an international and global phenomenon and that social inequality and disparity can only be removed by reclaiming the lost political and economic space through a protracted class struggle. This new understanding and resolve contributed both to strengthening their struggles on the ground and also to the actions that the movements took to demand and bring about the FRA in 2006.

Within the larger space of resisting state and corporate resource grab, we can today see that the struggles are becoming decentralised, and even delinked in many places, and that they are no longer led by middle-class activists or intelligentsia. The growing consciousness of the people has taken the movements forward, at times at the cost of their lives, and they have made sure that the neoliberals do not have an easy way forward. The struggles that have taken place over this past decade in Nandigram and Singur in the state of West Bengal (now Paschimbanga), in Mundra (on the coast of Kutch, in Gujarat), in Raigad in Maharashtra, in the hilly terrains of Himachal and Uttarakhand, in Latehar, Chengara, Haripur, and Nayachar, in the Odisha and Andhra coastal regions, and in the Kalinga Nagar, Jashpur, and Sonbhadra struggles led by the communities themselves, are exemplary examples of this. This truly is the most remarkable aspect of India's new movements and needs special mention and affirmative support. Another exceptional feature of these movements is the emergence of gender consciousness and the need for women to play an important role in leadership.[36] These struggles will definitely inspire and can give new directions to people's movement.

The emergence of a collective consciousness on a composite class basis can clearly be seen in the forest rights struggles, both at the political level and also at the level of economic production, as there is direct and common conflict with the companies in the forest areas. At the political level, new alliances of diverse communities are taking place and rapidly outpacing other more traditional political alliances of dominant groups and the state forces. These dominant forces are today facing serious crisis within themselves, but at the same time they are trying to divide the communities on traditional lines, especially caste and religion, though they are not succeeding. At the level of economic production, new relationships are coming up very strongly in some areas, such as in the form of collective production in agriculture and in forestry, again initiated and led by women. This has definitely helped the communities to sustain their production even during drought periods. The age-old system of bonded and wage labour is also in decline in some areas. Although it is difficult at this stage to predict the future outcome of this process, the collective process is definitely strengthening community-based leadership.

The new rejuvenated community leadership is also engaged in linking forest rights struggles with the other struggles and thus helping the forest rights struggles to come out from their traditional isolation. This could clearly be seen in the protest rally that took place in August 2011 in front of the Parliament House, called *Sansad Gherao* ('Surround Parliament'), against the then proposed Amendments to the Land Acquisition Act.[37] Since 2006, thousands of forest community members from different states have come together with other communities from across the country to protest against the draconian colonial law in New Delhi, organised by *Sangharsh* ('Struggle'), a joint platform of diverse struggling groups with a common agenda of resisting neoliberal aggression. Forest and land rights struggle is thus today at the threshold of a radical transformation from being separate, isolated movements in various less known interior areas to becoming a comprehensive social and political movement which relates to and includes other rights-based struggles, and especially those by natural resource–based communities like fishworkers, landless and poor peasants, and mining-based peoples.

People's control of natural resources and against displacement have now become a central demand of independent mass movements in India—and in fact marks one of the key differences with the 'Maoist' movement in the country. In the popular movements, this demand, and the struggles around these demands, are now increasingly initiated by local people's aspirations and their involvement. This is very different from Maoist-controlled movements which do not raise the question of people's control of resources, since they have no clear-cut position on these issues—and where all their movements' activities are strictly controlled by the armed Party militia. This is also why violence is the main theme in their conflict with the state, where this is not the case for people's movements. Crucially, the question of the alienation of tribal populations from their land and their resources is secondary in their movement. The central issue for Maoists is the capturing the state power through armed struggle. Thus, although they have a strong bias in favour of oppressed peoples, the role of people's movements in their controlled areas is subservient to armed struggle, which also cannot be led and owned by people's initiatives.

It is also important here to critically review the role of middle class and progressive forces in the process of the alienation of tribal and other marginalised working peoples, which was started in the colonial period and continued in the post-colonial period, and that has come to intensify in the present neoliberal regime, and in the struggles against this. During the anti-colonial freedom struggle and immediately after independence, progressive middle-class groups remained supportive of the mass struggles that were taking place. In the subsequent decades after the independence—the 1950s and 60s—although the majority of progressive groups and the middle class in general supported the 'mixed economy' development paradigm that had been formulated by the independent Indian state, and that came to be responsible for the massive alienation and displacement of tribal and other marginalised sections, some of the progressive groups played a significant role in the mass movements of the 1960s and 70s. And after 1975, when then Prime Minister Indira Gandhi imposed an 'Emergency' in the country, with the suspension of all civil liberties, many middle-class activists who got disillusioned with centrist politics and the mainstream left parties started working with marginalised peoples in the interior areas on critical issues like displacement, livelihood, human rights, environmental issues, health, the public distribution system, and so on, and over time came to play a major role in organising the labouring poor for achieving social and economic justice.

The subsequent period, from the 1980s onwards, has seen a new phase in social movement in India, the emergence of people's own assertions in the social and political arena. A new generation of community leadership is now developing through mass resistance against various projects undertaken by national and international capital, resulting in the closure or stoppage of many projects. In some of the areas, the resistance has been very militant and independent. Popular movements are emerging as an independent force and have started creating impacts in different political and social fields.

This development has had a serious impact on the political scenario in India, in different ways. On the one hand, the ruling and/or dominant political parties are facing the loss of their base in some areas of the country. On the other hand, the emergence of this new force has also started affecting the middle-class social activists. Such activists, many of whom played leadership roles in the movements they helped organise in part because of the particular skills they brought as well as their social and political contacts in the outside world, are today unsure about the emerging community-based leadership that believes in collective action and that is keen to be directly involved in all negotiation processes, and in evolving new methodologies for resistance. This new consciousness of course needs to be encouraged, in order to ensure the direct involvement of critical masses in political and social processes. But in this rapidly emerging context, middle-class activists in movement need to radically change their roles if they are to remain relevant to the social movements. They have to move to playing an actively and consciously supportive role to strengthen community and community-based leadership, and not assuming or wanting leadership itself.

Movements in India are today in a transitional phase. The middle-class leadership can, for instance, still write on behalf of movements, but they can no longer get into negotiations with the state by themselves. Equally, the ruling classes are also asking as to who has the right to speak on behalf of people. And finally, in many situations it has become clear that the ordinary people in movements are today ahead of their middle-class leadership, especially in the context of asserting their rights and of negotiating with the state.

Unity of Struggles around Natural Resources: Political Struggle for Justice

The movement to effectively implement the Forest Rights Act is an inalienable part of the struggles that are taking place today in India—and across the world—for democratic governance. The struggle for the implementation of forest rights is not important only for the forest-dependent people or communities, it is equally important for the other natural resource–based working people like fishworkers, mineral dependents, agriculturalists, bamboo workers, handloom weavers, and artisans who are partly or indirectly dependent on forest and other natural resources; and also society at large. In 2011, the fishworkers' struggle won a major battle against the government when they managed to repeal the notification of an amendment to the Coastal Management Zone (CMZ) and to bring back, through protracted struggles over the previous three years, the powerful Coastal Regulation Zone 2011 (though diluted relative to the 1991 version).

Based on this understanding, popular movements for forest rights felt that they needed to develop a larger framework for their fight for environmental justice. It was in this context that in June 2011 they organised a national consultation on these issues inside the Great Himalayan National Park in Banjar, in Himachal Pradesh. Thirty-six people's movements and twelve support organisations from different parts of India took part in the consultation. The meeting decided to call for a 'National Federation of Natural Resource–based Traditional Working Peoples / Communities'. It was agreed that such a federation, while attempting to bridge the vacuum between social movements and trade unions, could also give political direction and tie loose ends to the different natural resource–related struggles taking place across India.

As a follow-up to this, various movements came together in this context on December 15 2011 to march on Parliament in New Delhi to commemorate the day when the FRA was passed five years before, in 2006. The prime agenda of the meeting was the implementation of the FRA. The movements also agreed that their slogans must reach Parliament. Shaheed-e-Azam Bhagat Singh, India's great revolutionary leader, freedom fighter, and martyr in 1930s, once said, while defending the act of throwing a bomb in the Legislature's Central Hall, that "You need such explosions to open the ears of a deaf government." Even if the movements were now referring to the verbal bombs they would throw, this historical saying is still relevant for social movements given that the situation has not changed from the British period.

Along with this action, the movements also organised a national conference to come together to form a federation across several movements: The forest struggles, the fishworkers' forum, the anti-mining struggles of Jharkhand, the affirmative land struggles from South, North, East, and Western India, the Dalit movements from South and North India, and so on. The idea of a federation came as a part of preparing a platform to discuss, share, and brainstorm politics, movements, strategies, and alliances. In relation to this, the agenda within the forest movements has been not only to go with the FRA and to demand its implementation but also to go beyond the FRA and to move in the direction of community governance in forest areas. Equally, and after succeeding in their campaign to introduce a draft fishworkers' rights bill in Parliament, fishworkers also needed to learn from the experience of forest workers regarding legislation for gaining rights and about the challenges of such an approach. With this background, the movements agreed on December 16 2012 to form a federation of 'Natural Resource–Based Working People's Organisations', as a part of getting prepared for the larger struggle to take control over the natural resources by the communities.

This perspective, and this expression of struggle, had been spelled out clearly back in June 2009, in the Dehradun Conference of the National Forum of Forest People and Forest Workers, where more than 200 forest movements had gathered.

In the Declaration that was formulated and agreed upon at the Conference, they sent out a message to entire world that they wanted Climate Justice:

> This is no ordinary crisis. Not merely a climate crisis—or in your words, this magnified, self-created monster of a financial crisis. We believe it is a Crisis of Civilisations. It's no ordinary clash but a fundamental clash between our knowledge systems; of being, of nature and your wisdom, technology, and demonic tendencies. Your world rests on ideas of power, territories, boundaries, profit, exploitation and oppression and you try to own everything, including Mother Nature.
>
> Before demanding individual rights we will collectively struggle for claiming community implementation of the FRA. We have an inalienable right over our forest land. We will collect all those documents from government records where our rights have been registered. We will fight to stop all those companies that have attacked our forests. We will strengthen the struggle against commodification of forests. In order to reach our goal we will each strengthen our organisation in our area as well as bring together all such organisations such that we can together fight with strength.[38]

Conclusion

The forest rights movements have always taken place in the broader context of ecological justice. Within their understanding of the forests as their habitat and their heritage, their demand has been for sovereign rights over natural and productive resources for the indigenous and local communities, since their cultural, economic, and political identities are fundamentally intertwined with these resources.

With the advent of colonial interest in exploiting the resources for creating surplus, intense conflicts arose between local communities and colonial power during the mid-eighteenth century. This has only continued in post-colonial India, with the rise of the Indian nation-state. The transfer of political power from the British Raj to the newly independent state did not alter the fundamental issue, the control of resources the ruling class or the native elites through the exercise of the power of eminent domain that the state vests in itself. The conflict over the issue of ownership of natural resources continues, and has remained unresolved. This basic contradiction is also reflected in the Indian Constitution, in the section on Fundamental Rights. This situation has become only more serious now with the direct attack on these resources by global capital under neoliberalism, where the extraction of natural resources has increased manifold and capital has moved significantly from simple industrial production to actually taking over and acquiring the precious natural resources of land, forest, water, and minerals.

In order to protect the interest of the elites and of capital, the Indian state has always repressed people's resistance, no matter whether it is small or big movement. For this very reason, the many and very diverse forest and land right movements have always been militant mass movements in nature, and so also in their articulations. They have always had their roots in the communities, and hence the participation of local peoples in the movement has always been spontaneous and almost total.

Generally speaking, we are today seeing a significant increase in leadership coming from within the communities and not by party-sent vanguards or by independent vanguards. But since these diverse movements did not link up, they each remained isolated. Such isolation only helped the state attack the movements brutally and separately, and also helped it create divisions within and between movements. It was only in the 1970s that some left-radical groups and independent social activists started linking these peoples' resistance movements around specific issues like displacement, land and forest rights, the violations of human rights, and so on. With the initiation of the neoliberal economy by the Indian state in the 90s, the commodification of natural resources became rampant—but simultaneously, people's resistance against such policies also developed very strongly.

In this emerging context, the question of linkage between various diverse movements became very relevant, resulting in the emergence of diverse new social and political forces at different levels—local, regional, and national. Exposure to international experiences through various social and political forums like the World Social Forum has also helped this process immensely.

Among these diverse formations, two distinct categories of groups are playing crucial roles in the present socio-political scenario. One category can be identified as left-wing, non-parliamentary radical groups—like the Maoists—who want to settle the conflict between the people and the Indian state through armed struggle, with the support of people's movements and also of sections of the middle-class intelligentsia. The other category is collective fora of militant, democratic, mass movements who do not subscribe to any particular political ideology but are strongly rooted in militant mass mobilisation for collective negotiation with the state for the settlement of constitutional and democratic rights. While the left radical groups are focused in certain geopolitical regions, the democratic mass movement groups are spread all over the country. But the principal operators of the Indian state find it convenient not to make any distinction between these two categories. Instead, they are trying to brand both sections as 'Maoist', or 'left extremist', so that they are then enabled to crush all the movements through violent repression. The state, and even the dominant political class, does not have the confidence in settling issues through participatory and democratic negotiations. Political parties of the mainstream are becoming increasingly irrelevant in this important political discourse.

At this critical juncture of our history, the challenges before militant democratic movements are very clear. On the one hand, they have to fight the repression they are facing from the ruling forces of capitalism, feudalism, and patriarchy, and also fight to retain their independent identity. On the other hand, they have to work for creating alternatives for establishing a democratic polity, which can ensure peace, justice, and dignity through a sustainable development process. Put precisely, this is a struggle between two political systems—or between two civilisations.

References

All India Union of Forest Working People, June 2013—'Puri Declaration, June 2013'. Passed unanimously by the Founding Conference of the All India Union of Forest Working People (AIUFWP), June 3–5 2013, Town Hall, Puri, Odisha, India, at http://ntui.org.in/what-we-do/nrega/affiliate-updates/all-india-union-of-forest-working-people/ (Accessed April 2017)

Anon, April 2010a—'Peoples Agreement' from the 'World Peoples' Conference on Climate Change and Mother Earth's Rights' organised by the Plurinational Government of Bolivia in Cochabamba, Bolivia, in April 2010, at http://pwccc.wordpress.com/support/ (Accessed April 2017)

Estebancio Castro Diaz, nd, c.2008—'Climate Change, Forest Conservation and Indigenous Peoples Rights'. Discussion paper for the International Expert Group Meeting On Indigenous Peoples And Climate Change, Darwin, Australia, April 2–4, 2008. Published by the Global Forest Coalition, Paper 2007/WS.6. Available at https://www.un.org/esa/socdev/unpfii/documents/EGM_cs08_diaz.doc (Accessed April 2017)

Mamata Dash, August 2008—*The World Social Forum ... as movement groups in India see it*. Paper prepared as CACIM Forum Fellow 2007–8. Volume 6 in *Critical Engagement*—CACIM's Occasional Publications Programme. New Delhi: CACIM, at http://www.cacim.net/twiki/tiki-index.php?page=Publications (Accessed April 2017)

Delhi Forum, NFFPFW, Jharkhand/Save the Forest Movement, NTUI, WALHI/FoE (Indonesia), et al, January 2005—'Global movement for peoples' rights and forest conservation: The Mumbai-Porto Alegre Forest Initiative', Porto Alegre, January 30 2005, at http://www.wrm.org.uy/statements/Mumbai/ (Accessed April 2017)

Government of Bengal, 1908—*Chota Nagpur Tenancy Act of 1908* (Bengal Act VI of 1908)

Government of India, Ministry of Tribal Affairs, 2006—*Forest Rights Act 2006*, at http://tribal.nic.in/index1.asp?linkid=376&langid=1 (Accessed April 2017)

NAPM (National Alliance of People's Movements), July 2011—'*Sansad Gherao! Delhi Chalo!* Repeal Land Acquisition Act Now!'. Invitation to a National Action Against Forced Displacement & Land Grab and for Community Control Over Natural Resources and Livelihood Rights, August 3–5 2011, Jantar Mantar, New Delhi, at http://unitedblackuntouchablesworldwide.blogspot.ca/2011/07/fwd-initiative-india-august-3-5.html (Accessed April 2017)

NFFPFW (National Forum of Forest People and Forest Workers) and others, 2004—'Mumbai Forest Rights Initiative Declaration'. Declaration issued from the World Social Forum held in Mumbai, India, January 2004

NFFPFW (National Forum of Forest People and Forest Workers), June 2009—'Dehradun Declaration 2009', a Declaration by the Indigenous and Forest Peoples of India, taken at the Second National Conference, held in Dehra Dun, India, June 10–12 2009; dated June 12 2009. Posted by Delhi Forum on June 19 2009, 4:43:32 pm GMT+05:30, as 'Important—Dehradun Declaration of Forest Peoples on Environment Justice', at http://www.wrm.org.uy/countries/India/Dehradun.html (Accessed April 2017)

The Telegraph, February 2012—'Chotanagpur Tenancy Act: What next', in *The Telegraph*, February 23 2012, at http://www.telegraphindia.com/1120223/jsp/jharkhand/story_15169375.jsp#.UoqKEY05Taw (Accessed April 2017)

World Commission on Environment and Development, October 1987—'Report of the World Commission on Environment and Development: Our Common Future'. Chairperson of the Commission, Gro Harlem Brundtland, at http://www.un-docu-ments.net/wced-ocf.htm (Accessed April 2017)

World Rainforest Movement, January 2005—'The Mumbai—Porto Alegre Forest Initiative', at http://wrm.org.uy/all-campaigns/the-mumbai-porto-alegre-forest-initiative/ (Accessed April 2017)

Notes

1. Ed: I want to take this chance to very specially thank Roma and Ashok Choudhary for preparing this essay for this book, and for bearing with the repeated revisions I made them, as activists, go through over all too many years. But I would like to think that they—and readers—will agree that the result is a deeply textured and great essay, and a great contribution to this book.

    Just as a footnote, readers will sometimes elsewhere find Ashok Choudhary's name spelt as 'Ashok Chowdhury' (and his eddress also uses this spelling). This is the same person; but 'Choudhary' is the correct spelling.

2. The 75 million hectares include forest land, water bodies, and areas containing mineral deposits.

3. Correctly used, the term 'Maoist' refers to those who are followers of Mao Zedong, and in the context of this essay, to those who believe in the people's organisations, as did Mao. From more recently however, the term has come to be popularly used in India—in the media and the government but also among 'progressive' circles—for referring to armed political groups active in many parts of central India who say they are fighting on behalf of oppressed peoples, but who are in fact not following Mao's strategy of creating popular organisations and of challenging the idea of the modern liberal 'nation-state', but who are instead acting as a vanguard, towards creating another state. (This question is complicated by the fact that some of the groups call themselves the 'CPI—Communist Party of India—Maoist', but this is just a name.) These groups have come out of what was originally formed in 1969 as the 'CPI (Marxist-Leninist)'—which in turn was a breakaway from the CPI (Marxist)—and who were known as 'Naxalites' since the first outbreak took place from a village in West Bengal called Naxalbari ('home of Naxals'). Ashok Choudhary: "As someone who comes from the 1967 generation, I do not accept the new groups as Maoists."

4. The Indian government claims that 'left wing armed radical groups' are operating in about 200 districts of India, out of a total of 640 districts—in other words, in nearly

one-third of the country—and that they constitute the 'gravest threat to the nation'; thus attempting to justify the use of extreme powers in such areas.

5. The term 'forest peoples' includes (i) the original Adivasis (literally, 'original dwellers') who have always lived in the forests; (ii) the enslaved bonded labour—mostly Dalit agricultural workers—who were brought into the forests from the plains by the British in the nineteenth century to work as labour in logging and for clearing the forests (the *Taungiyas*), just as was also the case all over the world, such as in the Caribbean, the Pacific Islands, etc; and (iii), also peoples from the plains who came into the forests in the pre-colonial period and worked as metal workers and leatherworkers, and who were included and absorbed by the indigenous peoples in many forest regions (and who are today called the *Moolnivasis*). This is why the first organisation we helped form and worked with, the NFFPFW—the National Forum of Forest People and Forest Workers—used the terms 'forest people' and 'forest workers' to describe these communities as its constituency; as inclusive terms. See note 21 below for more details on the *Taungiyas*.

6. Ed: The term 'subcontinent' includes Bangladesh, Bhutan, India, Nepal, and Pakistan.

7. Prabhat Patnaik, a renowned left-wing political economist.

8. The untouchables or scheduled castes communities in India (and more generally across South Asia).

9. Ed: For details of the NFFPFW, see http://delhisolidaritygroup.wordpress.com/category/nffpfw/; and for the formation of the AIUFWP, see http://ntui.org.in/what-we-do/nrega/affiliate-updates/all-india-union-of-forest-working-people/.

10. This point was made in the course of presentations by such peoples at meetings at the World Social Forum meeting held in Mumbai, India, in January 2004, and continues to be made by them today, such as during meetings of the NFFPFW and now the AIUFWP with government officials, etc.

11. For details, see http://pwccc.wordpress.com/ (Accessed April 2017)

12. Ed: See: Anon, April 2010a (the 'Peoples Agreement' from the 'World Peoples' Conference on Climate Change and Mother Earth's Rights' organised by the Plurinational Government of Bolivia in Cochabamba, Bolivia, in April 2010).

13. Ed: See also the so-called 'Bruntland Report', the report of the World Commission on Environment and Development (October 1987). The Chairperson of the Commission was Gro Harlem Brundtland of Norway.

14. Indian forests are spread across the Himalayan region, the central region, the southern region, and on international borders such as Pakistan, Nepal, Bhutan, China, Burma, and Bangladesh.

15. The colonial period continued in India till 1947. It was during this period that, for the first time, the forests of India came to be used to serve the interests of a foreign empire. The British looked at forest resources only as a revenue-earning source and ruthlessly looted these resources for around a hundred years—but where in order to do this, they had to fight tough battles with tribal and indigenous communities. The resistance they faced made clear to them that they would not succeed in looting the resources, so ultimately in 1865 they created a 'Forest Department' to legitimise this looting, and in 1927 brought in a draconian 'Indian Forest Act'. (The looting of forest resources for the previous hundred years had been done without the cover of any law.) The Act of 1927 made the local people outsiders and enemies of the forest,

and the forest resources became the property of the state. The government of India continued this colonial legacy after the country gained independence in 1947, and in fact the Forest Department (FD) used the 1927 Act to increase the land under its control through unscrupulous means.

16. These were all legendary revolutionary tribal leaders who gloriously fought with British and never succumbed to the tyranny of British. Tilka Majhi killed the British Collector in his office in 1782, saying that "the forest belongs to *singh bongha* (Sun God) and not to the British".

17. The 1927 Act was enacted to earn revenue from the forest and had nothing to do with saving the forest and wildlife. The first line of the Act makes clear its intentions by saying that it is "An Act to consolidate the law relating to forests, the transit of forest-produce, and the duty leviable on timber and other forest-produce".

18. The Korean Posco steel company has the highest FDI investment in the state of Odisha, which in return has given illegal forest clearances to this company.

19. A report prepared as a result of an order passed by the High Court in the state of Himachal Pradesh to probe the viability of major projects in the state—the hydro projects, the cement projects, and also the mega Renuka dam that is located in a highly sensitive, extremely seismic Himalayan zone—concluded that none of the projects are environmentally viable.

20. Hegemony of the upper caste elites of India.

21. Government of India, Ministry of Tribal Affairs, 2006.

22. *Taungiya* villages are the villages settled by the British to plant commercial trees by using silvicultural techniques. *Taungiya* is basically a system to plant trees in rows along with the crops. The villagers were generally lower caste Dalit and other backward people brought in by the Forest Department from nearby villages, who—as they had historically been exploited by the feudal landlords—were lured by the FD's promises of agricultural plots and land for houses. They however now entered into another system of bondage, now by the State, which acted as a feudal landlord. Now, they were provided land for five years for cultivation and plantation, and then shifted to another area after the trees attained good height. They were not allowed to construct *pucca* [permanent] houses, and they were also not entitled to any health, education, and other basic services. This remains the case even till now in various parts of India. There are around 7,000 such villages that still exist. For the first time, the FRA passed in 2006 talked about the conversion of these forest villages into revenue villages.

23. Landlords and rent collectors dating from the colonial period, and from the Mughal period before that.

24. Forest lands are areas within forests that are without trees, on which forest peoples have settled. But because the 'settlement'—demarcation and registration—of these areas has never been done, even the boundaries between the forest lands and the actual forest areas are not clear.

25. The CNT Act was enacted in 1908 after a long struggle by tribals (Government of Bengal, 1908; for some history, see also *The Telegraph*, February 2012). The Act ensured control over forests and lands by the tribal *Munda manki*. In the Chhota Nagpur region of central India, where the Munda tribals predominate, the *Munda mankis* together form a kind of council that has the authority in all land and forest-related matters. The system is known as *khutkatti*.

26.   Unpublished notification; copy in authors' files.

27.   One of the key arguments of the NFFPFW in campaigning for the FRA was that the term 'traditional rights'—which was widely used by the government and by political parties, but only in a populist way—had no legal strength. Its demand was that the FRA had to give legal definition and backing to this customary concept.

28.   Garhwal is now a district in the state of Uttarakhand.

29.   This fact has been regularly referred to by local movements, as documented by our organisation at the field level. It was also mentioned in the Forest Working Plan (that is periodically prepared and issued by the Forest Department).

30.   To say this is not to say that the FD officials did not react, and there is indeed a long history of brutal and violent repression by FD officials, and especially against local communities who resisted their actions. But it was precisely the exposure of this history and tradition of brutality by government officials, and the violation of minimum human rights resulting in the alienation of local communities from forest governance, that—among other things—in time led the European Union and the World Bank to become uneasy and so to put pressure on the government.

31.   A 'revenue village' is a legally constituted village. With the term dating from colonial times—and referring to defined areas from which the colonial administration extracted revenue according to norms it set—the term has continued to be used by the government of independent India and recognised under Panchayati Raj legislation and under the 73rd and 74th Amendments to the Constitution of India.

32.   'Joint Forest Management', a programme of afforestation run by the World Bank and other IFIs through the Forest Department, is in serious conflict with the provisions of the Forest Rights Act.

33.   REDD = Reducing Emissions from Deforestation and Forest Degradation in Developing Countries, a UN and World Bank-promoted strategy.

34.   NFFPFW (National Forum of Forest People and Forest Workers) and others, 2004. (Ed: Document not available at the time of going to press, but references to and some details on this meeting and Declaration can be found in: Castro Diaz, nd, c.2008; Dash, August 2008; and: World Rainforest Movement, January 2005.)

35.   Delhi Forum, NFFPFW, Jharkhand/Save the Forest Movement, NTUI, WALHI/FoE (Indonesia) et al, January 2005.

36.   Our experience is that this has been the case because when conflict situations arose, men were often confused as to what to do, whereas the women were more clear, and confident; and over time, the leadership that they offered also became clear and assertive. We believe that this is the case because whereas men tend to be linked with and integrated into the outside world and economy, and to see that world as their reference point, women are more rooted in the forests and in the land, and their concern for nature and for nurturing the forest is far stronger. From the beginning, our organisers at NFFPFW recognised this, and we worked with the women to develop their leadership. Their leadership has definitely been resisted—by the men, by the state, and by the traditions of feudality—but women stood firm even when facing physical attack from state forces. This has changed the face of the movement qualitatively, as the value of their leadership has become clear.

37.   NAPM (National Alliance of People's Movements), July 2011.

38.   NFFPFW (National Forum of Forest People and Forest Workers), June 2009.

OpenWord

Open Space in Movement:
Reading Three Waves of Feminism[1]
Emilie Hayes

"Feminism" is a loaded term, shifting and negotiated over time, and taking on different shapes and understandings depending on one's perspective and location. A study of feminism thus requires a careful negotiation of complex ideas, of which I have only been able to take up a few. I am only too aware that I have managed to just begin this exploration.

As a starting point for managing the issue's complexity, I am settling on a definition of feminism drawing from both second- and third-wave writers. According to Jennifer Baumgardner and Amy Richards, "feminism [is] a word that describes a social justice movement for gender equity and human liberation".[2] bell hooks also provides a well-known definition of feminism as "a movement to end sexism, sexist exploitation, and oppression".[3] The term 'the women's movement', which is used widely and interchangeably with feminism, can be harnessed by a variety of groups who do not necessarily acknowledge the existence of sexism or engage in a struggle for the equitable redistribution of power.[4] Antrobus's distinction between feminism and the feminist movement is helpful. According to her, feminism can be conceptualised as a consciousness of women's subordination, whereas the accompanying 'movement' is concerned with changing social conditions, and emerges as a process of "individual women becom[ing] aware of *their separateness as women*, their alienation, marginalisation, isolation or even abandonment within a broader movement for social justice or social change".[5]

My exploration will be situated in those movements that "reject patriarchal privilege",[6] are concerned with social change, and struggle for gender equity and liberation from sexist oppression. As such, I will be using the term 'feminist movement' throughout this paper, conceptualised through the writings of Baumgardner, Richards, hooks, and Antrobus.

Using the framework and metaphor of waves to describe the three main phases of the feminist movement in North America, I argue that the second-wave feminist movement created both figurative and literal manifestations of open space that allowed expressions of dissent, which ultimately contributed to the emergence and shape of the third-wave feminist movement and the advancement of the feminist project overall. I will begin with an overview of the first, second, and third waves of feminism, briefly addressing the appropriateness of using the term 'waves' for conceptualising the feminist movement. I will follow with an examination of the notions of 'open space' and dissent within the feminist movement, focusing specifically

on dissenting perspectives from women of colour and generational dissent. I will offer a brief exploration of the World March of Women, a global movement that originated in Québec, to demonstrate how dissent in the feminist movement has contributed to its growth and evolution, and how notions of open space in the feminist movement have persisted and evolved over time. I will conclude with a brief examination of the ways in which these dissenting perspectives contributed to the growth of the feminist movement, and by addressing potential future directions.

Before beginning this exploration, however, it should be noted that a study of feminism is a daunting and complex task. As such, I have limited the scope of this investigation to the North American context, and I do not explore the many-layered effects and influences of sexualities, ethnicities, and even anti-feminist theories and practices on the evolution of the feminist movement, which are subjects in themselves.

In this discussion, I will focus on the Canadian feminist movement, and bring in the US perspective where relevant. This makes sense to do because as Lisa Young has argued, the Canadian and US feminist movements are more similar than any other national movements in North America due to their shared roots in the student movement of the 1960s, a shared resistance to rigid postwar gender roles, and the consumption in the two countries of similar, and sometimes identical mass media.[7]

Waves of Feminism

First-wave feminism is commonly identified as women's struggle for a legal identity, including the right to own property, form contracts, vote, run for political office, and sit in the Senate.[8] Between 1880 and 1920, increased activism and awareness among Canadian women propelled them out of the isolation of their homes with a sense of religious duty and spirit of expanding opportunity, combined with apprehensions about the state of Canadian society and their special place within it.[9] Indeed, it was concern over Canada's social ills and the need to save Canadian society that motivated women to fight for the vote.[10] Women received the national franchise in 1918, and although women continued to struggle for social change thereafter, minimal attention was paid to feminist activity by those outside of the movement thereby creating the impression that the first wave receded shortly after women secured the right to vote.[11]

While this waning of the movement was the common perception, it is also a fact that women acquired increased education, affluence, and awareness throughout the subsequent period, and especially during the 1940s and 1950s. While this process may not be perceived as feminist activism, and though women continued to be subjected to significant gender inequality, this period laid the foundation for "a new wave of feminism to emerge in the 1960s".[12]

This second wave of feminism coalesced around the belief that women and men were not inherently different, and that gender differences were socially constructed.[13] Women began to question the very foundation of society as paternalistic and male-dominated, and began to pressure men for support at home, and also the government for more supportive policies on childcare, maternity leave, and for higher wages.[14]

Women from diverse backgrounds and locations engaged in this second wave of the feminist movement. As a result, perspectives, interpretations, demands, and actions related to gender inequality and power varied according to social location, and shifted depending on the context and issues of the time.[15] While some feminists focused on the centrality of the home and the family as the locus of feminist struggle, women of colour, differently-abled, poor, lesbian, and minority women claimed that their experiences as women were quite different from that of the white, middle-class woman, and that their struggles centred around much more than just the home and family.[16] Second-wave feminist action also focused on sexuality and reproductive rights—women's right to sexual pleasure, control of their own bodies, policy issues around male sexual violence, legal issues around divorce and pornography, and political and legal struggles around rape and sexual assault.[17]

Third-wave feminism emerged in the 1990s. Its theorising focuses on concepts of multiple identifications, complexities, and ambiguities, and cautions against thinking in dichotomous terms.[18] Third-wave feminism's priority is the inclusion of various genders, sexualities, ethnicities, races, and classes through grassroots modes of organising.[19] This is represented in the use of personal narratives, the Internet, and zines, all with the constant thread of practicing feminism at the individual, personal level.[20] Heywood and Drake provide a useful summary of third-wave feminism as "the development of modes of thinking that can come to terms with the multiple, constantly shifting bases of oppression in relation to the multiple, interpenetrating axes of identity, and the creation of coalition politics based on these understandings".[21]

Many however, have noted problematic elements in compartmentalising the larger feminist movement by using the concept of waves. The wave model evokes a sense of surges and ebbs that does not properly describe the life of feminism. Moreover, the attempt to define feminism and delineate its boundaries is complicated since feminism is expressed in a variety of ways from "militant political activism, to silent volunteerism, to academic research and writing, to the creation of works of art, to so much more".[22] It also risks essentialising generations of feminists in predetermined categories[23] and oversimplifying feminism by glossing over its complexities.[24] Moreover, since second-wave feminists are "neither dead nor silent",[25] and since many of the goals set by the second wave have not yet been accomplished, identifying a third wave is perceived by some as problematic.[26]And beyond this, many younger women today identify with the second wave, and there are also older, baby boomer women who identify more strongly with the third wave.[27]

While there is some understandable uneasiness in using the concept of waves to categorise feminist debates, I feel that it is nevertheless useful in that it denotes that feminist movements have been informed by particular locations and struggles. The notion of waves also seems to adequately describe feminism's fluidity and its lack of definable boundaries, and it also reflects the movement's continual growth and change.[28] Moreover, using the term 'waves' to depict the feminist movement may contribute towards a sense of solidarity and identity among young feminists with earlier feminist activity,[29] since ultimately all these waves are of the same water.

Open Space and Dissent in the Feminist Movement

In the context of the World Social Forum (WSF), the notion of open space is conceived as a space that is "socially horizontal" with "no leaders", and relatively undirected "without an owner".[30] There is no official spokesperson, no central hierarchy, and the only shared commitment is an opposition to neoliberal globalisation.[31] Whitaker likens this concept to a "factory of ideas or an incubator" where participants can work towards their goals and give life to new movements with more specific aims, which also amplify the wider struggle.[32] Indeed, it is its open and horizontal formulation that both challenges traditional and unequal power structures, and also allows the WSF to serve as a tool for struggle.[33] Keraghel and Sen add that an open space also allows for the "celebration of diversity and plurality",[34] so that participants feel respected, and ideas can be freely exchanged.[35]

Using this concept of open space as a framework, I will examine how both figurative and literal open spaces that fostered the sharing and development of ideas were created within the feminist movement, thereby further advancing the feminist project. As I see it, these spaces, in their quest for openness and inclusiveness, provided an opportunity for dissent, thus allowing for new movements with more specific aims to emerge—and in turn spurring on new ways of feminist thinking, such as anti-racist feminist thought and a feminist project that was more inclusive of women with diverse identifications.

The first and perhaps more striking feature of the second wave is that those involved in it created various kinds of spaces marked by a horizontal make-up, with no leaders or official spokespeople, in which all women were viewed as equal, and committed to opposing patriarchal oppression. Examples include woman-centred collectives and forums that allowed women to share information, challenge patriarchal notions, and resolve women's oppression;[36] and consciousness-raising groups that offered a space for women to discuss their personal experiences and feelings, allowing them to discover that the challenges they faced were reflective of a larger patriarchal system of oppression.[37] In Canada, hundreds of groups met weekly in the early 1970s, providing women with the opportunity to "recognise, reinterpret, and change" their living conditions, priorities, identities, and careers.[38]

Over time, this form of organising, and the spaces created for this kind of exchange, changed women's consciousness of their identity. During the 1970s women's centres began to emerge, to provide places for women to connect with other women involved in the feminist movement and come together to organise for social and political change.[39] In the 1980s, new, often small and local, women's groups emerged to represent the needs of specific categories of women, which allowed women from marginalised groups to voice their concern that the majority, white, heterosexual feminists must begin to take into account the differences in race, religion, ethnicity, different abilities, ages, and sexual orientations.[40]

Spaces with more specific purposes such as women's shelters, rape crisis centres, and organisations that serve particular populations such as immigrant women, domestic workers, ethnic groups, and women with disabilities were also created.[41] Feminist-inspired women's caucuses surfaced within trade unions and political parties, seeking to exert pressure for gender equity in leadership positions, and the inclusion of women's issues on organisational agendas.[42] On university campuses, women's studies classes began to materialise, offering feminist courses and a space for young women to examine the role of women in society.

Jo Freeman, writing in the midst of the second wave, reflected critically on the open structure of the younger section of the feminist movement. These small, decentralised groups with a "lack of formal organisation, an emphasis on participation, a sharing of tasks, and the exclusion of men"[43] shared many common traits with the WSF's much later notion of open space; following a general policy of "structurelessness" and advocating a lack of hierarchy.[44] With its foundations in participatory democracy, the movement assumed all women were equally capable, and the contributions of all participants were encouraged and equally valued.[45] These small groups spread widely and the concept of "leaderless, structureless groups" eventually dominated this section of the movement.[46] For instance, this open structure permeated the National Organization for Women (NOW) in the US; local chapters disregarded the structure proposed by the national office and simply developed their own organisational processes.[47] This translated into "loose chairing of meetings, unstructured, occasionally irrelevant, discussion, expression of personal feelings and enthusiasm, avoidance of authoritarian and domineering styles, and decision making by consensus".[48]

'Rap groups' also emerged from these gatherings, in which women discussed and analysed their experiences.[49] These groups were easy to organise and eventually became the most widespread practice of this younger branch of the second wave, bringing increased numbers of women into the feminist movement.[50]

The 1970s also saw the creation of women's collectives—including in book, magazine, and newspaper publishing—to bring to the wider public women's issues that might have been rejected by mainstream publishers.[51] This arguably provided a foundation by which the third wave was able to utilise texts as a tool for raising awareness and practicing activism. Zines, usually self-published and self-distributed alternative and non-commercial publications, later emerged as an important outlet in the third wave, through which many women share personal stories, and reclaim their culture and language from mainstream characterisations of women; and have provided an avenue for critiquing the mainstream media.[52] Zines allow for an accessible space in which young feminists can share ideas and political views on feminist activities, while also serving as 'incubators' for ideas by inspiring other forms of activism.[53]

Along with zines, hybrid publications such as *Bust* have been produced to fill a gap between zines and mainstream publications.[54] The Internet, particularly email, websites, and chat groups, has also served as an important space for the feminist community, where women and girls can communicate with others as well as organise and share information.[55] Both the use of zines and the Internet have provided a relatively safe, supportive, and accessible space for women to express themselves and discuss feminism.[56]

However, these various spaces are not without limitations. Freeman notes how a "tyranny of structurelessness" was represented in the uneven distribution of tasks, roles, and resources among participants.[57] While no official structures of authority existed, decision-making processes continued to occur in an informal manner with the decision-making rules known only to those few who belong to the informal group. Because rules of decision-making were closed and not accessible to all, circuits of power were simply masked by the appearance of structurelessness.[58] Freeman claimed that structurelessness actually served as a "smokescreen" for naturally emerging structures, and the perception of horizontality provided a means to exercise hegemonic power.[59] This "myth of structurelessness" meant that no attempts could be made to challenge the use of power within the movement because there were no mechanisms by which to do so.[60] Interestingly, this issue has also emerged within the seemingly non-hierarchal structure of the WSF, as important decisions are made with a lack of transparency about why, how, and by whom they are made.[61]

Moreover, while the rap groups of the 1970s were conceived of as open spaces for women, they were explicitly closed to men, thus transforming an open space into a closed one. As such, the notion of open space in the feminist movement was contradictory—although women from diverse backgrounds and perspectives were welcome, anyone who did not fit into the mainstream conceptualisation of 'woman' was excluded. This has come under particular scrutiny by some third-wave feminists who recognise that the category of 'woman' is fluid and unfixed, and seek to include the transgendered community in the feminist movement.[62] Again, Keraghel and Sen have noted a similar challenge within the WSF, which is ultimately restricted to those with a "clear and defined position" and where they have therefore questioned whether it is indeed an open space.[63]

Similarly, while these structureless groups attempted to be more participatory, they were reliant on friendship networks to keep them afloat and could often be exclusionary for those not tied into a particular network.[64] Freeman also critiques these unstructured groups for taking a great deal of time, energy, and patience in long and exhausting decision-making processes;[65] their focus being spent on "group processes rather than group ends".[66] As a result, smaller rap groups suffered when participants wanted to go beyond simply expressing their own experiences to taking action.[67] In discussing some of the central critiques of the notion of open space in the WSF, Wallerstein notes that the WSF has experienced similar challenges, being perceived as nothing more than a "talk fest" which stops short of acting on its reflections and discussions.[68] This reflects "the classic dilemma of social movement organisations"—that social change requires "tightly" organised and hierarchal organisation, which conflicts with the "participatory style" required to nourish and support the democratic ideals of the movement's goals.[69]

The textual and technological strategies of the third wave also challenge genuine openness. Though the Internet has provided an important space for many feminists, it requires access to computers, software, and a particular set of language skills, and is therefore not accessible to all people, and particularly to marginalised groups.[70] Several zines and hybrid magazines have also been criticised for their shift towards mainstream publication standards, complete with advertising and glossy pages. Bell notes how this trend undermines the genuine expression of ideas as these publications become obliged to their corporate sponsors, and seek to meet professional standards that are determined by that very mainstream culture to which they were striving to provide an alternative.[71]

While the openness of women-centred spaces can be challenged, literal spaces such as women's centres, consciousness-raising groups, and rap groups, as well as textual spaces such as zines, hybrid publications, and the Internet nevertheless fit well within Whitaker's and the WSF's notion of open space.[72] Many scholars have noted how such spaces provided a relatively open and accessible space for women to share information and ideas, and mobilise and organise for change.[73] Characteristics such as an emphasis on participation, the valuing of all contributions, and lack of formal organisation created space for specific needs to be raised. Akin to Whitaker's notion of the incubator, smaller groups were formed as a result of these open spaces, to meet the needs of specific groups such as women immigrants, domestic workers, differently-abled women, as well as women who suffered abuse, and ultimately provided a venue for the expression of dissent, which contributed to forming the third wave. Indeed, many third-wave writers note that they owe a great deal to their second-wave sisters for bringing issues of sexuality and sexual diversity to the fore[74] and awakening many to the deeply rooted issue of gender inequality.[75] Walker also acknowledges that both second-wave and Third-World feminists have provided third-wave feminists with the language and images that allow for an examination of diversity, expose contradictions, and pay heed to the politics of hybridity and coalition.[76]

Both the first and second waves have been criticised for their failure to document the histories of women of colour and to identify racism as an issue for feminist organising. In fact, first-wave feminism perpetuated stereotypes of women of colour as corrupted victims of their culture, unable to function as real mothers, and thus "active agents" in society's degeneration.[77] This positioning allowed white women to capitalise on their privilege and elevate their status, arguing for the right to vote based on their greater morality and purity, thereby excluding women of colour from first-wave feminism.[78] By depicting themselves as the 'mothers of the race', first-wave feminists used racist assumptions to secure a distinctive role in the public sphere as protectors of 'the race', while also depicting women of colour as a homogenous group inferior due to racial characteristics, not gender.[79] Indeed, one of the most prominent Canadian first-wave feminists, Emily Murphy, outlined her views that "Nordic races were inherently superior" in her book *The Black Candle*; and the Woman's Christian Temperance Union's (WCTU) version of feminism was narrowed to include only those women from dominant cultures who viewed themselves as innately morally superior.[80]

However, racism within feminist discourse is not a fixture of a bygone era. Indeed, Brand argues that feminist themes so far have "refused to be informed by Black women's lives", instead lending themselves to racist, capitalist, and imperialist ideologies.[81] Cooper adds that feminists remain implicated in reproducing the marginalisation of women of colour by continuing to reconstruct a particular version of history that relies on mainstream sources, which omit women of colour.[82] Women of colour in both advanced capitalist states as well as former colonies are thus still constantly pushed to the margins of Western feminist discourse, depicted as "monolith, pitied as passive, dismissed as tradition-bound" in a discourse that "mirrors the Empire ... and ... global capitalism".[83]

Another common critique of all three waves of the feminist movement is that they have all been taken over by white, middle-class women who focus on the privatisation of the family. This white, middle-class version of feminist thought focuses on how women have been relegated to the domestic sphere of the household, and posits gender oppression as the central cause of women's inequality, yet sidesteps analyses of how race and class impact women's experiences both inside and outside the house, and how it was white privilege that allowed some of them to engage in the struggle in the first place.[84] This focus on domestic gender relations overlooks the experience of many women around the world who have not only had to work both inside and outside the home in order to survive (and often in the homes of privileged white women), but are also overrepresented in domestic work in hospitals and hotels.[85] The feminist discourse universalises women's experiences by lumping the multiple identifications of women of colour into the category 'gender'. Though feminist discourse claims to empower women, it simultaneously ignores the discrepancies between their lives. In other words, the feminist movement in Canada has been dominated by white and middle-class women who often focused on gender oppression as the central cause of women's inequality, ignoring how race interacts with one's experience as a woman.[86]

Anti-racist feminist thought has emerged to challenge this dominant feminist discourse, claiming that women of colour experience gender in very different ways from white, middle-class women.[87] These women began to question the essentialist and universal category of 'woman', and advanced the notion that gender, race, class, ethnicity, and sexuality intersected in their identity formation, and that they experienced oppression on many levels, not just as women.[88] Wane notes how Black Canadian feminists seek out a liberatory practice where the historical, social, cultural, and economic relationships of women of African descent can be analysed and illuminated.[89] For example, in contrast to white, middle-class women who do not have a class consciousness and thus focus their struggle in relation to white middle-class men, emancipatory feminism relevant to Black women must confront the conditions of capitalism and production that have impacted Black women.[90] Ultimately, anti-racist feminist thought advocated a feminist project that developed a "self-conscious politics of partiality", and one that was not conceived as a "political home" for all women.[91] This translates into a precarious balance between the necessity to reach out and include all women, yet simultaneously "tokenism and further marginalisation".[92]

The literature of the third wave interrogated mainstream feminism for its role in perpetuating racial differences between women and examined the ways in which the interests of white, middle-class women shaped the contours of mainstream feminist thought.[93] Young women began pushing the boundaries of who and what constitutes feminism and critiquing the second wave for universalising the experience of women and for advancing theories centred on the sameness of women.[94] The rejection of gender as a transcendental force over multiple identities such as race, sexuality, or ability "sets [third-wave feminists] at odds with the previous generation of feminists".[95] Third-wave feminists represent a desire to openly address the contradictions of second-wave feminism and challenge its repressive and restrictive nature, thereby forcing a break in, and a reformulation of, feminism.[96]

There is also another layer of complexity. The third wave, often described as including young women, is replete with familial metaphors and noted for its generational differences.[97] The relationship between the second and third wave is particularly well-suited to generational comparison due to its adherence to the thirty-year model of generational birth—the second wave emerged in the 1960s and the third in the 1990s—resulting in identifying second-wave feminists as mothers to their third-wave daughters.[98] This is reflected in Baumgardner and Richards's critique of second-wave feminists who attempt to "[treat] us like daughters ... who need to be moulded".[99] In some cases, the relationship between second- and third-wave feminists is characterised as "pervasive and debilitating",[100] "confrontational and uncooperative, even hostile".[101]

On the other hand, second-wave feminists have critiqued the third-wave feminist movement for forgetting their struggles and ungratefully homogenising the second-wave movement into a definable set of ideas that distort a varied social movement.[102] Others have noted that some of the tactics and theories that the third wave attempts to reinvent may already exist, resulting in a loss of valuable information and resources from assuming that current challenges faced by women have no historical precedents.[103] Moreover, second-wave feminists are critical of the individualist trend within third-wave feminism, characterised as a "feminist free-for-all": The perception that everything and everyone can fit within the third wave without a core set of beliefs or shared goals, thus creating a sense that the third wave is less activist, with no definable sense of a movement.[104] Similarly, some have argued that while the voices and perspectives of the so-called third wave are valued and important, they may not constitute an "essentially new" movement,[105] being more representative of the process of growing into adulthood as young women attempt to determine their particular version of feminism.[106]

Although a prevalent theme within the feminist movement, such dissent has provided valuable opportunities for growth and development towards a more inclusive feminism. As noted by bell hooks, feminism is "a theory in the making" which needs criticism, deeper analysis, and the exploration of new possibilities.[107] In considering feminism in this way, it becomes clear that dissenting views that challenge homogenous or universalistic notions of a woman's experience help to both deconstruct feminism as well as add layers to it, thereby contributing to the process of critique, analysis, and opening of new possibilities.

Anti-racist feminists dissented against dominant white, middle-class, heterosexual feminism and illuminated the ways in which feminists may be implicated in the oppression of other women. Moreover, by reproducing ethnocentric historical narratives, feminists may continue to be implicated in a racist feminism, replicating the history of a 'white' Canada. To counter this, anti-racist feminist thought has allowed for the questioning of whether a universal notion of gender exists, or ever did; brought feminists a step closer to confronting and coming to terms with racialising processes in which they may have participated; placed the experiences of women of colour at the centre; confronted the ways in which conditions of capitalism and production have differentially impacted women of colour; and contributed to a liberatory practice where the voices, spaces, and histories of women of colour can be reclaimed.[108]

In their attempt to reject the universal woman, third-wave feminists have deconstructed second-wave feminist thought and added new complexities to feminism by resisting boundaries, labels, or categories, and pushing the limits of what constitutes feminism. As a result, third-wave feminism attempts to include women of all identifications and seeks to acknowledge and investigate the ways in which women's identities intersect. While the second wave focused more exclusively on women's issues, such as violence against women, access to jobs, and reproductive choices, third-wave feminists have taken up issues that intersect with women's experiences, such as anti-poverty work due to women's high representation among the homeless and the poor, or anti-globalisation activism to protest the exploitation of women in the Global South from economic corporate globalisation.[109]

Resisting the notion of the universal woman, the third wave has also expanded the second wave's motto "the personal is political" by inserting personal narratives into feminist theorising and using their subjectivities to provide personal elements to feminist theory and action.[110] Third-wave feminists have also attempted to synthesise what has been gleaned from second-wave theories, expose what doesn't work, and combine them into new theories and strategies for feminist organising; and take second-wave feminism a step further by making institutional gains in law, legislation, and policy in those areas advocated by the second wave.[111]

Bridging the Gaps: The World March of Women

The World March of Women (WMW) exemplifies how dissent in the feminist movement has fostered its evolution and growth, and how successful practices of open space have persisted over time. Moreover, the WMW provides an example of a feminist project not categorised in a particular 'wave', bridging regional, national, and international feminist movements, involving women of diverse identifications and ages from around the globe. This is exemplified in the Canadian Women's March Committee's commitment in 2000 to bringing together women of diverse identifications and from across regions and organisations in Canada, as well as to connect Canadian women to the international activities of the March.[112]

The WMW was initiated by the *Fédération des Femmes du Québec* ('Québec Federation of Women') in the early 1990s as a ten-day *Marche du pain et des roses* ('March for bread and roses') and is now a permanent and worldwide movement involving thousands of women's groups unified for a common purpose.[113] The first march, in Québec, made demands on the provincial government, attempted to make connections across divisions in the movement, and hoped to boost grass-roots feminism.[114] The success of the Québec march led to the introduction of a World March at the UN Conference on Women in Beijing in 1995, and eventually to the first World March in 2000, and to the articulation by the WMW of a Women's Global Charter for Humanity in 2005.[115]

The WMW is an important demonstration of how feminists have learned from the past and determined successful strategies, thereby contributing to the growth and development of the feminist project. Conway notes that the debates of second-wave feminism regarding how women experience their gender depending on their geographical location have led to a greater sensitivity to these differences, as well as a commitment to fighting inequality not only between women and men, but also among women. These debates contributed to a "transnational feminism that was also anti-imperialist, anti-colonial, anti-racist, and anti-capitalist".[116] This transnational feminism is represented in the WMW, where the diversity of feminist movements is recognised, respected, and valued; as well as by the leadership of women from the Global South in new international networks and conferences.[117]

Moreover, particular strategies and philosophies of open space have persisted and developed over time. Lorraine Guay, a member of the WMW strategic committee, notes that the March is part of a long history of feminism and a tribute to previous feminist struggles.[118] This is reflected in the goals, values, Constitution, and By-laws of the WMW. The goals of the WMW were reached through "tried and true" practices present in earlier feminist waves, such as talking together, sharing stories, and finding common interests.[119] Guay also notes that the deployment of third-wave strategies, such as using the Internet, has offered an important space for the World March to mobilise, share information, participate in discussion, and engage in networking.[120]

Similar to the WSF's notion of open space as socially horizontal and without an owner, the WMW is self-initiated, without support from any outside authority or agency, and rooted in women's groups and associations.[121] The WMW also encourages and fosters independence and autonomy for participating groups, and emphasises the need to be "transparent", thereby reflecting a movement that attempts to be open and horizontal.[122] Moreover, it seeks to ensure that action is led by all participating groups and that leadership remains in the hands of ordinary women.[123] The Constitution and by-laws for the WMW also stress autonomy for its members, and a flexible decision-making structure.[124] This is apparent in its consensus-based model for decision-making, and the openness of its international meetings to observers from other networks and movements.

The WMW encourages and facilitates national or territorial coordinating bodies in order to maintain diversity and multiply efforts in new and creative ways.[125] This process can again be compared to Whitaker's notion of the incubator, where participants can give life to new movements with more specific aims, which also help to develop the wider struggle. Although participating groups, viewed as central to the March, are united in a shared set of articulated goals, they are autonomous in terms of how they translate these goals into local action.[126] Not only have these participating groups enabled the mobilisation of women from around the world, they also have the potential to become permanent fixtures in varying localities.[127]

However, as with previous waves of feminist activity, the open nature of the WMW has some limitations. Most significantly, the WMW insists that participating groups must subscribe to the purpose, values, and objectives of the March's overall plan.[128] As such, while participating groups are encouraged to be autonomous, they are simultaneously required to support goals and values set by an International Committee composed of eleven elected representatives.[129] Moreover, Guay outlines several points of conflict within the World March, including issues of sexuality, reproductive rights, prostitution, and disagreements around strategy.

However, the WMW is also an expression of global solidarity. This movement, along with the participation of feminists at the WSF, provides a ripe opportunity for the construction of partnerships and coalitions between both feminists as well as others active in global social movements, thereby fostering the growth of the feminist project overall.[130] As noted by Miles, Canadian feminists must recognise that women's needs, perspectives, opinions, and priorities vary in diverse and often divergent ways.[131] As such, the system as a whole must be challenged in order to uncover common interests in social change, ensuring solidarity among women of diverse identifications and geographic areas, so they may "play a role in the vibrant and multi-centered global feminist movement".[132]

In transnational feminism, it is of central importance to learn from the history of the feminist movement how to reject approaches that privilege "one form of power globally", recognise how power intersects many spheres of social life, and avoid universalising theories of feminism.[133] This will necessitate new strategies for ensuring open space to facilitate dialogue across linguistic and cultural differences, address power relations between participants, and enable the poorest to participate.[134] According to Eschle these discussions, initiated in the feminist movement and continuing today, point to a "more democratic future for feminism".[135]

Conclusion: The Challenges of Open Space and Dissent

While open space within the feminist movement has allowed for the expression of dissent, which has in turn helped to build a more inclusive feminism, it has also created fractures within the movement. However, the strength of second- and third-wave feminism has been their self-awareness and self-criticism, which has allowed for the identification of shortfalls and the continued revitalisation of feminism and feminist theory. It is when all feminist voices are part of the dialogue that feminism will truly be able to move forward.[136]

As noted at the beginning of this essay, a study of feminism is both daunting and a complex task. There are many holes in this exploration, including the fact that it is limited to explorations of only select instances of open space and dissent, and then only within a North American context. Sexuality was also a significant source of dissent within the second wave, and persists in the third wave with the exclusion of lesbians, transgendered women, and women of other sexual orientations.[137] In addition, in discussing dissent from feminists of colour, I have risked further homogenising these women into monolithic categories. Aboriginal, African-Canadian, Arab-Canadian, Central- and South American-Canadian, and Asian-Canadian women each experience their identities in different ways. While this essay has paid particular attention to dissent by women of colour in the second wave of feminism, the diversity of experience based on ethnicity deserves further study and discussion in relation to how they differently experience or identify with their gender and with feminism. Finally, although I have not discussed dissent by anti-feminists—because of their complete rejection of the feminist project—these "feminist dissenters"[138] should be analysed for the ways in which they have both negatively impacted the feminist movement, and the ways in which they may have served hooks's call for critique, analysis, and exploration for the development of feminist theory.

Although dissent within the feminist movement has caused conflict and fractures, it has also allowed for—indeed, encouraged—the expansion, growth, and development of the feminist movement, for instance as exemplified in the emergence of anti-racist feminist thought and in the advent of third-wave feminism, both of which strive to include women from diverse backgrounds and encourage women's multiple identifications. Third-wave feminism has also allowed for an expansion of our vocabulary of dissent, with third-wavers using "textual communities" to resist through personal narrative.[139] Zines, hybrid publications, and anthologies have served as 'open spaces' that have allowed women to resist mainstream gender characterisations, share information, and build feminist movements. The use of new conceptualisations of space in textual and online formats has allowed for new kinds of organising, which may result in the incubation of new movements and ideas that should be followed closely. bell hooks's notion of feminism as a theory in the making will be important to pay heed to as we observe the directions of the third wave, and continue to critique, deconstruct, and analyse in hope of the formulation of new possibilities.

References

Rita Alfonso and Jo Triglio, 1997—'Surfing the Third Wave: A Dialogue Between Two Third Wave Feminists', in *Hypatia*, vol 12 no 3, pp 7–15

Jennifer Allyn and David Allyn, 1995—'Identity Politics', in Rebecca Walker, ed, 1995—*To Be Real: Telling the Truth and Changing the Face of Feminism.* Toronto: Anchor

Sonia E. Alvarez, with Nalu Faria and Miriam Nobre, 2004—'Another (Also Feminist) World Is Possible: Constructing Transnational Spaces and Global Alternatives from the Movements', in Jai Sen, Anita Anand, Arturo Escobar, and Peter Waterman, eds—*World Social Forum: Challenging Empires.* Translation by Arturo Escobar (New Delhi: Viveka), pp 199–206, at www.choike.org/documentos/wsf_s313_alvarez.pdf (Accessed April 2017)

Ien Ang, 1995—'I'm a Feminist but ...: 'Other' Women and Postnational Feminism', in Barbara Caine and Rosemary Pringle, eds, 1995—*Transitions: New Australian Feminisms.* Sydney: Allen and Unwin

Peggy Antrobus, 2004—*The Global Women's Movement: Origins, Issues and Strategies.* Black Point, Nova Scotia: Fernwood Publishing

Cathryn Bailey, 1997—'Making Waves and Drawing Lines: The Politics of Defining the Vicissitudes of Feminism', in *Hypatia*, vol 12 no 3, pp 17–28

Jennifer Baumgardner and Amy Richards, 2000—*Manifesta: Young Women, Feminism, and the Future.* New York: Farrar, Straus, and Giroux

Brandi Leigh-Ann Bell, 2001—'Women-Produced Zines: Moving into the Mainstream', in Canadian Woman Studies, vol 20 no 4, at http://cws.journals.yorku.ca/index.php/cws/article/view/6907 (Accessed April 2017)

Dionne Brand, 1999—'Black Women and World: The Impact of Racially Constructed Gender Roles on the Sexual Division of Labour', in Enakshi Dua and Angela Robertson, eds, 1999—*Scratching the Surface: Canadian Anti-Racist Feminist Thought.* Toronto: The Women's Press

Canadian World March of Women, 2000—'It's Time for Change! The World March of Women 2000', in Canadian Woman Studies, vol 20 no 3, at http://cws.journals.yorku.ca/index.php/cws/article/view/12658 (Accessed April 2017)

Linda Carty, 1999—'The Discourse of Empire and the Social Construction of Gender', in Enakshi Dua and Angela Robertson, eds, 1999—*Scratching the Surface: Canadian Anti-Racist Feminist Thought.* Toronto: The Women's Press

Janet Conway, March 2006—'Alternative Globalizations and the Politics of Scale: Considering the World Social Forum and the World March of Women'. Manuscript submitted for publication, March 17 2006

Afua Cooper, 2000—'Constructing Black Women's Historical Knowledge', in *Atlantis*, vol 25 no 1 (Fall–Winter 2000), pp 39–50

Angela Y Davis, 1995—'Afterword', in Rebecca Walker, ed, 1995—*To Be Real: Telling the Truth and Changing the Face of Feminism.* Toronto: Anchor

Katherina Deliovsky, 2002—'The More Things Change ... Rethinking Mainstream Feminism', in Njoki Nathani et al, eds, 2002—*Back to the Drawing Board: African-Canadian Feminisms.* Toronto: Sumach Press

Jeannine DeLombard, 1995—'Femmenism', in Rebecca Walker, ed, 1995—*To Be Real: Telling the Truth and Changing the Face of Feminism.* Toronto: Anchor

Rene Denfield, 1995—*The New Victorians: A Young Women's Response to the Old Feminist Order*. Australia: Unwin & Allen

Madelyn Detloff, 1997—'Mean Spirits: The Politics of Contempt Between Feminist Generations', in *Hypatia*, vol 12 no 3

Rory Dicker and Alison Piepmeier, eds, 2003—*Catching a Wave: Reclaiming Feminism for the 21st Century*. Boston: Northeastern University Press

Jennifer Drake, 1997—'Third Wave Feminisms', in *Feminist Studies*, vol 23 no 1

Enakshi Dua, 1999—'Canadian Anti-Racist Feminist Thought: Scratching the Surface of Racism', in Enakshi Dua and Angela Robertson, eds, 1999—*Scratching the Surface: Canadian Anti-Racist Feminist Thought*. Toronto: The Women's Press

Enakshi Dua, 2005—'Canadian Anti-Racist Feminist Thought: Tension and Possibilities', in Barbara Crow and Lise Gotell, eds, 2005—*Open Boundaries: A Canadian Women's Studies Reader*. Toronto: Pearson Prentice Hall

Enakshi Dua and Angela Robertson, eds, 1999—*Scratching the Surface: Canadian Anti-Racist Feminist Thought*. Toronto: The Women's Press

Jane Errington, 1993—'Pioneers and Suffragists', in Sandra Burt, Lorraine Code, and Lindsay Dorney, eds, 1993—*Changing Patterns: Women in Canada* (Toronto: McLelland and Stewart Ltd), pp 59–91

Catherine Eschle, 2002—'Engendering Global Democracy', in *International Feminist Journal of Politics*, vol 4 no 3

Barbara Findlen, ed, 1995—*Listen Up: Voices from the Next Feminist Generation*. Seattle: Seal Press

Jo Freeman, 1970—'The Tyranny of Structurelessness', at http://flag.blackened.net/revolt/hist_texts/structurelessness.html (Accessed April 2017)

Jo Freeman, 1975—'Political Organization in the Feminist Movement', in *Acta Sociology*, vol 18 no 2–3

Lorraine Guay, 2002—'The World March of Women: A Political Action to Transform the World', background paper presented at the 'Citizenship and Globalization: Exploring Participation and Democracy in a Global Context Symposium', June 14–16, Vancouver, BC

Roberta Hamilton, 2005—'The Feminist Movement(s)', in Roberta Hamilton, ed, 2005—*Gendering the Vertical Mosaic*. Toronto: Pearson Prentice Hall

Emilie Hayes, December 2006—'Wading into the Waves of Feminism: Explorations in Open Space and Dissent in the Second Wave Feminist Movement and Its Contributions to the Emergence of Third Wave Feminism'. Paper presented at 'Revisiting Critical Courses @ Carleton', a Symposium in Ottawa, Canada, June 20–22 2007. Available at http://critical-courses.cacim.net/twiki/tiki-index.php?page=RCCSHome (Inactive April 2017)

Astrid Henry, 2003—'Feminism's Family Problem: Feminist Generations and the Mother-Daughter Trope', in Rory Dicker and Alison Piepmeier, eds, 2003—*Catching a Wave: Reclaiming Feminism for the 21st Century*. Boston: Northeastern University Press

Leslie Heywood and Jennifer Drake, eds, 1997—*Third Wave Agenda: Being Feminist, Doing Feminism*. Minneapolis: University of Minnesota Press

Christine Hoff Sommers, 1995—*Who Stole Feminism?: How Women Have Betrayed Women*. New York: Touchstone Press

bell hooks, 1984—*Feminist Theory: From Margin to Center*. Boston: South End Press.

bell hooks, 2000—*Feminism is for Everybody: Passionate Politics.* Cambridge, MA: South End Press

Chloé Keraghel and Jai Sen, 2004—'Explorations in Open Space: The World Social Forum and Cultures of Politics', in International Social Science Journal, vol 182, pp 483–493, at http://onlinelibrary.wiley.com/doi/10.1111/j.0020-8701.2004.00510.x/abstract (Accessed April 2017)

JeeYeun Lee, 1995—'Beyond Bean Counting', in Barbara Findlen, ed, 1995—*Listen Up: Voices from the Next Feminist Generation.* Seattle: Seal Press

Angela Miles, 2000—'Local Activisms, Global Feminisms and the Struggle against Globalization', in *Canadian Woman Studies*, vol 20 no 3

Angela Miles and Geraldine Finn, eds, 1992—*Feminism in Canada.* Montreal: Black Rose Books

Allyson Mitchell and Lara Karaian, 2004—'Third Wave Feminism', in Nancy Mandell, ed, 2004—*Feminist Issues: Race, Class, and Sexuality.* Toronto: Pearson Prentice Hall

Brenda O'Neill, 2003—'On the Same Wavelength? Feminist Attitudes Across Generations of Canadian Women', in Manon Tremblay and Linda Trimble, eds, 2003—*Women and Electoral Politics in Canada.* Toronto: Oxford University Press

Catherine M Orr, 1997—'Charting the Currents of the Third Wave', in *Hypatia*, vol 12 no 3

Michal Osterweil, 2004—'A Cultural-Political Approach to Reinventing the Political', in *International Social Science Journal*, vol 182 , at http://onlinelibrary.wiley.com/doi/10.1111/j.0020-8701.2004.00511.x/abstract (Accessed April 2017)

Natasha Pinterics, 2001—'Riding the Feminist Waves: In with the Third?', in *Canadian Woman Studies* vol 21, no 4 (Winter–Spring 2001), at http://cws.journals.yorku.ca/index.php/cws/article/view/6899 (Accessed April 2017)

N Reid-Maroney, 2004—'African Canadian Women and New World Diaspora, circa 1865', in *Canadian Woman Studies*, vol 23 no 2, at http://cws.journals.yorku.ca/index.php/cws/article/view/6313 (Accessed April 2017)

Candis Steenbergen, 2001—'Feminism and young women: Alive and well and still kicking', in *Canadian Woman Studies*, vol 21 no 4, Winter / Spring, at http://cws.journals.yorku.ca/index.php/cws/article/view/6898 (Accessed April 2017)

Gloria Steinem, 1995—'Foreword', in Rebecca Walker, ed, 1995—*To Be Real: Telling the Truth and Changing the Face of Feminism.* Toronto: Anchor

Mariana Valverde, 1992—'"When the Mother of the Race is Free": Race, Reproduction, and Sexuality in First-Wave Feminism', in Franca Iacovetta and Mariana Valverde, eds, 1992—*Gender Conflicts* (Toronto: University of Toronto Press), pp 3–26

Rebecca Walker, 1995—*To Be Real: Telling the Truth and Changing the Face of Feminism.* Toronto: Anchor

Immanuel Wallerstein, 2004—'The Dilemmas of Open Space: The Future of the WSF', in *International Social Science Journal*, vol 182

Njoki N Wane, 2004—'Black-Canadian Feminist Thought: Tensions and Possibilities', in *Canadian Woman Studies*, vol 23 no 2, at http://cws.journals.yorku.ca/index.php/cws/article/view/6321/5509 (Accessed April 2017)

Chico Whitaker, 2004—'The WSF as Open Space', in Jai Sen et al, eds, 2004—*World Social Forum: Challenging Empires* (New Delhi: Viveka Foundation), pp 111–121

World March of Women, 2007a—'Goals of the World March of Women', at http://www.worldmarchofwomen.org/qui_nous_sommes/objectifs/en (Accessed April 2017)

World March of Women, 2007b—'Declaration of Values', at http://www.
    worldmarchofwomen.org/qui_nous_sommes/valeurs/en/base_view (Accessed April
    2017)
World March of Women, 2007c—'Constitution and By-Laws', at http://www.
    worldmarchofwomen.org/qui_nous_sommes/statuts/en/base_view (Accessed April
    2017)
Lisa Young, 2000—*Feminists and Party Politics*. Vancouver: UBC Press

Notes

1. Ed: This essay is based on a paper written by the author while a student at Carleton University in 2006, initially titled 'Open Space and Dissent in Movement: Understandings and Lessons from the Canadian Feminist Movement', and then developed and presented at a Symposium in 2007 as 'Wading into the Waves of Feminism: Explorations in open space and dissent in the second wave feminist movement and its contributions to the emergence of third wave feminism' (Hayes 2006). I would like to warmly thank her for agreeing to revise what was a Master's student's initial exploration into the field into this great essay for this book.
2. Baumgardner and Richards 2000, p 50.
3. hooks 2000, p viii.
4. An example of this is REAL Women of Canada who identify themselves as an alternative women's movement yet view the family as the most important unit of Canadian society, view women's role as squarely within the family, and who support "traditional family values".
5. ibid, p 14, emphasis in original.
6. ibid.
7. Young 2000.
8. Dicker and Piepmeier 2003; O'Neill 2003.
9. Errington 1993
10. ibid.
11. ibid.
12. ibid, p 85.
13. Dicker and Piepmeier 2003
14. Errington 1993; Hamilton 2005
15. Hamilton 2005.
16. ibid.
17. Black 1993; Steenbergen 2001
18. Pinterics 2001; Steenbergen 2001; Bailey 1997; Dicker and Piepmeier 2003; O'Neill 2003
19. Heywood and Drake 1997.
20. Pinterics 2001; O'Neill 2003.
21. Heywood and Drake 1997, p 3.
22. Steenbergen 2001.
23. Dicker and Piepmeier 2003.
24. Mitchell and Karaian 2004.
25. Bailey 1997, p 19

26. Dicker and Piepmeier 2003.
27. Alfonso and Trigilio 1997.
28. Drake 1997; Mitchell and Karaian 2004.
29. Dicker and Piepmeier 2003.
30. Whitaker 2004, p 113; Sen and Keraghel 2004.
31. Wallerstein 2004.
32. Whitaker 2004.
33. Whitaker 2004; Osterweil 2004.
34. Keraghel and Sen 2004, p 484.
35. Whitaker 2004.
36. Steenbergen 2001.
37. Dicker and Piepmeier 2003.
38. Hamilton 2005.
39. ibid.
40. Black 1993.
41. ibid.
42. ibid.
43. Freeman 1975, p 224.
44. ibid.
45. ibid.
46. ibid, p 235.
47. ibid.
48. ibid, pp 230–231
49. ibid, p 235
50. ibid.
51. Hamilton 2005.
52. Bell 2001; Pinterics 2001.
53. Pinterics 2001.
54. Orr 1997.
55. Orr 1997; Pinterics 2001; O'Neill 2003.
56. Orr 1997.
57. Freeman 1970.
58. Freeman 1975.
59. Freeman 1970.
60. Freeman 1975, p 238.
61. Wallerstein 2004.
62. Mandell 2004.
63. Keraghel and Sen 2004, p 488.
64. Freeman 1975.
65. ibid, p. 231.
66. ibid, p 240.
67. ibid.
68. Wallerstein 2004, p 635.
69. Freeman 1975, p 233.
70. Orr, 1997.
71. Bell 2001.

72. Whitaker 2004.
73. Orr 1997; Freeman 1970; Steenbergen 2001; Dicker and Piepmeier 2003; Hamilton 2005; Pinterics 2001; O'Neill 2003; Bell 2001.
74. Delombard 1995, p 33.
75. Allyn and Allyn 1995.
76. Walker 1995.
77. Valverde 1992, p 13.
78. Dua 1999; Valverde 1992; Carty 1999.
79. Valverde 1992, p 6.
80. ibid, p 15.
81. Brand 1999, p 84.
82. Cooper 2000.
83. Carty 1999, p 41.
84. Carty 1999; Cooper 2000.
85. Carty 1999, p 42.
86. Cooper 2000.
87. Carty 1999; Pinterics 2001; Dua 1999.
88. Dicker and Piepmeier 2003.
89. Wane 2004.
90. Brand 1999.
91. Ang 1995, p 57.
92. Lee 1995, p 205.
93. Dua 1999.
94. Pinterics 2001.
95. O'Neill 2003, p 179.
96. Dicker and Piepmeier 2003; O'Neill 2003.
97. Bailey 1997; Henry 2003.
98. Henry 2003.
99. Baumgardner and Richards 2000, p 233.
100. Detloff 1997, p 78.
101. Dicker and Piepmeier 2003, p 15.
102. Detloff 1997; Pinterics 2001; Bailey 1997; Dicker and Piepmeier 2003.
103. Steinem 1995, p xix; Bailey 1997; Orr 1997; Davis 1995.
104. Dicker and Piepmeier 2003, p 17; Pinterics 2001.
105. Bailey 1997, p 23.
106. Pinterics 2001; Henry 2003.
107. hooks 1984.
108. Dua 1999; Wane 2004; Brand 1999.
109. ibid.
110. ibid, p 66.
111. ibid.
112. Canadian World March of Women, 2000.
113. Conway 2006. *Ed*: In 2008, and only underlining this intention, the Secretariat of the World March of Women was shifted from Montréal in Canada to São Paulo in Brazil.
114. ibid.

115. ibid.
116. ibid.
117. World March of Women 2007a; Miles, 2000.
118. Guay 2002.
119. World March of Women 2007a.
120. Guay 2002.
121. ibid.
122. World March of Women 2007b.
123. ibid.
124. World March of Women 2007c.
125. ibid.
126. Guay 2002.
127. ibid.
128. World March of Women 2007a.
129. World March of Women 2007c.
130. Alvarez et al 2003.
131. Miles 2000.
132. ibid.
133. Eschle 2002, p 330.
134. ibid.
135. ibid, p 333.
136. Henry 2003.
137. Mitchell and Karaian 2004.
138. Orr 1997, p 34.
139. Mitchell and Karaian 2004, p 64.

International Feminisms:
New Syntheses, New Directions[1]
Virginia Vargas

*The content of transnational action by social movements transcends the content
and contexts in which national dynamics take place, although they are closely
linked to them, influencing each other, empowering or disconnecting each other,
exchanging strategies, reinventing others, broadening or narrowing the spaces of
action. There is a "mutually constructed relationship between the national and
the international which suggests that transformations in one ought to bring about
transformations in the other."*
—James Goodman[2]

International Feminisms in the Making

Since the beginning of the second wave of feminism,[3] Latin American feminists
have developed rich regional and international patterns of interaction. The
content, successes, and contradictions of these patterns reflect the increasing
complexity of feminist goals and practices and the tensions or 'knots' that have
accompanied them since the beginning. The different approaches to development
in the region that have succeeded one another over time have also produced
changes—economic, political, and subjective—that influence feminist strategies.
The most dramatic and visible of these is the shift of the development paradigm
from industrial capitalism to a global information capitalism, which has had profound economic, social, and cultural effects on societies worldwide. In response to
this shift, feminists have been tailoring their strategies, making them more subtle
and complex, widening the content of their struggles in order to address the new
risks and exclusions, and nurturing new subjectivities and new spaces of transformation. The fact that feminisms faced the same situation as did movements
for sexual diversity only contributed to them—separately and together—tailoring
new sensibilities, forging new rights, and creating more democratic horizons.

Latin American feminisms have taken multiple forms, through innumerable organisations, collectives, action networks, themes, and identities. These
networks and collectives have given rise to a rich internationalist dynamic, generating new forms of thought and expression. On the regional level, the most important are the Feminist Encounters (*Encuentros*), which were held every two and
then every three years from 1981 to 2005, the last in Brazil. The dynamics of the
Encuentros reflect feminist advances, shared strategies, conflicts of perspectives

and meanings, and different discourses that have produced multiple and intense linkages between the national and the international.[4]

During the 1980s, when Latin American countries were under dictatorial or authoritarian governments and then moved toward democratic governments that proved to be far from fully democratic, feminist political strategies did not connect very well with the institutions of governance, either on the national or the global level. Instead, feminisms were oriented more toward politicising the conditions of women in the private sphere,[5] re-createing collective practices, and making the invisible visible. Latin American feminists devised new categories of analysis and even new languages to name things that had thus far gone un-named—sexuality, domestic violence, sexual assault, rape in marriage, and the feminisation of poverty, among others—and put them at the centre of democratic debates. The symbolic dimension of change, a kind of cultural ferment, was a part of feminist action, creating new dates to celebrate, and recovering leaders, histories, and symbols. These transcended national boundaries and gave regional feminisms a broader, Latino-Caribbean significance.

Feminist dynamics on the regional and international levels changed dramatically from the 1980s to the 90s. First, the return to democratic governments created new and complex political contexts, with varying effects on the development of feminisms and feminist strategies. The struggles for democracy where feminisms were actively involved, also brought forward the presence of new actors and identities. One of the main changes was that it became impossible to speak of feminism in the singular, not only because of its expansion across the region but also because of the differences in strategies and positions and also in the ways in which feminists in different contexts confronted the new uneasinesses that began to emerge within what had previously been considered classically feminist positions.

Second, the successive UN world conferences of the 1990s, on the Environment (1992), Human Rights (1993), Population (1994), and then the Fourth World Conference on Women in Beijing (1995), opened new spaces for feminist expression and new arenas for action and debate at the global level, broadening the exchanges with feminists from other parts of the world. A new, rich, and *international* feminist praxis began to emerge. Latin American feminisms, which had developed a rich regional articulation of different feminist expressions, were confronted with the construction of and contestation within the global arena. While in the 1980s contacts among Latin American and Caribbean feminists had largely been directed toward constructing a region-wide movement that would connect civil society groups across national borders, in the 1990s regional and global relations drew on two streams: One based on civil societies (primarily represented by the *Encuentros*), and one based on the interactions of feminists working in official state capacities. In Beijing, both groups were able to cooperate while also confronting each other, making similar demands yet following their own distinct dynamics. The feminists who came to Beijing arrived with experiences gained in key civil society organisations, and with the gains that had been achieved in previous UN conferences, where organised networks with expertise in each of these issues helped shape the Conference agendas and platforms.

In particular, Beijing brought together expert networks as well as identity groups and NGO feminists who came with little experience in lobbying governments and even less with global institutions. It thus provided an enormous opportunity for learning, but it also revealed the new tensions arising out of 'NGO-isation', or the increasing institutionalisation of feminist organisations.

So, a third feature of these processes refers to the contradictions that started to set in. The new incidence in national, regional, and global official state-oriented arenas also brought a new risk: That the relations between feminists and national governments as well as international institutions might become too intimate.[6] The new emphasis placed on lobbying contributed to changing the relations—from a movement logic to an institutional one, and towards an increasing fragmentation and individuation of collective actions as movement.[7] Some of the more radical demands of feminisms did not disappear but they are weakened, because, as Sonia Alvarez has said, the feminisms focused on what was possible rather than on what was desirable.[8] Moreover, during the first years of the 1990s, and as networks became more specialised and institutional strategies took precedence, there was the emergence of the 'me culture' promoted by the competitive and consumerist values of neoliberalism,[9] which had begun to install themselves in the social imagination.

In the new millennium, the complex developments that had taken place in the feminist movement as well as the paradigmatic shift to neoliberal capitalism altered possibilities for feminists as it did for other movements facing the challenges of neoliberal economic and political hegemony. The increasing power of conservative and fundamentalist economic, political, cultural, and religious forces deepened patterns of exclusion for the majority and directly challenged women's rights and sexual diversity. The United Nations, which from the start of the International Decade for Women (1975) to the Beijing Conference (1995) had provided ample space for debate and negotiation to global feminisms and had made it possible to broaden the meaning of 'women's rights', was no longer the organisation it was in the 1970 and 80s. Its autonomy was now severely weakened, overtaken by the scandalous unilateralism of the United States and the domination of global politics by the powerful economies. It has lost credibility. At the same time however, strong new movements of global solidarity emerged during this period, many seeking an alternative globalisation to the one promoted by neoliberalism. Many feminist groups played, and are today playing, active roles in this effort.

Feminist Dynamics for a New Millennium

The international world today is ... a series of levels and spaces in which the women's movements of Latin America have a permanent and challenging presence. The intensity of commitment and the seriousness of reflection around globalization have lessons for other radical democratic movements, theories and ideologies.[10]

... [B]efore, the inequalities among women in different social classes and geographical locations seemed like unchanging facts to be mediated through the political system and the economy. The increasing density of transnational connections has transformed the grounding of social movements as many movements combine. In this way, the apparently hard and fast 'facts' of inequality are converted into sets of direct experiences with relations of power among allies, male and female, who are part of a larger pattern of global inequalities and geographic distances.[11]

In the new millennium, feminists across the world are experiencing fundamental modifications in their ways of thinking and acting, and are becoming more complex and diverse in the struggles they take on. There are new interpretive frames for action that have affected both the content of feminist agendas and the spaces from which feminists choose to act.[12] This has broadened the global transformational horizons of the various strands of feminism.

This new political cultural climate is more flexible and inclusive. The historical conjuncture that brought forward the hegemony of global neoliberalism has also produced the disintegration of old paradigms.[13] There is an urgency to create a new reality by envisioning radical new approaches to address global change. This can be seen in new thinking about the state and capital at both national and global levels, which is opposed to the messianic, universal narratives of past movements. Conditions are ripe for the emergence of new forms of political culture or, better yet, for countercultural proposals that challenge the neoliberal logic of power that now exists at the global level and strongly impacts the local.[14]

One fundamental aspect of this new political culture is that it assumes that the transformation of the world depends on what Beck calls the "transformation of vision".[15] For me, this new way of looking at the world implies changing one's imaginative focus from the nation state to a more cosmopolitan view. This does not limit but relocates the global/local scale, avoiding the loss of social experience characteristic of abstract models.[16] In contemporary international society the levels of local, national, and global sociability are interconnected, and privileging one level over another is a political not an empirical decision. For his part, Beck assumes that these levels are complementary, which allows us to dissolve the fiction that any one of them represents 'reality'.[17] Instead, the cosmopolitan vision is closest to reality because it opens possibilities that a national perspective, taken alone, excludes.

This cosmopolitan vision is the key to understanding the new ways in which social movements are acting and interacting in global/local space, with a range of struggles and emancipatory concerns. It has been said that these movements have produced fragmentation and localised conflicts; they have been accompanied by what Norbert Lechner has called the "privatisation" of social conduct (which is seen in the resistance of people to involve themselves in collective action).[18] It is also true that new forms of interaction are occurring in what Manuel Castells calls the "networked society".[19] These are expressed not by unified actors in a well-defined social or even multicultural context, but rather as dimensions of a broad 'field' of social interaction, which is diverse and constantly expanding and transforming itself, producing new frameworks of meaning.[20] In this field, the radical break that many have posited between 'old' and 'new' social movements is no longer so clear. There are other dynamics which have just begun to be felt: Campaigns for global justice arising from new and different sources and efforts to free ourselves from obsolete paradigms without yet knowing what will replace them.

These struggles do not erase the differences among groups; on the contrary, what emerges is a multiplicity of meanings, as the social space of experience expands both locally and globally. And all these struggles, except for those that arise from an essentialist viewpoint, shape only a part of one's identity. In the case of feminism, the classical campaigns calling for a different view of sexuality and for changing the relations of power between men and women are merged with other struggles in order to oppose neoliberalism, militarisation, and fundamentalisms of various kinds. Our frameworks are constantly widening, responding and closely linked to global processes of transformation encompassing many emancipatory projects.

In relation to the question of the spaces from and within which feminisms now act, there are two significant and promising changes. The first is the possibility of recovering a politics that is not located solely in 'the state', but also in society and in daily life. The second is the prospect of transcending one's own location in order to connect and debate ideas with other groups oriented toward change, which broadens the emancipatory horizon and has the potential to create a 'counter-power' to confront (and offer alternatives to) the hegemonic power and discourses we face.

As for the content of feminist agendas, feminists have begun to widen political categories, such as democracy, for example, and make them more complex. The search for a concept of democracy that is plural and radical is central to their thinking and recovers the diversity of experiences and aspirations that the neoliberal model denies. It nurtures democratic, secular, untutored visions that are transcultural rather than Western and works on different scales and dimensions.

It incorporates subjectivity into the transformation of social relations and generating multiple sites from which emancipatory democratic agendas can emerge. In this process, struggles *against* material and symbolic exclusions and *for* redistributive justice and recognition create a new politics of the body. Dialogues among diversities are one of the ways in which feminist and women's movements are seeking to have an impact.

This perspective has also expanded the human rights paradigm, incorporating new rights to respond to new risks, subjectivities, and citizen demands. Countercultural strategies put the recovery and broadening of economic rights (those most devalued by neoliberalism) and sexual and reproductive rights (those usually resisted by official governing bodies) at the centre of feminist praxis. At the same time, various feminisms seek to impact the many dimensions of global transformation, resisting the neoliberal model, with its exaggerated individualism and consumerism, and opposing the growing militarism that is increasingly attributable to actions of the US government.

And there is a sustained battle against fundamentalisms. One critical effort is to show how discriminations by race, ethnicity, class, gender, age, and sexual orientation are linked as constitutive elements of a 'nucleus' of domination. To do this, feminists seek to understand and draw attention to the interpretive frameworks used by other social movements, but also to engage them in dialogue to raise issues that are insufficiently incorporated into their transformational agendas. Women's "impertinent forms of knowledge"[21] can undermine traditional discourses and must be present in the efforts to bring about change.

The fight against fundamentalisms is a shared goal among the many feminisms that are interacting internationally. In their multiple expressions—whether in the name of God, the market, or tradition—fundamentalisms defend a set of immutable ideas about the world that are held up as norms for society, often with horrendous consequences for the lives and bodies of women. In the struggle against fundamentalisms, the body is one of those "impertinent forms of knowledge" that can broaden the terms of transformation. The body has become an "endowed space of citizenship".[22] The rights of the body are what is in dispute in the struggle for sexual and reproductive rights; in the battle against AIDS, which is also a battle against patents and the transnational pharmaceutical companies; in the fight against militarism, which makes women's bodies war booty on all sides; and against racism, real and symbolic discrimination based on skin colour that has perverse consequences for women's sexual bodies. It is the battle against injustice and hunger, which permanently limit the bodily capabilities of new generations.

The body thus conceived recovers the connections between the public and the private; it confronts capital and the state, and national and international institutions. The body is a concept with democratic normativity,[23] confronting commonly held traditional meanings and supporting a new subjectivity that reclaims personal politics as integral to global emancipatory strategies. Examining the impacts of global forces on bodies provides a central fulcrum of analysis, although it has not yet produced a shared transformatory meaning for all groups.

The World Social Forum: Contested Space in the Construction of Counter-Power

"Another world is possible" is the motto of the World Social Forum. Seen from a feminist perspective, the task is much larger than it appears. Nevertheless we are making the dominant ways of thinking uncomfortable. But are we also making ourselves uncomfortable with our machismo, racism and other forms of intolerance? The purpose of the World Social Forum is to establish a dialogue among diverse perspectives. This gives the Forum its originality and power in the construction that globalizes the various citizenships of Planet Earth. But the road is long and full of obstacles. I hope that women will make us radical, acting as they have up to now: asking what is due and making us uncomfortable.[24]

The World Social Forum is a new global space that, slowly but surely, has become an arena for the construction of linkages, knowledges, and global democratic thought among social movements. As Betania Ávila writes, this is a space where feminism finds a fruitful place to weave its alliances and connect with others who are seeking change, and to contribute to the democratisation of politics. Movements and this global space are in "a dialectical relation, in which the movements produce a process that reconfigures the shape of each movement and of all movements together".[25]

Feminisms have contributed to this alternative process of globalisation. With a long and rich history of international solidarity, which has grown cumulatively out of the feminist *Encuentros* and involvement in expert networks and identity groups, feminisms express themselves at regional and global levels. Many interactions began at the UN Conferences, weaving the fabric of international connection. As Waterman says, there is no doubt that the support of feminist thinkers of the 1970s and 80s was critical to what is now considered a global movement for social justice. Their internationalist experience and their roles in new movements today can be traced back to earlier feminist practices on the international level.[26]

Many feminisms come together in the World Social Forum, which opens spaces for a variety of approaches and emphases in confronting neoliberal globalisation. In the Forums held to date (six world social forums, three polycentric forums, and innumerable regional, thematic, and national forums), feminists have had different kinds of presence and expression.[27] They are active in the organisation of workshops, panels, in interchanges and alliances with other movements, in the development of global campaigns, and in the management of the Forum, including the International Council.[28]

Regional and global networks of women connect with each other and with other movements. They have supported important 'global campaigns' in each of the Forums, including the Campaign of the *Marcha Mundial de Mujeres* (the World March of Women) calling for a 'Global Women's Map', and the campaign 'Against Fundamentalism, People are Fundamental' brought forward by the Latin America–based Feminist Articulation Marcosur (AFM) to broaden the concept of fundamentalism to include "all religious, economic, scientific or cultural expressions which deny humanity its diversity and legitimize the violent mechanisms by which one group subjects another, or one person subjects another".[29]

The Forum puts fundamental aspects of women's struggles onto democratic agendas. Over the years, feminists have organised panels including 'Abortion in the Democratic Agenda', 'The Effects of Neoliberalism on the Lives of Women', and 'Women Against War; War Against Women'. Special mention should be made of the panel 'Dialogue Among Movements' that has been organised by a group of networks from different regions in the most recent Forums,[30] beginning in Mumbai in 2004 and repeated in Porto Alegre in 2005. This panel brought trade unionists, 'untouchables', peasants, homosexuals, lesbians, and transsexuals into dialogue with one another to discuss their differences but also to share reflections on how to expand each group's perspective on transformation and thereby enrich their common ground for action.[31]

In 2007, at the Sixth World Social Forum in Nairobi, the feminist organising group, Feminist Dialogues, which is made up of twelve regional and global networks, organised several actions. A march co-organised by the Women's March for Freedom and various African feminist groups was the Forum's largest and most visible demonstration. The Young Feminists, along with the African Committee and African feminist organisations, co-organised the Central Panel of Women (a series of large thematic panels) and organised the Panel of Dialogue and Debates that brought feminist anti-war and anti-fundamentalist perspectives onto the agenda. On the fourth day of the Forum, the Young Feminists presented proposals to the WSF for actions to be carried out during the rest of the year.

Are there aspects of the feminist presence that make the Forum more radical, as Cândido Grzybowski has argued it should be? Perhaps the most evident have been making visible other dimensions of the political, bringing onto the stage new social and political actors, and incorporating new transformative dimensions, drawn from everyday life. All these dimensions are not always present in the social movements that converge in the forum. In other words, feminisms have taken full advantage of the basic feature of the World Social Forum, which is that it provides an umbrella for a multiplicity of movements whose common concern is the struggle against the catastrophic consequences of neoliberalism for the world's people. There is no single view on how to act and from what point of view as a univocal vision, whether on the impact of neoliberalism or with regard to the dynamics of social change more broadly, can exclude important debates and contestations over meanings and cultures, and the subversive ways which democratic change is occurring locally and globally. A univocal vision can also deny recognition to new social actors who have the capacity to carry on the struggle in different arenas.

Resisting Diversity

The statements of Frei Betto, a well-known progressive theologian committed to social movements, are an example of a problem the Forum faces in this regard. In a panel at the World Social Forum in Porto Alegre in 2005, he argued that feminism rose and fell in the twentieth-century, and that feminists should no longer be considered international actors or as committed to the transformations that the struggle against neoliberalism proposes. An open letter from Brazilian feminists, presented at the Forum, objected that his words had arbitrarily condemned a vibrant movement, active in the Forum, to oblivion. "To make a political subject invisible is a serious sign of an enormous arbitrariness, and goes against the democratic practices of social struggle".[32]

Perspectives that disregard the existence of movements like feminism reinforce the idea that some actors are more politically significant than others. But this narrow viewpoint cannot erase the experiences of feminists, homosexuals, lesbians, and transsexuals, or dismiss the specific struggles that, for example, the black feminists of Latin American have carried out in their own communities and cultures. To think in this way is to employ frameworks about emancipation that are profoundly contradictory to emancipatory goals.

Against these exclusionary dynamics, feminists within the WSF and the International Council have carried on a tenacious struggle to increase their visibility, democratise participation in panels and activities of the Forum, and to make gender and diversity basic principles on which the Forum rests. Their vision is not partial but global. Openness to diversity identifies new dimensions of struggle, not only for 'a better world', in the singular, but for other better *worlds* that will reflect many emancipatory perspectives.[33] Confronting exclusionary viewpoints is important to feminists, but it is also important for other actors. This became clear in the tensions that emerged in the Youth Camp of the 2005 World Social Forum where issues and perspectives were debated that had not been anticipated by the Forum's coordinating groups.[34]

Differences also exist in regard to the place from which one speaks. If the different groups and social movements agree on the need to struggle against neoliberalism and militarism, then ways to approach this agenda can be better grasped by reflecting on the impact of neoliberalism and militarism on women and on gender relations.[35] Other feminist issues are not as easily taken up by other movements, and therefore require further discussion and explanation. This has been the case for the struggle against fundamentalisms, which focuses on the relation between sexuality, production, and reproduction as questions relevant at both the symbolic and the material levels of the social relations of exploitation and domination.[36] The struggle against fundamentalisms recognises a diversity of connections life experiences and subjectivities.

But these perspectives are not yet recognised as important dimensions of the transformative proposals put forward by both men and women in the World Social Forum. In 2005, this issue was taken up in a statement to the press put out by AFM on the last day of the Forum. Speaking from the 'Women's Ship' (*Barco de las Mujeres*), AFM declared that:

> The fight for sexual freedom and abortion is one of the most advanced forms of opposition to fundamentalisms within the framework of the WSF. ... Until now it has not succeeded in making the Forum equal; the focus on the 'important' activities of the 'important' men shows how necessary it is to make the Forum more democratic. ... The AFM believes that the WSF should be a place of lived radical democracy, with equality among diverse people.[37]

A dramatic confrontation occurred at the 2007 Forum in Nairobi, where there was an exceptional presence of church groups from Africa and around the world, including a US-based pro-life organisation. Several of these groups organised an anti-abortion march inside the Forum. Later, in the closing ceremony, there was a verbal attack on a speaker who was a lesbian activist. In response, a group of networks and institutions sent a statement to the International Committee, which said in part:

> By this document we affirm that the struggles of our sisters (nuestr@s herman@s) for sexual and reproductive rights throughout the world are also our struggles. And therefore, calling on the principle of diversity that we believe is fundamental to the goal of constructing other possible worlds that are more solidary and just ... [and] given that the struggles to create these other worlds can only be successful if they recognize the diversity of identities and political positions, we affirm that the WSF is open to all who recognize this diversity. Organizations and individuals who promote the marginalization, exclusion, or discrimination of others cannot be part of this process. ... We call upon the International Council, and on the various Organizing Committees, to promote and support the integration of the struggles for sexual and reproductive rights in each Social Forum that takes place around the world. We understand the diversity of cultural and

political contexts, but the right to fight for the autonomy and liberty of nuestr@s herman@s is not negotiable.[38]

Diversity and Democracy

Providing space for debate is one of the most precious founding principles of the WSF. The tensions and contradictions and the different levels at which these are expressed are fundamental to the recovery of the diverse sensibilities and interrogations of the new stages of globalisation. Inequalities perceived and named become the basis for more daring proposals that can broaden and connect particular viewpoints.

These debates have expanded our understanding of democracy. Boaventura de Sousa Santos speaks of "demo-diversity" as a useful antidote to rigid and univocal conceptions of democracy. Demo-diversity is "the peaceful or conflictive existence, in a given social field, of different models and practices of democracy".[39] In order to have an impact on this new construction of democracy, it is necessary to make one's own position clear. Multiple feminist strategies arise from difference, as we support and commit ourselves to the struggles that have given rise to other social movements, the process that drives the Forum. Feminist political visions of democracy and change must be incorporated in this debate, creating a space for dialogue that is sensitive to differences and seeks points of convergence. This democratic vision incorporates struggles for recognition. For recognition to have space, Marta Rosenberg maintains, it is necessary to politicise differences, celebrating equality as the vehicle of justice while protecting expressions of differences as acts of freedom.[40]

For feminists representing many feminisms, democracy from diversity implies recognising that all the multiple democratic forms of fighting for justice and for emancipation—in the public and in the private—are valid, and that their expression broadens the democratic soil. Once this idea is accepted, the subjectivities and recognitions vital to diversity can be transformed. Differences perceived and named rather than ignored or repressed become the raw material for audacious proposals. The acceptance of diversity through recognition can subvert the fragmentation resulting from neoliberalism, which maintains that "there is no other alternative" to its view of the world and its future. All of these processes also reflect the ambivalent and still unexpressed ways in which feminist thought and action is being constructed on the global level.

Feminist Dialogues from Difference

A group of feminist networks, *articulaciones*, and organisations from different regions of the world took on the task of organising a space for recognition and dialogue among feminists in the Forum. A meeting under the trees, organised by AFM during the 2003 World Social Forum, led to the Feminist Dialogues initiated in 2004 in Mumbai and continued in Porto Alegre and Nairobi. Women from all over the world meet together for three days prior to the Forum: We were 180 in Mumbai, 260 in Porto Alegre, and 180 in Nairobi. Although most of these women had regional or transnational feminist connections, few had engaged in such discussions before at the global level. One of the constants of the Dialogues is the goal of finding feminist ways to approach the basic goals of the WSF—to confront neoliberalism and militarism—while also emphasising the importance of opposing all fundamentalisms. Making the body an analytical focus has the potential to integrate disparate views and inspire a radical democratic vision.

This idea was expressed as follows in the following 'Concept Note' for the 2005 meeting:

> Conscious as feminists that our bodies are full of cultural and social significance, we also experience our bodies as key sites of political and moral struggles. Through the bodies of women, the community, the state, the family, fundamentalist forces (state and non-state), religion, and markets define themselves. These forces and institutions, using a plethora of patriotic controls, transform the bodies of women into expressions of relations of power. The bodies of women, therefore, are at the centre of authoritarian or democratic projects.[41]

Building on this, in 2007 the Feminist Dialogue process issued a Concept Note on 'Feminist Perspectives on Radical Democracy' for the Third Feminist Dialogue:[42]

> The feminist movements of the new millennium are committed to the enrichment of the radical political-democratic project, in which diversity must be recognized, internalized and negotiated in ways that create subjects, rather than be considered something merely to be tolerated. We look for spaces where women can express and enrich themselves by a process of learning and experimenting with change, giving rise to the mutual recognition of and relations among other local, national, regional and global democratic struggles. This in turn will enrich the emerging democratic cultures, which will express themselves in an explosion of new themes, identities and social actors. ... A different world will not be possible without a different conception of democracy. And a different democracy is possible only through a process of personal and subjective revolution, involving both men and women, which actively recognizes diversity and takes the intersectionalities of these different struggles as a collective end.

Feminists who participate in the Forum, from their multiple differences and without any prior relationship among them, share a referential horizon that is expressed in their choice of the WSF as a place of participation and action. With different emphases, they share a commitment to struggles for redistribution and for recognition, and to interacting in pluralist spaces with other social actors, male and female. They want to "strengthen feminist political organization beyond borders", in the words of the Global Report of the Second Feminist Dialogue in 2005.[43] In the Forum, as we have seen, feminists are in dialogue and dispute to transcend their limits, democratising their interactions and avoiding their own 'fundamentalist' or single-minded versions of what is possible.

Those who participate in the Feminist Dialogues are active in many networks and organisations in addition to the WSF. Yet the Forum offers a distinct space for ongoing learning and interchange that can create new visions of democracy and strengthen global democratic forces. We are inspired by mobilisations within the Forum, like the March for Freedom in Nairobi.

The fact that women had interacted in feminist spaces before coming together in the Forum facilitated our discussions and aided our vision, but it has also made our interactions more complex. The reflections that nurture the Feminist Dialogues are part of a critical repositioning within feminism. As Gandhi and Shah put it,

> For us, feminism goes further than the popular liberal understanding of equality between men and women. ... Feminism as an ideology sees the oppression and agency of women within a patriarchal structure and within neoliberal economic, social and political systems. It is a feminism that is against fundamentalisms, global capitalism, and imperialism ..., which allies itself with the marginalized and the indigenous ..., [and] which develops its practices every day of our lives and seeks to work collectively and democratically. ... We believe that it is not necessary to privilege either the particular or the universal; rather we would accentuate and emphasize the relation between the two. Instead of universalizing our experiences, we need to universalize our visions and goals as women's movements.[44]

We also recognise that the dramatic changes we have lived in the last few decades have rendered obsolete the paradigms that used to inform our thinking and acting; that it is necessary to raise new questions and re-create or reconstruct new concepts and connections that take account of today's complexities; and that, facing the hegemony of neoliberal globalisation today, it is necessary to work with other actors to find ways to construct an alternative globalisation from a radical democratic standpoint. In these processes, gender identities cannot be viewed in isolation but must be seen in constant interaction and articulation with other identities. Discriminations based on race, ethnicity, age, sexual orientation, and geographical location are all expressions of global systems of domination.

We must be clear: There are many struggles. Rather than make differences invisible, we must use them to provoke a multiplicity of responses that can expand the space of social experience at the local and global level. The old distinction between local and global has lost much of its meaning, and this in turn requires a change of perspective, as Beck argues, from the national to the cosmopolitan. As Beck observes, conflicts over gender, class, ethnicity, and sexual preference have their origins in the nation, but they have long escaped that frame, and now overlap and interconnect globally.[45]

For Latin American feminists who participate in the WSF, the Feminist Dialogues have added a new dimension to their international experience, which has moved from the regional level of the Latin American and Caribbean *Encuentros* to the global spaces of the UN world conferences on women, to this new arena in which they interact with feminists and with other social movements at the global level. Their strategies are shifting from advocacy to the creation of counter-power and counter-narratives against neoliberal ideology. Both strategies were present at Beijing, but advocacy, not opposition, characterised the second half of the 1990s.

In contrast to the regional *Encuentros*, however, where all feminists who wanted and were able to participated, in these new global spaces we are not as many as we have been in other forums, nor all that we could be. We are a small group, which is due as much to the low levels of activist interest in global issues as to the cost of travel. The advances, new understandings, and new questions gained from these experiences still lack channels of expression and analysis at the national-global level. It is important for us to infuse our actions with insights from these multilevel discourses. Seen from any particular point on the planet, the global is always local.

In these four years, the Feminist Dialogues have changed. From the beginning, it was difficult to find a way to proceed, and we learned as we went, helped by the criticisms of the feminist participants and the self-criticism of the organising team. Seeing that the approaches we had used in previous meetings had failed to provide an environment in which we could express our similarities and differences and work toward future perspectives,[46] for the 2007 WSF in Nairobi we proposed that more attention be given to the discussion of feminist political agendas in relation to the goals of the WSF, and to the construction, from many perspectives, of global feminist agendas. The call to participate in the Feminist Dialogues was directed to "feminists with a strong interest in the political project of constructing a movement ... recognizing, of course, that the notion of 'a movement' is dynamic and filled with diversity and contradictions".[47]

In addition to discussions of democracy, citizenship, and neoliberal, fundamentalist, and militarised states, the meeting emphasised the goal of creating global feminist strategies, hoping to generate critical perspectives and diverse reflections from the different feminisms represented by the participants.[48] There was another contrast. For the first time the organising team decided to take positions within the Forum, supporting some of the initiatives already discussed, including the Women's Freedom March, the Feminist Youth Tent, and the opportunity (during the fourth day of the Forum) to collect and propose ideas for the list of actions the Forum as a whole would agree to carry out during the rest of the year.

There were also important changes in the WSF itself. The Forum moved toward greater democratisation and more effective inclusion of different perspectives within the framework of the Charter of Principles, making strategic spaces like that of the Feminist Dialogues and others more relevant. Feminists reacted to the active presence of participants linked to conservative churches by entering into many dialogues on many issues; they challenged conservative agendas using their feminist focus on the body to argue their case. Various panels were organised by the Feminist Articulation Marcosur (AFM) to focus on "the body in the democratic agenda". Church representatives were invited, and they accepted, which is a positive expression of the type of dynamic the Forum facilitates.

But this new church presence, which at Nairobi brought a narrow perspective of human rights, a moralism positioned against humanistic and emancipatory thought, and a commitment to denying the rights, liberty and autonomy of women, gays, lesbians, bi and transsexuals to the Forum, affected not only women and homosexuals, but also diluted the spirit of democratic pluralism that had been the mark of the WSF. For the first time, there was a 'pro-life' exhibit and an antiabortion march. And for the first time, a speaker was verbally attacked in the closing ceremony, because she was a lesbian and opposed by a significant sector of Forum participants. The visible presence of African groups supporting sexual diversity in Nairobi was a welcome counterbalance, but it is clear that sexual and reproductive rights have become one of the disputed divides at the global/local level that the Forum represents.

Conclusions

The Feminist Dialogues have been an intense learning experience for the group that first promoted them, which has now grown.[49] Political and practical lessons have been learned: The discovery of other perspectives and knowledges, new ways to interrogate reality, and awareness that the same strategies can produce different effects in different contexts. A significant example, which emerged from discussions in Mumbai, is the contrasting ways in which the right to abortion is seen in different contexts. For Latin American feminists, the right to have an abortion is the strongest expression of the struggle to broaden the margins of choice women have in their lives; it is an important political goal because it remains illegal in most of the region. But in India, abortion has been decriminalised, and Indian feminists must confront the fact that this opening of greater space for choice has also been used against women, because families overwhelmingly choose to abort female embryos. And beyond this, reproductive rights are recognised by law in India, but this has given further power not to women but to the state, which uses them to impose wide-reaching policies of birth control.

Other cultures, other resources, and other 'lacks' mean different problems; and for problems that women have in common, there are often different solutions with different risks. It is enriching to know that the common goals of justice and liberty cannot necessarily be pursued using the same strategies, and that similar strategies often produce quite different results. This knowledge extends the limits of what we can imagine as possible, which complicates feminist proposals at the global level. It also raises the fundamental question of whether there can ever be universal solutions—or universal ways of thinking about them.

References

Sonia E. Alvarez, 1998—'Latin American Feminisms "Go Global": Trends of the 1990s and Challenges for the New Millennium', in Sonia E. Alvarez, Evelina Dagnino, and Arturo Escobar, eds, 1998—*Cultures of Politics, Politics of Cultures: Re-visioning Latin American Social Movements.* Boulder, CO: Westview Press

Articulación de Mujeres Brasilera, 2005—'*Carta Abierta a Fray Beto*' ['Open Letter to Frei Betto', in Spanish], World Social Forum 2005, Porto Alegre, Brazil, at www. articulacaomulheres.org.br (Inactive April 2017)

Articulación Feminista Marcosur, 2002—'*Documento de la Campaña contra los Funda-mentalismos*' ['Document on the Campaign Against Fundamentalisms', in Spanish]. World Social Forum 2002, Porto Alegre, Brazil, at www.mujeresdelsur.org.uy (Inactive April 2017)

Articulación Feminista Marcosur, 2005—'*Nota de Prensa desde el Barco de las Mujeres*' ['Press Note from the Women's Ship', in Spanish], World Social Forum 2005, Porto Alegre, Brazil, at www.mujeresdelsur.org.uy (Inactive April 2017)

Articulación Feminista Marcosur, 2007—'*Diálogos Feministas. Nairobi 2007: Celebrar la diversidad, Construyendo estrategias globales*' ['Feminist Dialogues, Nairobi 2007: Celebrating Diversity, Constructing Global Strategies', in Spanish], at www.mujeres-delsur.org.uy/fsm/2004/diálogos (Inactive April 2017)

Betania Ávila, 2001—'*Feminismo y ciudadanía: La producción de nuevos derechos*' ['Feminism and Citizenship: The Production of New Rights', in Spanish]. Lima: Flora Tristán, AGENDE, Equidad de Género. (*Mujeres al Timón: Cuadernos para la incidencia política feminista*, n.2)

Betania Ávila, 2003—'*Pensando o Forum Social Mundao: A través do feminismo*' ['Thoughts on the World Social Forum: Cutting Across Feminisms', in Portuguese], in *Revista Estudos Feministas*, vol 11 no 2 (July–December 2003). Florianópolis

Ulrico Beck, 2004—'*Poder y Contrapoder en la Era Global: La Nueva Economía Política Mundial*' ['Power and Counterpower in the Global Era: The New Global Political Economy', in Spanish]. Paidós Estado y Sociedad 124. Barcelona, Buenos Aires, México

Manuel Castells, 1999—'Los efectos de la globalización en América Latina por el autor de "la era de la información"' ['The Effects of Globalisation in Latin America for the author of "The Information Age"', in Spanish], in *Insomnia: Separata Cultural* (Uruguay), vol 247 (Spring), June 25 1999

Feminist Dialogues Coordinating Group, July 2006—Feminist Dialogues 2005 Report. Manila: ISIS International

Feminist Dialogues Coordinating Group, 2006—'Concept Note for the Feminist Dialogues', Annex 2 in the *Feminist Dialogues 2005 Report*, pp 72–76

Feminist Dialogues, January 2007—'Concept Note: Feminist Perspectives on Radical Democracy', prepared for the Feminist Dialogues 2007 held at the 7th World Social Forum in Nairobi, Kenya, January 16 2007, at http://feministdialogues.isiswomen. org/index.php?option=com_content&view=article&id=51&Itemid=135 (Accessed July 7 2009, inactive April 2017)

Feminist Dialogues Coordinating Group, 2007—'Global Feminists Strategies—Challenges and Common Approaches', Feminist Dialogues, Nairobi 2007. Concept Note for Subtheme 3. www.feministsdialogues.isiswomen.org

Nandita Gandhi and Nandita Shah, 2007—'Un Espacio Interactivo para Feministas' ['An Interactive Space for Feminists', in Spanish], at http://www.mujeresdelsur-afm.org. uy/dialogos-feministas/85-3er-dialogo-feminista-nairobi-2007-un-espacio-interactivo-para-feministas (Inactive April 2017)

James Goodman, 1998—'Transnational Integration and "cosmopolitan nationalism"'. Paper presented to the Colloquium on 'The Possibilities of Transnational Democracy', organised by the Centre for Transnational Studies, University of Newcastle, UK (unpublished)

Cândido Grzybowsky, 2002—'¿Es posible un mundo más femenino?' ['Is a more feminine world possible?', in Portuguese], on the WSF / FSM website, January 31–February 5 2002

Wendy Harcourt and Feminist Dialogues Coordinating Group, 2007—'A note on the Feminist Dialogues 2007 Methodology', in Wendy Harcourt and Feminist Dialogues Coordinating Group, 2007—*Transforming Democracy: Feminist Visions and Strategies*, Report of the Feminist Dialogues 2007 held at the 7th World Social Forum in Nairobi, Kenya, January 2007, pp 9–11

Emilie Hayes, 2017—'Open Space in Movement: Reading Three Waves of Feminism', in Jai Sen, ed, 2017a—*The Movements of Movements, Part 1: What Makes Us Move?*. Volume 4 in the *Challenging Empires* series. New Delhi: OpenWord, and Oakland, CA: PM Press

Elizabeth Jelin, 2003—'*La escala de la acción de los movimientos sociales*' ['The scale of the social movement actions', in Spanish], in Elizabeth Jelin, compiler, 2003—*Mas allá de la nación: Las escalas múltiples de los movimientos sociales* ['Beyond the Nation: The multiple scales of social movements', in Spanish]. Buenos Aires: Libros del Zorzal

Jeffrey S Juris, 2012a—'Social Forums and Their Margins: Networking Logics and the Cultural Politics of Autonomous Space', in Jai Sen and Peter Waterman, eds, 2012—*World Social Forum: Critical Explorations*. Volume 3 in the *Challenging Empires* series. New Delhi: OpenWord

Norberto Lechner, 1996—'*La transformación de la política*' ['The transformation of the political', in Spanish], in *Revista Mexicana de Sociología*, vol LVIII, no 1, pp 5–17

Diana Mafia, 2000—'*Ciudadanía Sexual: Aspectos legales y políticos de los derechos reproductivos como derechos humanos*' ['Sexual Citizenship: Legal and political aspects of reproductive rights as human rights', in Spanish], in *Feminaria*, year XIV, vol 26/27–28 (Buenos Aires)

Rodrigo Nunes, 2012—'The Intercontinental Youth Camp as the Unthought of World Social Forum, Revisited', in Jai Sen and Peter Waterman, eds, 2012—*World Social Forum: Critical Explorations.* Volume 3 in the *Challenging Empires* series. New Delhi: OpenWord

Program of Democracy and Global Transformation of the University of San Marcos, Lima, the Feminist Articulation Marcosur, the Flora Tristan Center (Lima), ABONG, the Paulo Freire Institute, et al, 2007—'*En Diversidad, Otro Mundo Es Posible*' ['In Diversity, Another World Is Possible', in Spanish]. Open Letter to the International Council of the WSF

Marta Rosemberg, 2002—'¿Which Other World Is Possible?', in *Women's Global Network of Reproductive Rights Newsletter*, Amsterdam, vol 75, pp 5–8

Mari M Santiago, 2004—'Building Global Solidarity through Feminist Dialogues'. Manila: Isis Women's Resource Centre

Boaventura de Sousa Santos, October 2002—'*Para uma Sociología das ausencias e uma sociología das emergencias*' ['For a Sociology of absences and a sociology of emergences', in Spanish], in *Revista Critica de Ciencias Sociales* ['Critical Review of the Social Sciences', in Spanish], no 63, pp 237–280

Boaventura de Sousa Santos, 2006a—'*Conocer desde el Sur: Para una cultura política emancipatoria*' ['Learn from the South: For an emancipatory political culture', in Spanish]. Colección Transformación Global of the Programa de Estudios sobre Democracia y Transformación Global ['Study Programme on Global Democracy and Transformation'], Universidad Nacional Mayor de San Marcos, Lima, Perú

Giulia Tamayo, 1998—'Re-vuelta sobre lo privado / re-creación de lo publico: La aventura inconclusa del feminismo en América Latina' ['Re-turn on the private / Re-creation of the public: The unfinished adventure of feminism in Latin America', in Spanish], in Cecilia Olea, ed, 1998—*Encuentros (des) Encuentros y Búsquedas: El Movimiento Feminista en América Latina* ['Encounters with (mis) Encounters and Searches: The Feminist Movement in Latin America', in Spanish]. Lima: Ediciones Flora Tristán

Millie Thayer, 2001—'Feminismo transnacional: Re-lendo Joan Scott no sertao' ['Transnational Feminism: Re-reading Joan Scott in the wilderness', in Portuguese], in *Estudios Feministas*, vol 9 no 1CFH/CCE/AFSC (Florianópolis-SC-Brasil), p 12

Virginia Vargas, 2009—'International Feminisms: New Directions', Chapter 7 in Jane Jaquette, ed, 2009—*Feminist Agendas and Democracy in Latin America* (Durham, NC: Duke University Press), pp 145–164

Virginia Vargas and Lilian Celiberti, 2005—'Los nuevos escenarios, los nuevos / viejos sujetos y los nuevos paradigmas de los feminismos globales' ['The new scenarios, new / old subjects, and new paradigms of global feminisms', in Spanish] at www.mujeresdelsur.org (Accessed April 2017)

Peter Waterman, 2000—'17 tesis acerca del viejo internacionalismo, la nueva solidaridad global, una futura sociedad civil global' ['17 theses on the old internationalism, the new global solidarity, a future global civil society', in Spanish], at the Universidad

de San Marcos, Lima, Peru, on January 11 2000, at http://www.antenna.
nl/~waterman/17tesis.html (Accessed April 2017)

Peter Waterman, 2002b—'What's Left Internationally? Reflections on the 2nd World
Social Forum in Porto Alegre', Institute of Social Studies, The Hague, Working Paper
Series no 362, 38 pp

Peter Waterman, 2005a—'Feminism, Globalisation, and Internationalism: The State
of Play and the Direction of the Movement', at https://www.researchgate.net/
publication/228812434_Feminism_Globalisation_Internationalism_The_State_of_
Play_and_the_Direction_of_the_Movement (Accessed April 2017)

Peter Waterman, 2006—*Los Nuevos Tejidos nerviosos del internacionalismo y la solidaridad* ['New neural tissues of internationalism and solidarity', in Spanish], in the
Colección Transformación Global series, published by the Programa de Estudios
sobre Democracia y Transformación Global, Universidad Nacional Mayor de San
Marcos, Lima, Perú

Notes

1. This is a slightly edited version of an essay of the same title that appeared as Chapter 7 in Jane Jaquette, ed, 2009—*Feminist Agendas and Democracy in Latin America* (Chapel Hill, NC: Duke University Press), pp 145–164. Copyright 2009, Duke University Press. All rights reserved. Used by permission of the publisher. For further reproduction permission, contact permissions@dukepress.edu.

2. Goodman 1998.

3. Ed: For a discussion of the concept of waves of feminism, see the chapter by Emilie Hayes in this volume (Hayes 2017).

4. The regional-global connections and interrelations have become more complex to the degree that the number of feminisms in the region also multiplied. Initially more homogeneous, seeing similarities and congruities among recently discovered themes, ways of contesting, and having similar perceptions of autonomy, as time passed there were more differences among feminists, less in their strategies and more in the ways in which they incorporated diversity as well as the different moments when groups became active, sometimes strongly affected by national and subregional characteristics (among those in South America, which were more developed and hegemonic, and those in Central America, who emerged from the region's civil wars). Others were increasingly differentiated by their opportunities and access; by their urban or rural bases; by the degree to which they recognised diversity (lesbian feminists began to hold their own *Encuentros*, often preceding the regional ones). The tensions that were seen at the end of the 80s between 'institutionalised' (NGO) and 'voluntary' feminists were a foreshadowing of what would be a more tenacious conflict in the 90s.

5. Tamayo 1998.

6. Waterman 2005a.

7. Lechner 1996.

8. Alvarez 1998.

9. Lechner 1996.

10. Waterman 2000.

11. Thayer 2001, p 106.

12. Jelin 2003.

13. Waterman 2006.

14. Ed: This essay was finalised in 2009. The "neoliberal logic of power" that Vargas refers to still exists and dominates at the global level, but as most readers know, resistance to this logic—and the emergence and assertion of new cultures of politics—has exploded in the subsequent years, and especially from 2011 on. Her words therefore—"Conditions are ripe for the emergence of new forms of political culture or, better yet, for countercultural proposals that challenge the neoliberal logic of power that now exists at the global level"—now seem prophetic, but were the result of decades of struggle.

15. Beck 2004.

16. Santos 2002.

17. Beck 2004.

18. Lechner 1996.

19. Castells 1999.

20. Jelin 2003.

21. Mafia 2000.

22. Ávila 2000.

23. The Campaign for the Inter-American Convention of Sexual and Reproductive Rights is part of this strategy, reflecting new forms of interaction and dispute with international organisations. The initiative does not come from the UN but from organised feminist groups and with argumentative force.

24. Grzybowski 2002.

25. Ávila 2003, p 3.

26. Waterman 2002b.

27. As mentioned above in endnote 14, this essay was finalised in 2009 (and written in the years before). Three more world editions of the WSF have been held since then (in Belém, Brazil, in 2009, in Dakar, Senegal, in 2011, and in Tunis, Tunisia, in 2013), along with several regional and national-level fora.

28. In the IC there is an active presence of feminist networks that support democratisation and the permanent broadening of the World Social Forum. Among them are the Articulacion Feminista Marcosur, the World March of Women, Red Mujeres Transformando la Economía ('Women's Network to Transform the Economy'), the Dawn network, Red de Educación Popular entre Mujeres (REPEM), the Akshara network, and the LGBT South-South Network, among others.

29. Articulación Feminista Marcosur 2002. Initiated in the 2002 World Social Forum by the Articulación Feminista Marcosur, the Campaign Against Fundamentalisms is now a global campaign.

30. The organisations and networks that initiated this experience are: Akshara (from India), WICEJ, Articulación Feminista Marcosur de America Latina, FEMNET (in Africa), DAWN, red global (global network), and INFORM (Sri Lanka).

31. This experience is in keeping with the new methodology of the Forum, which seeks precisely to put different networks in dialogue and cement relations among groups interested in the exchange of strategies and proposals.

32. Articulación de Mujeres Brasilera 2005.

33. This dispute has been evident since the first World Social Forum, where the presence of women was quantitatively greater than that of men, and yet only a few individual

women participated in all the panels. In the second Forum, some feminists succeeded in organising some panels, but the responsibility for organising the themes or 'axes' (each one of which groups 6 or 7 large panels) remained in male hands. At the third Forum, of the 5 axes, two were organised by feminist networks: The Articulación Feminista Marcosur and the World March of Women.

34. See Nunes 2012, Juris 2012a.
35. In the case of militarism, besides confronting a warlike culture that privileges war, women point out what the logic of war implies for women's bodies. Neoliberalism not only flexibilises work but makes the private sphere responsible for social welfare obligations that states ought to provide, which increases the burden of women's work and their responsibilities as caretakers of the family, health, etc.
36. Ávila 2003.
37. The Ship was organised by the Campaign against Fundamentalisms, providing a space for diverse activities, workshops, discussion groups, and presentations over topics as varied as water as a scarce resource to discussions with and about transvestites and transsexuals.
38. Program of Democracy and Global Transformation of the University of San Marcos, Lima, the Feminist Articulation Marcosur, the Flora Tristan Center (Lima), ABONG, the Paulo Freire Institute et al, 2007. This open letter, initially signed by the above organisations, subsequently received a significant number of additional signatories.
39. Santos 2006.
40. Rosenberg 2002.
41. Feminist Dialogues Coordinating Group, 2006.
42. Feminist Dialogues Coordinating Group, January 2007.
43. Feminist Dialogues Coordinating Group, July 2006.
44. Gandhi and Shah 2007.
45. Beck 2004.
46. The fact that the organising team did not want to seek consensus on actions or agendas helped produce this outcome.
47. Harcourt and Feminist Dialogues Coordinating Group 2007b.
48. Feminist Dialogues 2007.
49. The initial group included the AFM, Inform, NNAWG, DAWN, WISEJ, Isis Manila, and FEMNET. To this first group have been added: Akina Mama wa A'frica—AmWA, The Latin American Committee for the Defense of Women's Rights—CLADEM, Latin American and Caribbean Network of Young People for Sexual and Reproductive Rights—REDLAC, and the Popular Education Network of Women of Latin America and the Caribbean—REPEM, Women Living Under Muslim Laws—WLUML, and Women in Development—WIDE.

Re-Creating the World:
Communities of Faith in the Struggles for Other Possible Worlds
Lee Cormie

... religious and imperial traditions remain constitutive dimensions of modern societies.
—Willfried Spohn[1]

When conservative evangelical Christians call for action on global warming, Hindu holy men dedicate themselves to saving sacred rivers, and Buddhist monks work with Islamic mullahs to try to halt the extinction crisis, boundaries are clearly being redrawn in the ongoing struggle for the political hearts and minds of the world's believers.
—Jim Motavalli[2]

Today, we can only oppose fundamentalism effectively if we engage with spiritualities and forms of art and liberation cultures, with their capacity to relate to the majority of our populations. These dimensions of spirituality and of the arts were badly interpreted in the formulations of [the] classical left. So there is a great challenge to open up the scope of who we talk to.
—Moema Miranda[3]

Introduction: Faith Communities in Global Justice Movements and the World Social Forum

The vast majority of the world's peoples are 'religious' in a rich variety of expressions. But so far 'religion' has only ambiguously been present in the discourses of the global social justice movement (GSJM[4]) and the World Social Forum (WSF). One kind of religion—'fundamentalism': Christian, Hindu, Muslim (and market)—is frequently referred to, and condemned. More generally, the prevailing attitude echoes classic modern discourses framing 'religion'—along with 'pre-modern' civilisations and indigenous traditions—as backward and 'conservative', part of the 'primitive' or 'traditional', 'pre-scientific' past.

But backward and fundamentalist expressions of religion are only part of the story. For there have also been modernising movements within religious communities, some of them progressive, radical, even revolutionary. And, since the eruptions of progressive social movements in the 1960s, religious activists and organisations have been involved in many progressive social movements, in some

contexts at the forefront.[5] And this presence has been increasingly recognised in activist discourses, for example in lists of activist communities, organisations, and coalitions sponsoring events and campaigns.

Concerning the WSF in particular, faith-based individuals and organisations have also been central from the beginning.[6] But they too have generally framed their participation in the secular discourses of progressive political cultures, for example concerning hunger or Third World debt. And they have generally omitted reference to the specifically religious dimensions of their communities and commitments, and of the debates and struggles within them.

In recent years, though, the religious dimensions of the struggles for another world have been slowly emerging from the shadows. A poll of WSF participants in 2003 revealed that over 60 per cent identified themselves as 'religious', startling organisers and helping to make 'religious' issues more visible.[7] The WSF's move to Mumbai in 2004, home of Hindu fundamentalism but also of great religious traditions centring on liberation, intensified this development. Thereafter, organisers included a thematic focus on 'Ethics, Cosmovisions, and Spiritualities' in the fifth WSF in Porto Alegre, in 2005. In the seventh WSF in Nairobi, in 2007, religions / spiritualities were clearly at the forefront, reflecting African realities and provoking new rounds of intense debate.[8] And in Belém, in 2009, the centrality of indigenous peoples intensified concern with spiritualities and cosmovisions.

However, these developments in the practices of the GSJM have not yet been worked out in the theoretical discourses of global capitalism or world-system or in the debates about the WSF as 'space' or 'movement'. Moreover, in many ways the borders and dynamics of 'religion' and 'culture', 'economy', and 'politics', along with the scholarly discourses addressing these realities, are shifting. So in these pages I propose broadening GSJM and WSF dialogues with reference to rapidly expanding discussions on five fronts:

- The proliferation across the world of faith-based resistances to the projects of neoliberal globalisation (NLG) and empire;
- The cultural / religious dimensions of the project of neoliberal globalisation, and of capitalist discourses and practices more generally;
- The world historical transitions underway around the world, transforming society, civilisation and nature, history and evolution, disrupting the reigning discourses of the natural and social sciences, and re-opening classic religious / philosophical / scientific questions concerning creation, human nature, freedom, and destiny;
- The transmodern (rather than modern, premodern, or postmodern) character of the religious and cultural traditions of the majorities of the world's peoples, and their continuing relevance as sources of resources, wisdom, and inspiration; and—

- The chaotic, uneven, non-linear, long-term, and open-ended character of world historical transitions, their implications for re-inventing twenty-first century politics, and the contributions of the WSF in nurturing intercultural dialogue, solidarities, and coalitions incarnating hope that "another world is possible".[9]

Globalisation, Empire, and Idolatry

Here I can note only a few instances in the proliferation of faith-based communities, centres, organisations, networks, and coalitions over the last forty years. I will begin with Christian initiatives, because I know them best, but will also point to initiatives which have emerged in other faith communities.

The development of critical Christian stands on social issues over the last forty years is marked by the profusion of programmes, centres, offices, networks, and coalitions linking different groups within specific Christian churches (denominations), across them in ecumenical coalitions, and increasingly with secular movements and other faith communities in coalitions, at every scale within countries and internationally.[10]

There are also networks and coalitions of church-based NGOs, and offices and programmes in national and international ecumenical councils of churches. Two deserve special note:

World Alliance of Reformed Churches (WARC)
WARC is a fellowship of 75 million Reformed Christians in 216 churches (Congregational, Presbyterian, Reformed, and United Churches with roots in the sixteenth-century Protestant Reformation) in 107 countries, with a small office in Geneva. After its 22nd General Council in Seoul, Korea (1989), WARC members wrestled with the issues of global economic justice in the light of Christian faith, through a programme of regional conferences. And, in 1997, the delegates at the 23rd General Council of the WARC meeting (at Debrecen, in Hungary) unanimously passed a resolution launching a *processus confessionis* (confession process), expressing their conviction that the time had come to write a confession of faith which rejects injustice and struggles against it, in the name of faith in the triune God who promises a new creation in Christ. They called upon WARC and its member churches "to give special attention to the analysis and understanding of economic processes, their consequences for people's lives, and the threats to creation, [and] to educate church members at all levels about economic life, including faith and economics".[11] After additional international consultations, participants in the 24th General Council concluded that "the current world (dis)order is rooted in an extremely complex and immoral economic system defended by empire".[12] And they committed member churches to "work together with other communions, the ecumenical community, the community of other

faiths, civil movements and people's movements for a just economy and the integrity of creation".[13]

World Council of Churches (WCC)

The WCC brings together more than 340 churches, denominations, and church fellowships in over 100 countries and territories, representing some 550 million Christians, with the majority in the South. Since its origins in 1948, it has been a global centre for dialogue among Christian churches worldwide, with special concern for issues of social justice. As 'globalisation' moved to the centre of debates in the 1980s, the WCC has been actively promoting research, dialogue, and participation of church members, with other movements and NGOs, in important international dialogues, like United Nations assemblies and summits, and lobbying the World Bank and the World Trade Organization.

At the WCC's 8th Assembly (at Harare, in Zimbabwe, 1998) delegates affirmed that they had heard the cries of the poor that "globalisation is not simply an economic issue. It is a cultural, political, ethical and ecological issue", and they recommended that "the challenge of globalisation should become a central emphasis of the work of the WCC".[14] They expressed appreciation for WARC's "committed process of recognition, education and confession (*processus confessionis*) regarding economic injustice and ecological destruction", and encouraged WCC member churches to join this process. In Potsdam (in Germany, 2001) the WCC's Central Committee recommended that member churches and the WCC "develop a comprehensive ecumenical theological analysis of economic globalisation and its impact on the churches, and provide a theological basis for the search for alternatives".[15] And, at the WCC's 9th General Assembly (Porto Alegre, 2006) participants focused on 'alternative globalisation'.[16]

The WCC has also collaborated with other groups in organising international consultations on globalisation. A major collaborator in these ecumenical initiatives has been the Lutheran World Federation (LWF), a global communion of 140 member churches in 78 countries, representing nearly 66.7 million Christians. In 2001, the LWF launched a programme for churches around the world to engage with 'economic globalisation' as faith communities.[17]

And for many Christians the WSF itself has become a major point of reference, in terms of their evolving understanding of NLG and growing opposition to it, their own educating and organising efforts among church members, and their networking efforts with other religious and secular movements.[18]

Muslim, Hindu, Buddhist, and Jewish Communities

For the last 500 years, since the beginnings of European modernisation and colonisation, there have been many movements of resistance and transformation within the world's faith communities. But they have articulated their positions in the terms of their own traditions, including specifically religious or spiritual concerns. These have been targeted by secularist Western scholars and many political activists on the left as primitive, irrational, and conservative, relegated to the past, marginalised in the present, and banished from the future. So recovery of these absent traditions is central in the emergence of post-Eurocentric scholarship.[19] Meanwhile, in terms of contemporary activism, there are proliferating signs of creativity and renewal within many communities, of multiplying faith-based NGOs, networks, and movements, and of their convergence and collaboration with other movements and coalitions in GSJM—global social justice movement—struggles. Here it is possible to cite only a few significant voices and coalitions.

Writing from a European perspective, for example, Muslim activist and scholar Tariq Ramadan insists that:

> Islamic teachings are intrinsically opposed to the basic premises and the logic of the neoliberal capitalist system, and Muslims who live in 'the system's head' have a greater responsibility, with others who are working toward the same goal, to propose solutions that could create a way out and lead to a more just economy and more equitable trade.[20]

In a similar spirit, from an Indian perspective, Muslim activist and scholar Ali Asghar Engineer wrote:

> the Quran lays great emphasis on distributive justice. It is totally against accumulation and hoarding of wealth. It condemns accumulated wealth as strongly as possible. It also exhorts the people to spend to take care of orphans, widows, needy and the poor.[21]

He added that it "strengthens the social roots of peace by emphasising the role of need based economy and resolutely opposing greed based one",[22] and insisted that "social, political and economic justice is very essential for fighting religious fundamentalism" like that evident in Hindu nationalism.[23]

The Buddhist Peace Fellowship (BPF), with programmes in the US and Asia, articulates a vision of Buddhism as "a path of spiritual transformation and liberation", to "free beings by ending contemporary suffering: racism, sexism, militarism, species-ism, economic oppression, caste and class, and the many other ways that society creates a collective me and mine, the sickness of grasping for which Dharma is the cure".[24] The BPF's mission includes raising "humanitarian, environmental, and social justice concerns among Buddhist communities", bringing "a Buddhist perspective to contemporary peace, environmental, and social justice movements", and offering concrete "public witness through our practice, for peace and protection of all beings".[25] Occasionally, the BPF also issues public statements on pressing issues, like the war in Iraq and the dictatorship in Burma.[26] The BPF also collaborates with DharmaNet International in promoting "engaged Buddhism" among groups around the world on a broad range of issues (including addiction recovery, ecological issues, gay and lesbian issues, women's issues, and solidarity with Burma and Tibet).[27]

In Thailand, the Sathirakoses-Nagapradipa Foundation (SNF) is the legal body for five organisations committed to "struggle at the grassroots, national, regional and international levels for freedom, human rights, traditional cultural integrity, social justice and environmental protection". Central to this mission is the conviction that "inner change (personal development) and outer change (political, economic, and structural changes) must go hand in hand to bring about a transformation of society". And, with the people of Siam (hybridised and anglicised as Thailand) and other concerned citizens from around the world, this network is "working to cultivate the seeds of peace and to lay the foundation for meaningful social transformation".[28] As SNF's founder Sulak Sivaraksa insists, "religion is at the heart of social change, and social change is the essence of religion".[29] Member groups address issues like "peace reconciliation, ecology, women issue and empowerment, health, education, human rights, community building, alternative development, role of spiritual leaders in modern world context".[30]

In India, Swami Agnivesh has been committed "to bring[ing] spiritual values in politics and social responsibility in religions". He has been central in movements like the Bandhua Mukti Morcha (Bonded Labour Liberation Front), Naari Sudhar (Women's Emancipation), and the Baal Mukti Aandolan (Movement Against Child Labour). He has also helped found the Adhyatma Jagaran Manch (Movement for Spiritual Awakening), to fight against the communal agenda of the Sangh Parivar, the 'family of associations' in India that includes the political party the Bharatiya Janata Party and that promote Hindu nationalism, communalism, and racism. Over the years, he has led mass campaigns on "bonded labour, child labour, modern consumerist trends, ecological destruction of Third World in general and India in particular, religious fundamentalism, casteism, racial feelings and slavery of all kinds".[31] And, along with Ali Asghar Engineer, he was awarded The Right Livelihood Award (the alternative Nobel prize) in 2004 for "[his] outstanding vision and work on behalf of our planet and its people".[32]

In Jewish communities around the world there are initiatives, drawing on Jewish traditions, to engage in GSJM struggles, and to inspire and renew their communities. In the US, the Shalom Center "is dedicated to inspiring the Jewish community to greater attention and action on questions of peace and justice for the planet and all who dwell on it", with programs on immigration, globalisation and economic justice, gender justice, environmental justice, justice and peace in the Middle East, and the spirituality of justice.[33] In the UK, the Jewish Socialists' Group share "a commitment to building the kind of socialism that will encourage minorities to express and develop their historical and cultural identities and that will liberate ordinary people of all communities from poverty, racism, sexism, oppression, and war".[34] In Israel and Palestine, Bat Shalom is "a feminist grass-roots organisation of Jewish and Palestinian Israeli women working together for a genuine peace grounded in a just resolution of the Israel-Palestine conflict, respect for human rights, and an equal voice for Jewish and Arab women within Israeli society".[35]

Aboriginal Spiritualities and Politics

For hundreds of years, and in many countries around the world, indigenous resistance to colonialism and 'development' has been grounded in spiritual traditions that do not distinguish between 'spiritual' / 'religious' and 'material' / 'economic' concerns.[36]

For example, at the second international summit of aboriginal peoples from Abya Yala (Mexico, the Caribbean, Central and South America), participants affirmed that "our ancestors, our grandparents taught us how to love and revere our bountiful Mother Earth (Pacha Mama) and how to live in harmony and freedom with the natural and spiritual beings that inhabit Her". They criticised national governments that are following guidelines emanating from the IMF and World Bank, which are devastating them in order to repay "external debt and are disregarding our collective rights to our land, changing legislation to allow privatisation, corporative alliances, and individual appropriation". They insisted that indigenous peoples "have our own models which guarantee the reproduction of our Peoples and Nationalities in harmony with nature, and are rooted in our ancestral cultural heritage", and pledged "to establish alliances with other civil society sectors", in particular other social movements, and "to participate in international fora such as the World Social Forum and the Americas Forum with common proposals reflecting the position of the Indigenous movement".[37]

Interfaith Dialogue and Collaboration

Increasingly, for faith-based activists around the world, there are interfaith initiatives to dialogue, network, collaborate in campaigns, and build movements. For example, in the US Tikkun has launched a 'Network of Spiritual Progressives' supporting a broad range of GSJM struggles, including Jubilee 2000 demands for debt cancellation for poor nations, reparations to Native Americans and African Americans, LGBTQ rights, halting and reversing climate change, and ethical consumption, along with recognition of the spiritual dimensions of every struggle.[38] Traditional interfaith dialogue initiatives like the Parliament of World Religions are expanding their agendas "to enhance the interreligious movement for peace, justice and sustainability".[39] And more and more spokespeople, like Brazilian Christian theologian Marcelo Barros, affirm that growing appreciation of cultural / religious diversity makes the experience of dialogue and collaboration in gatherings like the World Social Forum "fundamental for a new theology of cultural and religious pluralism", which is crucial in the ongoing renewal of these communities and their traditions.[40]

These few examples of religious communities and activisms confirm that, unseen in the secular discourses of the modern social sciences and politics, struggles of resistance and transformation have been underway within faith communities too. Far from being simply 'traditional', 'premodern', 'conservative', and / or 'fundamentalist', these communities are internally diverse, including progressive currents too. These activists are probing their own sacred stories and traditions for insight and inspiration. They are developing increasing literacy and sophistication in technical, economic, and political debates. They are challenging their own communities towards conversion and renewal, and collaboration with other groups—religious and secular—in struggles for another world. They are denouncing the "false gods of empire and war" and daring "to live our hopes that a new world is not only possible but is being built through people's movements".[41] In doing so, they are helping to transform the discourses of religion and of economy, ethics, and politics. And they are helping to change the course of history.[42]

They are also helping to expose the 'religious' dimensions of the discourses and practices of capitalism, and of modernity more generally.

Religious Dimensions of Neoliberal Globalisation

There is a tendency in scholarly and activist circles, especially those influenced by Western liberal and Marxist traditions, to regard neoliberal discourse as a single unchanging doctrine, which 'naturally' and 'inevitably' flowed from existing structural logics and historical trends. This presumption has contributed to widespread neglect in the study of the multiple facets, different audiences, and shifting discourses of neoliberalism.[43]

But the project of NLG did not fall from the sky as a single, coherent, comprehensive, even revolutionary (or counter-revolutionary) project. Nor did it fall into the hands of a single united 'ruling class' or group of elites united with a single mind about the challenges facing them, their shifting interests, most promising prospects, key choices, and coherent strategies for moving forward conveniently situated across a broad range of institutions and capable of acting effectively on many fronts. Nor was there a broad and compliant public in every country ready to believe every claim and endorse every policy.

Because it centred so clearly on renewing classic liberal faith in the wonders of the 'free market', some of the key architects of this movement, which brought together liberals and conservatives, opted for the label 'neoliberal'.[44] However, from the beginning this movement has been a coalition, with different spokespeople articulating variations of central doctrines tailored to them. And recognising its cultural / religious dimensions is central to understanding the politics and economics of the rapidly evolving struggles over it.

In the early stages of their efforts to respond to proliferating challenges from labour unions and new social movements erupting in the 1960s, falling corporate profits, and increasing global competition, liberal and conservative elites mobilised vast resources to clarify their positions and reframe the terms of public debate.[45] They sought to enshrine economics as the single most authoritative, 'scientific' discourse, allegedly providing neutral, objective, universally relevant interpretations of what is happening in the world. They decreed that 'private property', 'free markets', 'competition', and 'globalisation' are natural, inevitable, and good. By the early 1990s, after the tearing down of the Berlin Wall and the dissolution of the Soviet Union, they announced that a consensus prevailed—the 'Washington Consensus'[46]—indeed, a universal 'common sense',[47] marking the "end of history".[48]

However, as baptised in the agendas of the Thatcher and Reagan administrations after 1979, this neoliberal project has been much more than 'economic'. Rather, it has been 'global', aiming to transform society—family life, culture, politics, economy, religion—as well as the whole world; to create nothing less than a 'new world order' in the words of Bush I.[49] Here, I can only note some central religious features of this project as it emerged and developed in the US.[50]

In opposition to critics' charges of the amorality (absence of values) or immorality (wrong values, such as individualism and narrow self-interest, lack of concern for the common good, the environment, or peace), key spokespeople of the project have insisted that their agenda was explicitly religious and moral, that 'democratic capitalism' was founded on Judeo-Christian principles, and that this agenda that was naturally good in both economic and religious / ethical terms, was, indeed, God-given.

For example, Michael Novak of the American Enterprise Institute, who served as the Reagan administration's representative to the UN Commission on Human Rights, insisted that "no society in the long history of the Jewish and Christian people owes more than our own to the inspiration of Jewish, Christian, and humanistic traditions".[51] Indeed, he claimed, "the Bible was decisive for the invention of the system we enjoy in the US".[52] And, he insisted, "liberal society, benefiting from centuries of reflection upon biblical themes such as sin, creativity, and a new conception of community ... has set a benchmark for other societies".[53] Similarly, sociologist Irving Kristol, widely recognised as "the standard-bearer of neo-conservatism"[54] and sometimes referred to as its 'godfather',[55] insisted that, in modern society, Judeo-Christian values are the foundation on which capitalism has been built. Specifically, these values have been incarnated in the good bourgeois citizen, being "a good parent, a good husband or wife, a good citizen, earning a living and keeping a family together, obeying the laws".[56] In other words, Kristol argued, "the bourgeois is the link between Judeo-Christianity and capitalism".[57]

Intellectually and politically, the evolving neoliberal / neoconservative agenda centrally involved targeting left Christians and liberation theologies.[58]

It involved forging and mobilising cadres of zealous fundamentalist Christians to capture the Republican Party, to mobilise key fractions of voters to swing elections, and to sweep their candidates to power.[59]

Indeed, its architects declared that, in the words of President Reagan, the "real crisis we face today is a spiritual one; at root, it is a test of moral will and faith", insisting that the "renewal of America" involves "a great spiritual awakening in America, a renewal of traditional values that have been the bedrock of America's goodness and greatness".[60] As George Gilder insisted in *Wealth and Poverty*, widely regarded as the bible of the Reagan administration (and heavily subsidised in its worldwide distribution by the CIA),[61] "faith in man, faith in the future, faith in the rising returns of giving [ie, investments], faith in the mutual benefits of trade, faith in the providence of God are all essential to successful capitalism".[62] In a more fundamentalist tone, Falwell, the leader of a movement called the Moral Majority, insisted that support for the free enterprise system of profit and for a strong US American military presence in the world was linked to Christian faith in God.[63]

Moreover, in their efforts to mobilise support in the face of continued opposition, the high priests of this movement regularly raised the spectres of "the evil empire"[64] and "axis of evil"[65] to reframe debates in religiously apocalyptic terms, seeking to simplify issues, polarise positions, overwhelm doubt, stampede people in support of their options, and brand resistance as treasonous, even demonic.

And as they fanned the flames of demonic threats to 'Western Christian civilisation', they also proclaimed hope—if only people would reject the false promises of 'world communism'—for 'a new golden era' accompanying breakthroughs in science, new technologies, the emergence of the 'information economy', and globalising markets.[66]

So, neoliberals and neoconservatives radically expanded the horizons of debate to include economics and politics, but also religious, cultural, and ethical matters. In their most ambitious expressions, they vastly expanded the boundaries of human agency and of hope for the future to include the elimination of scarcity and want, the transcendence of ignorance and human limitations, and great leaps forward in the evolution of life on earth, even in the cosmos.[67] They focussed especially on mobilising 'born-again' liberals and 'born-again' conservatives, with a reformulated faith transforming the God of traditional Christianity into the God of the market, free trade, and empire.

In these terms, economic doctrines of the 'free market' and 'free trade' functioned not as empirical science, whose propositions are tested against experience in dialogue open to all, but as 'market fundamentalism' involving blind faith in idols, deafening its adherents to the cries of its victims, and blinding them to the suicidal consequences of their own actions.[68]

More generally, we are learning to recognise that the actual functioning of corporations and markets, and international financial institutions—socially constructed in ongoing processes of construction, contestation, and re-construction in each context[69]—have had cultural and religious dimensions.[70] The World Bank is as much a producer of specific discourses of development as an instrument for enforcing a certain regime.[71] The advocates of 'free markets' preach with the fervour of missionaries about the sole road to salvation.[72] Disputes over 'economic' matters take on the appearance of morality wars.[73] Consumerism, reflecting the trappings of cults and spiritualities associated with past empires—and most visible in the US especially in the ritualised shopping frenzy around Christmas—became the central driving force of late capitalism.[74] In many respects, Bush II's administrations took on the character of a theocracy, indeed, of Christian fascism.[75] And in the wake of global financial meltdown, "faith in neoliberal orthodoxies has imploded"[76] and their disciples confess to feelings of blasphemy in recommending nationalisation of banks.[77] So, seeing beyond the 'economic' dimensions of NLG and other capitalist projects is essential to understanding them, the evolving coalitions mobilised in support of and in opposition to them, and the broad challenges facing every hope for 'another world'.

Re-Creating the World

Critics of NLG have tended not only to blame it for all that is wrong in the world, but to treat it as the most significant force changing the world. In the process, they have tended to overlook the expanding scales of human agency, reflected in developments in knowledge/'science', new technologies, and scales of social organisation, and the great proliferation of popular social movements, which are transforming the dynamics of societies everywhere, and the relationships of their civilisations to (the rest of) nature. This neglect contributes to a vast underestimation of the complexity, scope and scales of progressive politics. It also contributes to profound misreadings of the character of 'hopes' for 'another world' and of the 'faiths' which sustain them.

More precisely, in a world of great disparities in power and capacities to act, the agency of some humans is vastly expanding. But, regardless of initial responsibility, these developments are drawing all people everywhere into the effects of these decisions, and responsibility for them. Indeed, they are opening horizons of possibility—for good and ill—on historic, even evolutionary, scales.

Humans are major geological, biological, environmental, atmospheric, climatological, and ecological, as well as political and economic, forces. Groups of people are manipulating matter at the nanoscale, creating new forms of matter, as well as new evolutionary niches, life forms, and processes for creating life, and engineering projects altering the face of the earth, transforming land, air, water, and local and planetary ecosystems. In the process, we are becoming "the planet's most potent evolutionary force, far greater in impact than anything in history, except perhaps the asteroid that wiped out the dinosaurs" 65 million years ago.[78] Dynamics of epochal change on multiple scales—civilisational, geological, climatological, ecological, and evolutionary—are accelerating, and on the horizons appear radically different possibilities for the future of all of life on the planet.

Two major poles have emerged in the rapidly proliferating scenarios for the future.

At one pole, experts point to seemingly endless signs of progress. Announcements appear in the news every day: Scientific breakthroughs promising radically new technologies, medical miracles, communications marvels, expansions of the new realm of virtual realities. Especially among middle and upper classes, some of these promises are becoming realities, and inspiring bigger dreams of a new golden era in human history, indeed in the history of the solar system, perhaps even the history of the cosmos. These dreams include visions of improved humanity, literally of posthuman or transhuman successor species enhanced by bio-, info-, pharmo- and cogno-technologies, interfacing with artificial intelligences, globally linked in an emergent world brain.[79] In these visions, humanity is reaching out to other planets in the solar system, and into the star-filled heavens beyond. And some commentators wonder if human nature has already become obsolete,[80] if new and improved post-humanities are already emerging.

On the other hand, as the histories of marginalised peoples repeatedly confirm, new knowledge, technologies, and scales of social organisation are often appropriated by reigning elites and turned to their own ends. The elixir of scientific breakthroughs and expanding power deafens them to the victims, blinds them to the consequences of their choices, and contributes to civilisational crisis, even collapse.[81] And in the early years of the twenty-first century, images of apocalypse are becoming mainstream, as reports stream in concerning unfolding catastrophes and darkening horizons for the future.

A partial list includes: Global pandemics suddenly killing millions, perhaps tens of millions, of people, producing waves of fleeing refugees, and expanding turmoil regionally and globally;[82] spreading militarism,[83] led by the US despite enormous costs in terms of the quality of life for ordinary Americans, fiscal health, and ongoing development,[84] and the widespread pollution and ecological disruption associated with it, along with multiplying wars, especially over natural resources like oil and water,[85] intensified by chemical, biological weapons, and smaller nuclear weapons; enviro- or energo-fascism, as governing elites demand more powers to act in the face of emergencies [86] on broader and more fundamental scales; runaway biotechnologies, nanotechnologies, nanobiotechnologies,[87] and / or artificial intelligence in robots[88] (most likely triggered by corporations and governments reacting in panic to some climate change or other catastrophe, and launching an ill-conceived major geo-engineering project (indeed, the first battles against geo-engineering have already been fought[89]); and climatic cataclysms, mutually reinforcing and generating widespread destruction and social turmoil, waves of refugees and immigrants, conflicts, and wars.[90]

So, along with new knowledge, technologies, and scales of social organisation, increasing numbers of commentators are pointing to a world already in transition. A few, mostly privileged groups, regularly enjoy enhancements in their lives, and dreams of transcending the historic limits of being human.

In contrast, vast numbers of others face growing suffering, turmoil, and conflict. And many face extinction: For example, many indigenous communities are declining; communities in Sub-Saharan Africa are devastated by HIV / AIDS—"our nation is dying of AIDS", in the words of a South African children's chorus;[91] and thousands of insect, plant, amphibian, and animal species disappear in what is already the sixth mass extinction event in the history of life on earth.[92]

And increasingly experts like James Lovelock, formulator of the Gaia hypothesis, are warning about the future of humanity as a whole: "[B]efore this century is over, billions of us will die and the few breeding pairs of people that survive will be in the Arctic where the climate remains tolerable".[93] Indeed, some are crying out about the prospect of the extinction of the human species ('humanicide'), with God knows what implications for the evolution of the cosmos.[94]

So, in more ways than we can see, we are caught in world historic processes of re-creating ourselves, our civilisation, and (the rest of) nature, in nothing less than a "fierce struggle to re-create the world".[95]

In this world in transition, the ancient symbols of heaven and hell have come to life again, tempting us and terrifying us, as we confront many fundamental choices, and our choices are helping to tip the balance along various paths into the future.

Transmodern Spiritualities and Politics

These developments are also disrupting the boundaries of certain knowledge, hope(s) (eg, which transcend conventional expectations reflecting historical constellations of power and trends), and faith(s). In particular, doubts about the alleged certainties of Western modes of natural and social science, especially economics, are spreading like wildfire;[96] 'faiths' and 'religions' are being seen in new light.[97]

Indeed, the word 'religion' is at the heart of widespread confusion about 'religion'. Historically and cross-culturally, there have been many diverse 'religions', woven in different ways with other cultural, economic, and political strands into the psychic and cultural fabrics of particular peoples. Some, though, have been more visible than others, especially those of elites, who have tended to frame their outlooks in more 'spiritual' / 'otherworldly' terms, centring on personal meaning and beliefs, allegedly separate from economics and politics. With their role in creating and preserving public documents, these religious expressions have predominated in historical records. With the great expansion of the middle classes in the modern world, and of universities with their Westernised middle-class professors and students, these expressions have been enshrined in the dominant discourses as 'religion'.[98] And the 'history of 'religion' has been framed as 'progress': From 'primitive', 'irrational', 'superstitious', and 'magical' religions to highly individualised, spiritualised, rational, and ethical modern religion, or, in secularist accounts, to the disappearance of religion altogether.[99]

But, as the voices of oppressed groups and communities repeatedly confirm, the experiences, sufferings, and hopes of the majority differ from those of elites. As we have seen, religious communities include great internal diversity, with different, even conflicting, interpretations of their traditions and their significance in addressing contemporary debates. There is growing recognition of the myriad forms of religiosity, indeed of the fact that many languages do not even have a word for 'religion'.[100] In the shifting scholarly and activist landscapes around the world, efforts are underway to radically reframe 'religion', along with those other pivotal concepts of Eurocentric frameworks: 'Culture', 'economy', and 'politics'.

There is also growing recognition that religious traditions have never been static and unchanging. Other peoples and their traditions are not closed and static. They have continued to evolve. And they are not in any simple sense pre-modern, or modern, or postmodern.

Rather, they are transmodern.[101] Without converting to modernity, they have engaged in "transforming tradition in a traditional way".[102] Traditional communities, as Sardar says of Islam, "reinvent and innovate tradition constantly. Indeed, a tradition that does not change ceases to be a tradition".[103] And in the process these religious traditions have contributed to multiple modernities.[104]

Today these traditions, with their strong religious and cultural links to the past, do not in any simple sense contain 'answers' to questions in a world being so profoundly reshaped. As at other turning points in history, all traditions of knowledge, hope, and faith are challenged to radical conversions and renewal.[105] But, within these traditions, there are many diverse strands, including many creative expressions of "critical and open traditionalism that uses the historic past to create a bright future".[106] The boundaries between mystery, ignorance, knowledge, uncertainty, probability, hope, and faith are shifting.[107] People are experimenting with alternative epistemologies beyond methodological modernism,[108] which, far from refusing the advances of modern sciences, place them "in the context of the diversity of knowledges existing in contemporary societies".[109] They are drinking deeply from the wellsprings of other ways of seeing, values and ethical frameworks, modes of collective identity, discipline, solidarity, and activism. They are weaving other discourses of hope, and expressions of 'faith' in a being / force / spirit transcending historical trends and constellations of power, and pointing to other possible futures.

World Historical Transitions

These developments are also calling into question modern notions of progress, including revolutionary progress, leading to more complex readings of the past, of the present, and of transitions to the future.

With the proliferation of other voices long marginalised in political and scholarly circles, other pasts, other histories, other sufferings and hopes, other end times and new beginnings have begun to (re)appear in mainstream debates,[110] disrupting Western linear views of history, turning "'the' past into a plurality of worlds",[111] revealing multiple histories and senses of history.[112] They are contributing to radically different perceptions of change in natural and human history, as involving, along with linear developments in certain periods, sudden, catastrophic disruptions, chaos, collapse, and non-linear transitions.[113] They are transforming our visions of social change, pointing to more complex, contradictory, uneven, chaotic, and long-term processes of change to another world. And they are transforming the horizons of progressive politics for the twenty-first century.

In particular, they are also helping to make clear the irreducibly local character of politics. Still largely unaddressed in the discourses of the GSJM and WSF, politics in particular places, while increasingly linked to 'global' dynamics, remains uniquely shaped by local languages and traditions, histories of struggle, distinctive conjunctures of pressures and possibilities, each with its own pace of change. In this light, local cultural / religious / political traditions remain central in local struggles, and 'translation' across the ignorance, gaps, and divisions which have marked the world is becoming increasingly central in progressive politics at every scale.[114] Thus, we are slowly coming to grasp the scope and magnitude of changes involved in re-creating the world, and the long time lines involved.

We are slowly coming to grasp the frequency, range, and depth of challenges to conversion to new insights and perspectives, values, and identities within individuals, communities, and movements, as irruptions of still newer voices challenge old identities, politics, and faiths.[115]

And we are slowly coming to the depth of challenges to faith in the 'progress' of 'science', 'technology', 'the economy', even 'revolution'.

Especially for the middle classes of the world, and all those seduced by this dream, the spiritual, psychic, and political traumas are profound, as awareness is dawning that "a retreat of the rich from overconsumption is the necessary first step towards improving the lives of an increasing number of people".[116] And the implications of this insight are very radical indeed:

> if we hope to survive as a species, and if there is to be hope for millions of other creatures, we need to shrink the human enterprise. Economic contraction may be bitter medicine, but it's part of the cure for what ails our planetary home.[117]

In this light, 'spaces' like the WSF have a unique and central significance in hopes for a better world: Where marginalised peoples and groups and those seeking to be in solidarity with them can meet on their own terms, probe the limits of different traditions and epistemologies, and experiment with new ecologies of knowledge; where new and renewed modes of education and formation of consciences can be nurtured; where bonds of solidarity can be forged; where new disruptions, chaos, and shifting horizons of reality and possibility can be anticipated and engaged with; where unanticipated, new soul-shaking, identity-changing, and movement-redefining challenges to conversion can be addressed; where dangerous memories of past suffering and martyrdom—and of many subsequent resurrections of hope from the grave—can be nurtured; and where hopes and faiths, ethics and politics, movements and coalitions can be re-invented.

Along these paths into the future, transmodern traditions offer many stories of apocalypse harbouring memories of social and ecological catastrophes in the past.[118] But they also harbour memories of navigating these past transitions from end times to new beginnings. And they offer deep wellsprings of insight and inspiration as we navigate the shoals of world historical transitions in our own places, in our own time.

We are slowly coming to recognise "what a radically transformed world we live in, one that has been transformed not only by such nightmares as global warming and global capital, but by dreams of freedom, of justice, and transformed by things we could not have dreamed of".[119] And, as gatherings like the WSF help to make clear, another world is not only possible in the future, but is emergent every day in countless expressions of GSJMs around the world.

Conclusion

At the dawn of the 21st century, in the wreckage of global (dis)order, across the South especially but also in the North, "life continues, reborn and organised even in the displaced, persecuted, blocked and exterminated people".[120] In coming together, marginalised peoples and their allies are redrawing the boundaries of identity and self-interest, forging bridge identities[121] and bonds of broader pluricultural, plurireligious solidarities[122] and politics, and generating countless concrete alternatives.

These developments are disrupting conventional Western categories of religion, economy, and politics, and challenging older frameworks and modes of left politics too, requiring us "to divest ourselves of old frameworks and habits if we really want to build a new world", having "to learn to unlearn what we have been taught for so long",[123] concerning 'religion' and many other matters.

And, in GSJM coalitions and gatherings like the WSF, these developments are shared and celebrated, in a "fiesta of ideas and networking"[124] among the oppressed and all those in solidarity with them and with the Earth, bringing people together to creatively experiment with "a new way of doing politics"[125] and to celebrate experiences of a shared Spirit along the paths to "a world where all worlds fit".[126]

These peoples and movements are creating, in the words of a recent WARC consultation,

> visions of a civilisation of convivial life of all living beings ... which contain revitalised wisdom from their philosophical, cultural and religious traditions of past and present. Buddhist wisdom to overcome greed, Hindu dharma of the cosmos, Confucian wisdom of Li/Ki, Taoist wisdom of the Way (Tao), Islamic wisdom of justice, and many African, Asian, Native American and Pacific original peoples' cultural and religious wisdom provide reservoirs for the foundation of visions of a new civilisation.[127]

References

Swami Agnivesh, nd—at http://www.swamiagnivesh.com/Swamiji.htm (Accessed April 2017)

S Anand, Nivedita Menon, and Aditya Nigam, 2007—'Secularism Has Become Another Religion', interview with Étienne Balibar, in *Tehelka*, October 6 2007, at https://kafila.online/2007/10/02/%E2%80%98secularism-has-become-another-religion%E2%80%99-%E2%80%93-etienne-balibar/ (Accessed April 2017)

Talal Asad, 1992—*Genealogies of Religion: Discipline and Reasons of Power in Christianity and Islam*. Baltimore: Johns Hopkins University Press

Marcelo Barros, 2008—'Cultural and Religious Pluralism: A Pivotal Point for Liberation Theology', in José M Vigil, Luiza Tomita, and Marcelo Barros, eds, 2008—*Along the Many Paths of God* (Berlin, Germany: Lit Verlag), pp 85–102

Bat Shalom, nd—'Women with a Vision for a Just Peace', at http://www.batshalom.org (Accessed April 2017)

Sharon Beder, 2006—*Free Market Missionaries: The Corporate Manipulation of Community Values*. Sterling, VA: Earthscan

Bret Benjamin, 2007—*Invested Interests: Capital, Culture, and the World Bank*. Minneapolis: University of Minnesota Press

'Biography of Sulak Sivaraksa', nd—at https://sivaraksa.wordpress.com/about/ (Accessed April 2017)

Debra Black, 2008—'To the Rescue of AIDS Orphans', in *Toronto Star*, May 25, p A6, at http://www.thestar.com/article/429657 (Accessed April 2017)

Fred Block, 1990—*Postindustrial Possibilities: A Critique of Economic Discourse.* Berkeley: University of California Press

Fred Block, 2006—'A Moral Economy', in *The Nation*, March 20 2006, at https://www.thenation.com/article/moral-economy/ (Accessed April 2017)

Agnes Brazal, 2004—'Beyond the Religious and Social Divide: The Emerging Mindawawon Identity', in *Focus* vol 2 no 3, pp 7–26

Neil Brooks, 1995—*Left Vs Right: Why the Left Is Right and the Right Is Wrong.* Ottawa, ON: Canadian Centre for Policy Alternatives

Buddhist Peace Fellowship, 2003—'Upon the Start of War', at http://www.bpf.org/html/current_projects/peace_pages/statement.html (Accessed lc on May 15 20, inactive April 2017)

Buddhist Peace Fellowship, 2007—'Statement in Support of Monks' Protest in Burma', at http://www.bpf.org/html/resources_and_links/statements/burma_9–07.html (Accessed lc on May 12 2008, inactive April 2017)

Buddhist Peace Fellowship, nd—'Vision and Mission', at http://www.bpf.org/html/about_us/mission/mission.html (accessed lc on May 12 2008, inactive April 2017)

President George W Bush, 2002—'State of the Union', Washington, DC at https://georgewbush-whitehouse.archives.gov/news/releases/2002/01/20020129-11.html (Accessed April 2017)

Kurt M Campbell, ed, 2008—*Climatic Cataclysm: The Foreign Policy and National Security Implications of Climate Change.* Washington, DC: Brookings Institution Press

Caritas Africa-All Africa Conference of Churches, 2007—'Ecumenical WSF Platform', at http://www.aacc-ceta.org/wsf/default.asp?active_page_id=1 (Accessed lc on July 20 2007; inactive April 2017)

José Casanova, 1994—*Public Religions in the Modern World.* Chicago: University of Chicago Press

Central Committee of the World Council of Churches, 2001—*Economic Globalization: A Critical View and an Alternative Vision*, Report of Policy Reference Committee II, Potsdam, Germany, January 29—February 6 2001. Geneva, Switzerland: World Council of Churches, at http://www.oikoumene.org/en/folder/documents-pdf/dossier6.pdf (Accessed April 2017)

Centro Ecuménico Diego de Medellín ('Diego De Medellín Ecumenical Centre'), at https://www.facebook.com/diegodemedellin/ (Accessed April 2017)

John Brown Childs, 1994—'The Value of Transcommunal Identity Politics', in *Z Magazine*, July 1994

John Brown Childs, 2003b—'Emplacements of Affiliation', in John Brown Childs, 2003a—*Transcommunality: From the Politics of Conversion to the Ethics of Respect* (Philadelphia: Temple University Press), pp 21–45

David Christian, 2005—*Maps of Time: An Introduction to Big History.* Berkeley: University of California Press

Churches' Center for Theology and Public Policy—at http://www.cctpp.org/index.htm (Accessed on lc June 23 2008, inactive April 2017)

Lee Cormie, 2004—'CEJI and Ecumenical Coalitions: Hope for a New Beginning in History', in Derek Simon and Don Schweitzer, eds, 2004—Intersecting Voices: Critical Theologies in a Land of Diversity (Ottawa, ON: Novalis), pp 300–322

Harvey Cox, 1999—'The Market as God: Living in the New Dispensation', in *The Atlantic Monthly*, 283 (March 1999), pp 18–23, at https://www.theatlantic.com/magazine/archive/1999/03/the-market-as-god/306397/ (Accessed April 2017)

Benjamin Danji 2005—'Samba and Revolution: Dispatches from the International Youth Camp', in *Upside Down World*, February 5 2005, at http://upsidedownworld.org/main/content/view/95/63/ (Accessed April 2017)

Mike Davis, 1996—'Cosmic Dancers on History's Edge?', in *New Left Review* I / 217 (May-June 1996), pp 49–73, at https://newleftreview.org/I/217/mike-davis-cosmic-dancers-on-history-s-stage-the-permanent-revolution-in-the-earth-sciences (Accessed April 2017)

Mike Davis, 2004—'Planet of Slums', in *New Left Review 26* (March–April 2004), pp 5–34, at http://newleftreview.org/II/26/mike-davis-planet-of-slums (Accessed April 2017)

Vine Deloria Jr, 2002—*Evolution, Creationism, and Other Modern Myths: A Critical Inquiry*. Golden, CO: Fulcrum Publishing

Departamento Ecuménico de Investigaciones ('Ecumenical Department of Research'), at http://www.deicr.org/#&panel1-1 (Accessed April 2017)

Charles Derber and Yale Magrass, 2008—*Morality Wars: How Empires, the Born Again, and the Politically Correct Do Evil in the Name of Good*. Boulder, CO: Paradigm Publishers

Jared Diamond, 2005—*Collapse: How Societies Choose to Fail or Succeed*. New York: Viking Press

Sara Diamond, 1989—*Spiritual Warfare: The Politics of the Christian Right*. Boston: South End Press

Enrique Dussel, 2002—'World-System and 'Trans'-Modernity', translated by Alessandro Fornazzari, in *Nepantla*, vol 3 no 2, pp 221–244

Esther Dyson, George Gilder, George Keyworth, and Alvin Toffler, 1994—'Cyberspace and the American Dream: A Magna Carta for the Knowledge Age (Release 1.2, August 22 1994)', in *The Information Society*, vol 12 no 3, pp 295–308

Niles Eldredge, 2001—'The Sixth Extinction', in *ActionBioscience*, June 2001, at http://www.actionbioscience.org/evolution/eldredge2.html (Accessed April 2017)

Engaged Buddhism, nd—at http://www.dharmanet.org/engaged.html (Accessed April 2017)

Asghar Ali Engineer, 2000—'Muhammad (PBUH) as Liberator', in *Islam and Modern Age* (July 2000)

Asghar Ali Engineer, 2001—'On Developing Theology of Peace in Islam', in *Islam and Modern Age* (October 2001)

Asghar Ali Engineer, 2002—'Islam, Globalization and Fundamentalisms', in *Islam and Modern Age* (August 2002)

Gustavo Esteva, 2001—'The Meaning and Scope of the Struggle for Autonomy', in *Latin American Perspectives*, vol 28 no 2, pp 120–148

ETC Group, 2003—'Green Goo: Nanobiotechnology Comes Alive!', in *Communiqué*, 77 (January–February 2003), at http://www.etcgroup.org/sites/www.etcgroup.org/files/publication/174/01/comm_greengoo77.pdf (Accessed April 2017)

ETC Group, 2008—'The World Torpedoes Ocean Fertilization: End of Round One on Geo-Engineering', Press release, in *ETC Group News Release*, May 30 2008, at http://www.etcgroup.org/sites/www.etcgroup.org/files/publication/694/01/etcnrworldtorpedoesof1may08.pdf (Accessed April 2017)

Ana Maria Ezcurra, 1984—*Ideological Aggression Against the Sandinista Revolution: The Political Opposition Church in Nicaragua*. Translated by Elice Higginbotham and Bayard Faithfull. New York: New York CIRCUS

Heba Raouf Ezzat, 2004—'Beyond Methodological Modernism: Towards a Multicultural Paradigm Shift in the Social Sciences', in Helmut Anheier, Marlies Glasius, and Mary Kaldor, eds, 2004—*Global Civil Society 2004/5* (London: Sage), pp 40–58, at http://www.lse.ac.uk/internationalDevelopment/research/CSHS/civilSociety/yearBook/chapterPdfs/2004-05/Chapter2.pdf (Accessed April 2017)

Jerry Falwell, 1981—*Listen America!*. New York: Bantam Books

Michael Ferber, July 1985—'Religious Revival on the Left', in *The Nation*, vol 241 (July 6–13 1985), pp 9–13

Ann Ferguson, June 1998—'Resisting the Veil of Privilege: Building Bridge Identities as an Ethico-Politics of Global Feminisms', in *Hypatia*, vol 13 no 3 (June 22 1998), pp 95–114

First People's Forum for Peace for Life, 2004—'A Call to Solidarity and Action', Final conference statement from 'Sowing Seeds of Peace in the Era of Empire: Christians in Solidarity with Muslims', Davo City, Philippines, at http://www.peaceforlife.org/aboutus/2004/statement.html (Accessed lc on April 30 2007, inactive April 2017)

Francis Fukuyama, 1989—'The End of History?', in *The National Interest*, vol 16 (Summer), pp 3–18, at https://ps321.community.uaf.edu/files/2012/10/Fukuyama-End-of-history-article.pdf (Accessed April 2017)

Joel Garreau, 2005—*Radical Evolution: The Promise and Peril of Enhancing Our Minds, Our Bodies—and What It Means to Be Human*. New York: Random House

General Command of the Zapatista Army of National Liberation–Clandestine Revolutionary Indigenous Committee, 2001—'Words of the EZLN in Puebla', Puebla, Mexico, at http://flag.blackened.net/revolt/mexico/ezln/2001/ccri/ccri_puebla_feb.html (Accessed April 2017)

Susan George, 1997—'How to Win the War of Ideas', in *Dissent* vol 44 no 3, pp 47–54, at http://www.globallabour.info/en/Dissent%20Summer%201997%20-%20George.pdf (Accessed April 2017)

Susan George and Fabrizio Sabelli, 1994—*Faith and Credit: The World Bank's Secular Empire*, Boulder, CO: Westview Press

Alan Geyer, 1997—*Ideology in America: Challenges to Faith*. Louisville, KY: Westminster John Knox Press

George Gilder, 1981—*Wealth and Poverty*. New York: Bantam Books

Newt Gingrich, 1996—*To Renew America*. New York: HarperCollins

Ramón Grosfoguel and Ana Margarita Cervantes-Rodríguez, 2002—'Unthinking Twentieth-Century Eurocentric Mythologies: Universalist Knowledges, Decolonialization, and Developmentalism', in Ramón Grosfoguel and Ana Margarita Cervantes-Rodríquez, eds, 2002—*The Modern/Colonial/Capitalist World-System in the Twentieth Century: Global Processes, Antisystemic Movements, and the Geopolitics of Knowledge* (Westport, CT: Praeger), pp xi–xxix

Ramachandra Guha, 2003—'How Much Should a Person Consume?', in *Vikalpa: The Journal for Decision Makers*, vol 28 no 2 (June 2003), pp 1–11

Sandra Harding, 1986—*The Science Question in Feminism*. Ithaca, NY: Cornell University Press

Chris Hedges, 2007—'The Rise of Christian Fascism and Its Threat to American Democracy', in *AlterNet* 8 (February 7 2007), at http://www.alternet.org/story/47679 (Accessed April 2017)

Richard Heinberg, 2008—'Making the Most of a Global Depression', in *Hope Dance* 67 (March–April 2008), at http://www.resilience.org/stories/2008-03-18/making-most-global-depression/ (Accessed April 2017)

Franz Hinkelammert, 1983—'The Economic Roots of Idolatry: Entrepreneurial Metaphysics', in Pablo Richard et al, 1983—*The Idols of Death and the God of Life*, translated by Barbara Campbell and Bonnie Shepard (Maryknoll, NY: Orbis Books), pp 165–193

Eric Hochstein and Ronald O'Rourke, 1981—*A Report on the Institute on Religion and Democracy*, prepared for the General Board of Global Ministries and the General Board of Church and Society of the United Methodist Church and the United Church Board for Homeland Ministries of the United Church of Christ

Christopher Hook, 2004—'The Techno Sapiens Are Coming', in *Christianity Today* (January 2004), pp 36–40, at http://www.christianitytoday.com/ct/2004/001/1.36.html (Accessed April 2017)

Richard Horsley, 2003—'Religion and Other Products of Empire', in *Journal of the American Academy of Religion*, vol 71 no 1, pp 13–42

Richard Horsley and James Tracy, eds, 2001—*Christmas Unwrapped: Consumerism, Christ, and Culture*. Harrisburg, PA: Trinity Press International

Sohail Inayatullah, 2005—'Islamic Civilization to Globalization: From Islamic Futures to Post-Western Civilization', in Metafuture.org, at http://www.bcasas.org.pe/h1.html (Accessed April 2017)

Instituto Bartolomé de Las Casas—at http://www.bcasas.org.pe/h1.html (Temporarily inactive April 2017)

International Network of Engaged Buddhists, nd—'About Us', at http://inebnetwork.org/about/

Jewish Socialists' Group—at http://www.jewishsocialist.org.uk (Accessed April 2017)

Chalmers Johnson, November 2003—'Sorrows of Empire', in *The Project Against the Present Danger*, Foreign Policy in Focus special report, at http://www.uslaboragainstwar.org/Article/8828/project-against-the-present-danger-sorrows-of-empire (Accessed April 2017)

Chalmers Johnson, February 2008—'Why the US Has Really Gone Broke', in *Le Monde Diplomatique*, at http://mondediplo.com/2008/02/05military (Accessed April 2017)

Bill Joy, 2000—'Why the Future Doesn't Need Us', in *Wired*, vol 8 no 4, at http://www.wired.com/wired/archive/8.04/joy_pr.html (Accessed April 2017)

Jubilee Debt Campaign, Jubilee Research, and CAFOD, nd—'The Birth of Jubilee 2000: A Brief Account of the Origins of the Jubilee 2000 Campaign', in *Jubilee Debt Campaign*, at http://old.jubileedebtcampaign.org.uk/The20birth20of20Jubilee202000+282.twl (Accessed April 2017)

Jubilee South—at http://www.jubileesouth.org (Accessed April 2017)

Jubilee USA—at http://www.jubileeusa.org (Accessed April 2017)

Justice, Peace, and Creation Team, 2006—'Alternative Globalization Addressing Peoples and Earth (AGAPE)'. A Background Document prepared for the World Council of Churches 9th Assembly. Geneva, Switzerland, 2005, at http://www.wcc-assembly. info/fileadmin/files/wccassembly/documents/english/agape-new.pdf (Accessed April 2017)

Kairos—at http://www.kairoscanada.org (Accessed April 2017)

Kairos Europa—at http://www.kairoscanada.org (Accessed April 2017)

Michael Klare, 2007—'Is Energo-Fascism in Your Future: The Global Energy Race and Its Consequences (Part 1)', in TomDispatch.Com (January 14 2007), at http://www. tomdispatch.com/post/157241/klare_the_pentagon_as_an_energy_protection_ racket (Accessed April 2017)

F H Knelman, 2006—'"Soft" Fascism Is Getting Harder', in *CCPA Monitor*, February 1 2006, at https://www.policyalternatives.ca/publications/monitor/february-2006-soft-fascism-getting-harder (Accessed April 2017)

Irving Kristol, 1979—'The Disaffection from Capitalism', in Michael Novak, ed, 1979— *Capitalism and Socialism: A Theological Inquiry* (Washington, DC: American Enterprise Institute for Public Policy Research), pp 15–29

Ray Kurzweil, 2005—*The Singularity Is Near: When Humans Transcend Biology*. New York: Penguin

Vinay Lal, 2002—'The Disciplines in Ruins: History, the Social Sciences, and Their Categories in the "New Millennium"', in *Emergences: Journal for the Study of Media and Composite Cultures*, vol 12, no 1, pp 139–155

Irene León, ed, 2006—*La Otra América en Debate: Aportes del I Foro Social Américas* ['Debate in the Other America: Contributions to the First Americas Social Forum', in Spanish]. Quito, Ecuador: Foro Social Américas

Charmaine Levy, 2012—'Influence and Contribution: Brazilian Liberation Theology, the Progressive Church, and the World Social Forum', in Jai Sen and Peter Waterman, eds, 2012—*World Social Forum: Critical Explorations*. New Delhi: OpenWord

James Lovelock, 2006a—'The Earth Is About to Catch a Morbid Fever That May Last as Long as 100,000 Years', in *The Independent*, January 16 2006, at http://www. independent.co.uk/voices/commentators/james-lovelock-the-earth-is-about-to-catch-a-morbid-fever-that-may-last-as-long-as-100000-years-5336856.html (Accessed April 2017)

David Loy, 1997—'The Religion of the Market', in *Journal of the American Academy of Religion*, vol 65 no 2, pp 275–90, at http://www.religiousconsultation.org/loy.htm (Accessed April 2017)

Lutheran World Federation (The Church and Social Issues—Department for Theology and Studies), 2001—*Engaging Economic Globalization as a Communion*, A working paper intended to stimulate a process in member churches of the Lutheran World Federation, and in their relationships (with other churches, faiths, sectors in society), for reflecting on the dynamics and effects of economic globalisation and discerning how to respond in light of the faith we confess, the values we uphold, and the communion which we embody, Geneva, Switzerland: Lutheran World Federation, at https://www.lutheranworld.org/content/resource-engaging-economic-globalization-communion (Accessed April 2017)

Marc Luyckx, 1999—'The Transmodern Hypothesis: Towards a Dialogue of Cultures', in *Futures*, vol 31 no 9, pp 971–82, at https://repository.berkleycenter.georgetown.edu/RD-19990528-Luyckx-Transmodern.pdf (Accessed April 2017)

Eduardo Mendieta, 1997—'From Christendom to Polycentric Oikonumé: Modernity, Postmodernity, and Liberation Theology', in David Batstone, Eduardo Mendieta, Lois Lorentzen, and Dwight Hopkins, eds, 1997—*Liberation Theologies, Postmodernity and the Americas* (New York: Routledge), pp 253–272

Zia Mian, 2004—'At War with the World: Nuclear Weapons, Development and Security', in *Development*, vol 47 no 1, pp 50–57

Daniel L Migliore, 2004—*Faith Seeking Understanding: An Introduction to Christian Theology*. Grand Rapids, MI: W B Eerdmans

John Mihevc, 1995—*The Market Tells Them So: The World Bank and Economic Fundamentalism in Africa*. Penang, Malaysia: Third World Network

John Mihevc, 1998—'The Idolatrous Theology of the International Monetary Fund', in Canadian Ecumenical Jubilee Initiative, ed, 1998—*Making a New Beginning: Biblical Reflections on Jubilee* (Toronto: Canadian Ecumenical Jubilee Initiative), pp 87–93

John Mohawk, 2006—'Surviving Hard Times: It's Not for Sissies', in *Yes Magazine* (Summer 2006), at http://www.yesmagazine.org/article.asp?ID=1466 (Accessed April 2017)

Jim Motavalli, 2002—'Stewards of the Earth: The Growing Religious Mission to Protect the Environment', in Emagazine.Com, vol 13 no 6 (November–December 2002), at https://www.thefreelibrary.com/Stewards+of+the+earth%3A+the+growing+religious+mission+to+protect+the...-a094011497 (Accessed April 2017)

Movimiento Continental de los Cristianos por la Paz con Justicia y Dignidad ['Continental Movement of Christians for Peace with Justice and Dignity'], 2004—'*Mensaje a los Cristianos del Continente*' ['Message to Christians on the Continent', in Spanish], *Encuentro Continental y Internacional* ['Continental and International Encounter'], Bogotá, Colombia, at http://web.archive.org/web/20041210205746/www.cristianosporlapaz.org/mensaje2.htm (Accessed April 2017)

Ashis Nandy, 1995—'History's Forgotten Doubles', in *History and Theory*, vol 34 no 2, pp 44–66

Michael Novak, 1982—*The Spirit of Democratic Capitalism*. New York: American Enterprise Institute for Public Policy Research / Simon and Schuster

Michael Novak, 1986—*Will It Liberate? Questions about Liberation Theology*. New York: Paulist Press

Onyango Oloo, 2007—'Critical Reflections on WSF Nairobi 2007', on *CADTM*, March 29 2007, at http://www.cadtm.org/IMG/article_PDF/article_2544.pdf (Accessed April 2017)

Stephen Palumbi, 2001—*The Evolution Explosion: How Humans Cause Rapid Evolutionary Change*. New York: Norton

Raimon Panikkar, 1995—'Is History the Measure of Man? Three Kairological Moments of Human Consciousness', in Raimon Panikkar, 1995—*Invisible Harmony: Essays on Contemplation and Responsibility* (Minneapolis: Fortress Press), pp 134–44

Leo Panitch, 2009—'Thoroughly Modern Marx', in *Foreign Policy*, May–June 2009, at http://foreignpolicy.com/2009/09/30/thoroughly-modern-marx/ (Accessed April 2017)

Parliament of the World's Religions, nd, c.2004—'Pathways to Peace: The Wisdom of Listening, the Power of Commitment'. Report of the 2004 Parliament. Barcelona, Spain, 2004, at https://parliamentofreligions.org/content/pathways-peace-wisdom-listening-power-commitment (Accessed April 2017)

Richard Peet, 2003—*Unholy Trinity: The IMF, World Bank, and WTO*. New York: Zed Books

Kevin Phillips, 2006—*American Theocracy: The Peril and Politics of Radical Religion, Oil, and Borrowed Money in the 21st Century*. New York: Viking Press

Dennis Pirages, 2005—*'State of the World 2005'—Containing Infectious Disease*, Washington, DC: WorldWatch Institute, at http://www.worldwatch.org/node/68 (Accessed April 2017)

Lewis F Powell, Jr, 1971—'Attack of American Free Enterprise System'. Confidential memorandum to Eugene Sydnor, Jr, Chairman, Education Committee, the US Chamber of Commerce, distributed to its national membership of leading executives, businesses, and trade associations, 1971, at http://reclaimdemocracy.org/powell_memo_lewis/ (Accessed April 2017)

The Progressive Conservative Party of Ontario, 1994—*The Common Sense Revolution*, Toronto: The Progressive Conservative Party of Ontario, at http://www.ontariopc.com/feature/csr/csr_text.htm (Accessed lc on September 9 2002, inactive April 2017)

Adam Przeworski, 1986—*Capitalism and Social Democracy*. New York: Cambridge University Press

Tariq Ramadan, 2004—*Western Muslims and the Future of Islam*. New York: Oxford University Press

Ronald Reagan, 1982—'The Evil Empire', Speech to the British House of Commons, London, at https://www.mtholyoke.edu/acad/intrel/evilemp.htm (Accessed April 2017)

Ronald Reagan, 1983—'Remarks', Annual Convention of the National Association of Evangelicals, Orlando, FL, at https://reaganlibrary.archives.gov/archives/speeches/1983/30883b.htm Accessed April 2017) (Accessed April 2017)

Martin J Rees, 2003—*Our Final Hour: A Scientist's Warning—How Terror, Error, and Environmental Disaster Threaten Humankind's Future in This Century on Earth and Beyond*. New York: Basic Books

Hubert Reeves, Joel De Rosnay, Yves Coppens, and Dominique Simonnet, 1998—*La plus belle historie du monde* ['The most beautiful history of the world', in French]. Editions du Seuil, 1996, translated from French and published as *Origins: Cosmos, Earth, and Mankind*, New York: Arcade Publishing

António Sousa Ribeiro, 2004—'The Reason of Borders or a Border Reason: Translation as a Metaphor for Our Times', in *Eurozine*, January 8 2004, at http://www.eurozine.com/the-reason-of-borders-or-a-border-reason/ (Accessed April 2017)

Matthew Richardson and Nouriel Roubini, 2009—'Nationalize the Banks! We're All Swedes Now', in *Washington Post*, February 15 2009, B3, at http://www.washingtonpost.com/wp-dyn/content/article/2009/02/12/AR2009021201602.html (Accessed April 2017)

Richard H Roberts, 2002—*Religion, Theology and the Human Sciences*. New York: Cambridge University Press

Douglas Robinson, 1990—*American Apocalypses: The Image of the End of the World in American Literature*. Baltimore: Johns Hopkins University Press

Mihail Roco and William Sims Bainbridge, eds, 2002—*Converging Technologies for Improving Human Performance: Nanotechnology, Biotechnology, Information Technology and Cognitive Science*, draft report of a National Science Foundation and Department of Commerce workshop of leading experts from government, academia, and the private sector, with subsequent contributions of members of the US science and engineering community, Arlington, Virginia, at http://www.wtec. org/ConvergingTechnologies/Report/NBIC_report.pdf (Accessed April 2017)

Marshall Sahlins, 1999—'What Is Anthropological Enlightenment? Some Lessons of the Twentieth Century', in *Annual Review of Anthropology*, vol 28 no 1 (October 1999), pp i–xxiii

John Saloma, 1984—*Ominous Politics: The New Conservative Labyrinth*. New York: Hill and Wang

Irene Santiago, 2004—'A Fierce Struggle to Re-Create the World', in Jai Sen, Anita Anand, Arturo Escobar, and Peter Waterman, eds, 2004—*World Social Forum: Challenging Empires* (New Delhi: Viveka Foundation), pp xiv–xvi, at http://www.choike.org/ documentos/wsf_foreward_santiago.pdf (Accessed April 2017)

Boaventura de Sousa Santos, 2005—'The Future of the World Social Forum: The Work of Translation', in *Development*, vol 48 no 2, pp 15–22, at http://www.ces.fe.uc.pt/bss/ documentos/The_Future_of_the_WSF_Develop.pdf (Accessed April 2017)

Boaventura de Sousa Santos, 2006—*The Rise of the Global Left: The World Social Forum and Beyond*. New York: Zed Books

Boaventura de Sousa Santos, João Arriscado Nunes, and Maria Paula Meneses, 2007—'Introduction: Opening up the Canon of Knowledge and Recognition of Dif- ference', in Boaventura de Sousa Santos, ed, 2007—*Another Knowledge is Possible: Beyond Northern Epistemologies* (London: Verso), pp xix–lxii

Ziauddin Sardar, 2004—'Islam and the West in a Transmodern World', in *IslamOnline*, August 18 2004, at http://www.islamonline.net/english/Contemporary/2002/05/ Article20.shtml (Accessed April 2017)

Sathirakoses-Nagapradipa Foundation—'Who We Are', at http://www.sulaksivaraksa. org/en/index.php?option=com_content&task=view&id=46&Itemid=92 (Accessed lc on March 15 2006, inactive April 2017)

Wolf Schäfer, 1993—'Global History: Historiographical Feasibility and Environmental Reality' , in *Conceptualizing Global History* (Boulder, CO: Westview Press), pp 47–69

Peter Schwartz and Peter Leyden, 1997—'The Long Boom', in *Wired* (July 1997), pp 115–129 and 168–173, http://www.wired.com/wired/archive/5.07/longboom.html (Accessed April 2017)

Second Continental Summit of the Indigenous Peoples and Nationalities of Abya Yala, 2005—'Kito Declaration', Quito, Ecuador, July 21–25 2004, at http://www. cumbreindigenabyayala.org/index_en.html (Accessed April 2017)

Alan Senauke, nd—'A History of the Buddhist Peace Fellowship: The Work of Engaged Buddhism', in *Buddhist Peace Fellowship Web Page*, at http://www. buddhistpeacefellowship.org/about-bpf/history/ (Accessed April 2017)

Shalom Center—https://theshalomcenter.org/ (Accessed April 2017)

Christian Smith, 1996—*Resisting Reagan: The US Central America Peace Movement*. Chicago: University of Chicago Press, at https://books.google.ca/books/about/ Resisting_Reagan.html?id=ZnPY5D6rX4cC&redir_esc=y (Accessed April 2017)

Rebecca Solnit, 2004—*Hope in the Dark*. New York: Nation Books, available at: http://www.kcrw.com/dialabook/Hope_in_the_Dark.htm (accessed lc on May 1 2006)

Willfried Spohn, 2003—'Multiple Modernity, Nationalism and Religion: A Global Perspective', in *Current Sociology*, vol 51 nos 3–4, pp 265–286

Peter Steinfels, 1979—*The Neoconservatives: The Men Who Are Changing America's Politics*. New York: Simon and Schuster

Chris Stewart, 2005—'Humanicide: From Myth to Risk', in *Journal of Futures Studies*, vol 9 no 4 (May 2005), pp 15–28, at http://jfsdigital.org/wp-content/uploads/2014/01/94-A02.pdf (Accessed April 2017)

Cecile Surasky, 2004—'Anti-Semitism at the World Social Forum?' in *The Electronic Intifada*, February 19 2004, at http://electronicintifada.net/v2/article2436.shtml (Accessed lc on June 10 2009, inactive April 2017)

Göran Therborn, 2003—'Entangled Modernities', in *European Journal of Social Theory*, vol 6, no 3, pp 293–305

Tikkun, nd—'*Tikkun*/NSP Core Vision', at http://www.tikkun.org/nextgen/tikkuns-core-vision (Accessed April 2017)

United Church of Canada, 2006—*Living Faithfully in the Midst of Empire*, Report to the 39th General Council 2006. Toronto: United Church of Canada, at goo.gl/imMFX8 (Accessed April 2017)

Hilary Wainwright, Oscar Reyes, Marco Berlinguer, Fiona Dove, Mayo Fuster Morell, and Joan Subirats, 2007—*Networked Politics: Rethinking Political Organisation in an Age of Movements and Networks*. Amsterdam: Transnational Institute

WARC and CWM Consultation, 2006—'An Ecumenical Faith Stance Against Global Empire: For a Liberated Earth Community', Manila Declaration, International Consultation on Theological Analysis and Action on Global Empire Today, by the Covenanting for Justice Project of the World Alliance of Reformed Churches, Manila, at http://warc.jalb.de/warcajsp/side.jsp?news_id=809&part_id=0&navi=6 (Accessed April 2017)

Peter Waterman, February 2005—'Fred Halliday, Come Down from Your Mountain!', in *OpenDemocracy*, February 3 2005, at http://www.opendemocracy.net/globalization-world/article_2328.jsp (Accessed April 2017)

Peter Waterman, 2005b—'The Old and the New: Dialectics Around the Social Forum Process', in *Development*, vol 48, no 2, pp 42–47

George Weigel, 1995—'The Neoconservative Difference: A Proposal for the Renewal of Church and Society', in Mary Jo Weaver and Scott Appleby, eds, 1995—*Being Right: Conservative Catholics in America* (Bloomington: Indiana University Press), pp 138–162

Hans Weiler, 2004—'Challenging the Orthodoxies of Knowledge: Epistemological, Structural, and Political Implications for Higher Education'. Colloquium on Research and Higher Education Policy of the UNESCO Forum on Higher Education, Research, and Knowledge, held in Paris, France, 2004, at http://www.stanford.edu/~weiler/Unesco_Paper_124.pdf (Accessed April 2017)

Chico Whitaker, 2007—*A New Way of Changing the World*. Nairobi: World Council of Churches

John Williamson, 1994—'In Search of a Manual for Technopolis', in John Williamson, ed, 1994—*The Political Economy of Policy Reform* (Washington, DC: Institute for International Economics), pp 9–28

World Alliance of Reformed Churches, 2004—'Covenanting for Justice in the Economy and the Earth', As agreed by the General Council, 24th General Council, Accra, Ghana, at https://perspectivesjournal.org/blog/2006/05/16/covenanting-for-justice-in-the-economy-and-the-earth/ (Accessed April 2017)

World Alliance of Reformed Churches, 1997—*Processus Confessionis: Process of Recognition, Education, Confession and Action Regarding Economic Injustice and Ecological Destruction*, Background Papers No 1: Milan Opocensky—'Reformed Faith and Economic Justice'; Bob Goudzwaard—'Concept paper about the *Processus Confessionis*'; Gordon Douglass—'The Globalization of Economic Life'; and Section II Report, 'Justice for All Creation' of the 23rd WARC General Council, Debreccen, Hungary, August 1997. Geneva: World Alliance of Reformed Churches, at http://www.stichtingoikos.nl/WARC%20Background%20doc%20Debrecen%201997.doc (Accessed April 2017)

World Council of Churches, 2006—'Alternative Globalization Addressing People and Earth—AGAPE'. Official Working Document, World Council of Churches 9th Assembly, Porto Alegre, RS, Brazil, at https://www.oikoumene.org/en/folder/documents-pdf/agape-new.pdf (Accessed April 2017)

World Council of Churches, 1998—*Together on the Way: 5.3. Globalization*, Report of the Eighth Assembly of the World Council of Churches, Harare, Zimbabwe. Geneva: World Council of Churches, at http://www.wcc-coe.org/wcc/assembly/fprc2d-e.html (Inactive April 2017)

Robert Wuthnow, 1988—*The Restructuring of American Religion*. Princeton, NJ: Princeton University Press

Notes

1. Spohn 2003, p 268.
2. Motavalli 2002.
3. Moema Miranda, in Wainwright, Reyes, Berlinguer et al 2007, p 26.
4. In the WSF, in particular, there is an increasingly shared sense of convergence among 'left' or 'progressive' social movements. But there is no widely accepted list or terminology about the relationships between 'old' (socialist, labour, Marxist) and 'new' movements, including feminist, ecological, anti-racist, indigenous, LGBTQ (lesbian, gay, bisexual, transsexual, queer), movements of the disabled or differently-abled, etc. In this essay, GSJM includes this rapidly expanding list of movements, discovering shared interests in opposing neoliberal globalisation and in forging another world. See also Waterman 2005; Santos 2006.
5. For example, the Civil Rights Movement in the US was largely based in black churches. And at the height of the Reagan counter-revolution, one commentator insisted, "the religious left is the only left we've got" (Ferber 1985, p 10); see also Smith 1996. Similarly internationally: "With the collapse of socialism, liberation theology seemed the only 'International' that was left" (Casanova 1994, p 3).
6. Levy offers insights into the influence of Brazil's Christian liberation movements in shaping Brazilian contributions to the launching of the WSF (Levy 2008).
7. See Santos 2004, p 65.

8.   The big tent in the exhibition area and many activities on the WSF programme made the collaboration of Caritas Africa (an international Catholic NGO) and the All Africa Conference of Churches highly visible in Nairobi. Traditional left suspicions about religion haunted many expressions of concern about NGO dominance at this forum. Less obvious were the commitments of resources, months of planning, and preparation to educate people about the WSF, to raise funds, and to promote participation in the WSF. See Caritas Africa-All Africa Conference of Churches 2007. And one member of the Nairobi organising committee judged "the collaboration between progressive Christians, Muslims, and radical civil society organisations in supporting the full participation of the slum dwellers, evictees and street kids" a "major success" (Oloo 2007, 7).

9.   In this paper, I am reporting on discussions underway around the world, especially in the circles of GSJMs and their scholarly supporters, which are expanding the horizons of progressive politics, and re-inventing justice / emancipation / liberation. I am aware, though, that no one has God's point of view—or the one true 'scientific' view—on these developments. As Grosfoguel and Cervantes-Rodríguez point out, "there is no objectivist, neutral, god-eye view above and beyond the geopolitical 'situatedness' of knowledge production in the colonial horizon of modernity" (Grosfoguel and Cervantes-Rodríguez 2002, p xix). I realise my perspective is shaped by my experiences living in Canada and the US, and that other people in other contexts, drawing on other traditions, will articulate these developments in different ways. But my perspective has also been deeply influenced by my commitments over three decades to listening to many historically marginalised 'others' in the Global South and my participation in various initiatives at cross-cultural and international dialogues and solidarity, including many international and local WSF events. I deeply believe that authentic hopes for the future—if there is to be a future for humanity—must be stitched together, shared, and concretely embodied in coalitions and campaigns.

10.   For example: ecumenical coalitions like the US Churches' Center for Theology and Public Policy in Washington, DC (Churches' Center for Theology and Public Policy); the thirteen Canadian ecumenical inter-church social justice coalitions developed through the 1970s and 1980s and recently folded into Kairos; the Institute for Contextual Theology in Johannesburg, South Africa; Instituto Bartolomé de Las Casas ('Bartolomé de Las Casas Institute') in Lima, Peru; Centro Ecuménico Diego de Medellín ('Diego De Medellín Ecumenical Centre') in Santiago, Chile; Departamento Ecuménico de Investigaciones ('Ecumenical Department of Investigations') in San José, Costa Rica; Kairos Europa; international movements like Jubilee 2000 and local movements linked to them, like Jubilee 2000 UK, Jubilee South, the Canadian Ecumenical Jubilee Initiative, and Jubilee USA.

11.   World Alliance of Reformed Churches 1997.

12.   World Alliance of Reformed Churches 2004, para 11.

13.   ibid, para 41. See also WARC's 'An Ecumenical Faith Stance Against Global Empire: For a Liberated Earth Community' (WARC and CWM Consultation 2006). Likeminded spirits in the United Church of Canada, who had been following the WARC process, produced a similar document, *Living faithfully in the midst of empire*.

14.   World Council of Churches 1998.

15.   Central Committee of the World Council of Churches 2001.

16.   World Council of Churches 2006.

17.   Lutheran World Federation (The Church and Social Issues—Department for Theology and Studies) 2001.

18.   See Justice, Peace and Creation Team. "Alternative Globalization Addressing Peoples and Earth (AGAPE)." (A Background Document). World Council of Churches 9th Assembly. Geneva, 2005, at https://www.oikoumene.org/en/folder/documents-pdf/agape-new.pdf (Accessed April 2017).

19.   See the fourth section, "Transmodern Spiritualities and Politics", below.

20.   Ramadan 2004, p 177.

21.   Engineer 2000. Ed. Asghar Ali Engineer died in May 2013.

22.   Engineer 2001.

23.   Engineer 2002.

24.   Senauke nd.

25.   Buddhist Peace Fellowship nd.

26.   Buddhist Peace Fellowship 2003, 2007.

27.   Engaged Buddhism nd. For a critical Buddhist perspective on capitalist economics and consumerism as the "religion of the market", see Loy 1997.

28.   Sathirakoses-Nagapradipa Foundation nd.

29.   Quoted in Biography of Sulak Sivaraksa nd.

30.   International Network of Engaged Buddhists nd.

31.   Swami Agnivesh nd.

32.   "Presentation to Swami Agnivesh." The Right Livelihood Award, 2004, at http://www.rightlivelihoodaward.org/?s=Swami+Agnivesh (Accessed April 2017); "Presentation to Asghar Ali Engineer." The Right Livelihood Award, 2004, at http://www.rightlivelihoodaward.org/?s=Asghar+Ali+Engineer (Accessed April 2017).

33.   The Shalom Center nd.

34.   Jewish Socialists' Group nd.

35.   Bat Shalom: Women with a Vision for a Just Peace nd. For a response by a Jewish activist to the charges that the GSJM and the WSF are "anti-semitic" in opposing the policies of the Israeli government, see Surasky 2004.

36.   As Childs notes, "the very distinction between 'spiritual' and 'material' does not apply to many such outlooks" (Childs 2003, p 28).

37.   II Continental Summit of the Indigenous Peoples and Nationalities of Abya Yala 2005. Indigenous movements and concerns formed a major axis of the first Americas Social Forum, in Quito, Ecuador (2004); see León 2006.

38.   Tikkun/NSP core vision nd.

39.   Parliament of the World's Religions 2004.

40.   Barros 2008, 99.

41.   First People's Forum for Peace for Life 2004.

42.   Indeed, Davis suggests, in the burgeoning slums of megacities around the world today religious movements like "populist Islam and Pentecostal Christianity (and in Bombay, the cult of Shivaji) occupy a social space analogous to that of early twentieth-century socialism and anarchism" (Davis 2004, p 30).

43.   George 1997.

44. Weigel, one of the architects of neoliberal / neoconservative convergence, has insisted that "the origins of political 'neoconservatism' ... had far more to do with ideological developments within the liberal camp than with a natural evolution of conservative political thought" (Weigel 1995, pp 144). See also Novak 1982.

45. For an early effort to mobilise resources in responding to the world revolution of 1968 and the increasing squeeze on corporate profits, see the Powell Manifesto (Powell 1971).

46. Williamson 1994.

47. The Progressive Conservative Party of Ontario 1994.

48. Fukuyama 1989.

49. On the 'revolutionary' character of this project, see Przeworski 1986, p 219.

50. For a description and analysis of the religious dimensions of Thatcherism in the UK, see Roberts 2002.

51. Novak 1982, p 21.

52. Novak 1986, p 37.

53. ibid, p 43.

54. Steinfels 1979, p 81.

55. Saloma 1984, p 9.

56. Kristol 1979, p 26.

57. ibid, p 25.

58. Hochstein and O'Rourke 1981; Ezcurra 1984; Geyer 1997.

59. S Diamond 1989.

60. Reagan 1983.

61. Wuthnow 1988, p 261.

62. Gilder 1981, p 97.

63. Falwell 1981.

64. Reagan 1982.

65. Bush 2002.

66. Dyson, Gilder, Keyworth et al 1996; Gingrich 1996; Schwartz and Leyden 1997; Roco and Bainbridge 2002.

67. As De Rosnay has proclaimed: "After the cosmic, chemical, biological phases, the curtain is going upon the fourth act, an act covering the next thousand years in which humanity will play the starring role" (De Rosnay, in Reeves, De Rosnay, Coppens, et al 1998, p 194).

68. Hinkelammert 1983; Loy 1997; Mihevc 1998.

69. See Brooks 1995; Block 1990.

70. Cox 1999; Block 2006.

71. As Benjamin notes: "the work of producing confidence in the Bank and in development—and thereby producing faith in capitalism—has been one of the few constants for the Bank during its sixty-year existence" (Benjamin 2007, p 10). See also; Mihevc 1995; Peet 2003.

72. As Susan George (long prominent in the alter-globalisation movement and in the WSF since the beginning) and Fabrizio Sabelli have noted: There are no societies without religion, even, or especially, those which believe themselves to be entirely secular. In our century, in our society, the concept of development has acquired

religious and doctrinal status. The [World] Bank is commonly accepted as the Vatican, the Mecca or the Kremlin of this twentieth-century religion" (George and Sabelli 1994, p 6). See also Beder 2006.

73. Derber and Magrass 2008.
74. Horsley and Tracy 2001.
75. Phillips 2006; Hedges 2007.
76. Panitch 2009.
77. Richardson and Roubini 2009.
78. Palumbi 2001, p 10.
79. Garreau 2005; Kurzweil 2005.
80. Hook 2004.
81. J Diamond 2005.
82. Pirages 2005.
83. Mian 2004.
84. Johnson 2008.
85. Klare 2007.
86. Johnson 2003; Knelman 2006; Klare 2007.
87. ETC Group 2003.
88. Joy 2000.
89. ETC Group 2008.
90. Campbell 2008.
91. Black 2008.
92. Eldredge 2001.
93. Lovelock 2006a; Stewart 2005.
94. Rees 2003, p 181.
95. Santiago 2004.
96. Lal 2002; Weiler 2004.
97. The resurgence of 'religion' is part of what Waterman describes as the shift "from the nineteenth to twentiethcentury era of primarily institutional power to the 21st century of an increasingly communicational and cultural one" (Waterman, 2005).
98. Horsley 2003.
99. Casanova has pointed to the extraordinarily wide scope of secularist dogma: "The theory of secularisation may be the only theory which was able to attain a truly paradigmatic status within the modern social sciences" (Casanova 1994, p 17), serving as a virtual orthodoxy among Westernised intellectuals, and influencing political discourses everywhere.
100. As French Marxist philosopher Étienne Balibar has confessed: "I have my doubts about the significance of religion in today's political discourse. I fear this can be a very western—I am wondering if the category of 'religion' itself is not part of what Edward Said called Orientalism" (Balibar in Anand, Menon, and Nigam 2007). See also Asad 1992, 29.
101. Dussel 2002.
102. Esteva 2001, p 122.
103. Sardar 2004.
104. Therborn 2003.

105. The fact that their own traditions have changed radically in the past is also often neglected in progressive Christian documents like those referred to in the first section, "Globalisation, Empire, and Idolatry".
106. Inayatullah 2005. Accordingly, as Luyckx reports, "today we observe all over the world a new kind of conflict inside each religion, inside Marxism, inside science" (Luyckx 1999, p 378).
107. As Harding has noted: "Coherent theories in an obviously incoherent world are either silly and uninteresting or oppressive and problematic" (Harding 1986, p. 164).
108. Ezzat 2004.
109. Santos, Nunes, and Meneses 2007, p xx.
110. Of course, apocalypse has been central to the culture and ideology of the Christian right, wielded to grossly oversimplify issues, polarise groups, and usher people along prescribed political paths. But it has been more widely pervasive too. As Robinson points out, concerning American literature:

    "the ideology that American writers at their most mythic invariably engage is *apocalyptic*: it is an ideology very much concerned with the end of old eras and the beginning of new eras, with the transition in space and time from an Old to a New World, from the Age of Europe (decadence, decay, death) to the Age of America (rebirth, return to primal innocence), in which America becomes the messianic model for the world" (Robinson 1990, p 2).

    Indeed, as Mendieta argues, apocalypse has been central to the images and philosophies of modernity:

    "Modernity ... has always been in crisis. Crisis is its essence. Crisis is the possibility of the imminent rupture of the new into the established, the settled, the sedimented. This is the ineluctable consequence of its temporal regime(s). As long as we have to disavow the old in order to remain at the foremost boundary of time, crisis is but the necessary haste to shade the ancient or primitive in order to remain modern. Indeed, we are defined by our complete orientation towards the future" (Mendieta 1997, p 256).

    It is important to stress, though, that as powerful as these modern right-wing versions of apocalypse have been and continue to be, they are very different from the biblical images of apocalypse; indeed, in the view of some theologians, they are profound distortions (Migliore 2004, pp 330–336). And they are radically different from the visions of apocalypse increasingly central in progressive circles, and in their implications for choice and action.
111. Schäfer 1993.
112. Nandy 1995; Panikkar 1995.
113. Davis 1996; Christian 2005.
114. Childs 1994; Ribeiro 2004.
115. See Santos 2005, p 17.
116. Guha 2003.
117. Heinberg 2008.
118. Deloria 2002; Mohawk 2006.
119. Solnit 2004, p 2.
120. Movimiento Continental de los Cristianos por la Paz con Justicia y Dignidad ['Continental Movement of Christians for Peace with Justice and Dignity' in Spanish], 2004.

121. Ferguson 1998.
122. Brazal 2004.
123. Whitaker 2007, p 20 fn 6.
124. Danji 2005.
125. Whitaker 2007, p 74 fn 9.
126. General Command of the Zapatista Army of National Liberation–Clandestine Revolutionary Indigenous Committee 2001. As Sahlins says of indigenous communities around the world, they are contributing to "a new planetary organisation of culture. Unified by the expansion of Western capitalism over recent centuries, the world is also being re-diversified by indigenous adaptations to the global juggernaut" (Sahlins 1999).
127. WARC and CWM Consultation 2006.

OpenWord

Mahmoud Mohamed Taha:
Islamic Witness in the Contemporary World[1]
François Houtart

From the 1930s through to his execution in the 1980s, Mahmoud Mohamed Taha—a theologian, engineer, and political figure in Sudan, and co-founder of the Sudanese Republican Party—not only played an important role in Sudan's independence struggle, but was also significant for his support of liberal reform within Sudanese society and within Islam.

A particularly negative view of Islam has spread around the world, based on the bent of political Islamism, which is a reaction to the cultural aggression of the West and particularly its military strikes in Iraq and Afghanistan. It is therefore important to know that Islam cannot be reduced to this single component. It is a constant in the history of religions that their relationship with political power influences the content of their message. We have seen this with Christianity when it became the ideological support of the feudal system. We can see this in Buddhism when it gets associated with power, the government necessarily being a 'bodhisattva', or when it binds itself to a narrow nationalism, as with certain monasteries in Sri Lanka. And what about Judaism, that some associate with the exclusion of the other, based on a notion of Israeli territory that is historically frozen and considered sacred? Does all this mean that we should forget the founding values of these religious movements?

This is precisely what Mahmoud Mohamed Taha aimed at: To rediscover the prophetic character of Islam, to underline what it could provide in a world of deepening inequalities, suffering under the blows of global capitalism, and to contribute to peace and reconciliation in torn and ravaged countries. Obviously however, such a project collided head on against the harshest currents of Islam, which in a number of countries in the Middle East is closely associated with political power. That is why, like many other prophets, Taha paid with his life for his intellectual courage and political commitment, working towards a humanistic socialism and an opening for a multicultural state in his country, Sudan.

To fully understand the life and work of Mahmoud Mohamed Taha, one must retrace the essential elements of his biography, recall the historical context of the Sudan of his era, and consider certain characteristics of the genesis of Islam.

Mahmoud Mohamed Taha and Sudanese Society

He was born, according to sources, in 1908,[2] or between 1909 and 1911,[3] in Rufa, a city situated on the Blue Nile in the centre of Sudan. Having lost both his parents at a young age, he obtained his engineering degree in 1936 from the University of Khartoum. His grandfather had taken part in the Mahdi Revolt against the English. After briefly working on the railroad, he was employed in the Gezirah cotton farms.

Starting at the end of the 1930s, Taha participated in the nationalist movement in favour of independence, opposing foreign occupation as much as the traditional elites. This would lead him to found the Nationalist Party in 1945, which was socialist inspired and held a moderate vision of Islam. A year later, he was jailed. Just after being freed, Taha undertook the defence of a Rufa woman who had circumcised her daughter. While he did not support the practice, he opposed the punishment, which to him was an expression of colonial power. He was jailed once again.

After this experience, he devoted himself to the study of Islam's mystics, Hallaj Ghazâli and Ibn Arabi. Following the Sufi tradition, he gave himself over to fasting, prayer, and even meditation. He deepened his study of the Koran. He also studied Western philosophy. Following his religious experience, he named his party the Republican Brothers, distinguishing them from the Muslim Brothers, another Islamic political organisation. This lost him a number of supporters who joined other political parties of the period. However, Taha's new direction was both deeply religious and political. His conviction was that the inspiration of a prophetic Islam had to make viable the political option of a socialist and republican orientation: More justice and more democracy.

He continued in his profession of engineering, all the while teaching his ideas of Islam until 1973, when he was forbidden to teach publicly. The community he had formed lived by the principles of Islam adapted to the modern world, calling for equality between women and men, refusing male privilege in marital law, and abolishing the practices of dowries and expensive weddings that characterised marriages at the time.

Forbidden to teach, he would address groups of listeners in public parks, a common practice at the time and one that I witnessed in 1968 at a Khartoum gathering in solidarity with the liberation movements of the Portuguese colonies, South Africa, and Namibia. People swarmed to the event, and popular participation was intense once the orator began to speak. One can well imagine that such activities by Mahmoud Mohamed Taha were not to the taste of the religious and political authorities of the time.

Despite the restrictions on the activities of the Republican Brothers, they supported the regime of President Gaafar Nimeiry during the 1970s and 80s.

Nimeiry maintained a nationalist line without imposing *Shari'a*, as fundamentalist currents demanded, and preserved unity between the north (Muslim) and the south (non-Muslim, Animist or Christian) of the country. However, the regime gradually gave in to religious conservative elements. In 1977, Mahmoud Mohamed Taha was jailed again. And in 1983, an article in which Taha criticised the Vice President for his politics of religious representation and discrimination against the south formed the basis for his detention without trial, which lasted 19 months. Upon his release from prison, he moved directly against President Nimeiry's policy of Islamisation and demanded guarantees of democratic freedoms, notably for the south, which provoked another incarceration.

Mahmoud Mohamed Taha's final trial began on January 8 1985, based upon a critical document he had published on December 25 1984. The judge accused him of propagating unorthodox views of Islam, liable to trouble believers, and of promoting sedition. Five defendants were condemned to death, the primary being Taha. The Court of Appeal, solicited not long after, confirmed the double accusation of apostasy and harm to state security. The sentence was immediate execution for Mahmoud Mohamed Taha and a delay of one month for the other four, to give them the chance to amend. The decision of the Court of Appeal was passed down on January 15. President Nimeiry ratified it and announced it publicly on radio and television on January 17. He gave only three days for Mahmoud Mohamed Taha's companions to repent, which they did, following the execution. This led to the release of all Republican Brothers.

In the meantime, on January 18, all security forces in the city had been mobilised and the army surrounded the central prison of Khartoum. Parachute soldiers infiltrated the prison. Hundreds of people were allowed into the court where the gallows had been erected. Mahmoud Mohamed Taha was brought in, his head covered in a veil, which was lifted before the execution. Smiling, he looked around at the crowd, then the veil was replaced on his head and he was hanged.

President Nimeiry did not last much longer. He was overthrown on April 6 of the same year. Based on the new constitution of October 1985, Mahmoud Mohamed Taha's daughter requested a review of his trial. On November 18 1986, the Supreme Court declared the trial of January 1985 null and void.

Mahmoud Mohamed Taha published his book, *The Second Message of Islam*, in 1967. It was reissued five years later and went through five successive editions in Sudan. The importance of this publication is twofold. First, the author adopts a critical distance from the Koran, resituating it in its historical and social context. Its interpretation, he argues, must be a process of social science. Secondly, the work uses Islam to support a social and political position that defends simultaneously the socialist option and calls for equality in law for Muslims and non-Muslims, judging such a position to be more true to authentic Islam than the fundamentalist methods calling for *Shari'a*.

While recognising their differences in approach, one could draw a parallel between his method and that of Ali Shariati in Iran. Both sought an Islam better able to meet the challenges of the contemporary world. Both opted for democratic socialism. Both paid with their lives for the ideals they defended, Ali Shariati having been assassinated in London in the late 1970s.

Return to the Origins of Islam

To place in perspective what Mahmoud Mohamed Taha calls the second message of Islam, we must distinguish between *Shari'a*—the law adapted to the social and cultural conditions of seventh-century Arab societies—and the *Sunna*—or the spiritual experience of the Prophet as a man of God (Nabî).[4] *Shari'a*, in Taha's view, is a transitory mission for its time, whose great principles should be drawn out, without applying to the twentieth-century prescriptions that were meant for the seventh. On the other hand, the *Sunna* represents an ideal to live by, "never attained, towards which all of humanity must strive".[5]

The revelations of Mecca are thus closer to the founding principles of Islam than those of Medina that followed. "The fundamental message of the Mecca preaching," writes Etienne Monard, "became in some sense occult when it came to founding a community incarnated in space and time, by the necessities of adaptation to local conditions".[6]

The Arabian Peninsula had undergone profound alterations over the centuries preceding the time of the Prophet. Cosmopolitan merchant cities (with many Christians and Jews) had developed along the coasts, ensuring commercial links between the Mediterranean and the Orient, facing the indigenous tribes of the north, for whom Mecca was the religious centre. Until the beginning of the sixth century the kings of Kinda had maintained their hegemony over all of Central Arabia, but they were replaced by the Hymiarites of the South. All these changes, accentuated by the rivalries between Persia and Byzantium, transformed the traditional social structure, notably creating profound inequalities. The universal and egalitarian message the Prophet introduced to Mecca disturbed the city's merchants and Mohamed was forced to leave the city to find refuge in the Oasis of Yathrib (the future Medina).

This did not happen without conflict between the dominant Arab groups and the Jews who had settled there. Mohamed came out the victor in the seventh year of Hijra (period calculated since the migration from Mecca to Yathrib). This rallied the inhabitants of Mecca to his cause. He also won the loyalty of most of the Bedouin clans, who accepted having to pay the *zakât* (tribute). Thus, Islam, which had been the religious expression of a social protest, progressively formed the cultural basis for a new political entity, playing a major role in constructing its norms, in justifying its practices, and in legitimising its power. These are two periods that Mahmoud Mohamed Taha is keen to differentiate.

To appreciate this distinction is to understand the significance of Mahmoud Mohamed Taha's contribution, as described by Samir Amin in the preface to the French version of his writings:

> Mahmoud Mohamed Taha reads in Islam two messages from God (from the Arabic word *risâla*), one which is immediate (the first *risâla* in the words of Taha), the other which is ultimate (the second *risâla*). Knowing at the start the second *risâla* illuminates the debate, allows one to seize the purport of the first and to understand why dominant Islam contents itself with it.
>
> True faith does not exist without adhesion to the second *risâla*, which is summarised in one sentence: *man was created in God's image.* He is therefore free, responsible and perfectible. The life of individuals is a permanent struggle that has no meaning except when viewed from the perspective of struggle towards divine perfection, pushing aside the permanent dangers of moving away from it. The life of societies, as well, has no other meaning than that of their fight to progress in the direction of perfection.
>
> Mahmoud Mohamed Taha deduces from this essential message a radical conclusion: the ideal society that must be the objective of social struggle, the society that creates the most favourable conditions allowing for the individual human being to undertake his own fight to move closer to God, the society without which faith will remain a victim of the limits society imposes upon the blossoming of responsible individual freedom, can only be a socialist and democratic society.
>
> Socialism, according to Mahmoud Mohamed Taha (who uses the Arabic term *'ishtirâkiyya*) is synonymous with equal access for all to all material wealth that the human spirit can create. His definition is, in reality, closer to the concept of communism (in Arabic *shuyûiyya*) than the experiments and programmes of modern historical socialism. However, in the view of Mahmoud Mohamed Taha, so long as these social conditions are not created, the individual remains a prisoner to the egoist compulsions that push him and limit his potential capacities to move further on the path of perfection in the divine image.
>
> In his definition of material wealth, Mahmoud Mohamed Taha considers the issue of *man-nature interaction*, in the terms of the second message of the theology of Islam that he propounds. Nature is also a creation of God, like human beings who are a part of nature. Nature thus is not a collection of things placed at the unlimited disposal of humanity. By consequence, humanity cannot move closer to divine perfection unless it establishes a balanced relationship with nature, deepening consciousness of belonging to the universe in its whole form. This rule defines, therefore, the ends and conditions for the organisation

of the production of material wealth that promotes the fulfilment of societies and individuals.

In turn, this socialism (or communism), as an ideal social system is senseless unless it is democratic, that is, in the words of Mahmoud Mohamed Taha, founded on the absolute freedom of individuals. This absolute freedom is the condition of responsibility, the guarantee that the choices that individuals are led to make at any time, in all their relations, can move them closer to (or further from) God.

This is the 'second message' (the ultimate message) of Islam, in the theology proposed by Mahmoud Mohamed Taha. This message, furthermore, *Islam shares with all the religious expressions of humanity* across time and space. For, Islam, thus conceived, has always existed, according to Mahmoud Mohamed Taha. It does not 'date' to the Koranic revelation. It is *the religion of God* (in Taha's own words), that is, the religion that has existed at all times and is expressed by Judeo and Christian revelations, among others.

In the Koranic revelation, as in the Tradition (the *Sunna*), one must therefore *distinguish the ultimate message of Islam from its situational commandments.* In his learned and fine analysis of the texts, Mahmoud Mohamed Taha indicates that the ultimate message occupies a dominant place at the beginning of the revelation, in the Mecca *suras*. Here, the revelation is not concerned with the problems of managing society, but only in the essence of the faith (free and responsible human beings were created in the image of the one and only almighty God). On the other hand, the occasion being available to organise a slightly better society than that of contemporary Arabia, around the Prophet in Medina, a society capable of taking some steps in the right direction, to open a door for the advancement of the faith, God did not miss the opportunity to help men to structure it. Mahmoud Mohamed Taha consequently considers that the commandments made to this society must be seen as situational, not as the final image of the ideal society, the realisation of the absolute. He deals here with eight issues in succession that Muslims generally consider to be dealt with by the law (*Shari'a*) as expressed in the Medina community:

1. Holy war (*jihad*),
2. Slavery (*ar-riqq*),
3. Capitalism (*ar-ra'sumâliyya*) which we can interpret as the issues of economic management of society by means of private property and legal commerce,
4. Inequality between men and women,
5. Polygamy,
6. Divorce/repudiation (*al-talâq*),
7. Women's veil (*al-hijâb*), and—
8. Separation between men and women in social life.

Through an attentive analysis of the holy texts, Mahmoud Mohamed Taha defends his theology, emphasising the nuances that demonstrate, in his interpretation, the situational character of the solutions brought by the law at the exact time and place. Each of the chapters concerning the eight issues has the same, significant title ... Holy war is not fundamental to Islam ... Polygamy is not fundamental to Islam, etc.

Mahmoud Mohamed Taha consequently dedicated himself to actively preaching, through his writings and his words, and through organising militant students around him. He preached against a conservative, ritualistic, and formal interpretation of Islam that respects only the immediate message in favour of an interpretation emphasising the ultimate message, calling for action to transform society to favour the spread of the faith.[7]

In the present political circumstances, Taha's message has a tough time being heard. On the one hand, Islamist movements have hardened, leaving little space for differing orientations. They have established strong, popular social foundations, thanks to actions of immediate assistance. On the other hand, authoritarian powers in the Islamic world got built on a monolithic and orthodox Islam that allows no room for religious pluralism. As for the nationalist regimes that emerged strongly after the Second World War, their secular character distanced them from religious references and their transformation into authoritarian—sometimes hereditary—regimes did not facilitate the existence of critical initiatives either. The Marxist movements, in their criticism of the structures of oppression, including cultural ones, entailed a rejection of Islam in all its forms.

That new currents exist today, partly inspired by the thought and testimony of Mahmoud Mohamed Taha, is undeniable—but they have been pushed down to the catacombs. It is therefore difficult to detect them and to report on them accurately. However, it is important to know this reality, both for the outsider, to reduce prejudice, and for the insider, to encourage the world of Islam to draw from its traditions the necessary force to play a role that is both critical and forward-looking, in a world threatened by the destruction of the planet and of millions of human beings pillaged by capitalism. Finally, like liberation theology in Christianity, Taha's thinking can help all those struggling for justice and equality for human beings to take into account the religious dimension as a source of inspiration for social and political commitment.

But for providing this inspiration—through a religious and social struggle worthy of the great prophets in human history—Mohamed Mahmoud Taha paid with his life.

References

Samir Amin, 2002—'Préface', in Mahmoud Mohamed Taha, 2002—*Un Islam à vocation libératrice* ['The Second Message of Islam', in French]. Paris: L'Harmattan

Samir Amin, nd, c.2012–13—'Towards an Islamic Theology of Liberation', translated from the original in French by Anthony Mansueto, at http://www.alfikra.org/article_page_view_e.php?article_id=1019&page_id=1 (Accessed April 2017)

Abdullahi Ahmed An-Naim, 1996 [1987]—'Translator's Introduction', in Mahmoud Mohamed Taha, 1996—*The Second Message of Islam*. (Syracuse, NY: Syracuse University Press)

Etienne Renaud, 1997—'À la mémoire de Mahmud Mohamed Taha' ['In Memoriam, Mahmoud Mohamed Taha', in French], in *Prologues*, no 10 (Summer 1997), pp 14–21

Notes

1. The first draft of this essay was translated from the original French by Jonathan Williams, of Ottawa, Canada, and proofed by Dima Saab, July 27 2009. Ed: I have taken the liberty of making some minor further adjustments in the language, to make it flow more freely, and for the quotation from Amin 2002, referring also to another essay by Samir Amin where he covers very similar ground (Amin, nd, c.2012–13).

   Ed: As noted elsewhere in this book, the author of this essay, François Houtart, walked on on June 6 2017, shortly before the publication of this book, and therefore of this essay. I had known François since the early 1990s, but more substantively from the early 2000s, through the World Social Forum. Even if he and I had our occasional disagreements over the subsequent years over policy and strategy, I think we always retained our mutual respect and regard, and I would therefore like to put on record here my great admiration for the grace and modesty with which he always conducted himself despite his extraordinary track record—and my gratitude to him for always agreeing to my requests for an essay, including this one; and where every one of which has expanded my understanding of the world of movement.

2. Renaud 1997.
3. An-Naim 1996.
4. Renaud 1997, p 15.
5. ibid.
6. Renaud 1997, p 16.
7. Amin 2002.

Local Islam Gone Global:
The Roots of Religious Militancy in Egypt and Its Transnational Transformation[1]
James Toth

It is hard to imagine a social movement that spans the entire spectrum from the local and microscopic to the grand, global, and macroscopic. The Islamic movement is an exception. Since June 1967—when Israel won the Six Day War—radical and militant Islamic movements have appeared in country after country throughout the Middle East and South Asia. Yet, to US Americans, and perhaps to most people across much of the world, they remained essentially remote, localised affairs, until, on September 11 2001, this detachment suddenly dissolved and the entire world came to realise the full global extent of Islamic militancy.

This essay chronicles the emergence of local Islamic militancy in southern Egypt, concluding that its genesis in the grassroots of the Egyptian Sa'id[2] is critically important to understanding its subsequent transnational transformation. Only once its parochialism is well established and understood can we begin to conceptualise how such a local oppositional movement articulated with the worldwide al-Qa'ida network headed by Usama bin Ladin,[3] and in that sense how local movement transmogrifies into a global one. From a small but important insurrection in one region of one Arab country, Egypt, to a globally connected web of holy warriors—this is the movement that I document here.

What follows is a study of one small, contributing portion of the Islamic movement as it emerged in the Sa'id and as it was revealed through anthropological fieldwork conducted in one of this region's major cities. In and by itself, it did not simply transform into al-Qa'ida, which is a river fed by multiple tributaries. Nor can this one study be justifiably generalised to include all Islamic movements, which vary from militant to moderate, political to cultural, pragmatic activism to doctrinaire orations. It does, however, pinpoint the political economy, the social and community base, the theological and ideological justification, and the government actions and deeds that, duly multiplied and amplified, fed into the formation of the group that eventually attacked New York City and Washington, DC.

Many have argued that 'terrorism' is born of poverty and resentment. However, this begs the question why such religious militancy is not pandemic throughout the Third World, or at least among Islamic nations. Poverty and domination, of themselves, do not breed violence; just as often they produce the opposite—submission. In this case, however, it is the perceived *injustice* of the distribution of wealth and power, not the actual allocation per se. Poverty and political powerlessness have been around for some time, yet seldom do they generate the resentment and anger that are provoked when individuals believe these have been begotten in illegal or immoral ways. Accusations of corruption are not merely economic or financial indictments; they are first and foremost moral criticisms. Allegations of arrogance are not simply political grievances; they are also principled arguments against the misuse of authoritarian power. Participants say these ethics and principles derive directly from the Qur'an and the universal theory of Islam. In Muslim societies where outright secularists still constitute a minority and where the eighteenth-century Enlightenment separation of religion and politics became a colonially-imposed doctrine, Islam still strongly colours the beliefs, actions, and perceptions of movement activists. Thus, this focus on poverty and power, and on corruption and arrogance, gives the Islamic movement its peculiar sense of frustration but also its uncommon appeal and strength. As with so many social movements, then, purely economic or sociological analyses are necessary, but insufficient. The doctrines and cultural beliefs, too, must be examined to fully understand how local movements erupt into global campaigns, and why.

Social Justice in Islam

Accusations of 'terrorism' often deny the legitimacy of the grievances that perpetrators harbour against the targeted hegemon, or else recode them as no more than so-called innate or primordial emotions like jealousy, anger, and hate. Yet the Islamists I spoke with—activists and fellow travellers alike—agree that many devout and pious Muslims do have strong moral and political objections to their own governments and their Western supporters. These grievances fall squarely under the label of injustice and tyranny, in an ironic re-enactment of David and Goliath.

Sayyid Qutb, considered by many the grandfather of the contemporary Islamic militant movement, authored *Milestones*,[4] which, in concert with Qutb's own 1966 martyrdom, became the 'Islamist manifesto' because of its harsh, bitter, and aggressive demands for an unequivocal Islamist victory. Yet, Qutb also wrote a more studied tome many years before he shifted to advocating radical violence, a 1948 book called *Social Justice in Islam*,[5] which contains the morals and political principles that underlie his later, more revolutionary rant. It was the repeated and egregious violation of social justice in Islam that, in the end, warranted the high level of militancy Qutb advocated.

Qutb considered the Islamic orthopraxy that God laid down in the Qur'an—the Right Path, or *Sharia*—to comprehensively embody social justice such that a strict adherence to Islamic law by both rulers and ruled guaranteed justice and obedience. Moreover, he considered Islamic justice so beneficial for all—Muslim and non-Muslim alike—that he did not hesitate to advocate universalising Islam in much the same way as the West universalised modernity, a secularised disguise for Calvinist Christianity.[6]

Yet, in terms of social justice Qutb need not have worried. The notions of social justice and fair play that he diligently derived from Islam's venerable documents—the Qur'an, the *Sunna*—are well established and understood in the other Middle East monotheisms, Judaism and Christianity. Whether it be nationalist or communist revolutions, civil wars or wars of independence, liberation theology or Islamic militancy, radical social movements are often permeated by a common concept of social justice which is coloured by Middle East religions that have affected a wide portion of the globe.

In 833, in the reign of Caliph al-Ma'amun (813–833) during the Abbasid dynasty when Islam, Baghdad, and the Muslim world were at the pinnacle of their civilisation, a political battle broke out between the liberal Mu'tazilite philosophers and their caliphal supporter, and the conservative People of the Hadith (traditional Prophetic stories) led by Ahmad ibn Hanbal. When al-Ma'amun arrested and imprisoned ibn Hanbal, the people in Baghdad did a very strange thing. They didn't demonstrate in the streets for the liberals, radicals, or progressives who had the caliph's ear. Instead, they protested against the incarceration of the conservative jurisconsult. Ibn Hanbal had advanced a very strict interpretation of Islamic law, and his supporters astutely understood that the liberals' counter-interpretation left far too much room for al-Ma'amun to insert his own rules and stray from the social justice God had incorporated into Islamic law. Thus, the stricter the interpretation, the stricter the justice people could expect from their rulers. In what may have been the Islamic equivalent of the Protestant movement—only eight centuries earlier—the people chose Islamic law as the embodiment of justice. Eight hundred years later, in the definitive and secularising English Civil War, the Calvinist Roundheads triumphed over the Anglican Cavaliers, and the legal system became secular, modern, more adaptable—especially to the interests of rulers and their elite supporters. The popular classes in England followed a direction opposite to the wisdom of the Baghdad crowds. Since then, modern European working classes have opted for increasing liberalism—the more, the better; such that Marx counted on them as the fuel for the progressive revolutions executed in the name of economic and political justice. In both moments—the Puritan experiment and the Mu'tazilite ordeal—society stood at the threshold of choosing either modernity or tradition. England preferred the former, the Abbasids the latter. In ninth-century Baghdad, and in today's Islamic movement, safekeeping traditional legal interpretation was and is considered the safest way of preserving social justice. It binds the popular classes and regulates what they can and cannot do, thereby limiting their freedom. In exchange, it does the very same for those in power, so their rule doesn't exceed their authority. This better ensures obedience from the ruled and better guarantees social justice from the rulers.[7] One of the key demands in contemporary Islamism is the re-insertion of Islamic law into Muslim societies.

Michael Walzer's recent book on Just War theory—*Arguing about War*—promptly acknowledged its roots in an Augustinian Catholicism adopted by Europe's eleventh-century Crusaders.[8] But Walzer just as hurriedly declared his intentions to secularise and universalise these Christian ideas. Yet, before banishing religion altogether, he began to sound very much like Hasan al-Banna (1906–1949) in his undated piece 'On Jihad',[9] which laid down a familiar set of 'do's-and-don't's' about religious violence, or like Sayyid Qutb (1906–1966) in his *Islam and Universal Peace*,[10] which indicated when peace could actually be abrogated. These three comparable creeds prescribed defensive wars and proscribed offensive wars except under certain conditions, one of which is when people are afflicted by tyranny, oppression, and injustice.[11]

Does a universal notion of social justice extend beyond the horizon determined by the three Middle East monotheisms? Thirty years ago, Barrington Moore asked a similar question in *Injustice: The Social Bases of Obedience and Revolt*.[12] When do people rise against injustice? Yet instead of a definition of justice based on historically contingent religious and, later, national imperialism, he characterised this fairness as anchored in a universal human nature and psyche that appeared biologically based. This certainly makes justice as universal a concept as the human body. But it also makes it a concept that can be biologically determined—some people have more of it, just like some people have more pigment—and therefore borders on the racialist.

However, Moore refined his definition by tying it more firmly to "problems of social coordination" (or relationships) located at three levels—political (authority), social (status), and economic (class). This parallels Qutb's own version that considered the foundation of justice to include freedom of thought, social equality, and social responsibility. The author of *Islam and Universal Peace* further refined this foundation to embrace:

- Individual civil rights and social obligations or collective civil rights;
- Equality of social classes and social origins;
- Political and governmental issues such as democracy, consultation, compliance, equity, and ruler-ruled relations; and—
- Economic issues such as property ownership, income and income distribution, consumption, usury, and taxation.

Qutb's earlier book concluded that it took the establishment of all four to genuinely produce Islamic justice; the absence or even shortage of one or more could indicate a social injustice that, he wrote later, may well be worth fighting against.

Moore himself went on to propose a Durkheimian theory where social movements are initiated when suffering and oppression—which, after all, are the norms, he argues—go beyond bearable and justifiable limits and are thus rejected and removed. This functionalist approach corresponds closely with such social movement theorists as Eric Hobsbawm,[13] Frances Piven and Richard Cloward,[14] and Charles Tilly.[15] Moral outrage and grievances, however, must derive from *social* relationships, since unlike Durkheim's *Suicide*,[16] it is not enough for one person to feel the unbearable pain and misery but it requires a collective consensus. Resource Mobilisation and Rational Choice theorists such as Mancur Olson,[17] Sidney Tarrow,[18] and Doug McAdam, John McCarthy, and Mayer Zald[19] have explained such anger and grievances by focusing on the political opportunities and constraints, social mobilisation and organisation, and perceptional framing processes found in constituting social movements.

There seems to be a syllogism in Moore's argument whereby the emergence of social movements means, *ipso facto*, that tolerable limits of injustice have been trespassed, whatever these are. Saying injustices occur when social contracts are violated merely defers analysis and avoids inherent subjectivism: "Injustices take place when we say they take place. And we're going to reverse them".

This syllogism is a safe bet in the Islamic movement however, for it is difficult to document the exact date that injustices and grievances begin and the growing awareness of them by leaders and rank-and-file. Here, countless small, individual choices get made, often framed at or after the Friday noon sermon by radical and demagogic preachers who wrathfully challenge government authority and international hegemony. But these choices are not automatic—for there is no Oriental Despotism here of unquestioning fidelity to a charismatic leader—but rather involve reflection, discussion, and multiple family conferences and consultations. The choices and discussions I heard were certainly logical, but often engineered by a withering away of legal and non-violent alternatives. In the end, there was only one choice a devout Muslim could really make, with the consequences of a massive rise in Islamic militancy in Egypt from 1967 to 1992. Here, then, is the story of what they decided to do.

Egypt's Underdevelopment: Midwife to Contemporary Islamism

The rise of the current Islamic movement in Egypt took place at a conjuncture of three different trends in the global economy and regional politics that critically shaped Egypt's growing underdevelopment, and the outbreak of violence that emerged as a militant attempt to halt it.

First, there was a twenty-year worldwide recession induced by the 1974 and 1979 oil price hikes. Within the Third World, these trends were exacerbated by declines in petrodollar investments after the 1985 oil price collapse. This generated a realignment in the international division of labour whereby businesses in the First World de-industrialised their production facilities and relocated them to more favourable cheap-labour sites within the Third World.

After the economic recession of 1967 and the oil price shock of 1974, industrial investment declined in the First World but increased throughout the Third. These areas became the Newly Industrialising Countries (NICs) that included Singapore, Taiwan, South Korea, and Hong Kong. Financing such investments came from oil revenues recycled through multinational corporations and offshore banks. Their principal markets lie in trading with other Third World countries and in re-exporting to the West.[20]

However, this development polarised the new economic order. While some countries benefited from the transfers of First World capital, others, like Egypt, were further impoverished. Egypt was not an NIC, and only sporadically benefited from transfers of First World capital. Like many Third World countries, Egypt suffered a debt crisis in the 1970s owing to energy costs, worldwide inflation, overvalued currency, stagnant public-sector industrialisation, and a deteriorating agricultural sector.[21] Farming was squeezed of crops, capital, and labour, but agricultural exports that could earn hard currency were low, and government-appropriated profits from crop sales subsidised a growing urban labour force instead of financing industrialisation.[22] Import substitution industrialisation (ISI) failed owing to lack of investment, especially in new technology. Despite attempts to privatise throughout the 1970s, new capital-intensive competition from foreign markets, rigid government regulations, and outmoded production facilities kept Egypt's public sector moribund.[23] Moreover, what little investment entered the country was overwhelmed by the doubling of Egypt's population from 19 million in 1947 to 37 million in 1976, specifically among the 15–45 age group, most in need of jobs and social services.[24]

Finally, Egypt's humiliating defeat in the Six Day War of June 1967 led to disenchantment with centralised, state-led development, and a popular rejection of the secular Arab nationalism and radical modernisation programme initiated by President 'Abd al-Nassir.[25] The disenchantment led to increasing dependence on private investors, and the rejection to a turn towards religion.

Unable to accumulate foreign currency from agricultural or industrial exports, Cairo turned increasingly to international finance. At first Egypt attempted unsuccessfully to attract foreign investment by relying on its ties with neighbouring Arab petroleum exporters. But its efforts were stymied as petrodollars moved first to regional rivals like Lebanon, later into First World banks, and then to more profitable peripheral economies elsewhere. The 1979 Camp David treaty further advanced Egypt's estrangement. Until a regional reconciliation could be achieved, Egypt relied on revenues from domestic oil production, declining cotton exports, canal fees, and tourism.[26]

Throughout the 1970s and early 1980s, these conditions were insufficient to fuel economic growth. Instead, Egypt depended on US assistance and foreign aid, international bank loans, and remittances from emigrant workers. In particular, it capitalised on its large labour force. Seeing that emigration abroad had become a major new source of income for Egyptian workers, it thought that such labour remittances should also become a potential source of foreign currency for the state. High incomes earned abroad, however, were converted into consumer purchases, real estate, and housing; and later, returning emigrants established small, informal businesses. Many also sought to finance pious deeds and charitable acts as ways of demonstrating their momentary success and eternal gratitude.

So, rather than financing employment-generating industrial projects, much of this private hard currency fuelled 'soft' investments in commerce, banking, real estate, and tourism.[27] Therefore, to generate the jobs needed for a growing population, the government was forced to borrow. But, because of its unsatisfactory credit rating, Cairo's only recourse was the International Monetary Fund (IMF), whose austere lending conditions, in turn, aggravated the impoverishment of individual workers and consumers.

Soon, many urbanites became more vocal in demanding higher incomes and more employment as their already precarious standard of living was further eroded by the steep rise in consumer costs and the burden of unemployed dependants. As a result, their anger became more intense and their opposition more prominent.

By the early 1990s, economic disorder came to overwhelm Egypt's consuming public, including the rural and urban working classes, and even the heretofore comfortable middle class. Unable to influence government policy through recognised channels, many of the disaffected turned to other outlets. The secular Left, already neutralised by two decades of marginalisation, was unable to provide the leadership to shape and transform such disaffection. Instead, such guidance came from middle-class radicals who joined the Islamist movement and galvanised mass discontent into a serious challenge to the state. The proletarian core of their support came from the unorganised multitudes who had flocked to small district towns, provincial capitals, and urban interstices where they had found jobs in small construction crews, unregistered workshops, and informal service activities.

Religious Insurrection

The rise of the current Islamic movement builds on a hundred-year history that began with Muhammad Abduh, head of al-Azhar in the late nineteenth century. Abduh called for ridding Islam of centuries of Sufi and superstitious accretions, rejecting the intermediaries between worshippers and God that had crept into

Sufi Islam, and returning to the practices and beliefs of a Golden Age of the *salaf*, or ancestors.

The ideas of this 'grandfather' of the Islamic movement were among those adopted by Hasan al-Banna when he established the Muslim Brotherhood in 1928, which thereafter (in the 1930s and 1940s) became the prototype for later Islamist organisations in Egypt and elsewhere. Under Abduh, Salafiya Islam paralleled the growth of nationalism and evolved into what most Egyptian Muslims today practice and believe. Under al-Banna, however, Salafiya Islam was radically reinterpreted in defence against modernists and secularists.

One major intellectual of the Brotherhood, Sayyid Qutb, who was jailed and martyred by Jamal 'Abd al-Nassir, wrote what I would call the 'Islamic Manifesto' while he was in prison from 1954 to 1965, which radicalised this defensive rhetoric and preached an interpretation of Islam that became the intellectual foundation of contemporary Islamist associations.

These Islamist organisations proliferated after the Six Day War, principally among college students throughout Egypt. At first they were encouraged by the government, until Anwar al-Sadat's visit to Jerusalem in November 1977 turned them against a state that could forgive and make peace with its enemies. Thereafter, the government became the principal target as these associations raised a moral and ethical campaign against what they saw as official corruption and injustice.[28]

Since its inception in the late nineteenth century, the social base of the Islamic movement in Egypt had changed, becoming less elitist and more populist.[29] By the 1970s and 1980s, even the lower middle and working classes split between those who considered themselves 'authentic' (*ibn al-balad*) or as Westernised Egyptians (*ibn al-zawwat*).[30]

Those who considered themselves genuine and authentic but had become strongly disaffected from their secular and Westernised counterparts joined a movement that was difficult to distinguish from the religion itself. Islam is a radically monotheistic religion, which requires both correct belief (orthodoxy) *and* correct practice (orthopraxy),[31] believing in one single God and practicing the code of conduct revealed in the Qur'an. Its profession of faith, the Shahada— "There is no god but God, and Muhammad is His Messenger"—unites these two aspects. When carried to its logical conclusion—some would say, its extreme— the Shahada presents a programme for revolutionary action in today's modern world: Reject as polytheism all authority that is elevated to the level of God, and reject as unbelief all codes but those contained in the Qur'an.[32]

Activists in the Islamic movement see the world as a society in crisis, a crisis arising from a deterioration in traditional religious values, beliefs, and practices.[33] But more than experiencing mere decline, these traditional doctrines are also under vigorous attack, both from outside society by foreign elements (principally Western), but also (perhaps more importantly) from within, by 'agents' of those foreigners who have become secular collaborators under their influence. Consequently, corruption, dishonesty, impropriety, poverty, injustice, and personality cults appear not only pervasive, but flourishing. The degeneration of religion that produced this crisis is similar to the ignorance, or *jahiliya*, that prevailed before the rise of Islam.

The Islamic movement's explanation for the general cause of this crisis rests on the accusation that Muslim society has deviated from the Shahada, bringing about the elevation of false gods and the replacement of His precepts with man-made laws. But what specifically causes this degeneration varies with time: First, the colonial domination of Christian Britain, then the adoption of French legal codes and the secularist abolition of the Caliphate, later nationalism and its elevation of leaders to godlike status, and, more recently, assaults by crusaderism, Zionism, communism, and others hostile to Islam.

Based on this interpretation, Islamist leaders concluded that in order to overcome this crisis of ignorance and deviation from the Right Path, the movement must strive to re-establish both God's sovereignty over Muslim practices and the fierce unity and monotheism of Muslim belief. This means, primarily, to reinstitute divine *Shari'a* law and to abolish all that is worshipped besides God. Exactly how these goals are to be achieved varies, however, and herein lie a number of different approaches that lead to organisational distinctions within the Islamic movement. These different approaches can all be grouped under the rubric of jihad, but then it is no longer possible to define jihad as just 'holy struggle'. Jihad is not just the violent or militant implementation of correct Islamic practice and belief, although this is certainly one important approach. Instead I prefer to define jihad as 'activism' and then to distinguish three types: *Jihad bi al-qalb*, or 'activism of the heart'; *jihad bi al-kilma*, or 'activism of words'; and *jihad bi al-haraka*, or 'jihad of action', of proper deeds and achievements as well as violence and militancy.[34]

Thus the Islamic movement includes a wide range of participants and activists based on which tactics they choose to implement their goals. Not all Muslims are even in the movement, and instead may follow modern, secularised understandings of Islam, or pursue the more mystical teachings of Sufism.[35] Of those who identify with the movement, the vast majority advocate a jihad of the heart, where personal practices, beliefs, and identity are subjectively but privately reoriented in order to conform to the movement's definition of what is correct.

A much smaller number go further and advocate *da'wa*, or preaching in missionary fashion, implementing a *jihad bi al-kilma* to achieve the movement's aims though an educational approach. These moderates advocate a gradual realisation of correct practice and belief, perform good deeds and pious acts, and provide a 'demonstration effect' of what proper Muslims should be like. Radicals

Islamists, however, call for more immediate results. The difference between *kilma* and extreme *haraka* is similar to that between reform and revolution. When jihad by action (or sword) involves violence and armed struggle, then radicals become militants, often discouraged by the slow pace of establishing God's sovereignty through *da'wa*, or disillusioned when religious deeds and projects are destroyed by police action.

The Underdevelopment of Southern Egypt

The recent growth of the Islamic movement has been particularly intense in the Sa'id. From 1994 to 2000, I conducted anthropological fieldwork in one of the area's major cities,[36] which had already become a notorious hotbed of Islamic radicalism and militancy. Actual field research into radical and militant Islam is rare, for obvious security reasons.[37] Here, I capitalised on an informal network of old friends, acquired while managing an international programme of community development in the mid-1980s. Because of tight state security, the research remained somewhat restricted. Nevertheless, I was able to delineate the contours of this religious movement and the government's response to it. I should in fact say 'movements' here, in the plural, for here, as elsewhere, the Islamic campaign was not homogenous but contained a profusion of small, local, uncoordinated, autonomous associations. In the process of interviews and informal discussions, certain patterns emerged that cast a new light on the shape and substance of this well-known but not well-understood religious campaign.

The Sa'id is less developed than the rest of Egypt—not only compared to Cairo and the urban provinces but even when measured against the Delta.[38] For example, while the Sa'id is more urban than the Delta, with a higher proportion of its population in cities and towns, it has fewer people actually engaged in industrial production. Its urban areas, then, become centres for commerce and services—value-added, but not value-created—as villagers migrate from a prevailing pattern of estate and large-plot farm production that contrasts sharply with the peasant arrangements found farther north. Of those Sa'idis remaining in the countryside, a far greater proportion work just in agriculture rather than engaging in the wider variety of non-farm occupations available within the Delta.[39]

Moreover, the Sa'idi population is more distant from Cairo, Alexandria, and the Canal Zone cities, and more dependent on the smaller cities and towns located within the region. In fact, while many Egyptians from the Delta commute to their urban worksites while still residing in their villages, Sa'idis are forced to move permanently in order to access urban employment.

Reinforcing this physical and economic distance, Sa'idi mythology claims this region has long remained outside Cairo's purview, whereas the Delta has been subdued for a longer time. The perennial irrigation known for centuries in the

Delta came more slowly to the Sa'id. The Sa'id remained more tribal, clannish, and conservative whereas the more flexible nuclear family became the norm much earlier in the north.[40]

The Sa'id also displays a pattern of sectarian distribution different from the rest of the country. In the Sa'id, the Coptic population is much larger and more rural than in the Delta.[41] It is said that when the Muslim general Amr ibn al-'As conquered Egypt in 640, he ordered the Copts into the cities. This command was, by and large, implemented in the Delta, but never to the same degree in the south. The result is that in the Sa'id, the Copts represent a more visible and more conservative community. This ensured that inter-faith hostility was not likely to be absent.

Thus the Sa'id is socially, economically, and politically remote, if not downright isolated, from the rest of the country. Like elsewhere, this south, too, has developed at a slower pace, and is even perceived as being slower, a southern drawl if you will, that stigmatises it as intellectually and culturally backward. Pejorative Sa'idi jokes fill the repertoire of most Cairene comedians. Most of the Sa'idi jokes I know were told me by Sa'idis themselves. They point to both the stigma and the pride that Sa'idi identity endures.

Since the rise of the regional petro-economy after 1974, skilled workers and white-collar employees in towns and cities along the southern Nile valley emigrated abroad much sooner and in greater proportion than those from the rest of the country. But the larger share of Sa'idis working in Libya, Saudi Arabia, the Gulf, and Iraq made their return after the 1985 oil-price drop even more problematic: Local labourers bumped out by repatriates did not return to their villages, nor did they easily find new jobs in cities.[42] Thus poverty became much more acute in the south than in the rest of the country. In the early 1990s, the number of those Sa'idis living below the poverty line reached as high as 40 per cent.[43]

Meanwhile, state budgets and investments had consistently neglected the Sa'id. IMF pressure reduced government spending even further. Then, as reports of government corruption and dishonesty multiplied, many Sa'idis saw this depleting what little was left for services and development. Endemic poverty combined with smaller budgets, discrimination, and improbity generated an outrage against injustice that pauperism alone could not have provoked, and led to a higher incidence of social turmoil in the south in the 1980s. Even so, by the early 1990s, this unrest had begun to spread to the rest of Egypt.

The Rise of an Islamic Movement

The Islamic associations found throughout the Sa'id were outgrowths of university campus organisations that had arisen in the 1970s. They first grew out of the requirement, I was told, to practice a more devout and pious Islam by providing development, charity, and guidance to those in need. But their popular appeal and success seriously alarmed Egypt's government and threatened the routine way it operated. Unwilling or unable to change, the administration instead sought to eliminate this challenge. As state persecution and government corruption deepened, the battle to establish a moral campaign based on Islam intensified.

Those who found these radical Islamist associations appealing and inspiring fell into two social classes that had both experienced the dislocation of rural-to-urban migration:[44] Middle-class professionals and working-class indigents.

The middle-class Islamists I met were, generally, university students from rural farm families who had benefited from the new free education policies implemented by the 'Abd al-Nassir administration in the 1960s, and had since graduated to an uncertain urban job market. These included well-educated but nonetheless frustrated white-collar professionals[45] who were highly motivated and accomplished; among the best and brightest students in their class; but also the first-time college students in their families. Bereft of the family connections and parlour mannerisms of upper-class urban Egyptians, they achieved their brilliance through hard work and demonstrated merit. Many had participated in the state-supported campus Islamic associations of the 1970s.

On graduation, however, these students from the stigmatised south discovered that despite their costly education—dearly paid for not only in money but also in the personal sacrifice of their families—the road to gaining better professional employment and achieving higher class status that leads inevitably to the capital was essentially blocked by the ascriptive wall of elite Cairene society. Frustrated when wealthy family connections took precedence over merit, they migrated to Libya, Iraq, and the Gulf to acquire the better incomes unavailable at home.

However, after 1985, when regional oil revenues began to decline, these professionals returned home to the Sa'id. They reactivated the piety and spirituality learned during their college days and reinforced while working abroad. They chose to emulate the life of the Prophet Muhammad, to grow beards and dress in white robes, and to perform charitable acts and good deeds. But they also remained thwarted in their quest for upward mobility, and therefore they channelled their frustration into mobilising an equally discontented ex-rural working class. The tone was one of moral outrage; their adversary became those corrupted by opportunism and contact with Western authorities.[46]

Those who followed these middle-class leaders included disgruntled members of the working class employed irregularly in construction, services, and informal businesses.[47] As ex-rural workers coming from a depressed agricultural sector, they had had to migrate from the village to the city but were still unable to change the misfortunes and hardship caused by Egypt's faltering economy.[48]

Constrained by high prices, low wages, and unemployed kin, they came to rely heavily on the largesse of private benefactors to get them through tight times.

Proletarianisation and rural-to-urban migration had been taking place in Egypt for some time, but in the 1970s, this process accelerated rapidly after the seven years of economic stagnation following the Six Day War.[49] This exodus was not so much a torrent of rural workers and ex-peasants moving abroad as an immense flow into urban communities to replace those who did emigrate. Yet, after 1985, fewer skilled urban workers travelled abroad, and those who did came home sooner. Back in the Sa'id, they mixed with their unskilled colleagues who had never emigrated, and both groups sought work in an informal sector whose investments were already declining.

These ex-rural workers and ex-rural professionals became strongly linked through the pervasive mutuality of paternalism—the favours and privileges that workers first get from employers in exchange for services and commitments.[50] These reciprocal, personalised relations were first forged in the countryside, and later, when employment shifted to the city, they enabled patrons to maintain a readily available workforce and allowed clients to guarantee future employment opportunities.[51] These loyalties were then readily transferred to other benefactors even when they appeared outside the actual labour process, so that critical services from middle-class professional patrons were exchanged for faithful support from working-class client beneficiaries.

They both joined religious associations that re-created and reinforced the intimacy of an imagined but bygone village community. Middle-class village students attending urban universities for the first time in the history of their families were unfamiliar with the impersonality of large campuses, crowded classrooms, and indifferent professors. Rural workers moving into the city and finding employment in construction crews, workshops, and services were unaccustomed to the detached bureaucracy of government offices and large companies, and the rapid transactions of commercial exchange. This shared sentiment and uncertainty drove both groups into the more familiar, intimate surroundings of the Islamic associations. These contrasted sharply with urban organisations such as professional syndicates, labour unions, and political parties whose anonymity and coldness alienated these potential members. Instead, these impersonal—and secular—organisations attracted the urban-born activist.[52]

Yet, ironically, the doctrines of these religious associations were not the same as those which these villagers had left behind. Village Islam had been textured by the passive and tolerant quietism of Sufism, saint shrines, and miracles. Urban Islamist associations rejected such 'superstition', and instead exhibited the indignant political activism of Salafiyism, legalism, and self-righteousness.[53] The shift from rural to urban had been paralleled by a transformation from 'traditional' to 'modern'. However, this was not a secular modernity based on the

European Enlightenment but rather a religious one inherited from the doctrines of Muhammad Abduh, Hasan al-Banna, and Sayyid Qutb.

Very few of these associations ever reached the violent intensity practiced by such well-known organisations as al-Jihad or al-Jama'a al-Islamiya.[54] Instead, most enthusiasts embraced a non-militant religiosity that advocated performing good deeds and pious acts on the one hand, and bestowing devout blessings and grateful loyalty on the other. Their militancy, if it came, would arise later. Hostile action required shifting to formally organised militant associations like al-Jihad or al-Jama'a al-Islamiya.

Since the start of skilled labour emigration abroad after 1971, many devout, university-trained professionals remitted their ample salaries home and allocated a significant portion toward performing Islamic pious acts, and funding community development and charity projects. In the early 1980s, such financing increased with the profit-sharing and monetary transactions routed through Islamic investment companies. Moreover, supervision by like-minded colleagues over the religious *zakat* (Islamic alms or tithes) donations to local private mosques guaranteed that the bulk of these contributions reached those in need.[55]

Islamic investment companies appealed to devout Egyptian Muslims because they applied the principles of Islamic finance. They were also attractive because they earned higher rates of return than regular banks. Islamic companies operated on the basis of Islamic commercial law, similar to the profit-sharing of a small private stock exchange or mutual fund. Depositors did not receive interest, which is forbidden in Islam, but instead shared the profit or loss incurred on money-making activities.[56] Since dividends, when paid, were not technically a form of interest, they were not subject to strict state regulation. In the mid-1980s, depositors were receiving shares that, when computed as rates of return, earned dividends as high as 25 per cent annually—twice what the public banks offered.[57] Together, both individual and company donations generated ample funds that were used to finance numerous community development projects implemented through recipient mosques by local Islamic associations.

The quantity and quality of these small development projects far outweighed the meagre efforts of government programmes, or even the lavishly funded attempts by state-authorised foreign agencies. In 1985, while directing a US-based community development programme in the Sa'id, I attended a regional conference of local development organisations that revealed the large proportion of Islamic efforts. Of thirty participating agencies, three were foreign-funded. The rest consisted of privately financed local associations that operated on a very small scale and budget, but had a very high success rate. These associations provided hospital beds for the poor, low-cost health clinics, affordable housing, after-school tutoring, complimentary textbooks, clothing exchanges, veterinarian services, small-scale business assistance and low-cost credit, and guidance through the labyrinthine state bureaucracy for permits, licenses, and tax abatements. All of these constituted critically important services that the government in Cairo simply could not, or would not, provide.[58]

Nor was the foreign community any more successful, despite its ample resources. Most foreign development agencies (NGOs) were located in the Sa'id. Very few operated in the Delta, although a few programmes were active in the poorer neighbourhoods of Cairo. Placing these NGOs in the south had not simply been a serendipitous decision by government officials in Cairo: These agencies seemingly offered impressive showcase examples of secular development in a region where the alternative was strongly identified with Islam. But, since secular foreign operations like the one I managed lacked the political insight and clout necessary to successfully implement their programmes, the smaller but more astute Islamic organisations were much more effective.

The vast scope of these Islamic development activities, subsumed under the name of good deeds and pious acts, delivered a wide range of social benefits otherwise considered the duty of the state. For example, by the early 1990s, government schools here had become so ineffective that many parents who had foregone family income to give their children an education were forced to sacrifice even more by enrolling them in after-school tutorial programmes that might improve their chances for better scores on the Thanawiya 'Amma examination.[59] In order to provide better instruction, a number of Islamic associations built and operated five private, comprehensive schools. In a separate project, fifteen devout Muslim teachers joined under the auspices of the Jama'iya al-Da'wa al-Islamiya[60] to offer private lessons at a nominal cost.

Other associations had similar projects. A group of Muslim doctors, pharmacists, and clinicians established the Jama'iya al-Muhamadiya al-Islamiya and staffed an Islamic clinic. In 1994, they charged a £E3 fee for examinations, treatment, and prescriptions when other doctors were charging £E15 for examinations alone. They also admitted patients "regardless of what was on their wrist"—a reference to the Coptic custom of etching a cross on their lower arm—an indication that the clinic was open to both Christians and Muslims. Jama'iya al-Tawhid wa al-Nur al-Khairiya built an entire dormitory near the local university campus for rural students. Jama'iya al-Huda al-Khairiya added a twenty-four-bed wing to one of the city's private hospitals reserved exclusively for indigent patients. Every month, the Jama'iya al-Sahwa al-Islamiya distributed clothes, food, textbooks, and prescription medicines to neighbourhood families. These charitable activities provided a wide range of services otherwise unavailable from large government or foreign offices. Many of the latter's activities, despite sophisticated planning, deteriorated from mismanagement and improper funding, while those undertaken in the name of Islamic charity continued for as long as their endowment remained viable and their donors free.

The Sa'id was not alone in receiving Islamic philanthropy. In October 1992, an earthquake caused unusual devastation throughout Egypt, including Cairo. When the populace recovered from its shock, shelter, clothing, and food were foremost on people's minds. Yet the government was particularly slow in providing aid. Local Islamic organisations, on the other hand, rushed immediately to the stricken areas to deliver material assistance. Government officials defended their delay by pointing out that they needed time to investigate all the requests since many petitioners would present fraudulent claims. The Islamic groups, however, had little need to investigate supplicants since they felt that few would lie before God.[61] Observers I talked to noted that both sides were probably correct.

A year later, when a long-term instability brought about by the earthquake caused large mud slides beneath the Muqattam hills east of the capital, government troops were ordered to assist the victims without delay, worried that another public relations blunder would help expand the influence of the Islamic opposition. The state then declared private aid and assistance illegal except through the Egyptian Red Crescent.[62] This effectively eliminated any Islamic philanthropy.

All these Islamic achievements clearly surpassed government and foreign undertakings in people's minds. Poor Egyptians gained tangible benefits from such programmes, unlike from the ineffective efforts of government offices or international agencies, which mostly served the middle-class bureaucrats who staffed them. It was clear to me from visiting these projects and associations, and talking to their staff and members, that these professionals were Muslims seriously committed to easing the lives of those they served.

The religious benefactors who helped the poor and needy benefited in turn from the allegiance they won from doing so. The devotion and loyalty these workers were accustomed to bestowing on their patrons in the workplace flowed beyond the worksite, and even spilled over from the evening-school lessons and the medical check-ups, to embrace the realm of radical activism within and outside the community. Whether these devout but déclassé professionals participated legally in community politics or unlawfully in militant action, their supporters found it easy to transfer their paternal loyalty to them.

When Islamist technocrats entered political contests in numerous provincial-, city-, town-, and district-level election campaigns and partisan appointments, they received overwhelming support and loyalty from those they had once assisted. When pious but alienated professionals exhorted their followers to berate and attack the government for its fiscal corruption, which had eliminated social services, working-class clients obliged and joined them to actively promote their agenda, and to establish what they saw as a virtuous and honest administration. So, when the burning question turned to radically refashioning what many saw as a profoundly corrupt and dishonest government, the fundamental reply simply became 'Islam'.

After 1985, permanent labour repatriation, steady decreases in overseas remittances, and the government crackdown on Islamic investment companies generated major declines in funding for vital services. As the government took over local private mosques and appointed new clerics,[63] it did more than just silence oppositional preachers. Before such takeovers, the local finance committees of private mosques, composed of educated, middle-class members, decided how the *zakat* donations were to be distributed. However, once the state controlled these mosques, I was told, it deposited most *zakat* donations into government banks and decided where the little that remained was to be distributed, frequently resulting in a precipitous decline in financing local social services.

Then, when the state reduced its budget, especially in social services, under pressure from IMF bailouts, many Sa'idis felt particularly upset and indignant. They felt even more powerless and frustrated when the political system prevented them from even voicing their concerns or further pressuring officials for better treatment.

A number of Sa'idis told me that a legal, religious-based political party could contain the angry and disaffected factions of young, provincial white-collar professionals and ex-rural workers. What they envisioned was an Islamic party that paralleled the Christian Democratic parties in Germany and Italy. Yet, so long as the Egyptian government denied this movement a legitimate channel for influencing state policy, they argued, the more its collective alienation would turn to unlawful acts of violence.

Nationally, political participation remained limited, continuing a government policy that had begun shortly after the July 1952 revolution. One of the first edicts issued by the new republican government was to abolish political parties, seeing them as both corrupt remnants of a decaying monarchy as well as likely avenues of counter-revolution. Egypt then witnessed a number of one-party organisations to mobilise and lead the country towards greater development, culminating in the Arab Socialist Union (ASU).[64]

Immediately after the Corrective Revolution of May 1971, al-Sadat reorganised the ASU in order to make it less threatening. But the triumph of the October 1973 war gave him a wider latitude, previously unimaginable. In April 1974, he proposed major modifications in the ASU that essentially expelled recalcitrant factions—workers, peasants, students, academics, and their advocates—who opposed his new Open Door policy.[65] Since the state was abandoning the public sector and relying instead on private-sector investments to generate jobs, profits, and commodities, those segments harmed by this new policy who might protest and raise objections could prove embarrassing to the administration. This would also displease Cairo's benefactor, the United States, which had insisted not only on opening Egypt's trade door to the West but also on erecting a US American-style, party-based democracy. By implementing a multiparty system, the administration won acclaim from Washington and still effectively silenced all but the most agreeable opposition.

Since they were too large to be censured outright, these troublesome factions were muzzled by affiliating them with new political parties too weak to influence government policies and operations. Before the 1952 revolution, politics had been permeated by patron-client relations, but during the period of one-party organisations, this paternalism had ceased. It now reappeared, such that political success once again depended on displaying the right, servile deference to access powerful government officials. Those not in the new ruling party were denied such access and therefore neutralised. So silenced, many members of the underclass who had previously spoken out through various ASU departments (*amanat*) were no longer able to bring attention to their critical conditions.

Then, throughout the late 1980s and 1990s, the growing political gap between elite secular parties and frustrated provincial professionals and the unorganised urban working classes was filled in the Sa'id by local Islamic associations that posed a serious challenge to the state.

In 1992 the government and its secular supporters mounted a major campaign against the Islamists who openly threatened its complacent and comfortable position underwritten by what activists saw as fraud and corruption. Already religious opponents dominated an impressive number of formal professional and university organisations. But discontent from the bottom of the social pyramid was beginning to incite the unorganised and provoke even greater turmoil throughout the Sa'id and even in Cairo. The government responded defensively but ruthlessly,[66] with arrests and detention, extra-judicial executions and torture, and official denunciations. Compromise seemed unthinkable.

Providing good deeds, charitable acts, and material welfare seemed far removed from senseless demagoguery or wanton terrorism. Indeed, the spiritual attitude and religious demeanour of the devout professionals I met appeared beyond reproach. Yet, the accumulative effects of constant government arrest, torture, and humiliation in the Sa'id, I was told, pushed pious activists across the thin line that had separated them from those committed to mayhem.

Such a transition from pacifism to militancy sometimes seemed more a response to state persecution than due to any planned strategy for violence. The situation in Mallawi, a district town in the southern province of al-Minya, illustrates how good intentions changed into destruction.[67] In 1991, al-Jama'a al-Islamiya—and here it is difficult to distinguish between the generic term and the specific organisational offshoot of al-Jihad[68]—began as a non-political charitable association. At first its relationship with the local government was benign as its religious education and material welfare programmes hardly constituted crimes. In May 1994, however, local security forces arrested two prominent members of the association and, while no mention of police misconduct was reported, the association's leader, Rajab 'Abd al-Hakim, was provoked enough to warn security officers to stop interfering with the group's activities. A month later, security forces "stormed Abdel Hakim's house and shot him". He died that evening in hospital. Three months later, association members attacked the local police headquarters, launching what became a small civil war.[69] Throughout 1994 and 1995, Mallawi remained under strict martial law and a harsh twelve-hour curfew. What had once been harmless good deeds and charitable acts had been transformed into militancy and bloodshed.[70]

Throughout the Sa'id, men wearing full beards and white robes, and women in the dark *naqab*, the complete Islamic covering, were routinely arrested, questioned, tortured perhaps, and humiliated. Homes of suspected militants were bombed and burned. Few Sa'idi militants came to trial—such luxury was reserved mostly for their more prominent Cairene counterparts—but instead were either fatally shot in police crossfire or jailed indefinitely without appearing in court.[71] Many families became heartbroken and terrified by such government action. Neighbourhoods became divided, sympathising with those whose piety had earned them great admiration, frightened, however, that their sympathy might make them suspect as well. Anger swelled, and, in response, many acts of police misconduct were repaid by outraged relatives—not through organised retribution but by individual acts of revenge. That most religious violence erupted in the Sa'id may be more a testimony to this region's 'tribal' practice of seeking revenge for the dishonour of family members—*al-th'ar*—than to an exceptional concentration of state force.[72] Police misconduct also occurred in Cairo, Alexandria, and the Delta, but without this remnant of tribal tradition, such acts elsewhere went unavenged.

Thus Islamic radicals took up the cause of opposing what they saw as the ignorance, corruption, and injustice committed by the government and its representatives. Pushed to the extreme, they crafted an ideology based on religion that justified what the state called terrorism, but what the militants called holy combat against abuse and persecution. Based on the writings of Sayyid Qutb, Muhammad 'Abd al-Salam Faraj, Umar 'Abd al-Rahman,[73] and others, a militant Islam arose that appealed to those harshly persecuted for enacting the compassion decreed by the basic tenets of their religion.

Of course, not all attacks against government forces were merely individual acts of retaliation. Nor were they simply reactions provoked by the police harassment of otherwise blameless non-militant Islamic radicals. Informants reported that there may well have been clear cases of organised, intentional violence, perhaps even funded by foreign governments and sympathetic collaborators from outside Egypt.[74] Firearms and ammunition certainly flooded the Sa'id, yet this was not altogether new since old tribal vendettas, antedating the rise of Islamic militancy, had once required such weapons.[75] Nevertheless, a significant portion of the violence that erupted in southern Egypt, it seemed to me, happened first in resisting arrest by those who desired just to practice their faith in a more devout and concrete way, and, second, in retaliation for the abuse and suffering that occurred when these pious Muslims were taken into police custody.

The Stir Spreads

Immediately after the October 1992 earthquake, as religious violence began erupting in the Cairene suburb of Imbaba—which state security had deemed a 'state within a state' for assuming many of the functions of government otherwise unavailable to local residents—the government chose to mount a full-scale military attack against the Islamists.

In an ironic sense, Imbaba and nearby neighbourhoods, such as al-Munira al-Gharbiya, had experienced 'reverse colonialism', as Sa'idis had migrated north to carve out impoverished replicas of their homeland.[76] Then, because the government was unable or unwilling to provide social and welfare services here, Islamic development activities emanating from local mosques filled the gap with schools, clinics, and workshops, much as they had done back home.[77] This assistance then served as a base for further mobilising residents to a programme of Islamic ethics and social justice that contrasted greatly with what were considered the decadent surroundings of unscrupulous wealth and secular power. The state claimed that Islamist leaders incited followers to attack cinemas, nightclubs, hotels, and other instances of moral corruption, like bawdy weddings or unveiled women. It also accused them of such crimes as petty theft, drug trafficking, and extortion.

To crush the Islamic movement in Imbaba, the government ordered 15,000 troops to "invade" this Islamist semi-state on December 8 1992, declaring war against al-Jama'a al-Islamiya which had, according to officials, "seized control of the district", and the government intended to "take it back".[78]

> The police broke into the houses of suspected militants, destroying the possessions inside. Dozens of Imbaba residents were arrested off the streets merely because their beards and Islamic dress looked suspicious. The wives, mothers, and sisters of wanted militants were arrested and detained for up to a month at a time. They complained of being tortured at the Imbaba police station and ordered to strip naked before giving forced confessions for crimes they had never committed. Children between eight and fifteen years old were beaten by security police aiming to coerce information from them about their wanted relatives.[79]

The 'Battle of Imbaba' all but silenced militant Islamists, leaving the field (in Cairo at least) to apolitical moderates who aspired simply to establish (or re-establish) neighbourhood services but who shunned the popular mobilisation for radical programmes. This siege may well have been the last gasp of organised Islamic militancy, at least domestically. It would, thereafter, rise to new heights (or sink to new depths), but outside Egypt's borders and far from the immediate problems of state corruption and injustice. Shortly after the government withdrew from Imbaba, followers of Shaykh Umar Abd al-Rahman in New York City attempted to topple the World Trade Center (February 26 1993). Two years later, on June 26 1995, al-Jama'a attempted to assassinate President Mubarak in Addis Ababa, Ethiopia. And six months after that, the Egyptian embassy in Islamabad, Pakistan, was truck-bombed.

Only on one more occasion did Islamic militancy rear its ugly head inside the country, when six men killed fifty-eight tourists and four Egyptian guards at the Pharaonic sites in Luxor, and it was not clear if this was by order or from disorder. That is, was attacking foreigners a new strategic policy for devastating Egypt's tourist economy, or was it, as many claimed, a confusion between foreign-based, prison-based, or locally based leaders? Since such horror, however, concerted Islamist attacks have ceased.

This has not stopped the government from arresting its opponents, primarily from the more staid Muslim Brotherhood, nor has it discouraged prison-based leaders from both al-Jihad and al-Jama'a al-Islamiya from declaring a "unilateral and unconditional cease-fire".[80]

But the field of battle had shifted. And while the militants' goals and objectives had not changed, there were fewer now willing to achieve them. Perhaps this was due to arrest, perhaps to simple exhaustion, or perhaps it was merely a lull, the eye of a hurricane. Or, conceivably, there was the growing realisation that such efforts were a waste, given the international political and economic forces of the times. A more thoughtful analysis might have produced a much more wide-ranging approach.

From among the hundreds of Sa'idis who were arrested in Imbaba and elsewhere that year,[81] a significant but unknown proportion crossed the line from non-violence to militancy. Further, arrests and mistreatment intimidated and silenced many among those who participated in Islamic development associations. As successful programmes and services closed for lack of funds and authorisation, the government did nothing to compensate by providing its own. This, in turn, provoked even more anger and anxieties among those who had benefited from these charitable acts. Many said that the termination of these religiously charged development projects had made life even more difficult and precarious for the working classes.

Yet state policies continued to generate poverty and anger at the bottom, and corruption and opportunism at the top, which together eroded the state's ability to sustain solid economic growth and wore down its legitimacy in creating a national consensus. Increasingly, the state's security forces were called upon to buoy up the government's sagging authority. The Islamic opposition, unable to share power and peacefully alter the current configuration of economic policies and policy-makers, turned instead to more militant means to achieve its political goals.

Globalising the Islamic Movement

On September 11 2001, Islamism viciously and violently catapulted itself to the top of the agenda of the US. Nineteen Muslim members of a shadowy Islamist organisation known before only for a few scattered attacks outside the US now burst upon the US scene and burned their version of militant Islam into the minds of somnambulant US Americans. Usama bin Ladin's al-Qa'ida network was a spin-off of the umbrella group, the World Islamic Front for Jihad Against Jews and Crusaders. The Front combined a number of disparate and desperate national organisations such as al-Jihad and al-Jama'a al-Islamiya from Egypt, the Armed Islamic Group from Algeria, the Ulama Association of Pakistan, and an assortment of other freelance militants and militant groups from Sudan, Morocco, Saudi Arabia, Yemen, and Somalia. First it established a base of operation in Afghanistan and then raised a counterattack against the paradoxically godless and godlike United States. As we know, they commandeered four aircraft and piloted two of them into the World Trade Center in New York City and a third into the Pentagon in Washington DC. The fourth apparently crashed prematurely in the Pennsylvania countryside.

September 11 was not the first attack by al-Qa'ida. The organisation was also held responsible for the August 7 1998 attack on US embassies in Kenya and Tanzania. Earlier, constituent groups had also conducted daring attacks against what they considered enemy targets. Al-Jama'a had been held responsible for the massacre of tourists in Luxor, in Egypt, in November 1977; an aborted attack on Greek tourists in April 1996; a suicide truck-bombing of the Egyptian embassy in Pakistan in November 1995; an attempted assassination of Egyptian President Mubarak in Addis Ababa, Ethiopia, in June 1995; and at least eight minor attacks in Cairo and southern Egypt from 1993 to 1995. The Egyptian al-Jihad also mounted assaults, more against government officials than against the tourists targeted by al-Jama'a. It has also been held responsible for the first attempted attack against the World Trade Center in February, 1993.[82]

The roots of September 11 go back to 1979, when two important events took place just a month apart and, although thousands of miles from each other, ultimately became strongly joined together and to the US. In November 1979 the Grand Mosque of Mecca was taken over by Saudi militants disgruntled by the moral corruption of the ruling regime despite its austere Wahhabi Islam.[83] In December, the Soviet Union sent troops to Afghanistan upon invitation by the ruling party, the People's Democratic Party. What connected these two events was one person: Usama bin Ladin.

Shortly after the Soviet Union entered Afghanistan, bin Ladin moved from his native Saudi Arabia to Peshawar on Pakistan's northwest frontier. For the next ten years he set about bankrolling and then actively leading a jihad against the USSR. Using his family's resources amassed through lucrative construction contracts with the Saudi state, bin Ladin financed the building of schools and shelters for Afghan refugees in Pakistan. His role soon shifted, however. In 1986, he and Abdalla Azzam, the Jordanian representative and recruiter for the Muslim Brotherhood in Pakistan, defeated a Soviet military operation in the village of Jaji, an event that is now a legend in the chronicles of the war. Bin Ladin began attracting a personal following of fighters, financed through family money, Muslim charitable donations, official Saudi finance, and US funds funnelled through Pakistani intelligence agents. Huband reports that after the Battle of Jaji, the number of Afghan Arabs jumped from 300 to around 7,000.[84]

Bin Ladin returned to Saudi Arabia a hero and a recruiter of more *mujahidin* fighters. His success on the lecture circuit was interrupted, however, by the 1990 Gulf War. Bin Ladin's fervent and outspoken opposition to basing US troops in his country forced him to flee to Sudan in 1991. There he stayed as a businessman and militant organiser until the US forced Sudan to evict him in 1996. He then returned to Afghanistan.

The Soviets withdrew in 1989 and the government it supported fell three years later. For the next five years, various Afghan factions fought a deadly civil war to capture control of the state. First Gulbeddin Hekmatyar, and later Burhanuddin Rabbani, presided over little more than poverty, chaos, and a weak factional army. They were more than outmatched by the well-financed, well-armed civilian army of Afghan refugees from Pakistan, the Taliban. In 1996, when bin Ladin returned to Afghanistan, the Taliban took control of Kabul and declared Afghanistan an Islamic emirate. The leader of the Taliban, Muhammad Umar Akund, and bin Ladin soon became partners in furthering their Islamist political agenda. Although the principal focus of the programme was defeating the Northern Alliance and subduing local tribes, a small contingent of zealous fighters were trained specifically to extend this jihad to global proportions.

There seems to be quite some distance between Mallawi and Rajab 'Abd al-Hakim—as mentioned before—and the World Trade Center, the Pentagon, and Usama bin Ladin. Given what we know about the very local nature of Islamic militancy in southern Egypt, how can we explain this sudden international prominence? A number of models have attempted to explain this complex shift. Here, I wish to explore these different accounts. No one single model is absolutely correct; a combination of all these versions seems the best overall answer.

Perhaps the most attractive explanation is that bin Ladin and al-Qa'ida represent the globalisation of militant Islam.[85] Bin Ladin himself appears as the Manichaean antithesis of today's George Soros, not so much because bin Ladin challenged capitalism (he did not), but because both men generated devastating world-scale consequences, though of opposite valorisation, as the tentacles of their capitalist financial dealings reached out well beyond the personal and national borders that physically contained them. Similarly, but organisationally, al-Qa'ida becomes the contemporary equivalent of the Abraham Lincoln Brigade that operated in the 1930s in the Spanish Civil War. Like the brigade, al-Qa'ida attracted volunteers from all over the Muslim world to converge on Afghanistan, a magnet for those thirsting for adventure, purpose, and employment. In its heyday in the 1980s, and particularly after 1986, when US funds channelled through Saudi Arabia and Pakistan were plentiful, bin Ladin and his jihad against the Soviet Union proved rather successful. "In the 1980s, the war in Afghanistan enjoyed fervent, almost giddy support across the Arab world, inspiring poetry, song and glowing accounts of courage and bravery in the name of Islam".[86]

Perhaps it was too successful, for it continued to attract adherents well after the Soviets admitted defeat in 1989 and went home. Thereafter, the Afghan Arabs grafted themselves on to the more indigenous Taliban, and together they carved out a government and state limited only by a parcel of territory in the northwest still controlled by the Northern Alliance. As with many other groups trained to incite mayhem, the Afghan Arabs radicalised once they lost their raison d'être, much like US-trained Cubans after the Bay of Pigs. Many analysts employ the term 'blowback' to describe the reversal as al-Qa'ida members shifted their gunsights from the Soviets to the US.

But perhaps this simplistic volte-face is far too mechanical and therefore suspect. After all, why wouldn't jihadists just declare victory and go home, much less decide to bite the hand that fed (and financed) them? Another explanation, then, would be to see al-Qa'ida's mandate as a reflection of a home-grown anger and resentment that had become diverted from local concerns to suspected collaborators beyond national boundaries. "Frustrated by repression at home, bleak economies and a helplessness bred by the close watch of security forces, they went to Afghanistan to take a place on the front line of a war for Islam".[87]

Thus, even as Islamic associations were crushed in Egypt, Algeria, Palestine, and Saudi Arabia, their members popped up in Afghanistan with renewed zeal and more intense anger. In a sense, then, this becomes a hydraulic model: Pushed down 'there', militancy popped up 'here'. Al-Qa'ida appears, then, the outcome of Middle East governments being all too successful in stamping out domestic religious militancy. Many Islamists, of course, were arrested and jailed; some were killed, and others simply dropped out and returned to 'civilian' life. A fourth cluster, however—perhaps the most zealous and vehement of all—disappeared underground and escaped the country. Stripped of all perspective and sense of community, they turned to the only organisation left open. Then, it is not difficult to imagine militants condemning the only remaining superpower for supporting and even encouraging the shortcomings of their own comprador governments. As bin Ladin noted later, why waste time with attacking autocratic Arab governments or even Israel, "the Zionist entity", when striking the US at its core could be more effective?

These two models assume, then, a straight extrapolation from the horrors of Mallawi to the terrors of Kandahar. But it would be folly to assume that these account for all Islamists, particularly those who stayed home. Two other models provide a more nuanced perspective of a globalising Islamic movement. Anthony Shadid[88] employed a Durkheimian maturation model whereby militant organisations develop an increasingly more sophisticated programme. The trajectory he envisioned went from militancy to welfare to participation in the formal political system. Shadid offered Lebanon's Hezbollah as an archetype; the Palestinian Hamas and the Egyptian Muslim Brotherhood also come to mind. Thus al-Qa'ida and its constituents appear as stunted organisations, retarded in their development by their incapacity to achieve local goals but also limited by the regional politics of Arab authoritarianism and Israeli intimidation from growing into 'mature' democratic associations.

But the Muslim Brotherhood and its history in Egypt provides yet a fourth model. Its moderate leaders and members gained dominance in the organisation and marginalised the militants. The reasons for such marginalisation may be the arrest and death of militants, or the state's support of moderates. In any event, internal machinations within various militant organisations take advantage of a growing polarisation between radicals and moderates to oust the former and install the latter. Those who 'lose', however, do not simply sulk; instead, they leave to establish more militant offshoots that disagree as much with their former colleagues as with their declared enemies. The result is that even while the Muslim Brotherhood professed its desire to participate legally in Egyptian politics, its disaffected progeny stayed local or expanded internationally to wreak havoc on both its parent and its adversaries.

A final model is a variation of the last. It suggests that such moderation is not just an evolutionary outcome but the result of government manipulation. This becomes an *agent provocateur* thesis whereby the state surreptitiously encourages false radicals and demagogues whose subsequent faulty planning and implementation outrage others and discredit the movement. At the same time, the government may well placate moderates in order to buttress the latter's claims to authority within their organisation. The result is a weaker militant campaign but a stronger moderate organisation.

Thus we see a variety of different models that explain the transformation of Egypt's Islamist movement from a local campaign to a global crusade: Globalisation, Hydraulic, Immaturation, and Manipulation. But Usama bin Ladin does not simply reflect a distorted version of the demands of Egypt's al-Jihad or al-Jama'a al-Islamiya. In addition to ending support for Arab dictators, his other demands include ending the occupation of Islam's holy places—the US military presence in the Arabian peninsula and the Zionist-Israeli presence in Palestine. These, then, become a distillation, and hence a lower common denominator for militant movements from all over the Muslim world. At the same time, the anger that stokes such a global movement is still forged in individual states. Even as some moderate religious activists hope to integrate into the system—organising, perhaps, the local equivalent of the Christian Democratic parties that participate in Germany and Italy[89]—others have turned their backs on such secular modernity and continue to espouse their radical version of Islamic politics. Conspiracy theorists, remnants of the corporatist Nasserist state who remain ever cognisant of the government's involvement in all political machinations, see behind this evolution a marginalisation, exporting and globalising Cairo's desire to crush its domestic opponents even if this means shifting the struggle to other, external venues. Egypt's government is all too ready to join the war against terrorism—a war it had been waging well before September 11—and, in the process, to even teach the US a few lessons.

Conclusions

Since 1995, government repression in Egypt has prevailed and domestic militancy has gone into remission.[90] But it would be foolish to rule it out locally even as it erupts internationally. Government forces may have momentarily silenced the state's religious opponents, but they have not resolved the key economic, political, and ethical problems that gave rise to this movement in the first place. As long as there remains a shortage of good jobs and steady incomes, a narrow range of legitimate avenues for political dissent, and a desire for an honest and virtuous government, Islamic activists will continue to mount a jihad of the heart, tongue, and hand.

If those who undertake militant jihad constitute a small tip of a huge iceberg, then it also seems important to consider that mass of people lying below this tip, those ordinary Muslim men and women who live quite ordinary lives and have quite ordinary jobs and who, like the militants, also oppose the state and its corruption and injustices, but do not subscribe or resort to their violent methods and techniques. Although they condemn such tactics and pursue, instead, a jihad of words and good deeds, their grievances and goals strongly converge with those of a more militant persuasion.

Meanwhile, in the last two decades, as the world has become phenomenologically smaller,[91] with advances in communication and transport technology, local Islamic conflicts against secular opponents have been able to expand to envelope the entire global community. Local militants, pushed out by both government repression and moderate colleagues carried with them the anger and discontent fashioned at home, and took advantage of the political chaos of Central Asia to emerge as a global movement.

Today, the battle lines seem even more starkly drawn, with the US, Israel, and secular Middle East governments like Egypt on one side, and Islamic militants, ranging from the local urban neighbourhoods of southern Egypt to al-Qa'ida at a global scale, on the other. But while the contestants are clearly identified, the outcome is far less marked. It may well become the major clash of the twenty-first century.

References

Geneive Abdo, 2000—*No God but God: Egypt and the Triumph of Islam*. Oxford: Oxford University Press

Ziad Abu-Amr, 1994—*Islamic Fundamentalism in the West Bank and Gaza: Muslim Brotherhood and Islamic Jihad*. Bloomington: Indiana University Press

Ahmad Abu Zayd, 1965—*al-Th'ar: Dirasah Anthrupulujiyah bi-Ihda Qura al-Said*. Cairo: Dar al-Maarif

Hasan al-Banna, 1978—*Five Tracts of Hasan Al-Banna (1906–1949): A Selection from the Majmu'at Rasai'l al-Imam al-Shahid Hasan al-Banna*. Berkeley: University of California Press

Hamid Ansari, 1986—*Egypt: The Stalled Society*. Albany: State University of New York Press

Hasan Bakr, 1994—*al-'Unf al-Siyasi fi Misr: Asyut: Bura al-Tawtir: al-Asbab wa al-Duwafiya'* ['Political Violence in Egypt: Asyut as a Site of Tension—The Reasons and the Motives, 1987–93', in Arabic]. Cairo: Markaz al-Mahrusa li al-Bahuth wa al-Tadrib wa al-Nashr

Asef Bayat, 1988—'Revolution Without Movement, Movement Without Revolution: Comparing Islamic Activism in Iran and Egypt', in *Comparative Studies in Society and History*, vol 40 no 1

Asef Bayat, 1997—*Street Politics: Poor People's Movements in Iran*. New York: Columbia University Press

Jacob David Bleich, Spring 1983—'Preemptive War in Jewish Tradition', in *Tradition*, vol 21 no 1

Michael J Broyde, 1996—'Fighting the War and the Peace: Battlefield Ethics, Peace Talks, Treaties, and Pacifism in the Jewish Tradition', in J Patout Burns, ed, 1996—*War and Its Discontents: Pacifism and Quietism in the Abrahamaic Traditions*. Washington, DC: Georgetown University Press

François Burgat, 1997—*The Islamic Movement in North Africa*. Austin: University of Texas Press

CAPMAS (Central Agency of Public Mobilization and Statistics), 1978a—*The General Census of Residents and Residences, 1976. Population Census. Detailed Results.* Cairo: Arab Republic of Egypt

CAPMAS, 1978b—*Population and Development: A Study of the Population Increase and Its Challenge to Development in Egypt.* Cairo: Arab Republic of Egypt, September

CAPMAS, 1990—*Statistical Yearbook.* Cairo: Arab Republic of Egypt, June

Eric Davis, 1987—'The Concept of Revival and the Study of Islam and Politics', in Barbara Freyer Stowasser, ed, 1987—*The Islamic Impulse.* London: Croom Helm

R Hrair Dekmejian, 1995—*Islam in Revolution: Fundamentalism in the Arab World*, second edition. Syracuse, NY: Syracuse University Press

Emile Durkheim, 2006—*On Suicide.* Translated by Robin Buss. New York: Penguin Books

EOHR (Egyptian Organization for Human Rights) c.1994—*Aliyat Intaj al-'Unf fi Misr: Asyut, Hala Numazhajiya* ['Tools of the Production of Violence in Egypt: the Asyut Case Study', in Arabic]. Cairo: EOHR

John L Esposito, 1998—*Islam: The Straight Path*, third edition. New York: Oxford University Press

Mamoun Fandy, Winter 1994—'Egypt's Islamic Group: Regional Revenge', in *Middle East Journal*, vol 48 no 4

Nadia Ramsis Farah, 1986—*Religious Strife in Egypt: Crisis and Ideological Conflict in the Seventies.* New York: Gordon & Breach

Robert Fisk, February 1995a—'Terror Stalks Egypt's Forgotten Towns', in *The Independent*, February 8 1995

Robert Fisk, February 1995b—'"Might of the Sword" Menaces Christians', in *The Independent*, February 9 1995

Robert Fisk, February 1995c—'Cairo Puts Faith in Bullet and Bulldozer', in *The Independent*, February 10 1995

Patrick D Gaffney, 1994—*The Prophet's Pulpit: Islamic Preaching in Contemporary Egypt.* Berkeley: University of California Press

Anthony Giddens, 1990—*The Consequences of Modernity.* Cambridge: Polity Press

Michael Gilsenan, 1992—*Recognizing Islam: Religion and Society in the Modern Middle East.* New York: I B Tauris

Ellis Goldberg, 1992—'Smashing Idols and the State: The Protestant Ethic and Egyptian Sunni Radicalism', in Juan R I Cole, ed, 1992—*Comparing Muslim Societies: Knowledge and the State in a World Civilization.* Ann Arbor: University of Michigan Press

Joel Gordon, 1992—*Nasser's Blessed Movement: Egypt's Free Officers and the July Revolution.* New York: Oxford University Press

Laila Shukry El-Hamamsy, 1975—'The Assertion of Egyptian Identity', in George DeVos and Lola Romanucci-Ross, eds, 1975—*Ethnic Identity: Cultural Continuities and Change.* Palo Alto, CA: Mayfield Publishers

Iliya Harik, 1994—'Pluralism in the Arab World', in *Journal of Democracy*, vol 3 no 5, pp 43–56

Nigel Harris, 1986—*The End of the Third World: Newly Industrializing Countries and the Decline of an Ideology.* London: I B Tauris

David Harvey, 1989—*The Condition of Postmodernity: An Enquiry into the Origins of Cultural Change.* Oxford: Blackwell

Eric Hobsbawm, 1959—*Primitive Rebels.* New York: W W Norton

Mark Huband, 1998—*Warriors of the Prophet: The Struggle for Islam*. Boulder, CO: Westview Press

Saad Eddin Ibrahim, 1980—'Anatomy of Egypt's Militant Islamic Groups: Methodological Note and Preliminary Findings', in *International Journal of Middle East Studies*, vol 12 no 4, pp 245–266

Saad Eddin Ibrahim, 1996—'Cairo: A Sociological Profile', in Saad Eddin Ibrahim, 1996—*Egypt, Islam, and Democracy: Twelve Critical Essays*. Cairo: American University in Cairo Press

Reuven Kimelman, 1992—'War', in Steven Katz, ed, 1992—*Frontiers of Jewish Thought*. Washington, DC: B'nai B'rith Books

Timur Kuran, 1993—'The Economic Impact of Islamic Fundamentalism', in Martin E Marty and R Scott Appleby, eds, 1993—*Fundamentalisms and the State: Remaking Politics, Economies, and Militance*. Chicago: University of Chicago Press

Bruce B Lawrence, 1998—*Shattering the Myth: Islam Beyond Violence*. Princeton, NJ: Princeton University Press

Michael Lerner, 1996—*The Politics of Meaning: Restoring Hope and Possibility in an Age of Cynicism*. Reading, MA: Addison-Wesley

Michael Lerner, 2003—*Healing Israel/Palestine: A Path to Peace and Reconciliation*. San Francisco: Tikkun Books

Michael Lerner, ed, 1992—*Tikkun: To Heal, Repair, and Transform the World*. San Francisco: Tikkun Books

Brynjar Lia, 1998—*The Society of the Muslim Brothers in Egypt: The Rise of an Islamic Mass Movement, 1928–1942*. Reading, MA: Ithaca Press

Moses Maimonides, 1949—*Mishnah Torah, Book 14: Book of Judges*. New Haven, CT: Yale University Press

George M Marsden, 1991—*Understanding Fundamentalism and Evangelicalism*. Grand Rapids, MI: William B Eerdmans Publishing Company

Richard C Martin and Mark R Woodward, with Dwi S Atmaja, 1997—*Defenders of Reason in Islam: Mu'tazilism from Medieval School to Modern Symbol*. Oxford, UK: Oneworld Publications

Doug McAdam, John McCarthy, and Mayer Zald, 1996—*Comparative Perspectives in Social Movements: Political Opportunities, and Cultural Framing*. New York: Cambridge University Press

Barrington Moore, 1978—*Injustice: The Social Bases of Obedience and Revolt*. White Plains, NY: ME Sharpe

David Novak, 1974—'A Jewish View of War', in *Law and Theology in Judaism*, vol 1, pp 125–135. New York: Ktav Publishing House

Mancur Olson, 1965—*The Logic of Collective Action: Public Goods and the Theory of Groups*. New York: Schocken Books

Frances Fox Piven and Richard Cloward, 1977—*Poor People's Movements: Why They Succeed, How They Fail*. New York: Vantage Books

Sayyid Qutb, 1978—*Milestones*. Translated by M Siddiqui, Salimiah, Kuwait: International Islamic Federation of Student Organizations. (The title is also translated as *Signposts on the Road* from the Arabic *Ma'alim fi al-Tariq*. First published in Cairo in 1964.)

Sayyid Qutb, 1993—*Islam and Universal Peace*. Plainfield, IN: American Trust Publications

Sayyid Qutb, 2000—*Social Justice in Islam* ['al-'Adala al-Ijtima'iya fi al-Islam']. Translated by John B Hardie. Oneonta, NY: Islamic Publications International

Alan Richards and John Waterbury, 1998—*A Political Economy of the Middle East*, second edition. Boulder, CO: Westview Press

Martin Riesebrodt, 1993—*Pious Passion: The Emergence of Modern Fundamentalism in the United States and Iran*. Translated by Don Reneau. Berkeley: University of California Press

Yahya Sadowski, 1991—*Political Vegetables: Businessman and Bureaucrat in the Development of Egyptian Agriculture*. Washington, DC: Brookings Institution

Anthony Shadid, 2001—*Legacy of the Prophet: Despots, Democrats, and the New Politics of Islam*. Boulder, CO: Westview Press

Denis J Sullivan, 1994—*Private Voluntary Organizations in Egypt: Islamic Development, Private Initiative, and State Control*. Gainesville: University Press of Florida

Denis J Sullivan and Sana Abed-Kotob, 1999—*Islam in Contemporary Egypt: Civil Society vs the State*. Boulder, CO: Lynne Rienner

Sidney Tarrow, 1994—*Power in Movement: Social Movements, Collective Action, and Politics*. New York: Cambridge University Press

Charles Tilly, 1978—*From Mobilization to Revolution*. Reading, MA: Addison-Wesley Publishing Co

James Toth, 1999—*Rural Labor Movements in Egypt and Their Impact on the State, 1961–1992*. Gainesville: University Press of Florida

James Toth, March 2000—'Rural-to-Urban Migration and Informal Sector Expansion: Impediments to Egyptian Development', for First Mediterranean Social and Political Research Meeting, Robert Schuman Centre of the European University Institute, Florence, Italy, March 22–26 2000

Michael Walzer, 1997—*Arguing about War*. New Haven, CT: Yale University Press

John Waterbury, 1978—*Egypt: Burdens of the Past, Options for the Future*. Bloomington: Indiana University Press, American Universities Field Staff

John Waterbury, 1983—*The Egypt of Nasser and Sadat: The Political Economy of Two Regimes*. Princeton, NJ: Princeton University Press

Mary Anne Weaver, 2000—*A Portrait of Egypt: A Journey through the World of Militant Islam*. New York: Farrar, Straus & Giroux

Max Weber, 1992—*The Protestant Ethic and the Spirit of Capitalism*. New York: Routledge

Raymond L Weiss, ed, with Charles E Butterworth, 1975—*Ethical Writings of Moses Maimonides*. New York: Dover Publications

Eric Olin Wright, 1997—'Rethinking, Once Again, the Concept of Class Structure', in John R Hall, ed, 1997—*Reworking Class*. Ithaca, NY: Cornell University Press

Notes

1. Ed: This essay was published earlier, with the same title, in June Nash, ed, 2005—*Social Movements: An Anthropological Reader*, Oxford, UK: Blackwell, pp 117–145. This essay was however finalised before the irruptions in Egypt of January 2011 and—importantly for the discussion here—before the Muslim Brotherhood came out again into the open and its subsequent coming to power in the 2012 elections

(and its toppling in 2013). But in a way therefore all the more because of what has more recently happened—including the swings that are taking place today, and the resistance that is coming from all sides—this essay, aside from being a fascinating essay on movement and the globalisation of movement, also provides an extraordinarily rich and vivid background to subsequent and contemporary developments. I warmly thank the author, the editor, and the publisher for their generous respective permissions to publish it here in an edited form. For further reproduction permission, contact RRobertson@bos.blackwellpublishing.com.

2. In Egypt, the region south of Cairo is called the Sa'id, as distinguished from the region north of the capital called the Delta.

3. This essay follows the transliteration scheme of the US Library of Congress.

4. Qutb 1978.

5. Qutb 2000.

6. Marsden 1991, pp 91–92; Weber 1992, chapter 2, pp 13–38.

7. Martin and Woodward, with Atmaja 1997, chapter 1, pp 1–21.

8. Walzer 2004.

9. al-Banna 1978, chapter 6, pp 133–161.

10. Qutb 1993, chapter 2, pp 5–15.

11. Judaism also has a tradition of just and fair warfare. Most scholars begin with Moses Maimonides (1135–1204) (Maimonides 1949). (Also see Weiss and Butterworth 1975.) More recent contributions to this discussion include Kimelman 1992; Novak 1974, pp 125–135; Broyde 1996, pp 1–30; and Bleich 1983, pp 3–41. Michael Lerner, editor of *Tikkun* magazine (*Tikkun Olam* in Hebrew means 'repairing the world'), has written considerably on justice in Judaism. Besides the pages of his magazine, there are two authored books—Lerner 1996 and 2003—and an edited volume, Lerner 1992.

12. Moore 1978

13. Hobsbawm 1959.

14. Piven and Cloward 1977

15. Tilly 1978.

16. Durkheim 2006.

17. Olson 1965.

18. Tarrow 1994.

19. McAdam, McCarthy, and Zald 1996.

20. Harris 1986, pp 114–117.

21. ibid, p 165; Richards and Waterbury 1998, p 27.

22. Toth 1999, chapter 5.

23. Richards and Waterbury 1998, p 184.

24. CAPMAS 1990, pp 7, 18; 1978a, p 54.

25. Farah 1986, pp 21–22.

26. Waterbury 1983, pp 402–404.

27. ibid, pp 132–133.

28. François Burgat (1997) treats the Islamic movement as a newly emerging crusade (p 1: "a new voice from the South") that absorbed activists disenchanted with the failures of the Arab socialism that had dominated this part of the world throughout the 1950s and 1960s. But the movement did not rise *de novo* in the 1970s, nor was it

a reincarnation of a dispirited left. The current movement only seems to have arisen from nothing—actually from its ashes—because it was crushed in Egypt from 1954 to the early 1970s by the secular nationalist government of Jamal 'Abd al-Nassir, a regime considered by many activists to be godless. Before that came the Muslim Brotherhood founded by Hasan al-Banna in 1928 and the Salafiya movement under Muhammad Abduh in the 1880s. Thus the 'current phase' appears only after a momentary hiatus.

29. Davis 1987.

30. See El-Hamamsy (1975, pp 276–306) for details of these cultural categories.

31. John Esposito (1998, p 68) claims that the appropriate question in Islam is not what people believe (as in Christianity) but what they do (as in classical Judaism as well). That is, what counts is orthopraxy, not orthodoxy. While he is correct to say that classical Judaism is primarily a set of laws, and Christianity a set of beliefs, Islam, as the last of the three Abrahamic religions, combines both belief and practice. Yet, as Ellis Goldberg concludes (1992, p 206), citing material from Hasan al-Banna and Sayyid Qutb, Islamic radicals and militants consider "good deeds" more important than "good words" in their efforts to re-establish *Shari'a* law and the Right Path. This shift from 'words' to 'deeds' also paves the way, if necessary, for a shift in strategy from mere talk to militant action. On the other hand Sufi Islam, condemned by radicals and militants, reverses this emphasis, focusing instead on spiritualism and inner conviction.

32. Qutb 1978, chapter 5.

33. Qutb 2000, p 262.

34. Many activists employ this triptych, based on a Hadith, or authentic report, about the Prophet Muhammad, who said: "Whoever among you sees any evildoing, let him change it with his hand; if he cannot do that, let him change it with his tongue; and if he cannot do that, let him change it with his heart; and that is the minimum faith requires" (ibid, p 87). Sayyid Qutb also defined a fourth type, a jihad of the sword, although this is a minority opinion (Qutb 1978, p 110).

35. Gaffney 1994, pp 36–43.

36. This ambiguity is more than just following the standard anthropological tradition of keeping field-site names anonymous. It also avoids identifying specific localities because of the real security risks to my informants whose residence and identity could be readily recognised from my work.

37. I know of three instances of such fieldwork in Egypt—Ibrahim 1980, Gaffney 1994, and Ansari 1986. Other analysts rely on these firsthand accounts, as well as secular commentators, government officials, and newspapers and journals, none of which appear particularly neutral or objective. Ibrahim and Ansari's material dates from the 1970s, when the government encouraged radical (but non-militant) Islamists on Egypt's college campuses to organise and mobilise, but before 1985, when middle-class radicals began to reach down and mobilise disaffected members of Egypt's working classes. Gaffney's information appears incidental to his principal intention of documenting various types of preachers and sermons. Visits to southern Egypt involved constant government surveillance. Upon being escorted by state security officers and left at the residence or business of a small number of friends ('key informants'), I was able, however, to chat and interact with some latitude. Conversations ('interviews') with visiting activists were conducted at the sole discretion of these key informants—truly 'gatekeepers' in the literal sense. Background information

about these partisans was gathered later. Formal research techniques were difficult, if not impossible, to follow. There was no universe of respondents, no sampling, and no formal interview schedules. Patterns did appear, however, which were consistent enough that an overall order eventually emerged.

38. When the Muslim Brotherhood began to expand its organisation in the 1930s, after its founder, Hasan al-Banna, had moved from Ismailiya to Cairo, new branches and sub-branches were located primarily in the Delta. In the 1930s, the Delta was experiencing some of the same developmental forces—commercialisation, urbanisation, industrial, and occupational specialisation—now affecting the Sa'id. In listing new locations, Brynjar Lia mentions only one new branch in the Sa'id, in the relatively developed city of Asyut. Otherwise, he records Delta provinces as the sites when new offices were opened outside of the major metropolitan areas. Lia 1998, pp 121–122, notes 5, 8, 10.

39. In the 1976 census, 30.5 percent of Sa'idis lived in cities as compared to 26.4 per cent of people in the Delta. At the same time, 24 per cent of Sa'idis engaged in agriculture and 2.4 per cent in industry, as compared with 19.8 and 3.7 per cent, respectively, in the Delta. CAPMAS 1978b, pp 85–96.

40. See Bakr 1994, p 101. Although Bakr focuses exclusively on Asyut Province, many of his conclusions can be generalised to other provinces within the Sa'id.

41. The proportion of the Coptic population in the Delta is 1.9 per cent outside the large metropolitan areas along its perimeter. Approximately two-thirds of these are urban-based. In the Sa'id, the Coptic population is much higher—rising up to 14 per cent in 1976, when the percentage in the entire country was 6.2. Of these, a little under two-thirds live in the Sa'idi countryside, a pattern opposite that of the Delta. CAPMAS 1978b, pp 73–84.

42. Bakr 1994, p 194. Bakr lists unemployment as the single most important factor underlying organised political violence. As accurate as this might be, it is also the injustice of not having a job because government corruption reduced job-generating investment, or because social connections prevailed over expertise, that also infuriates frustrated job seekers.

43. al-Wafd, February 19 1995.

44. Riesebrodt (1993, p 186) concludes that the rural-born, urban-bound migrant constitutes one of the global components of religious fundamentalist movements, at least in the two case studies he investigated, the United States and Iran. It certainly is the case in Egypt as well, to the extent that I would call Islamism the politics of rural-to-urban migration.

45. The notion of frustration here captures what appears to be a contradictory movement: migrants desire, and expect, upward mobility when they move. Instead, once in the city, they experience—and resent—downward mobility, often due to a stigmatisation over which they have no control. This is the Durkheimian revolution of rising and thwarted expectations. See Goldberg 1992, pp 211–213; Farah 1986, p 34; and Bakr 1994, pp 172, 205.

46. Ibrahim 1980, pp 430–432; Ansari 1986, chapters 9, 10.

47. The reasons behind working-class participation in such ideological movements have been questioned. Riesebrodt (1993, p 158) argues that in the Iranian Revolution, lower-class involvement was based less on abstract religious ideology and more

on cliental ties to charismatic, middle-class leaders. Asef Bayat (1997, chapter 3; 1998, pp 136–169) further claims there were even two separate revolutions in Iran because class-segregated neighbourhoods and the lack of "meaningful formal associations", such as mosques, inhibited any cohesion between these two classes. However, urban Egypt lacks the occupational homogeneity found in Tehran neighbourhoods. Moreover, mosques, schools, clinics, and coffee houses constitute important sites where both middle- and working-class men meet. Also see Toth 2000. Thus in Egypt, working-class participation was greater than in Iran, but like in Iran, its involvement was based on cliental ties, not religious ideology. However, it was largely the effectiveness of this mobilisation, more than any previous 'populist' movement, that worried government officials with fears that lower-class eruptions, like those in January 1977, would (again) capsize their plans and policies.

48. Toth 1999, chapter 7.

49. Ibrahim 1996, p 100; Waterbury 1983, pp 112–117.

50. Riesebrodt (1993, p 9) concludes that fundamentalism involves a struggle over the shift from personal, paternalistic ties to impersonal, bureaucratic relations involved in modernisation. My earlier work on Egyptian rural workers (Toth 1999) confirms this.

51. Toth 1999, chapter 7.

52. Ibrahim 1980, p 452.

53. Gilsenan 1992, chapter 10.

54. Al-Jihad ["(Religious) Struggle"] was the organisation responsible for the assassination of President al-Sadat and holds sway primarily in Cairo. Al-Jama'a al-Islamiya ["(the) Islamic Association"] was its organisational offshoot that dominated the Sa'id, although earlier organisations have claimed ancestry as well (see note 51). Both believed in a jihad of militant action to overcome ignorance, or *jahiliya*, although al-Jihad pinpointed just government officials as unbelievers, while al-Jama'a al-Islamiya included the larger Egyptian society as possible apostates. For an insightful examination of these and other militant organisations, see Bakr 1994.

55. *Zakat* is among the five mandatory obligations of Muslims. Islamic activists regard *zakat* a part of Islam's social justice. It constitutes an income tax, which in Egypt is a voluntary donation at the rate of 2.5 per cent. Contributors told me they paid their portion either directly to the mosque, if it was privately controlled, or directly to known beneficiaries, if the mosque was government staffed. Islamic investment companies also automatically withheld a 2.5 per cent deduction on all monetary transactions for *zakat* donations.

56. Kuran 1993, pp 308–310.

57. Sadowski 1991, p 231.

58. See also Bakr 1994, p 49; Sullivan 1994; Abu Zayd 1965; and Sullivan and Abed-Kotob 1999.

59. The Thanawiya 'Amma is the large comprehensive examination held at the end of high school that determines the discipline of college students and hence their subsequent occupation.

60. This and other association names are pseudonyms.

61. Supplicants were also endorsed by two witnesses personally known to both benefactors and beneficiaries.

62.   al-Sha'b, October 20, 1992.

63.   Gaffney 1994, pp 44, 91.

64.   Gordon 1992.

65.   Waterbury 1978, pp 253–254.

66.   EOHR c 1994, p 1.

67.   *Middle East Times*, 5–11 February 1995.

68.   Gaffney (1994, pp 329–330) notes that the Islamic Association, al-Jama'a al-Is-lamiya, in al-Minya was preceded by the al-Jam'iya al-Islamiya, also translated as the Islamic Association, but with a slightly different nuance in the Arabic. This is also the generic term for any Islamic association. The confusion is not just among foreign speakers; my informants also found it difficult to distinguish between these two organisations and the generic term.

69.   See Fisk 1995a, p 15; 1995b, p 14; 1995c, p 13.

70.   Today, the Hamas organisation in Gaza and the West Bank of Palestine is in a similar contradictory position. It is engaged in so-called terrorist attacks against Israel while simultaneously operating charitable programmes. Hamas is an acronym for the Islamic Resistance Movement and is an offshoot of the Muslim Brotherhood. See Abu-Amr 1994. By US law, its funds have been frozen and donations to Hamas are prohibited. Yet fungibility makes this financial situation difficult: it may well reduce violent attacks by cutting off funds budgeted for weapons and ammunition, but it also hurts those benefiting from its numerous non-violent programmes. The situation in Palestine is much worse than in Egypt, for the Israeli government has much less interest in the welfare of Palestinians and the number of alternative agencies is much smaller.

71.   See Fisk 1995a, b, c.

72.   Bakr 1994, p 38.

73.   The last two are the ideologues behind al-Jihad and al-Jama'a al-Islamiya, respectively. Muhammad 'Abd al-Salam Faraj was executed as a result of the assassination of President al-Sadat in 1981. He argued that a militant jihad of the sword was imperative for all Muslims who otherwise were unbelievers for rejecting it. Umar 'Abd al-Rahman is in prison in the US for his part in the World Trade Center bombing in 1993. While teaching at Asyut University, he issued a number of fatwas, or religious pronouncements, justifying a militant jihad against Egyptian officials and civilians.

74.   Bakr 1994, pp 236–238.

75.   Abu Zayd, *al-Th'ar*. Interestingly, Abu Zayd's ethnography about *th'ar* retaliation in the Sa'id alludes to local Copts as armaments suppliers to rival Muslim tribal clans. This indicates that perhaps some of the sectarian violence in the Sa'id between Christians and Muslims was not altogether without cause, as militants targeted those who profited from equipping the violence. Bakr (1994, pp 173–174) also points out the preponderance of Christians among Asyuti elites in more recent times.

76.   Abdo 2000, p 26.

77.   Weaver 2000, p 147.

78.   Abdo 2000, p 20. It appears impossible to verify government reports of a single, overarching organisation rather than a multitude of independent associations.

79.   ibid, p 24. Abdo cites a March 1993 report of the Egyptian Organization of Human Rights as the source of this information. Elsewhere, Weaver (2000, p 149) quotes

an Islamist lawyer, Ali Ismail, whom she interviewed in November 1994: "[w]omen were tortured with electroshocks and beaten in the streets—dragged by their hair, after their *hijabs* were savagely torn off their heads". He goes on to tell her that no fewer than 5,000 people were arrested, of whom 4,500 were released over the next year. Of the remaining 500, only 100 have been brought to trial (ibid).

80. Abdo 2000, p 197.
81. EOHR c 1994, p 2.
82. This may well indicate the fluidity and confusion of these groups. Most US government officials attribute the first World Trade Center bombing attempt to al-Jihad, but under the leadership of Shaykh 'Abd al-Rahman. However, Shaykh Umar 'Abd al-Rahman is the spiritual leader of al-Jama'a al-Islamiya.
83. Wahhabi Islam is similar to Salafi Islam in that both condemn the worship of intermediaries between believers and God. But the overall doctrinal basis of each is different, as is the social milieu—one tribal and nomadic, the other urban and bureaucratic. Neither forms the basis of militant Islam until its adherents feel attacked by non-Muslims. See Riesebrodt 1993.
84. Huband 1998, p 3.
85. ibid, p 12.
86. Shadid 2001, p 80.
87. ibid, p 82.
88. ibid, chapter 8.
89. See Ibrahim 1996 and Harik 1994. This is also Shadid's conclusion (2001).
90. Ed.: Again, this essay was revised for this book in 2009, two years before the 2011 uprising (and even if the militancy of 2011 was of a very different nature to that discussed in this essay).
91. What Anthony Giddens has called time-space distanciation or what David Harvey called time-space compression. Giddens 1990 and Harvey 1989.

Fighting for Another World:
Yusuf al-'Uyairi and His Conceptualisation of Praxis and the Permanent Salafi Revolution[1]
Roel Meijer

Introduction: The Islamist Movement and Yusuf al-'Uyairi

The Islamist movement is today well known as a world movement, and within this broader movement al-Qaeda—and more generally, Jihadi Salafism, in practice if not in name—is all too infamous. Studies on the ideological development of the al-Qaeda and Jihadi Salafism, however, have been relatively limited compared to the enormous attention paid to their organisational capacity.[2] This is all the more puzzling, as there exists a huge Salafi library and a substantial Jihadi Salafi one.[3]

Studies that do focus on ideology fall into four groups. The first argues that Islam is unable to cope with the modern world.[4] The second states that radical Islamic thought should not be regarded as an Islamic phenomenon but as part of globalised modernity, and analysed as part of modern political thought.[5] The third argues that radical Islamic currents are not political at all. They lack a programme, are no longer connected to a certain cause, and do not mobilise Muslims on the bases of political goals.[6] Politics has been reduced to ethics. In the case of al-Qaeda, some argue that its ideology is part of a 'debased, millenarian and nihilistic' strand of Islamic radicalism.[7] Others of this current hold that it has adopted much of its rhetoric from left-wing Third Worldism.[8] In contrast, the fourth group regards it more seriously as a social movement.[9] It emphasises its rational character, taking advantage of the emerging opportunities, gaining access to power; its organisational capacity; and that it is creating a new ideology however much it might lay claim to authenticity.[10]

Of these four currents, I believe the second and fourth are the most fruitful approaches to analysing the broader Islamist movement, of which al-Qaeda is a part.[11] This essay intends to support their arguments in favour of looking at al-Qaeda as a modern political ideology and movement by examining the vivid and powerful writings, life, and life practice of Yusuf al-'Uyairi, a key activist, strategist, and theorist in the radical Islamic movement. By doing so, I hope to make comprehensible—for the average reader, in all parts of the world—the ideology and ideological development of this major contemporary phenomenon.

Yusuf al-'Uyairi is usually known as the founder and first leader of al-Qaeda on the Arabian Peninsula. Although he is regarded as among the foremost ideologues of Jihadi Salafism by both Jihadis themselves and terrorism experts,[12] he is less well known for his extensive political writings.[13] Most of his work concentrates

UYAIRI

CRITIQUE PEOPLE BATTLE
CURRENTS GENERAL SAUDI THEREFORE RELIGION
ACTIVIST AL-QAEDA CLASH CIVILISATIONS ESPECIALLY
STRATEGIC INVASION SHAYKHS
WORK TRUTH AFGHANISTAN MARTYRDOM BASED CAUSE FOREIGN
CULTURAL IDEOLOGY
SUPERIOR ULAMA SECOND PART AWDA
CALLED PRINCIPLE AMERICAN PRACTICE
LIFE WORKS IMPLEMENTATION AL-WALA RELIGIOUS
STATES AL RESISTANCE POLITICAL ARGUES
TAWHID TERMS AL AL
TAIBIQ SOCIETY NEW SALAFISM WRITINGS ONE MEANS UMMA
YOUTH ARGUMENT MUJAHID UNDERSTANDING INDIVIDUAL
CONCEPT MUSLIM CRUSADERS TAKE QUIETIST SALMAN
BECOME THEORY OPERATIONS AQIDA GOD PRINCIPLES SOCIAL
CREED WA-L-BARA STRUGGLE PROGRAMME ENEMY IMPORTANT
HOWEVER ARGUED ISLAM SAHWA IRAQ ANALYSIS LIKE
ISLAMIST RIGHT CORRUPT MUST ALSO REVOLUTIONARY PRAXIS JIHADI FORM KNOWLEDGE MILITARY SUPPORT DIFFERENT
STATE MUJAHIDIN SALAFI WORLD AMONG GROUP IMPERIALISM MUCH
GOAL ULTIMATE WEST MOVEMENT STATED
MUSLIMS ISLAMIC ARABIA WAR ALTHOUGH
SENSE VIOLENCE ACCORDING MANHAJ THOUGHT FRAMED BIN
REGARDED LEVEL REALITY YUSUF JIHADIST MAIN ABU
JIHAD WESTERN IDENTITY WAY END
EVEN LEADERS POLITICS FIRST REGION
CHECHNYA TRUE FACT TWO 9/11 TAKING

on political, economic, and cultural relations between the West and the Islamic world. This preoccupation with politics finds expression in the central role the term 'reality' (*waqi'*) plays in his works. For him, transforming reality (*taghyir al-waqi'*) is the real goal of *jihad*. According to 'Uyairi, understanding reality along with having a pure religious intention (*niyya*) is a precondition for devising an appropriate strategy to fight the enemy and establish God's rule on earth. Fighting in the way of God (*fi sabil Allah*) is, in fact, an Islamic revolutionary praxis.[14] This essay's main goal is to trace 'Uyairi's construction of this praxis and its form.

To this ideological analysis, one must supplement the value of the fourth approach, that of social movement theory. The combination is necessary because most attention in social movement theory has been paid to group dynamics and less to individual thinkers and strategists. 'Uyairi fits the figure of the activist-strategic thinker who mobilises a social movement, defined by Sidney Tarrow as 'collective challenges, based on common purposes and social solidarities in sustained interaction with elite, opponents and authorities'.[15] It is with this intent that 'Uyairi framed his ideology to resonate with the grievances of the group he was trying to activate, mostly Saudi Arabian youth—followers of the Sahwa movement, the main politically reformist Salafi movement in Saudi Arabia—but also Muslim youth globally. Social movement theory has been applied to Saudi Arabia and the Islamist movement extensively,[16] but few attempts have connected the Jihadi movement to the larger Sahwa reform movement that emerged in the 1990s.[17] From 'Uyairi's work it is obvious that he was constantly in dialogue with the broader Sahwa and other Islamist movements, whose followers he tried to win over to the Jihadist camp by criticising their leaders and presenting a more consistent alternative. In his attempt to establish his credentials and gain hegemony over the larger reformist movement, he linked Jihadist discourse with other mainstream Islamist and Salafist tropes, appropriating them for the Salafist cause.[18]

Generally, 'Uyairi's framing can be divided into three levels.[19] At the highest level of the grand narrative, which is analysed in the second section, 'A Clash of Civilisations', a general explanation of the problem is framed. 'Uyairi appropriated the concept of the clash of civilisations for the Jihadi Salafist cause. The battle, on this abstract level, is a clash between two programmes or methods, the programme of truth (*manhaj al-haqq*) and the programme of falsehood (*manhaj al-batil*).

On the second level, a solution is provided. The third section, 'A Revolutionary *Manhaj*: The Only Path to Change', includes the general theoretical solution 'Uyairi provided, and his contention that Salafi Jihadism is better equipped to tackle the enemy than other currents because it has a superior understanding of reality and a deeper religious belief (*'aqida*), leading to a better and more effective method or practice, a *manhaj*. At this level, 'Uyairi not only formulated a theoretical solution to the problem but also the tools to interact with reality and change it.

A remark on Salafism in its quietist form is necessary here. As such Jihadi Salafism is opposed to the officially sanctioned form of Salafism as expounded by the Saudi religious establishment, the main source of Salafism and Wahhabism.[20] This so-called purist, or apolitical, quietist Salafism rejects contentious activism and opposes critique of the status quo, sanctioning the legitimacy of the ruler according to the doctrine of *wali al-amr* (loyalty to the ruler), even if he is iniquitous, as long as he does not work against Islam and become an apostate. The goal of Salafism is the return of Islam to the pristine purity of the pious forefathers (*al-salaf al-salih*) and the purification (*tasfiya*) of creed (*'aqida*) and practice (*manhaj*) of the individual and the collective by means of education (*tarbiyya*), not political activism. The central concept of Salafism is *tawhid*, the Oneness of God, and the major sin is giving associates to God (*shirk*) by accepting intermediaries or venerating other human beings or objects (such as trees). All Islamic movements that participate in politics, such as the Muslim Brotherhood, are vilified as 'activists' (*harakiyyun*), 'deviants' (*munharifun*), or 'innovators' (*mubtadi'un*), who threaten the Muslim community's unity through instigating 'dissension' (*fitna*), a major sin in conservative Islam, and supporting 'extremism' (*ghuluw*), or worse venerating their political leaders, which is considered a sin in the form of *shirk*, i.e. giving God associates. As an antidote to politically activist, 'extremist' movements, quietist Salafism has concentrated on laying down the guidelines for correct, respectful, pious behaviour by promoting a highly conservative moralism (*akhlaq*), with its origins in medieval rules governing Islamic conduct, having a deeply anti-revolutionary political meaning. The key element in the creation of this law-abiding attitude is the avoidance of 'passions' (*ahwa'*); thus, members of deviant movements are called 'the people of innovation and passions' (*ahl al-bid'a wa-l-ahwa'*).[21]

In contrast, 'Uyairi defines a revolutionary Salafi *manhaj*, akin to both the Marxist and, in some respects, Sayyid Qutb's concepts of praxis.[22] Jihadi Salafism shares with Salafism an abhorrence for the West and innovation (*bid'a*) in doctrine, but, in opposition to quietist Salafism, argues that one can only be a true Muslim by actively opposing local regimes, the West, and the 'establishment' *'ulama*, who have become stooges of the regimes, have accepted a 'false consciousness', and in fact are themselves innovators because they worship the state instead of God. If quietist Salafism argues that purification of doctrine and living according to the right *'aqida* and *akhlaq* will lead to a just and perfect society, activist Salafism believes that purification should not only include educating Muslim in following the correct doctrine but also fighting against those who corrupt it. It demands commitment and self-sacrifice for the purification of society in order that it submits to the Oneness of God (*tawhid*).

Two practices are crucial for the Salafi Jihadi praxis for purifying Muslim society and fighting the enemy: *al-wala' wa-l-bara'*, loyalty to God and dissociation from unbelievers is meant to strengthen the will; while *jihad* is violent resistance of the enemy both indigenous and foreign. In theory 'Uyairi did not differ so much in the utopian end vision of quietist Salafism, the idea that the perfect society and social justice will be obtained when Muslims live according to the pious ancestors (*al-salaf al-salih*); he differed in the method to reach this goal. Jihad is seen as the essential form of self-fulfilment as a Muslim. In fact, fighting for God is the only means of self-realisation as a Muslim in Jihadi Salafism. From his writings, this end stage is never touched upon except in the sense of total self-purification and striving for this goal is important, not so much reaching that end stage.

In the fourth section of this essay, 'Revolutionary Practice', I deal with the implementation (*tatbiq*) of the revolutionary praxis of *jihad*. On this more strategic level, 'Uyairi focuses on the direct battle and shows how, in a dialectical process of interaction between theory and practice, a revolutionary praxis is formed, exercised, and adapted during its implementation at different international fronts. The form of this revolutionary praxis depends on how 'reality' and the threat of the enemy are framed.[23] Again, while I emphasise the political and revolutionary content of Yusuf al-'Uyairi's works, this does not mean that he actually had a political programme. His programme was formed in the ongoing dialectical process of implementing revolutionary *jihad* and 'transforming reality'. The goal was a just society but this can be more readily conceived of as a utopia based on religious injunctions than on a clear model and ways to achieve this. If he had a sense of justice and exploitation (of oil wealth, and of people by imperialism and local rulers), it was formulated in the awkward Salafi terminology of corruption (*fasad*) and giving associates to God, or recognising intermediaries between God and man (*shirk*), in quietist Salafism regarded as the gravest sin because it undermines monotheistic character of Islam and the all-powerful nature of God. It is perhaps the Salafi distaste for accepting politics, except in general terms such as liberation, that prevents Jihadi Salafism from formulating a clear programme. Comparing Yusuf al-'Uyairi's approach to say, Che Guevara's, is perhaps apt when it is concerned with their shared revolutionary fervour, but is beside the point in regard to their divergent programme and end goal.

The second remark concerns the relationship between theology and politics in 'Uyairi's writings. In his informative article on Salafism, Quintan Wiktorowicz argues that there exist three Salafi currents, the purist, the political, and the Jihadist, which differ in their programme, their *manhaj*, but share the same '*aqida*, basic creed.[24] I argue that 'Uyairi's writings do not support this view. In both its *manhaj* and '*aqida*, Jihadi Salafism differs from political and purist groups. The activist form of Jihadi Salafism is ultimately based on a different interpretation and definition of the '*aqida*, and reflects, therefore, on the specific jihadi praxis which is determined in a dialectical process between theory (*tanzir*), implementation (*tatbiq*), and interaction with 'reality'. This is apparent from the importance the different groups attach to their *'aqida:* Having the right *'aqida* means having access to the correct interpretation of 'reality.'[25] This accounts for an interminable and vehement debate between different currents within the Salafi movement, some of which I explore below.

A Clash of Civilisations

The Life of a Third-Generation Saudi Mujahid

Reading the biographies of Yusuf al-'Uyairi it is clear that he devoted his life to *jihad* and defending Islam.[26] Yusuf bin Salih bin Fahd al-'Uyairi, *nom de guerre* Abu Salih or Shaykh al-Battar, was born on April 24 1974 in the Saudi city of Dammam.[27] He left school at 18, before completing secondary school. He arrived in Afghanistan in 1991, during the last phase of the war against the Najibullah regime. He was trained in the al-Faruq camp, where he later became a trainer himself. At the time, this camp did not belong to al-Qaeda. He does, however, seem to have been acquainted with bin Laden, who appointed him his bodyguard for four months and whom he accompanied to Sudan in 1992. From there, we are told, he was sent to help organise the anti-US struggle in Somalia, led by Abu Hafs al-Misri, bin Laden's military leader. Afterwards he returned to Saudi Arabia and worked as volunteer in Dammam, gathering donations for the struggle in Bosnia and Kosovo. During this stay, he met Salman al-'Awda twice. During this period he married the sister of the wife of Shaykh Sulayman al-'Ulwan, with whom he had three daughters. After the bomb attack on the compound of the US American military base at Khobar in 1996, he was arrested and incarcerated in Dammam, where he was reportedly tortured.[28]

After his release in 1998, Yusuf al-'Uyairi became involved in Chechnya and Daghestan, where he seems to have been in contact with the Saudi guerrilla leader Khattab. 'Uyairi also played an important role as fundraiser, which was the starting point of his growing estrangement with Salman al-'Awda, who was released from prison in 1999. As he became more independent, Yusuf al-'Uyairi started to publish his own works in support of the transnational Jihadi cause. His works on Chechnya dealt with prisoners of war,[29] 'martyrdom operations,'[30] and hostage taking, using as example the Moscow Theatre hostage taking of October 2002.[31] Some of these works were published by his newly founded research institute, the Institute for Islamic Research and Studies (*Markaz al-Buhuth wa-l-Dirasat al-Islamiyya*), which acted as a forum for Jihadi ideas. In addition, he posted his works, often issued in series, on Saudi websites. Other causes he picked up were those of the Taliban, which had taken over Afghanistan in 1996,[32] and the Moro movement in the Philippines.[33] His growing estrangement from the Sahwa *shaykhs* was marked by their condemnation of 9/11, which he defended in *The Truth about the New Crusades.*[34] It was in this period that he became webmaster of al-Qaeda's site, *al-Nida'.*

To the general public in the world, Yusuf al-'Uyairi became known as the founder and first leader of al-Qaeda on the Arabian Peninsula.[35] It seems bin Laden asked him to organise a cell in Saudi Arabia after he left Sudan and returned to Saudi Arabia in 1992. But the project only took off after his release from Dammam prison in 1998, when bin Laden assigned him to recruit and train leaders for the organisation. He recruited most of the leaders, like Khalid Hajj and 'Abd al-'Aziz al-Muqrin, from among his acquaintances in Afghanistan. Like the second echelon, they were on the List of 19 that the Saudi state published in May 2003.[36]

Yusuf al-'Uyairi was killed on May 31 2004 during a clash with the police ten kilometres northwest of the town of Turba, near Hail, the capital of the northern province of Saudi Arabia.[37] He was just thirty years old. In the short span of twelve years, which included two years in prison, he was therefore a bodyguard (to someone no less than Osama bin Laden), an activist on the ground and a movement builder, a war strategist, an internationalist, and a religious theorist and polemicist at a time of major ferment in one of the world's great faiths—and also the builder of a research institute and a webmaster. In short, a complete contemporary warrior. His having to die as and when he did is perhaps also tragic, because from a pamphlet he wrote just before his death, in which he accused the US of being behind the attack on his group, he seems to have been opposed to the timing of the attacks in Saudi Arabia during which he was killed.[38]

Zero-Sum-Game

Tawhid stands at the heart of Salafi ideology in general but, like Samuel Huntington, Yusuf al-'Uyairi adopts the clash of civilisations as the overarching concept for an activist and dramatic ideology.[39] 'Uyairi's starting point was that the West is engaged in a war on all fronts against Islam—economic, political, religious, and cultural. But the struggle is especially directed on the level of identity. This struggle is a zero-sum-game, for Islam is equal to one's identity and humanity. Losing one's religion means losing one's identity, morals (*akhlaq*), and principles (*mabadi*). One is literally dehumanised, for it leads to debauchery (*da'ar*), and corruption (*fasad*) 'in all its forms', with the result that Muslims are degraded to lead the life of 'animals' (*bahimi*), and, in fact, lose the right to exist.[40]

A war of civilisations is in itself not strange to the Islamist movement. What distinguishes the Salafi Jihadi version is its uncompromising character. It is a war waged until the bitter end, founded on a conviction that Islam has almost been vanquished. Following the standard line, also upheld by bin Laden, Yusuf al-'Uyairi propagates the main apocalyptic theme of the Jihadis—that the Muslim community has been humiliated and become 'the most despised *umma*' (*adhalla umma*).[41] It is a battle between a Western programme / method (*manhaj al-gharb*) of deception and deviation, and the Muslim programme of truth (*manhaj al-haqq*).[42] In this apocalyptic vision, 'Muslims everywhere are threatened in their religion (*din*), soul (*nafs*), honour (*'ird*), money (*mal*), rationality (*'aql*) and off-spring (*nasl*).'[43] If Muslims lose this war of principles (*mabadi'*) and creed (*'aqida*), 'Uyairi argues, they will have forfeited their right to exist.[44]

Apart from being ubiquitous and eternal, he argues that this Western 'crusade' against the Islamic world is also well planned. It aims to destroy the identity of Muslims, corrupt their morals, and terminate any religious feelings in order that Muslims lose faith in their creed (*'aqida*), the very basis of their resistance. This is a precondition for ruling over Muslims.[45] The most important means to defeat Islam is to corrupt it, by promoting free sex and stimulating the 'corruption of women' (*ifsad al-mar'a*). Other means are the imposition of 'diversionary curricula' at school, spreading drugs, and permitting the sale of alcohol.[46]

Although Yusuf al-'Uyairi's accusations fed on the basic Islamist diatribe against the West, they were also based on his extensive reading and knowledge of contemporary Western sources. He shored up his arguments by referring to such prominent US American intellectuals involved in the debate on Islam as Bernard Lewis, Thomas Friedman, and Samuel Huntington, who, he said, claim to be 'objective' and 'neutral' but in reality incite public opinion to support the US American 'crusade'.[47]

Typical of radical Islamism and Salafism was his rejection of 'well intended' attempts by the West to spread democracy in the Muslim world. Regarded as part of the battle of civilisations, democracy and secularism are distrusted on account of the distinction these concepts make between church and state, and their pro-motion of the sovereignty of the people. Besides leading to the worship of humans instead of God (*shirk*), secularism leads to the 'bestialisation of all activities of life,' the rise of 'odious capitalism, the liberation of women, the equality between man and woman, equality between religions, and non-discrimination on the basis of religion and belief'. Its fundamental flaw is that 'it promotes total freedom: Freedom of belief, freedom of expression, freedom of science, and freedom to change man from a servant of God into a low animal.'[48] This, he argued, was also an important reason for the US American invasion of Iraq:

> [The invasion of Iraq] will ensure American hegemony by imposing American democracy, American politics, American education, and American culture and American morals and even American Islam on all countries except Israel. It is a comprehensive plan that will transform the region entirely, if it includes the heads of government. ... This dangerous project will enslave the region and destroy the last remains of Islam from life in its entirety. It is a corrupt and cor-rupting plan (*mubadara al-fasad wa-l-ifsad*). It is a plan of unbelief (*kufr*) and of atheism (*zandaqa*).[49]

Simultaneously, according to 'Uyairi, the West tries to undermine the *umma's* will to resist this cultural and political invasion by injecting into it the idea that violence (*'unf*) and *jihad* should be rejected. This is the main assignment of moderate *'ulama* who, under influence of rationality (*ta'aqqul*), spread the idea that violence and resistance endangers the *umma* because it is too weak to combat the enemy. They condemn the *mujahidin* as impatient (*ta'ajjul*), irresponsible (*tahawwur*), and a threat to the internal Muslim front, leading to friction (*fitna*). 'Uyairi believed that these *'ulama* had been co-opted into the state and that they destroyed the strength of creed (*'aqida*) in the name of coexistence (*ta'ayush*), tolerance (*tasamuh*), and mutual understanding (*taqarub*). By claiming that Islam was a religion of peace and admonishing Muslims to limit their discourse to theoretical generalities (*'umimiyyat nazariyya*) they instilled impotence (*ghayr al-istita'a*) in the struggle with the hypocrites (*munafiqun*) and even Shiites (called *rawafid*, 'rejecters', by 'Uyairi), Jews, and Christians.[50]

Rejection of Politics

Despite his appropriation of the master narrative of the clash of civilisations and its cultural connotations, Yusuf al-'Uyairi's writings are predominantly a critical analysis of the political situation in the Muslim world. He prided himself on knowing 'reality' (*waqi'*). In these texts 'interests' (*masalih*) are as, or even more important, than creed and religion. Rather than just condemning the adversary for his religion, and framing the struggle as a clash of religions, he 'demonstrated' the corruption and falsehood of the adversary by referring to information he obtains from news stations like Fox News, the BBC, or English newspapers, as well as policy reports of renowned think tanks.[51] 'Reality' and his political analysis confirmed the threat of Western civilisations to Muslim identity.

Yusuf al-'Uyairi's main concern was with foreign, especially US, interference in the Middle East, which he called 'colonialism' (*isti'mar*). For instance, in his analysis of the stationing of US troops in Saudi Arabia in 1991, he argued that it is US interests that keep them in the region, not their inherent character as 'crusaders'.[52] This is 'proven' by the subordination of international treaties and bodies to imperialist goals. 'Uyairi concluded that neither alliances nor treaties are important; only power, and in the final analysis, military power. Therefore, 'Uyairi considered all Western rhetoric of justice and respect for human rights as worthless propaganda.[53]

Similarly, his critique of democracy was not only based on democracy as a godless, secular system that rejects *tawhid* in favour of the will of the people, transparency, and accountability, nor as a way to dominate the region culturally by introducing new values. He also condemned it because it was used as a pretext for political and economic domination of the region, and a means to undermine the resistance to that domination. He questioned the US support for democracy, because 'if the people of the region could choose a political power freely they would choose Islamists, as they did in Algeria; and this is what the Americans reject'.[54]

He also rejected Western political projects because he believed Israel dictates US foreign policy. He stated that 'one can even say that America is Greater Israel' or that 'Israel is a lesser America'.[55] Referring to articles in *The Observer* and *Ma'arif,* which analysed Israeli influence on US policy, he believed that the real goal of the war on Iraq was to liberate Iraq for the Jews, not for the Iraqis as the US claimed.[56]

In his analysis, the final reason why politics had become tarnished was that local regimes collaborate with imperialism and are not based on their own peoples' support. In fact, these local despotic regimes, that he termed *tawaghit* (idols, despots), and the official *'ulama*—called 'establishment *'ulama'*—are deemed even more loathsome than the 'crusading forces' because they claim to be Muslim and mislead the youth. As he saw it, these governments make alliances with 'Zionist-Crusading forces' and support 'the crusading campaign' (*al-hamla al-salibiyya*), as was apparent from the war in Afghanistan and Iraq, whose governments 'will agree to implement American education and Westernise the *umma* in its totality and wipe out Islam'.[57]

This long history of political and economic dominance by the US, supported and implemented by local states and *'ulama,* instilled in 'Uyairi a fundamental distrust of politics, expressed in his rejection of all political institutions, much like the Taliban in Afghanistan:

> To end this situation it is necessary for the Arab states to stop deceiving their people. It is necessary to dissolve the Arab League, the Gulf Cooperation Council, the Ministry of Foreign Affairs, in fact the whole ministry and all that is related to foreign affairs. It suffices to appoint a representative who relays the debates on the issue to the American president and the Foreign Secretary. Neither these ministries nor the ministers have had any positive consequences for the region.[58]

Under these conditions, politics is the root of the problem rather the means to change it. 'Calls for tolerance (*tasamuh*), closer relations (*taqrib*), and mutual understanding (*tafahum*) with the killers (*qatala*) of the *umma*, the crusaders,' he condemned as hypocritical. 'We are surprised that every time their killing increases, the call for debate (*hiwarat*), closer relations (*taqrib*), mutual understanding (*tasamuh*), and coexistence (*ta'ayush*) becomes louder.'[59] For him, the only way to stop their power was to fight them and to call for a *jihad*.[60] Political rather than cultural dissonance between Islam and the West seemed to him to be the root of the problem.

Rationalism and the Westernised Muslim 'Intellectual'

'Uyairi's framing of the enemy was also directed against the influence of Western thought and their promoters in the Islamic world, the moderate reformers, the Westernised intellectuals (*muthaqqafun*), whom he regarded as a Fifth Column. While they claimed to 'enlighten' (*tanwir*) Islamic thought and pretend to lead Muslims to a renaissance, 'Uyairi accused them of supporting imperialism by undermining the true Islamic intellectual heritage. This clash was framed as a struggle between the programme of truth (*manhaj al-haqq*) and the programme of falsehood (*manhaj al-batil*), or the Western programme (*manhaj al-gharb*) called rationalism (*mu'tazilism*).

He highlighted the dangers of rationalising (*'aqlaniyya*) and Westernising (*taghribiyya*) Muslim thought.[61] He stated that during the past century Westernised Muslims (*al-mutagharbiyyun*) called for a rational interpretation (*tafsir*) of the Qur'an and Sunna, subjecting them to materialist principles to bring them closer to the Western model (*manhaj al-gharb*). They were based on Westernising ideas (*afkar taghribiyya*), imported values (*qiyam wafida*), and secular programmes (*al-manhajiyya al-'ilmaniyya*).[62] 'Uyairi regards modernisers (*'asraniyyin*) as especially dangerous because they practice innovation (*bid'a*) and import Western thought (*al-afkar al-wafida*), while pretending to be Islamists and reforming Islam. 'Uyairi stated that modernism (*'asriyya*), modernisation (*'asraniyya*), and Westernisation (*taghribiyya*) are, by definition, opposed to Islamic law (*Shari'a*). He accused intellectuals of being hypocrites (*munafiqun*) and practicing dissimulation (*taqiyya*): 'They form the bridgehead of Western imperialism and culture that is opposed to the Islamic culture in its origin, legacy (*turath*), and history, and mislead (*tadhlil*), corrupt (*tazyif*), and cheat (*khid'a*) the *umma*'.[63] The goal of imperialism is to 'corrupt their deep rooted creed' (*tazyif 'aqidatihim al-rasikha*).[64]

'Uyairi appropriated the discourse of other currents of Islam, radicalised them, and turned them against their original thinker. He used them against prominent thinkers of the Muslim Brotherhood and the more liberal-minded, or former leftists representatives of the Salafi movement.[65] His ire was especially directed at thinkers who called themselves *al-Wasatiyya*, 'the Muslims of the middle of the road', such as the Egyptian Fahmi Huwaydi, who condemned Salafis as 'idolaters, who are worshippers of the text' (*wathaniyyun hum 'abd al-nusus*).[66] He vilified others, such as Hasan al-Turabi, for developing a flexible doctrine, by calling for 'the necessity of a new *fiqh* for a new reality'. As he saw it, what united all these reformers was their call for 'enlightened religious thought' (*al-fikr al-dini al-mustanir*) and that, like the *mu'tazila*, 'they give rationality absolute sovereignty'. In his opinion, their punishment for innovation (*bid'a*), arrogance (*istikthar*), and bad intentions (*su' niyyatihim*) must be excommunication (*takfir*).[67]

426 | The Movements of Movements, Part 1

This does not mean that Yusuf al-'Uyairi was against *tajdid*—reformism—in itself. In fact, 'Uyairi affirmed that Wahhabism was also a reform movement, but he rejected *tajdid* as Muhammad 'Abduh and other 'rationalists' had applied it, on the basis of foreign principles and foreign-inspired programmes (*manahij*).[68] Reform, he argued, cannot be based on replacement (*tabdil*).[69] It can only be based on the pious forefathers, the *salaf al-salih*. Classical terms like *ijtihad*, therefore, have more legitimacy than modern terms like *tajdid*, which are linked to secularism.[70] Similarly, for him terms such as culture (*thaqafa*), intellectual (*muthaqqaf*), and thinker (*mufakkir*) are part of the secular project to drive back and confine Islamic terms like religious scholar (*'alim*, *muta'allim*) and individual reasoning (*ijtihad*) to a separate religious realm of *fiqh*. 'Uyairi believed it was the Salafi Jihadi task to retrieve the original meaning of *tajdid* to regain direction and create a renaissance (*nahda*) and progress (*taqaddum*) that can only be based on an Islamic identity (*huwiya*).[71]

Weakening and Dilution of the *Sahwa manhaj*

If the above actors were enemies in the clash of civilisations, Yusuf al-'Uyairi's relationship with the most important reform movement in Saudi Arabia in the 1990s, the Sahwa movement, was more ambivalent.[72] On the one hand, 'Uyairi praised the Sahwa movement as 'the most important reformist (*tajdid*) movement in Arabic thought and society at the present moment.'[73] In an open letter he even lauded one of its leaders, Safar al-Hawali, for 'your guidance of the Sahwa youth' (*tawjihuka li-shabab al-sahwa*).[74] To another leader, Salman al-'Awda, 'Uyairi wrote 'Dear *shaykh*, may God protect you, you know how much we love you, honour you, and respect you ...'[75] As a sign of respect for Salman al-'Awda, the critique in his open letter is framed as 'advice' (*nasiha*).[76]

On the other hand, it is clear that the purpose of these writings was to castigate the Sahwa *shaykh*s. Two issues stand out. One is the accusation that the *shaykh*s had become part of the 'establishment' *'ulama* when criticising the *mujahidun* for leaving the *manhaj* on account of their extremism (*ghuluw*), violence (*'unf*), and practise of excommunication (*takfir*).[77] Further, they had let the *mujahidin* down by refusing to instruct them during the *jihad* in Bosnia, Afghanistan, and Chechnya.[78] He accused Salman al-'Awda of, specifically, leaving them in the lurch, not just lacking in courage.[79]

Above all, Yusuf al-'Uyairi criticised the Sahwa *shaykh*s for the weakening of their *manhaj* during their stay in prison from 1994 to 1999. Safar al-Hawali was especially castigated for directly attacking the *mujahidin* in his *Address to the Umma Concerning Recent Events*.[80] How 'Uyairi attacked them however, is especially interesting, in terms of the way he approaches his ideological battles within the Islamist movement and for the light it throws on his own revolutionary programme of 'changing reality'. He framed their deviation from the right path in terms of 'orbiting around a new star of a *manhaj*' (*darat fi falak manhaj jadid*), leading to a new way of 'interacting with reality' (*ta'amul ma'a al-waqi'*), which results in abandoning hope of 'changing reality' (*taghyir al-waqi'*). He accused Salman al-'Awda of giving in to the state and having 'submitted to reality' (*rudukh li-l-waqi'*), acquiescing merely in its 'modification not its production' (*tahwiruhu la sina'atihi*), with the result that their *manhaj* is corrupted and weakened.[81]

As an example of separating theory (*tanzir*) from practice (*tatbiq*), Yusuf al-'Uyairi directed his attack on the participation of the Sahwa *shaykh*s in an international campaign in 2003 to protest the US invasion of Iraq.[82] His argument was that the campaign, based on Christian-Muslim dialogue, was based on 'slogans without meaning' and 'images without content'.[83] Instead of devising concrete plans (*al-baramij al-'amaliyya*) for change, the campaign concentrated on 'raising the consciousness of the masses' (*taw'iyat al-'amma*), which, he comments, is already quite aware of the situation.[84] In another essential section where he demonstrated the link between revolutionary praxis (*manhaj*) and creed (*'aqida*), he stated that once one cooperates with the state, one's independence is compromised and one's *manhaj* is 'diluted' (*tamyi'*), which threatens the very creed (*'aqida*) it is based on. Working with 'client governments' means supporting imperialism, leading to coordination (*tansiq*) and cooperation (*ta'awun*) with churches and such Islamic reformists as Fahmi Huwaydi.[85] By betraying the transformative potential of the '*manhaj al-sahwiyyin*' the Sahwa *shaykh*s have become mere 'intellectuals' (*muthaqqafun*), who talk without effect.[86]

If 'Uyairi's critique of the Sahwa *shaykh*s gives an insight into their differences, his willingness to work with them, despite his critique, shows how he tried to include them in a more principled movement of resistance. He ascribed their lack of commitment to ignorance, not wilful rejection, and believed the role of the Sahwa *shaykh*s had not yet ended if they showed themselves 'more enthusiastic (*akthar hamasan*), more perseverant (*akthar sumudan*), and clearer in their *manhaj* (*akthar wuduhan fi-l-manhaj*).' He believed they could still join the *manhaj* of truth if they kept their *manhaj* simple, undiluted, and rejected coexistence (*tasamuh*), tolerance (*tasahul*), pliability (*lin*), and mitigation (*talyin*).[87] He added, in true activist fashion: 'We want to mobilise (*taf'il*) the Islamic people, whose wings are clipped, whose wealth is plundered, and who suffer under governments who refuse them everything, even the right of demonstration.'[88] By rejecting reality (*rafd al-waqi'*) instead of submitting to it, and by adopting the revolutionary programme of the Jihadis, he argued that the Sahwa *shaykh*s could regain their credibility.

In the end, however, the Sahwa *shaykh*s' attitude towards 9/11 and their support for the US constituted a watershed. 'We warn them [that we will condemn them] for apostasy on the grounds that they are helping the crusaders by word or by *fatwas* in favour of the Arab states, condoning the participation in the fight against terrorism.' For 'Uyairi, and the 'aqida of the al-Qaeda on the Arabian Peninsula, any form of cooperation (mu'awana) and assistance (musa'ada) of the kuffar against Muslims either by mouth, deed, or money in lesser or greater form, was unacceptable. Anyone who provided this assistance in any form or degree was an apostate (murtadd).[89]

A Revolutionary Manhaj: The Only Path to Change

The 'Victorious Group' as Vanguard

The concept of a revolutionary praxis (manhaj) and of the instruments of its implementation on the second level derive from the general principles of the 'aqida, which, as we have seen, 'Uyairi claimed to be purer and stronger than of the Sahwa movement. It is also buttressed by the general culturalist master narrative of the clash of civilisations and its corollary of political and economic imperialism. The second level of the revolutionary manhaj forms, as it were, an intermediate stage between the Salafi Jihadist 'aqida and direct application of its principles in reality, providing the agency (the vanguard) and the instruments (al-wala' wa-l-bara' and jihad) for the implementation (tatbiq) of the Jihadist revolution. The previous section sketched the main problem and how other agencies and practices failed to solve it; this section will deal with the solution 'Uyairi provided and the revolutionary manhaj he presented as the only means to obtain revolutionary change.

He did this by, first, asserting the religious legitimacy of the mujahidin. To counter the Sahwa shaykhs' critique, he stated that 'the mujahidin do have a manhaj, a route (tariq), and a concept (fikr), which are in complete agreement with the manhaj of mainstream Sunnism (ahl al-sunna wa-l-jama'a) in their beliefs and fiqh.'[90] He was careful to stress they were not fanatics, or khawarij, as they were called by their enemies.[91] Moreover, he referred to their venerable intellectual tradition.[92] In fact, 'Uyairi argued that the mujahidin, as people of the jihad (ahl al-jihad), have a superior knowledge than religious scholars (ahl al-'ilm).[93] At the heart of this argument is that one can only acquire a true understanding of the world and become part of the victorious group (al-ta'ifa al-mansura) if one is active in the resistance and participates in the jihad.[94]

Having the right religious knowledge, thus, is not enough. Other preconditions are crucial for joining the 'victorious group' who, as leaders of the revolution, must 'enlighten' the people and 'assert its belief (iman) and creed ('aqida) in this matter.'[95] Besides having knowledge, a true Muslim also must be pure himself (tazkiya), and engage in the highest form of activism, jihad.

'Uyairi gave three reasons why the mujahidun are better suited to lead the umma than the Sahwa shaykhs. Firstly, they hold principles supreme, higher than friendship or politics.[96] Secondly, they are self-effacing and willing to sacrifice themselves for the higher goal. 'They will sell their land, and leave their wives and children and money, and they will trample on all forms of opulence (*taraf*) and comfort (*rafahiya*) [to achieve their goals].'[97] Thirdly, the *mujahidun* are independent: They are 'the only ones who say and do what they believe in'. In other words, in contrast to hypocrites, 'the *mujahid* is only afraid of God' and submits to *tawhid*.[98]

These characteristics of the *mujahid* will also lead, he argued, to that other element in revolutionary praxis, the attainment of a superior knowledge of 'reality' (*waqi'*). Yusuf al-'Uyairi states his case for the superiority of revolutionary epistemology in his treatise on martyrdom operations in Chechnya. In this tract he stated that, 'it is not possible to judge this operation and other ones like it, without knowledge of reality (*ma'rifat al-waqi'*)', or the science of reality ('*ilm al-waqi'*)'. More than any other issue of *fiqh*, questions of *jihad* should be based on reality, he argued. But this knowledge is not based on a disinterested analysis of the situation. Neutral knowledge in this phase of a deep crisis of the world is not possible, and knowledge of reality has been transferred to those who have a higher understanding of reality than anyone else: 'Those who want to judge specific instances of *jihad* should first of all ask the people of the *jihad* (*ahl al-jihad*) about the truth of their reality (*haqiqat waqi'ihim*), and only then can they judge. The reality of the *jihad* is taken from the *mujahidin* not from the apostates'. Those who attain consciousness of the highest reality may determine what is true and false.[99]

This Leninist and Maoist logic of praxis, the eulogy of the revolutionary will and knowledge whose incontestable logic is based on the moral superiority of self-sacrifice, and as having a privileged access to truth during the struggle, forms the core of Yusuf al-'Uyairi's formulation of Jihadi Salafism.[100] By stating that revolutionary praxis is the source of religious and scientific truth, all neutral objective criteria for its evaluation are swept aside. It posits the activist *mujahid* as holder of the absolute truth against the ineffective scholar or reformer, who is misled by a 'false consciousness', the arrogant intellectual deluded by rationalism, and the corrupt dictator (*taghut*) in the pay of imperialism. Moreover its claim to superior knowledge, surprising in a martyrdom culture often regarded as irrational, is meant to disarm the moderate reformers who condemn violence as counterproductive and counsel moderation, accusing the *mujahidin* of jeopardising Islam through their fanaticism and irrationalism.

Socially, Jihadism has the additional advantage of ending alienation. By being an individual achievement in resisting temptation and overcoming personal trials, Jihadism leads to a personal salvation and redemption, while simultaneously submitting the individual to superior forces, the collectivity following the will of God, or embodied in laws of history—in the Marxist case—or the general good (*al-maslaha al-'amma*), *tawhid*, or *'aqida* in the Salafist case. In this sense, like Marxism, the Salafi cause constitutes a form of sublimation, liberation, or, in a more mystical sense, self-abnegation, self-transcendence, and redemption.[101]

Al-Wala' wa-l-bara' *and the Training of the Revolutionary Will*

One of the most important means of joining the chosen group and pursuing the *manhaj al-haqq* is to exercise the practice of *al-wala' wa-l-bara'* ('loyalty to Muslims and dissociation from infidels'). *Al-Wala' wa-l-bara'* is part of the Jihadi Salafist *'aqida*. In Yusuf al-'Uyairi's work, this concept acquires an activist dimension and is regarded as a means of steeling the revolutionary will and exercising the revolutionary muscle. It is a mental operation that can be practised in 'reality' and precedes *jihad*. It is also a trial by God of the *mujahid* and the non-*mujahid* to strengthen their resolve to stay away from forces that corrupt, both Muslim and non-Muslim, proving the purity of their intention (*niyya*) and demonstrating their total submission to *tawhid*, thereby becoming a tool in God's hands.

In political terms, it is akin to a boycott. It is allied with the concept of *takfir*, excommunication, and functions as a means of defining the boundaries between good and evil, although *takfir* has a much more (inter)active dimension and is directed against Muslims alone. The *'aqida* of the Jihadist leads to a broadening and radicalising of these concepts, giving them a political meaning in contrast to the social meaning it has for official, state-sanctioned Salafism.[102]

In several places, 'Uyairi elaborated on the disciplining function of *al-wala' wa-l-bara'* and its relation with the *'aqida* and *manhaj*. For instance, he criticised the Sahwa *shaykh*s for distinguishing between neo-conservatives in the US, from whom they believe one should stay away, and liberals, who are acceptable as partners. 'Uyairi stated that the majority of US Americans have applauded the invasion of Iraq and 'this means that the whole of the West is extremist'.[103] In hierarchy, he stated, the rules of *al-wala' wa-l-bara'* are part of the *'aqida* and therefore have the authority of a 'theoretical statement' (*taqrir nazari*) and not that of a 'practical project' (*mashru' 'amali*). Therefore 'as *al-wala' wa-l-bara'* is part of the *'aqida* it applies to all enemies and one must stay away from them, warn against them, and announce one's enmity against them, without distinction between right and left'.[104] Likewise, in another place 'Uyairi argued it is forbidden to participate in elections. In his critique of Salman al-'Awda he states that if they compromise their *manhaj* in this regard, 'they destroy ... the principle of *al-wala' wa-l-bara'*, dilute ... the *'aqida* (*ma'i'u al-'aqida*), and appease ... the *tawaghit* (*dahanu al-tawaghit*)'.[105]

In other words, the principle of *al-wala' wa-l-bara'* functions as a barrier to 'diluting of the identity' (*tamyi' huwiya*) of the Muslim, [in turn undermining his sense] of his belonging (*intima'ihi*) and the fragmentation of his loyalty (*tashtit wala'ihi*).[106] Indeed, 'Uyairi argued that it is one of the central aims of the West to attack the concept and practice of *al-wala' wa-l-bara'*, like *jihad*, and to replace it with concepts that emphasise cooperation and mutual understanding.

Unleashing the Jihadi Revolution

If *al-wala' wa-l-bara'* is a disciplining force, *jihad* is the ultimate embodiment of the activist Islamic project, and is therefore a concept at a higher level. For 'Uyairi it unites all the best qualities a Muslim must have to become a real Muslim, and is the ultimate test of faith (*iman*), commitment (*iltizam*), and perseverance (*sabr*).

Jihad is also the ultimate source of knowledge (*ma'rifat al-'ilm*), experience, and the final means of measuring success in the application (*tatbiq*) of the *manhaj* and strategic thinking.[107] As such, it is both spiritual and physical,[108] intellectual, and practical. *Jihad* is the ultimate proof that one has not been tempted by wealth, political power, and corruption (*fasad*), bribery (*rashwa*), innovation (*bid'a*), and ascribing associates to God (*shirk*), all of which stand in the way of total submission to God and installing a true Muslim society. In particular, *jihad* is a political struggle against all those who participate in the war on Islam as collaborators, 'crusaders', and 'Zionists', politicians, rulers (*tawaghit*), scholars, and hypocrites (*murji'iyyin*). It affects all levels of religious belief and practice, from the spiritual (*ruhiyya*) and the ideational (*fikriyya*), to the method and strategy (*manhaj*) and its practical implementation (*al-tatbiqiyya al-'amaliyya*).[109] Finally, by participating in it the *mujahid* wipes away both the humiliation (*madhilla*) and hypocrisy of the world and the corrupt international order based on man-made laws that benefit imperialism. In this crisis, *jihad* is an individual duty (*fard 'ayn*) on every Muslim to defend the *umma*. All these levels of participating in *jihad* are embodied and represented by the concept of ritual practice, a rite (*sha'ira*), which is regarded as a form of worship (*ta'abbud*).[110]

In general political terms, *jihad* is the ultimate creative modernist project of total destruction in order to build a new world of total submission to an ideal, a concept of absolute purity. Its violence creates a *tabula rasa*.[111] For instance, in his work on Iraq, 'Uyairi stated that to wipe the slate clean violence is imperative: 'The redressing of this humiliation can only be done through *jihad*', for it is impossible for the 'tree of this religion to strike roots in our land until it is irrigated by the blood of its sons, like the first *mujahidin* irrigated it. We will not be able to achieve anything unless we exert ourselves in the same way they did.'[112]

That this principle is not directed at a distant or abstract enemy but at rulers and society close by is clear from how *jihad* becomes the embodiment of *tawhid*. In 'Uyairi's terms, submission to *tawhid* means practising *jihad*. This is both an individual and a social exercise. To achieve total submission to *jihad*, all Muslims must participate in it in one form or another, by 'exercising *jihad* through money' (*jihad bi-l-mal*), 'by the tongue' (*jihad bi-l-lisan*), 'by the hand' (*jihad bi-l-yad*), or 'by means of the heart' (*jihad bi-l-qalb*).

Interestingly, 'Uyairi calls this last aspect of *jihad* 'the very cornerstone of Islam', adding, 'you cannot accept the God of Islam without it'.[113] In fact, it coincides with the practice of *al-wala' wa-l-bara'* and the creed (*'aqida*) as it aims at distancing oneself from the *kuffar*.[114] Moreover, the social aspect of *jihad* as a way of life is also clear from a chapter he devotes to the role parents must play in the *jihad*. 'For this, every father and mother must realise that they carry a heavy responsibility for the victory of this religion. And they must take part in the *jihad* with their sons, their money, their tongues for the victory of Islam and the dignity of the *umma*.' He states that 'obedience of the two parents is a *fard 'ayn*' (individual obligation).[115] As a means of social disciplining, *jihad* aims both to combat fear in society and instil heroism in the *mujahidan*.[116]

For 'Uyairi the ultimate theoretical challenge in this project was to unleash its creative powers. 'Our goal of writing on the principles of *jihad* is to liberate (*tahrir*) the *manhaj* of *jihad* from the chains (*quyud*) and the shackles (*aghlal*) which have enveloped it in darkness (*zulman*) and lies (*juran*).' His goal was to 'correct' (*tashih*) the concept of *jihad*.[117]

To keep faith in victory, he drew up six principles (*thawabit*).[118] The first principle is that *jihad* is eternal and that it will continue 'until God has inherited the earth and all that is on it.'[119] He dismissed as a sign of weakness the argument that Muslims cannot fight the enemy because he is much stronger—an argument found among establishment '*ulama*.[120] The second principle is that *jihad* is not connected to a specific person, as this too can lead to defeatism.[121] The third principle is that *jihad* is not limited by space. '*Jihad* is transnational and is not restricted by boundaries and restrictions.' 'Uyairi also did not recognise the distinction between defensive *jihad* and offensive *jihad*, or the *dar al-islam* and the *dar al-harb*. This does not mean that *jihad* should be carried out everywhere simultaneously. '*Jihad* is not limited territorially but [is based] on legal and practical preconditions.'[122] The fourth principle is that *jihad* is not dependent on the vagaries of the battlefield. 'To connect the ritual of *jihad* to a certain battle [and possible defeat] is one of the reasons for a psychology of defeatism (*inhizamiyya*) and one of the major reasons for the weakness of Muslims today.'[123] The fifth principle is also related to the issue of mental steadfastness. In that sense, the *jihad al-nafs*, struggle against the self, is the pillar of a successful struggle against the enemy. One must become a 'slave of the *jihad*' (*'abd al-jihad*) to succeed. It is in this regard that the intention (*niyya*) must be pure for an action to succeed.[124] And the sixth is that defeat is only related to a weakening of faith.[125]

'Uyairi, who was widely associated with violence and the martyrdom attacks of the al-Qaeda on the Arabian Peninsula, only mentions martyrdom operations as a subsection of the fifth principle, as *jihad al-nafs*, and not as a main component of *jihad*. He justifies these actions when 'the goal is sincere' (*sidq al-qasd*), the 'resolution is firm' (*tasmim al-'azm*), and the *mujahid* has 'the purity of intention of gaining martyrdom' (*ikhlas al-niyya fi talab al-shahada*).[126] But for 'Uyairi, it was only one element among others, one that came as a reward at the end of the clash of civilisations. In his conception this total war is mostly waged in the field

of ideas, in the battle between the way of truth (*manhaj al-haqq*) and the way of
the West (*manhaj al-gharb*) or falsehood (*batil*). Ultimate defeat is ideological
defeat, in which Muslims lose their faith and identity and become animals.[127]
Jihad is therefore both a mental exercise of the elite and a collective duty of all
society to retain its discipline and identity.[128]

Revolutionary Practice

The Permanent Revolution

'Uyairi offered a radical *manhaj* as a response to the clash of civilisations on the first
level. On the second level, he proposed the transforming instruments of *al-wala'
wa-l-bara'* and *jihad*. On the third level of praxis, the phase of implementation (*tatbiq*) by means of 'operations' (*'amaliyyat*), the dialectic with reality is most marked.
Here, the ultimate proof of the efficacy of Jihadism is tested and analysed. This level
is primarily dominated by a strategic analysis, which draws up the means to analyse
the outcome of the struggle of the zero-sum-game. In social movement theory, it is
based on the opportunity structure: When is it feasible and advisable to wage *jihad*,
and by what means and tools? What are the benefits (*masalih*) and disadvantages
(*mafasid*) of particular 'operations' (*'amaliyyat*) and how are they justified?

The analysis of 'reality' is crucial to this. But, of course, this is not a neutral
analysis of cause and effect, for the ultimate criteria of analysis are informed by
the *'aqida* and the zero-sum-game of the clash of civilisations, and basically by
the experience of the *mujahid* as the ultimate arbitrator in determining the 'truth'
by virtue of his purer intention and superior insight into reality. However, on
this level, more than on the other two, there is also room for debate, because it is
here that a tension exists in the dialectical process of the praxis between theory
(*tanzir*) and implementation (*tatbiq*) and the nature of reality.

Although 'Uyairi claimed that *mujahidin* can reach a higher level of knowledge
(*'ilm*) and purity in faith (*niyya*), changing reality in the civilisational struggle is the
ultimate proof of their effectiveness. The Salafi Jihadist cause is rooted in success
on the ground. Praxis is localised and flexible and dependent on a host of elements,
although the criteria of benefits (*masalih*) and disadvantages (*mafasid*) are determined by the crisis of Islam and measure of damage they inflict on the enemy and
the benefits they provide the *umma*. 'Uyairi contributed to this debate and extended
the revolutionary praxis by justifying martyrdom operations and hostage-taking.
And, although this had been done before, the force of his arguments is based on his
command of the 'facts' and how he uses them to justify the revolutionary program.

Martyrdom in Chechnya

Yusuf al-'Uyairi's initial exercises in strategic thinking were probably first applied
in Chechnya, where he encountered martyrdom operations and defended them.

It was also a step in his estrangement from the Sahwa *shaykh*s. 'Uyairi's used the example of Hawa (Eve) Basayev, who is 'one of the small number of women whose glorious name history will remember', to defend suicide missions.[129] In accordance with the principles of *masalih wa mafasid* (benefits and disadvantages), 'Uyairi meticulously explained his justification for martyrdom operations. He stated that it is impossible to reject all martyrdom operations in principle. At the same time, a universal acceptance is also not possible. One must look at each case separately and take into account all the military, political, and religious aspects. Issues he mentions are the position of the enemy, the phase of the war (*wad' al-harb*), personal position (*hal al-shakhs*) of the future martyr, and the circumstances and effects of the operation (*mulabasat al-'amaliyya*).[130] Interestingly, he bases his ultimate jurisprudential argument on *qiyas*, analogy. The main problem is that the *salaf*, the forefathers, did not know this phenomenon.[131] However, the principle of damaging the enemy and gaining paradise remains the same: 'This difference has no effect on the nature of the judgement on the issue.'[132]

The main justification is therefore not religious. Martyrdom only becomes fully legitimate on condition that it is connected with the practical level of inflicting damage on the enemy (*wujud al-nikaya bi-l-'adw*), terrorising them (*irhabuhum*), and strengthening the souls of the Muslims.[133] In the end, the personal level of redemption must coincide with the general interest (*al-maslaha al-'amma*) of the collective.[134] In that sense, the individual purity of intention also serves a public purpose. For only if his or her intentions are pure (*khalisa*) can the martyr mobilise public opinion (*'ala ra'y al-jumhur*).[135] This is the decisive mobilising factor by example for 'it must encourage the Muslims to fight the enemy.'[136] In sum, the strategic benefits of martyrdom operations must outweigh the disadvantages in all these fields for it to be permissible. According to 'Uyairi this was the case in Chechnya because the material and psychological damage caused to the enemy more than compensated for the death of a *mujahid*, who is a *shahid* anyway.[137]

The fact that he did not object to women taking part in the *jihad*, and indeed actively promoted it, is interesting. Whether this means that he saw women as being equal to men is unclear, but it is certainly a deviation from a purist Salafi perspective.

Hostage-Taking in the Philippines and Chechnya

'Uyairi's treatise on the Abu Sayyaf group in the Philippines highlights another aspect of revolutionary praxis.[138] The immediate motivation for his analysis of the Abu Sayyaf group was an article on www.islamtoday in which Salman al-'Awda criticised the Abu Sayyaf group for taking hostages, which, he claimed, has tarnished the name of Islam and damaged the chances of the Islamic Front of Moro in its negotiations with the government. 'Uyairi tried to break down the case of the reformists by demonstrating with 'facts' that the Islamic Front's power is highly inflated and that it lacks infrastructure. His superior knowledge of 'reality' shows that it hardly has any influence for the Abu Sayyaf group to jeopardise.

He moreover 'demonstrated' that the actions of the Abu Sayyaf group were more than justified, legally. In an alarmist analysis of the plight of the Moro, 'Uyairi compared their situation to that of the Palestinians, threatened by systematic colonisation of Muslim lands—in this instance, by Christians. While Christians obtained support from the government, Muslims were forced to resettle and emigrate, which destroyed their livelihood, religion, honour, and offspring. 'Uyairi argued that in these extreme circumstances all means of resistance are allowed, and that the taking of hostages is among the more moderate means of defending oneself. For this he uses the analogy of Muslims who are allowed to eat pork and drink wine to save their lives. Another argument was that Christians who invaded Muslim land have become part of the *dar al-harb* and therefore can be taken hostage.[139]

While 'Uyairi's analysis of Abu Sayyaf was mostly juridical and based on his definition of reality, his treatise on the Moscow Theatre hostage-taking was argued entirely in strategic military and political terms of taking advantage of opportunities.[140] Aside from the general remark that it is allowed to kill Russians because they are at war with Muslim Chechnyans, his analysis focused on the practical level of costs and benefits. The benefits are the expansion of the war into enemy territory and lessening the pressure on the Chechnyan population; heightening the sense of insecurity within the Russian population and increasing its opposition to the war; raising the cost of the war for the Russian state; and last but not least, fermenting divisions between the Russian politicians and military. 'Uyairi even took into account international public opinion that would be moved by the plight of the Chechnyan people and sympathise with them from a human rights perspective. 'Uyairi did not believe in human rights but did not desist from using it in the service of *jihad*.[141] As an important asset of the action, 'Uyairi mentioned that it was composed of all sections of the Chechnyan population.[142] In the rest of his article, in a dubious representation of facts, he enumerates the results of the action in weakening the Russian state and society.[143]

9/11

Yusuf al-'Uyairi's conceptualisation of Jihadi praxis comes into its own with his view of 9/11 in his *The Truth about the New Crusades*[144] and *Questions about the New Crusades*.[145] In the first book, Yusuf al-'Uyairi addressed the jurisprudential issues involved in 9/11, whilst in the second he mostly counters the criticisms directed against the 'operation' (*'amaliyya*).

In both works he showed himself to be a spokesman of al-Qaeda, repeating many of the theological and strategic arguments presented elsewhere. For instance, on a juridical level, he rejected the idea that the US is protected by a 'covenant' (*'ahd*) with the Islamic world because it has 'breached the contract' (*naqd al-'ahd*) with the *umma* by its support of Israel,[146] in addition to committing acts of aggression against Muslims: 'Today it bombs and boycotts Iraq, the Sudan, and Afghanistan and is aggressive towards Muslims.'[147] In his reading, the US is therefore squarely at war with the Muslims, and its territories must be regarded as the abode of war (*dar al-harb*).[148] The argument that among the victims of 9/11 were the elderly, women, and children, all protected categories in Islamic law, is also rejected because their protection is not absolute. Typical of al-Qaeda is the argument that people are no longer innocent when part of a populace involved in war (*ahl al-harb*).[149] Even the accidental killing of Muslims is allowed, for otherwise it would not be possible to wage *jihad* against the West.[150]

Although he frames these issues in theological arguments, the basic principle is strategic: According to him, the advantages (*masalih*) far outweighed the disadvantages (*mafasid*).[151] He sweeps aside the counter-argument that 9/11 jeopardised the *jihad* in Palestine, provoked the destruction of the Taliban regime in Afghanistan, and thereby hampered the spread of Islam.[152] Afghanistan would have fallen sooner or later, he argues, and the sympathy for Muslims has been spurious. He is even willing to sacrifice the lives of Muslims living in the US for the survival of the rest of the *umma*: 'How can we let the interests of five hundred Muslims in the US prevail over those of 300 million Muslims who are being repressed [in the rest of the world] by the United States [?]' In this context of total war, the bad image Muslims have acquired is irrelevant: 'This is the mentality of the fatalist and the feeble-hearted. ... How can the Muslim relinquish the *Shari'a* and the rules of his religion and the example of the Prophet? Our religion is the religion of the slaughtering (*dhabh*) of the *kuffar*, the religion of wiping them out if they do not submit.'[153] Accepting these arguments is in fact falling prey to the strategy of the West to undermine the Muslim resolve to fight the enemy.

'Uyairi gives three reasons why 9/11 should be regarded as successful in the long term. The first is that the *mujahidin* took the initiative and caught the enemy off guard, forcing it to respond while it was unprepared. Secondly, it unmasked the true face of the US as an aggressive country, which in the long run will contribute to the *jihad* against it. Third, he expresses the hope that the US will be bogged down in Afghanistan in a long drawn-out struggle that it cannot win.[154]

Iraq

For the same strategic reasons, Yusuf al-'Uyairi welcomed the invasion of Iraq.[155] For 'Uyairi, Iraq is the ultimate battleground, where all the experience of the *mujahidin* in Afghanistan, Bosnia, Chechnya, and the Philippines comes together. Although 'Uyairi only lived during the first two months of the US invasion of Iraq, he followed events closely and kept a diary on the invasion on the Institute for Islamic Research and Studies website. In this diary, he is mostly concerned with the possibilities of US failure. In the first entries, he believes the real battle still has to occur in the cities, especially Baghdad, which the US Americans are approaching and where he hopes they meet their demise. He expects their technological superiority will not be useful in the cities, where their helicopters and bombs are ineffective, and calculates that it might take eight months for them to take the cities.[156] He advises, for instance, the Iraqi people to adopt the strategy of a guerrilla war, for it 'is a revolutionary war (al-harb al-thawriyya) in which civilians or at least a part of them are mobilised'.[157] Like in the Gaza Strip, where Palestinians hold down a superior Israeli force, he expresses the hope 'that Iraq presents a tremendous opportunity for Muslims to turn Iraq into a hell for the crusaders and to inflict upon them a humiliating defeat, even if that may take some time'.[158]

This opportunity arises when the regime collapses in April, and he is convinced that Iraq has become a golden opportunity to defeat the US: 'Our battle with the crusaders has not ended and will not end after the fall of Baghdad or Iraq as a whole. Our battle with the crusaders is a continuous battle and we as an Islamic umma will continue struggling to evict the crusaders from every place'. In fact, 'fighting them by means of guerrilla [in Iraq] and bleeding them and destroying them is the best means to defend the umma'.[159] Foreshadowing the later influx of youth from surrounding countries, 'Uyairi calls upon the youth to take part in this jihad. Every means of resistance is allowed in this war, including martyrdom operations, and poisoning of food and water. Most of the rest of the series is concerned with detailed guerrilla tactics.[160]

Conclusion: Building Another World— An Alternative Modernist Project?

For liberal Westerners, and perhaps to all those who consider themselves civil, cosmopolitan, and / or progressive, Yusuf al-'Uyairi's thought is not very pleasant. Jihadi Salafism is among the most challenging ideologies of the moment, completely opposed to everything liberalism stands for. As he projects it, Jihadi Salafism rejects debate, tolerance, mutuality, equality of religions, equality of men and women, rationalist philosophy, and freedom of thought. In politics, it is opposed to democracy, pluralism, representative government, international covenants and institutions, and human rights. As politics is corrupt and corrupting, and all political institutions suspicious, only violence remains as a form of resistance. These ideas are anchored in the 'aqida, evolved into instruments of waging the jihad in the manhaj of Jihadi Salafism and implemented in a dialectic between the manhaj and 'reality'.

Becoming the complete Other is, however, not a result of Islam. Nor is it an accident. Although 'Uyairi based himself on the principles of Wahhabism / Salafism, his ideology is framed to meet modern circumstances and challenges. It is a response to repression, war, and destruction that the West has wrought on the Middle East, and in which local regimes participate. It is also a response to how the Sahwa *shaykh*s have been forced to compromise their programme of reform.

In itself, 'Uyairi's work is thoroughly modernist. It is a total worldview that tries to cover all aspects of modern life, framing an ideology for changing reality in all spheres of life. This is done in constant competition with other political, cultural, and religious currents and leaders, especially the Sahwa movement, to demonstrate their weakness on all levels, from their *'aqida* to their *manhaj* and implementation. In contrast to the opinion of some researchers, Jihadi Salafism is not Third Worldist, lacking intentionality, or founded in an individualist mysticism. Rather, it attempts to formulate a response on ideological, cultural, and strategic levels to threats or perceived threats to the Muslim world that emanate from the complete dominance of that world by the West. If these threats are framed as a clash of civilisations, it is buttressed by an elaborate analysis of 'reality', and how the West has ruthlessly manipulated that reality politically, economically, and culturally with the intention of destroying Muslim identity.

'Uyairi's originality lies in his ability to create a revolutionary praxis that enables Muslims to counter this threat uncompromisingly, by establishing a Jihadist culture and politics that mobilises the population under the leadership of a vanguard in a war to the bitter end. The strength of this revolutionary praxis is that it is based on a fixed ideology of confrontation, which is also practical and flexible. Combining both unchanging principles of struggle laid down in the *'aqida*, reformulated as general concepts and instruments of battle in *al-wala' wa-l-bara'* and *jihad*, this revolutionary praxis is tested and adapted in a dialectical process with 'reality'.

However dismaying this might be for those living out other realities, the experience of this past decade and more has shown that this seemingly 'closed' worldview has tremendous appeal for youth in both the Middle East and the West who feel humiliated by their marginalisation in the world that is emerging around them today. It simultaneously contends to be an objective, rational analysis of reality, which it explains in a political, cultural, and religious language, even as it provides instruments with which to change that reality. The worldview put forward promises the redemption of the Muslim world. Though the concept of praxis shows similarities in its broad action-oriented approach to that of Sayyid Qutb, its appeal is perhaps even stronger as it is more elaborate in its theological definition of *'aqida*, its more thorough conceptualisation of resistance and revolution by means of *al-wala' wa-l-bara'*, martyrdom missions, and *jihad*, and its far more detailed analysis of the current relations between the West and the Muslim world. Indeed, 'Uyairi's life as lived is itself in many ways a book that is available for us to read and re-read, to understand how our world, which—to take a phrase from the Zapatistas—is a world in which many worlds fit, is today emerging.

Note on sources

This essay is based on an analysis of the standard texts that are ascribed to Yusuf al-'Uyairi. All of these were found on the Internet, but it is never certain that they were his own works. The only indication that they were so is that the same collections of his texts are found in different formats on different authoritative websites.[161] Nevertheless, some works are very different from others. In addition, it is not certain that some texts are complete or that they have not been edited afterwards, such as the series on Iraq. It is also unclear whether he is the only author, or that other authors have contributed to these works. He certainly copied sections or adopted ideas from others and transformed them—which is also a way to appropriate them. Although I have tried to indicate how he appropriated the themes and tropes of other currents, I have not attempted to certify their originality. In itself, it is interesting that the collections are now regarded as his work. I have tried not to include his military writings, nor the whole imagery of al-Qaeda, much of which probably Yusuf al-'Uyairi was responsible for when he was webmaster of its website, *al-Nida'*.

References

Hannah Arendt, 1970—*On Violence*. New York: Harcourt Brace & World Inc

Raymond W Baker, 2003—*Islam without Fear: Egypt and the New Islamists*. Cambridge, MA: Harvard University Press

Paul Berman, 2004—*Terror and Liberalism*. New York: W W Norton & Company

Leonard Binder, 1988—*Islamic Liberalism: A Critique of Development Ideologies*. Chicago: University of Chicago Press

François Burgat and Muhammad Sbitli, 2002—'Les Salafis au Yémen … la modernisation malgré tout' ['The Salafis in Yemen … Modernisation despite everything', in French], in *Chroniques Yéménites* ('Yemeni Chronicles), vol 10, at https://cy.revues.org/137?lang=en (Accessed April 2017)

Jason Burke, 2003—*Al Qaeda: Casting a Shadow of Terror*. London: I B Tauris

Michael Burleigh, 2006—*Sacred Causes: Religion and Politics from European Dictators to Al Qaeda*. London: Harper Press

Natana Delong-Bas, 2004—*From Revival and Reform to Global Jihad*. Oxford: Oxford University Press

Faisal Devji, 2005—*Landscapes of Jihad: Militancy, Morality, Modernity*. London: Hurst & Company

John L Esposito, ed, 1983—*Voices of Resurgent Islam*. New York: Oxford University Press

Roxanne L Euben, 1999—*Enemy in the Mirror: Islamic Fundamentalism and the Limits of Modern Rationalism—A Work of Comparative Political Theory*. Princeton, NJ: Princeton University Press

Mamoun Fandy, 1999—*Saudi Arabia and the Politics of Dissent*. New York: Palgrave

François Furet, 1995—*Le passé d'une illusion: Essai sur l'idée communiste au XXe siècle* ['The Passing of an Illusion: An Essay on the Idea of Communism in the 20th Century', in French]. Paris: Editions Robert Laffront

Fawaz A Gerges, 2005—*The Far Enemy: Why Jihad Went Global*. Cambridge: Cambridge University Press

Safar al-Hawali, nd—'Bayan li-l-umma 'an al-ahdath' ['Communiqué to the Umma Concerning the Recent Events', in Arabic], at http://www.alhawali.com/main/ (Accessed April 2017)

Faris bin Hazzam, 2005a—'Qissat ta'sis al-Qa'ida fi al-Sa'udiyya', Part I ['The Story of the Founding of al-Qaeda in Saudi Arabia', in Arabic], in *al-Riyad*, September 27 2005

Faris bin Hazzam, 2005b—'Qissat ta'sis al-Qa'ida fi al-Sa'udiyya', Part II, ['The Story of the Founding of al-Qaeda in Saudi Arabia', in Arabic], in *al-Riyad*, October 6 2005

Thomas Hegghammer, 2006a—'Global Jihadism after the Iraq War', in *Middle East Journal*, vol 60 no 1 (Winter 2006)

Thomas Hegghammer, 2006b—'Terrorist Recruitment and Radicalization in Saudi Arabia', in *Middle East Policy*, vol 13 no 4 (Winter 2006)

Thomas Hegghammer and Stéphane Lacroix, September 2004—'Saudi Backgrounder: Who Are the Islamists?', International Crisis Group *Middle East Report*, no 31 (September 21 2004)

Thomas Hegghammer and Stéphane Lacroix, 2007—'Rejectionist Islamism in Saudi Arabia: The Story of Juhayman al-'Utaybi Revisited', in *International Journal of Middle East Studies*, vol 39 no 1

Samuel P Huntington, 1996—*The Clash of Civilizations and the Remaking of World Order*. New York: Simon and Schuster

Toby Jones, Fall 2003—'Seeking a "Social Contract" for Saudi Arabia', in *Middle East Report*, vol 228 (Fall 2003), at http://www.merip.org/mer/mer228/seeking-social-contract-saudi-arabia (Accessed April 2017)

Toby Jones, November 2003—'Violence and the Illusion of Reform in Saudi Arabia', in *Middle East Report*, at http://www.merip.org/mero/mero111303 (Accessed April 2017)

Toby Jones, 2005—'The Clerics, the Sahwa, and the Saudi State', in *Strategic Insights*, vol 4 no 3 (March 2005), at http://www.ccc.nps.navy.mil/si/2005/mar/JonesMar05.asp (Accessed April 2017)

Farhad Khosrokhavar, 2005—*Suicide Bombers: Allah's New Martyrs*. Translated by David Macey. London: Pluto Press

Bruce B Lawrence, ed, 2005—*Messages to the World: The Statements of Osama bin Laden*. London: Verso

Bernard Lewis, 2002—*What Went Wrong? Western Impact and Middle Eastern Response*. London: Phoenix

Rabi' bin Hadi al-Madkhali, 2007—'al-Bahth 'ala al-muwadda wa-l-i'tilaf wa-l-tahdhir min al-firqa wa-l-ikhtilaf', at www.rebee.net/show_des.aspx@ pid=3&d=263.12/21/1429/2007 (Accessed rm January 22 2009, inactive April 2017)

William McCants and Jarret Brachman, 2006—*Militant Ideology Atlas, Executive Report*. West Point, NY: Combating Terrorism Center, at https://www.files.ethz.ch/isn/26189/Atlas-ExecutiveReport.pdf (Accessed April 2017)

Roel Meijer, 2005—'The "Cycle of Contention" and the Limits of Terrorism in Saudi Arabia', in Paul Aarts and Gerd Bauman, eds, 2005—*Saudi Arabia in the Balance: Political Economy, Society, Foreign Affairs*. London: Hurst & Company

Roel Meijer, ed, 2009—*Global Salafism: Islam's New Religious Movement*. New York: Columbia University Press

Abu Bakr Naji, 2006—*Idara al-tawahhush, Akhtar marhala satamarra bihi al-umma* ['The Management of Savagery: The Most Critical Stage through which the Umma Will Pass', in Arabic]. Translated by William McCants. John M Olin Institute for Strategic Studies, Harvard University, at https://azelin.files.wordpress.com/2010/08/abu-bakr-naji-the-management-of-savagery-the-most-critical-stage-through-which-the-umma-will-pass.pdf (Accessed April 2017)

Gwenn Okruhlik, 2001—'Understanding Political Dissent in Saudi Arabia', in *Middle East Report Online*, at http://www.merip.org/mero/mero102401 (Accessed April 2017) (Accessed April 2017)

Gwenn Okruhlik, nd—'Networks of Dissent: Islamism and Reform in Saudi Arabia', on SSRC site, 'After Sept 11', at http://essays.ssrc.org/sept11/essays/okruhlik.htm (Accessed April 2017)

Peter Phillips, 2002—'Report from Cairo on the International Campaign against US Aggression on Iraq'. Centre for Research on Globalisation, at http://www.globalresearch.ca/articles/PHI212A.html (Accessed April 2017)

Madawi Al-Rasheed, 2007—*Contesting the Saudi State: Islamic Voices from a New Generation*. Cambridge: Cambridge University Press

Olivier Roy, 2004—*Globalised Islam: The Search for a New Umma*. London: Hurst & Company

Alfred Schmidt, 1974—'Praxis', in H G Backhaus et al, eds, 1974—*Gesellschaft. Beiträge zur Marxschen Theorie*, Part 2['Society: Contributions to Marxist theory', in German] Frankfurt: Suhrkamp

Stuart R Schram, ed, 1969—*The Political Thought of Mao Tse-tung*. New York: Frederick A Praeger

David A Snow and Robert D Benford, 1988—'Ideology, Frame Resonance, and Participant Mobilization', in *International Social Movement Research*, vol 1

Sidney Tarrow, 1998—*Power in Movement: Social Movements and Contentious Politics*. Cambridge: Cambridge University Press

Joshua Teitelbaum, 2000—*Holier than Thou: Saudi Arabia's Islamic Opposition*. Washington, DC: The Washington Institute for Near East Policy

Wikipedia, nd—'February 15, 2003 anti-war protests', at http://en.wikipedia.org/wiki/February_15,_2003_anti-war_protests (Accessed April 2017)

Quintan Wiktorowicz, 2001—'The New Global Threat: Transnational Salafis and Jihad', in *Middle East Policy*, vol 8 no 4

Quintan Wiktorowicz, 2004—'Framing Jihad: Intramovement Framing Contests and al-Qaeda's Struggle for Sacred Authority', in *International Review of Social History*, vol 49 supplement 12

Quintan Wiktorowicz, ed, 2004—*Islamic Activism: A Social Movement Theory Approach*. Bloomington: Indiana University Press

Quintan Wiktorowicz, 2006—'Anatomy of the Salafi Movement', in *Studies in Conflict and Terrorism*, vol 29 no 3

Yusuf al-'Uyairi—A select bibliography

[Note for those not familiar with the transliteration of Arabic into English: Titles starting with '*al-*' are cited in the endnotes according to the first subsequent word. For consistency and ease of access therefore, the full citations are also listed / ordered here accordingly—by the initial of the subsequent word.]

- *'Amaliyyat 'al-Masrah fi Muskuw', madha rabiha minha al-mujahidun wa madha khasaru?* ['The "Moscow Theatre" operation: What did mujahidun benefit and what did they lose?' , in Arabic], nd, np
- *Hal intaharat Hawwa' am istashhadat? bahth mutawwal fi hukm al-'amaliyyat al-ishtishhadiyya* ['Has Eve committed suicide or has she martyred herself? An elaborate study on martyrdom operations', in Arabic], nd, np
- *al-Hamla al-'alamiyya li-muqawamat al-'udwan: Zayf, khida', wa-sha'arat kadhiba* ['The global campaign for resisting aggression: Deception, treachery, and false slogans', in Arabic], nd, np
- *Haqiqat al-harb al-salibiyya al-jadida* ['The truth of the new crusade', in Arabic]. Second issue published in Rajab, 1422 (September 2001), np
- *Hasan Farhan al-Maliki wa zahira naqd usul al-shar'iyya* ['Ḥasan Farhan al-Maliki and the phenomenon of the critique of the roots of legitimacy', in Arabic]
- *Hidayat al-hayara fi jawaz qatl al-asara* ['Guidance for the perplexed on the permissibility of killing prisoners', in Arabic], nd, np
- *Hukm al-jihad wa-anwa'ihi* ['The Pronouncement / Judgment of *Jihad* and its forms', in Arabic], nd, np
- *Ida'at 'ala tariq al-jihad* ['Illuminations on the road of *jihad*', in Arabic], nd, np
- *al-'Iraq wa-l-Jazira al-'Arabiyya ba'd suquṭ Baghdad* ['Iraq and the Arabian Peninsula after the Fall of Baghdad', 2003', in Arabic], np
- *Ma hakadha al-'adl ya fadila al-shaykh! Difa'an 'an Jama'a Abi Sayyaf al-Filbiniyya* ['This is not justice, oh honoured Shaykh. In defence of the Society of Abu Sayyaf of the Philippines', in Arabic], nd, np
- *al-Mizan li-haraka Taliban* ['The Taliban movement in balance', in Arabic], nd, np
- *Munasahat Salman al-'Awda ba'd taghyir manhajihi* ['Advice to Salman al-'Awda after he changed his *manhaj*', in Arabic], nd, np
- *Risala maftuha ila shaykh Safar al-Ḥawali* ['Open letter to Shaykh Safar al-Hawali', in Arabic] nd, np
- *Risala min Yusuf al-'Uyairi, ahad al-maṭlubin al-tis'a 'ashar ila 'umum al-muslimin* ['Letter from Yusuf al-'Uyairi, one of the List of 19, to the Muslims, 2003', in Arabic], np
- *Risalat al-shaykh Yusuf li-ra'is qism da'irat al-raqaba 'ala al-sujun fi al-mantiqa al-sharqiyya 'an awda' sijn al-Dammam* ['The letter of Shaykh Yusuf (al-'Uyairi) to the director of the department of inspection of the prisons in the southern region on the conditions of the prison of Dammam', in Arabic], nd, np
- *al-Riyada al-badaniyya qabla al-jihad* ['Physical exercises before participating in the *jihad*', in Arabic], nd, np

- *Silsilat al-harb al-salibiyya 'ala al-'Iraq* ['Series on the crusade war in Iraq', in Arabic] (March–April 2003), np
- *Tasa'ulat hawla al-harb al-salibiyya al-jadida* ['Questions about the new crusades', in Arabic], nd, np
- *Tawajud al-Amrika fi al-Jazira al-'Arabiyya: Haqiqa wa-ahdaf* ['The Presence of America in the Arabian Peninsula: Truth and Goals', in Arabic], nd, np
- Thawabit 'ala darb al-jihad ['The principles of jihad', in Arabic], nd, np

Notes

1. This essay is a slightly changed version of an article that appeared earlier, 'Yusuf al-Uyairi and the Making of a Revolutionary Salafi Praxis', in *Die Welt des Islams* ['The World of Islam', in German] vol 47 nos 3–4 (2007), pp 422–459. I want to thank the editors of *Die Welt des Islams* for their kind permission to republish it here in a slightly different version.

    Ed: I would like to add my warm thanks to the author for his immense patience in addressing all the small revisions that I requested for this edition of this marvellous essay, and also the editors of *Die Welt des Islams* for their permission to the author to republish it here. For further reproduction permission, contact the author at roel-meijer@planet.nl.

2. The exceptions are Wiktorowicz 2001, pp 18–38; Lawrence 2005; and Gerges 2005. See also Burgat and Sbitli 2002. Ed: This essay was completed by the author in 2009, and therefore does not take into account subsequent publications (or developments).

3. The most extensive collections of articles on Salafism is the book I have edited, Meijer 2009. For an extensive analysis of the differences in doctrine and practice between the different currents within Salafism, see my introduction 'Genealogies of Salafism', pp 1–32. For specific analyses of Jihadi Salafism, see Hegghammer 2006a, pp 11–32. For an analysis of earlier forms of Salafism, see Hegghammer and Lacroix 2007, pp 103–122. Much of the research on the intellectual background of Jihadi Salafism is of a strategic nature, geared to finding the underlying aims and methods Jihadi Salafi thinkers propagate in their works. See, for instance, the translation of Abu Bakr Naji's *Idara al-tawahhush, Akhtar marhala satamarra bihi al-umma* (Naji 2006).

4. See, for instance, Lewis 2002.

5. Euben 1999; Berman 2004.

6. Roy 2004; Devji 2005.

7. Burke 2003, p 82.

8. Roy 2004, p 50.

9. See for an interesting compilation of this approach, Wiktorowicz 2004.

10. See Quintan Wiktorowicz's 'Introduction: Islamic Activism and Social Movement Theory', in Wiktorowicz 2004, pp 1–33.

11. By 'Islamist' I mean political Muslim movements that strive for the establishment of an Islamic state and want to implement the *Shari'a*, such as the Muslim Brotherhood before its reformation in the 1990s. The non-political, quietist Salafist current of Nasir al-Din al-Albani is not Islamist in this sense. There is also a difference in the adoption of ideas of non-Salafi or semi-Salafi Islamist movements such as the

Egyptian al-Jama'at al-Islamiyya and Tanzim al-Jihad. Whereas the purist Salafis reject these political currents, the political and Jihadist Salafi movement have been influenced by them.

12. See the biography of Yusuf al-'Uyairi written by Reuven Paz, in Meijer 2009, pp 441–442.

13. Yusuf al-'Uyairi is usually called a 'Jihadi strategist'; see McCants and Brachman 2006, p 9; Hegghammer 2006a, p 16. This designation, however, neglects 'Uyairi's non-strategic works and his worldview, into which his military strategy must be located to give it meaning.

14. See, for a good review of the concept praxis, Schmidt 1974, pp 264–308.

15. Tarrow 1998, p 4.

16. Okruhlik nd and 2001; Jones 2003a and 2003b.

17. For the exception, see especially the outstanding work of Madawi Al-Rasheed (Al-Rasheed 2007). See also my article, 'The 'Cycle of Contention' and the Limits of Terrorism in Saudi Arabia' (Meijer 2005, pp 271–311). For an overview of the different currents and their interaction see Hegghammer and Lacroix, September 2004.

18. For more on framing, see Snow and Benford 1988, pp 197–217; Wiktorowicz 2004, pp 159 177.

19. Tarrow 1998, pp 106–122.

20. Salafism has its origins in Wahhabism, the doctrine propagated by the eighteenth-century reformer from the Arabian Peninsula, Muhammad ibn Abd al-Wahhab. His followers have laid claim to the term 'Salafi', which refers to the first three generation of Muslims, the last dying around 810, the so-called *al-salaf al-salih*, in order to hide their sectarian character and represent the true Islam.

21. al-Madkhali 2007, p 13.

22. See especially the reading of Sayyid Qutb by Leonard Binder, 'The Religious Aesthetics of Sayyid Qutb: A Non-Scriptural Fundamentalism', in Binder 1988, pp 170–105. It is not clear whether Yusuf al-'Uyairi was directly influenced by Qutb. He does not mention him in the line of thinkers who developed the Jihadist *manhaj* in his *Risala maftuha ila shaykh Safar al-Hawali* ('Open letter to Shaykh Safar al-Hawali'). In my view, every revolutionary or political movement has to deal with the interaction between theory and practice to devise a method of changing reality. This is the similarity with the Marxist and Leninist movements. The ideological similarities between 'Uyairi and Qutb are that both regard current regimes as *kufr*. The differences are that 'Uyairi does not condemn all of society, and that his concept of praxis is much more detailed and strategic. In the Salafist tradition, he musters a much more elaborate theological apparatus than Qutb to justify the Islamic revolution against the West and local authoritarian regimes. It is therefore also more legalistic and less 'emotional' than Qutb's promotion of *jihad*, as Binder argues. In his attempt to unleash the creative forces of *jihad* 'Uyairi propounds a much more elaborate concept of *jihad* as a means to change society as a whole into a Jihadist force that is imbued with its activist spirit. In this sense, his work is both more abstract and theoretical and more detailed and concrete, although he tries to mobilise the same forces and refuses to provide a political programme and an end goal, except in such vague terms as creating a Muslim society. Partly, 'Uyairi's more elaborate concept of praxis stems from the long experience the Jihadist movement

has had and the evolution of the Jihadist ideology since Qutb wrote *Signposts* in the 1960s. Its shift to include the West and the concentration on very specific issues of Western interference in the Middle East and elsewhere also reflects the globalisation of Western culture and politics, and the transnationalisation of the Jihadist movement.

23. There are parallels with Mao Zedong's concept of praxis, which is also an adaptation of those of Lenin's to the local circumstances. See 'On Practice', in Schram 1969, pp 190–194.

24. Wiktorowicz 2006, pp 208–213. He states: 'Salafis are united by a common creed, which provides principles and a method for applying religious beliefs to contemporary issues and problems', and 'The splits are about contextual analysis, not belief' (p 208).

25. This is confirmed by the enormous importance they ascribe to their distinct *'aqida*, often published as a separate document that demonstrates their principles. Due to the importance and nature of these documents, they should be regarded as a manifesto of their religious and political programme. See for instance the manifesto of al-Qaeda on the Arabian Peninsula, *'aqidat al-ta'ifa al-mansura*, published by their electronic magazine, *Ṣawt al-Jihad*, or that of al-Qaeda in the Land of the Two Rivers, *Hadhihi 'aqidatuna*, or that of Abu Muhammad al-Maqdisi of the same title. *Kitab al-tawhid*, written by Muhammad ibn 'Abd al-Wahhab, has also been called his manifesto (cf Delong-Bas 2004, p 57). While the *Sawt al-Jihad* manifesto enumerates its basic principles, such as the political struggle against the idol / despot (*taghut/tawaghit*), unbelievers (*kafir/kuffar*), international political system, and democracy, in which *jihad* and *takfir* figure prominently, the manifesto of Abu Muhammad al-Maqdisi is far more classical. See also the *'aqida* of al-Qaeda in Bernard Haykel's 'On the Nature of Salafi Thought and Action', in Meijer 2009, pp 33–57. It seems that Wiktorowicz's model as presented in Wiktorowicz 2006 is too schematic.

26. See for a biographical account of 'Uyairi's life and others associated with his organisation, Hegghammer 2006b, pp 39–60.

27. There is basically one biography, published in two issues of *Sawt al-Jihad*, no 1, pp 15–18 and no 2, pp 15–18, written by Muhammad bin Ahmad al-Salim. It has subsequently been republished as *Man huwa al-shaykh al-Battar?* on the website www.tawhed.ws, which has been copied in an abridged version as *Muqtataf min sira Yusuf al-'Uyairi* ('Selections from the life of Yusuf al-'Uyairi'), and completely as *Siyar a'lam al-shuhada* ('The lives of the outstanding martyrs' published by the radical website *al-Qa'idun* in 1427 / 2004. (Inactive April 2017).

28. 'Uyairi—*Risalat al-shaykh Yusuf li-ra'is qism da'irat al-raqaba 'ala al-sujun fi al-mantiqa al-sharqiyya 'an awda' sijn al-Dammam* ('The letter of Saykh Yusuf [al-'Uyairi] to the director of the department of inspection of the prisons in the southern region on the conditions of the prison of Dammam').

29. 'Uyairi—*Hidayat al-hayara fi jawaz qatl al-asara* ('Guidance for the perplexed on the permissibility of killing prisoners').

30. 'Uyairi—*Hal intaharat Hawwa' am istashhadat? bahth mutawwal fi hukm al-'amaliyyat al-ishtishhadiyya* ('Has Eve committed suicide or has she martyred herself? An elaborate study on martyrdom operations').

31. 'Uyairi—'Amaliyyat "al-Masrah fi Muskuw", madha rabiha minha al-mujahidun wa madha khasaru? ('The "Moscow Theatre" operation: What did mujahidun benefit and what did they lose?').

32. 'Uyairi—al-Mizan li-haraka Taliban ('The Taliban movement in balance'). According to the biographies he finished this book after 'The truth of the new crusade' (see note 19).

33. 'Uyairi—Ma hakadha al-'adl ya fadila al-shaykh! Difa'an 'an Jama'a Abi Sayyaf al-Filbiniyya ('This is not justice, oh honoured Shaykh. In defence of the Society of Abu Sayyaf of the Philippines'). It is a open letter addressed to Salman al-'Awda after he attacked the Abu Sayyaf group of un-Islamic activities by taking hostages.

34. 'Uyairi—Haqiqat al-harb al-salibiyya al-jadida ('The truth of the new crusade'). Second issue published in Rajab, 1422 (September 2001).

35. Bin Hazzam 2005a.

36. Bin Hazzam 2005b.

37. See al-Sharq al-Awsat, June 4 2003 and July 30 2003.

38. 'Uyairi—Risala min Yusuf al-'Uyairi, ahad al-matlubin al-tis'a 'ashar ila 'umum al-muslimin ('Letter from Yusuf al-'Uyairi', one of the List of 19, to the Muslims, 2003).

39. Huntington 1996

40. 'Uyairi—al-'Iraq wa-l-Jazira al-'Arabiyya ba'd suqut Baghdad ('Iraq and the Arabian Peninsula after the Fall of Baghdad', 2003), p 5

41. 'Uyairi—Risala maftuha ila shaykh Safar al-Hawali ('Open letter to Shaykh Safar al-Hawali'), p 10.

42. al-'Iraq wa-l-Jazira al-'Arabiyya, p 16.

43. This is a common but also specific theme that he uses, for instance, to legitimise kidnapping in the Philippines by the Abu Sayyaf group. See: 'Uyairi—Ma hakadha al-'adl, p 16.

44. 'Uyairi—Thawabit 'ala darb al-jihad ('The principles of jihad'), p 41f.

45. 'Uyairi—al-'Iraq wa-l-Jazira al-'Arabiyya, p 5.

46. ibid, pp 5ff.

47. ibid, p 9.

48. ibid, p 13.

49. ibid, p 50.

50. ibid, pp 16f.

51. 'Uyairi—Tawajud al-Amrika fi al-Jazira al-'Arabiyya: Haqiqa wa-ahdaf ('The presence of America in the Arabian Peninsula: Truth and Goals'), pp 16ff; al-'Iraq wa-l-Jazira al-'Arabiyya, pp 28f.

52. ibid, pp 1–24. See also his al-'Iraq wa-l-Jazira al-'Arabiyya, pp 22f.

53. ibid, pp 43f.

54. ibid, pp 50–53.

55. ibid, pp 46f.

56. ibid, p 8.

57. ibid, p 11.

58. ibid, p 45.

59. ibid, p 11.

60. Tawajud al-Amrika, p 15.

61. 'Uyairi—*Hasan Farhan al-Maliki wa zahira naqd usul al-shar'iyya* ('Ḥasan Farhan al-Maliki and the phenomenon of the critique of the roots of legitimacy').

62. ibid, p 5.

63. ibid, p 5.

64. ibid, p 9.

65. For a broader analysis of the discourse of authenticity and Islam, see: Baker 2003; *Ḥasan Farhan al-Maliki*, pp 23–34.

66. 'Uyairi—*Hasan Farhan al-Maliki*, p 26.

67. ibid, p 36.

68. ibid, pp 39f.

69. ibid, p 19.

70. ibid, p 4.

71. ibid, p 42.

72. For a general overview of the movement in the 1990s, see Fandy 1999 and Teitelbaum 2000. For an analysis of the Sahwa movement since its leaders have been released from prison and co-opted by the state, see Al-Rasheed 2007, pp 59–101 and Jones 2005.

73. 'Uyairi—*Hasan Farhan al-Maliki*, p 12.

74. 'Uyairi—*Risala maftuha*, p 2.

75. 'Uyairi—*Ma hakadha al-'adl*, p 1.

76. 'Uyairi—*Munasahat Salman al-'Awda ba'd taghyir manhajihi* ('Advice to Salman al-'Awda after he changed his *manhaj*') was published as an open letter on August 15 2000, eight months after the release of Salman al-'Awda from prison. Interestingly, the form of discrete advice, *nasiha*, was also used by the Sahwa *shaykhs* in their critique of the state in 1991.

77. 'Uyairi—*Risala maftuha*, p 21f.

78. ibid, pp 15 and 21.

79. 'Uyairi—*Ma hakadha al-'adl*, p 3.

80. Safar al-Hawali, *Bayan li-l-umma 'an al-ahdath* (accessed on the website of Safar al-Hawali, May 2006).

81. Munasahat Salman al-'Awda, p 4.

82. See: Phillips 2002; Wikipedia nd. It is not entirely clear which campaign 'Uyairi is referring to when he is dealing with the campaign the Sahwa shaykhs participated in.

83. 'Uyairi—*al-Hamla al-'alamiyya li-muqawamat al-'udwan: Zayf, khida', wa-sha'arat kadhiba* ('The global campaign for resisting aggression: Deception, treachery, and false slogans'), p 4.

84. ibid, p 8.

85. ibid.

86. ibid, p 4.

87. Munasahat Salman al-'Awda, p 6.

88. 'Uyairi—*Hamla*, p 8.

89. 'Uyairi—*Haqiqat al-harb al-salibiyya al-jadida*, pp 11f. See also *'Aqidat al-ta'ifa al-mansura* issued by Sawt al-Jihad.

90. 'Uyairi—*Risala maftuha*, pp 18, 22.

91. 'Uyairi—*Hamla*, p 9.

92. 'Uyairi—*Risala maftuha*, p 18. In the debate around whether Salafism and Jihadi Salafism are indigenous or influenced by 'foreigners', Yusuf al-'Uyairi responds to Safar al-Hawali and gives an account of the genealogy of the Jihadi Salafi' foundation of the programme (*ta'sil al-manhaj*) that includes much more 'foreigners' than Saudis: Abdallah 'Azzam, 'Umar 'Abd al-Rahman, Shaykh Tamim al-'Adnani, Shaykh Abu Talal al-Qasimi, Ayman al-Zawahiri, Shaykh Rifa'i Ahmad Taha, Shaykh 'Abd al-Qadir 'Aziz, Shaykh Abu Yasir al-Misri, Shaykh Abu Hafs al-Muritani, Shaykh Abu 'Abdallah al-Muhajir, and Shaykh Abu Ibrahim al-Misri. Interestingly, Sayyid Qutb is not included.

93. I have derived the notion that he believed that Jihadis are superior from his work on Chechnya, but this is also clear in the open letters to Safar al-Hawali and Salman al-Awda. The term *ahl al-jihaad* is used in his work on Chechnya, *Istishhadiyya*, p 5, and Iraq, *Silsilat al-harb al-salibiyya 'ala al-'Iraq*, p 43. The term *ahl al-'ilm* is also used throughout his work.

94. This is also the central Marxist, especially Leninist and Maoist, concept of praxis related to the idea of the vanguard.

95. 'Uyairi—*Hamla*, p 12.

96. 'Uyairi—*Ma hakadha al-'adl*, p 1.

97. 'Uyairi—Risala maftuha, p 12.

98. ibid.

99. 'Uyairi—*Hal intaharat Hawwa'*, p 5.

100. For a comparison with the Bolshevik Party and Lenin's concept of the vanguard, which also has origins in sectarian Christian origins and community of faith, see Burleigh 2006, pp 75–86.

101. Khosrokhavar 2005, p 44; Faisal Devji 2005.

102. See Al-Rasheed 2007, chapter 1, pp 22–58.

103. 'Uyairi—*Hamla*, p 11.

104. ibid.

105. 'Uyairi—Munasahat Salman al-'Awda, p 4.

106. 'Uyairi—*Hasan Farhan al-Maliki*, p 51.

107. 'Uyairi has written three works on *jihad*. The most important is *Thawabit 'ala darb al-jihad* ('Principles of *Jihad*'). His other works are *Ida'at 'ala tariq al-jihad* ('Illuminations on the road of *jihad*') and *Hukm al-jihad wa-anwa'ihi* ('The Pronouncement / Judgment of *Jihad* and its forms').

108. It is interesting that Yusuf al-'Uyairi has also written a manual on physical exercises for *jihad*: *al-Riyada al-badaniyya qabla al-jihad* ('Physical exercises before participating in the *jihad*').

109. 'Uyairi—*Thawabit*, pp 3f.

110. 'Uyairi—*Thawabit*, p 2.

111. For a comparison with communism and modern 'constructivism' and the urge to see the social as a product of the will, the rejection of traditions, and the passion for the future, see Furet 1995. Self-realisation through violence is also found in Sartre's introduction to Franz Fanon's *Wretched of the Earth* where he states that 'irrepressible violence … is man recreating himself'. It is through 'mad fury' that the 'wretched of the earth' can 'become men'. See Arendt 1970, p 12.

112. *Ba'd suqut Baghdad: Mustaqbal al-'Iraq wa-l-Jazira al-'Arabiyya*, p 2. Furet argues that communism exerted tremendous attraction for claiming the truth of its praxis,

because it simply was revolutionary, shortened the path to the future, trusted only action, and announced the new citizen liberated from egoism as the only legitimate participant in the social contract. It was universal and had history on its side (Furet 1995, p 124). Like communism, Jihadi Salafism is highly abstract and has shorn Salafism of its mundane practices and rituals, transforming it into a totalising concept that demands total submission and commitment.

113. 'Uyairi—*Ida'at*, pp 3ff.
114. ibid p 5.
115. ibid, p 15.
116. 'Uyairi—*Tasa'ulat hawla al-harb al-salibiyya al-jadida* ('Questions about the new crusades'), pp 6f.
117. 'Uyairi—*Thawabit*, p 2.
118. ibid, p 18.
119. ibid, p 5.
120. See also this argument in *Tasa'ulat*, pp 6f.
121. 'Uyairi—*Thawabit*, pp 12–20.
122. ibid, pp 22f.
123. ibid, pp 26f.
124. ibid, pp 29–33.
125. ibid, pp 41–46.
126. 'Uyairi—*Hal intaharat Hawwa'*, p 24.
127. 'Uyairi—*Thawabit*, pp 42–45.
128. It is instructive to make a comparison with another revolutionary Islamist, Sayyid Qutb. Although there are many similarities, 'Uyairi's works are much less concerned with a broad vision and theory and more with revolutionary praxis and interaction with reality. See for instance, Yvonne Y. Haddad's 'Sayyid Qutb: Ideologue of Islamic Revival', in Esposito 1983, pp 67–98. See especially the section on Qutb's concept of *manhaj* (p 90), which, in contrast to 'Uyairi's highly practical use of the term, is abstract and ritualistic, and proceeds through four stages: forming a community (*jama'a*), being prosecuted in a *jahiliyya* society, migration, and the final victory and consolidation of power.
129. 'Uyairi—*Hal intaharat Hawwa'*, p 2.
130. ibid, p 5.
131. 'The difference between the period of the *salaf* and the contemporary period is not that now we are able to penetrate deeply in enemy lines individually or as group, but in the past that martyrs were killed by the hands of the enemy [by swords and spears] whereas today they are killed by their own hands [explosives].' See ibid, p. 20.
132. ibid, p 20.
133. ibid, p 28.
134. ibid, p 30.
135. ibid.
136. ibid, p 45.
137. ibid, p 7.
138. 'Uyairi—*Ma hakadha al-'adl*.
139. ibid, p 18.

140. 'Uyairi —*'Amaliyyat 'masrah Muskuw', Madha rabiha al-mujahidun minha wa madha khasiru?* ('The Moscow Theatre' operation: What benefit did the *mujahidun* reap and what losses did they incur?').

141. ibid, pp 2f.

142. ibid, p 4.

143. ibid, pp 6–12.

144. 'Uyairi—*Haqiqat al-harb*.

145. 'Uyairi—*Tasa'ulat*.

146. 'Uyairi—*Haqiqa al-harb*, pp 4f.

147. ibid, p 5.

148. ibid.

149. ibid, pp 5ff. The most famous case is the case of *tatarrus*, but 'Uyairi mentions another six instances in which 'innocents' can be killed in battle: In retribution; in revenge when unbelievers target children, elders, and women; when they cannot be discerned from the attackers; when they help the attackers in deeds or words; when it is impossible to make a difference between them and the enemy with heavy weapons, as happened in Ta'if; when they form a shield (*tatarrus*) for the enemy with their women, children, and the enemy, and could not be fought without killing the shield (*turs*); when they violate (*nakatha*) the treaty (*'ahd*) and they are punished in retribution, exemplary punishment (*tankil*), as happened with the Bani Qurayza.

150. ibid, pp 7f.

151. ibid, pp 8f. and *Tasa'ulat*, p 3.

152. 'Uyairi—*Haqiqat al-harb*, p 10f.

153. ibid, p 11.

154. 'Uyairi—*Tasa'ulat*, p 9.

155. 'Uyairi—*Silsilat al-harb al-salibiyya 'ala al-'Iraq* ('Series on the crusade war in Iraq') (March–April 2003).

156. ibid, pp 18–23.

157. ibid, p 30.

158. ibid, p 32.

159. ibid, p 43.

160. ibid, p 44.

161. These include www.tawhed.ws of Abu Muhammad al-Maqdisi and www.ozooo.tk (Both links inactive April 2017).

The Networked Internationalism of Labour's Others[1]

Peter Waterman

In March 2002, the UK-based International Union of Sex Workers (IUSW), London, became an affiliate of the General Municipal and Allied Workers Union, one of Britain's oldest. It should be noted that, although networked internationally, the IUSW is formally a trade union, and that it is actually a national or even local (London) union of international (ie cross-national) sexworkers. Therefore, like other such new kinds of collective worker self-expression, this is less a case for celebration, more one for investigation.

Photo: Fredderico D'Ammicci

We peasants, artisans, and others
Enrolled among the sons of toil
Let's claim the earth henceforth for brothers,
Drive the indolent from the soil!
On our flesh too long has fed the raven,
We've too long been the vulture's prey.
But now farewell the spirit craven,
The dawn brings in a brighter day!

Then comrades come rally!
And the last fight let us face.
The Internationale
Unites the human race!
(Chorus, 2x)
(From an English translation of Eugène Pottier's *L'Internationale*)[2]

The Internationalism/s of Labour's Others

Although long considered the anthem of international union, labour, socialist, and communist movements, Potier's words nowhere refer to any of these. It stands more in the tradition of Flora Tristán's 'Workers' Union' of 1843,[3] in which the uprising and emancipation of labouring people (in France? anywhere? everywhere?) would lead to universal liberty, equality, and solidarity. In Potier's French original there is a first verse reference to *"les damnés de la terre"* (thus "the *damned* of the earth", and not, as in the English, "wretched"). There was, therefore, added licence for Frantz Fanon to use the phrase for the title of his book and make it apply to the poor of the Third World.[4] But he thereby laid another *particular* claim on a *universal* appeal to internationalism on behalf of all the poor. With the end of state, and decline of party, communisms (and the often compulsory singing of a song emptied of all emancipatory significance), Potier's words may now speak to a new international movement—but this time on behalf of all labouring people and in the name not of an ideology, nor a state (present or future), but of the principle of human solidarity. As suggested by the lines above, and as spelled out in the French original: The international will *be* the human race.

The major international movement of our day is, of course, one that has many names—none of which refers to either the proletariat in particular nor the people in general: 'Anti-Globalisation', 'Anti-Corporate', 'Anti-Capitalist', 'Global Justice and Solidarity'. I still prefer the last of these, not because I am lacking in either anti-neoliberal spirit or anti-capitalist desire, but because it seems to me to better capture the present nature of this amorphous but many-splendoured and many-prickled thing. 'Global Justice and Solidarity' has other characteristics which may recommend itself as a name. One is an explicit reference to the global, another is an implicit reference to economic and socio-cultural rather than solely political rights, a third is the *absence* of class-specificity—surely appropriate to the multi-class composition of the movement.

Yet there is good reason to return to the sons (not to speak of the daughters) of toil. Indeed, there are several good reasons.

The first is that *L'Internationale* was, for many decades and much of the world, *the* anthem of the international labour movement.

The second is because of the specific reference in the above verse to those enrolled amongst the toilers—the artisans, peasants, and others. Given that the inter/national union movement has, with exceptions, forgotten the song and abandoned any *emancipatory* sense of internationalism, could it be that the notion of an emancipatory internationalism, if not the song itself, has migrated to other categories of the popular sectors, historically less incorporated into twentieth-century capitalism? Could it be that these are the *new* bearers of the old internationalism, or the popular bearers of a *new* internationalism within the Global Justice and Solidarity Movement (GJ&SM)?

The third reason for addressing labour's others is that these are the (growing) majority of the working class, understood as a global phenomenon. In a 'Shining India' for instance (to paraphrase a $20 million promotional claim by the Indian government in early 2004), with a labour force of over 370 million, they represent 83–93 per cent of the workforce, and only 3.5 per cent are in any way unionised!

A fourth is that, whilst the Third Worldist internationalisms of the 1960s and 70s have passed into history, there is new theory suggesting a much broader and more complex notion of the working class.[5] This might not privilege the marginalised, in the way that some 'new theories of revolution' did after 1968. But it certainly refers to, broadens, and loosens the old narrow conceptualisation, image, or assumptions about this class.

There is, finally, a wave of new writing that does at least suggest that such 'marginal' sectors do have their own autonomous international relations and might have more affinity with or demonstrable contact with the GJ&SM than the unionised working class.

To what kinds of workers am I here referring? Broadly the same categories as those in an old piece of my own from 1981, exploiting the same words of the *Internationale*.[6] At that time I was talking about the interrelationship of working classes only within 'peripheral capitalist societies'. What I actually said was "workers, peasants, artisans, and (m)others"—the latter to the distinct chagrin of one feminist just recruited to lead a 'Women and Development' Programme at my institute. Let me today suggest the following often overlapping categories: Casual/ised workers; urban residential communities; child workers; rural labour / communities; indigenous peoples; im/migrant workers; petty-producers / traders / service-providers; the un/under-employed; the high- and low-tech 'precariat';[7] and, obviously, the women housekeepers, rural labourers, homeworkers, sex workers, factory workers, domestic workers, amongst the above.

What's Networking Got to Do With It?

There is no need to assume a new privileged bearer of social emancipation and global emancipation—as might be suggested by the concept of the 'precariat'. No more is there a necessity to assume a privileged relational form for the expression of such—as might be suggested by some of the literature around networking. In the first case one would be reproducing the notion of such a privileged agent. In the second case one would be reducing 'networking' from a way of understanding human and social relationships to an empirical form (that might reproduce within itself characteristics of the hierarchical, bureaucratic institution, or of charismatic leadership).

It will be sufficient if we recognise the following: First, the subversive effect of considering seriously the networking form—the variety of networking forms—taken by new worker movements; second, the emancipatory effect of not considering such relational forms as temporary (in the absence of) or transitional (on the way), in relation to 'real' union forms; and third, that the customarily middle-class initiated or staffed labour network—local, national, regional, global—is not necessarily less 'working class' than a traditional union that produces its 'middle class' internally, out of its own institutional dynamics or as a result of external demands / attractions.

But, in any case, as the next section will surely suggest, the common form taken by the self-articulation of new worker interests, identities, or concerns internationally is the network.

A Problematic Case: Organising Cleaners Internationally

There is not yet much literature on the 'networked internationalism of labour's others'. Four pieces come to mind—the first on peasants / farmers; the second on fishworkers; the third on women garment workers; and the fourth on the Euromarches, starting 1997, against unemployment and poverty.[8] I will here present a fifth case that really has none of the above characteristics but is nonetheless relevant to research on the topic. This is a campaign which started in 2007 and which I observed the beginnings of.

I'm referring to a union campaign to organise cleaners in the Netherlands, which actually has its inception around two decades earlier with Justice for Janitors (J4J), a campaign by the Service Employees International Union (SEIU) in the USA. The term 'janitor' in the US covers doorkeepers, cleaners, and related 'property services staff'. These are, in the US, mostly migrants, often illegal. The work is customarily outsourced, but not necessarily to small companies: The property services providers are often MNCs. For example, the Danish-based ISS claims 200,000 customers worldwide, and maybe 250,000 workers, from Brunei to Iceland and Uruguay. Not forgetting, of course, the Netherlands. In this country there are between 150,000 to 200,000 company-employed cleaners. Many of them like their work but certainly not the low pay, the increasing workload, the insecurity, the arbitrary or discriminatory behaviour of immediate supervisors, the denial of sick leave, the uncertainties when 'their' company loses its contract to a competitor (which has undercut its offer and needs to recover this from the workers). In Schiphol Airport, there are some 60,000 such workers, but only 2,000 or so work for the airport authority itself, the rest for numerous subcontractors.[9]

The campaign to organise cleaners is in the hands of FNV Bondgenoten, the major Dutch industrial workers union. However, the idea of organising this dispersed and largely immigrant force comes from the USA. The methods it is using are US American. And an experienced SEIU / J4J organiser was sent to the Netherlands to animate the exercise, train the Bondgenoten organisers, and advise on the mobilisation methods. There is some kind of understanding between SEIU in the USA, Bondgenoten in the Netherlands, and their joint international, the Union Network International (UNI). This now refers to itself as the "global union for skills and services with 15 million members in 900 unions".[10] UNI has a Property Services department, which also covers the growing security guards industry. UNI, which is itself one of the newer and more dynamic of the internationals, is now calling itself UNI Global Union, and its Property Services department, UNI Property Services Global Union!

We are here, admittedly, considering the organisation and expansion of institutionalised union bodies, national, regional, and international or global. The word 'global' may be much in evidence, but what does it have to do with the 'networked internationalism of labour's others'? Certainly such workers have been marginal to the organised working class. And as immigrants they are customarily marginalised in the places where they live. So much for 'others'. But it seems to me that this internationally-linked organising campaign actually lies in the ambiguous zone between union institution-building and labour networking. The case suggests the extent to which the previously hidebound and immobile unions have taken on the methods of community organising of the US, of the new social movements of the 1980s–90s, and even the global justice movement of the present day. And it invites us to consider whether what we are witnessing is union instrumentalisation of social movement networking, or movement penetration and transformation of international unionism as we have known it.

This overlapping or interpenetration became evident to me at the three cleaners' campaign meetings I attended in the Netherlands in October and November 2007. The first was held in the cellar of a community centre in Amsterdam, hosted by a political club of young left activists and students; the second was held in a multicultural community centre in a working-class / immigrant area of The Hague; the third was the first national rally of the cleaners, organised by the union, but supported by one or two left political parties. Even the third one, the clearly union-organised meeting one, was more like a celebration of, or community-building exercise amongst, the 300–400 multi-cultured cleaners (and families) present.

This 'social movement' aspect of the campaign is suggested even more strongly by an exchange between Valery Alzaga and Rodrigo Nunes, two J4J organisers. It appears that this new labour-organising strategy is about as far from traditional unionism as it is possible to get. These are some of the new elements, from experience in the US, in London, in Berlin, and in Milan: One, the involvement of allies from community organisations, autonomist social movements, and friendly political parties; two, the centrality of research to campaigning (identifying the relevant industrial / employment structure and key worker communities); three, developing worker-approved organisers from amongst the cleaners; four, establishing effective media contacts; five, identifying meaningful periods or dates for mobilisation and protest; six, making connections with immigrant rights movements; and last, moving—after initial victories on wages, conditions, and recognition—from external to internal campaigning (recruiting to the union).

Much of this kind of activity belongs to the repertoire of 'organising' as distinguished from 'service' unionism. Much of it belongs to familiar forms of community organising. These organisers both use the word 'network'. The awareness of the two organisers goes further:

RN: ... This is the most important element of J4J, I'd say. A campaign in itself could be described as business unionism, but it is part and parcel of the J4J model that you activate the community, you create new, transversal connections—which is what you could call social unionism. For me that's the most important element: At the end of the day, with J4J as with anything else, there's no guarantee that relations won't become crystallised, that you won't just create a new representative class [layer of representatives?—PW]. But if a campaign successfully feeds into a lively movement around it—a movement that can also, to some extent, reclaim the union as its own—then you have more chances of there always being enough pressure 'from below' to keep things moving.

VA: Not just that; the movement can do things that the union can't. The union is limited in various ways by legal or structural constraints. So if something needs to be done that the union can't do, it's important to have the support of those who can. Almost all our members are migrants, often with an irregular status. They can't do a sit-in and risk being arrested, but others can. If there are housing problems in a place, it's not our direct job to start a campaign, but we can support those who do. At the same time, it's important that these relations are very clear and open. I helped organise J4J marches supported by the Black Bloc, and they knew there could be no trouble because of people's legal status—so you had all these kids in black marching alongside Mexican grandmothers, pacifists, American Indian Movement members, university and high school students, migrant rights organisations.

Also, what you say about reclaiming the union. ... A union victory has the effect of spreading this feeling of possibility to everyone else. This was certainly one of the things that led to such a vibrant migrant movement in the US in the last few years—people saw their friends and family organise and win, and started organising too. J4J has had an important role in the struggle for migrant legalisation in the US. A direct role, by participating in coordinations, co-organising marches, building alliances.[11]

Nunes and Alzaga (both involved with the World Social Forums and / or other transnational solidarity movements) do mention campaigns in different countries but hardly mention the relations between cleaners or movements *internationally*. Yet, in so far as Nunes is a Brazilian and Alzaga a Mexican-American, and both have been active with their communities of birth, they themselves embody the new internationalisms and belong to a new generation of internationalists.[12]

However, it appears from all available sources that there is little if any horizontal connection between the cleaners in the UK, the US, and the Netherlands.[13] And this despite the cleaners commonly being bilingual or trilingual, and often sharing such languages as English and Spanish. Cross-border connections seem to so far depend on international union relations. In the case of the Netherlands, these would seem to be between the FNV-Bondgenoten, the SEIU, and the UNI. And this triangular institutional model seems to be energised by SEIU and informed by its discourse. There is, of course, no reason to object if a good idea or experience comes from a US union that is itself responding to pressures from above in the form of a globalised neoliberalism, and from outside or below in the form of the civil rights movement, low-paid worker dissatisfaction, immigrant self-mobilisation, and the global justice movement—particularly if, like Alzaga and Nunes, one is aware of the dangers of demobilisation or bureaucratisation. One has to further remember that any 'horizontal' solidarity relationship is more likely to occur between organisers / communicators than between the workers themselves. In UK English terms, it is more likely to be an equivalent to 'shop steward internationalism' than 'shop floor internationalism'. The matter will be settled over time by the workers and activists involved, by whether they are more satisfied to be 'represented by' than 'present in' the international.

One further qualification has to be borne in mind. This has to do with the leader/ship that, more than any other, has been behind this new wave and type of worker organisation. In the present case, this is the SEIU and its president, Andy Stern. SEIU claims to be the fastest-growing union in the US and Stern is identified with globalising US unionism. Moreover, he has been a leading critic of the old AFL-CIO (American Federation of Labor and Congress of Industrial Organizations), marked by its model of "service-unionism", "business-unionism", "state-corporatism", and "trade union imperialism"—as also its secular decline in numbers and influence. As against these, Stern has championed "organising unionism", reduction of the myriad existing unions into industrial ones, and "global partnerships".[14] These are supposed to involve both globalised unionism and the global justice and solidarity movement! Stern suggests where the Netherlands fits into this picture:

> With a mandate from the SEIU's 2004 convention delegates to build a global union, followed by UNI's adoption of global unionism, SEIU assigned staff to Australia,

Poland, England, India, France, Switzerland, Germany, the Netherlands, South America and, soon, Africa.[15]

However, this brave new world of unionism is marked by tensions and contradictions, from the lowest level to the highest. There have been, within SEIU unions, complaints that in the face of local worker truculence the leadership will negotiate over their heads, or even merge difficult locals (branches) out of existence. From the title of his book onwards, Stern reveals his own sympathy for US Americanism and the US American (Capitalist) Dream. His notion of international militancy includes negotiations with the state-controlled All China Trade Union Federation. And he is apparently even prepared to consider *paying* Third World workers to strike on behalf of US ones.[16]

The contradictions in Stern's discourse could lead one to simply dismiss the new SEIU / Bondgenoten / UNI strategy as 'Business Unionism on a World Scale', and thus to throw doubt on the J4J strategy, nationally and globally. This would be to fail to recognise, however, the concessions that SEIU is also making toward 'shop floor' and community mobilisation and to the global justice movement, as well as the risk taken in employing young educated organisers, likely to have been infected by new movements and ideas. It would, moreover, require us to consider the organised cleaners as a manipulable mass rather than as possessing agency.

To return to the matter of international networking between cleaners. Whilst in this particular case any relationship between such workers, in the Netherlands, the USA, and—hypothetically—China, would seem to be mediated by national and international union structures, and motivated by the aim of re-creating a twentieth-century social partnership (this time at global level), the matter does not have to end where it may have begun. Union leaderships propose, but workers, communities, and critically-minded activists dispose. Given the existence of the other networks mentioned, given cleaners' simple curiosity or need for direct horizontal contacts, given the widespread common knowledge of English and / or Spanish, given the decreasing cost and increasing ease of communication, I would be surprised if an international network of property service workers did not develop during the next five years. Whether this would be part of the union structure, an independent 'shop floor' initiative within the union, or an independent network, is yet to be seen. The matter practically begs for a participatory action research (PAR) project.

Theoretical / Ideological / Strategic Resources

How are we to conceptualise the phenomena revealed in such cases? Let me make some suggestions based on past work and recent reading. Here I would like to mention writing on the following: 'Social movement' or the 'new social'; new forms of, or new wave, labour organising; labour or social movement networking; and the emancipation of labour and global social emancipation.

Social Movement Unionism

The literature on *social movement unionism* is both growing and varied, as suggested in an earlier overview.[17] Based on a recognition of the revolution within capitalism represented by its globalised and networked phase, this approach combines certain traditional Marxist and other socialist insights with those of the European / Latin American New Social Movement theory of the 1970s–80s. It assumes the necessity of surpassing the traditional understandings of work, the labour movement, and internationalism. And then of recognising both the variety of work for capital, the consequently varied kinds of worker and labour protest, of workers as bearers of other significant identities, and of the labour movement as just one expression of a struggle against growing human alienation and for a new social emancipation.

New Wave Labour Organising

The conceptualisation of 'social movement unionism' has been criticised by Anthony Ince, who considers it to be an over-general and homogenising category.[18] In a wide-ranging international review, he prefers to talk of 'new wave labour organising' and to consider, critically, the relevant types and sub-types. These include 'New Union Organising' (subtypes: Organising Unionism, Partnership and Bargaining to Organise), 'Network Unionism' (Social and Community Organising Unionism, Radical Organising Unionism), and 'New Worker Organising' (Worker Centres, Solidarity Networks, and 'Cyber-Unionism'). Without going into each of his categories it would appear that the typology makes room for much, if not all, of what we have been earlier considering. Where it might not, it could be fine-tuned or extended. He says:

> The New Labour Organising strategies discussed here do not represent the full scope of possibilities for new (or rediscovered) forms of worker mobilisation, and they do display some significant problems that need to be overcome. The next decade will be pivotal for the long-term future of the labour movement, since these new ideas have brought with them new challenges and difficulties that need to be addressed if they are to be successful and sustainable. What is imperative now is to consolidate the moderate gains that have been made, and build upon them positively without losing sight of the ultimate goal. This goal should be ambitious, not simply recruiting workers, nor empowering them, but the facilitation of our collective self-empowerment as a whole, accompanied by the recognition that every struggle is intimately connected to every other. A strong labour movement is built upon such connectivity, democracy, and solidarity.[19]

Here three caveats. The first has to do with his attitude toward the international, about which he says:

> In an era of increasingly globalised labour and capital markets, it is important that strategic co-ordination should reflect this. As such, unions and organisations that believe in New Labour Organising strategies need to assert this on the world stage, lest they remain isolated from the majority. There is a significant amount of already-existing labour internationalism, but this must move beyond statements of solidarity towards a more concrete sense of mutualism and skill sharing. Bodies such as the ILO and ICFTU may hold the key to this.[20]

I would consider the ILO-ICFTU nexus proposed here to be a part of the problem. The International Labour Organisation (ILO) is an interstate body, within which labour (actually, of course, *unions*) have only a 25 per cent representation. Capital and state have the other 75 per cent. The inter/national unions, themselves representing under 20 per cent of the world labour force, are content to be considered to represent labour globally—and to broadcast top-down the (at best) liberal-reformist ideology of the ILO. The nexus has only been reinforced since other inter/national unions joined the ICFTU (International Confederation of Free Trade Unions) to form the International Trade Union Confederation (ITUC) in November 2006. Whilst this does not necessarily rule out the possibility of either the ITUC or the ILO being part of the solution, I would like to hope that this would be in the form of a radically democratised ITUC, mobilising workers for a radical democratic reform of the ILO.

The second caveat follows from this and it is a question of whether, in an otherwise admirable pluralism, Ince enables us to move from sensitive analysis to effective strategy. This, for me, requires some kind of policy proposal, with relevance, obviously, for the internationalism of labour's others.

The third caveat might therefore be that, although Ince recognises the practical significance of networking, he does not seem to consider this as itself an emancipatory field or force.

Overlapping with the Ince conceptualisation is the literature on *new forms of labour organising*. Much of such work is carried out within the far-reaching institutional or ideological parameters of the International Labour Organisation and the traditional union internationals. One could include here the 'one-size-fits-all' campaign for 'Decent Work', promoted by the ILO and uncritically endorsed by the ITUC. This campaign certainly allows for the autonomous organising of 'informal sector' workers, and seems to be approved of by, for example, StreetNet. 'Decent Work' is implicitly based on the European capitalist welfare state developed in the post-World War Two period. It therefore wants us to go back from the bad capitalism of the present day to the good capitalism of the past (though the word 'capitalism' does not appear in this discourse). It is therefore unable to consider the political-economic, ideological, or socio-geographic limitations to that dying utopia. Why, for example, did it disappear? Was the collapse of capitalist social partnership not written into the terms of the original understanding? 'Decent Work' is moreover promoted as the single answer, simultaneously, for the regularly employed and unionised in the North / West, and the casual, subcontracted, temporary, part-time, and unemployed of the Global South. And it is dependent on its promotion or imposition worldwide by such inter-state bodies as the ILO and the EU.

Finally, one should recognise a body of literature that seems to possibly overlap with the autonomist orientation of Ince on the one hand and the institutional one of traditional Northern unions on the other. Kloosterboer is interesting not only for his reporting on a wide range of union and other forms of worker organising worldwide but for his at least implicit assumption that these are part of a *broad new labour movement*—and further, for the implied recognition that Dutch unions have something to learn from such.[21]

Labour or Social Movement Networking

This brings me to my next theoretical resource, the literature on *labour/social movement networking*. Recognition of the extent to which a computerised and globalised capitalism is networked is now widespread.[22] Well established, also, is the capitalist think-tank literature on 'netwars'.[23] Less common is argument for *labour* networking, national or international. But it is well represented, I think, in the long quotation below from Charles Heckscher:

> Networks have advantages on two fronts: In confronting modern flexible and decentralised management systems, and in mobilising the energy of new movements. In the past, corporations were able to crush networks. But the changing context has given networks a new life. They are potentially stronger than before, both because of growing understanding of how they work best, and because of technological advances that speed decentralised communication. ...The type of organisation and leadership needed to build and sustain networks and netwars is in many ways the opposite of that needed for traditional mass action and large-scale hierarchies. ...The network approach ... requires that labour think of itself as a coordinator rather than a power, as a player in a complex force field rather than as the leader of the forces of social justice. It is in many ways an attitude of humility, but it may be now that in humility there is strength ... in the world of new movements and netwars, it is not always clear who is a member and who is not. The key question is not how many members you have, but who you can mobilise. ...The real problem for labour is to grow in influence—in the ability to unite groups outside its own boundaries. With influence, labour could help to

bring together different and shifting communities around key campaigns. With influence, it could concentrate its efforts on the weak points of the relations among firms. Influence comes from vision and from the ability to listen without dominating. It comes from understanding how networks work—the logic of swarms and identities and campaigns—and being able to reflect the values of a large range of social justice groups. The pursuit of influence would put energy and resources into meetings with far flung groups, into building alliances, into structuring consistent communications systems across diverse organisations, and into Internet capability. It is a way of acting that is as different from industrial union organisation as industrial unions were different from crafts in the 1930s—and as continuous as both with the core mission of labour.[24]

I find this a rather rich specification and as relevant to the global as to the national. It has been spelled out—or at least imagined—for migrant sex workers, for instance, by Laura Agustín.[25] She tells a tale in which the hero is … a mobile phone! And imagines a future in which sex-worker activists would provide sex workers with not simply tea and sympathy but access to an expanding range of audio-visual resources. The problem, she would seem to imply, is not that labour's others cannot speak, but that they have not so far been heard. Imaginative and critical use of new technology enables this. It also, of course, puts into question the traditional need for the *organisation*, with its hierarchy and its leaders—bureaucratic, charismatic, or both.

Against the kind of argument mentioned above, we should, however, recognise the objections of Andy Mathers.[26] Self-identified with an indubitably networked and international labour campaign, Mathers prefers to dismiss networking theory and to at least imply that the movement he is analysing is partial or temporary—a moment before the return or development of an organised labour movement—with a Marxist or even Trotskyist leadership. Having castigated some of the world's innovative social theorists—including at one point myself!—as the "new social democratic left",[27] Mathers prefers to explain his network in terms of US social movement theory—much criticised by Marxists for its liberal-pluralistic assumptions and reformist aspirations. His case, it appears to me, runs ahead of his theoretical and political framework. Which by no means implies that the Euromarches he studies should be considered exemplary or non-problematic. Nor does it mean that Mathers's criticism is to be dismissed. Rather does it require us to find more adequate resources for understanding or strategising the relationship of the new networked social (movements) with the traditionally political (state, law, parties, unions).

Although not specifically addressed to the relationships here under consideration (those of the international labour networks with either the hegemonic order in general or the hegemonic labour organisations in particular), the Argentinean scholar-activist Ezequiel Adamovsky certainly focuses on an aspect crucial to such relationships. This is expressed in terms of the tension between the autonomous social movements and the 'heteronomous' political sphere. He points to two extreme (though not uncommon) errors of emancipatory movements—of either a purist self-isolation from the political sphere; or of entering this sphere and losing radical social energies to a process of assimilation to the 'heteronomous' ruling class forms and practices. Adamovsky proposes a kind of institutionality that might avoid both horns of the contemporary social movement (and network!) dilemma:

> Contrary to the usual belief, autonomous and horizontal organisations are more in need of institutions than hierarchical ones; for these can always rely on the will of the leader to resolve conflicts, assign tasks, etc. I would like to argue that we need to develop institutions of a new type. By institutions I do not mean a bureaucratic hierarchy, but simply a set of democratic agreements on ways of functioning, that are formally established, and are endowed with the necessary organisational infrastructure to enforce them if needed.[28]

Global Social Emancipation and Reconceptualising Work

Finally, in terms of theoretical / ideological / strategic resources, we might consider this position of Boaventura de Sousa Santos on 'global social emancipation':

> The paradigm of social emancipation developed by western modernity is undergoing a deep and final crisis. Social emancipation must, therefore, be reinvented. It must be understood as a form of counter-hegemonic globalisation relying on local-global linkages and alliances among social groups around the world which go on resisting social exclusion, exploitation, and oppression caused by hegemonic neoliberal globalisation. Such struggles result in the development of alternatives to the exclusionary and monolithic logic of global capitalism, that is to say, spaces of democratic participation, non-capitalistic production of goods and services, creation of emancipatory knowledges, post-colonial cultural exchanges, new international solidarities.[29]

Appropriately enough, this comes out of a research project which addresses itself both to 'alternative production' and to international labour solidarity.[30] It also relates to the kind of issues being raised, though certainly not settled, within the World Social Forum process.

I am not aware of projects of 'labour's others' that really go into the question of alternative production, or what, within today's global justice movement, comes under the rubric of the 'solidarity economy'. This is, however, allowed for, I think, in the reconceptualisation of 'work' by André Gorz.[31] Gorz produces a challenging critique of the ideology of work that still dominates the international trade union movement as much as it does the capitalist (or statist) media. This ideology holds first of all that the more each works, the better off all will be; second, that those who do little or no work are acting against the interests of the community; and third, that those who work hard achieve success and those who don't have only themselves to thank or blame. Gorz points out that today the connection between more and better has been broken and that the problem now is one of producing differently, producing other things, working less.

Gorz distinguishes between three kinds of work: First, work for economic ends (the definition of work under capitalism / statism); second, domestic labour and work for 'oneself' (reproductive work, care work, primarily the additional task of women, for whom 'self' customarily means 'the family'); and third, autonomous activity (artistic, relational, educational, mutual aid, etc). He argues, or at least allows for, a movement from the first type to the third, and for the second one to be increasingly articulated with the third rather than subordinated to the first. If the trade unions are not to be reduced to some kind of neo-corporatist mutual protection agency for the skilled and privileged, they will, Gorz argues, have to struggle for liberation *from* work:

> Such a project is able to give cohesion and a unifying perspective to the different elements that make up the social movement since 1) it is a logical extension of the experience and struggles of workers in the past; 2) it reaches beyond that experience and those struggles towards objectives which correspond to the interests of both workers and non-workers, and is thus able to cement bonds of solidarity and common political will between them; 3) it corresponds to the aspirations of the ever-growing proportion of men and women who wish to (re) gain control in and of their own lives.[32]

All of the foregoing needs to be studied in depth. In researching our particular subject matter, it would be necessary to synthesise such elements or offer a consistent alternative theoretical framework. But it does seem to me that we already have the minimal theoretical resources to begin.

References

Ezequiel Adamovsky, 2006—'Autonomous Politics and its Problems: Thinking the Passage from Social to Political', at http://www.choike.org/documentos/adamovsky_autonomous.pdf (Accessed April 2017)

Ezequiel Adamovsky, 2017—'Autonomous Politics and its Problems: Thinking the Passage from the Social to Political', in Jai Sen, ed, 2017b—*The Movements of Movements, Part 2: Rethinking Our Dance*. Volume 5 in the *Challenging Empires* series. New Delhi: OpenWord, and Oakland, CA: PM Press

Laura Agustín, 1999—'They Speak, But Who Listens?', in Wendy Harcourt, ed, 1999—
Women@Internet: Creating New Cultures in Cyberspace (London: Zed Books), pp
140–155

Valery Alzaga and Rodrigo Nunes, 2007—'Organise Local, Strike Global', in *Turbulence*,
at http://turbulence.org.uk/turbulence-1/organise-local-strike-global/ (Accessed
April 2017)

Manuel Castells, 1996—*The Rise of the Network Society: Vol 1.* Oxford: Blackwell

Gabriele Dietrich and Nalini Nayak, 2006—'Exploring Possibilities of Counter-Hegemonic Globalisation of the Fishworkers' Movement in India and Its Global Interactions', in Boaventura de Sousa Santos, ed, 2006—*Another Production Is Possible:
Beyond the Capitalist Canon* (London: Verso), pp 381–414

Mark Edelman, 2003—'Transnational Peasant and Farmer Movements and Networks', in
Helmut Anheier, Marlies Glasius, and Mary Kaldor, eds, 2003—*Global Civil Society
2003* (London: Oxford University Press), pp 185–220

Dan Gallin, 2007—'Looking for the Quick Fix: Reviewing Andy Stern'. Global Labour
Institute

André Gorz, 1999—'A New Task for the Unions: The Liberation of Time from Work', in
Ronaldo Munck and Peter Waterman, eds, 1999—*Labour Worldwide in the Era of
Globalisation: Alternative Union Models in the New World Order* (Houndmills, UK:
Macmillan), pp 41–63

Michael Hardt and Antonio Negri, 2004—*Multitude: War and Democracy in the Age of
Empire.* New York: Penguin

Charles Heckscher, 2006—'Organisations, Movements, and Networks', in *New York Law
School Review*, vol 5, no 2, pp 313–36

Anthony Ince, 2007—'Beyond "Social Movement Unionism"? Understanding and
Assessing New Wave Labour Movement Organising', at https://www.netzwerkit.de/
projekte/waterman/ince (Accessed April 2017)

Dirk Kloosterboer, 2005—*De Vakbeweging van de Toekomst: Lessen uit het Buitlenland*
['The Union Movement of the Future: Lessens from Abroad', in Dutch]. Amsterdam:
Federatie Nederlandse Vakbonden

Dirk Kloosterboer, 2007—*Innovative trade union strategies: Successful examples of how
trade unions meet the challenges of the 21st century.* Amsterdam: Federatie Nederlandse Vakbonden, at http://www.newunionism.net/library/organizing/FNV%20
-%20Innovative%20Trade%20Union%20Strategies%20-%202007.pdf (Accessed April
2017)

Andy Mathers, 2007—*Struggling for a Social Europe: Neoliberal Globalisation and the
Birth of a European Social Movement.* Aldershot: Ashgate

Boaventura de Sousa Santos, ed, 2006c—*Another Production Is Possible: Beyond the
Capitalist Canon.* London: Verso

Peter Waterman, 1981a—'*Obreros, campesinos, artesanos y madres: Hacia un enten-
dimiento de las interrelaciones de la clase trabajadora en las sociedades capitalistas
periféricas*' ['Workers, Peasants, Artisans, and Mothers: Towards an Understanding
of the Working Class in Peripheral Capitalist Societies', in Spanish], in *Revista Mexicana de Sociología*, vol 43 no 1, pp 63–103

Peter Waterman, 1981b—*Workers, Peasants, Artisans and Mothers.* Occasional Paper no
91. The Hague: Institute of Social Studies

Peter Waterman, 1999—*Of Saints, Sinners and Compañer@s: Internationalist Lives in the Americas Today*. Working Paper no 286. The Hague: Institute of Social Studies

Peter Waterman, 2004d—'Adventures of Emancipatory Labour Strategy as the New Global Movement Challenges International Unionism', at http://jwsr.pitt.edu/ojs/index.php/jwsr/article/view/315/327 (Accessed April 2017)

Peter Waterman, 2007f—'The Networked Internationalism of Labour's Others: A Suitable Case for Treatment', at http://www.choike.org/documentos/waterman_others2007.pdf (Accessed April 2017)

Notes

1. This is a work in progress that has been through various redrafts. Bibliography and resources have been cut to the bone. For a longer version see Waterman 2007f.

   Ed: As noted elsewhere in this book, the author of this essay, Peter Waterman, walked on on June 17 2017, shortly before the publication of this book, and therefore of this essay. The reality is that almost as a matter of course, and as a co-editor, he contributed a fresh essay to every one of the volumes in what he and I together conceptualised as the *Challenging Empires* series (see the Note from OpenWord at the end of this book on the series), starting from CE1 in 2004, *World Social Forum: Challenging Empires*. The publication of this essay is therefore almost certainly the end of a long and wonderful collaboration, and often very creative dance, that we have shared. I'm not sure who led when, but that doesn't matter!

2. See http://en.wikipedia.org/wiki/The_Internationale.

3. Tristán 1843.

4. Fanon 1986.

5. Hardt and Negri 2004, chapter 2.1.

6. Waterman 1981a, 1981b.

7. A neologism for the growing number of subcontracted, casualised, part-time, and temporary workers.

8. Edelman 2003; Dietrich and Nayak 2006; Hale and Wills 2005; and Mathers 2007, respectively.

9. The campaign continued, with strike action, achieving a victory in early 2009. See http://unionrenewal.blogspot.com/2009/04/victory-for-amsterdam-airport-cleaners.html.

10. See http://www.uniglobalunion.org/ (Accessed April 2017).

11. Alzaga and Nunes 2007.

12. Waterman 1999.

13. It seems that at one point ISS workers from Denmark did come over to support a J4J campaign in the USA (Kloosterboer 2005, p 34). There are likely to have been other cases.

14. Stern 2006, pp 111, 113. My quotes from Stern 2006 are dependent on Gallin 2007.

15. Stern 2006, p 112.

16. Gallin 2007.

17. Waterman 2004d.

18. Ince 2007.

19. ibid, pp 48–49.
20. ibid, p 44.
21. Kloosterboer 2005, 2007.
22. Castells 1996.
23. See http://www.rand.org/pubs/monograph_reports/MR1382/index.html.
24. Heckscher 2006.
25. Agustín 1999.
26. Mathers 2007.
27. ibid, p 3.
28. Adamovsky 2006; see also the revised version included in the companion volume to this book, Adamovsky 2017.
29. See http://www.ces.uc.pt/emancipa/en/index.html.
30. Santos 2006c.
31. Gorz 1999.
32. ibid, p 45.

OpenWord

From Anti-Imperialist to Anti-Empire:
The Crystallisation of the Anti-Globalisation Movement in South Korea
Cho Hee-Yeon

Introduction: From Protesting Dictatorship to Protesting Globalisation

"Down the US, stop pushing us to open!", yelled angry peasants during a rally condemning the US for forcing the Korean agro-livestock products market open, held in Seoul from April 22–23 1985. Some 100 of the rallyists attempted a march to the US Embassy. Ten years later, on 13 December 1995, Korean peasants again gathered but this time at Victoria Park in Hong Kong, voicing their hearts during a Via Campesina International Peasants Rally—but this time they said "Down Down WTO!", "No No Globalisation!" and "WTO kills farmers!". The difference in wording between the two sets of slogans well demonstrates how the path of Korean peoples' movements, including labour and agrarian movements, was charted and changed, in their awakening and practice.

Korean popular movements have had quite a peculiar career when compared to others that have arisen in the Third World. After its liberation from Japanese colonial rule in 1945, after the surrender of Japan to the US and its allies marking the end of World War II, Korea went through a civil war fought by political and social forces over the nature of the nation-state. The war, which took place from 1950–53, concluded with the division of the nation into South and North Korea. North Korea rushed forward on the road of nationalist socialism and was ruled by a strong anti-US ideology, while the South was realigned into an ultra anti-communist society under overwhelming US influence. In the process, the South Korean progressive movement, which had grown in the struggle against Japanese colonialism, was dismantled and many progressive activists were killed. As a result, the movement had to make a fresh start, from a 'ground zero' of some sort. The 1961 military coup and the military developmental dictatorial regime that arose in consequence[1]—like in so many other Asian countries—must be seen against this backdrop. The military dictatorship under General Park Jung-hee gripped control over labour and people using anti-communist propaganda on the one hand, and on the other it propelled the nation towards a pro-bourgeoisie industrialisation, which mainly involved funnelling economic resources strategically into the export industry and mobilising an 'economic nationalist' mentality.

This however had its own consequences. Resistance against the developmental dictatorship grew into a popular progressive movement in Korea.[2] The

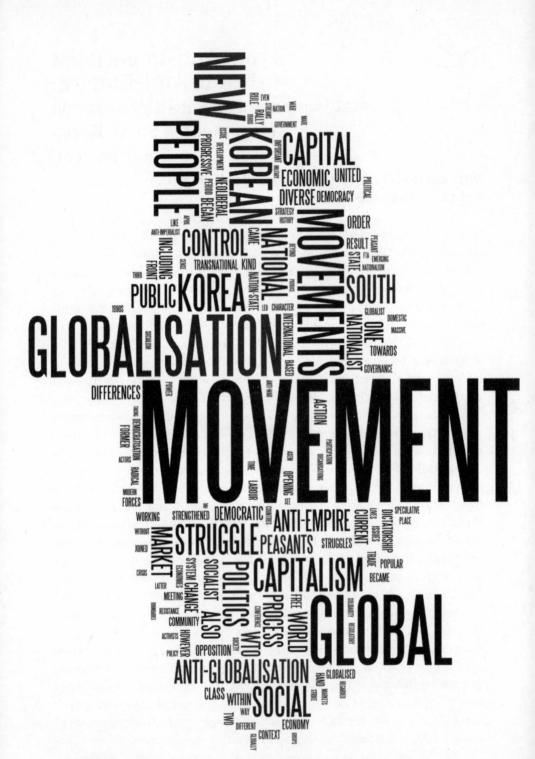

developmental dictatorship mobilised people on the platform of 'economic nationalism', towards industrialisation and modernisation, which was partly successful. People were reshaped as 'industrial soldiers', responding to the call from the top for a 'modernised nation'. This meant that just as in the case of some other Third World countries in Asia in the 60s, dictatorial and right-wing forces appropriated the cause of nationalism.

Popular people's resistance emerged in the mid- and late 70s, when Korea witnessed a surge of mass-based, anti-dictatorial, pro-democracy activism. The massacre that followed the Gwangju uprisings in 1980, conducted with the US's support, radicalised the movement. *The peasantry, especially the lower peasantry, which had so far been a major foothold of the dictatorship, turned into a 'resistant class' in the process.* This change was a direct result of the government's policy of disregarding agriculture and opening up the produce market. Moreover, with the population's political consciousness rising, people increasingly cold-shouldered the government's persistent, hate-mongering, and divisive anti-North Korea policy. Nationalism came to be reappropriated by the resistance movement and, in the process, the 'industrial soldiers' that had till then been sweating for the nation's development turned into a 'resistant people' armed with nationalism.

One of the expressions of the change that took place was the anti-US movement of the 1980s, triggered when the US attempted to open up Korea's produce market. The movement had two streams: The National Liberation group, with a clear-cut anti-US position, and the People's Democracy group, which followed Leninist revolutionary ideology and the doctrine of class contradiction. Both represented a strong protest against the US and its steps to (neo)colonise South Korea. This nationalist resistance became mainstream and spread so widely that strong nationalist struggles against the US appeared across the country, and through this to a situation where the majority of the population—which had till then supported the dictatorship—came to see the US as an obvious obstacle to democracy and national reunification. In particular, the resistant peasants' movement, and its fundamental stance against the "US forcing us to open", slowly created a national consensus. The 1980s saw regular protests, including the occupation of places such as the US Embassy and the US Cultural Centre.

Up to the 1970s, the US had generally been regarded in South Korea as a 'liberator', protecting the South from the threat of North Korea. This was reflected in the use of the expression 'blood ally' in both countries. Maintaining sturdy ties with the US was the state's most important business. The massive radicalisation of Korea's new nationalist resistance movements however, including the peasants' movement, made the US look like a 'super imperialist', marshalling its imperialist machinery to control the South.

The movements in this period were basically aimed towards democracy and the reform of the state of South Korea, and so were based on resistance against the

US and its allied ruling classes in Korea, which were blocking both. This peaked in June 1987 when Korean society entered into democracy through a large-scale anti-dictatorship people's democratic movement that caused the dissolution of dictatorship and the start of democratisation of the South Korean state. In the early stages of democratisation, from the mid-1980s to the mid-1990s, the main focus was given to democratisation of the state and capital, especially the Korean Chaebol as the biggest conglomerate, and the effects of globalisation on domestic democratisation was not seriously considered. The next phase came in the mid-90s when the movement, which had so far been a nationalist statement against the US, but was now facing a slew of challenges from globalisation, began to have issues with the global order itself.

The Korean people's movements had long been anchored on a strong nationalist base, as a result of their long-standing struggle against dictatorship, and so focused mainly on domestic issues. Even among activists with a revolutionary mindset, it was difficult to find an internationalist identity or recognition of the transborder dimension of the movement.[3] But the peasants' and people's movements in Korea soon realised that their struggles—in the context of the new phase of globalisation, and the emerging anti-globalisation movements against the global order itself—were no longer to grapple with the US alone, but with large-scale transnational capital.

The economic crisis of 1997 was the turning point that led to this transformation of popular consciousness. The government had to swallow the IMF's policy conditions (high interest rates, restructuring of financially distressed firms, layoffs, etc), which created massive bankruptcy of marginal companies and made millions of people jobless. As this happened, people came to understand that globalisation was something that could touch their lives very directly. The Kim Dae-jung government pressed ahead with opening capital and finance markets as widely as possible to get over the crisis, which strengthened the hold of foreign capital on Korea's stock market, in turn awakening the public to the fact that the Korean economy hinged not only on domestic factors but also on huge amounts of speculative funds. They also came to see that the neoliberal restructuring being forced on the country by IMF policy conditionality was devastating their lives, including the massive layoff of workers and the bankruptcy of the companies on the margin.[4]

Against this backdrop, and in a series of steps, Korea's popular movement became part of the anti-globalisation movement. The first step was during 1994–95 when the Korean peasants' and people's movements joined in a rally against the Uruguay Round (UR), which was deemed to be on the side of developed countries. It became routine for Korean peasants to go to rallies to protest the forced opening of the South Korean produce market that was taking place. In time, this anti-UR struggle turned into a movement against the multilateral and bilateral negotiation and trade system when the World Trade Organization (WTO) came into being in

1995. At the forefront were peasant movement groups such as the Korean Peasants' League (KPL) and a coalition called People's Action to Save Our Agriculture.

Korean peasants' movements were at first solely concerned with the policy opening up (or 'liberalising') of the country's economy, which they could see would have an obviously negative influence on their prospects. But the process of the struggle jolted them into also having a critical view of the global-scale neo-liberal economic order, instances of which were mushrooming everywhere. The situation of the working-class movement, especially the trade union movement, was the same. Until the economic crisis of 1997, the working-class movement focussed on domestic labour issues and fought for higher wages and expansion of social benefits and against the detrimental revision of labour laws. Now it changed. Similarly, the student movement, which had led the militant struggle against dictatorship, shifted its focus to the reunification issue. Like the change in the peasants' movement, most Korean movements changed themselves to confront globalisation from the mid- and late 1990s, through confronting the 'liberalisation' policies of the government.

Emergence and Development of the Anti-Globalisation Movement in the Mid-1990s

Spurred by the shock of the breakdown of the socialist bloc, the 1990s can be characterised as a mad dash towards unbridled capital or global free markets. All the restraints that had been put on the market in the name of welfare, labour rights, citizenship, human rights, etc were broken to pieces in the name of global competitiveness. After socialism crumbled and there began a limitless competition toward a single global market, ordinary people began overwhelmingly tending towards a TINA (There Is No Alternative) perspective: That there was no alternative to liberalisation.

Against this popular atmosphere, the progressive movements, supposedly keeping the socialist idea, seemed to wither away, and a market-fundamentalist stream seemed to sweep across the globe. But, diverse movements dispersed globally began to stage a counter-attack from the mid-1990s onwards. The 1990s also saw a series of struggles: The armed struggle of the Zapatista EZLN against the North American Free Trade Agreement (NAFTA) that started in January 1994; the 1995 French general strike of the public sector; the Korean general strike in 1996–97 to protest the retrogressive revision of the Labour Law; and Seattle's anti-WTO rallies in November 1999, which halted the second ministerial meeting of the WTO. The 1999 Seattle struggle, in fact, was a clear signal that diverse movements from the global community had come together in a symbolic turn through which individual popular movements from across the globe joined in the spirit of anti-globalisation. This was even more obvious in the case of Korea, where the people gave themselves the momentum for an epistemological revolution by transforming their old local nationalist struggle into a global anti-globalisation one.

The leading campaigns related to the anti-globalisation movement in Korea grew stronger and drew larger and larger numbers of participants, which culminated in the formation of an umbrella organisation called the Korean People's Action against Investment Treaties and the WTO (KoPA). From this point on KoPA led the struggles sparked by WTO-related conferences or trade and investment-related negotiations.

An interesting aspect of what happened was that in South Korea, the anti-globalisation movement was led by groups seen as radical in the Korean social movement community. These radical groups clearly defined the character of the globalisation taking place as 'neoliberal.'[5] On the other hand, the moderates within the movement community didn't take the issue of privatisation of public corporations seriously, and even regarded it as a way of reducing the dictatorship's control over them.

At this juncture, the diverse kinds of opposition forces that had gathered in Seattle in 1999 also joined the struggle against the Davos Economic Forum in January 2000, and then the struggle against the IMF-WB meeting in Washington, DC in April 2000. In this process, the anti-globalisation movement took shape as a new dominant stream of opposition against ongoing neoliberal globalisation.[6]

Just as there are different orientations on the global movement scene, different orientations in the anti-empire movement in South Korea also emerged. It was during the movement confronting the Asia-Europe Meeting (ASEM) in Seoul, in October 2000, that the anti-globalisation movement became an important action agenda in the Korean social movement community—influenced by the emerging global anti-globalisation struggle. The South Korean social movement, encouraged by the worldwide anti-globalisation movement, accepted this chance to join the global opposition to neoliberal globalisation. In the process, several movement organisations in Korea created a network called 'Civil Forum for ASEM 2000', which convened a counter-forum to ASEM in which more than 130 Korean, and several foreign, organisations took part, discussing different movement issues such as the environment, migrants issue, and so on.

Soon after, in 2003, a Korean peasant named Lee Kyung-hae performed a kind of public suicide strike in the course of anti-WTO protests taking place in Cancún, in Mexico, which became a very symbolic action against globalisation at the time. Considering that he was not a leading peasant activist but an ordinary peasant, his act showed how widely and deeply the opposition to the global order was shared by Korean peasants.[7]

During this period, the oppositional militancy of the Korean peasant movement continued to develop and take a position not only against the US as a predominant imperialist nation demanding the opening of the Korean agricultural market, but also against the global order. In December 2005, more than 1,000 peasants, labourers, and activists went to Hong Kong to resist the Doha agenda negotiation of the seventh ministerial meeting of the WTO. They performed a militant and well-organised struggle, another clear sign that the Korean people's movements were becoming an active militant force against globalisation, in Asia. To cement this impression, from early 2006 on there was a long-running anti-Korea-US Free Trade Agreement (FTA) struggle. It was a very popular campaign in which relatively moderate citizens' movements including environmental, women's and human rights' movements, and radical grassroots-people's movements came together with basically the same agenda.

Along with the anti-globalisation struggle against the opening of markets, there also sprang up a new movement that problematised speculative international financial capital. In August 2004, some labour activists and progressive economists sat together to establish a centre called Spec Watch Korea to monitor speculative capital, following the ATTAC model in France and in alliance with it. It monitored the activities of speculative finance, demanding that it be taxed and regulated. One of its successful campaigns drew public attention to the sale of the Korean Exchange Bank to a foreign speculative fund named Lone Star, during the turmoil of the economic crisis in 1997. The campaign criticised the bargain sale and sought to bring the persons involved in the sale to court. In the course of this the issue of speculation by international financial capital also became an important issue for Korea's opposition community and its populace.

The following table shows clearly how the South Korean people's movements got connected to, and participated in, diverse globalisation-related struggles:

Date	Event
September 28 1990	People's Action to Reject the UR Negotiations for Produce (a coalition of 36 groups) formed; became the start of the anti-UR movement (led by the Korean Peasants' League, etc). (UR refers to the Uruguay Round of WTO negotiations.)
1993	People's Action to Safeguard our Agriculture formed. (In April 1994, the UR bill was passed by the National Assembly)
April 23 1995	National Peasants' Rally to appeal for a Special Act on the Procedures of the WTO
September 15 1999	People's Action to Reject Investment Agreement in WTO's New Round formed
October 6–9 1999	Daegu Round of the WTO
December 10 1999	National Peasants' Rally to appeal for solving the problem of farm household debt and to reject the market opening following WTO negotiations
February 2000	Rally organised by Korean People's Action against Investment Treaties and the WTO (KoPA)

October 20 2000	People's action against neoliberalism, ASEM 2000, in Seoul
March 2001	National Council of Peasant Representatives against Korea-Chile FTA agenda
November 2002	Struggle against the Special Economic Zone (Free Economy Zone)
January 2003	Participation in the Asia Social Forum (ASF), in Hyderabad, India
February 2003	Rally organised by Korean People's Action against Investment Treaties and the WTO (KoPA)
October 2003	Participation in the struggle to halt the WTO ministerial meeting taking place in Cancún, Mexico, including the public suicide by Lee Kyung-hae
2004	Participation in the anti-World Economic Forum struggle in Davos, Switzerland, and in the World Social Forum (WSF) in Mumbai, India
April 26 2004	Massive rally to appeal for the halting of the Korea-US FTA negotiations
June 13 2004	East Asia meeting of the WEF, massive anti-war and anti-globalisation rallies
August 2004	Spec Watch Korea formed to regulate and tax foreign speculative finance
September 6 2004	Massive rally to "Safeguard our Rice"
November 2004	Struggle to stop the Korea-Japan FTA
November 2005	Anti-APEC meeting struggle in Busan
December 2005	Struggle against the seventh WTO ministerial meeting in Hong Kong
February 2006	Movement against Korea-US FTA
April 2006	Formation of People's Action to appeal for thorough investigation into Lone Star Gate and to reverse the illegal sale of the Korea Exchange Bank

Note: Adapted from Seonmee Kim 2008.

Increasing Sensitivity to the Transnationality of the Movement Acquired through Participation in World Conferences

The experience of participating in world conferences with global agendas also gave important impetus to strengthening sensitivity to the transnational and globalist nature of the movement emerging in Korea. The UN Conference on Environment and Development in Rio de Janeiro (1992), the UN Conference on Human Rights in Vienna (1993), the World Summit on Social Development in Copenhagen (1995), the UN World Women's Conference in Beijing (1995), the

UN Conference on Human Settlements (HABITAT II) in Istanbul (1995), the World Summit on Sustainable Development (Rio+10) in Johannesburg (2002), and the World Social Forums from 2001 to 2004 provided good opportunities for South Korean social movements to accept transnational issues related to globalisation as their own. This change was reflected in the increasing number of participants: Whereas only twenty Koreans joined the 1992 conference in Rio de Janeiro, 500 participated in the Rio+10 conference in Johannesburg in 2002. Similarly, whereas only ten Korean activists attended the first WSF in Brazil, but more than 400 joined the fourth WSF in India in 2004.

This stance of 'anti-globalisation' can be said to have developed along two lines: As expressed in the form of struggles against international forces and organisations driving economic globalisation such as the WTO or IMF on the one hand, and through diverse forms of alternative discussion and communication between different movement streams such as at the WSF on the other.[8] The participation of Korean social movements in the latter spurred an epistemological change towards a new globalism. Through the experience of these world conferences, the sensitivity and awareness of self-accountability for global solidarity has expanded beyond the national orientation.

Expansion of the Global Anti-War and Peace Movement

Similarly, and in addition, the global expansion of the anti-war peace movement against the US invasion of Iraq and the participation of the Korean movement community in it provided an important driving force for its transformation from a domestic issue-oriented movement to a new movement confronting the so-called "armed globalisation".[9] As is well known, the unjustifiable Iraq War and the aggressive militaristic policy expressed in the so-called pre-emptive strike strategy gave momentum to expanding and strengthening the transnational anti-war peace movement.[10] Similarly, and somewhat ironically, the anti-terror war—which was launched with the intention of preventing so-called terrorist attacks—only served to intensify struggles against the predominance and hegemony of the US as led by the Bush administration.

In a sense, the movement in Korea experienced a leap in awareness of transnational solidarity. In South Korea, which had long been a US ally and was asked to send troops to Iraq, the 'anti-dispatch movement' came to be strengthened and popularised. The movement against the dispatch of Korean troops to Iraq attracted large crowds, and most of South Korea's movement organisations joined a nationwide network to fight against the dispatch. This movement utilised diverse tactics, including a hunger strike, a strike by shipping workers, demonstrations, and media propaganda. It was one of the most enduring united campaigns.

The South Korean movement thus actively now joined both the transnational anti-war global action for peace on the one hand, and also the anti-dispatch movement on the other hand. One can say that by joining these two processes the South Korean movement was reborn as an organic part of the global movement. In this way, the opposition movement in South Korea, which had so far focused on domestic issues, began confronting the globalised order itself, changing from being based on oppositional nationalism to being based on a progressive new globalism.[11]

From Anti-Imperialism to Anti-Empire

I would like to define this kind of change in the Korean opposition movements as a change from an *anti-imperialist* movement to an *anti-empire* one.

This change in South Korea has diverse factors. Among them, two are most important. The first is that people began to feel the objective impact of globalisation in their everyday lives, and second that the movement actors progressively changed their perspective or approach to practical issues from a nationalist to a globalist one. Concerning the former, the globalisation process began to exert an impact, usually negative, on real lives, which created fertile ground for anti-globalisation movements. The opening up of the agricultural produce market began in the early 1980s due to pressure from the US. At that time peasants regarded this pressure for opening markets as a bilateral issue, restricted to the very particular relationship between the US and South Korea. However, during the struggles against the UR and WTO, the peasants came to realise that this pressure was coming from the general process of globalisation. Because of this, peasants came to stand at the forefront of the anti-globalisation movement.

Structurally speaking, the democratisation process in South Korea accompanied globalisation. The 1980s onward has been a period of both democratisation and globalisation. The globalisation process implies processes such as the opening of domestic markets, privatisation, flexibility of the labour market, and downsizing of the government and public sector. In this sense, I would say that the 1980s and 1990s have been a period of 'overlapped progress of democratisation and globalisation'. This is not unique to South Korea. Generally speaking, the process of the 'Third Wave' of democratisation, to use Huntington's term,[12] occurred in the international context of globalisation.

Concerning the second factor, I want to emphasise that the internationalist or globalist perspective began to be strengthened within the movement community. Influenced by the objective changes coming as a result of globalisation, there occurred a subjective change in the perception of it. If the activists in the 1980s had maintained a kind of *nationalist*—and especially a kind of *oppositional* nationalist—approach on the presupposition of nation-state order, those in the 1990s and thereafter began to adopt, increasingly, a *globalist* approach on the presupposition of global integration.[13] If we can say that the nationalist ethos was dominant in the former, we can also say that the globalist ethos dominates the latter. This kind of *anti-empire* movement became popular on the global scene after the 1999 Seattle struggle, and after the start of the WSF in 2001. Through increasing awareness of the importance of transnational solidarity, the struggle against the transnational capital driving globalisation has been perceived as a new horizon for movement activities. As a result, the character of the anti-empire movement has been strengthened from the 1990s onwards in South Korea, just as it has grown globally.

The current anti-globalisation movement is a united front composed of diverse kinds of orientations and ideas in some tension. Different streams have converged in the common battle against neoliberal globalisation, with the anti-globalisation movement including streams as diverse as socialist, anarchist, Third World nationalist, social democratic, etc. This diversity can also be found in terms of their collective agendas: Trade imbalance, discrimination against women, foreign debt, reform of disintegrating international financial organisations, regulation of speculative financial capital, sustainability of the global environment, anti-war, anti-racism, rights of indigenous peoples, and so on.[14] The differentiation between the anti-imperialist and anti-empire movements highlights the fact that the internationalism of the working class and socialist movements should be revived and reconstructed in the new spirit and in the new context of neoliberal globalisation, but recognising that we also have to admit the diversity and complexity of the composition of the anti-globalisation movement. Even Third World nationalism, if it wants to keep some progressive meaning, has to be reconstructed in the new globalist spirit, which is getting necessarily more progressive because of the globally integrated reality.[15]

Moreover, sometimes actors from within anti-imperialist and anti-empire movements join the same campaign. For example, the movement against the dispatch of Korean combat troops included both kinds of actors. In addition, the movement organisations at the front in the anti-imperialist movement have been performing an important role even in the anti-empire movement.[16] However, since the 1990s, that aspect of the anti-empire movement that focused on the globalised order itself has been strengthened. Many Korean social movements are trying to bring this globalist character to the fore, while also trying to retain the positive elements of the nationalist movement.[17]

Anti-Empire Movement: Differences and the Global United Front Movement

Radical anti-globalisation activism all over the world was strengthened after the Seattle struggle, and as mentioned above this also influenced the preparatory process of the movement in South Korea against the ASEM. But this process also divided the South Korean movements into two groups, with one organising street rallies against ASEM and the other relatively moderate group organising a counter-forum.[18] The latter can be characterised as being based on a strategy of the critical correction of current globalisation, and the former as based on a strategy of anti-globalisation. For the most part, this difference was between a 'civil movement' camp and a 'grassroots people's movement' camp. The strategy of critical correction of current globalisation was based on the discourse of global governance, which does not refuse the globalisation process itself but regulates and corrects the diverse negative outcomes of globalisation. In contrast, the strategy of anti-globalisation, which is completely against globalisation and has been adopted by grassroots people's movements everywhere, including labour and peasant movements, is based on the characterisation of globalisation as capital-driven and harming the interest of people at the grassroots, and favouring only business. This strategy is represented by KoPA, which includes most grassroots people's movement camps in South Korea, including the Korean Confederation of Trade Unions (KCTU), which—significantly—was established during this period, in September 1999. Its main stands are anti-neoliberal globalisation, anti-Free Economic Zones, and anti-Free Trade Agreements.

There are moreover differences in views even within the anti-empire movement, on issues such as the necessity of globalisation and alternatives to it. Whether the main agenda should be globalisation itself or the neoliberal character of globalisation is one example. Equally, and in relation to alternatives, there is a cleavage over separating from globalisation entirely and returning to the national economy or founding a globalised alternative.[19] Despite such differences, the bottom line of the movement camp—with its strategy of radical confrontation of globalisation—is that the current globalisation process is against people's interests.

To borrow Patrick Bond's expression, the former is oriented towards *fixing* the current global governance system, while the latter towards *nixing* it.[20] Of course, these two possibilities are not predetermined, but determined by the result of the struggle between dominant and opposition forces, like the anti-globalisation movement. If neoliberal globalisation proceeds in a way that is dominated by capital and accompanied by destructive impacts on people's lives, there is a high possibility that the different forces, whether nix-oriented or fix-oriented, will converge into one common stance. However, if the pro-globalisation forces turns its way to adopt some reformative measures to mitigate the current destructive effects of globalisation, and—as its result, the fix-oriented stream is co-opted by it—there will be a lower possibility of changing the current global governance system and contemporary globalisation will go forwards with a somewhat transformed character. And when the nix-oriented and fix-oriented streams are constrained within a nationalist frame, this possibility will get higher.

Here I would underline that the anti-empire movement is—and needs to be—a global united front of diverse kinds of heterogeneous movements. It should be a new global united movement based on differences, respecting differences. This inherits, in some sense, the spirit of the united front movement against Fascism in the 1930s and 1940s, in which formerly hostile forces like social democratic and revolutionary communist forces came together to combat the common 'fascist enemy'.

The modern history of the working class shows that it is an ongoing process that continuously reconstructs itself to have a political unity, bridging regional, sectoral, occupational, and other differences. In the current globalisation context these kinds of differences are increasing. In the twentieth century, these differences were regarded as needing to be overcome and removed, as we saw in the experiences of state socialism and anti-fascist movements. Now, in the new context, we have to make a new global solidarity of differences, acknowledging both the tension between the real differences and the necessity of forming a new global solidarity that extends beyond them. Such a unity is not a sameness but a commonness, in which the differences are a rich source of dynamics and not mere hostile confrontation.

In this sense, I would define the anti-empire movement as a new global united front movement of differences. Globalisation brings with it increasing heterogeneity in movements, because it creates diverse opposition subjects with differences in nationality, ethnicity, sex, religion, cultural identity, class, race, and so on. The new global united front movement from below can be formed and strengthened when diverse oppositional potentials and streams converge onto a new common identity,[21] when the working class and the people overcome national and other divisions and achieve the transnational consciousness of commonness—which I would call an 'anti-empire identity'.

The Anti-Empire Movement: A New Global United Front for Public and Social Control of Globalised Capitalism

Here I want to describe the relation between the anti-empire movement and capitalism, that is the structural meaning of the anti-empire movement. I would define it as a global united front movement for public and social control of capitalism. This united movement confronts globalised capitalism, or the globalised movement of capital, while the anti-imperialist movements have confronted the nationalised movement of capital beyond the local. This public and social control of the globalised movement of capital can take diverse shapes, from revolutionary reconstruction to reformative regulation of capitalism.

From a progressive point of view, neoliberal globalisation means the globalisation of the movement of capital. Such a globalisation of the movement of capital, which results in strengthening international competition between capital and in bringing "crisis" to individual capital,[22] tends to weaken the leverage of the national state and push it towards becoming a market-friendly or pro-business state, characterised by neoliberalism. Such a globalisation process is composed of the international accumulation regime of capital, global integration of markets, and international communication through the development of information and communication technology (ICT).

The problem is that this globalisation of capital movement is breaking away from social regulatory mechanisms created through social and class struggles within nation-state boundaries, and integrates all the former fragmented areas into the global free market. In this process, poor Third World countries are bearing the brunt. When external attacks and internal structural problems were united, many such countries rushed into IMF bailouts, which highlighted the possibility of international capital dictatorship without any public or social control mechanism.

The most visible phenomenon of the globalisation of capital movement is the 'violent' and destructive movement of global financial capital. The violence of such movements is making speculativeness, as an inherent character of capitalism, more threatening. Such concepts as casino or Rambo capitalism reflect the violent aspect of contemporary capitalism. This kind of change can be defined as transformation and reorganisation of the former domination of capital by way of globalisation of capital movement. We are confronted with the necessity of a new reorganisation of opposition to this kind of reorganisation of domination.

The History of Capitalism as a Process towards Public Regulation of the Free Market

Because capitalism is regarded as the free market order, the history of capitalism is generally regarded as that of forming and strengthening the 'free' market. However, when we see that same history from below, it has been a history of creating public and social regulatory measures to control the inhumanity and exploitativeness of the free market (for example, minimum wage), which otherwise has the unlimited maximisation of profit as its only goal.

In the nineteenth century, the demand and struggle for this kind of public control was overshadowed by the overwhelming ideological influence of 'successful' capitalism. But the crisis and over-accumulation of capitalism itself, and the struggle against that brutal accumulation process, necessitated change in the 'free' market. So-called 'modified capitalism' is the result of such change. The social democratic welfare state system signals the emergence of a class-compromise system with a certain, if limited, public regulatory mechanism. This welfare state system was made possible by maintaining the equilibrium of class power within the boundaries of a nation-state as the terrain for struggle.

However, this kind of system began to be disorganised by the globalisation of capital movement, facilitated by such factors as the breakdown of socialist systems, bringing with it a new power disequilibrium between the ruling and ruled, and scientific-technological development, bringing with it a new infrastructural condition that favoured 'free' global movement. In this process, the former public control mechanisms, made within a nation-state's terrain, began to lose their power and to disintegrate. As Dirlik says, capitalism has kept a global vision of movement, although its real working has been kept within national boundaries. However, "de-territorialisation"[23] and de-nationalisation of capital movement now became possible.

The globalisation of capital movement disintegrates the territorial base of democratic rule and weakens the 'social' character of democracy, which has been obtained through struggle. For example, the functions of social security and economy management are being increasingly limited by global conditions, and thus becoming empty shells. 'Politics' and the market are divided, and the future of the nation is no longer decided by the will of the voters, but thrown to the mercy of the floating global market. This is a reason to argue that neoliberal globalisation threatens democracy.

We have to keep in mind that such democratic control has been instituted by long-term struggles against the miserable situations made by violent movements of capital. In this context, I would say that the bottom line of the anti-empire movement with diverse orientations should be the public and social control of globalised capitalism, resulting in radical reconstruction of the global governance regime.[24]

Socialist and Democratic Movements to Control Capitalism

In other words, we can say that there have been two movements that have aimed to exercise public and social control over capitalism, in the 1900s and 2000s, within the national terrain: One is the movement for *socialist control of capitalism* and the other for *democratic control of capitalism*. We can say that there has been a war between capitalism and socialism, on the one hand, and between capitalism and democracy, on the other. The former aimed to overcome capitalism and construct communist planned economies, while the latter aimed to regulate the market. Both interacted with each other. The former—socialist control—has helped the latter—democratic control—strengthen. Within the working-class movements, there has been the revolutionary communist movement, on the one hand, and the so-called 'general democracy' (GD) movement to control capitalism by way of democratic measures like the eight-hour workday, minimum wage, and so on, on the other.

However, in the late 2000s, two changes have broken down the bases of these two 'national' movements. On the one hand, capital began a new global movement as a result of disempowering national democratic measures to control capitalism; and, on the other hand, the state socialist regimes that aimed at socialist control of capital collapsed. In addition, the democratic principle is still constrained by national boundaries, without any vision of its extension onto the global level,[25] and the socialist idea hasn't been liberated fully from the nationalist frame.

Helped by this situation, capitalism has been able to move globally without any serious opposition, which means that the power accumulated by socialist and democratic control of capitalism has been lost. The anti-empire movement thus must be seen as an effort to revive movements for the socialist and democratic control of capitalism in the new globalisation context, in a new spirit and form. We might yet see new wars developing between capitalism and democracy,[26] and between capitalism and socialism at the global level. The radical actors in the war between capitalism and socialism may also be active in the one between capitalism and democracy. In this sense, the anti-empire movement is the global united front movement for democratic control of capitalism, including socialist control movements as active parts.

Conclusion: Globalisation not as the Extinction of Politics but as a Chance for a New Global People's Politics to Emerge

Jean-Marie Guenno, a famous French intellectual, wrote *La fin de la democratie* ('The End of Democracy'), on the supposition that the world founded on the nation-state system is experiencing a new structural disintegration.[27] In his view, the period in which the territorial boundary was the main criterion is over, and politics will not survive in this kind of revolution. When the state does not exist any more, politics will not exist. In addition, he says, the presupposition that politics as a field of 'social contest and universal interest' exists, and that actors with their own unique energy of action also exist—which are the factors that made possible the modern nation-state—has broken down. As a result, we will see a new society which is fragmented infinitely, without any consensual memory and solidarity consciousness, and integrated only by images constantly broadcast by mass media. This leads to a society without citizens, and to society as—as Guenno terms it—'non-society'.

I predict a totally different picture of the world from the one Guenno has depicted, and would say that we should make it real from the bottom. As globalisation proceeds, the need for a new global politics is getting increasingly urgent. I think that we should create a new global politics and the people currently engaged with national and territorial spatial limitations should be the new actors trying to realise it. If not, the world imagined by Guenno will work, in reality, as a world of capital without any public mechanism to guarantee people's needs and interests, dazzling with colourful images. From a progressive view from below, the globalised order emerging in the wake of the disintegration of the nation-state should not merely be seen, in Guenno's expression, as "non-society", and should instead be reconstructed as a new global political community, in which the people living in that order and suffering by it form new public and social regulatory rules and mechanisms for their economic lives. In this sense, the 'end' of national politics should result in not 'the end of politics' but in the emergence of a new *global* politics.

If we look back on the history of the modern state and capitalism, we can recognise the relations between new emerging economies, politics, and states. In the pre-modern period, there existed localised economies, locally fragmented political and military power, and pre-modern people loyal to a feudal order. However, as localised economies expanded beyond local community boundaries, the 'national' bourgeoisie grew and national economies emerged, integrating the former localised economies. Thus, a new integration of political power and national concentration of military power proceeded forwards—which I would call 'national politics from above', based on economic integration. In response to, and in struggle against, this change, a new modern working-class and socialist movement emerged, in the form of a new people's political movement from below, acting within the national spatial terrain. Those movements have helped force a new public and social regulatory rule onto the nation-state, to control the new nationally integrated economy. In other words, this is a new national politics from below.

In the same way, I expect that the interaction between economic globalisation and people's movements will follow a similar trajectory, although this might be a political imaginary at the moment. As national economies get integrated globally, as expressed in the emergence of the WTO regime, a new global governance system, an incipient global politics from above, will emerge and work beyond the nation-state order. The issue for the progressive movements in response to this new change is how to organise new global people's politics from below, beyond national boundary limitations, as a driving force to construct anew a global public and social regulatory mechanism for a globally integrated economy, which will define people's everyday lives in new forms, just as the movement during the transition to modern society did, in its time.

In the modern period, the people's movements comprised and strengthened people's politics from below, in confrontation with national politics from above managed by the capitalists, bureaucrats, and market-friendly politicians. The new people's movements, expressed in diverse forms and fragmented along differences including nationality, etc, should also form and strengthen new people's politics from below in the current neoliberal globalisation context.

Currently, there is taking place a new competition and struggle over the hegemony over global politics, or global governance, that is mandated to provide a rule for letting the global economy work. In fact, it is not that there is no global rule for global politics in the current economic globalisation. To the contrary, there exists a global rule, that is the 'maximal market autonomy'—oriented rule (or global politics) to regulate the global economy as little as possible, as expressed in the current WTO protocol or in the FTA. It is a kind of economistic global politics or laissez-faire style global politics, which considers any public and social rule that aims to regulate economy as evil.

If the struggle against the current economic globalisation is strengthened, a new possibility will be opened for the disintegrational reconstruction of the current economistic global governance system, including the IMF, WTO, and so on. It ranges from the radical nix of the current global governance to the reformist fix of the maximal market autonomy–oriented rule.[28]

In this context, it is clear that transnational global politics is not headed for extinction but, to the contrary, is emerging strongly. One of the main elements of the new global politics is to realise a new public and social control over the global movement of capital. The anti-empire movement as a global united front movement is a key actor for waging and spreading such a global politics.

References

Patrick Bond, 2003—*Against Global Apartheid*. London: Zed Books

Alex Callinicos, 2003—*An Anti-Capitalist Manifesto*. London: Polity

Cho Hee-Yeon, 2004—'Defeat-Bush Campaign as the Coupling of the Anti-Globalization and Peace Movement against "Armoured Globalization"', in *Inter-Asia Cultural Studies: Movement* vol 2. London: Routledge

Cho Hee-Yeon, 2005—'"Second Death" or Revival of the "Third World" in the Context of Neo-liberal Globalization?', in *Inter-Asia Cultural Studies: Movement* vol 6 no 4 (London: Routledge)

Cho Hee-Yeon and Kim Eun Mee, 1998—'The State and Class in the Economic Development in South Korea and Taiwan—Focused on "State Autonomy" and Its Social Conditions', in Eun Mee Kim, ed, 1998—*The Four Asian Tigers, Economic Development, and The Global Political Economy*. San Diego: Academic Press

Chun So-hee, Autumn 2003—'Anti-WTO Struggle announcing the possibility of leap of the internationalist practices', in *Progressive Review*, vol 17

Arif Dirlik, 1994—*After the Revolution: Waking to Global Capitalism*. Lebanon, NH: University Press of New England

John Feffer, 2003—*North Korea/South Korea: US Policy at a Time of Crisis*. New York: Seven Stories Press

Jean-Marie Guenno, 1995—*La fin de la democratie* ['The end of democracy', in French]. Translated by the Institute of International Society and Culture. Seoul: Koryowon

Michael Hardt and Antonio Negri, 2000—*Empire*. Cambridge, MA: Harvard University Press

Michael Hardt and Antonio Negri, Fall–Winter 2001—'Adventures of the Multitude: Response of the Authors', in *Rethinking Marxism* vol 34, p 237

Martin Hart-Landsberg and Paul Burkett, September 2001—'Economic Crisis and Restructuring in South Korea: Beyond the Free Market-Statist Debate', in *Critical Asian Studies*, vol 33 no 3

David Held, 1995—*Democracy and the Global Order: From the Modern State to Cosmopolitan Governance*. Stanford, CA: Stanford University Press

Samuel P Huntington, 1991—*The Third Wave: Democratization in the Twentieth Century*. Norman: University of Oklahoma Press

International Forum on Globalization, 2002—*Alternatives to Economic Globalization: A Better World Is Possible*. San Francisco: Berrett-Korhler Publishers, Inc

Jung Jong-kwon, October 2000—'The Review of ASEM Struggle, One Step Forwards and Two Steps Backwards', in *Solidarity or Social Progress*, vol 10

Seonmee Kim, 2008—'The Response of the Korean Civil Society to Globalization', in Sohn Honchul and Kim Won, eds, 2008—*Globalization and Korean State-Civil Society* (Seoul: Imagine Publishers), p 166

Thomas H Marshall, 1964—'Citizenship and Social Class', in Thomas H Marshall, 1964—*Class, Citizenship, and Social Development*. New York: Doubleday and Company

Marxism 21, vol 1, 2003. Kyungsang University: Institute for Social Sciences

Kim Moody, September–October 1997—'Towards an International Social-Movement Unionism', in *New Left Review*, vol 225

Ronaldo Munck and Peter Waterman, eds, 1999—*Labour Worldwide in the Era of Globalization: Alternative Union Models in the New World Order*. New York: St Martin's Press

George E Ogle, 1990—*South Korea: Dissent within the Economic Miracle*. London and New Jersey: Zed Press

Rethinking Marxism, vol 34, Fall–Winter 2001

Claude Serfati, 2002—'Armed Globalization', at goo.gl/naiZRC (Accessed April 2017)

Gary Teeple, 1995—*The Globalization and the Decline of Social Reform*. Atlantic Highlands, NJ: Humanities Press

Peter Waterman, 1997—'More than Marxism Is Necessary for an "International Social-Movement Unionism"'. The Hague: Institute of Social Studies

Peter Waterman, 2004a—'The Global Justice and Solidarity Movement and the World Social Forum: A Backgrounder', in Jai Sen, Anita Anand, Arturo Escobar, and Peter Waterman, eds, 2004—*World Social Forum: Challenging Empires* (New Delhi: Viveka), pp 55–66, at http://www.choike.org/nuevo_eng/informes/1557.html (Accessed April 2017)

Peter Waterman, 2007e—*Globalisation, Social Movements, and the New Internationalisms*. London: Cassell

Kurt Weyland, 2003—'Neo-liberalism and Democracy in Latin American: A Mixed Record', in *Latin American Politics and Society*, vol 46 no 1

Won Yeong-Su, Autumn 2003—'Stream and Prospects of the Anti-Globalization Movement', in *Progressive Review*, vol 17

Ellen Meiksins Wood, February 1997—'A Reply to A Sivanandan', in *Monthly Review*, vol 47 no 9

Yoon Jeong-eun, November 2000—'Global People's Solidarity in the Action Day in Seoul', in *Participatory Society*, vol 48

Irish Marion Young, 2000—*Inclusion and Democracy*. New York: Oxford University Press

Eddie Yuen et al, eds, 2004—*Confronting Capitalism: Dispatches from a Global Movement*. New York: Soft Skull Press

Notes

1. In the 1950s, after independence, a civilian government ruled South Korea. However, the military captured state power by way of a military coup d'état in 1961. At the time, South Korean capitalism was in its incipient stages, and the bourgeoisie was weak. The military established a kind of 'developmental dictatorship', and drove strong developmentalist policies in favour of the weak bourgeoisie, in the name of

achieving so-called modernisation and industrialisation, until 1987 (Cho and Kim 1998).

2.   In the early stages of the developmental dictatorship, ordinary people were mobilised from above to support it. However, as the contradictions of development expanded and diverse kinds of victims were created by the violence and repressiveness of the dictatorship, they became angry and began to join the anti-dictatorship movement. The people who had earlier said 'Democracy doesn't feed us' changed to saying 'We can't live only on bread. We are thirsty for democracy'. In its early stages, the opposition was joined by students, church ministers, journalist, and other intellectual groups, but it spread to the grassroots gradually (See Ogle 1990).

3.   In the economic crisis in 1997, South Korea rushed for an IMF bailout, just like other East Asian countries. Capitalising on this, the IMF made policy conditions, including a high interest policy and opening the financial market, in order to 'readjust' East Asian economies to fit into the Washington Consensus. At this point, a vocal opposition demanded a renegotiation of the bailout. However, such voices were stigmatised as national traitors. Uncritical, pro-American consciousness had settled in ordinary people's minds during the hot Cold War and, as a result, the recommendations of the Western international economic organisations were accepted as necessary and as not needing critical reflection. This was a kind fetishised consciousness.

4.   Hart-Landsberg and Burkett 2001.

5.   The character of global neoliberalism implies diverse orientations such as the promotion of the primacy of private property rights, of the market as panacea; free economic zones, deregulation of the economy, and the privatisation of public corporations; the transformation of the tax structure in favour of business, the reduction of national debt, the downsizing of government, the restructuring of local government, and dismantling welfare; the promotion of charities; the circumscription of civil liberties and human rights; and the circumscription of trade union powers (Teeple 1995).

6.   The chronology can be found in Eddie Yuen et al 2004, pp xxxix–xlviii.

7.   In the Korean movement tradition, this kind of public suicide strike has been a symbolic way of struggle adopted by activists at critical conjunctures to deliver their cause to ordinary people and to the powerful. For example, Chun Tae-il, the labour activist, burned himself to deliver the message of resistance to capitalists and the government, in November 1970.

8.   Won 2003.

9.   Armed globalisation is expressed in diverse forms. Serfati uses the concept (Serfati 2002); John Feffer speaks about 'gunboat globalisation' (Feffer 2003). I have elsewhere also used the term 'armoured globalisation' (Cho 2004).

10.   The main reason behind strengthening transnational solidarity is the aggressive militaristic policy of the US as expressed clearly in the Iraq War, which has made 'armed globalisation' an essential characteristic. This means that globalisation proceeds with heightened militarism and amplifies that militarism. In a way, the globalisation of capital movement is closely intertwined with global militarisation; and the expansion of the anti-globalisation movement has been closely intertwined with the growth of the anti-war peace movement.

11.   Traditionally, the Korean people's movement has focussed on domestic issues, which continues to be the case. Most activists accept the global governance system and the policies of the IMF and the World Bank. In this sense, their participation in WSF has given them a chance to look at these institutions as changeable and dominated by powerful countries' economic interests. Some groups within the movement community wanted to take advantage of the WSF to expose young student activists to global movements, and thus to active participation in global common actions like that against the Iraq War. The high militancy and mobilisation capacity of the Korean movement, especially labour and peasant movements, is helping it play a very important role in fighting neoliberal globalisation. However, the consciousness of unity of the global justice movement, that is the anti-empire movement, is still weak and has far to go.

12.   Huntington (1991) differentiated three 'waves' of democratisation. The 'third wave' means the wide change for democratisation from the mid-1970s onwards. Although he does not stress this, the third wave proceeded in the international context of rapid neoliberal globalisation, which has however weakened democratic governance by the way of creating tighter external economic constraints for democratic and social policies of governments and political parties (Weyland 2003).

13.   The concept of politica is borrowed from different sources. The first is Hardt and Negri's idea (2000). In their usage, 'empire' is differentiated from the former predominant imperialist state. The empire is a kind of transnational order driven by globalisation of the market, not allowing "the outside". Although their concept still shows obscurity and abstractness, it brings to the fore the exploitation and repression in the newly globalised. (Concerning diverse kinds of critique on thoughts in *Empire*, refer to the special issue of *Rethinking Marxism* 2001 and responses to it by Hardt and Negri 2001) The second usage can be found in the sense of the predominant or super-imperialist state. It might be exemplified in the expression 'American Empire'. This implies that the militaristic and economic dominance of American imperialism expanded to cover the globe. In either case, it means that the globally-integrated new domination transcends boundaries of nation-states.

14.   Alex Callinicos classified the anti-globalisation movement, defined by him as "anti-capitalist movement", into "reactionary anti-capitalist", "bourgeois anti-capitalist", "localistic anti-capitalist", "reformative anti-capitalist", "autonomist anti-capitalist", and "socialist anti-capitalist", taking advantage of the dichotomy in *The Communist Manifesto* by Karl Marx (Callinicos 2003). Peter Waterman sorted different positions on globalisation and anti-globalisation against pro-Washington Consensus currents and resurgent rightwing currents into "post-Washington consensus current", "Third World nationalist current", and "global justice movement" (Waterman 2004a, pp 64–65).

15.   In imagining Asia, the Bandung Conference of 1955 is a very important historical resource of oppositional perception. When we want to revive its spirit in the current context, it can be differently approached—either by a "nationalist Bandung" approach or a "'globalist Bandung" approach (Cho 2005).

16.   In Korea, there are two main camps within the movement community: National Liberation (NL) and People's Democracy (PD). The former stands on the presupposition that the US, as the main imperialist force, strives to colonise South Korea—so,

overcoming this imperialist country's domination is necessary for people's liberation. However, the NL is also actively involved in anti-globalisation movements like the anti-WTO struggle.

17. There are different views on the WSF within the Korean movement community. Many Korean activists think the WSF is approaching a turning point. It has provided a global public sphere for diverse kinds of movements to meet and identify common grounds. However, the problem is that the common ground is so narrow. The WSF has helped diverse movements converge on a common enemy, that is neoliberal globalisation. However, it is functioning just as a meeting place, and participants are too heterogeneous to agree on higher levels of action against globalisation. In this sense, the task of how to substantiate global solidarity lies ahead for the global movement. For this, diverse sectoral and regional solidarities should be strengthened—transborder regional solidarity is a stepping stone for transborder global solidarity.

    In East Asia, the South Korean movement community is in a good position, as compared to in Japan and China, to contribute to strengthening transborder solidarity, because Japan is a former imperialist country and China has dominated neighbouring countries in the pre-modern period. Capitalising on this advantage, many groups in the South Korean movement are trying to strengthen transborder solidarity in diverse areas such as the peace movement, environmental movement, and so on. However, the popular nationalist atmosphere and lack of regional community consciousness among East Asian countries and their movement communities is restricting the substantiation of transborder solidarity.

18. Yoon 2000; Jung 2000.

19. This difference reminds me of the debate between dependency theorists and the position that the 'orthodox' Marxist Bill Warren takes. He criticises dependency theory, emphasising the effect of imperialist domination on industrialisation. In *Empire*, Negri argues that 'We have to precipitate globalisation, not block it'. This sparked a hot critique from orthodox Marxists. To me, what Negri wanted to say is that the struggle against capitalism has already changed from the nationally fragmented one to globally integrated one, and it should be performed on the presupposition of one globalised scene, coming out of the nationalist frame. There was a debate in Korea on the effect of globalisation and Negri's position (refer to special issue on 'imperialism or empire', *Marxism 21* 2003).

20. Concerning the "fix-it-or-nix-it" debate, refer to Bond 2003, pp 193–214.

21. The debate between Waterman and Moody is suggestive of this. The debate had several important issues, theoretical and practical, over the centrality of the working-class and labour movements, and on the relation between the labour movement and other social movements (Waterman 1997; Munck and Waterman 1999; Moody 1997). For more information, refer to Waterman 2007e. In my view, the so-called centrality of the labour movement exists not as an existential prerogative but in initiatives in practical struggles in the global justice and solidarity movements.

22. Wood 1997.

23. Dirlik 1994, p 155.

24. The principle of public control can be posited differently, depending on political positions. However, its lowest common denominator was elaborated by the International Forum on Globalization as follows: Democracy, subsidiarity, ecological

sustainability, common heritage, diversity, human rights, jobs, livelihood, employment, food security and safety, equity, the precautionary principle, commons, and so on (International Forum on Globalization 2002).

25. Until now, democracy has been regarded as a principle to manage a national political regime. Nowadays, theoretical efforts attempt to extend the democratic principle to the global governance level. According to I M Young, modern democracy stands on the principle that the range of democratic institutions should be identical to the range of obligations of justice. As globalisation proceeds, transnational processes are influencing people living in national boundaries, but they can't influence political decisions related to it. Young argues that the democratic principle should be extended onto the global level, and that the scope of relations in which the principle of justice is applied is global (Young 2000, p 249). More positively, David Held, as a global social democrat, argues that the Westphalian model that defined the modern nation-state regime has been disintegrated by the emergence of diverse kinds of power centres and networks outside the jurisdiction of the nation-state. The UN model from 1945 on is not working as a transnational governance regime to regulate conflict among nation-states. In this sense, he tries to theorise the "cosmopolitan democracy model". In the current globalisation process, democracy can't be constrained within national boundaries. He argues for a global system of regulatory regimes to which regions relate in a federated system, and imagines concrete global democratic institutions such as the introduction of parliamentary institutions into UN and global referendums—and even a world army as a regulator of the world military conflicts (Held 1995). Negri does not try to construct the theory of global democracy directly. However, he argues that national forms of sovereignty have been replaced by imperial forms (Hardt and Negri 2000). He positively defines this as the empire. In this sense, this global imperial new order can't be understood by imperialism based on national forms of sovereignty. This empire is characterised by heterogeneous composition, no unified power centre, and no outside. In response to this change of global reality, he suggests global citizenship as one of the new agendas of global movements. These effort of theorisation representing the transnational global movement from below are opposite to such imperialist action as the US invaded Iraq in the name of constructing democracy there. George Bush took advantage of the democracy discourse to legitimise the immoral and illegal war against Iraq. The US has dismissed the popular demand for democracy to legitimise its support for dictatorship in the name of security in the 1960s and 1970s. However, as democracy spread to all around the world through popular struggles from below, it is using it to legitimise its aggressive action against the so-called 'evil axis', which does not obey its influence.

26. T H Marshall said that the twentieth century has been one of warfare between citizenship and the capitalist class system, and that the equality orientation within citizenship has weakened the class system, which is characterised by inequality (Marshall 1964).

27. Guenno 1995, pp 80–81.

28. Chun 2003, pp 52–53.

The Weakest Link?
Neoliberalism in Latin America[1]
Emir Sader

The new century is off to a surprising start. The continent that had been a privileged territory for neoliberalism, Latin America, and where it was first applied—in Chile and Bolivia—has rapidly turned into the leading arena not only for resistance but for construction of alternatives to neoliberalism. Two faces of the same coin: Precisely by having been the laboratory for neoliberal experiments, Latin America is now having to deal with the consequences. The 1990s and the 2000s have been two radically opposite decades. During the 90s, the neoliberal model was imposed to varying degrees in virtually every country on the continent–with the exception of Cuba. The then US President Clinton, who did not even cross the Rio Grande to sign the first North American Free Trade Agreement (NAFTA), was forced not long after to approve a super-loan from Washington when the first crisis of the new model broke out in Mexico. The US went on to press for a hemisphere-wide Free Trade Area of the Americas (FTAA), presenting this as the natural outcome of the seamless extension of free trade policies.

At an Americas summit meeting in Canada in 2000, Venezuela's Hugo Chávez was the only leader to vote against Clinton's proposal for an FTAA, while Cardoso, Menem, Fujimori, and their colleagues fell meekly into line. On the occasion of his first Ibero-American Summit, Chávez reported, Fidel Castro—President of Cuba—passed him a piece of paper on which he had written: "At last I'm not the only devil around here". It was thus with some relief, too, that Chávez—himself elected president of Venezuela in 1998—attended the investiture as president of Lula (Luiz Inácio Lula da Silva) in Brasilia and Néstor Kirchner in Buenos Aires in 2003, before moving on to that of Tabaré Vázquez in Montevideo in 2004, that of Evo Morales in La Paz in 2006, and in 2007 those of Daniel Ortega in Managua and Rafael Correa in Quito; followed in 2008 by Fernando Lugo in Asunción. Meanwhile the US free trade proposal that had been approved almost unanimously in 2000 was dead and buried by 2004. Since that date, Chávez himself has been re-elected, as was Lula in 2006; in April of 2008, Kirchner was succeeded by his wife, Cristina Fernández, and Lugo triumphed in Paraguay, putting an end to more than sixty years of rule by the Colorado Party.[2]

What is the meaning of this radical reversal, faster than any the continent has experienced before, producing a greater number of progressive governments, whether left or centre-left, than it has seen in its entire history? It is true that the continent displays the highest levels of inequality in the world, an income gap aggravated by the neoliberal decade; and yet the hard blows that punished past popular struggles, along with the solidity of the neoliberal establishment, made such a rapid turn quite unexpected. In what follows we shall attempt to understand the conditions that transformed Latin America into the weakest link in the neoliberal chain.

Imposing the Model

A precondition for the privatisation programmes imposed across successive Latin American countries in the 1980s and 90s was the defeat and disarming of earlier movements of the left and organised labour. During the decades of development (the 1950s through to the 1970s), the emphasis was on import-substitute industrialisation—in particular in Mexico, Argentina, and Brazil, but also to a lesser extent in Colombia, Peru, Chile, Uruguay, and Costa Rica. These developments were underwritten by broad politico-ideological projects that encouraged the strengthening of the working class and its trade unions, backed by local party formations and democratic national blocs, in a context of nationalistic ideologies and identities. The potential this built up burst onto the political scene in the 1960s as a radical force, when the long cycle of growth petered out in conflicts over workers' rights, at a time when the Cuban example was pointing towards alternatives that transcended the limits of capitalism and US imperial domination. The response to these struggles was an era of military coups, first in Brazil and Bolivia in 1964, in Argentina in 1966 and 1976, and in Uruguay and Chile in 1973.

The combined and closely related processes of military dictatorship and the application of neoliberal models acted together to yield an extreme regression in the balance of power between social classes. It would have been impossible to implement the wholesale sell-offs of national industrial resources that unfolded most drastically in Chile, Uruguay, and Argentina without first crushing the people's ability to defend their interests. These three countries had been remarkable for their achievements, possessing advanced systems of social protection under states that assumed a regulatory capacity and a role in expanding the domestic market, guaranteeing the social welfare of the population, and providing public services. The most brutal repression they had ever known was needed to clear the way for neoliberal policies that privatised state functions—in the case of Argentina, transferring virtually all public resources into the hands of private capital—and abolished hard-won social rights. In short, three of the most enlightened states on the continent found themselves completely dismantled.

In the course of the 1990s, neoliberalism penetrated Latin America right across the political spectrum. The programme was originally implemented by the far right, in Pinochet's Chile. It found other right-wing followers—such as

Alberto Fujimori in Peru—but also absorbed forces that had historically been associated with nationalism: The PRI (Institutional Revolutionary Party) in Mexico; Peronism in Argentina under Carlos Menem; and in Bolivia, the Nationalist Revolutionary Movement—the party that had headed the nationalist revolution of 1952 under Víctor Paz Estenssoro. The next target was social democracy, as neoliberalism gained the adherence of the Chilean Socialist Party, Venezuela's Acción Democrática, and the Brazilian Social Democracy Party. It became a hegemonic system across almost the entire territory of Latin America.

Nevertheless, the neoliberal model failed to consolidate the social forces necessary for its stabilisation, resulting in the early onset of crises that would check its course. The three largest Latin American economies were the theatre for the most dramatic crises: Mexico in 1994, Brazil in 1999, and Argentina in 2002. The programme crumbled without delivering on its promises. The ravages of hyperinflation were checked, but this was only achieved at tremendous cost. For a decade or more, economic development was paralysed, the concentration of wealth grew greater than ever before, public deficits spiralled, and the mass of the population had their rights expropriated, most notably in the domain of employment and labour relations. On top of this, national debt expanded exponentially and regional economies became highly vulnerable, helplessly exposed to attack from speculators, as these three countries each discovered to their cost.

It was neoliberalism's poor economic performance in Latin America that in many instances led to the defeats of the governments that pioneered it. These include Alberto Fujimori in Peru, Fernando Henrique Cardoso in Brazil, Menem in Argentina, Carlos Andrés Pérez in Venezuela, and Gonzalo Sánchez de Lozada in Bolivia; also gone are the PRI in Mexico, the alternation of the two traditional parties in Uruguay, and the politicians who tried to perpetuate neoliberalism even beyond its collapse, including Fernando De la Rúa in Argentina, Lucio Gutiérrez in Ecuador, and Sánchez de Lozada in Bolivia. It is also important to note the isolation of those leaders who struggle to keep it going, such as Felipe Calderón in Mexico, Michelle Bachelet in Chile, Alan García in Peru, or Alfonso Uribe in Colombia. (Uribe, incidentally, lost recent local elections revolving around issues of governance; his prestige derives from the uncompromising deployment of 'democratic security policies' against 'terrorism', a position which earns him a steady 80 per cent domestic support.) As of 2008, a growing number of presidents have been elected, or in some cases re-elected, in response to the failure of the neoliberal economic model.

Rapid Cycles of Reversals

We can trace a series of upswings and downswings, triumphs and setbacks, in Latin American politics since the victory of the Cuban Revolution in 1959. Their rise and fall have come in quick succession, compared to the time-spans of the

European left. The result has been a series of recalibrations in the balance of power, which itself reflected the prolonged crisis of hegemony that overtook the region when the import-substitution model that had held sway since the crash of 1929 finally ran out of steam.

The first cycle, from 1959 to 1967, saw the triumph of the Cuban Revolution and the spread of the rural guerrilla movement to Venezuela, Guatemala, and Peru, in emulation of those of Colombia and Nicaragua. The period saw mass mobilisations in several countries, including Brazil during Goulart's 1961–64 government, and broad resistance to the dictatorship that followed the military coup there in 1964. For the Latin American left this was a period of upswing, directly influenced by the success of Cuba, but cut short by the death of Che Guevara in Bolivia in 1967.

The second cycle runs from 1967 to 1973. It saw the decline of the rural guerrilla movements and the rise of new urban guerrillas in Uruguay, Brazil, and Argentina. Allende was elected president in Chile (1970–73); the same years saw the government of Juan José Torres (1971) in Bolivia, and nationalist governments under Juan Velasco Alvarado in Peru (1967), and Omar Torrijos in Panama (1968). In summary, this was a mixed period inaugurating an era of reverses, marked by military coups and dictatorships.

The years 1973 to 1979 saw the consolidation of military dictatorships across the Southern Cone. As in Brazil, juntas came to power in Bolivia in 1971, Chile and Uruguay in 1973, and Argentina in 1976. Velasco Alvarado was overthrown in Peru. The neoliberal model was rolled out in Pinochet's Chile. This was a period of unmitigated downturn. By contrast, the long decade of 1979 to 1990 brought Sandinista victory in Nicaragua, revolution in Grenada, and a nationalist government in Suriname. Castro was elected president of the Movement of Non-Aligned Countries, and guerrilla forces expanded in El Salvador and Guatemala. The 1980s were a period of overall progress.

In another switch, the years from 1990 to 1998 saw the Sandinista defeat, the start of the 'special period' in Cuba, and the entrenchment of neoliberal hegemony across the continent, with the collaboration of the PRI, Menem, Pérez, Cardoso, and Fujimori in their respective countries, and the continuation of Pinochetist economic neoliberalism in Chile under the Concertación coalition of Socialists and Christian Democrats. This was definitively a period of net regression. Yet from 1998 onwards, the wind turned in the other direction with the election of Chávez in Venezuela, followed by the launch of the World Social Forums in Porto Alegre in 2001, Lula's election victory in 2002, and further gains for the left and centre-left in Argentina, Uruguay, Bolivia, Nicaragua, Ecuador, and finally Paraguay. Mercosur ('Southern Common Market') was expanded to incorporate Venezuela, Bolivia, and Ecuador, while the Alternativa Bolivariana para las Américas (Bolivarian Alternative for the Americas)—or ALBA, 'dawn'—brought together a new left grouping of the Andean-Caribbean axis. So far, this has been a period of appreciable progress.

This rapid-fire succession of upswings and downswings testifies to the continent's instability, and its poor capacities for consolidating alternative programmes; and yet it is also a sign of the left's astounding ability to recover from its defeats, no matter how crushing these seem to be—Che's murder, the coup in Chile, the rout of the Sandinistas, or the tightening grip of neoliberal processes. Like a mole, the popular movement repressed in one country has popped up elsewhere. It tunnelled from the south to the north of the continent, from the country to the city, from the discourse of the old left to new forms of expression, from party structures to looser social movements, and from these to new political and ideological forces. In other parts of the world, defeats on the scale experienced here led to long periods of abeyance, for example after the loss of Germany and Italy in the wake of World War I, or the crushing of republicanism after the Spanish Civil War. Not so in Latin America.

The brevity of the cycles is also surprising: Only three years passed between the death of Che and the ebbing of the first *guerrillero* wave in 1967, and the election of Allende in 1970. Between the 1973 military coups in Chile and Uruguay, and that of 1976 in Argentina, and then the 1979 victory of the Sandinistas—six and three years respectively. And from the collapse of the socialist world, the beginning of the 'special period' in Cuba, the 1989 overthrow of the Grenada government, and the end of the Sandinista regime in 1990, it was only eight or nine years until the election of Chávez. The neoliberal model was just beginning to put down roots when its first crisis erupted in Mexico in 1994—the year that NAFTA was signed and the Zapatista rebellion broke out, while Cardoso was taking office in Brazil. Notably, the three progressive cycles together add up to 29 years, encompassing the victory of the Cuban and Nicaraguan Revolutions and the governments of Allende, Chávez, Morales, and Correa. By contrast, the periods of retreat make up a total of 14 years, including the death of Che, the Chilean coup, and the Sandinista defeat.

Three Strategies of the Left

Cross-cutting these political cycles, three overall strategies of the Latin American left can be discerned. The first sequence, dating back to the 1940s, was one of major structural reforms contemporaneous with the hegemony of the import-substitution model. The left opted for an alliance with sectors of the national business elite in the name of economic modernisation, agrarian reform, and a certain autonomy with respect to Northern imperialism. This strategy was implemented by legendary nationalist leaders such as Getúlio Vargas of Brazil, Lázaro Cárdenas of Mexico, and Juan Perón of Argentina, in concert with parties of the left or centre-left. In Chile, textbook cases of this approach were the Popular Front of 1938 and the Allende administration in 1970–73. But the programme failed at the same time as the industrialisation effort, when the internationalisation of economies pushed the corporate elites into solid alliance with international capital, laying the groundwork for the eventual neoliberal model. These same entrepreneurs also supported the military dictatorships of the Southern Cone, making no secret of their readiness to liquidate the popular movement for the sake of an export-centred economy geared to luxury domestic consumption by way of intense labour exploitation.

Allende's government, based on the Communist and Socialist parties, with a programme that envisaged the nationalisation of 150 leading corporations, constituted the most advanced example of the attempt to progress from reformist policies to a socialist overcoming of capitalism. Among the multiple reasons for its defeat, there can be no doubt that the fact that Allende started out with just 34 per cent of the vote, and that three years later his government's share had only risen to 44 per cent, was a major obstacle in implementing such a radical programme. Unidad Popular also underestimated the class nature of the state. It neglected therefore to institute an alternative power outside the traditional apparatus, which ultimately cornered and smothered the executive. The Chilean and Uruguayan military coups were carried out in the year that marked the transition from a long, expansive cycle to a recessive one, triggered by the oil crisis of 1973. A page of history had been definitively turned, and with it one strategy of the Latin American left was now closed.

A second great strategy emerged with the Cuban Revolution. Any revolutionary victory—above all when it is the first of its kind in a whole region—carries charismatic persuasive force, as we know from the Russian and Chinese experiences in 1917 and 1949. The Cuban triumph coincided with the end of the cycle of Latin American economic expansion under the popular governments and democratic regimes that had prevailed over much of the continent during the 1940s and 50s. The first Argentine coup was carried out in 1955, the second in 1966; the Brazilian and Bolivian coups took place in 1964, and already by 1954 Guatemala was in the throes of counter-revolution. It seemed that the cycle of democratic governments had run its course, in parallel with the economic crises.

It was then that Cuba unexpectedly presented an alternative route, in contrast to the impasse that popular struggles in other countries had reached under their traditional leaderships. Latin America was no stranger to guerrilla movements; it had known rural insurgencies such as those of Nicaragua and El Salvador in the 1930s, as well as the national-revolutionary struggles in Mexico in the 1910s, or in Bolivia in 1952. Yet events in Cuba radiated a special appeal, pointing the way to a new epoch for the left. Due to the similarity of levels of development reached at that period by most of the countries of Latin America, the Cuban Revolution was immediately more influential in the region than the Russian Revolution had been in Europe in its day. All the more so, thanks to the way it was presented by such—attractive, if misguided—codifications as Régis Debray's account of the Cuban experience and how it might be replicated in other countries and continents.[3] The massive congresses hosted by Cuba—Tricontinental in 1965 and OLAS (Latin American Solidarity Organisation) in 1967—were instrumental in giving huge momentum and worldwide publicity to the new strategy, which was also exemplified by the activities of Che Guevara in Africa and Latin America.

The guerrilla struggles played out in three distinct phases over the next decades. The first, in the 1960s, had a rural character, with hubs in Venezuela, Guatemala, and Peru; it ended with Che's death in Bolivia just as he was attempting to coordinate these with other movements that were beginning to appear in Uruguay, Brazil, and Argentina. The second phase was that of the urban guerrillas in the three latter countries, which operated between the late 1960s and early 1970s. The third phase was once more based in the countryside, inspired by the victory of the Sandinistas in 1979, and centred throughout the 1980s chiefly in Guatemala and El Salvador. The Sandinista electoral defeat in 1990 coincided with the shift to a unipolar world under the imperial hegemony of the US, which put an end to the viability of guerrilla strategies. The impossibility of military victory in other countries forced Guatemalan and Salvadoran fighters to reinsert themselves into mainstream political institutions, and the heyday of *guerrillero* strategies was basically over.

At the same time, the global realignment after 1990 had far-reaching consequences for the parties of the traditional left, both nationalist and social democratic. Their adherence to neoliberal policies, and the effects of these policies themselves, disabled the trade union movements and the broader gamut of left-wing forces. The collapse of the USSR and the socialist camp precipitated a conclusive crisis for Communist parties across the continent. Several changed their names and even their natures, as was the case with the Brazilian Communist Party; others simply faded away, while those that survived were left in social, political, and ideological quarantine.

The other forces of the left were variously affected by the new conditions. The Brazilian Workers' Party (PT), the Uruguayan Frente Amplio, and the Nicaraguan Frente Sandinista all evolved into parties of the centre-left, accepting when in power the economic models they had fought against in opposition. Of the former guerrilla groupings, only the Frente Farabundo Martí of El Salvador has managed to survive as a significant political force since laying down its arms. The MIR (Movimiento de Izquierda Revolucionaria—Revolutionary Left Movement) in Chile, the Montoneros and the PRT-ERP (Partido Revolucionario de los Trabajadores–Ejército Revolucionario del Pueblo—Workers' Revolutionary Party—People's Revolutionary Army) in Argentina, the ALN (Ação Libertadora Nacional–National Liberation Action) and the VPR (Vanguardia Popular

Revolucionaria–Popular Revolutionary Vanguard) in Brazil, and the guerrilla groups in Peru and Venezuela have all been dissolved, whilst the Tupamaros in Uruguay have reinvented themselves as a political force that bears no relationship to their past as a guerrilla movement.

The Rise of Social Movements and the 'Autonomy of the Social'

The entire framework of political and ideological struggle in Latin America has thus been remodelled under neoliberal hegemony. The radical reversal of the balance of power imposed by the dictatorships of the preceding decades was further reinforced by the new world order. The abandonment of popular forces by former nationalist or social democratic allies, together with the harsh social consequences of free-market economics, have propelled social movements into the forefront of the resistance to neoliberalism—the third and latest strategy from below. The Zapatistas, the landless peasant movement (MST) in Brazil, the indigenist movements of Bolivia and Ecuador, the *piqueteros* or unemployed workers' activists (or pickets) in Argentina—these are just some of the groups that have pioneered the new militancy. They have resisted to the best of their ability while neoliberalism stripped the state of its functions, pushed through the wholesale privatisation of public enterprises, and expropriated rights to formal employment, health, and education. Opposition to NAFTA was the central plank of the Zapatista platform unveiled in 1994. Landless peasants in Brazil have taken action against sell-offs, and the resistance to water privatisation in Cochabamba in 2000 was the starting point for a remarkable new phase in the history of the Bolivian left. Something similar took place in Ecuador, where indigenist movements demonstrated their power of veto against two neoliberal administrations—under Abdalá Bucaram in 1997 and Jamil Mahuad in 2001—forcing both presidents from office. Later mobilisations, this time led by urban movements formed to defend citizens' rights, overthrew a third government, that of Lucio Gutiérrez, in 2005.

The difficulties experienced by the neoliberal model itself in Mexico, Brazil, and Argentina, combined with the pressure of popular resistance to it, opened the door to a new phase, in which the left camp formulated urgent alternatives in the context of the crisis of hegemony across the continent. This posed dilemmas in relation to the state and political power, to which some movements responded proactively, whereas others held back.

A common position among the latter was to use their critiques of the traditional left, the neoliberal state, and standard political practices to justify a sweeping repudiation of parties, state, and politics in general, taking refuge in what they called 'the autonomy of social movements'. At a time when neoliberalism was sharpening its assault on the state in favour of the market, on politics in favour of economics, and on political parties, in favour of corporations, a certain ambiguity crept into the distinction between the neoliberal arguments and these new movements that championed the 'social' dimension to the detriment of politics, parties, and states. A new tendency arose within the left or the overall resistance to neoliberalism, embodied in social movements and NGOs, and articulated around the dichotomy of 'state versus civil society'. The World Social Forum reinforced this tendency by welcoming social movements and NGOs but remaining closed to political parties, arguing that this space belonged to civil society.

There are two main problems with this position. Firstly, it blurs the boundaries with neoliberal discourse, as pointed out above, which likewise regards the state and party politics as its great enemies. Secondly, given that neoliberalism is characterised by the wholesale expropriation of rights, it can only be overcome in the political sphere: Through the universalisation of rights enacted by the governing authority of the state. Otherwise, the struggle against neoliberalism would remain perpetually on the defensive, having discarded the political instruments necessary for its own realisation. Some movements have remained trapped in this paradox, ostensibly embodying hubs of resistance yet unable to move forward into challenging neoliberal hegemony, via a fresh articulation of the social with the political. Their critique of the state is subordinated to the terms of the theoretical discourse of neoliberalism, structured around the polarisation of state versus private. This polarity is designed to demonise the state, take control of the private sphere (in which market relations are embedded), and abolish the indispensable framework for the democratisation and defeat of neoliberalism: The public sphere.

The real polarisation is between the public sphere and the market sphere. Insofar as the neoliberal project is committed to the infinite extension of market relations, the state is not so much a pole as a space of hegemonic dispute between the two spheres. The construction of an anti-neoliberal alternative must begin with the reorganisation or recasting of the state in favour of the public sphere, universalising citizens' rights while divorcing the state and general social relationships from the market. To democratise means to de-marketise, to recuperate for the terrain of people's rights, which neoliberalism has delivered into the hands of the market. Limiting the field of action to the 'social' as opposed to the 'political', proclaiming the autonomy of social movements as a principle, means condemning oneself to impotence, and ultimately to defeat.[4] The cases of Bolivia on the one hand, and of Ecuador and Argentina on the other, provide instructive examples of these alternatives.

La Paz, Quito, Buenos Aires

In Bolivia, the new left was constructed upon a critique of the blind economism of the traditional left, which classified indigenous peoples solely as *campesinos*—peasants—because their means of subsistence could be defined as small-scale rural production. This economism had robbed the Aymara, Quechua, and Guaraní peoples of their deep and ancient identity. The new critique—explicitly voiced by Alvaro García Linera, current vice president of Bolivia—empowered the construction of a new political subject: The indigenous movement. In alliance with other social forces, the movement went on to found the MAS—Movimiento al Socialismo—in order to unite the forces built up since 2000 towards effective action in the political sphere and hegemony at the national level, through the candidacy and presidency of Evo Morales.

Since 2000, and leading up to Evo's election six years later, the militant activism of indigenous movements succeeded in preventing the privatisation of the water supply that was to be exploited by a French company, and overthrew the neoliberal governments of Sánchez de Lozada and Carlos Mesa. Morales was elected on a platform that pledged to nationalise natural resources, undertake agrarian reform, and convene a Constituent Assembly charged with redefining Bolivia as a multinational, multi-ethnic, multicultural state. The indigenous movement progressed from specific issues—such as water—through a struggle against the national government, to the creation of a party rooted in social movements, and finally to the construction of an alternative anti-neoliberal project for Bolivia to be implemented by a state refounded on new lines.

Similar events took place in Ecuador, where the resistance to neoliberalism spearheaded by indigenous movements brought down two governments. Movements such as Pachakutik and CONAIE placed their trust in a military man, Lucio Gutiérrez, who had played a role in the fall of the second government and participated in the World Social Forum at Porto Alegre; there were to be several indigenous representatives in his cabinet. But even before taking office, Gutiérrez travelled to Washington to sign agreements with the Bush administration, betraying his campaign pledges on economic policy and the military base at Manta, where US troops were stationed. The indigenous movements withdrew their support and pulled out of the government, but they were divided. Some leaders remained loyal to Gutiérrez until the end, and the indigenous forces were so weakened by the process that they played little part in the 2005 uprisings that led to his fall, which was the work mostly of urban movements.

During the 2006 presidential election, the left was represented by Rafael Correa, a young Christian economist who had briefly served in the government of Gutiérrez's vice president and campaigned on an anti-neoliberal platform which presented itself as the political continuation of all the grassroots mobilisations of recent years. At first the indigenous movements did not stir, mistrustful of institutional participation after their experiences in the Constituent Assembly and Gutiérrez's government. When they finally fielded a candidate in the shape of their leader, Luis Macas, the space of the left was already occupied by Correa and his largely urban followers, although Correa also attracted the support of the indigenous population.

The movement in Ecuador proved unable to transcend the dilemma between the 'autonomy of the social' and the need to reconnect with the political sphere, remaining split between three options: The traditional form of supporting and participating in governments; withdrawal from the institutional political fray; and the belated fielding of an assertive but isolated candidate who took only 2 per cent of the vote. And so a movement with an extraordinary history failed to progress from the path of pure resistance to that of the construction of alternatives, and found itself excluded when the time came to plan for post-neoliberalism.

In Bolivia, by contrast, indigenous movements did prove equal to the task of making this transition. The foundation of MAS and the candidacy of its leader, Evo Morales, expressed a new way of linking social movements to the political sphere. Evo continued as president of the Coca Growers' Federation of Cochabamba, his native province, at the same time as he became the leading candidate of the Bolivian left and won election as President of the Republic. This achievement is a milestone in the history of the Latin American left, and more specifically in the history of anti- and post-neoliberal struggles.[5]

The *piqueteros* (pickets) of Argentina also illustrate the dilemma facing the new movements. These groups sprang to prominence during the terminal crisis of peso-dollar parity—an extreme and radical example of financial neoliberalism—by organising mass demonstrations, pickets, and road blocks, attracting many who had been pauperised by the effects of the currency peg. There was also a proliferation of factory takeovers, in which workers successfully rescued concerns that had been abandoned or closed by their proprietors. This early conflict with the De la Rúa government—which had inherited the dollar-parity policy from the Menem administration, and stuck with it until it blew up in their faces—marked the beginning of the deepest crisis ever faced by the Argentine state. In December 2001, after angry demonstrations against his government, De la Rúa fled from the Casa Rosada, the presidential palace, in a helicopter. Over the following days, several more presidents came and went. The bankruptcy of the economic model was obvious, and the possibility of a non-neoliberal government openly discussed. When new elections were called, Carlos Menem came up with an even more radical proposal: Full dollarisation of the Argentine economy. This would imply severing the country from processes of regional integration, a blow from which it might not have recovered. Further damage would have been caused by Menem's plan to boost US free trade ambitions by signing a bilateral treaty between the two countries.

Faced with this crisis of hegemony for the traditional political parties—the Partido Radical in disarray after De la Rúa's resignation, the Peronists bitterly divided—the social movements coined the famous slogan, *¡Que se vayan todos!*:

Out with the lot of them! This amounted to a refusal to take part in the electoral process, yet without suggesting any way in which power might be rethought or reorganised. It was a quintessential expression of the 'autonomy of social movements', disdainful of politics but lacking any alternatives. From a position of strength, one can indeed get rid of 'the lot of them'. Without organised political forces, the slogan was merely a way to bow out from the fight for an alternative hegemony. In the Argentine case, this enabled Menem to win the first electoral round in 2002 and a relatively obscure provincial governor, Néstor Kirchner, to win the second. Kirchner set out to project, from within Peronism, the image of a moderate alternative to Menem in the mould of Lula or Tabaré Vázquez. Thus the crisis of hegemony was overcome. Kirchner capitalised on the fury of the streets, and the contempt for the Menem and De la Rúa governments. From a centre-left position, he set about repairing the cracks in state legitimacy and winning over many sectors of the *piqueteros*, whose more radical wings were thus isolated and weakened.

In all these instances, the notion of the autonomy of the social served neither to help the regrouping of mass forces intent on organising new forms of political action, nor as a way of constructing alternative forms of power, but rather as a refusal to confront the issue of power altogether. The clearest theoretical expositions of such tendencies are to be found in the works of Toni Negri and John Holloway.[6] They argue explicitly for the abandonment of power, of the political sphere, on grounds that power corrupts everything since its forms of representing the popular will are intrinsically tainted and distorting; the will of the people can only be legitimately represented within the social sphere. Furthermore, Negri portrays the state as a conservative brake on globalisation. Yet neither makes any attempt to construct concrete anti-neoliberal strategies; their prescriptions lead only to the inertia of the social movements. The WSF, for its part, made the need to regulate flows of finance capital one of its founding theses; yet this can only take place—as, for example, in the case of Venezuela—through state action.

Another approach to the crisis of hegemony besetting Latin America—with the exhaustion of the neoliberal model but the continuation of free trade policies—can be found in Zapatismo. This movement was born of the demands of indigenous groups in Chiapas and enjoyed a high national profile for a while, but it remained confined to the southeast of Mexico and the demands of a single sector. Rather than profit from the crisis of the PRI, the Zapatistas took no part in the institutional jousting—which they condemned—and the PAN (National Action Party) stepped into the breach instead, as another right-wing option. Nor did they participate in the 2006 presidential elections, preferring to conduct the 'Other Campaign', parallel to the official race: An occasion for pouring more venom on the mainstream left candidate, the PRD's (Party of Democratic Revolution) Andrés Manuel López Obrador, than on his rivals. Once more the winner was the PAN, although by a tiny margin this time, and amid well-founded accusations of fraud. Felipe Calderón has continued with the neoliberal policies of his predecessor. He has also challenged the state monopoly of oil with a project that paves the way for the privatisation of Pemex, while intensifying the crackdowns on popular protest.[7]

Centre-Left Inflexions

A further response to the crisis of hegemony is that of the traditional left, embodied in governments like those of Lula, Kirchner, Vázquez, or Ortega, which enjoy some form of critical support from the social movements of their countries—trade unions, rural movements, public-sector employees in health or education. These governments maintain the neoliberal model, but attempt to develop more flexible social policies—notably in Brazil, but also in Argentina, Uruguay, and Nicaragua—that distinguish them from orthodox neoliberal administrations. Their foreign policies, moreover, are firmly committed to regional integration, with the accent on Mercosur and the more recently created UNASUR (Union of South American Nations), in preference to free trade agreements with the US. This is the fundamental issue that divides Latin America today: The line that separates countries such as Chile, Mexico, Peru, or Costa Rica, which have signed deals of this kind, from others such as Argentina, Brazil, Uruguay, Paraguay, Venezuela, Bolivia, Ecuador, Nicaragua, or Cuba, that are more interested in regional integration. This is a completely different distinction to that between a 'good' or 'moderate' centre-left, and a 'bad' or radical left, cultivated by the Western media and formulated by figures such as Jorge Castañeda, spokesman of the Latin American right, in order to divide the left by co-opting the moderates and isolating the radicals.[8]

Meanwhile, four Latin American governments have taken the priority of regional integration a step further, aiming to break with the dominant model and begin the construction of what we might call the post-neoliberal alternative. Venezuela, Bolivia, Ecuador, and Cuba are committed—Ecuador only unofficially so far—to building the Bolivarian Alternative for the Americas (ALBA), whose integration process is more far-reaching; it now also includes Haiti, Nicaragua, and Honduras. ALBA has attempted to combat the neoliberal model by creating de-mercantilised spaces and promoting what the World Social Forum has called 'fair trade', that is, exchanges not governed by market rates or WTO norms of free trade.

This experiment is unique for its practice of alternative modes of exchange, prefiguring what that 'other possible world' that the WSF speaks of might look like. Here, each country gives according to what it has and receives according to its needs. Thus ALBA's two founding countries, Venezuela and Cuba, swap the oil of the first for the second's expertise in education, public health, and sports, in line with their respective wants and possibilities. Thanks to these transactions, Venezuela has become the second country in Latin America to claim the status of an 'illiteracy-free territory', according to UN criteria. This achievement was obtained in a public, de-mercantilised space, not under market conditions or subject to the educational budgets of traditional governments, even those of relatively more developed countries like Argentina, Mexico, or Brazil; and it was not the product of a highly developed government-sponsored literacy method such as that of the Brazilian Paulo Freire.

Bolivia has announced that by the end of 2008 it expects to join Venezuela and Cuba as another illiteracy-free territory, thanks once more to the direct input of Cuban specialists. Other successes include 'Operation Miracle', a project that has restored the eyesight of hundreds of thousands of Latin—and indeed North— Americans by means of free operations in Cuba, Venezuela, and Bolivia; in the latter country, for example, thousands of Argentineans have benefited from the scheme. Meanwhile the Latin American School of Medicine is training the first generation of doctors from humble backgrounds, North Americans included, free of charge. Venezuela is using its oil revenues to construct a space of solidarity exchanges—Petrocaribe—that helps fund poor sectors in the US, just as ALBA runs solidarity programmes in Haiti, Bolivia, Nicaragua, and elsewhere on the continent. Regional integration projects, like the Banco del Sur (Bank of the South) scheme, the transcontinental gas pipeline, and teleSUR (New Television Station of the South), are other attempts to alter the relation of the region to the world market, by devoting financial resources and commodities to the fulfilment of its own objectives.

Vanguard States

Why, despite all this, has a full-fledged challenge to capitalism not emerged yet in Latin America? The answer must be sought in the global balance of forces following the victory of the West in the Cold War. The extensive processes of deregulation and marketisation that this unleashed did not produce an era of sustained economic growth; instead, productive investment was in large part transferred to the speculative financial sphere. The social and geographical concentration of wealth has intensified. The limits and contradictions of the capitalist system are revealed on a greater scale than ever before. Yet the subjective factors necessary for the construction of alternatives—forms of collective organisation and of consciousness, politics, and the state—have been weakened by these same processes. The state and the public domain have withered under the onslaught of rent-seeking capital, backed by international agencies that relentlessly preach the doctrine of free trade. Ideologically, the triumph of liberalism has imposed its own interpretation of the world as a hegemonic monopoly: Democracy could only mean representative parliamentarism; the economy could only mean the capitalist market economy; the client and the consumer eclipsed the citizen and the worker; competition replaced rights and the market subsumed the public sphere.

This is why the successive crises of the neoliberal economic model have not prompted an overt challenge to capitalism as such. In Latin America, the countries that have gone furthest in combating neoliberalism are those in which it was least entrenched. In Venezuela the advance of free market policies was halted by the failure of the Carlos Andrés Pérez and Rafael Caldera administrations; in Ecuador, by the fall of three governments in a row. In Bolivia, indigenous communities managed to preserve their identities not only in the countryside, but also in the urban districts where they are most highly concentrated, cities like La Paz, El Alto, and Cochabamba. Ideologically, neoliberalism has put down deeper roots in the relatively more developed countries: Mexico, Brazil, Chile, Argentina. Brazil was ruled by an unbroken sequence of neoliberal governments for ten years; in Argentina, Menem also ruled for ten years; and neoliberal orthodoxy was fully implemented in Mexico as much under the PRI as under the PAN. In Brazil and Argentina the neoliberal model continues to hold sway, despite certain areas of flexibility.

The governments that, by analogy to post-capitalism, might be called 'post-neoliberal'—those of Venezuela, Ecuador, and Bolivia—did not emerge in any of the classic bastions of the Latin American left, such as Brazil, Chile, Argentina, or Uruguay. They did not appear in countries where the working class and workers' movements had gained most ground, thanks to advances in the industrialisation process and the historical experiences of the political left. They emerged as new historical subjects, forged in the struggles against privatisation and in popular protests at neoliberalism's social costs. In Bolivia this subject is clearly the indigenous movement, following the disappearance of the mine workers' movement. In Venezuela it is an anti-imperialist nationalist movement with military origins. In Ecuador it is a hybrid subject, the sum of several contingents formed by great waves of popular mobilisation, from indigenous movements to urban democratic campaigns, sweeping up many other sectors along the way including trade unionists, students, and members of the critical intelligentsia.

These are all anti-neoliberal social forces, but not necessarily anti-capitalist.[9] They might become so, depending on the ability of the social and political leadership to bend the struggle in that direction, lending an anti-capitalist dynamic to the anti-neoliberal alliance. The project of twenty-first-century socialism, launched by Hugo Chávez and developed by many other forces, is after all an unprecedented historical construct which seeks to merge the anti-neoliberal struggle with an anti-capitalist one. The most advanced political processes in

Latin America—in all the world, in a sense, considering it is here that this project has gone furthest—are attempting to design political projects that can be called post-neoliberal. We use this term to denote approaches that combine the restoration of several state functions: Its regulatory capacity to defend national sovereignty over natural resources; its ability to carry out universally inclusive social policies, as the representative of the great working mass of society; its scope for creating new mechanisms of political participation and for redefining the links between the social and the political. In such economies the recast state will exercise its hegemony, but in cohabitation with a sizeable private sector, and socialised properties may take different forms—cooperatives, small family concerns, etc. The goal is to create a new model of socialisation by reconceptualising the state around the public sphere, with the idea that twenty-first-century socialism means the rehabilitation of the public domain, the universalisation of rights, and thoroughgoing de-marketisation. The success of this will ultimately depend on the degree of de-marketisation achieved in the post-neoliberal model.

Challenges

Following an initial period of euphoria, it is possible to discern the signs of an imminent new phase which these Latin American governments must prepare themselves to confront. In Paraguay the triumph of Fernando Lugo—ending decades of dictatorial rule by a party-state regime—has added to the list of new types of government in the region. Lugo has broad social support which will provide him with substantial legitimacy as he confronts a series of difficult issues: Agrarian reform, corruption, tax reform, and the renegotiation of treaties on hydroelectric power with Brazil and Argentina. In El Salvador, there are favourable odds on Mauricio Funes of the Frente Farabundo Martí for president in March 2009.[10]

Yet these developments have coincided with the emergence of new obstacles. Chávez's defeat in Venezuela in the referendum of November 2007 and the foreseeable difficulties in his winning the municipal elections of November 2008 in the face of a united opposition, suggest that significant losses could be inflicted on his government.[11] And despite Morales's victory in the August 2008 recall referendum in Bolivia—68 per cent, on an 84 per cent turnout—the problems besetting his government remain; negotiations will have to be resumed in an attempt to solve the intractable issues of the new constitution. Nonetheless, popular support for these governments is substantially greater than appears in the media.

As for Lula, although the crisis provoked by accusations of corruption has not entirely gone away, he has won a second term and still enjoys an approval rating of 70 per cent. This popularity is the reward for a comparatively steady economic expansion, but most of all for the appreciable effects of the government's social policies, suggesting that it will be hard to settle on a candidate to succeed Lula for 2010. In Uruguay, Tabaré Vázquez should find it easier to choose a successor, although the Frente Amplio is split between those supporting his moderate chancellor and those preferring a more left-wing candidate.

Like Morales and Chávez, Cristina Fernández in Argentina has been under fierce attack from the right. After taking over from her husband, Néstor Kirchner, in April 2008, the president's popularity nosedived during the first months of her administration, as the traditional urban middle-class opposition joined forces with meat and grain producers in their campaign of road blocks and lockouts.

Cuba is beginning to relax the rigid policies it was obliged to put in place to get through the 'special period'. However, the first government reshuffle reconfirmed the old revolutionary guard, as though to signal that reforms would only be undertaken within the ideological framework of the revolution. The Party Congress scheduled for 2009 must be an opportunity to refresh the leadership, indicating the possible future shape of a post-Fidel Cuba.

Hegemonic Contestations

What kind of place will Latin America be after this wave of progressive governments? How irreversible are the current changes? Into what kind of regression might it drift, should present political processes fail to be secured? Counter-neoliberal strategies in the present scenario imply a protracted dispute for hegemony: Neither an unequal alliance with dominant bourgeois sectors (the reformist strategy), nor the annihilation of the enemy (the premise of armed struggle). Instead, these strategies involve restating the dispute over hegemony in terms of the conquest of power, including legislation to reverse the processes of marketisation and empower the reconstitution of social subjects 'for themselves'. Beyond this, at a higher stage, it will require the foundation of a new state, able to embody the new balance of power between major social blocs.

In Bolivia, for example, the conquest of power through the ballot box was achieved in the wake of one of the most thorough bids to dismantle a state that the continent had ever seen. This began with the liquidation of the tin mines and culminated in the privatisation—'capitalisation', in the language of Bolivian neoliberalism—of the principal state-owned companies, rescinding state control of natural resources, and crippling the government's power to impose any form of regulation. This was the situation inherited by the Morales government, which at once began to implement its strategic counter-platform: Nationalisation of natural resources, the most urgent being gas; convocation of the Constituent Assembly; and first steps toward agrarian reform.

The nationalisation scheme was unable to dispense with the collaboration of foreign firms, because the state could not shoulder the investment burden and the Bolivian gas company had been thoroughly stripped of technical and managerial expertise. The best the government could do was to raise gas export taxes from

18 to 84 per cent, creating an essential fund to cover the bulk of government spending on social programmes, particularly aimed at children and the elderly.

With respect to the design of the Constituent Assembly, the government's had originally planned for direct representation of indigenous peoples and all the social movements, but excluding political parties, which would have guaranteed a crushing victory against the opposition. But Bolivia is not Venezuela, where the state is strong— and all the stronger for retaking control of the national oil company—and the corporate sector relatively weak, so that its attempts at a political boycott fell flat and had no economic repercussions beyond limited shortages and inflation. In Bolivia, economic power is overwhelmingly in private hands and concentrated in the eastern provinces, the fiefdom of the right. There was reason to fear that the opposition, faced with the prospect of outright defeat, might launch a damaging economic boycott against the government, deepening the risk of the country splitting up. Thus the Assembly was finally structured around existing parties, with an outcome that gave the government an absolute majority but not the two-thirds it needed to legitimate its constitutional project.

A lot of manoeuvring in a lengthy war of entrenched positions subsequently played itself out.[12] It is a war that the left in these countries is fighting at the government level, with broad popular mandates and plenty of scope for initiative, even when confronting the economic and media power of the opposition. No gains are irreversible. Yet the setbacks experienced by the right, with the isolation and fall of the most orthodox neoliberal governments, allow us to suppose that were they to return to power, displacing today's left and centre-left, they would make sure to maintain some of the present governments' social schemes or implement versions of their own, something that was unthinkable before. There is no doubt, though, that they would resume the privatisation programme, halt the regional integration process, and seek rapprochement with the US and the North as a whole. The sole alternatives to the progressive governments now in power, including the most moderate, lie to the right of them: The left as it stands today nowhere displays a high enough level of strength and support, or a clear enough alternative discourse.

Some region-wide projects would be very hard to undo however, if they advanced significantly under present governments: The continental gas pipeline or the Banco del Sur, for example. There is greater popular support for the left, in more countries at once, than this continent has ever known, owing to social policies that contrast with those of neoliberal administrations. This support has outweighed all the economic and media power of the elites, in a scenario that has repeated itself in elections right across the region. Whether radicals like Chávez, Correa, and Morales, or moderates like Lula, Vázquez, Néstor and Cristina Kirchner, Ortega, Lugo, and López Obrador, these candidates were all faced by a neoliberal bloc that has been bolstered by the powerful private monopoly of the media, 'manufacturing consensus'. And yet when it comes to an election, we have seen that people—in Venezuela, Argentina, Bolivia, Brazil, Ecuador, and Uruguay—have voted the other way.

In the World Context

What impact might Latin American developments have in the world at large? We could examine the question with regard to three great pillars of contemporary power: The power of arms, the power of money, and the power of words. On the question of arms, it seems unlikely that Latin America could do more than play a passive role, refusing to back the military expansionist plans of the US empire, as it did in Iraq. As for the global economic situation, Latin America can have little impact beyond the alliances with India, China, Russia, and South Africa, which Brazil in particular has forged. The growth of South-South exchanges—chiefly with China and India, but also with Iran—are steps toward a different mode of international trade relations, in which the weight of the US counts less than before. Moreover, the regional integration projects unique to Latin America offer a path to relative independence from the US, and an alternative to the free trade agreements peddled by Washington. Here, too, are found some of the very few governments in the world that openly defy North American imperial hegemony: Cuba, Venezuela, Bolivia, Ecuador.

None of this, of course, suffices to build a political and military counterweight to the US. At best the continent is resisting. The founding in May 2008 of UNASUR, a project for the integration of all the countries of South America, and the proposal for a South American Defence Council—both initiatives US-free—point toward a new space and model for continental integration.[13]

The importance of the region as a whole derives from its energy resources, primarily oil, and from its exports of cash crops, soya in particular. But domestic markets are becoming more attractive as their capacity for consumption increases, while regional integration reinforces political negotiating muscle, as has been seen in the dealings of the G-20 with the WTO. The process of breaking with the neoliberal model and founding alternative spaces for trade has turned the continent into an indispensable reference in any debate around the alternatives to neoliberalism. It is partly for these reasons that Chávez's leadership has become celebrated beyond continental borders. Yet one of the more vulnerable aspects of post-neoliberal processes is their global isolation; in the absence of other allies Venezuela has been forced to cultivate any governments that are in conflict with the US, such as those of Russia, Iran, Belarus, and China. In addition, the Latin American countries that have made concrete moves to break with the model are not the most developed, relatively speaking; their greatest economic asset is to be able to count on Venezuela's oil.

On the ideological plane, Latin America is better placed to table issues for debate: The plurinational, pluriethnic state; the notion of twenty-first-century socialism; and alternative formulas for regional integration such as ALBA. However, there are few platforms for disseminating the new ideas and raising them against the *pensée unique* and its theories, incessantly propounded by the mass media. And in turn, Latin American critical thought, which can boast a long tradition of far-sighted interpretations and theoretical innovations, is faced with fresh challenges in response to issues such as the new nationalism, the rise of indigenous peoples, the new model of accumulation, processes of socialisation and de-marketisation, and the historical and political future of the continent. In some countries—most importantly Bolivia—the experiments underway are accompanied by a rich process of reflection and theoretical elaboration. In others, there is a considerable dissociation, not to say contradiction, between much of the intelligentsia and the process the rest of the country is embarked on: The most striking example is Venezuela. In countries with a strong university-based intelligentsia such as Brazil, Argentina, and Mexico, a significant part of the educated elite will not commit itself to participating in the principal areas of social and political struggle, even if it maintains a high standard of intellectual elaboration. The existing theoretical potential may play an important role in the construction of post-neoliberal models.

The Next Phase?

In retrospect, the international rise, consolidation, and jeopardisation of neo-liberalism falls into three distinct phases. The first was marked by the Thatcher-Reagan tandem, corresponding to the strongest and most openly reactionary ideological expressions, with Pinochet in Chile and Jeffrey Sachs in Bolivia as its most authentic regional equivalents. The second phase corresponded to the governments of the so-called Third Way, represented by Clinton and Blair, which pursued a supposedly 'light' version, a consolidation of the model, given that the heavy lifting—privatisations, unlimited predominance of the market, opening-up of the economy—had already been carried out. It was as if the green light had been given for governments of similar tendencies in Latin America—social democratic and nationalist—to set out on the same path: From Buenos Aires to Mexico City, the Washington Consensus swept the board. The third phase was inaugurated with the Mexican peso crisis and the onset of turbulence in the globalised economy, while the Bush-Cheney White House imposed a harsher, more conservative tone in response to the attacks of 2001; aggressive policies from Washington combining with an economy in stagnation.

This was the background, in the late 1990s and early 2000s, to the overthrow of one neoliberal government after another in Latin America. Incoming leaders took advantage of the relative weakening of US political and economic leadership to render the FTAA unviable, and began to develop alternative policies for regional integration. This phase also corresponded to a decline in the international preponderance of the US economy and rising demand on the world market from China and India—the former in particular developing large-scale direct exchange with many countries in the region.

What might the next phase bring? If some governments have encountered setbacks recently—in particular Venezuela, Bolivia, and Argentina—world developments are themselves producing further changes. Rising commodity prices and the international impact of the North American recession are favourable for the export of Latin American primary products—in which agriculture still plays an important role. A new Democratic administration in the US from 2009 might seek to change the discourse and break the unprecedented isolation that Washington faces in the region. This would represent a new challenge for the processes of regional integration and the construction of a post-neoliberal model. It is possible to envisage a new drive for cooptation by Washington, based around its traditional allies Colombia and Mexico, plus Alan García's Peru, which has recently signed a free trade agreement (FTA) with the US; but the White House would now also seek to attract the centre-left governments—those of Brazil, Argentina, and possibly Uruguay—away from the bloc of regional integration, while isolating those of Venezuela, Bolivia, Ecuador, and Cuba.

On the other hand, other processes underway—Mercosur, ALBA, UNASUR, Banco del Sur, the continental oil pipeline, among others—may well advance, because the North American recession favours the diversification of regional trade with countries such as China. This may reinvigorate the conditions for the consolidation of these governments and their projects of integration. It remains to be seen what pattern will result from the combination of economic recession and a Democratic administration. The internal development of Venezuela and Bolivia, crucial components of the bloc of integration, is in many ways fundamental for the future political scenario of the region; along with Ecuador, which is rapidly moving ahead with the construction of new constitutional institutions, and the new government of Paraguay. Overall, however, it is developments in Mexico, Argentina, and Brazil that will determine the outlook across the continent. If Cristina Fernández's government can succeed in overcoming its current crises and if Lula can choose his successor in 2010—thus preventing Brazil from shifting to the pro-FTA, anti-integrationist column—then there are strong indications for a second decade of rule by the new regionalist forces of Latin America.

References

Ezequiel Adamovsky, 2017—'Autonomous Politics and its Problems: Thinking the Passage from the Social to Political', in Jai Sen, ed, 2017b—*The Movements of Movements, Part 2: Rethinking Our Dance*. Volume 5 in the *Challenging Empires* series. New Delhi: OpenWord, and Oakland, CA: PM Press

Cho Hee-Yeon, 2017—'From Anti-Imperialist to Anti-Empire: The Crystallisation of the Anti-Globalisation Movement in South Korea', in Jai Sen, ed, 2017a—*The Movements of Movements, Part 1: What Makes Us Move?*. Volume 4 in the *Challenging Empires* series. New Delhi: OpenWord, and Oakland, CA: PM Press

Régis Debray, 1967—*Revolution in the Revolution?*. London and New York: Penguin

Guillermo Delgado-P, 2017—'Refounding Bolivia: Exploring the Possibility and Paradox of a Social Movements State', in Jai Sen, ed, 2017a—*The Movements of Movements, Part 1: What Makes Us Move?*. Volume 4 in the *Challenging Empires* series. New Delhi: OpenWord, and Oakland, CA: PM Press

John Holloway, 2005 [2002]—*Change the World Without Taking Power*. London: Pluto Press

François Houtart, 2017—'We Still Exist', in Jai Sen, ed, 2017b—*The Movements of Movements, Part 2: Rethinking Our Dance*. Volume 5 in the *Challenging Empires* series. New Delhi: OpenWord, and Oakland, CA: PM Press

Alex Khasnabish, 2017—'Forward Dreaming: Zapatismo and the Radical Imagination', in Jai Sen, ed, 2017a—*The Movements of Movements, Part 1: What Makes Us Move?*. Volume 4 in the *Challenging Empires* series. New Delhi: OpenWord, and Oakland, CA: PM Press

Xochitl Leyva Solano and Christopher Gunderson, 2017—'The Tapestry of Neo-Zapatismo: Origins and Development', in Jai Sen, ed, 2017a—*The Movements of Movements, Part 1: What Makes Us Move?*. Volume 4 in the *Challenging Empires* series. New Delhi: OpenWord, and Oakland, CA: PM Press

Notes

1. Ed: This article was first published in *New Left Review* 52, July–August 2008; http://www.newleftreview.org/?page=article&view=2730. I am grateful to the author and the publishers for their permission to reprint it here in an abridged and slightly edited form. For further reproduction permission, contact kheya@newleftreview.org.

    There are many important details in this grand sketch of the major changes that have been taking place in Latin America; simply to make the essay and the details more accessible to our readers, we have expanded and translated the many acronyms in the original, and added a few references. For the full version of the essay and of the author's arguments, see his books:

    Emir Sader, 2009a—*A nova toupeira: Os caminos da esquerda latinoamericana* ['The new mole: Paths of the Latin American left', in Portuguese]. São Paulo: Boitempo Editorial; and:

    Emir Sader, 2009b—*Caminos de la izquierda latinoamericana* ['Paths of the Latin American left', in Spanish]. Buenos Aires: Siglo XXI.

2. Ed: This essay was written and first published in 2008, and finalised for this book in 2009; so this narration of history stops here.

3. Debray 1967.
4. Ed: For another discussion of the 'autonomy of social movements' in the Latin American experience, see the essay by Ezequiel Adamovsky in the companion volume to this book (Adamovsky 2017).
5. Ed: For a discussion of the role and relationship of social movements in recent and contemporary Bolivia, see the essay by Guillermo Delgado-P in this volume (Delgado-P 2017).
6. Ed: For the latter, see Holloway 2005 [2002].
7. Ed: For other discussions of Zapatismo, see the essays in this book by Alex Khasnabish and by Xochitl Leyva Solano and Christopher Gunderson (Khasnabish 2017, Leyva Solano and Gunderson 2017) and by François Houtart in the companion volume (Houtart 2017).
8. This false distinction is reiterated by the *Economist*'s Latin American editor, Michael Reid, who fulminates against left alternatives to neoliberalism in his 2007 book, *Forgotten Continent*.
9. Ed: For a discussion of the dynamics of anti-imperialist forces during the same period in another part of the world, South Korea, see the essay in this book by Cho Hee-Yeon (Cho 2017).
10. Funes was indeed elected president in the March 2009 elections.
11. Ed: Chávez's party, the Partido Socialista Unido de Venezuela (PSUV), "won 17 of the 22 governorships up for grabs on November 24, when Venezuelans turned out in droves to vote." See http://www.as-coa.org/article.php?id=1356 (Inactive April 2017).
12. See the original essay for more details, citation in endnote 1.
13. Though Colombia's formal participation complicates matters, since Uribe has decided to allow the US to establish a military base on its territory.

The Return of Strategy[1]
Daniel Bensaïd[2]

Since the beginning of the 1980s, there has been an 'eclipse' in the debate about strategy in movement and in politics, in contrast with the intense discussions that took place in the 1970s, prompted by the experiences of Chile and Portugal (and later, Nicaragua and Central America). The neoliberal offensive that started in the early 80s made the 1980s a decade of social resistance at best, characterised by a defensiveness in class struggle, even in those cases when popular democratic pressure forced dictatorships to give way—notably in Latin America.

The withdrawal from politics found expression in what could be called a 'social illusion', analogous with the 'political illusion' of those criticised by the young Marx for thinking that 'political' emancipation through the achievement of civil rights was the last word in human emancipation. This illusion was reflected in, among other things, the talk of the self-sufficiency of social movements, as reflected in the experiences after Seattle (1999) and the first World Social Forum (WSF) in Porto Alegre (2001).

Simplifying somewhat, I call this the 'utopian moment' of social movements, which took different forms: Utopias based on the regulation of free markets; Keynesian utopias; and, above all, neo-libertarian utopias, in which the world can be changed without taking power, or by making do with counter-powers (for example, in the writings of John Holloway, Toni Negri, and Richard Day).[3]

The upturn in social struggles yielded political or electoral victories in Latin America—Venezuela and Bolivia. But in Europe the struggles ended in defeat, except for the movement in France against the CPE ('*Contrat première embauche*', or 'first job contract') attacks on the rights of young workers. The push towards privatisation, the reforms in social security, and the dismantling of social rights could not be prevented. This lack of social victories has caused expectations to turn once more towards political (mostly electoral) solutions, as recent Italian elections have demonstrated.[4]

This 'return of politics' has led to a revival in debates about strategy. Witness the polemics around the books of Holloway, Negri, and Michael Albert,[5] and the differing appraisals of the Venezuelan process and of President Lula's administration in Brazil. There has been the shift in the Zapatistas' orientation with the Sixth Declaration of the Selva Lacandona and the 'Other Campaign' in Mexico.[6] The discussions around the project for a new LCR (*Ligue Communiste Révolutionnaire, or* 'Revolutionary Communist League') manifesto and Alex

517

Callinicos's *Anticapitalist Manifesto*[7] belong in the same context. We are coming to the end of a phase of big refusals and stoic resistance—Holloway's 'scream' in the face of 'the mutilation of human lives by capitalism,'[8] slogans like 'The world is not a commodity' or 'Our world is not for sale' or 'Another world is possible'.[9] We need, now, to be specific about what the other 'possible' world is and—above all—to explore how to get there.

There Is Strategy and Strategy

Notions of strategy and tactics are military terms that were imported into the workers' movement, above all from the writings of Clausewitz and Delbrück.[10] However, the meanings of these terms have varied greatly. At one time, 'strategy' was the art of winning a battle, with tactics being no more than troop manoeuvres. Since then, there has been no halt to the expansion of the field of strategy over time and space, from dynastic wars to national wars, from total war to global war.[11] So, today we need to distinguish between global strategy operating on a world scale and 'limited strategy' concerned with the struggle for power within a particular area. In some ways, the theory of permanent revolution sketches out a global strategy. The revolution starts from the national arena (in one country) and expands to the continental and world level; it takes a decisive step with the conquest of political power but is prolonged and deepened by 'a cultural revolution'. It thus combines act and process, event and history.[12]

This dimension of global strategy is even more important today than it was in the first half of the twentieth century, faced as we are with powerful states whose economic and military strategies extend worldwide. The emergence of new strategic areas at the continental or world level shows this. The dialectic of the permanent revolution (as against the theory of socialism in one country), in other words the intertwining of national, continental, and world levels, is tighter than ever. One can seize the levers of power in one country (like Venezuela or Bolivia), but the question of continental strategy (and its various extrapolations) immediately becomes a matter of domestic policy—as in the Latin American discussions over Alba versus Alca,[13] the relationship to Mercosur, or to the Andes Pact. More prosaically, in Europe the resistance to neoliberal counter-reforms can be reinforced by the balance of forces at the national level, and by legislative gains. But a transitional approach to public services, taxation, social protection, and ecology has to be pitched at the European level from the outset.[14]

Strategic Hypotheses

In this essay, I confine myself to the question of what I have called 'the limited strategy'—the struggle for the conquest of political power at the national level. I focus on this because the framework of globalisation can weaken national states, and some transfers of sovereignty inevitably take place. But—I suggest—the national rung, which structures class relationships and attaches a territory to a state, remains the decisive rung in the sliding scale of strategic spaces.

Let us straight away put aside the criticisms—from writers like John Holloway and Cédric Durand[15]—that ascribe to us a 'stageist' vision of the revolutionary process, according to which we make the seizure of power the 'absolute precondition' for any social transformation. The argument is either a caricature or it stems from ignorance. Vaulting from a standing start is not something we have ever been keen on.

The concepts of a united front, of transitional demands, and of the workers' government—concepts that have been defended not just by Trotsky but also by Thalheimer, Radek, and Clara Zetkin[16] have a precise aim. This is to link the event to its preparatory conditions—revolution to reforms, the goal to the movement. Gramscian notions of hegemony and of a 'war of position' operate along the same lines.[17] The opposition between the East (where power would be easier to acquire but more difficult to maintain) and the West arises from the same concern.[18] We have never been admirers of the theory of the mere collapse of the system.[19]

As Trotskyites, we have insisted on the role of the 'subjective factor' (as against both the spontaneist view of the revolutionary process and the structuralist immobilism of the 1960s). Our insistence is not on a 'model' but on what we have called 'strategic hypotheses'.[20] Models are something to be copied; they are instructions for use. A hypothesis is a guide to action that starts from past experience but is open and can be modified in the light of new experience or unexpected circumstances. Our concern, therefore, is not to speculate but to see what we can take from past experience, the only material at our disposal. (Though, even if we do this, and if as revolutionaries we are to avoid the risk of doing what the generals are said to do—always still fighting the previous war—we must also recognise that the past is necessarily poorer, in terms of lessons, than the present and the future.)

Our starting point for putting forward our thesis lies in the great revolutionary experiences of the twentieth century: The Russian Revolution, the Chinese Revolution, the German Revolution, the popular fronts, the Spanish Civil War, the Vietnamese war of liberation, May 1968, Portugal, and Chile. We use them to distinguish between two major hypotheses, or scenarios: That of the *insurrectional general strike*, and that of the *extended popular war*. They encapsulate two types of crisis, two forms of dual power, and two ways of resolving the crisis.

As far as the insurrectional general strike is concerned, dual power has so far taken a mainly urban form, of the Commune variety—not just the Paris Commune, but the Petrograd Soviet, the insurrections in Hamburg in 1923, Canton in 1927, and Barcelona in 1936. But dual power cannot last long in a concentrated area. Confrontation therefore leads to a rapid resolution, although this may in turn lead to a prolonged confrontation: Such as the civil war in Russia, and the liberation war in Vietnam after the 1945 insurrection. In this scenario, the task of demoralising the army and of organising the soldiers plays an important part. Among the more recent and meaningful experiences in this respect were the soldiers' committees in France, the SUV ('Soldiers united will win') movement in Portugal in 1975, and the conspiratorial work of the MIR[21] in the Chilean army in 1972–73.

In the case of the extended popular war strategy, the issue is one of territorial dual power through liberated and self-administered zones, which can last much longer. Mao understood, and elaborated on, the conditions for this as early as 1927, in his pamphlet *Why Is It that Red Political Power Can Exist in China?*, and the experience of the Yenan Republic[22] shows how it operates.

According to the insurrectionary general strike scenario, the organs of alternative power are socially determined by urban conditions; according to the extended popular war scenario, they are centralised in the (predominantly peasant) 'people's army'.

There exist a whole range of variants and intermediary combinations of these two hypotheses. So, the Cuban Revolution made the guerrilla *foco* ('focus') a link between the kernel of the rebel army and attempts to organise and call urban general strikes in Havana and Santiago.[23] The relationship between the two was problematic, as shown in the correspondence of Frank Païs,[24] Daniel Ramos Latour, and Che himself about the tensions between 'the sierra' and 'the plain'. Retrospectively, the official narrative privileged the heroic epic of the Granma[25] and its survivors. This contributed to bolstering the legitimacy of that element in the 26 July Movement and of the ruling Castro group, but it was detrimental to a more complex understanding of the process.

This simplified version of history was set up as a model for rural guerrilla war and inspired the developments of the 1960s in Peru, Venezuela, Nicaragua, Colombia, and Bolivia. The deaths of De La Puente and Lobatòn in Peru (1965), Camillo Torres in Colombia (1966), Yon Sosa and Lucio Cabañas in Mexico, Carlos Marighela and Lamarca in Brazil, Che's tragic expedition to Bolivia, the near annihilation of the Sandinistas in 1963 and 1969, and the disaster of Teoponte in Bolivia in 1970 marked the end of that cycle.

The strategic hypothesis of the Argentinean PRT[26] and the MIR in Chile made greater use, at the beginning of the 1970s, of the Vietnamese example of extended popular war (and, in the PRT's case, of a mythic version of the Algerian war of liberation). The history of the Sandinista front until its victory over the Somoza dictatorship in 1979 reveals a mixture of different outlooks. The Prolonged People's War tendency of Tomàs Borge stressed the development of a guerrilla presence in the mountains and the need for a long period for gradually accumulating forces.

The Proletariat Tendency of Jaime Wheelock insisted on the social effects of capitalist development in Nicaragua and on the strengthening of the working class,
while also retaining the perspective of a prolonged accumulation of forces with a
view to an 'insurrectional moment'. The 'Tercerist' Tendency of the Ortega brothers was a synthesis of the other two tendencies, which allowed for coordination
between the southern front and the uprising in Managua.

Looking back, Humberto Ortega summed up the differences thus:

> The politics which consists of not intervening in events, of accumulating forces
> from [the] cold, is what I call the politics of passive accumulation of forces. This
> passivity was evident at the level of alliances. There was also passivity in the
> fact that we thought we could accumulate arms, organise ourselves, bring hu-
> man resources together without fighting the enemy, without having the masses
> participate.[27]

He recognised that circumstances shook up their various plans:

> We called for the insurrection. The pace of events quickened, objective condi-
> tions did not allow us greater preparation. In reality, we could not say no to the
> insurrection—such was the breadth of the mass movement that the vanguard
> was incapable of directing it. We could not oppose this torrent. All we could do
> was to put ourselves at its head in the hope of more or less leading it and giving
> it a sense of direction.[28]

He concluded, 'Our insurrectional strategy always gravitated around the masses
and not around some military plan. This must be clear.' In reality, having a strategic option implies a sequencing of political priorities, of when to intervene, of
what slogans to raise. It also determines the politics of alliances.

Mario Payeras's narrative of the Guatemala process[29] illustrates a return from
the forest to the town and a change in relationships between the military and the
political, the countryside and the town. Régis Debray's *A Critique of Arms* (or,
rather, a self-criticism) also provides an account of the start of this evolution in
the 1960s.[30] There were the disastrous adventures of the Red Army Fraction in
Germany and of the Weathermen in the US[31] (to say nothing of the ephemeral
tragi-comedy of the *Gauche prolétarienne* [Proletarian Left][32] in France and the
theses of July and Geismar[33] in their unforgettable *Vers la Guerre Civile* ['Towards
Civil War', in French] of 1969). All these and other attempts to translate the experience of rural guerrilla war into 'urban guerrilla' war came to an end in the 1970s.
The only instances of armed movements to have lasted successfully were those
whose organisations had their social base in struggles against national oppression
(Ireland and the Basque Country).[34]

These strategic hypotheses and experiences are not simply reducible to militarism. They set political tasks in order. Thus the PRT's conception of the Argentinean Revolution as a national war of liberation meant privileging the construction of an army (the ERP) at the cost of self-organisation in workplaces and neighbourhoods. Similarly, the MIR's orientation of emphasising, under Popular Unity, the accumulation of forces (and rural bases) led to its downplaying the threat of a coup d'état and, above all, underestimating its long term consequences. Yet, as the MIR's general secretary Miguel Enriquez clearly perceived, following the failure of the first, abortive, coup of June 29 there was a brief moment favourable to the creation of a combat government, during which the MIR could have prepared for a trial of strength.

The Sandinista victory in 1979 certainly marked a new turn. That, at least, is the view of Mario Payeras, who stressed that in Guatemala (as in El Salvador) revolutionary movements were not confronted by clapped out puppet dictatorships but by Israeli, Taiwanese, and US 'advisers' in 'low intensity' and 'counter-revolutionary' wars.[35] This increasing asymmetry has since gone global with the new strategic doctrines of the Pentagon and the declaration of 'unlimited' war against 'terrorism'.

This is one reason (in addition to the tragic hyper-violence of the Cambodian experience, the bureaucratic counter-revolution in the USSR, and the Cultural Revolution in China) why the question of revolutionary violence has become a thorny, even taboo, subject, whereas in the past the epic sagas of the Granma and of Che, or the writings of Fanon, Giap, or Cabral made violence appear innocent or liberatory. What we see is a groping towards some asymmetrical strategy of the weak and the strong, an attempt to synthesise Lenin and Gandhi,[36] or orient towards non-violence.[37] Yet the world has not become less violent since the fall of the Berlin Wall. It would be rash and otherworldly to bet on a 'peaceful way'. Nothing from the century of extremes that we have just come out of promises this scenario.

The Hypothesis of the Insurrectional General Strike

The guideline for our strategic hypothesis in the 1970s[38] was the insurrectional general strike, which, for the most part, bore no resemblance to the variants of acclimatised Maoism and its imaginary interpretations of the Cultural Revolution. It is of this hypothesis that we are now the 'orphans', according to Antoine Artous.[39] What might have had a certain 'functionality' yesterday is lost today. He does not deny, however, the continuing relevance of notions of revolutionary crisis and dual power. The hypothesis needs, he insists, serious reformulation—one that avoids wallowing in the term 'rupture' and in verbal trickery. Two points crystallise his concern.

On the one hand, Artous insists that dual power cannot be totally situated outside existing institutions and be made to spring from nothing in the form of a pyramid of soviets or councils. We may once upon a time have surrendered to this oversimplified vision of real revolutionary processes that we used to pore over in political study groups. But I doubt it. Be that as it may, other texts swiftly corrected whatever vision we may have had.[40] We may even, at the time, have been disturbed or shocked by Ernest Mandel coming round to the idea of 'mixed democracy' (a combination of parliament and workers' councils) after he had reassessed the relationship between the soviets and the Constituent Assembly in Russia. Yet, clearly, one cannot imagine a revolutionary process other than as a transfer of legitimacy that gives preponderance to 'socialism from below' but also interacts with forms of representation, particularly in countries with parliamentary traditions that go back over more than a century, and where the principle of universal suffrage is firmly established.

In practice, our ideas have evolved—as they did, for example, during the Nicaraguan Revolution. In the context of a civil war and a state of siege, organising 'free' elections in 1989 was open to question but we did not challenge the principle. Rather we criticised the Sandinistas for suppressing the 'council of state',[41] which might have constituted a sort of second social chamber and have been a pole of alternative legitimacy to the elected parliament. Similarly, though on a more modest scale, the dialectic over the budget in Porto Alegre in Brazil, between the municipal institution (elected by universal suffrage) and participatory committees, is worth consideration.

The problem we face today is not really that of the relationship between territorial democracy and workplace democracy (the Paris Commune, the soviets, and the Setubal popular assembly of Portugal in 1975 were all territorial structures), nor even that of the relationship between direct and representative democracy (all democracy is partially representative). The real problem is how the general will is formed.

Most criticism of soviet-style democracy, whether by the Eurocommunists[42] or by Norberto Bobbion,[43] is targeted at its tendency to corporatism: A sum (or pyramid) of particular interests (parochial, workplace, office), linked by a system of mandation, that cannot allow for the creation of the general will. But democratic subsidiarity, too, has its drawbacks. If the inhabitants of a valley are opposed to a road passing through it, or if a town is against having a waste collection centre, then there must be some form of centralised arbitration.[44]

Artous's second concern, notably in his criticism of Alex Callinicos, bears on the assertion that Callinicos's transitional approach halts at the threshold of the question of power, which is then left to be resolved by some unconvincing *deus ex machina*, a spontaneous tidal wave of the masses and a generalised outburst of soviet democracy. Though a defence of civil liberties figures prominently in Callinicos's programme, he appears to make no demands of an institutional nature (for example, the demand for proportional representation, a constituent assembly or single chamber, or radical democratisation).[45] Cédric Durand, on the other hand, conceives of institutions as mere intermediaries for autonomous protest strategies.[46] This, in practice, might boil down to a compromise between 'below' and 'above'—in other words, crude lobbying by the former of the latter, which is left intact.

In reality all sides in the controversy agree on the fundamental points inspired by *The Coming Catastrophe* (Lenin's pamphlet from the summer of 1917)[47] and the *Transitional Programme of the Fourth International* (inspired by Trotsky in 1937[48]): The need for transitional demands, the politics of alliances (the united front),[49] the logic of hegemony, and the dialectic (not antinomy) between reform and revolution. We are therefore against the idea of separating an ('anti-neoliberal') minimum programme and an (anti-capitalist) 'maximum' programme. We remain convinced that a consistent anti-neoliberalism leads to anti-capitalism, and that the two are interlinked by the dynamic of struggle.

We can argue about exactly how the balance of forces and existing levels of consciousness should structure transitional demands. Agreement is easy, however, on targeting the privatisation of the means of production, communication, and exchange—whether in relation to public sector education, humanity's common resources, or the increasingly important question of the socialisation of knowledge (as opposed to intellectual private property). Similarly, we can easily agree on exploring ways to socialise wages through systems of social protection as a step towards the withering away of the wages system. Finally, in opposition to the generalisation of the market, we open up the possibility of extending the free provision of not merely services but basic items of consumption (and thus of 'de-marketisation').

The tricky question about the transition is that of the 'workers' government'. The difficulty is not new. The debates during the fifth congress of the Communist International (1924) on the performances of the German Revolution and the Social Democrat-Communist governments of Saxony and Thuringia demonstrate this. They reveal the unresolved ambiguity of the formulae that came out of the early congresses of the Communist International and the range of interpretations which they could give rise to in practice. Albert Treint[50] emphasised that "the dictatorship of the proletariat does not fall from the sky; it must have a beginning and the workers' government is synonymous with the start of the dictatorship of the proletariat". Nevertheless he denounced the "saxonisation" of the united front: "The entry of the communists into a coalition government with bourgeois pacifists to prevent an intervention against the revolution was not wrong in theory", but governments of the Labour Party or Left Bloc type cause "bourgeois democracy to find an echo within our own parties".

The Czechoslovak Smeral declared during a debate on the activity of the International: "As far as the theses of our congress in February 1923 on the workers' government are concerned, we were all convinced when we drew them up that they were in line with the decisions of the fourth congress. They were adopted unanimously". But " what are the masses thinking about when they speak of a workers' government? ... In England, they think of the Labour Party, in Germany and in other countries where capitalism is decomposing, the united front means that the communists and social democrats, instead of fighting one another when the strike breaks out, are marching shoulder to shoulder. For the masses the workers' government has the same meaning and when we use this formula they imagine a united government of all the workers' parties". And, Smeral continued: "What deep lesson does the Saxon experiment teach us? Above all, this: That one cannot vault from a standing start—a run-up is needed".

Ruth Fischer's answer was that as a coalition of workers' parties the workers' government would mean "the liquidation of our party".[51] In her report on the failure of the German Revolution, Clara Zetkin argued:

> As far as the workers' and peasants' government is concerned I cannot accept Zinoviev's declaration that it is simply a pseudonym, a synonym or god knows what homonym, for the dictatorship of the proletariat. That may be correct for Russia but it is not the same for countries where capitalism is flourishing. There the workers' and peasants' government is the political expression of a situation in which the bourgeoisie can no longer maintain itself in power but where the proletariat is not yet in a position to impose its dictatorship.[52]

In fact, what Zinoviev defined as the "elementary objective of the workers' government" was the arming of the proletariat, workers' control over production, a tax revolution ...

One could go on and quote other contributions. But the resulting impression would be of enormous confusion. This expresses a real contradiction and an inability to solve the problem, even though it was raised in a revolutionary or pre-revolutionary situation.

It would be irresponsible to suggest a solution that could be universally valid; nevertheless, the following three criteria can be variously combined for assessing participation in a government coalition with a transition perspective:

a) The question of participation arises in a situation of crisis, or at least of a significant upsurge in social mobilisation, and not from a vacuum;

b) The government in question is committed to initiating a dynamic of rupture with the established order. For example—and more modestly than the arming of the workers demanded by Zinoviev—radical agrarian reform, 'despotic incursions' into the domain of private property, the abolition of tax privileges, a break with institutions like those of the Fifth Republic in France, European treaties, military pacts, etc;

c)   Finally, the balance of forces allows revolutionaries to ensure that even if they cannot guarantee that the non-revolutionaries in the government keep to their commitments, they have to pay a high price for their failure to do so.

In this light, participation in the Lula government in Brazil by the far left[53] appears to have been mistaken, for the following reasons:

> For ten years or so, with the exception of the landless movement, the mass movement has been on the retreat;
>
> The colour of Lula's social-neoliberal politics was clearly shown in his electoral campaign and in his 'Letter to the Brazilians' (promising to keep to the previous government's financial commitments). The financing of his agrarian reform and 'zero-hunger' programme was mortgaged in advance;
>
> Finally, the social balance of forces within both the party and the government was such that to be a half-minister in agriculture was not to support the government "like a rope supports a hanged man" but rather like a hair that clearly could not. That said, and taking into account the history of the country, its social structure and the formation of the Workers' Party (PT), we chose not to make this a matter of principle (though we expressed our reservations orally to the comrades about participation and alerted them to the dangers). We preferred to go along with the experiment so as to draw up the balance sheet alongside the comrades, rather than give lessons 'from a distance'.[54]

About the Dictatorship of the Proletariat

The question of a workers' government inevitably brings us back to the question of the 'dictatorship of the proletariat'. In 2004, an LCR conference decided by a majority of over two-thirds to remove mention of it from its statutes. That was fair enough. Today the term 'dictatorship' more readily invokes the military or bureaucratic dictatorships of the twentieth century than the venerable Roman institution of temporary emergency powers duly mandated by the Senate. Since Marx saw the Paris Commune as "the political form at last discovered" of this dictatorship of the proletariat, we would be better understood by invoking the Commune, the soviets, councils, or self-management, rather than hanging on to a verbal fetish that history has made a source of confusion.

    Generally speaking, the 'dictatorship of the proletariat' tends to carry the image of an authoritarian regime and to be seen as synonymous with bureaucratic dictatorships. But for Marx it was the democratic solution to an old problem—the exercise for the first time by the (proletarian) majority of emergency power, which till then had been the preserve of a virtuous elite, as with the Committee of Public Safety of the French Revolution, even if the committee in question emanated from the Convention and could be recalled by it. The term 'dictatorship' in Marx's time was often counterposed to 'tyranny', which was used to express despotism.

The notion of a 'dictatorship of the proletariat' also had a strategic significance, one often raised in the debates of the 1970s upon its abandonment by the majority of (Euro)communist parties. Marx had clearly grasped the idea that the new legal power, as an expression of a new social relationship, could not be born if the old one remained: Between two social legitimacies, "between two equal rights, it is force that decides". Revolution implies, therefore, a transition enforced by a state of emergency.

And Carl Schmitt,[55] who was an attentive reader of the polemic between Lenin and Kautsky, understood perfectly what was at issue when he distinguished between the "chief constable dictatorship", whose function in a state of crisis is to preserve the established order, and the "sovereign dictatorship", which inaugurates a new order by virtue of a constitutive power.[56] If this strategic perspective, whatever name we give it, remains valid, then there necessarily follows a series of consequences about how power is organised, about legitimacy, about how parties function, etc.

On the 'Broad Party'[57]

The structural situation in which we find ourselves today opens up a space to the left of the major traditional formations of the workers' movement (social democrats, Stalinists, populists). There are many reasons for this. The neoliberal counter-reform, the privatisation of the public arena, the dismantling of the welfare state, and the market society, have, between them, sawn off the branch on which sat social democracy—and populist administrations in certain Latin American countries. The communist parties in Europe have suffered the after-effects of the implosion of the USSR together with the erosion of the social bases they had acquired in the pre-war years and the period of liberation from the Nazis, without gaining new roots. There really does exist what we often call a radical 'space', which has found diverse expression in the emergence of new social movements and electoral formations. This is the present day basis for reconstruction and regrouping.

But this 'space' is not homogenous and empty so that all we have to do is fill it. It is a highly unstable force field, as shown spectacularly by the conversion in less than three years of Rifondazione from lyrical movementism, at the time of Genoa and Florence,[58] to government coalition with Romano Prodi. This instability stems from the fact that social mobilisations have suffered more defeats than they have won victories, and that their link to the transformation of the political landscape remains tenuous. In the absence of meaningful social victories, the hope of the 'lesser evil' ("anything but Berlusconi—or Sarkozy or Le Pen!") moves, for lack of real change, to the electoral terrain where the weight of institutional logic remains decisive (in France, that of plebiscitary presidentialism and a particularly anti-democratic electoral system). That's why the symmetry of a happy medium between an opportunist and a conservative danger is a false perspective: They don't carry the same weight. We must know how to dare to take risky decisions (the most extreme example being that of the October insurrection)—but we must also know how to weigh the risk and calculate our chances if we are to avoid pure adventurism. As the great dialectician Pascal said, we are already committed—we must wager. Yet race-goers know that a bet of two-to-one is small time, and that a bet of a thousand-to-one, though it may hit the jackpot, is a desperate throw. The margin is between the two. Daring too has its reasons.

The evolution from right to left of currents like Rifondazione or the Linkspartei remains fragile (even reversible) for the very reason that the effects of social struggle on the field of political representation remain limited. It depends in part on the presence and weight within them of revolutionary organisations or tendencies.

These are very general common factors. But over and beyond these, conditions vary enormously, depending on the specific history of the workers' movement (for instance, whether social democracy is totally hegemonic or whether important communist parties still subsist). It also depends on the balance of forces within the left. Apparatuses are determined not only by ideology, but by social logics. They cannot be transformed by whispering in the ears of their leaders, but only by modifying the real balance of forces.

The perspective of a 'new force' remains an algebraic formula for now (this was true for us before 1989–91, and is even truer since). Translating it into practice cannot be mechanically deduced from formulae as vague and general as 'the broad party' or 'regroupment'. We are only at the start of a process of reconstruction. What counts in the approach to this is our programmatic compass and strategic aim. This is one condition that will allow us to discover the organisational mediations we need and to take calculated risks. That way we avoid throwing ourselves headlong into some impatient adventure and dissolving ourselves into the first ephemeral combination that comes along. Organisational formulae are in reality very variable, depending on what's at issue: A new mass party (like the PT in Brazil in the 1980s, though this is an unlikely pattern in Europe), minority splits from a hegemonic social democracy, or parties that we might previously have termed centrist (Rifondazione, five years ago), or a coalition of revolutionary currents (as in Portugal). This last hypothesis remains, however, the most likely for countries such as France, where there is a long tradition of organisations like the Communist Party and the far left and where, without a really powerful social movement, for them to simply merge in the short or medium term is difficult to imagine.

But in every case, reference to a common programmatic background, far from being something that obstructs future reconstruction is, on the contrary, its precondition. Strategic and tactical questions can then be prioritised so that we are not torn apart because of this or that electoral outcome. We can distinguish the political base on which organising open theoretical debate makes sense. We can assess which compromises allow us to forge ahead and which pull us back. We can adjust to forms of organisational existence (whether to be a tendency in a shared party, part of a front, etc), depending on our allies and how their dynamic fluctuates (from right to left or left to right).

References

Kolya Abramsky, August 2008—*The Bamako Appeal and the Zapatista 6th Declaration—From Reorganizing the Existing World to Creating New Ones*. Volume 1 in Critical Engagement—CACIM's Occasional Publications Programme. New Delhi: CACIM, at http://www.cacim.net/twiki/tiki-index.php?page=Publications (Accessed April 2017)

Michael Albert, 2004—*Parecon: Life after Capitalism*. London: Verso

Tariq Ali, 2017—'Storming Heaven: Where Has The Rage Gone?', in Jai Sen, ed, 2017a—*The Movements of Movements, Part 1: What Makes Us Move?*. Volume 4 in the *Challenging Empires* series. New Delhi: OpenWord and Oakland, CA: PM Press

Perry Anderson, 1977—'The Antinomies of Gramsci', in *New Left Review*, vol 100

Antoine Artous, December 2005—'*Stratégie révolutionnaire. Quelques éléments clés*' [Revolutionary Strategy: Some key elements', in French], in *Critique Communiste* 179

Antoine Artous, January 2006—'The LCR and the Left: Some Strategic Questions', in the *International Socialist Tendency Discussion Bulletin* 7

Daniel Bensaïd, 2003—*Un monde à changer* ['A World to Change', in French]. Paris: Textuel

Daniel Bensaïd, 2006b—*Planète altermondialiste* ['Alter-Globalisation Planet', in French]. Paris: Textuel

Fausto Bertinotti, 2001—*Ces idées qui ne meurent jamais* ['Ideas that will never die', in French]. Paris: Le temps des Cerises

Luc Boltanski and Eve Chiapello, 2006—*The New Spirit of Capitalism*. London: Verso

Alex Callinicos, 2003—*An Anti-Capitalist Manifesto*. Cambridge: Polity Press

Carl von Clausewitz, 1984 [1976, 1873]—*On War*. Edited and translated by Michael Eliot Howard and Peter Paret. (Original edition—London: N Trübner, 1873). The 2006 Project Gutenberg edition at http://www.gutenberg.org/files/1946/1946-h/1946-h.htm (Accessed April 2017)

Richard J F Day, 2005—*Gramsci Is Dead: Anarchist Currents in the Newest Social Movements*. London: Pluto Press

Régis Debray, 1967—*Revolution in the Revolution*. London: 1967

Régis Debray, 1974—*La Critique des Armes* ['A Critique of Arms', in French]. Paris: Éditions du Seuil

Hans Delbrück, 1990—*Warfare in Antiquity: History of the Art of War*, Volume 1. Translated by Walter J Renfroe, Jr. Lincoln: University of Nebraska Press

Cédric Durand, December 2005—'*Qu'entend-on par stratégie révolutionnaire aujourd'hui?*' ['What is revolutionary strategy today?', in French], in *Critique Communiste* 179

Michael Hardt and Antonio Negri, 2004—*Multitude: War and Democracy in the Age of Empire*. New York: Penguin Press

John Holloway, 2005 [2002]—*Change the World without Taking Power*. London: Pluto Press

Stathis Kouvelakis, 2005—'France: The Triumph of the Political', in *International Socialism* no 108 (Autumn 2005)

Jean-Guillaume Lanuque et al, eds, 2006—*Révolution, Lutte armée et Terrorisme* ['Revolution, Armed Struggle, and Terrorism', in French], special edition of *Dissidence*, vol 1. Paris: L'Harmattan

V I Lenin, 1953 [1917]—'The Threatening Catastrophe and How to Fight It', published October 1917; reprinted in *The New International*, a Monthly Organ of Revolutionary Marxism, vols 19–20, 1953

Xochitl Leyva Solano, 2017—'Geopolitics of Knowledge and the Neo-Zapatista Social Movement Networks', in Jai Sen, ed, 2017a—*The Movements of Movements, Part 1: What Makes Us Move?*. Volume 4 in the *Challenging Empires* series. New Delhi: OpenWord and Oakland, CA: PM Press

Giacomo Marramao, 1979—*Il Politico e le trasformazioni* ['Politics and Transformation', in Italian]. Bari, Italy: De Donato

Roel Meijer, 2017—'Fighting for Another World: Yusuf al-'Uyairi's Conceptualisation of Praxis and Permanent Revolution', in Jai Sen, ed, 2017a—*The Movements of Movements, Part 1: What Makes Us Move?*. Volume 4 in the *Challenging Empires* series. New Delhi: OpenWord, and Oakland, CA: PM Press

Roel Meijer, ed, 2009—*Global Salafism: Islam's New Religious Movement*. London: Hurst & Company

Humberto Ortega, 1982 [1980]—'Nicaragua—The Strategy of Victory', interview with Marta Harnecker, in Tomás Borge et al, 1982—*Sandinistas Speak*, edited by Bruce Marcus. New York: Pathfinder Press

Mario Payeras, 1983—'*Los días de la selva*' ['Days of the jungle', in Spanish]. New York: Monthly Review Press

Mario Payeras, 1987—*El trueno en la cuidad* ['The thunder in the city', in Spanish]. México: Juan Pablos Editores

Carl Schmitt, 2000—*La Dictature* ['The Dictatorship', in French]. Paris: Seuil

Leon Trotsky, 1983—*The Death Agony of Capitalism and the Tasks of the Fourth International*. New York: Pathfinder Press

Notes

1. Ed: This is an edited version of an article earlier published in *International Socialism*, no 113, and posted on January 4 2007 at http://www.isj.org.uk/index.php4?id=287&issue=113. It is published here with the generous permission of the author and the publisher. For further reproduction permission, contact isj@swp.org.uk.

   This article, like the original, takes up issues arising in a discussion on revolutionary strategy that began in the LCR's theoretical journal *Critique Communiste* ('Communist Critique', in French), March 2006, and was continued at a seminar in Paris in June 2006. Other participants included the editor of *Critique Communiste* Antoine Artous, LCR members Cédric Durand and Francis Sitel, and Alex Callinicos of the British SWP (Socialist Workers' Party). The other participants' positions are available on the website of the ESSF (*Europe solidaire sans frontiers*; 'A Solidarious Europe without Borders', in French). In the interests of space, and also because the discussion in the second half of the original essay was very 'internal', debating specific points, we have omitted the whole of Part V and a part of Part VI, and refer interested readers to the original article.

2. Ed: As also mentioned in the blurb for him (see 'List of Contributors'), the author of this essay, Daniel Bensaïd, died in January 2010. Although I never had the privilege of actually meeting him in person, to my understanding he was a legend in his time both as activist on the ground—a street fighter—and as strategist and theorist. I therefore want to add here that it was my great privilege to first have the agreement of such a legend to include one of his essays on strategy in this collection on 'the movements of movements', and then to also have had the chance to work fairly closely with him in the revision and finalisation of his essay for this book. Since he did his final revisions in June 2009—just six months before he died, of an illness— this was perhaps one of his last essays. It is therefore all the more our great privilege to carry it here.

3. For example, Hardt and Negri 2004, Holloway 2005 [2002], and Day 2005.

4. This was Stathis Kouvelakis's emphasis in Kouvelakis 2005. Note: The original article on which this essay is based was written perhaps in 2005, and so the author is referring here to the Italian elections in that year.

5. Holloway 2005 [2002], Hardt and Negri 2004.

6. Ed: See Abramsky, August 2008.

7. Callinicos 2003.

8. Ed: As put forward in Holloway 2005 [2002].

9. Ed: The slogan adopted by the World Social Forum from about 2002 on.

10. Clausewitz 1984, Delbrück 1990.

11. Ed: See also the discussion of the new concept of 'netwar' in the essay by Xochitl Leyva Solano in this book (Leyva Solano 2017).

12. Ed: For a discussion of another concept of 'permanent revolution'—the Salafist—see the essay in this book by Roel Meijer (Meijer 2017), and for a more complete treatment, his book (Meijer, ed, 2009).

13. Ed: ALBA: the Bolivarian Alternative for Latin America and the Caribbean, proposed by Chávez. ALCA: the Free Trade Area of the Americas, proposed by the US.

14. I shall go no further on this aspect of the question. It is simply a reminder. (See in this respect the theses proposed in the debate organised by *Das Argument—Journal for Philosophy and Social Sciences*, at www.europe-solidaire.org (Accessed April 2017).
15. Durand appears to attribute to us a "stageist view of social change" and "a temporality of political action centred exclusively on the preparation of the revolution as a decisive moment" (to which he opposes "an altermondialist and Zapatista historical time"?!). See his article in *Critique Communiste* 179 (Durand, December 2005). For a detailed critique of John Holloway's approach, see Bensaïd 2003; 2006b; and his articles in *Contretemps*, at www.europe-solidaire.org (Accessed April 2017).
16. In the debate about the programme in the Communist International up till its sixth congress.
17. See Anderson 1977.
18. See the debates around the report on the German Revolution at the fifth congress of the Communist International.
19. See Marramao 1979 and Daniel Bensaïd's pamphlet '*Stratégies et parties*' ('Strategies and Parties', in French).
20. As Antoine Artous reminds us in his article in *Critique Communiste 179* (Artous, December 2005).
21. A Chilean Movement of the Revolutionary Left.
22. A remote region of China run by the Chinese Communists from the mid-1930s until they took Beijing in 1949.
23. Despite the simplified myth of the foco, notably in Debray 1967.
24. The leader of the urban resistance in Cuba, killed in 1958 shortly before the victory of the revolution.
25. The Granma was the boat from which a group of guerrillas led by Castro landed in Cuba at the end of 1956.
26. 'Revolutionary Workers Party', an Argentinean section of the Fourth International, with a guerrilla group, the People's Revolutionary Army (ERP).
27. 'The strategy for victory', interview by Marta Harnecker (Ortega 1982 [1980]). Asked about the date on which the insurrection was called, Ortega replied: 'Because a whole series of more and more favourable objective conditions arose: the economic crisis, the currency devaluation, the political crisis. And because after the September events we realised that it was necessary to combine simultaneously and within the same strategic space the rising of the masses at a national level, the offensive of the military forces at the front and the national strike in which the employers were involved or in practice acquiesced. If we had not combined these three strategic factors simultaneously and in the same strategic space, victory would not have been possible. On several occasions there had been a call for a national strike, but it had not been combined with the mass offensive. The masses had already risen, but the rising had not been combined with strike action and took place at a time when the military capacity of the vanguard was too weak. And the vanguard had already delivered several blows to the enemy but without the presence of the other two factors.'
28. ibid.
29. Payeras 1983; 1987.
30. Debray 1974.

31. A guerrilla group formed from a split in Students for a Democratic Society, led by Bernadine Dohrn and Mark Rudd.

32. A French Maoist organisation formed in 1969.

33. Serge July was editor of the daily *Liberation* from 1974 to 2006, steering it from Maoism to the neoliberal 'centre-left'; and Alain Geismar, secretary of the lecturers' SNE-Sup union during the events of May 1968, then a Maoist, is now (2006–07) Inspector General of Education.

34. See Lanuque, ed, 2006 (*Révolution, Lutte armée et Terrorisme* ['Revolution, Armed Struggle, and Terrorism']).

35. Payeras 1983, 1987.

36. This is notably the theme of recent texts by Balibar.

37. The debate about non-violence in Rifondazione Comunista's theoretical review (*Alternative*) is certainly not without a bearing on its present course.

38. Ed: As mentioned in the author's blurb and in endnote 2, the author of this essay Daniel Bensaïd was a legendary strategist, and especially in the 1968 uprising in France (on which see the essay by Tariq Ali in this book, Ali 2017), and subsequently. Here—in this essay, which is based on an intense 'internal' discussion on movement strategy (for details, see endnote 1)—he is referring to his own experience.

39. Artous 2006. Artous is the editor of the LCR's theoretical journal *Critique Communiste*.

40. Notably Mandel's, in his polemics against the Eurocommunists' theses. See his book in the Maspero little collection and above all his interview in *Critique Communiste* 179.

41. A body of around fifty people nominated from the political parties, the Sandinista defence committees, the unions, professional associations, and private enterprise organisations.

42. Communists who broke with Stalinism in the late 1960s and 1970s to embrace left-wing parliamentarianism.

43. A left-of-centre Italian political philosopher.

44. The experience of the participatory budget at the Rio Grande do Sol state level offers many concrete examples in this respect: credit allocation, ranking of priorities, territorial sharing of collective supplies, etc.

45. Callinicos 2003.

46. Durand, December 2005.

47. Ed: The reference we have found, following the death of the author, is Lenin 1953 [1917], which has a slightly different title, 'The Threatening Catastrophe and How to Fight It'. We are however leaving the text as he finalised it.

48. Trotsky 1983.

49. It may be worth coming back to a discussion of this notion of a united front, or *a fortiori*, the anti-imperialist united front that some revolutionaries in Latin America have made flavour of the month, in the light of the evolution of social formations, of the role and composition of political parties, etc.

50. Albert Treint was the leader of the pro-Zinoviev wing of the French Communist Party in the mid-1920s.

51. Ruth Fischer was the leader of the ultra-left in the German Communist Party in the early and mid-1920s. She later became a fervent cold warrior.

52. Ed: We do not have a reference for this quote. Unfortunately, we somehow missed asking the author for a citation for this quote when he was finalising this essay, and now—since after his death in 2010—we have not been able to find one, or one with even approximately this wording. Although there are many 'finds' on the web, they are all only to earlier versions of this essay. The quote, with this wording, therefore remains unsubstantiated, as of date (though the person cited, Clara Zetkin, clearly did speak on the issue, but in other words. If any reader can help us with a citation, we would very much appreciate that. Let me know at jai.sen@cacim.net.

53. By members of the DS current—which is part of the Fourth International—such as Miguel Rosetto, as minister of popular agriculture.

54. At stake here, as far as the orientation in Brazil is concerned, was a conception of the Fourth International and its relationship to the national sections. But this question goes beyond the context of this text.

55. Right-wing German legal theorist of the inter-war years, who joined the Nazi Party.

56. See Schmitt 2000.

57. Ed: As mentioned in note 1, the original version of this essay was a contribution to a discussion on revolutionary strategy that began in the LCR's theoretical journal *Critique Communiste* ('Communist Critique', in French), March 2006, and was continued at a seminar in Paris in June 2006. In the interests of space and given the nature of this book, we have omitted the first two paragraphs of this section.

58. See Bertinotti 2001, and a critical approach to it (which appeared at the time of the ESF in Florence) in Bensaïd 2003.

Localisation as Radical Praxis and the New Politics of Climate Change
Peter North and David Featherstone

Looking for Alternatives

The movement for global justice that emerged through and after the Seattle protest of 1999 has largely been characterised as a movement *against* neoliberal economic globalisation, rather than *for* specific aspects of global justice. First characterised as a "swarm",[1] what has been called a 'movement' could better be described as a series of overlapping networks or spaces where groups with different agendas converged[2] at high-profile demonstrations at WTO, G8, or EC / FTAA ministerial meetings.[3] The wider transnational global justice movement was made up of connections between different struggles in the Global South— such as the Zapatistas in Mexico, the Argentinian *piqueteros* (pickets), and the Brazilian *Movimento Sem Terra* ('landless workers' movement')—supported by protesters in the Global North, who saw themselves as citizens benefitting from an unequal global division of labour. Hardt and Negri claimed these groups for the 'multitude', part of a wider conception of the proletariat that includes all those who have to work to meet their needs.[4] John Holloway celebrated their resistance, their refusal to submit to an exploitative system, their shout 'No!'.[5] The protesters seemed clear about what they opposed: Neoliberal globalisation in general, and proposed deals on Trade Related Intellectual Property Rights (TRIPS), the Multilateral Agreement on Investment (MAI), the World Trade Organization (WTO), the Free Trade Area of the Americas (FTAA), and the European Union in particular. Over time, an imperialist war in Iraq and attempts to restrict civil liberties under the guise of the so-called war on terror moved up the agenda.

The problem was clear—but what was the alternative? Protesters in the Global South did have more concrete arguments for livelihoods based on solidarity and common ownership but, for the North, apart from the inspiration of Southern struggles and proposals for reform of global trade governance, proposals for alternatives to neoliberal globalisation seemed underdeveloped. The problem was encapsulated by a banner on the Mayday 2002 protests against the City of London's financial district: "Let's overthrow capitalism and replace it with something really nice". Witty, understated, perhaps typically British, and later exposed as a prank by the producers of a TV spoof, but it hit a nerve. What would Northern protesters do differently?

Then climate change and 'peak oil' became public issues. The contemporaneous publication during 2007 of the IPCC'S Fourth Report,[6] the Stern Review,[7] and Al Gore's *An Inconvenient Truth*,[8] and at the same time, observable extreme weather events ranging from Katrina and South Asian cyclones to European flooding, droughts in Sudan, Southern Africa, and Australia, and forest fires in Greece and California, all suggested that the planet was warming,[9] perhaps dangerously so.[10] Oil prices rose from US$ 10 per barrel in 1997 to US$ 147 in mid-2008,[11] with speculation about future rises to US$ 200 or even US$ 500; while the drive to replace fossil fuels with biofuels led to global food price inflation and widespread food riots. Northern-based neoliberal globalised capitalism was not only globally unjust, as the protesters saw it; it was destroying the very ecosystems on which life depends.[12]

While the global justice movement had always contested the unequal social and environmental relations produced by globalisation, observable extreme weather and a new understanding that we were close to, or at the moment of, 'peak oil'—when demand begins to outstrip supply, leading to much higher prices (for the rich) and shortages (for the poor)—made it clear that growth-based globalised capitalism had, at last, come up against the natural limits that had been erroneously forecast in the past.[13] While the price of oil dropped back to below US$ 50 in 2009, the underlying problem of a lack of new discoveries of oil to keep up with exploding demand from newly industrialising countries in the Global South remained. Worse, the volatile price of oil meant that research into renewable alternatives to oil was cut drastically, retarding the likelihood of a technological fix. If carbon-based global capitalism does not have a future, then democratic economies that are just and egalitarian but carbon-based and focused uncritically on 'growth' do not either. Again, however, climate change activists were stronger on what they opposed than on recipes for alternatives. They were, as inscribed on their banners, "armed only ... with peer-reviewed science".[14] Peer-reviewed science tells us that climate change is a non-negotiable reality and that we should stop our planet-killing ways. It is a different matter, however, to open up a set of political questions about how this situation is negotiated and how alternative futures are shaped.

Some would argue that the best approach is to focus on injustice and solvable present-day problems—malaria, AIDS—leaving prescriptions for a better world to future generations, once the battle for justice is won.[15] But we don't think that is good enough, especially given the immediacy of the need to avoid catastrophic climate change. Here, we argue that progressive, subaltern-generated responses to climate change and resource constraints might already be beginning to provide an answer to the question, "How would you do it differently?" We examine here the concept and practice of 'localisation', which rejects the movement of goods and capital as dictated by contemporary globalisation. Localisation was developed and put forward by some antiglobalisers as a *counter* to neoliberal globalisation rather than as a proposal for alternative, subaltern, and more liberated forms of globalisation, and has formed a minority strand within the wider movement.[16] We accept that a comprehensive, progressive programme to avoid dangerous climate change would need to focus more widely than only on localisation, and in particular on developing alternatives to unsustainable capitalism such as how to heat homes and power economic activities, grow food, etc. We also do not assume that emissions will automatically be reduced by producing more locally; it may, after all, be better to produce food in the open air in Southern countries than in a heated greenhouse in the North.[17] We therefore focus on localisation here because it seems an obvious way both to reduce emissions and also to promote social justice, since international trade is a major source of avoidable emissions.

We first examine what advocates of localisation mean by 'the local'. Are they isolationists? What connections do they promote? How can proponents of localism counter criticisms that this effectively means 'pulling up the ladder', the rich North cutting the South off from the possibility of developing prosperity? And, along with this, would the South be better off if it concentrated on meeting more of its own needs, rather than fuelling unsustainable consumption in the North?

Second, we examine how localisation can be combined with international solidarity—with globalisation from below through subaltern connection and networking to build a better world.[18] We ask: How might these subaltern internationalisms contribute to the development of livelihoods that are enjoyable, vibrant, and wholesome, and do not entail the emission of unsustainable levels of carbon? How can the counter-globalisation movement engage with the struggles *against* the unequal social *and* environmental relations that are generated through neoliberal globalisation?

We write this essay as colleagues, friends, academics, and activists from different parts of the counter-globalisation and climate change movements, bringing together our different emphases in what we hope is a constructive engagement.[19]

Localisation, Global Justice, and Climate Change

Proponents of neoliberal globalisation argue that:

1. Goods should be produced in the cheapest possible place regardless of environmental or labour standards, or of externalised carbon emissions;
2. There should be an unfettered right to invest, to commodify, and to own, but no similar right to livelihood, to citizenship, or to a healthy ecosystem; and that—
3. Goods and services, finance, and the means of production should be free to move around the globe, but people should not have the same rights.[20]

Against this, some have advanced localisation.[21] Localisation means economic decisions should not focus exclusively on profit maximisation and economic efficiency but on meeting needs as locally as possible. In contrast to neoliberal globalisers, who call for the deregulation of economic decision-making, localisers call for the re-regulation and re-embedding of economics into local communities. Economic assets should be locally or communally owned and controlled through local economic institutions like worker-owned and run community development trusts, local money systems, local banks, cooperatives, communal gardens and restaurants, and communal land ownership.[22] Major parts of the economy and ecosystems should be held in common, off limits to monetisation, privatisation, and commodification.[23]

Localisation "does not mean walling off the outside world" in a nationalist autarkic project.[24] Rather, it stands against an integrated world economy based on a global division of labour without the regulation of labour and environmental standards. Taking a position against unsustainable and unequal neoliberal globalisation, localists argue that decisions about where to locate any given economic activity should not be based on cost alone, subsidised by cheap fuel and with CO_2 emissions externalised. They argue for focussing on producing as much as locally as possible, with international trade only as a last resort for goods and services that really cannot be produced more locally (for example, tea or citrus in the UK). It is an argument for economic subsidiarity.[25] Localists do not argue against connections out of the locality *per se*: Rather, they argue against a reification of connection as always inevitable and always good.

Localisation has also been advocated by the ecological and environmental elements of the overlapping networks that make up the global justice movement for many reasons. Cavanagh and Mander argue that localisation is inherently a subversive project vis-à-vis neoliberal globalisation since it entails fewer opportunities for multinationals to generate superprofits for elites.[26] Localisation would be a simpler economic system, with fewer opportunities for 'middle men' to add value or pass goods or services or money on, taking their cut en route. Before the recent revival of neoliberal globalisation, they argue, much of the planet's economic activity was off limits to globalisation, such as the peasant subsistence economy in the South, or where many basic services remained nationalised in the South and under local government control in the North—for example, municipal electricity, gas, and water.[27] Their argument is that much of social and economic life should be off limits to globalisation. The radical project then becomes the defence of the global commons—un-monetised and collectively used for use value and not exchange value—from commodification. Localists object to the loss of local control associated with neoliberal globalisation and to decisions about local economies being made by distant elites uncommitted to or ignorant of the places they affect through their decisions.

The second reason why localisation is a key part of the more explicitly anti-global elements of the wider global justice movement is that it connects to arguments that the development and social justice potential of trade is overstated. While some communities in the Global South have undoubtedly benefitted from connection, the benefits cannot be assumed. The argument is that neoliberal conceptions of 'free' trade is a sham designed to keep the South poor and Northern elites rich through the destruction of (mainly manufacturing) livelihoods in the North as a result of competition with goods and services produced in places with lower labour or environmental standards in the South, while in the South, rural livelihoods are destroyed by the dumping of subsidised EU or US agricultural produce.[28]

Echoing an older critique developed by dependency theorists like Raúl Prebisch and André Gunder Frank, contemporary localisers like Martin Khor, Vandana Shiva, Maria Mies, and Helena Norberg-Hodge argue that elites in the North are not genuinely committed to advancing the position of the Global South through trade, but keep the South in a position of dependency whereby they have to export often niche or low value primary products on unfair terms, and where terms of trade can change rapidly to the detriment of Southern producers. States in the Global South that have broken out of this dependent relationship have done so with a judicious mix of state intervention and appropriate forms of protection for their nascent industries, removing it only when these industries can stand on their own two feet.[29]

Beyond this however, and in contrast to those committed to 'fair' rather than 'free' trade, localisers argue that trade from South to North, even on better, fairer terms, is not the solution. They argue that, for generations, village-level self-sufficiency has generated fulfilling livelihoods for millions through unmonetised, often communal economies, throughout much of the South.[30] They claim that localisation in the South would mean greater living standards by meeting basic needs, leading, in the long run, to more diverse livelihood opportunities rather than economic and ecological monocultures created by focussing on exports. Southern countries are prevented from charting an independent course by the need to attract hard currencies to repay debt, and can be destabilised by the periodic crises to which capitalism is prone and which open capital markets amplify. Localisation aims at "celebrating and aiming for diversity of production, diversity of economic activity, and retaining control over capital, rather than letting it flow around the world".[31] South-North trade may also generate unsustainable emissions. Even if South-North trade did involve fewer emissions than producing the same goods in the North, localisers would question its utility—do Northern consumers really need year-round flowers or fruit? Might not the South be better off meeting its own more pressing needs?

Localisers argue that local diversity and local distinctiveness are good in and of themselves. Globalisation is the 'McDonaldisation' of society and economy,[32] the domination of the global brand.[33] Drawing on conceptions of what is thought to be good about the natural world, localisers argue for societies and economies that are diverse, interdependent, and resilient. A variety of local economies mirrors nature's diversity, facilitating experimentation and the development of more effective practices and models. Localised economies connected to each other combine diversity with interdependence, without uniformity. Localisers claim that diverse localised economies across space have 'trips' that mean that problems in one place are not necessarily transmitted everywhere, meaning they are more resilient to external shocks. Places reliant on economic monocultures are vulnerable to price fluctuations and changes in demand. In diverse and connected but more localised economies, if demand for a product produced in one place breaks down, then that place also has many other ways of making a living that it can fall back on. The argument is then that localised economies North and South would provide a wider range of livelihoods than would a network of local monocultures integrated into one big global network based on the division of labour.

Localisation also bridges the politics of globalisation and climate change. Avoiding 'dangerous' climate change requires deep cuts in carbon emissions quickly—of 80–95 per cent by 2050.[34] This requires a fundamental restructuring of currently unsustainable capitalist economic practices.[35] Localisers argue against regions and countries exchanging similar produce that could just as easily be produced for local consumption without the associated carbon emissions.[36] For the past forty-odd years, the global economy has gone through a process of time-space compression, based on near-instantaneous global telecommunications, externalised CO_2 emissions, and cheap petroleum, which has enabled a "spatial fix", whereby capitalist firms relocate from parts of the world characterised by low rather than high production costs, precisely because transport costs are either low or (in the case of telecommunications) close to zero, and CO_2 emissions are externalised.[37] The need to reduce emissions and energy usage means that we in fact need to undertake a time-space re-extension, where transport costs again become significant in terms of both finance and emissions. Currently very cheap goods produced through globalised production networks will become, and remain, more expensive. The currently near will become further away, again.

For radical localisers, this process of re-extension will go very deep, as the price of global connections makes international trade unsustainable. Ted Trainer, radical localist and champion of a post-materialist, small-scale technology society, consequently argues for a society constructed from many highly self-sufficient small settlements and localised economies, inhabited by people living lifestyles characterised by significantly reduced personal consumption as compared with those currently practiced widely in the North and by Southern elites.[38] The higher price of fuel, and the need to reduce emissions, would mean that people would have to decide to travel less. Cities would be 'villageised' so people could meet more of their needs from their neighbourhood without commuting or trucking goods and services around urban areas, while avoidable long distance travel would be cut down drastically. The vast majority of goods and services needed would be produced locally in decentralised small workshops and through community businesses that people could walk or cycle to. Small businesses would multiply, becoming the norm, and staying small. Crumbling transport infrastructures would be given over to community-owned farms growing food, grazing livestock, or for fish farms. There will still be some importing and exporting of goods, but it would be insignificant. What he calls "the simpler way" is unavoidable if we are to avert dangerous climate change.[39]

Trainer's rather autarkic vision is one extreme of the localising perspective. Few localisers argue for either hairshirts or for the complete disconnection of places with each other, and they are generally not, therefore, 'isolationists'.[40] The response of the autarkic nationalist Myanmar military government to the devastation of Cyclone Nargis in 2008 graphically demonstrated the limits of autarkic localisation. When localisation is contrasted with actually existing autarky, its scope becomes clearer.

Localisation is thus not set at any specific scale, but it is "a relative term. It means different things to different people and depends on context".[41] Hines, like Woodin and Lucas, sees localisation as a sensible and pragmatic alternative to a globalisation that needlessly moves goods and services in ecologically damaging ways.[42] The economy needs to be pragmatically reorganised so things are done as locally as possible, and this will provide diversity, generate jobs, livelihoods, and small businesses, *and* reduce needless carbon emissions. Once things are produced as locally as possible, we will be able to make decisions about what kinds of international connections are reconcilable with avoiding dangerous climate change. Localists often claim that their proposals are little more than sensible, pragmatic, and technical reforms necessary to avoid climate apocalypse that an unspecified 'we' can all agree on. We contend, however, that localisation is a deeply political and contestable programme, and we now turn to this.

Critiques of Localisation

Critiques of localisation, especially those from the left, focus on four issues. First, they argue that localists conflate the 'local' with progress and sustainability. For André Gorz:

> [C]ommunal autarky always has an impoverishing effect: the more self sufficient and numerically limited a community is, the smaller the range of activities and choices it can offer to its members. If it has no opening to an area of exogenous activity, knowledge and production, the community becomes a prison ... only

constantly renewed possibilities for discovery, insight, experimentation and communication can prevent communal life from becoming impoverished and eventually suffocating.[43]

Radical social ecologist Murray Bookchin agrees:

> No community can hope to achieve economic autarky, nor should it try to do so. ... Divested of the cultural cross fertilisation that is often a product of economic intercourse, the municipality tends to shrink into itself and disappear into its own civic privatism. ... Small is not necessarily beautiful.[44]

Localities are differentiated by class, gender, and a range of other local oppressions, and the left has generally preferred international links with other subalterns to alliances with local elites. On the other hand, recognising that localisation should not be confused with autarky, Bookchin also argues:

> We cannot ignore the fact that relatively self-sustaining communities in which crafts, agriculture, and industries serve definable networks of confederally organised communities enrich the opportunities and stimuli to which individuals are exposed and make for more rounded personalities with a rich sense of selfhood and competence (than those produced in globalised sweatshops, for example).[45]

Cavanagh and Mander agree the local *can* be small-scale and oppressive, but argue that it need not be.[46] Even the radical localiser Trainer argues for an international exchange of ideas and culture, particularly through information technologies. Opportunities for cyber and teleworking would remain, once global carbon emissions have been brought down as much as possible by localisation and other "powerdown" processes.[47]

Secondly, ecosocialists like Kovel[48] and Wall[49] have little time for what they call a naïve neo-Smithian valorisation of small, local economies, arguing that capitalism and markets are intertwined, and that markets have an inbuilt tendency towards growth and monopoly—the classic Marxist position. A Smithian localised economy would soon grow into a conventional capitalist market: Firms would either grow out of the locality or die, since capitalism requires businesses to compete with each other. Unless *all* capitalists agreed not to grow their businesses, steady-state capitalism is an oxymoron. Cavanagh and Mander agree that local businesses *can* be exploitative[50]—but this cannot be assumed. The work of Gibson-Graham is useful here. It points out that arguing that all businesses are inevitably capitalist or growth-orientated is like assuming all women are maternal or child-orientated.[51] Some businesses do focus on growth, but there is a great diversity in economic forms. This allows a focus on how alternative economic practices such as worker-owned enterprises and co-operatives can make a significant contribution to climate change politics. We can do more to explore the contribution to climate change politics of worker-owned enterprises and co-operatives, working in solidarity economies rather than capitalist economies.[52]

A third problem for the left is identifying the localising agent. DeFilippis argues that "since localities are not agents ... they cannot own anything. Instead, forms of local ownership are created by collective ownership or ownership by institutions that are place bound or place dependent".[53] Localisation should be better thought of as community control of economic resources like credit unions, communal housing, and local money networks. Through localisation, local collective control would be put on local investment and disinvestment, and therefore facilitate control of the production in ways that local residents, rather than actors far away, want. This production, he argues, can be counter-hegemonic.[54] DeFilippis also understands that many community-based organisations that localisers put faith in often do not have an oppositional politics.[55] They see themselves as promoting social inclusion, or as practical non-political alternatives, and are often dependent on grants and loans, disconnected from a wider social change movement. Localisers may claim them, but they do not necessarily see themselves as part of an oppositional network. They may even defend their claims to be common-sense, non-political organisations, to win grants and respectability in the eyes of elites.

The question then arises as to *who* will localise an economy, especially if much of the productive wealth is held by private sector elites. Harman, for example, argues that what George Monbiot's

> generally excellent book *Heat* (2006) does not show is how to create the agency, the active mass force, that can compel the governments of the world's most polluting states to implement such measures. He puts forward a generally excellent political programme for a political force that does not exist.[56]

We agree that the question of agency is key to climate change politics, but argue that it is an issue with which the global justice movement has in fact long engaged and from which advocates of localisation can learn. Many climate change activists engaging in direct action *against* unsustainable capitalist practices draw much of their strategy and tactics from this experience.[57]

The Transition Towns movement in the Global North is an interesting case study of agency. It looks to build local movements, arguing for and prefiguring post-carbon economies.[58] It is an agent, and has inspired quite an impressive level of mobilisation in towns and cities across in the English-speaking Global North quite quickly. So the issue here is less the lack of an agent than the ability of subaltern groups to move beyond the politics of prefiguration and challenge local and global systems of domination. On the one hand, critics from the global justice movement argue that it is informed by an extremely optimistic conceptualisation of the possibility of transforming currently unsustainable economic practices through local, citizen-based action, without explicitly challenging global power relations.[59] On the other hand, Transition Towns groups educate their members about climate change and peak oil, and develop alternatives that, they argue, will enable their communities to be resilient when global capitalism becomes unsustainable. In John Holloway's terms, Transition Towns focus on developing their members' sense of agency, their power 'to' act, rather than spending time challenging forms of elite power that, they suspect, have a limited future.[60] In movements engaging in direct action and in prefiguration perhaps we are beginning to see nascent social actors meeting Harman's concerns.

The fourth critique is from geographers on the left, who argue that localisation is a worthy but ultimately limited 'militant particularism', unable to contribute to wider, 'universal' questions of emancipation.[61] It is not good enough to say that the global ('them', people we don't know, far away) is 'bad', while the local ('us', people we know, nearby) is 'good'. The emancipatory project is built on connection with others, localisation on disconnection. Harman, for example, points to the connection between Mexico's Tortilla March and Northern consumption: "Filling SUV fuel tanks in California was causing hunger in Mexico".[62] Localisation suggests that local elites are given preference over subalterns elsewhere. It could, therefore, be seen as a dangerous practice, against left conceptions built on the unity of the vast majority against a small oppressing, only perhaps local, minority.

Overall, we argue that these objections from the left are problematic as they conceptualise 'local' and 'global' political strategies as separate, even defined against each other: In this view, localisation always leads to xenophobia, and internationalism to connection and solidarity. We would argue for more *relational* accounts, which understand that the 'local' and the 'global' are co-constituted through particular places and sites. Arguing for local food production in Mexico understands that pressures against it are created globally, but that is not the same as arguing that because food chains are often global, it is foolish, reactionary, or misplaced to support rioting subaltern groups in Mexico in their call for more control of the means of life. Attempts to argue for *exclusively* local or global strategies are false and destructive of political possibilities.[63] What does this mean for international solidarity?

Climate Change and the Maintenance of North-South Solidarities

The global justice movement has brought into contestation the unequal relations of power produced through neoliberal globalisation. This has been a productive and important process, which, despite the many criticisms levelled at these movements and their political strategies, remains one of their most significant achievements. Debates around climate change alone, however, have frequently isolated processes like carbon emission and global warming from the wider, unequal social and environmental relations upon which neoliberal globalisation depends. This section explores the relations of localising practices to transnational elements of the diverse global justice movement. First, it explores how the global justice movement has shown how globalising processes that create dangerous climate change are produced in and through local places, where they can also be challenged. Second, it explores how localising experiments and practices are related to alternative ways of producing globalisations that do not entail unsustainable emissions of carbon. Lastly, it explores the tensions and possibilities produced through these political interventions.

The global justice movement has demonstrated that it is possible to localise and contextualise the power relations that comprise neoliberal globalisation. This has important implications for transnational organising in relation to climate change. The left has long argued that environmentalism ignores contested power relations. We contend, however, that the way that the geographies of power are being contested through activist politics is itself producing a more antagonistic politics of climate change. They are producing political interventions that have usefully been described as 'environmentalisms of the poor'.[64] Further, they are also generating alliances and constructions of environmental problems that contest assumptions that environmentalisms, and hence the politics of climate change, are a middle-class privilege only relevant to the North.[65]

Movements such as the transnational boycott of Esso[66] and the condemnation of George Bush's politics around the Kyoto Protocol[67] are useful examples. They illuminate how environmentalisms have engaged with struggles against the unequal social and environmental relations created through neoliberal practices. These cuts into the contested geographies of power associated with climate change have forged distinctive alternatives to unjust and wasteful social and environmental relations.

The South has also provided rich histories of alternatives to export growth-led development, going back to Gandhi's objection to the then hegemonic British-championed conception of free trade:

> Free trade for a country which has become industrial, whose population can and does live in cities, whose people do not mind preying on other nations and, therefore, sustain the biggest navy to protect their unnatural commerce, may be economically sound (though, as the reader perceives, I question it's morality). Free trade for India has proved her curse and held her in bondage.[68]

Contemporary Gandhian alternatives have been championed by major movement intellectuals such as Vandana Shiva, Walden Bello, and Martin Khor,[69] and by particular movements such as the Karnataka State Farmers' Union (KRRS), which organises small and middle farmers at a village levels.[70] There are similarities with the *Movimento Sem Terra* (MST), the Brazilian movement of the landless, which has sought to produce alternatives to neoliberal forms of agriculture.[71] Argentina's alternative currency networks challenged the hold of the global finance system on that country after the crisis of 2001,[72] while its recovered factories continued to produce for local markets, once their owners declared them unprofitable.[73] In Honduras, COMAL is a network of forty-six small co-operative producers and 30,000 consumers providing for basic needs locally, in opposition to the planned FTAA.[74] These alternatives produce forms of radical localisation that are not atavistic or bounded, but linked to internationalist struggles against neoliberal globalisation.

The strategies of the MST are a good example of how localising strategies can be generated in combination with internationalist political strategies and identities. While the MST initially adopted intensive methods of agriculture on the land gained through their occupations, it has begun to experiment with alternative forms of agriculture and produced the first organic seeds in Latin America.[75] Its allies in the North, such as the Confédération Paysanne, have backed alternative proposals for rural development based around 'solidaristic agriculture' related to radical non-agricultural actors in rural communities.[76]

For João Pedro Stédile, a central figure in the MST leadership, an important context for the MST's experiments with alternative forms of agriculture has been a shift in terms of its 'enemy', no longer 'the old *latifundiários*' ('landowners') but global agribusiness, which, over the last ten years, has progressively penetrated "firms and economic units working in agriculture".[77] Consequently, it has sought to provide existing alternatives to the exploitative modes of agriculture associated with global agribusiness.[78] Rocha noted, in 2002, that MST co-operatives remain enmeshed in global agribusiness networks in various ways, some rearing chickens for Sadia, a Brazilian food company that exports frozen poultry to Europe.[79] MST's subsequent actions, however, have opened up different possibilities and shaped more diverse forms of agriculture.

João Rockett, a self-educated agronomist who helped the MST produce organic seeds, has argued that rejecting 'chemical farming' can produce social and environmental benefits:

> For instance, we're cultivating three varieties of wheat—one that's good for noodles, another for bread and another for biscuits. The other day a settler came back with an old variety of wheat that produces excellent straw for hats. Imagine a multinational company letting you grow wheat for that! But people love it. It fosters their sense of community.[80]

This agenda for alternative agriculture is not defined by isolationist localisation: It is local *and* internationalist. Thus, Stédile notes how the MST is looking for support from Venezuela's Bank for Economic and Social Development for recovering 'creole seeds', which are adapted to local conditions, rather than the uniform transgenic varieties promoted through transnational agribusiness.[81] MST has also been prominent in the international peasant movement, Via Campesina. To see localisation strategies as isolated from different struggles and political projects is problematic; it is necessary to consider how these can be co-constituted through the struggles and political projects that make up subaltern forms of globalisation.

Connections between movements do not, however, necessarily produce smooth, consensual alliances. Even when acting in solidarity, different movements have different ways of connecting localisation and global practices. This is evident in the alliance formed between the MST and Confédération Paysanne in opposition to transgenic seeds. José Bové of Confédération Paysanne and Stédile of the MST offered markedly different ways of negotiating these geographies of power. Stédile disagreed with Bové's position of fighting the European Union's farm subsidies on the grounds of their "distorting international trade to the detriment of developing countries".[82] He argued that "the problem is not the subsidies in Europe ... but the lack of subsidies in Brazil and elsewhere", and he condemned "the transformation of food products into a simple tool for business and profits".[83]

There remain important questions, then, in relation to the ways in which these strategies of localisation are seen as part of a transnational politics of solidarity and connection, or are related to more bounded ways of seeing local or national politics. But, it is significant that political projects in support of localisation can produce alternative, sustainable forms of globalisation rather than opposing globalisation per se.[84] Bové argues for a valued locally-specific geography, that of his Roquefort-producing region. How Bové differentiates his politics from other opposition to globalisation, however, is instructive. He argues of "chauvinist" opponents of globalisation that "their idea of sovereignty relates to the nation-state, and theirs is a selfish, frightened and irrational response". As an alternative, he argues for a "concept of sovereignty" which "enables people to think for themselves, without any imposed model for agriculture or society, and to live in solidarity with each other". Further, he argues specifically against a fetishisation of the national or local. He argues that the globalisation of trade must be counteracted on a world scale rather than on a narrow-minded nation-state basis: "Nationalists worry about the mixing of races, whereas we welcome fair trade, cultural exchange and solidarity; we stand for a dignified and free life under real democracy".[85]

Conclusion

This essay has outlined how new concerns about resource constraints and climate change enable those fighting for global justice to begin to flesh out what an egalitarian and low carbon alternative to neoliberal globalisation might look like. Localisation initially developed as a counter to the capacity of transnational corporations to destroy places through relocating jobs and finance to cheaper, less regulated places in the Global South. Climate change suggests that the global justice movement still needs to understand the ecocidal, as well as exploitative and socially regressive, nature of neoliberal global capitalism. Thus, what originally developed as an argument against globalisation now becomes more powerful given the reality of climate change and peak oil, as the neoliberal utopia of the globally integrated economy built on cheap fuel and externalised emissions becomes untenable. Resource constraints and the ability of the ecosystem to absorb the emissions of industrialisation change the nature of the debate.

Dominant constructions of climate change politics continue to marginalise concerns of equity and justice. Left critiques of localisation, as we have documented, have often seen localising practices as antithetical to internationalist strategies and as isolated from questions of global justice and equity. We have argued that this is a redundant and politically destructive critique. We have demonstrated through the discussion of movements like MST that localising strategies can co-exist with internationalist strategies and perspectives and be reworked and strengthened through relations with such strategies. One of our convictions and hopes is that connections between the global justice and climate change movements can shape a politics where a move towards more localisation need not be xenophobic—and where localising strategies can be part of producing more equitable and sustainable forms of globalisation. It is possible to combine political action in the local places where globalisation is produced, and reproduced, with sustainable forms of transnational connection.

References

Sam Ashman, 2004—'Resistance to Neoliberal Globalisation: A Case of "Militant Particularism"?', in *Politics*, vol 24 no 2, pp 143–153

Muzaffar Assadi, 1995—'"Khadi Curtain", "Weak Capitalism", and "Operation Ryot": Some Ambiguities in Farmer's Discourse, Karnataka and Maharashtra 1980–93', in Tom Brass, ed, 1995—*New Farmers' Movements in India* (London: Frank Cass), pp 212–227

Walden Bello, 2002—*Deglobalization: Ideas for a New World Economy*. London: Zed

Veronika Bennholdt-Thomsen and Maria Mies, 1999—*The Subsistence Perspective: Beyond the Globalised Economy*. London: Zed.

Jagdish Bhagwati, 2004—*In Defense of Globalization*. Oxford: Oxford University Press

Ingolfur Blühdorn, 2007—'Sustaining the Unsustainable: Symbolic Politics and the Politics of Simulation', in *Environmental Politics*, vol 16 no 2, pp 251–275

Murray Bookchin, 1995—*From Urbanisation to Cities: Towards a New Politics of Citizenship*. London: Cassel

Jose Bové and François Dufour, 2001—*The World Is Not for Sale: Farmers Against Junk Food*. London: Verso

Sue Branford and Jan Rocha, 2002—*Cutting the Wire: The Struggle of the Landless Movement in Brazil*. London: Latin America Bureau

Jeremy Brecher, Tim Costello, and Brandon Smith, 2000—*Globalisation from Below: The Power of Solidarity*. Cambridge, MA: South End Press

Daniel Buck, 2006—'The Ecological Question: Can capitalism prevail?', in Leo Panitch and Colin Leys, eds, 2006—*Coming to Terms with Nature: Socialist Register 2007*. London: Merlin Press

John Cavanagh and Jerry Mander, 2004—*Alternatives to Economic Globalization*. San Francisco: Berrett-Koehler Publishers

Ha-Joon Chang, 2003—*Kicking Away the Ladder: Development Strategy in Historical Perspective*. London: Anthem Press

Ha-Joon Chang, 2007—*Bad Samaritans: The Guilty Secrets of Rich Nations and the Threat to Global Prosperity*. Random House: London

Partha Chatterjee, 1984—'Gandhi and the Critique of Civil Society', in Ranajit Guha, ed, 1984—*Subaltern Studies III* (Delhi: Oxford University Press), pp 153–195

James DeFilippis, 2004—*Unmaking Goliath: Community Control in the Face of Global Capital*. London: Routledge

David Demeritt, 2006—'Science Studies, Climate Change, and the Prospects for Constructivist Critique', in *Economy and Society*, vol 35 no 3, pp 453–479

Meghnad Desai and Yahia Said, 2001—'The New Anti-Capitalist Movement: Money and Global Civil Society', in Helmut Anheier, Marlies Glasius, and Mary Kaldor, eds, 2001—*Global Civil Society 2001* (Oxford: Oxford University Press), pp 51–78

Ana Cecilia Dinerstein, 2007—'Workers' Factory Takeovers and New State Policies in Argentina: Towards an 'institutionalisation' of non-governmental public action?', in *Policy and Politics*, vol 35, pp 529

Richard Douthwaite, 1996—*Short Circuit: Strengthening Local Economies for Security in an Uncertain World*. Totnes, Devon: Green Books

David J Featherstone, 2003—'Spatialities of Transnational Resistance to Globalisation: the Maps of Grievance of the Inter-Continental Caravan', in *Transactions of the Institute of British Geographers*, vol 28 no 3, pp 404–421

David J Featherstone, 2008—*Resistance, Space and Political Identities: The Making of Counter-Global Networks*. Oxford: Wiley-Blackwell

John Feffer, ed, 2002—*Living in Hope: People Challenging Globalisation*. London: Zed

Bernardo Mancano Fernandes, 2005—'The Land Occupation as a Form of Access to Land in Brazil: A theoretical and methodological contribution', in Sam Moyo and Paris Yeros, eds, 2005—*Reclaiming the Land: The Resurgence of Rural Movements in Africa, Asia and Latin America* (London: Zed Books), pp 317–340

John Bellamy Foster, 2002—*Ecology Against Capitalism*. New York: Monthly Review Press

Thomas L Friedman, 2006—*The World is Flat: The Globalized World in the Twenty-first Century*. London: Penguin Books

J K Gibson-Graham, 2006a—*The End of Capitalism (as we knew it): A Feminist Critique of Political Economy*. Minneapolis: University of Minnesota Press

J K Gibson-Graham, 2006b—*A Post Capitalist Politics*. Minneapolis: University of Minnesota Press

Ranajit Guha, 1997—*Dominance Without Hegemony: History and Power in Colonial India*. Cambridge, Mass: Harvard University Press

Michael Hardt and Antonio Negri, 2000 *Empire*. London: Harvard University Press

Michael Hardt and Antonio Negri, 2005 *Multitude*. London: Hamish Hamilton

Chris Harman, 2007—'Climate Change and Class Politics', in *Socialist Review* (July–August 2007)

David Harvey, 1989—*The Condition of Postmodernity: An Enquiry into the Origins of Cultural Change*. Oxford: Blackwell

David Harvey, 2001—*Spaces of Capital: Towards a Critical Geography*. Edinburgh: Edinburgh University Press

Richard Heinberg, 2004—*Powerdown: Options and Actions for a Post-Carbon World*. Gabriola Island, BC: New Society Publications

Patrick Herman and Richard Kuper, 2003—*Food for Thought: Towards a Future for Farming*. London: Pluto

Colin Hines, 2000—*Localisation: A Global Manifesto*. London: Earthscan

John Holloway, 2002—*Change the World Without Taking Power: The Meaning of Revolution Today*. London: Pluto

Rob Hopkins, 2008—*The Transition Handbook: From Oil Dependency to Local Resilience*. Totnes, UK: Green Books

David L Imbroscio, 1997—*Reconstructing City Politics: Alternative Economic Development and Urban Regimes*. London: Sage

IPCC, 2007—*Climate Change 2007: The Intergovernmental Panel on Climate Change Fourth Assessment Report*, at http://www.ipcc.ch/publications_and_data/ar4/syr/en/contents.html (Accessed April 2017)

Naomi Klein, 2000—*No Logo*. London: Flamingo

Naomi Klein, 2002—*Fences and Windows: Dispatches from the Front Line of the Globalisation Debate*. London: Flamingo

Joel Kovel, 2007 [2002]—*The Enemy of Nature*. London: Zed Books

Tim Lang and Colin Hines, 1993—*The New Protectionism: Protecting the Future Against Free Trade*. London: Earthscan Publications

Bjorn Lomborg, 2007—*Cool It: The Skeptical Environmentalist's Guide to Global Warming*. London: Cavendish House

James Lovelock, 2006b—*The Revenge of Gaia*. London: Allen Lane

Mark Lynas, 2007—*Six Degrees: Our Future on a Hotter Planet*. London: Fourth Estate

Joan Martinez-Alier, 2002—*The Environmentalism of the Poor: A Study of Ecological Conflicts and Valuation*. Cheltenham: Edward Elgar

Doreen Massey, 1994—'A Global Sense of Place', in D Massey, ed, 1994—*Space, Place and Gender* (Cambridge: Polity Press), pp 146–156

Doreen Massey, 2005—*For Space*. London: Sage

Bill McKibben, 2007—*Deep Economy: The Wealth of Communities and the Durable Future*. New York: Times Books

George Monbiot, 2006—*Heat: How to Stop the Planet Burning*. London: Allen Lane

MST, 2001—'Fundamental Principles for the Social and Economic Transformation of Rural Brazil', in *Journal of Peasant Studies*, vol 28 no 2, pp 153–161

Pierpaolo Mudu, 2004—'Resisting and Challenging Neoliberalism: The Development of Italian Social Centres', in *Antipode*, vol 36 no 5, pp 917–941

Jonathan Neale, 2002—*You Are G8, We Are Six Billion*. London: Vision

NEF (New Economics Foundation), 2007—*The European Unhappy Planet Index: An Index of Carbon Efficiency and Well-Being in the EU*. London: The New Economics Foundation and Friends of the Earth

Johan Norberg, 2003—*In Defense of Global Capitalism*. Washington, DC: The Cato Institute

Helena Norberg-Hodge, 1991—*Ancient Futures: Learning from Ladakh*. London: Rider

Helena Norberg-Hodge, 2001—'Shifting Direction—From Global Dependence to Local Interdependence', in Edward Goldsmith and Jerry Mander, eds, 2001—*The Case against the Global Economy, and for a Turn towards Localization*. (London: Earthscan Publications)

Peter North, 2007—*Money and Liberation: The micropolitics of alternative currency movements*. Minneapolis: University of Minnesota Press

Mario Osava, 2001—'Peasants Speak Out against Food Imports', in *Third World Network Website*, at http://www.twnside.org.sg/title/peasants.htm (Accessed April 2017)

George Ritzer, 2004—*The McDonaldization of Society*. Thousand Oaks, CA: Pine Forge Press

Paul Roberts, 2004—*The End of Oil*. London: Bloomsbury

Jan Rocha, 2002—'On the Frontier', in *The Guardian*, June 26 2002, at http://www.theguardian.com/society/2002/jun/26/guardiansocietysupplement (Accessed April 2017)

Paul Routledge, 2003—'Convergence Space: Process Geographies of Grassroots Globalization Networks', in *Transactions of the Institute of British Geographers*, vol 28 no 3, pp 333–349

Boaventura de Sousa Santos, ed, 2006c—*Another Production Is Possible: Beyond the Capitalist Canon*. London: Verso

Molly Scott Cato, 2006—*Market Schmarket*. Cheltenham: New Clarion Press

Vandana Shiva, 2005—*Earth Democracy: Justice, Sustainability and Peace*. Cambridge, MA: South End Press

Michael Shuman, 2001—*Going Local: Creating Self Reliant Communities in a Global Age*. London: Routledge

João Pedro Stédile, 2007—'The Class Struggles in Brazil: The Perspective of the MST', in Leo Panitch and C Leys, eds, 2007—*Socialist Register 2008*, pp 193–216

Nicholas Stern, 2007—*Stern Review of the Economics of Climate Change*. London: HM Treasury/The Cabinet Office

David Strahan, 2007—*The Last Oil Shock: A Survival Guide to the Imminent Extinction of Petroleum Man*. London: John Murray

Erik Swyngedouw, 1997—'Neither Global nor Local: 'Glocalisation' and the politics of scale', in K Cox, ed, 1997—*Spaces of Globalisation: Reasserting the power of the local* (London: The Guildford Press), pp 137–166

Erik Swyngedouw, 2007—'Impossible "Sustainability" and the Post-Political Condition', in D Gibbs and R Krueger, eds, 2007—*Sustainable Development*. New York: Guilford Press

Janet Thomas, 2000—*The Battle in Seattle*. Golden, Colorado: Fulcrum Publishing

Ted Trainer, 1995—*The Conserver Society*. London: Zed Books

Trapese, 2008—*The Rocky Road to a Real Transition: The Transition Towns Movement and What It Means for Social Change*. Leeds: Trapese Popular Education Collective

Gabrielle Walker and David King, 2008—*The Hot Topic: How to Tackle Global Warming and Keep the Lights On*. London: Bloomsbury

Derek Wall, 2005—*Babylon and Beyond: The Economics of the Anti-Capitalist, Anti-Globalist and Radical Green Movements*. London: Pluto

Peter Waterman and Jane Wills, eds, 2001—*Place, Space and the New Labour Internationalisms*. London: Blackwell

Martin Wolf, 2005—*Why Globalization Works*. New Haven, CT: Yale Nota Bene

Mike Woodin and Caroline Lucas, 2004—*Green Alternatives to Globalisation: A Manifesto*. London: Pluto

Notes

1. Klein 2002.
2. Featherstone 2003; Routledge 2003.
3. Brecher, Costello et al 2000; Thomas 2000; Neale 2002.
4. Hardt and Negri 2000; 2005.
5. Holloway 2002.
6. IPCC 2007.
7. Stern Review 2007.
8. Gore 2006.
9. Lynas 2007.
10. Lovelock 2006b.
11. June 2008
12. Foster 2002; Wall 2005; Kovel 2007.
13. Heinberg 2004; Roberts 2004; Strahan 2007.
14. See: http://theonetonners.blogspot.com/2007/08/climate-camp-14th-21st-august.html.
15. Lomborg 2007.
16. Ashman 2004.
17. Walker and King 2007, pp 242–244.
18. Brecher, Costello et al 2000; Waterman and Wills 2001; Featherstone 2003.
19. Dave has strong interests in the formation of transnational solidarity networks in both the past and present, and has been involved in various campaigns over land rights. Pete has been involved with peace and socialist groups since the 1980s, attended the Florence ESF, and has more recently worked within the green movement. Dave is broadly more sympathetic to perspectives focussing on subaltern globalisations and international solidarities, while for Pete, climate change and resource constraints mean we need to take localisation more seriously.
20. Norberg 2003; Bhagwati 2004; Wolf 2005; Friedman 2006.

21. Lang and Hines 1993; Trainer 1995; Douthwaite 1996; Hines 2000; Norberg-Hodge 2001; Shuman 2001; Cavanagh and Mander 2004; Woodin and Lucas 2004; Scott Cato 2006.
22. Imbroscio 1997; DeFilippis 2004.
23. Wall 2005.
24. Shuman 2001, p 6.
25. Scott Cato 2006.
26. Cavanagh and Mander 2005.
27. ibid, p 105.
28. Norberg-Hodge 2001.
29. Chang 2003, 2007
30. Norberg-Hodge 1991; Bennholdt-Thommsen and Mies 1999; Shiva 2005.
31. Lang and Hines 1993, p 13.
32. Ritzer 2004.
33. Klein 2000.
34. Monbiot 2006; McKibben 2007; NEF 2007.
35. Blühdorn 2007.
36. Blühdorn 2007; Woodin and Lucas 2004, p 148.
37. Harvey 1989.
38. Trainer 1995, pp 56–111.
39. See: http://futurepositive.synearth.net/2003/01/21
40. Contra the assertion of Desai and Said 2001.
41. New Economics Foundation, quoted by Woodin and Lucas 2004, p 69.
42. Hines 2000, Woodin and Lucas 2004.
43. Gorz, quoted by Frankel 1984, p 59.
44. Bookchin 1995, p 237.
45. ibid, p 248, our emphasis.
46. Cavanagh and Mander 2005, pp 160–163.
47. Heinberg 2004.
48. Kovel 2007.
49. Wall 2005.
50. Cavanagh and Mander 2005.
51. Gibson-Graham 2006a; 2006b.
52. See Santos 2006c.
53. DeFilippis 2004, p 33.
54. ibid, p 35.
55. ibid, p 148.
56. Harman 2007.
57. For example, see: http://www.earthfirst.org.uk/leaveitintheground/ or www.planestupid.com.
58. Hopkins 2008.
59. Trapese 2008.
60. Holloway 2002.
61. Harvey 2001, pp 158–187. A similar argument is made by Hardt and Negri 2002.
62. Harman 2007.
63. Featherstone 2008; Massey 2005.

64. Martinez-Alier 2002.

65. Featherstone 2008.

66. http://www.stopesso.com/pdf/esso_caseagainst.pdf (Inactive April 2017).

67. Demeritt 2006.

68. Gandhi 1936, quoted by Lang and Hines 1993, p 28.

69. Bello 2002; Feffer 2002; Shiva 2005.

70. There is not the space here to engage with the important critiques of Gandhian politics for being hierarchical and marginalising significant forms of subaltern political
practice, see Chatterjee 1984, Guha 1997. For some of the tensions of the KRRS's
politics and their ambiguous relations to the uneven power relations of the villages
which they organise see Assadi 1995, Featherstone 2008, chapter 7.

71. Branford and Rocha 2002.

72. North 2007, pp 149–173.

73. Dinerstein 2007.

74. See: http://www.cafod.org.uk/honduras/looking-for-alternatives (Inactive April
2017).

75. Branford and Rocha 2002, pp 211–239; MST 2001; on MST more generally, see
Wolford 2004, 2005, Fernandes 2005.

76. Herman and Kuper 2003, pp 106–107.

77. Stédile 2007, p 198.

78. MST 2001.

79. Rocha 2002.

80. Rockett, cited in ibid.

81. Stédile 2007, p 214.

82. Osava 2001.

83. ibid; see also Stédile 2004, p 434.

84. See Massey 2005.

85. Bové and Dufour 2001, p 159; see also Massey 2005, pp 169–172.

OpenWord

Refounding Bolivia:
Exploring the Possibility and Paradox of a Social Movements State[1]
Guillermo Delgado-P

Introduction: A Moment of Rupture

By the year 2008, world news had announced the emergence of at least eight administrations in Latin America that claimed to belong to the New Left, or were associated with 'socialism'. These administrations of Argentina, Brazil, Bolivia, Chile, Ecuador, Nicaragua, Paraguay, Uruguay, and Venezuela are left-leaning, recognising that government should answer to demands posed by civil society and social movements (SM).[2] They have been elected to challenge and question key points, weakening the purpose of the ailing Washington Consensus policies of the 90s that called for the neoliberal regionalisation of economies through the privatisation of means of production, of which the most recent results are Costa Rica, Chile, and Peru (which have signed Free Trade Agreements [FTAs] with the US). In the Americas, 'free trade' has focussed on strengthening capital's bid, and is widely considered a means of neocolonisation. As new publics or new citizens emerged discontented with the Washington Consensus, new administrations arose and proposed renegotiating foreign debts with transnational and international banks such as the Inter-American Development Bank (IDB). A counterproposal to establish an alternative trade system under a Latin American rubric—the Bolivarian Alternative for Latin America (ALBA)—is now unfolding in the region.[3]

This essay attempts to give a historical background to the many recent changes that have occurred as a result of the strengthening of SM in Bolivia and the region—the most recent of which is the talk of withdrawal by Bolivia from the World Bank, the IMF, and the International Centre for the Settlement of Investment Disputes (ICSID), as mentioned by economist Alejandro Reuss[4]—and to critically discuss them.

In Latin America, the most visible effects of the Washington Consensus were increasing de-peasantisation, population displacement, and land privatisation. Applied in areas 'untapped' till then, privatisation formulas also affected natural resources such as water, oil, and fine woods, and biodiversity itself. Today, internal rural to urban migration has increased significantly, and it is thought that between 10–15 per cent of Latin American national populations are found other than in their places of origin.[5]. In this immediate past, the protests led by SM of mostly ethnic peoples in Bolivia—individuals and collectivities that claim a pre-Columbian heritage—were related to natural resources, transnational corporations, and a perception of depredation and dispossession by the powers that be, materialised in further privatisation and over-concentration of arable land in a few transnational hands. Naturally, large, tangible processes of exclusion generate communal mobilisations that question the role of the state, seen as shirking its regulatory responsibilities, answering only capital's bidding.

Looking at Bolivia today, I argue that neoliberalism weakened the already fragile social contract between the state and civil society here, creating a dangerous and defining rift. In 1987, Law 21060 introduced neoliberalism to Bolivia, calling for the privatisation of the means of production, while a new process of re-democratisation began, substituting the previous authoritarian regime. This approach was sanctified when the Bolivian Parliament Assembly approved a Law of Privatisation in 1994. In trying to redefine itself, the state offered, as a new development strategy, nine of its *departamentos* (or states) to promote autonomy from the central government. This however was not as an act of democratisation by promoting regional power but to privatise local natural resources. From the perspective of a private citizen, such laws suggested a new top-down restructuring and budget planning, closely related to the emergence of new, regional political elites. But, the outcomes were not viable, because of corruption, mismanagement, or simply a lack of private or state funds to support new regional projects. Private citizens remained observant of such developments, but were purposely marginalised as social actors.

By 1994, the Law of Popular Participation had, indeed, reduced the state's administrative presence by redistributing resources to regions and *departamentos*. This decentralisation encouraged *departamentos* to manage their own natural resources and enter neoliberal competition. However, what appeared as a solution to poverty soon collapsed in disillusion. In large sectors of society, young people found themselves only eking out livelihoods, and protests increased exponentially. Deteriorating social conditions and hardships both expanded and radicalised social movements during the first five years of this new century, as the gorge between haves and have-nots deepened, since neoliberalism responded only to the elite.

The last straw was the proposed privatisation of water and gas.[6] This motivated the simultaneous uprising of consumers across the country, ready to fight for the right to drink water.[7] In particular, social movements learned that Bechtel, a transnational corporation based in California, had agreed to take on the business of privatising water, and proposed to raise water bills by 400 per cent. Similarly, gas was to be privatised, and exported through Chile. Social movements, at this point, poured on to the streets to defend natural resources. The protest went beyond water or gas, and became a dispute over the functions of the state, about surplus, redistribution, and social reproduction. Bolivian social movements emerged from this battle as aggressive critics of neoliberalism and the Washington Consensus.

It is often said that Bolivia has been an unhappy country. Because it is economically poor, its inhabitants represent the raw confrontation of labour and capital. Now, the social movement and as militant expression of civil society's *fury* expressed in multiple street and road mobilisations pushed the state into a crisis, whereupon it abdicated. This abdication materialised in the ousting of two democratically elected administrations, those of Sanchez de Lozada in 2003, and of Carlos Mesa in 2005, each followed by the emergence of an interim government. Bolivians eventually elected President Evo Morales in December 2005.[8]

Here, we should understand social movements as expressions of civil society and democratisation that generated participation outside traditional channels such as political parties and established institutions. Social movements enact past repertoires of resistance, re-adapting them to their current conditions, reinforcing their new oppositional collectivities and identities. In Bolivia, coalitions of urban and rural cadres that emerged from NGOs, neighbourhood associations, student movements, and Indigenous-peasants' and workers' unions merged in street barricades. The *politicisation of fury* as a material expression of discontent overflowed the platforms and the leadership of traditional social movements. It expressed itself in the massive irruption of 'the popular', a multitudinous subject that instantly occupied the streets, reminiscent of Castoriadis' *magma*: "A magma is that from which one can extract (or in which one can construct) an indefinite number of assemblist organisations, but which can never be reconstituted (ideally) by an assemblist composition (finite or infinite) of these organisations".[9] The ousting of two presidents by sustained mobilisations of social movements constituted a conjunctural situation that galvanised large social sectors affecting all society. Thus, under state crisis, an assembly of assemblies articulated popular demands such that a self-organising culture of unions and street mobilisations gave corpus to the emergent social movement.

New Citizens, New Publics: The Emergence of Social Movements in Bolivia

In 1952, the then government of Bolivia enacted laws nationalising the tin mining industry (at the time, the only source of tin in the Western hemisphere); declared and realised partial agrarian reform; eliminated serfdom of Indigenous peoples; and offered nominal citizenship and voting rights to all Bolivians. This social revolution is all too little known.[10] However, although the 1952 reforms were inspired by revolutionary nationalism, in practice Bolivia did not modernise its vast countryside, inhabited by peoples of pre-Columbian heritage—largely the Aymara and the Quechua, along with smaller ethnicities. Although ethnic peoples constituted as much as 70 per cent of the national population in 2000, this demographic and social reality of Bolivia was not understood by the revolutionary nationalists of 1952, who imposed class-oriented peasant unions (and, later, militarisation) on these peoples as the only way to 'incorporate' ethnicities into the nation-state—and therefore, in reality, offered only the erasure of cultural diversity. This strategy was unsustainable, as the early revolutionary nationalists depended on the mono-production of tin mines and a very small urban and industrial sector, inadequate to realise large-scale modernisation. Mono-production (silver, rubber, tin ores, coca) during most of the twentieth century linked the nation-state to the world system, but it was hard for such a country to diversify its economy and to fully industrialise. On the other hand, although unions remain small entities today, it is amidst this early proletarian ethos that revolutionary thought was found. And, in the past, their strategic location made it possible for them to contest state and capital. Highly dependant on this work force, Bolivia had to answer their demands.

Today, Bolivia is among the poorest countries of South America and was, until recently, largely rural, with only a few cities with populations of more than one million (La Paz, Santa Cruz, and Cochabamba). Yet, Bolivia's land tenure systems have been extremely distorted; and national and international agencies have failed to offer reliable methods to account for land ownership. Such conditions constitute another variable that hints at, if not fully explains, the more recent mobilisation of rural social actors.

To compound this situation, in 1971, then under a military dictatorship, Bolivia was offered by its military government as a possible outlet to resettle and 'save' white South Africans affected by the dismantling of apartheid.[11] Fortunately, intervention by the international community quashed the racist proposal; however, a few foreigners took advantage of the 'cheap land sales' sponsored by a corrupt dictatorship that was indirectly involved in both land speculation and early, small-scale drug trafficking. Rural areas were affected by drug production during the 1970s and 1980s, when the García Mesa dictatorship was found dealing in cocaine.[12] In 1986, the tin market collapsed due to cheaper substitutes, expelling miners from their camps, dislocating their unions, and forcing them to migrate to cities and to coca-producing areas. In the 1990s, the US asked Bolivia to eradicate coca leaf plantations (*Erythroxylum coca*), incorrectly arguing that coca leaves are equivalent to cocaine.[13]

All this came to a head in the 1990s. This decade saw the demise of traditional political parties that had come to be seen, by young ethnic citizens, as no longer representing their demands and interests. This disillusionment with both the Old Left and the Old Right transformed into the emergence of the multitudes of social movements. Evo Morales—the President of Bolivia since 2006—is himself a leader of the very combative sector of *cocaleros* (coca leaf pickers) from the hotbed of a rural area of El Chapare and Yungas targeted by the failed war on drugs sponsored by the US throughout the last two decades of the twentieth century. *Cocaleros* are Indigenous Quechua and Aymara peoples who were forced to migrate due to severe drought conditions as early as the 1960s from the high Andes to the inter-mountain Yungas valleys to make a living; their first encounters with state violence involved their defence of their right to plant coca bushes to make a living. After the collapse of the tin mining industry in 1986, moreover, displaced miners joined them, and helped rural unionists strengthen their tactics. Throughout the 90s, the state, pressed by the US, declared a 'war on drugs' against them, while they answered the impudent violence of a state that did not offer them any other effective survival alternative.

Historically, it can be said that the last quarter of the twentieth century corresponds to a process of re-democratisation in Bolivia, after a dictatorship that lasted about eighteen years, from 1971 until 1988. It saw the emergence of ethnically oriented social movements overlapping the decline of working-class unionism, which had dominated political life in Bolivia for much of the twentieth century. This process took place in complex and paradoxical ways. Neoliberalism and privatisation acknowledged Bolivia as a pluricultural nation but, by doing so, and by the fact that the traditional unions alone were not able to respond to the challenge before them, they galvanised the emergence of new ethnic social movements. What Nash wrote about theorists can be argued as true of the situation that unfolded in Bolivia: "By drawing attention to the ethnic, gender, and racial composition of movements that were suppressed by those that gave priority to class position, new social movement theorists opened the stage of history to many actors".[14] In Bolivia however, and in this way overturning social movement theory itself, it has not been the social theorists who have done this, but the actors themselves who have opened the stage.

Until then, self-identity and ethnic identity in Bolivia were subsumed under a classist paradigm and under the organisational form of unionism, both in the mining industry and in rural areas. Urban working-class resistance personified the tensions between labour and capital, with the Cold War as the background. It was only in the last quarter of the twentieth century that a new wave of ethnic social movements emerged, demanding a say in the construction of the nation. Commenting on this, Pilar Domingo said: "The tortuous process of state-building in Bolivia has been neither even nor linear".[15] Thus, relevant ethnic social movements worked first on cultural retrieval, centring their activities in the Andean area where most of the Bolivian ethnic population lives, and where earlier forms of unionism had emerged and thus formed part of the repertoire of resistance.

As processes of ethnogenesis—the emergence of ethnic groups—solidified, the debate over gender issues entered public consciousness in the 1990s. NGOs emerged for the first time to accompany neoliberalism in 1986, because they were considered to be partners with business. The World Bank suggested that these NGOs implement social compensation policies. Although gender did not at first motivate the emergence of social movements per se, the re-democratisation of the state was accompanied by the emergence of NGOs, which worked towards institutionalising a Secretary of Gender that materialised in the early 1990s. Ethnic NGOs took advantage of the space offered by the state, and feminists also confronted the ethnic variable within gender, since a large proportion of ethnic NGOs were composed of women. This tension between ethnic social movements and gender demands, helped women organise as social movements, taking over public spaces and contributing to the emergence of a small but vocal group of anarchist feminists who struggled to make their voices heard.[16] Women had always participated in class-based unions, but as service sector workers, nurses, teachers, etc. But when feminist debates offered concepts to articulate women's political demands, NGOs assisted in strengthening women's rights as part of the re-democratisation and modernisation of the state.

Today, social movements in Bolivia are civil conglomerates that emerge from a combination of NGOs, ethnic associations, neighbourhood federations, rural and urban unions, students, and individuals. The ability of social movements to emerge as a 'movement of movements' relies on a purely conjunctural situation, in which their memory of dismemberment and resistance articulates their sense of re/membering an epic triumph. Thus, social movements are generational, which does not mean that a clear secession with the revolutionary and resistance repertoire of the past is an option. Indeed, the symbolic capital of the social movement revolutionary repertoire is constantly recuperated and recast. Undoubtedly, the epic social movement incursion in the first part of the 2000s has to do with the citizenry's increasing awareness about how natural resources were raffled by previous administrations at very low prices. Most would quickly assert that Bolivia's two ousted heads of state pilfered unabashedly, which led social movements to accept nothing short of 'direct democracy'. This social movement perception about the relevance of natural resources as commodities that should strengthen national coffers, and help pull the country out of poverty, has been in the minds of young impoverished generations that form the multitude of such movement.

The fact that 'one of theirs' is at the helm of the state today means that social movements are accommodated and free to express their demands. One can go further and state that, under the Morales administration, social movements have entered the space of renegotiation and proposal. Discontented social movements whose demands have not yet been fulfilled under Morales speak to the fact that social movements, largely, see themselves supporting a slow but sure process of redefinition as a priority that requires postponing specific demands where, ultimately, the stake is to ensure that Bolivia is refounded. This refounding is related to the historical perception that a small 'white' elite has governed the country and that, today, its political class needs to represent the rest of the country.

However, while Bolivia is largely ethnic, historically speaking a very reduced 'white' elite has always controlled the government—consciously subverting the possibility for other ethnicities to participate under equal conditions. Evo Morales represents such change. But the shift is not easy, as we are witnessing the substitution of one class by another. Privilege is hard to let go and 'whites' have been troubled by the changes taking place, to say the least.

As 'white' class privilege has been challenged over this past period however, the reaction of these people has verged on desperation. Violence has become a way of performing their anger and isolation—with impunity. The deepening racial hate and bigotry against ethnic populations represents the true face of the right that, despite democratic practice, resorts to violence when its class and racial privilege is eroded. Thus, their militant resistance, linked to the bigotry of their fascist discourse, originates in their self-hate and their ontological insecurity—since they cannot be accounted for as 'true Europeans'—and they brandish a strange construction of racial purity reminiscent of phrenologists of the 1850s. In this world, the Indigenous population is blamed for backwardness, whereas the 'white' population is said to have brought about 'modernisation', 'progress', and 'globalisation'.

This is especially strong in the Media Luna *departamentos*, in the eastern part of the country, where the landed elites and entrepreneurs have retrieved a racist discourse of fascism and ethnic cleansing. There is even an isolated right wing in this region, the *grupos de choque*, a sort of opportunist paramilitary corps, which represents an extreme reaction and should be considered a sad historical aberration.

Not all *departamentos* in Bolivia have equal access to natural resources. In the Bolivian Amazon, and especially in the Media Luna *departamentos* there, 90 per cent of the land is 'owned' by 10 per cent of the families, though their 'estate titles' lack proper registration and are hard to locate in the municipal records office because they have been intentionally distorted.[17] In such areas, some *departamentos* carried out partial modernisation projects (by accepting foreign investments, mostly franchises), but others have remained marginal in their ability to profit from a neoliberal arrangement where impoverished municipalities received only 20 per cent of central government monies.[18] The result was polarisation. Especially given the legacy of the 1994 Law of Popular Participation, the rich *departamentos* in the Media Luna were interested in selling 'their' natural resources to foreign investors, whereas poorer *departamentos* in the west were forced to ask for central state assistance. This commodification of natural resources and the dispossession it brings inhibited the dreams of new generations, and created a socio-cultural rift. In the Media Luna, it is struggles over land and control over strategic natural resources that are the key issues. It is in the Media Luna, in pockets of cosmetic neoliberal enterprise, that the new urban gentrification has imitated the global franchised simulacrum known as 'the neoliberal barrio'.

These historical antecedents and socio-economic realities help us understand the emergence of Bolivia's social movements, civil society, and politics. Under neoliberal regimes, the state tried to redefine itself by encouraging civil society's participation. Today, by pursuing a politics of national integration, the state has declared Bolivia to be a pluricultural nation—basically a new label to deflate the tension caused by the social exclusion of large ethnic populations.[19] It has acknowledged the fact that all participating cultures of Bolivia should be seen as having the same contributing responsibility to the larger project of nation building. But this is a complex challenge. At first, Indigenous and young people liked the idea, because their previously ignored cultural particularities were recognised as integral to the nation. Pluriculturalism strengthened ethnic pride. But the movements soon discovered that pluriculturalism was an empty signifier; and, as a result, pluriculturalism has more recently been further politicised by the movements it produced.

The Struggle to Democratise Democracy

By December 2005, the electorate in Bolivia gained the upper hand by electing one of its own, in part as a consequence of greatly surpassing previous electoral participation rates that had dropped to elemental figures. This majority of young activists can be considered 'new citizens' in a country that had an estimated population of 9.2 million in 2005. Throughout 2007, by retaking authority over state property and renationalising natural resources (at least on paper), the new government of Bolivia dismantled neoliberal arrangements, and the administration of Evo Morales, an ethnic Aymara, worked to grant the state the role it once played. The strategy is portrayed by some as being only a populist measure; but it needs to be understood that he is not acting by himself but responding to a new majority.

A closer look at this multitude[20] helps understand recent activism. As we have seen, these 'new citizens' have provoked political upheavals that have successfully ousted two Bolivian presidents and elected the world's first Indigenous person as president. Their self-valorisation and autonomy shaped the space for ethnicity-based communal dissatisfaction with status quo politics. As tensions built, these new citizens and publics have shaped very strong grassroots social movements, with the capacity to paralyse the country. The political scientist Raúl Prada Alcoreza considers these social movements "molecular",[21] because as nuclei of sorts they reproduce a multiplicity of social movements, each with its own sense of how the country should regard integration into an increasingly globalised world. Such social movements are horizontal 'coalitions' that mix class, gender, and ethnicity. They are historical products of a nation struggling to acquire a sense of self. Marxism informed their early industrial unions; ethnicity and gender triggered the emergence of excluded and culturally defined communities; and environmentalism as a critique of dispossession and extractive capitalism reinforced the stands of social movements on the meaning of democracy, social justice, citizenship, and the defence of natural resources.

Social movements thus acquired a clear sense of their decentralised coordination and non-hierarchical consensus—whether as local, rural, urban, or transnational activists or as intercommunicated alterglobalists. This image perhaps gives the sense of a nation that is fully politicised as it expresses itself through complex nuclei of organised entities at all levels. In a sense, one could also say that by challenging the nature of the old state, these social movements keep a sharp eye on corruption, which is an ethical position that so far has provided such social movements with the strength and moral authority needed to intervene and to reinvent their nation. In turn, this challenge galvanised them to demand a new constitution, one that reconceptualised the state.

This process of the redefinition of the Constitution has not been easy, however, since it polarised society. The Constituent Assembly was transformed into an arena where all the social tensions of the country came to be confronted. Although representatives of social movements elected as constituents represented the complex society that Bolivia is, previous privileged sectors also fought for their rights, creating an image of impasse that was only later diffused.

What happened in Bolivia has led to the emergence of an idea that what has taken shape is "a government of social movement", led by Evo Morales. This presents important questions for the public interested in understanding how social movements reached the government itself—and are, arguably, heading the state; and how what has been labelled a 'social movement state' legitimises its actions by carrying out the goal of instituting a new Constituent Assembly (CA). Is this not a contradiction in terms? Although there are cases of social movements taking over the state (for instance, the PT in Brazil), in Bolivia there was talk that social movements once in power were not social movements anymore. And once their leaders were elected to become constituents of a new Constituent Assembly, those that remained as militants of social movements themselves, thought that newly elected leaders were compromising radical positions.

The term 'government of social movements' was in fact coined by the press because of the role social movements played in electing Evo Morales and because of the presence of social movements in the state today. Several members of the administration have roots in social movements. Some have remained, others have gone back to their organisations, yet others have ceded their leadership to new appointees.[22] Our understanding of social movements is further provoked by the fact that even the Bolivian state sees itself as a 'social movements' state'. According to Vice President Alvaro García Linera, "FEJUVE [the Federation of Neighbourhood Councils] is the country's strongest social movement, an instrument of national and state demands, which has led it to envisage political state power as a means of satisfying these demands. This points to the emergence of a new political system and a new economic regime".[23] New concepts are thus being articulated. For example, the notions of 'popular sovereignty', 'democratic revolution', and 'constituting power' (*poder constituyente*)—where the latter term seems to be a notion that implies an active, ongoing, formative process that indirectly institutionalises change.[24]

In the backdrop of this discussion we must introduce the fact that the emergence of social movements has much to do with how traditional political parties lost touch with their constituencies. FEJUVE, as a social movement, is a coalition of new Indigenous urban residents who have populated a new city in Bolivia, El Alto. This city was formed precisely when neoliberalism began affecting the welfare of rural populations who, lacking alternatives, migrated to cities like El Alto, which is now an activists' base. Like FEJUVE, other social movements, have also merged and coordinated their actions. They now constitute an array of active organisations constantly evaluating the way the state affects them, although affecting the state is also their objective.

By March 2006, the Morales government approved and promulgated a 'Special Law to Convene a Constituent Assembly'. Issuing this new foundational document should be seen as a triumph of the social movements, since their democratic vocation is encapsulated in their ability to press for real change at the state level. Between August 2006 and December 2007, the CA wrote a new Constitution, which has been approved by a majority of votes in February of 2008 and is now effectively the new foundational document that is the New Constitution of Bolivia.[25] By and large, the constituents who played leading roles in drafting this document originated in social movements, and it has been in the Assembly that class, ethnic, and gender interests have clashed, repeatedly. It is here that social movement representatives have struggled with conservative, anti-Morales voices in the ('white') minority. The sector that will potentially be most affected by the new Constitution is the Media Luna, where the Evo Morales administration will allocate resources for the promotion of alternative projects of development, especially in impoverished areas where the state has never asserted itself (or where, rather, the past dictatorship granted 'special economic arrangements' that explain the accumulation of wealth in the area).

Parallel to the CA, the Morales administration also enacted an agrarian reform law and nationalised the gas and oil industry to reinvest revenues in the country's well-being. The basic redistributive land reform proposed by Morales is, definitively, a call to activate growth and improve equity. Land redistribution will affect about 20 million hectares over the next five years, effectively ending in 2010 when, the new constitution will continue restricting the extension of land tenure to no larger than 10,000 hectares per unit. These structural changes will affect the privileged social classes, now dispossessed of influence and power but not inert, even as the Morales administration seeks sustenance from the social movements. Because of this not-so-silent revolution,[26] some describe the process as the Third Bolivian Revolution. In this process, the nation-state has revealed the depth of its racial and class divisions; and the right has reacted to the changes taking place by offering violence with impunity, and with its representatives characterising their interventions by regionalising debates.

Regionalisation is only exacerbated by neoliberalism, but it also makes reference to the convoluted aspect of the Bolivian nation-state. Here, regionalisation is stressed by *departamentos*, as each claims the possession of natural resources as its means to secure revenues. For the Media Luna, the results of the CA transform themselves in struggles for autonomy but, following the new definition of the nation-state, areas with access to strategic natural resources (read: gas) must remain under state jurisdiction.[27] The right's goal is to portray local autonomy as secession, use comparative advantages, and disregard the centrality of the state. The fragmentation of the nation into neo-regions could further marginalise impoverished *departamentos*. The country would be split in two, with one claiming rights over highly profitable lands and gas reserves (amounting to 53.4 trillion cubic feet), and the other defending a reformed state that should assert itself over a sovereign nation, debating how to best manage 'pro-autonomy regions' without losing taxation rights and / or ownership of natural resources, or threatening the nation's integrity.

But the issue is also the canny ability of social movements to constitute themselves in multitudes and vice-versa. Just as these issues of natural resources prompted the democratic election of Evo Morales, social movements today consider his administration as defending Bolivia's sovereignty. Commenting on the intricacies of social change, Vice President Alvaro García Linera—himself an activist and social theorist by background—has said that social movements, once 'in power', pose deep questions regarding the generation of leadership.[28] This is very necessary self-criticism, because after the democratic takeover by Morales, social movements have become active members within the structure of the modern state through the CA, and, by virtue of this new arrangement, SM movement leaders have also left their movements, creating a vacuum. Civil society now needs to be regenerated.

By managing national natural resources wisely, Morales foresees a redefined state playing a better regulatory role. The reader may wonder why Morales keeps a strong and vital linkage with social movements, or how such linkages operate. Morales is the first ethnic Aymara to be elected President since Bolivia's independence in 1825. Yet, his administration has been able to bring back a popular national discourse as a way to accomplish a nation-state where the ethnic is only one component amidst several. Like Morales himself, not a few of his secretaries and undersecretaries originate in the social movements and several continue to maintain relations with their own organisations. A radical change is today being enacted in Bolivia, a situation in which social movements, through their leaders, influential now at the state level, are implementing concrete changes to benefit the population. Yet, some of the social movement leadership in positions of state administration have been challenged because of their lack of bureaucratic expertise; a few have been fired due to corruption charges, while some are back to the rank-and-file.

This coupling of militancy and appointments to the bureaucracy explains an active come-and-go, but also encourages further participation from SM themselves. For example, SM candidates who weren't elected to the CA prompted the popular organising of a parallel Assembly of social movements, where other non-elected representatives aired their own proposals, or criticised the debates of the CA. Bolivian social movements leaderships have also established transnational networks and have been active participants in several editions of the World Social Forum (WSF).

In sum, and in the context of public life, social movements began a process of political conscientisation and militancy, first in reaction to state violence and then to the 'democratic neoliberalism' that had been imposed on them. Simultaneously, for the first time, the acknowledgement of gender, sexuality, and racial discrimination entered the public space along with the ability of movements to retrieve the politics of memory. Young Indigenous people confronted the classist conservatism of Bolivian society. World events also touched the hearts and minds of young people: The collapse of the Berlin Wall in 1989, the fading of the Soviet Union in 1991, and the collapse of real socialism, and also the Zapatista uprising in Mexico in 1994, the large marches of ethnic and gay people demanding their rights, the talking back of 'ethnic minorities' in the developed world, the challenge to the 'Quincentenary celebration of 1492' dealing with the so-called 'Discovery of the Americas', a historic event that persists in the memory of Indigenous peoples in the Americas; and, of course, 9/11 and its aftermath, along with the perception that 'democracy' has been curtailed at the very heart of a country that liked to see itself as its quintessential example.

This account of recent processes in Bolivia also poses a question regarding the issue of social movements in the post-Washington Consensus. The CA was democratically elected in 2006. Its mandate has been to write a more inclusive document, acknowledging Bolivia's pluricultural nature. The document has been prepared, and many social movement leaders have signed it.[29] Rewriting the Constitution has been a major challenge, lending credibility to the concept of 'practicing participatory democracy'. In a sense, neoliberalism itself has been challenged and, by rejecting defects of the past, 'a government of social movements' has elaborated a new Constitution to re-invent the nation-state.

For the nation-state to be refounded and redesigned, representatives of social movements in state functions are in an ideal position to debate and challenge previous 'elite owners' of the state apparatus. But, to do so, they are also asserting and deploying the politics of ethnicity and singular identity, and thereby contradicting the principle and supremacy of plurinationality. We must accept that Bolivia is caught in a very real challenge, created by its own democratic revolution. Acknowledging ethnicity does not mean eliminating racism, just as acknowledging gender and sexuality does not make Bolivia a feminist nation.[30] The reality is that a colonial background shapes Bolivia's character and, in a sense, decolonisation means redefining the state.

'*Somos Más*' ('We Are the Majority') Democracy

Bolivia is at a crossroads. Seen from the outside, capitalism needs a functional, 'stable' nation linked to the world system, even if it gains little from it. After the Morales administration nationalised the oil and gas industries and sought better exchange terms, Bolivia was, for the first time, able to obtain concrete gains. So it seems that, despite a problematic and uneven—let's say 'colonial'—relationship with the powers that be, Morales has been able to extract tangible gains for the national coffers. But even his sharpest critics, see his concession and compromise as propelling him towards 'saving the old state' and giving in to the demands of the old ruling class.[31] And his vice president García Linera remains a harsh critic of the Media Luna, a seceding regional block, troubled by its inability to conceptualise a new form of nation-state integration. Both Morales and García Linera analyse the voices of social movements and find themselves immersed in them, carrying on the not so easy task of 'democratising democracy', where one specific objective is to impede the return of prebendal and patrimonial arrangements.

These new processes are calling for meticulous discussions on the meaning of democracy in Bolivia. Assuming that consensus in democratic discussions is needed, what exactly does a new 'social pact' mean? The lesson of Bolivian social movements seems to be that tensions and uncertainties in governmentality are being clarified for the first time. In a sense, the reality of having social movements in government has triggered the need to focus on 'ethnic, class, and gender inclusiveness', on 're-territorialisation', on 'wealth redistribution', and on governmentality itself. This is all the more so given that "The human development gap between the richest and poorest departments in Bolivia will increase rather than decrease until 2015".[32] So, rather than providing answers, the Bolivian case illustrates the undoing of misleading neoliberalism. The radicalisation of democratic practices—what I term 'democratising democracy'—and the implementation of a CA that proposes reorganising the territorial-national conceptualisation by probing the meaning and viability of notions like 'autonomy' without secession, and 'regionalisation' without disintegration, should aid in 'reinventing the Bolivian state'. As García Linera has put it, "To the extent that there exists a strong culture of local self-government, these logics of power and assembly-based democracy can be projected onto the state-wide or national level".[33]

We are witnessing a unique process unfolding in front of our very eyes. If all social movement intentions coincide in willingness, we will indeed witness the refounding of a republic and a social revolution that "hopefully will not be raffled as it previously was, in 1952".[34] However, the emergence of the right, concomitant with the slow reaction of legal courts to their violence, will further radicalise social movements which, in times of tension, will support Morales disregarding their own internal divisions.

In the nineteenth and twentieth centuries, the last words of some Indigenous leaders who were to be executed for their resistance were "We will come back in our thousands". Today, we are faced with a situation where Indigenous social movements in Bolivia recall these words and memory to instil courage and a sense of own history. The phrase today is "*somos más*" ('we are the majority'), and they believe that the epic struggle they are today engaged in recalls their past, but where they are now present in their thousands.

The debate in Bolivia also has a lot to do with the blow that globalisation inflicts on small, peripheral countries—but where, paradoxically, resistance of epic dimensions can unexpectedly leap on to the stage of history. Throughout this last decade, and specifically due to the emergence of the World Social Forum as a platform, a more interconnected Bolivian social movement has digested the analytical tools offered by WSF forces that stress commonalities in a global struggle for social justice. Leaders are, as Hardt observes, "swept up in the multitude, which is capable of transforming all fixed and centralised elements into so many more nodes in its indefinitely expansive network".[35]

The WSF has offered social movement leaders analytical categories to propose notions of global justice. Mainly, it has permitted social movements to translate and 'glocalise' their agenda, placing the defence of natural resources as part of the alternative, 'glocal' platform. Young Bolivian social movement leaders have been exposed to the dynamics of global circuits of dissent, and previously isolated movements have come to see themselves, for the first time, as part of a complex network of critical activists that re-centre alternative agendas in which water, gas, oil, biodiversity, land, gender rights, and hope galvanise their igneous social consciousness radicalising democracy itself. The ability of Bolivian social movements to propose and to generate viable agendas will be watched closely in the forthcoming Belém Forum in Brazil in January 2009, where concrete praxis

Refounding Bolivia | 571

will surely inform sharper global coordination and action, rather than just local protest. As some say, *Protesta con propuesta:* Protest and propose!

Conclusions

In this essay I have tried to draw out the complexity of social change in Bolivia and the idea, and seeming paradox, of social movement as the refoundation of a state. My intention has been to stress the relevance of historical antecedents as ways to understand the motives, reasons, and inspirations of social movements. The movements that have emerged in Bolivia with such fury and incivility have been shaped by a historical repertoire of resistance, a layered social history attached to the epics of social movements that have been affected by waves of historical events and by 'decolonisation'.

At the centre of these social movements we find younger generations of Indigenous peoples. It is they, having suffered persistent exclusion from public life, who have become militants of newly emergent political parties such as *Movimiento al Socialismo* ('Movement toward Socialism', MAS), Morales's astute creation.

Having brought exclusionary politics to the fore, globalisation and neoliberalism can be considered directly responsible for provoking social upheavals and discontent. Yet, they have also led to the emergence of a new movement, a conjunction of different forms of historical inequality (class, ethnic, gender) that are competing with each other.[36] Social movements that pushed for the undoing of neoliberalism now hold a clear challenge in their hands.

Refounding a nation is not painless, however. Elite classes affected by the challenge to neoliberalism are now on the offensive. In their aggressive counter-attack, fascism and ethnic cleansing are celebrated as deeds, often with impunity. This racialised script of Media Luna neoliberal oligarchy obstructs Bolivia's attempt to redefine itself. Their obstinacy has delayed the referendum needed to adopt the new Constitution.

Will Bolivia be able to redefine its nation-state, making it as inclusive and equal as possible? Brought about by localised interests, will the neo-regionalist fragmentation answer only to external economic demands? Will social movements of new generations be able to offer viable proposals for a new process of national integration? It is clear that democracy has been radicalised in Bolivia; the nation has never been so close to it: "Real democracy would presuppose that the *demos* be constituted as a subject present to itself across the whole surface of the social body".[37]

References

Raúl Barrios Morón and Silvia Rivera Cusicanqui, 1993—*Violencias Encubiertas en Bolivia* ['Covert violence in Bolivia', in Spanish], La Paz: CIPCA/Aruwiyiri

Alejandro I. Canales, ed, 2006—*Panorama actual de las migraciones en América Latina* ['Current overview of migrations in Latin America', in Spanish]. Zapopan, Mexico: Universidad de Guadalajara, Asociación Latinoamericana de Población

Cornelius Castoriadis, 1977—'Ontology and the Political Project', in Dick Howard, ed, 1977—*The Marxian Legacy* (New York: Urizen Books), pp 262–301

Manuel de la Fuente, 2001—*Participación Popular y Desarrollo Local. La Situación de los Municipios Rurales de Cochabamba y Chuquisaca* ['Popular Participation and Local Development: The Status of Rural Municipalities of Cochabamba and Chuquisaca', in Spanish] (Cochabamba: EDOBOL), pp 11–35

Guillermo Delgado-P, 1994—'Indigenous Contestation and Ecological Plundering: Lumber Companies and Ranchers Challenged in Bolivia', in *First Nations, Pueblos Originarios*. Davis, CA: Occasional Papers of the Native American Organized Research Program (NAORP), pp 1–14

Pilar Domingo, 2003—'Revolution and the Unfinished Business of Nation and State-Building', in Merilee S Grindle and Pilar Domingo, eds, 2003—*Proclaiming Revolution: Bolivia in Comparative Perspective* (London: Harvard University Press), pp 364–379

James Dunkerley, 2007—'Evo Morales, the "Two Bolivias", and the Third Bolivian Revolution', in *Journal of Latin American Studies*, vol 39, pp 133–166

Maria Galindo, 2006—'*Indias, putas y lesbianas, juntas, revueltas y hermanadas. Un libro sobre Mujeres Creando*' ['Indians, whores, and lesbians, juntas, riots, and sisters: Creating a Book on Women', in Spanish], in E Monasterios-P, ed, 2006—*No pudieron con Nosotras. El desafío del feminismo autónomo de Mujeres Creando* ['We were unable to, ourselves: The challenge of building an autonomist feminism', in Spanish] (La Paz: Plural), pp 27–59

Alvaro García-Linera, 2004a—'*La Sublevación Indígena popular en Bolivia*' ["The Indigenous Popular Revolt in Bolivia', in Spanish], in *Revista Chiapas*, vol 16, pp 125–142

Alvaro García-Linera, 2004b—'The Multitude', in Oscar Olivera and Tom Lewis, eds, 2004—*¡Cochabamba!: Water War in Bolivia* (Cambridge, MA: South End Press), pp 65–86

Alvaro García-Linera, 2005—'The Indigenous Movements in Bolivia', in *DEP: Diplomacy, Strategy, and Politics*, April–June 2005, p 18

Latin American Bureau (LAB), 1980—*Bolivia: Coup d'Etat*. London: LAB

Jean-Pierre Lavaud, 1981—'*Bolivie: Le Retour des Militaires*' ['Bolivia: The Return of the Military', in French], in *Problèmes D'Amérique Latine*, vol 62 no 4, pp 79–109

Norman Lewis, 1978—*Eastern Bolivia: The White Promised Land*. Copenhagen: IWGIA Document 31

R S Carlos Milani and Ruthy Nadia Laniado, 2006—'Transnational Social Movements and the Globalisation Agenda: A Methodological Approach Based on the Analysis of the World Social Forum', Working Paper vol 5, Rio de Janeiro: The Edelstein Center for Social Research

George Gray Molina, 2008—'Bolivia's Long and Winding Road', Interamerican Dialogue, Andean Working Paper

June Nash, ed, 2005—*Social Movements: An Anthropological Reader*. Malden, MA: Blackwell Publishing

Julieta Paredes, 2006—'*Para que el sol vuelva a calentar*' ['For the sun returns to heat', in Spanish], in E. Monasterios, ed, 2006—*No pudieron con nosotras. El desafío del feminismo autónomo de Mujeres Creando* ['They were unable to defeat us: The challenge of the autonomist feminism of *Mujeres Creando* ('Women Creating')', in Spanish] (La Paz: Plural), pp 61–75

Raúl Prada Alcoreza, 2005—'La Batalla del Agua en El Alto y el Conflicto de los Carburantes en Santa Cruz' ['The Battle of Water in El Alto and the Conflict over Fuel in Santa Cruz', in Spanish], in *Bolivian Studies Journal*, vol 5 no 1, March 2005

Raúl Prada Alcoreza, 2006—*Genealogía del poder* ['The Genealogy of power', in Spanish]. La Paz: Pisteuma

Pablo Mamani Ramírez, 2007—'Bolivia antes de Evo Morales. Fractura del estado colonial y poder de los microgobiernos indígenas' ['Bolivia before Evo Morales: Fracture of the colonial state and power of the indigenous microgovernments', in Spanish], in *Bolivian Studies Journal*, vol 7 no 1, September–October 2007, at https://www.bolivianstudies.org/revista/7.1/7.1.003.pdf (Accessed April 2017)

Jacques Ranciere, 1995—*On the Shores of Politics*. London: Verso

Alejandro Reuss, 2007—'Anti-Neoliberal Backlash: Leaving the World Bank and IMF Behind', in *NACLA (North American Congress on Latin America)*, July–August 2007, p 3

Gregorio Selser, 1982—*Bolivia: El Cuartelazo de los Cocadólares* ['A Coca-dollars Coup d'Etat', in Spanish]. Coyoacán, México: Mex-Sur

Luis Tapia, 2007—'El triple descentramiento. Igualdad y cogobierno en Bolivia', in K Monasterios, Pablo Stefanoni, et al, eds, 2007—*Reinventando la nación en Bolivia. Movimientos Sociales, Estado y Postcolonialidad* ['Reinventing the Nation in Bolivia: Social Movements, The State, and Postcolonialism', in Spanish] (La Paz: Plural/Clacso), pp 47–69

Graham Thiele, 1995—'The Displacement of Peasant Settlers in the Amazon: The Case of Santa Cruz, Bolivia', in *Human Organization*, vol 54 no 3, pp 273–282

WOLA (Washington Office on Latin America), 1991—*Clear and Present Dangers: The US Military and the War on Drugs in the Andes*. Washington, DC: WOLA

René Zavaleta Mercado, ed, 1983—*Bolivia Hoy* ['Bolivia Today', in Spanish]. México: Siglo XXI

Notes

1. Ed: This essay was written during 2007–8 and finalised in 2009; a good deal has happened in Bolivia since then, but in our understanding the developments in fact only elaborate and illustrate the discussion here, and the essential focus of this essay remains as valid now as then.

2. 'New Left' as a term originates with the 1989 events that emerged after the collapse of the Soviet block and the Berlin Wall, but also because it opts to consider a post-ideological civil society where gender, race, ethnicity, and environmental issues are seen as interacting in a new cycle of struggles.

    Ed: The above is the author's take on the term 'New Left'. In other parts of the world, though, the term came into use in the 1960s, such as the founding of the

New Left Review in Britain in 1960. With thanks to friends at PM Press for pointing this out.

3. Ed: As mentioned in endnote 1, this essay was written in 2008–9. ALBA itself was formed in 2004, by Venezuela and Cuba; Bolivia joined in 2006, Nicaragua in 2007, and Ecuador in 2009, and in October 2009 leaders from ALBA agreed during a summit in Bolivia on the creation of a regional currency.

4. Reuss 2007, p 3.

5. Canales 2006.

6. Prada Alcoreza 2005.

7. Until the crisis, citizens had paid the state for their water supply.

8. Morales won 53.7 per cent of the vote, the highest ever in Bolivia's republican life.

9. Castoriadis 1977, p 297.

10. Grindle and Domingo 2003; Zavaleta Mercado 1983.

11. Lewis 1978.

12. Selser 1982, pp 110, 169; WOLA 1991.

13. Coca is only the raw material that after convoluted and tedious steps, is processed into cocaine. Processing it into cocaine, however, became a specialized labour arrangement, and by the year 2000 it involved major players, consumers in the developed world as well as producers scattered throughout Latin America.

14. Nash 2005, p 10.

15. Domingo 2003, p 367.

16. Galindo 2007.

17. The *New York Times* described it as follows: *"land titles are of murky provenance"* (Romero 2006, p A3; also Paredes Mallea 2003; Delgado-P 1994; Thiele 1995).

18. de la Fuente 2001, pp 13–34.

19. The official name of the country is the 'Plurinational State of Bolivia'.

20. Alvaro Garcia Linera has defined 'the multitude' as "a block of collective action through which the subaltern classes give rise to autonomous, organized structures in relation to hegemonic discursive and symbolic structures". (Garcia Linera 2004, p 85.)

21. Prada Alcoreza 2006, pp 131–143.

22. The only exception is Oscar Olivera, a factory worker and union organizer, who led the so-called 'Water Wars' in Cochabamba (2000). Olivera has opted to remain a movement activist, and often evaluates Morales on his actions.

23. García-Linera 2005, p 18.

24. Prada Alcoreza 2006, p 49–60.

25. Ed. This essay was finalised in 2008–9. A draft constitution was approved on November 24 2007, but only following intense conflict in the country including threats of secession by the eastern part of the country. In February 2008, the Constituent Assembly submitted the final version and a referendum approved its content in the same month.

26. Dunkerley 2007, p 146; Fuentes 2007, p 95.

27. Gas reserves in Bolivia are the second largest in Abya Yala (South America), after Venezuela.

28. Interview, Montreal, September 6 2007.

29. Ed: The new Constitution of Bolivia came into effect on February 7 2009, when it was promulgated by *President Evo Morales* after being approved in a *referendum*

with 90.24 per cent participation. The referendum was held on January 25 2009, and the constitution was approved by 61.43 per cent of voters (http://en.wikipedia.org/wiki/Constitution_of_Bolivia).

30. Galindo 2006, pp 41–44; Paredes 2006, pp 109–111.
31. Mamani-Ramírez 2007.
32. Molina 2008, p 12.
33. García-Linera 2004b, p 82.
34. Jesús Urzagasti, personal communication, La Paz, December 2006.
35. Hardt 2004, p 236.
36. Tapia 2007, p 69.
37. Rancière 1995.

OpenWord

Forward Dreaming:
Zapatismo and the Radical Imagination
Alex Khasnabish

*We continue to be in the way. What the theorists of neoliberalism tell us is false:
that everything is under control, including everything that isn't under control.*

*We are not a safety valve for the rebellion that could destabilize neoliberal-
ism. It is false that our rebel existence legitimizes Power. Power fears us. That is
why it pursues us and fences us in. That is why it jails and kills us. In reality, we
are the possibility that can defeat it and make it disappear.*
—Subcomandante Marcos[1]

Incubating Futures

The date is January 1 1994 and the message from the far southeast of Mexico is
clear: ¡Ya basta!—enough is enough! As the new year begins, an indigenous insurgent army calling itself the Zapatista Army of National Liberation (*Ejército Zapatista
de Liberación Nacional*, EZLN) warns that the age of global neoliberal capitalism
isn't the 'end of history', it's the Fourth World War.[2] In Canada, the United States,
and Mexico, political and economic elites celebrate the start of the North American
Free Trade Agreement (NAFTA). In the far southeast of Mexico, some 5000 EZLN
guerrillas—almost exclusively indigenous Mayan young men and women—emerge
from the highlands and jungle of the state of Chiapas and declare war on Mexican
President Carlos Salinas de Gortari and the Mexican Federal Army, while condemning NAFTA as a 'death sentence' to indigenous peoples. This insurgent force is the
product of ten years of clandestine organising in some of the poorest, most repressed,
and most remote communities in Mexico and it is also a manifestation of the more
than 500 year trajectory of indigenous resistance to colonialism, exploitation, racism, and genocide. Not just that—the Zapatistas will also become a vital element in a
new trajectory of resistance and alternative-building on a transnational scale marked
by a directly democratic, anti-capitalist, inclusive, and autonomist spirit.

The resonance the Zapatista struggle achieved amongst activists transnationally serves broadly as the frame of this paper. The reasons for and consequences of this resonance have been profound and unpredictable but I will not
reiterate that analysis here. Instead, my purpose is to explore the relationship
between Zapatismo as a new radical imagination of political possibility and the
socio-political action it has inspired. More broadly, this analysis is engaged in a
larger debate: What is the relationship between radical social change projects and

imaginaries of radically alternative social worlds? Is there a link between partic- ularly resonant radical imaginations and durable, resilient, and powerful social movements on the ground? If so, how can those of us engaged in social change projects and the creation of knowledge for and about them—particularly in the Global North where mass radicalised movements are conspicuous by their ab- sence and political inertia continues to hold sway—understand and make better use of this relationship to move out of the shadow of past failures and into a space where the possibility of things being different can be taken seriously once again?[3]

What do I mean by 'radical imagination'? My use of the term shares an af- finity with critical theorist Susan Buck-Morss's use of the 'political imaginary', which she describes as a "topographical concept ... not a political *logic* but a po- litical *landscape*, a concrete visual field in which political actors are positioned".[4] Imagination is of course implicated in all that we do as social beings; indeed, it is the capacity through which we reflect upon what was, understand what is, and extrapolate what might be. The radical imagination is thus the space within which the hope that things might be otherwise is incubated before it comes to animate radical action toward social change. Utopian Marxist theorist Ernst Bloch has called this kind of anticipatory cognition a "forward dream".[5] This anticipatory cognition—what I call the radical imagination—is much more than mere fantasy or escapism, precisely because lived realities are neither closed nor static, their futures are still very much 'up for grabs' and open to a multitude of possibilities. Because it is anticipatory and, at least potentially, unbounded, the imagination is thus the terrain for the cultivation of radical possibilities. Rather than being restricted to what is or what was, the imagination is a space where we play with the possibilities of what might be. In this piece I do not pretend to offer definitive answers to the questions I pose above; but I aim to shed critical illumination upon the terrain of radical imagination and its capacity—or lack thereof—to generate powerful movement toward social change.

The analysis presented here draws upon a year of interviews, fieldwork, and participant observation between September 2003 and October 2004 with al- ter-globalisation, anti-capitalist, and social justice activists in Canada, the United States, and Mexico. These activists have all experienced what I have referred to elsewhere as the resonance of Zapatismo.[6] Rather than simply importing the model of the Zapatistas' struggle, activists in other places in the north of the Americas have sought to translate this resonance in ways that make sense within their own contexts. The analysis I present here focuses upon two examples of radical rather than reformist manifestations of this resonance: Peoples' Global Action and Big Noise Tactical. While resonance and its consequences have been produced in part by physical encounters between the Zapatistas and a diversity of collectives and individuals, more frequently it has been constituted through an engagement with Zapatismo as a radical political imagination communicated via the writings of EZLN spokesperson Subcomandante Marcos, 'reality tours' and solidarity caravans to Zapatista territory, activist websites, DVDs, and CDs, as well as more conventional media.

In addition to the range of channels used to circulate Zapatismo's radical imagination, it is important to note that in many cases the resonance of Zapatismo has not led to the construction of some kind of Zapatista-inspired tactical toolbox. Indeed, this is one of the more interesting and ambivalent aspects of the resonance of radical imaginations. Radical imaginations are mythological apparatuses—central orienting stories that explain the necessity of struggle, offer socio-political horizons to be struggled toward, articulate the means by which the struggle is to be carried out, and help establish a sense of collectivity amongst those whom they inhabit. These imaginations are essential to any attempt to create ways of 'living otherwise' because, as Eric Selbin argues, "along with the material or structural conditions ... it is imperative to recognize the role played by stories, narratives of popular resistance, rebellion and revolution which have animated and emboldened generations of revolutionaries across time and cultures".[7] What they are not is models for political action.

Affinity versus Hierarchy

In large part, Zapatismo's emphasis on an unfolding, imaginative, and contextually-committed radical politics that builds links between struggles through a logic of affinity can be understood by examining its opposite. From the French Revolution on, modern revolutionary movements have sought to achieve radical transformations of socio-political and economic orders via the seizure of one of the most powerful and robust apparatuses of command: the state. The persuasiveness of this vision has been so powerful that many anti-colonial struggles have also adopted similar visions, logics, tactics, and end goals. Of course, while the vision of enacting a totalising revolutionary transformation through the apparatus of the state is tantalising, the realities have been less inspiring. Instead of regimes of social justice, revolutions enacted in this manner have all too often ushered in systems of power that have exercised their own forms of terror, coercion, and oppression in the name of the revolution.

The forms of discipline associated with such an orientation serve to capture people's radical energies and to bend them to a singular project intent on exercising 'power-over' the social rather than liberating people's 'power-to'. In such struggles, winning power is the primary objective, while devolving and decentralising that power becomes a goal, at best, deferred until after the revolutionary struggle is complete.

Of course, none of this is to say that the state is no longer a powerful apparatus of control or that meaningful victories cannot be won upon its terrain. What it does indicate, however, is that our understanding of the process of revolutionary change, and of the radical movements capable of bringing about such transformations, must be critically reconsidered if the failures of the past are to be overcome.

So where might one begin to uncover alternatives to the modernist dream-turned-nightmare of revolution through the seizure of the state? In his analysis of anarchist currents in the newest social movements, Richard Day locates just such an alternative in a politics of affinity.[8] Against the modern left revolutionary narrative of hegemony and the state, a politics of affinity does not inhabit any singular terrain of struggle or manifest in a privileged historical subject. Instead, a politics of affinity is focused upon building connections across difference without seeking to obscure it. Deeply marked by and circulated via these bonds of affinity, Zapatismo's resonance has provoked a reformulation of the way in which radical social change is understood and the projects dedicated to its realisation are envisioned.

Zapatismo

As I have argued elsewhere,[9] Zapatismo—a term referring to the political imagination and practice of the Zapatista movement—has had powerful and unanticipated effects far beyond the indigenous communities in Chiapas, Mexico from where it emerged. While it would be impossible here to fully explore the political imagination and set of practices that comprise Zapatismo on the ground in Chiapas—as well as the histories of struggle locally, regionally, and nationally which have so deeply informed it—as a preface to what follows I offer an orienting overview of some of the key points that define Zapatismo.

Without reducing the reasons animating Zapatismo's resonance across regional, national, and transnational scales to singular or romanticised factors, a key factor in Zapatismo's appeal is that it embodies and seeks to provoke entirely new ways of thinking about and practising political possibility. As such, issues of power, democracy, autonomy, and dignity are central to the Zapatista struggle and to Zapatismo as radical political praxis. Rather than approaching revolutionary struggle or social transformation in highly ideological or dogmatic ways, Zapatismo envisions social change expansively as an unfolding and dynamic process. In comments made in an interview in 2001, Zapatista spokesperson Subcomandante Marcos reflected:

> If the EZLN perpetuates itself as an armed military structure, it is headed for failure. Failure as an alternative set of ideas, an alternative attitude to the world. ... You cannot reconstruct the world or society, or rebuild national states now in ruins, on the basis of a quarrel over who will impose their hegemony on society.[10]

In the same interview, Marcos elaborated on this point by noting that "[t]he EZLN has reached a point where it has been overtaken by Zapatismo", drawing attention to the important distinction between Zapatismo and the EZLN.[11] What is the significance of this distinction? First, it points to the nature of the EZLN itself. The EZLN is the Zapatista Army which exists to defend rebel territory in Chiapas but, unlike modern nation-states and their standing armies, the EZLN is an armed force which is formally under the authority of the Zapatista civilian base communities. The EZLN is subordinated to the authority of the Indigenous Revolutionary Clandestine Committee—General Command (CCRI-CG) which is comprised of civilian Zapatista 'comandantes'. However, unlike modern political systems of centralised power and authority with due pretensions to popular 'democratic' participation, these comandantes are in turn beholden to the authority of their respective community assemblies, a relationship that exemplifies the Zapatista slogan of 'to lead by obeying'.

A second dimension to the distinction Marcos identifies is that Zapatismo is not a coherent ideology, it is not a codified set of rules or a party platform to which one can adhere. Marcos alludes to this when he calls Zapatismo an 'intuition', a characterisation elaborated upon by Zapatista scholar Manuel Callahan who contends that "Zapatismo is a political strategy, an ethos, a set of commitments claimed by those who claim a political identity".[12] In this non-dogmatic spirit, Zapatismo embodies a subversion of the 'politics-as-usual' of liberal democracies or revolutionary vanguards. While some observers have claimed that the Zapatistas only adopted a political stance that explicitly disavowed the desire to seize power and institute a centralised revolutionary regime once it became clear that the EZLN could not militarily defeat the Mexican Army, the consistency and integrity of their commitment to a new, radically democratic notion of social change is woven through the roots of the movement. In an interview with a journalist in the streets of San Cristóbal de las Casas, the colonial capital of the state of Chiapas, on January 1 1994, Subcomandante Marcos affirmed the radical and unconventional spirit animating the Zapatista rebellion:

> It fell to the lowest citizens of this country to raise their heads, with dignity. And this should be a lesson for all. ... This is what we want. We do not want to monopolize the vanguard or say that we are the light, the only alternative, or stingily claim the qualification of revolutionary for one or another current. We say, look at what happened. This is what we had to do.
>
> We have dignity, patriotism and we are demonstrating it. You should do the same, within your ideology, within your means, within your beliefs, and make your human condition count.[13]

Zapatismo espouses a vision of socio-political change based on the pursuit of "democracy, liberty, and justice"[14]—the banners of the Zapatista struggle from the moment of its public emergence—for all. The precise meaning of each of these terms is contextually specific but in no case are they limited to liberal democratic understandings of them. The concrete practice of 'democracy' may differ between autonomous Zapatista communities in Chiapas and people who have found themselves inspired by the movement elsewhere. Nevertheless, it is the desire to experience having direct, non-alienated control over a collectively-lived social life, in the face of political, economic, and socio-cultural regimes which constantly seek to deny this experience, to which Zapatismo speaks.

Dignity, autonomy, and interconnectedness are all deeply intertwined within Zapatismo and are underwritten by the Zapatistas' radical critique of power. Autonomy—the capacity to govern oneself—is central because dignity is only possible when individuals and collectives have the freedom *and* responsibility to govern themselves rather than being ruled over by others. The recognition of the interconnectedness of social existence is the necessary complement to autonomy because a world that does not recognise existence as interdependent is a world pitted against itself, one doomed to replicate exclusion, domination, and violence. Zapatismo thus speaks to the desire not to conquer the world but to create a new world—a world, as the Zapatistas say, capable of holding many worlds.[15]

A Revolutionary Indigenous Encounter

How and why has the Zapatista movement provoked a desire to re-imagine radical socio-political change on a transnational scale—perhaps more than any other movement in recent history?[16] In order to understand this, something of the roots of the Zapatista movement need to be understood. While this overview is meant to be cursory in nature, I aim here to identify some of the key political nodes that provoked not only an international solidarity response toward the Zapatistas but a transnational affirmation of affinity with them expressed by a diversity of others engaged in their own struggles.[17]

While the Zapatista uprising exploded dramatically onto national and international political stages in 1994, histories of the EZLN testify to the depth of the process that had gone into organising the insurgency and to the unique political praxis that would emerge from the movement.[18] The EZLN is a unique product of a particular socio-cultural and political matrix made up of, on the one hand, indigenous Mayan communities in the highlands, canyons, and jungles of Chiapas and, on the other, by the urban, Marxist revolutionary cadres who arrived in the jungles of Chiapas in the early 1980s to prepare the peasantry for a revolution. By all accounts, the encounter of these two groups resulted not in the 'revolutionising' of the indigenous communities but rather in the 'defeat' of Marxist dogma at the hands of these indigenous realities. It is this defeat that would ultimately allow for the emergence of the Zapatista struggle itself.

Forced to leave their established communities in the highlands of Chiapas in search of land and opportunity, the new communities in the Lacandón Jungle formed by Chol, Tzeltal, Tzotzil, and Tojolabal migrants practised a very different kind of politics than did their former communities. Separated from a political landscape marked by established channels of privilege and power, these new communities developed systems of politics based on the communal assembly and consensus-based decision-making.[19] In this setting the collective ruled their representatives, a relationship that would become the cornerstone to the Zapatista democratic notion of 'commanding obeying'.

In the early 1980s, cadres from the *Fuerzas de Liberación Nacional* (FLN, Forces of National Liberation), an urban and Marxist-inspired guerrilla organisation, arrived in Chiapas with the hope of fomenting revolution.[20] Indeed, it is to these urban revolutionaries that the EZLN owes its invocation of the legacy of General Emiliano Zapata, one of the greatest heroes of the Mexican Revolution (1910–1920).[21] Chosen by the FLN because his radical agrarian struggle for land, autonomy, and justice best embodied the true revolutionary struggle of the Mexican people, Zapata was not particularly well known in Chiapas until relatively recently.[22] By laying claim to Zapata's legacy, the new Zapatistas sought to reclaim the radical, grassroots, and national dimensions of the Mexican Revolution, thereby extending their struggle beyond the borders of Chiapas and the indigenous base communities of the nascent EZLN.

While the encounter between the urban revolutionaries from the FLN and the indigenous migrant communities ultimately provided the seedbed for the EZLN, this was by no means an uncomplicated matter. Arriving out of an urban context as socio-cultural, political, and intellectual products of Euro-American modernity, Subcomandante Marcos and other *guerrilleros* were confronted by realities with which they were ill-equipped to deal. The physical challenges of guerrilla life aside, the urban revolutionaries encountered indigenous communities who grounded their existence upon very different understandings of the world. Indeed, the rugged mountainous terrain where Marcos and the other guerrillas first lived upon their arrival in Chiapas was not merely a useful tactical position to occupy for the Mayan communities living there, it was also "a respected and feared place of stories, myths, and ghosts".[23] By living there, "[i]nstead of arriving directly from the city or the university, the EZLN emerged out of ... that magical world inhabited by the whole of Mayan history, by the spirits of ancestors, and by Zapata himself".[24]

As the encounter proceeded, Marcos and the other urban revolutionaries began to realise that indigenous notions of time, history, and reality were fundamentally different from what they had been taught to believe and upon which they had grounded so many of their own political beliefs and assumptions.[25] For example, while Marcos had come to teach politics and history to the indigenous communities, he quickly discovered that these ways of knowing and imparting knowledge—laden with their own epistemological and ontological assumptions—made no sense to the communities.[26] If it were to survive, the emergent politics of this encounter required a new language, one born out of the urban Zapatistas' critical reading of Mexican history and current economic and political context combined with the communities' own histories of genocide, racism, suffering, and exclusion.[27]

The inversion of the traditional vanguard-masses relationship that occurred during the formation of the EZLN provided a distinctive model of popular, grassroots, and radically democratic organisation. Nowhere is the significance and consequences of this relationship more clearly illuminated than by the way Zapatista base communities arrived at the decision to initiate their rebellion. In mid-1992, Zapatista communities voted to go to war "to coincide with 500 years of resistance".[28] Measured against the political context geopolitically at the time, the Zapatista uprising seemed hopeless and anachronistic. In interviews and communiqués published since the uprising, Marcos and other Zapatista leaders have repeatedly asserted the divergence of opinion between the leadership of the EZLN, who advocated a tactical patience, and the communities who wanted open rebellion.[29] Eschewing an 'objective' accounting of the relative favourability of the geopolitical context for their uprising, the indigenous base communities of the EZLN measured the necessity of rebellion "against the arc of their own lives",[30] a philosophy which would deeply infuse Zapatismo and its resonance transnationally in the years to come.

While the Mexican Army succeeded in driving the EZLN back into the jungles of Chiapas, the counter-insurgency proved much more difficult than the EZLN's military capacity indicated. Even with no significant channels of communication established with actors outside of their movement nationally or internationally, in the days following the uprising people from across Mexico and around the world mobilised in an effort to halt the hostilities and to compel the Mexican government to negotiate with the insurgents. Part of this mobilisation can be attributed to pre-existing networks of communication and information distribution organised around Latin American solidarity and human rights;[31] but a much more compelling reason for this response lay in the moral force of this indigenous rebellion. Carried via news media throughout Mexico, the image of columns of indigenous men and women taking control of San Cristóbal de las Casas evoked "the historical memory of the country, the memory transmitted in families or studied in school. Indians, those about whom the urban society bore an ancient and unconfessed guilt, had organized themselves and risen up with weapons in their hands".[32] Travelling through telecommunications pathways, "[i]n a single blow the rebellion had legitimated itself before Mexicans".[33] In the face of the sheer force and scale of national and international mobilisation against a military 'solution' to the Zapatista rebellion, only twelve days after the Zapatista uprising began the Mexican government was compelled to declare a unilateral ceasefire and to invite the EZLN to a dialogue aimed at reconciling the grievances animating the rebellion.

Since its inaugural appearance on New Year's Day in 1994, the Zapatista movement has brought unprecedented national attention to the 'Indian Question' in Mexico, provoking debate about the conditions of life and socio-political and cultural aspirations of indigenous peoples living within the Mexican state, and making these issues among the most important with respect to the national political agenda.[34] In addition to this, the Zapatistas have also succeeded in galvanising a broad range of democratic movements in Mexico and throughout the world through new and innovative political projects and encounters.

Resonances beyond Borders

The EZLN's uprising on January 1 1994 turned out to be a shot heard around the world, particularly because the Zapatistas explicitly linked their rebellion to NAFTA and neoliberal globalisation. At a political moment heralded by neoliberal ideologues as 'the end of history' the radical expression of resistance, hope, and dignity offered by the Zapatistas lit a new fuse of political possibility on a global scale. In the words of one of my research partners, "we were all waiting for them ... we were waiting to hear a word like this ... [on] the day that NAFTA became law, at the southern tip of the North American Free Trade Area, at the darkest moment for movements in the Americas ... it was a word we were waiting to hear".[35] With no pre-existing ties to activist groups beyond the borders of Mexico, the Zapatista struggle would spread virally on a transnational scale to infiltrate the political imaginations of diverse groups of people.

In the aftermath of the uprising, the EZLN, hemmed in by tens of thousands of Mexican troops, would remain limited to rebel territory in the state of Chiapas and the broader Zapatista movement would emerge and remain focused largely within the confines of Mexican national territory. In spite of this, Zapatismo as a radical political imagination would travel via activist solidarity delegations, conventional corporate news sources, academic analyses, independent journalists, and a variety of other—particularly digital—media far beyond these territorial borders. While the Zapatistas have sought from the first day of their uprising to galvanise Mexican civil society into a broad-based rebellion against the existing corrupt power structure in the country, nothing in the EZLN's initial statements or declarations indicated their rebellion was in any way aimed at attracting an international audience. Nevertheless, people the world over have responded passionately to the Zapatista rebellion.

The significance of this is twofold. First, it demonstrates that, despite critics' claims to the contrary,[36] the Zapatista uprising was not simply an event staged by a cabal of EZLN leadership seeking to appeal to the revolutionary appetites of an international audience and belatedly adorned with trappings of 'indigenousness' to parlay this into political currency. The rootedness of the Zapatista struggle in the indigenous realities of the Mexican southeast testifies to its 'authenticity'. Second, the transnational appeal of the struggle means that in spite of the absence of direct linkages and channels of communication, something in the very nature of the Zapatista struggle called out to a diversity of people around the world in a way that resonated within the context of their own lived realities.

At first, the transnational response mirrored that of Mexican civil society as diverse groups organised aid and solidarity caravans to Chiapas as well as protests outside of Mexican embassies. As time passed, however, the transnational engagement with Zapatismo has become more diverse, much less traditionally solidaristic in nature, and much more attuned to building what the Zapatistas have called an "international order of hope for humanity and against neoliberalism" in the midst of the Fourth World War.[37] This consciousness of being participants engaged in a collective struggle 'for humanity and against neoliberalism' *alongside* rather than simply *in support of* the Zapatistas is something that the Zapatistas would in turn recognise, respond to, and seek to amplify.

Several writers from the ranks of the alter-globalisation movement have rhetorically marked the profound significance of Zapatismo in relation to new ways of conceptualising and enacting radical struggle. As Paul Kingsnorth asserts, "[t]he Zapatistas would become the unwitting, but not unwilling, forgers of a truly global insurgency against history's first truly global system".[38] In the words of Manuel Callahan, "[i]n many respects the Zapatista uprising is the moment when the movement against globalization found its global audience, and it is perhaps the place where the tactics of that movement began".[39] In considering "the Zapatista effect", Naomi Klein asks, "what are the ideas that proved so powerful that thousands have taken it on themselves to disseminate them around the world?", and answers: "They have to do with power—and new ways of imagining it".[40] She characterises the "essence" of Zapatismo as "a global call to revolution that tells you not to wait for the revolution, only to start where you stand, to fight with your own weapon".[41] Nowhere is Zapatismo's significance to the alter-globalisation movement more powerfully captured than by the editorial collective Notes from Nowhere in the first entry of their timeline of global anti-capitalism entitled, 'The Restless Margins: Moments of Resistance and Rebellion'.[42] Of January 1 1994, the collective writes, "[t]he EZLN ... declares war against Mexico, bringing its inspirational struggle for life and humanity to the forefront of political imaginations across the planet".[43] While it would be a mistake to take these comments as a simple reflection of Zapatismo or its significance for the alter-globalisation movement, they do point to the powerful inspiring force generated by the Zapatistas as well as the radicalising effect of Zapatismo upon imaginations of struggle and change transnationally.[44]

From September 2003 until October 2004, I worked with a diverse range of activists in the north of the Americas who had experienced the resonance of Zapatismo and had sought to materialise it in specific ways within their own realities; to build their own pocket of rebellion as part of a larger 'international order of hope'. Their reflections on the significance of Zapatismo and their reactions to its resonance illuminate the landscape of the radical imagination of Zapatismo beyond the borders of the rebel territory in the far southeast of Mexico. Further in the essay, I engage with the broader political and social implications of Zapatismo, as well as with two particularly compelling examples of the possibilities animated by this radical political imagination: Peoples' Global Action (PGA) and Big Noise Tactical.

Experimenting with the Zapatista Hypothesis

From July 27 to August 3 1996, nearly 5,000 people from forty-two countries participated in the First Intercontinental Encuentro for Humanity and Against Neoliberalism held in the Zapatista territory in rebellion.[45] Convoked by the Zapatistas and held in the five Zapatista *Aguascalientes*—meeting spaces for the Zapatistas and national and international civil societies—in the communities of Oventik, La Realidad, La Garrucha, Morelia, and Roberto Barrios, the first Encuentro was an opportunity for people from around the world to directly express their solidarity with the EZLN and the Zapatistas. More importantly, the Encuentro was envisioned by the Zapatistas as an attempt to build a transnational network of resistances to neoliberal capitalism. As preeminent symbols of this kind of resistance, the Zapatistas sought to catalyse a broader movement 'for humanity and against neoliberalism' without seeking to lead it.

"The Encuentro sent Zapatismo global," in the words of Paul Kingsnorth. "The ... delegates returned to their countries with new ideas, new ways of thinking about the future, and above all, new links".[46] Building on the transnational resonance of the Zapatista rebellion two years earlier, the Zapatista Encuentro in 1996 provoked people from all over the world to return home and try to infuse their own spaces and practices with the same joy of rebellion and hope for another world that they had encountered in Chiapas and to form another node in this emerging network of resistances. Dave Bleakney, a member of the Canadian Union of Postal Workers (CUPW)[47] and an activist involved in the founding of PGA and its manifestation in North America, expressed during our interview the profound value of the lessons offered by Zapatismo to Canadian and US activists since 1994:

> [The] struggle [of the Zapatistas] and others have taught me that we have more
> to learn from movements like that than they have from us. [We] need to learn
> from the south as opposed to [believing that] we have the answers, that's a real

588 The Movements of Movements, Part 1

struggle and it gets disheartening sometimes because I think it's a real hard one to cross over. I know within the labour movement, people call it solidarity but in fact you look at it [and] it's like charity. Labour movements [in the North] have come to maintain the order. If you look at global bodies like the WTO there's a constant clamour to get a seat at the table as if somehow being present at your own execution, surrounded by executioners, is [an] achievement. It's a really crucial juncture because—let's face it—the unions in Canada are going to be a lot more excited about going to Geneva to meet with the WTO than ... to live off rice and beans in Chiapas for 3 weeks and not have any running water, but it's clear to me that the greatest lessons to be learned are from the Zapatistas but also the piqueteros in Argentina who occupy factories and the MST who occupy land in Brazil. Another thing that the Zapatistas teach us is to be resourceful and self-reliant, to not think that there's somebody that's going to take care of us. I think the Zapatistas open up a whole other area of relations around the importance of honesty, that you don't need to spin anything.[48]

The notion of the Zapatistas as teachers to political movements and activists elsewhere is a provocative one, particularly so because what is being taught here is not a series of lessons on 'how to make a revolution' but rather broader and more foundational lessons in political horizons, ethics, and possibilities. As Bleakney points out here, ever since the fall of the Berlin Wall and the proclamation of 'the end of history' political elites have heralded liberal democracy as the pinnacle of political expression. Through their ongoing rebellion, the Zapatistas have accomplished a powerful interrogation of that conclusion as well as a complete subversion of the dogma of 'there is no alternative.'

Friederike Habermann, journalist, activist, and a participant in both Zapatistas-inspired *Encuentros* as well as PGA, expressed the revelatory significance of Zapatismo as well as the tangible lessons Zapatismo has offered to movements elsewhere during our interview. Specifically, Haberman discussed the connection between new ways of speaking and thinking about politics and the strategies used to materialise these alternatives:

[A] new language is important because it's easily accessible and ... it's able to bridge between more theoretical discourse and a discourse everybody understands. This is another very interesting point for me because Marcos is saying this came out of a clash between the smaller group of left-wing intellectuals who came into the jungle and tried to explain to the indigenous about imperialism and the Indigenous said well what are you talking about? [Zapatismo] is what [has been] born out of [the clash of these traditions]. Subcomandante Marcos [is an interesting figure in this regard] because he speaks of "us", of "us indigenous", but of course he's not indigenous. It's not by [accident] that it's him who is the [Zapatistas' spokesperson] because he can reach the people of his identity, [people from the world] he has been born in, he has been educated in, but still he shifted his identity so he's not just a middle-class, white guy. For me, this is a good example of how politics can become fruitful because when you're working for a better world you're always in danger to know it better for others. ... [The Zapatistas make it clear that] you can't copy a [political] tactic or a [social change strategy] but what you can have are these resonances [between different struggles which can inspire you] to [take action] in a different way—and in your own way—inspired by the Zapatistas, to [act] in a self-organized way, not to expect anything from the state, not to do any lobby politics.[49]

As Haberman expresses, one of the most important lessons offered by Zapatismo's radical imagination is that it is possible to build a new world today in a collective and self-organised fashion without seeking concessions from power and without seeking the permission of the powerful to do so. What Zapatismo has not provided is a blueprint, toolbox, or guidebook to radical social transformation. In this sense, Zapatismo's radical imagination is a catalyst for rebellion and an inspiring example of social change, not a template to be exported to other contexts.

If Zapatismo is a catalyst for a revitalised radical imagination of social change, what of its material manifestations? Put another way, if efforts at radical social change are to have an impact, let alone be durable and resilient, do they not need to materialise themselves through institutions, practices, and other elements of lived reality? The simple answer to this question is undoubtedly 'yes' but the ways in which this basic principle gets actualised are not so clear-cut. On the ground in Chiapas, the Zapatistas have built a clear process for their revolutionary struggle. Since their public emergence on January 1 1994, the Zapatistas have advanced their struggle for autonomy through the construction of autonomous municipalities, developed relations with organisations like the Mexico Solidarity Network to facilitate the marketing of fair trade goods (particularly textiles and coffee), and have built institutions necessary to support life in rebel territory such as schools, clinics, and governance and conflict-resolution structures. Based on Zapatismo's core principles, which I outlined briefly earlier in this piece, the Zapatistas have successfully managed to consolidate the autonomy the Mexican state refused to grant them. In addition to this, the Zapatistas have sought to build links with a diversity of other marginalised, exploited, and oppressed groups within and outside of Mexico through a process of encounter grounded in a logic of affinity rather than a vanguardist approach to radical politics.

As I have already said, however, what the Zapatistas have not done is offer a model for radical social change that can be exported beyond the context within which it has been developed. From armed rebellion to the construction of autonomous municipalities, the Zapatista strategy for radical social change has been both durable and resilient because it has been grounded in and enacted by communities in resistance—communities with living traditions of struggle and alternative-building in which these strategies make sense. Outside of this context, and outside of the social base upon which a movement like that of the Zapatistas so intrinsically depends, these strategies make little or no sense. How can autonomous municipalities be consolidated in the absence of a mass movement willing not only to fight for them but to actually do what it takes to *live* these alternatives? For those activists—particularly in the North—who have romanticised the revolutionary violence of the Zapatistas, their clandestine organising, or their model of insurgency, the remarkable lack of resonance these spectacles have for the broader population should be cause for further critical reflection on the really valuable insights offered by Zapatismo rather than a facile and often very macho valorisation of its most superficial aspects. Even in the case of Peoples' Global Action and Big Noise Tactical, the significance of Zapatismo for these collectives has far less to do with tactical lessons and much more to do with the advancement of new and radical way of envisioning socio-political transformation.

Direct democracy, a deep and powerful critique of power and the fetish of the state, a logic of affinity, a renewed and expansive radical imagination of so-cio-political possibility, and a concrete, inspiring, and hopeful example of alterna-tive-building in a world in which such alternatives had supposedly been foreclosed upon, are all contributions of irreducible significance made by the Zapatistas to a new transnational fabric of struggle. Indeed, the alter-globalisation movement's commitment to direct action, deep sense of inclusiveness rather than sectarian-ism, espousal of a 'diversity of tactics', and radical spirit of socio-political change that does not aim to claim power over others in order to transform the world, can all be traced in large part to the Zapatistas. While some of these currents were present before 1994, it is only after the Zapatistas' explosive public appearance that a new wave of coordinated mass action aimed at building a globalised world 'from below' emerged in earnest.

When compared with the tangibility of political institutions and process-es such contributions may seem more ephemeral than concrete. However, the problem in such a way of thinking lies in looking for 'alternative' but similar insti-tutions, which results in the creation of 'new' institutions just like the old. As US radical Staughton Lynd explains, rather than a formula or programme, Zapatismo has offered us a 'hypothesis' and its effects have been felt and will continue to be felt through the myriad ways in which activists experiment with it:

> Does it work? Can a society be fundamentally changed without taking over the
> state? I don't think we know yet ... [but] the Zapatistas ... have given us a new

hypothesis. ... It rejects the goal of taking state power and sets forth the objective of building a horizontal network of centers of self-activity.

Above all the Zapatistas have encouraged young people all over the earth to affirm: We must have a qualitatively different society! Another world is possible! Let us begin to create it, here and now![50]

I now turn to a brief exploration of two compelling instances of collective experiments with the Zapatista hypothesis: Peoples' Global Action and Big Noise Tactical.

Peoples' Global Action

At the end of the first Encuentro, the EZLN issued the 'Second Declaration of La Realidad for Humanity and Against Neoliberalism', calling for the creation of a "collective network of all our particular struggles and resistances, an intercontinental network of resistance against neoliberalism, an intercontinental network of resistance for humanity".[51] Specifying that this would not be "an organizing structure", that it would have "no central head or decision maker", "no central command or hierarchies", the EZLN called for the formation of a network that would provide channels of communication and support for the diverse struggles "for humanity and against neoliberalism" around the world.[52]

In the 'Second Declaration', the Zapatistas also called for a second Encuentro to be held, this time outside of Zapatista territory and on another continent. The Second Intercontinental Encuentro for Humanity and Against Neoliberalism was held one year after the first in Spain, drawing 3,000 activists from 50 countries.[53] It was at the Second Encuentro that the shape of the network the Zapatistas had called for began to coalesce out of a "need to create something more tangible than the encuentros".[54] In this spirit, Peoples' Global Action (PGA) was born at a meeting in Geneva in February 1998 attended by 300 activists from 71 countries.[55] As Olivier de Marcellus, one of the participants involved in the founding meetings of PGA, explains:

> PGA is an offshoot of the international Zapatista movement, founded in a meeting that prolonged the Second Encuentro in southern Spain, and drawing a lot of its European support from people who also support the Zapatistas. There is also a certain ideological and organizational resemblance, both being rather unorthodox, eclectic networks attempting to stimulate radical opposition worldwide. The principle difference is that PGA aims beyond debate and exchange to propose action campaigns against neoliberalism, worldwide.[56]

Since its inception, Peoples' Global Action has been one of the most important transnational networks for coordination and communication amongst groups and individuals committed to direct, anti-capitalist, and alter-globalisation action. PGA has been involved in coordinating Global Days of Action—the spectacular summit protests—against the World Trade Organization, G8, and the World Bank as well as a variety of conferences, caravans, and workshops around the world.[57] While PGA is largely dormant right now, particularly in the Global North, it has operated, in essence, as a rebel network inspired by the rebellious spirit and example of the Zapatista movement.

Very clear in its role as a network of coordination rather than an organisation, at the height of its activity PGA brought diverse groups and struggles together in a spirit of explicit anti-capitalism and direct action. With no membership, representing no one, and with no one charged with representing it or speaking in its name, PGA existed only insofar as the diverse collectives and individuals who made it up agreed that it did. Even now, PGA should be considered dormant rather than dead as any network of its nature could be reconstituted at any moment. Indeed, the overall success and durability of PGA is rooted in a constant decentralisation of power and continual rearticulation of collective identity.[58]

PGA's Manifesto and Hallmarks are 'living documents', subject to revision at each collective gathering, and facilitate the continual reinvention of collective identity even as PGA's commitment to decentralising power and decision-making to the most immediate and immanent level—with regions responsible for deciding upon convenors and infopoints—has provided mechanisms for challenging power hierarchies that exist in so many activist groups.[59] Like so much of the alter-globalisation movement, PGA has struggled in the aftermath of 9/11 and is now more of a virtual presence linking communities of activists together via its web-presence and various e-mail listservs than a living 'international order of hope'. Nevertheless, the long list of dramatic actions coordinated under its banner remains impressive and the architecture of the network remains in place for its reactivation should people desire to do so.

Big Noise Tactical

While PGA is a compelling example of anti-capitalist networking and mobilising at the transnational level, the resonance of Zapatismo has also had considerable and unanticipated effects at the intersection of culture and politics. Big Noise Tactical (BNT), a radical film-making collective based in New York City, is perhaps one of the most interesting examples inhabiting this intersection. BNT released their first film, *Zapatista*, in 1998.[60] It was followed by a number of other feature documentaries, including *This is What Democracy Looks Like* (2000),[61] and *The Fourth World War* (2003),[62] in addition to a host of 'tactical media' pieces produced in collaboration with other artists / activists focusing on a diverse set of events and issues relating to the global anti-capitalist / global justice movement. BNT was also a part of the first Independent Media Centre video team at the

WTO protests in Seattle in 1999, providing unprecedented independent media coverage of the 'Battle of Seattle' and laying the groundwork for the Indymedia proliferation that has followed.

The activist media-makers who comprise BNT however repudiate their identification as 'documentary-makers', 'artists', or 'film-makers'; instead, they situate their work politically in the following way:

> We are not filmmakers producing and distributing our work. We are rebels, crystallizing radical community and weaving a network of skin and images, of dreams and bone, of solidarity and connection against the isolation, alienation and cynicism of capitalist decomposition.
>
> We are tactical because our media is a part of movements, imbedded in a history of struggle. Tactical because we are provisional, plural, polyvocal. Tactical because it would be the worst kind of arrogance to believe that our media had some ahistorical power to change the world—its only life is inside of movements—and they will hang our images on the walls of their banks if our movements do not tear their banks down.[63]

This radical commitment to producing cinematic interventions that are part of social struggle rather than simply 'about it' clearly animates BNT's films. From *Zapatista* to *The Fourth World War*, both documentaries profoundly connected to the Zapatista struggle in Chiapas and its significance beyond its own geopolitical location, BNT's films do not simply document events but participate actively and intentionally in them as vehicles for the transmission of radical acts, ideas, and imaginations to a wide diversity of viewers.

The origins of Big Noise Tactical are intimately bound up with Zapatismo. Rick Rowley, one of BNT's founding members, found himself in Mexico in 1995 just as the Zapatista rebellion, and the Mexican state's repression of it, were once more shaking the country. The rebellion and what it represented constituted a radical break for Rowley, personally and politically. During our interview, Rowley reflected upon the events of 1995 and the connections between Zapatismo and the formation of BNT:

> [W]e all accepted that invitation to become Zapatistas and we returned to the United States as Zapatistas looking for what that might mean in the North and trying to learn from their example of struggle, you know take it seriously, not just as an inspiration but to learn from their tactics and their strategy. One of the things that was most resonant to us at that moment was the famous Zapatista line "our word is our weapon", armed with our word and sticks against this machine we're winning, and so we thought about what our word would look like in the North, and we didn't think that communiqués and children's stories and

poems in the left-wing papers in the States was the move that would make sense. We thought video made sense as a language that could circulate through these circuits of American culture. None of us had ever held video cameras before [or] had any film training, but we got credit cards and we bought cameras and went down and started to shoot *Zapatista* and so that was the beginning of Big Noise, that was the beginning of the work that followed, the work that I've done since then. We've never thought of ourselves as film makers but as Zapatistas looking for forms of struggle that make sense in the North.[64]

Rowley and other activists with BNT have found ways not to 'import' Zapatismo to the US but to find in its resonance specific meaning relevant to struggles in their own context. Through their encounter with the Zapatista struggle, BNT has engaged in the innovative process of making sense of Zapatismo's lessons and inspiration in ways that are capable of moving powerfully and dynamically through the "circuits of American culture".

Jacquie Soohen, another key member of BNT, reflected upon her own encounter with Zapatismo and its consequences for herself and for her political commitments during our conversation. Building upon Rowley's comments about the search for weapons that would make sense for struggles in the North, Soohen elaborated upon the connections between politics, culture, and media, and their intersection with Zapatismo from the perspective of her own experience:

[I heard] about [the Zapatista struggle] and [I was] just amazed that you could take that inspiration, the idea of victory, the idea of standing up for something and fighting and winning. You knew that the demos didn't work, you knew that it had to be something else, beyond identity politics, and taking possession of a history that was both your own and expanded beyond [the] identity boundaries that were clearly marked for you inside a world of individualistic capitalism. I went down for the second half of that shoot, [I] hadn't even thought about making films, that's not what I'd ever trained to do or even thought about doing, but when we [finished] *Zapatista* we started thinking about this and imagining this, how is our word our weapon? It was when we finally started screening the film that it began to make sense as a weapon and became something that we decided to keep doing as long as it made sense because you'd go places and you weren't talking to people who had, for the most part, ever even heard of Zapatismo or for the most part they weren't politically active ... [but] people were so moved by it ... we came to realize that it was our weapon that we could use and something we could give over to a larger movement. ... It's arrogant to believe that any film or any piece of work like that is ever going to change things by itself 'cause that's not how it functions, all of these things function inside of movements. [*Zapatista*] came out and we were working in tune with a whole bunch of people who were being inspired by the Zapatistas because it was so different and new and because it was a victory that was something that people were winning.[65]

These compelling reflections by Rowley and Soohen illuminate some of the most interesting and unpredictable implications of the transnational significance of Zapatismo as a radical imagination. While conventional solidarity activism within and outside of Mexico has been essential in defending the Zapatistas and their project of radical socio-political transformation, Zapatismo has also inspired activists to search for new ways of practising politics in their own spaces. Indeed, the implications of the transnational resonance of Zapatismo may quite possibly be much more powerful, and much more enduring, than the solidarity marshalled over the years by national and international 'civil societies'.

Big Noise Tactical's film *The Fourth World War* is ostensibly about the diverse struggles that make up the 'movement of movements' that is the alter-globalisation movement. Named in explicit reference to the notion of "the Fourth World War" articulated by Subcomandante Marcos and the Zapatistas,[66] *The Fourth World War* is a film about nothing less than the power of collective action to remake the world. Not a conventional documentary that aims to 'objectively' narrate the alter-globalisation movement, the film traces the global circulation of anti-capitalist and radically democratic struggles "for humanity and against neoliberalism". It is also a powerful and provocative example of the materialisation of a radical new way of thinking about socio-political change deeply inspired by Zapatismo. The film takes the viewer on a whirlwind trip around the world, setting down frequently to explore an emerging movement that is self-consciously global, yet everywhere takes on its own unique shape. While it tells a powerful story of the hope and possibility that resides in people's power to collectively transform their own social realities, the film itself is an artefact of this story and a participant in this larger struggle, and is itself a vehicle for the making of new meanings and the cultivation of new forms of struggle deeply inspired by movements like the Zapatistas. As Rick Rowley explained during our conversation:

Films don't change the world, movements of people do, and our films succeed or fail inasmuch ... as they participate in movements that successfully challenge this system. On one level we were ... a tissue for communication across ... geographic, political, cultural distance, we're a tissue through which it is possible for rebellious and revolutionary images to circulate, for models and tactics to circulate ... but we're part of a process that movements ... are already undertaking. It was amazing in these last couple of years to work on *The Fourth World War* and to see the degree to which movements are already in communication with one another and are self-consciously articulating themselves as global. ... We're run through by each other's ... examples and we're given strength and hope by each other's examples of victory. That's one of the things I think that movements here now, in the States especially now, need to remember is that we're a global movement and we're a historical movement, that ... we're tied to people outside of our borders and to moments outside of our time ... we're part of something much bigger than any state that's locked down. One of our most important roles is to remind people over and over again to fight against what I think ... is the primary or most disempowering aspect of capitalist culture and the way that capitalist culture reproduces itself which is producing the feeling in each and every person that they're alone, that they're an isolated consumer who's ... capable of winning victories ... only alone ... you can get yourself a good education, get yourself a good job, you can raise yourself out of poverty ... the arc that *The Fourth World War* takes is that it begins at this moment of capitalist decomposition where everyone's alone ... it begins in the moment after war dissolves every form of human connection that you have and tries to bring the audience to a point at the end where ... Marcos ends the film saying, "You will no longer be you, now you are us", you're part of a global movement of people and you're connected to human beings all over the planet in a way that is deeper than the connection that exists between a consumer and a producer, between an oppressor and the oppressed, or between ... a victim and a criminal ... When those kinds of connections of solidarity are successfully articulated ... things can change.[67]

Now You Are Us!

Across arbitrary political borders, across geographic space, and across cultural difference, Zapatismo's resonance has built bridges of affinity, solidarity, and political innovation while exploding conventional horizons of socio-political possibility. As much imaginative as material, this encounter between Zapatismo and diverse communities of radical activists has produced novel ways of imagining and enacting struggle toward a more dignified, democratic, just, and peaceful future. Beyond this, these experiences and this consciousness are beginning to materialise the possibility for the articulation of a new political terrain and political practice rooted in a mutual recognition of dignity and humanity, an affirmation of diversity, and the reclamation of the capacity to build a world capable of holding many worlds precisely because we are the only subjects truly capable of bringing it into being.

The Zapatista struggle has yielded a transnationalised political imagination that is radical for the following reasons: It conceives of socio-political action as a grassroots rather than vanguardist project; it embraces a multilayered and dynamic understanding of socio-political change rather than as something dominated by ideological dogmatism; its political horizon is marked by radical social, cultural, economic, and political transformation rather than reformism; it is not a vision of radical social change cut from whole cloth, rather, it is a provocation offering glimpses of a multitude of possible futures without retreating to the logic of hegemony to make sense out of them.

Inspired by Zapatismo and the Zapatista struggle, this radical imagination that I have briefly explored here through two of its manifestations is marked by deep commitments to horizontality, direct democracy, a logic of affinity, an abandonment of the fetish of the state, and a foundational belief in direct action. It also represents what Richard Day has identified as a politics of "infinite responsibility" operating on a terrain of "groundless solidarity".[68] Blowing apart traditional conceptualisations of solidarity as a principle operating within particular identity boundaries and in particular ways, these concepts call into being a political ethic rooted in one's unending responsibility to live a politics of the act that is always grounded in the necessary mutual recognition of dignity.

For my own part, I have long been inspired by the resonance of Zapatismo in my life inside and outside the academy, as well as inside and outside of activist spaces. In my search for political hope and possibility I encountered Zapatismo at first through journalistic, academic, and activist accounts and the music of bands like Rage Against the Machine. Later, I would have the opportunity to encounter Zapatismo and Zapatistas on the ground in Chiapas as an academic, an activist, and an ally looking for ways to materialise my sense of solidarity and to help cultivate that same joy of rebellion in my own context. In my day-to-day experience both as an activist and academic, these encounters and the resonance of Zapatismo deeply informed the ways I have sought to engage with the world around me. Rather than a map or a formula defining the path toward radical socio-political transformation or the practice of engaged, critical social research, Zapatismo is a provocation that has compelled me to look past the familiarity of established structures and dominant narratives. Indeed, my research into the phenomenon of the radical imagination and its significance for revolutionary social transformation, my pedagogical approach as university instructor, and my political commitments and activity inside and outside of the university all owe a profound debt to the Zapatista struggle. It is through Zapatismo and the concrete example of the Zapatista struggle that I have come to autonomy, anti-capitalism, and dignity as key principles in my own political constellation.

What I have attempted to provide here is only a glimpse of the possibility of this terrain seen through the lens of Zapatismo's transnational resonance. Zapatismo is by no means the only radical political imagination inhabiting this terrain but it has given rise to powerful manifestations of a new politics rooted in affinity rather than hegemony, and which offer at least the hope—to echo a famous Zapatista slogan—not of conquering the world but of making it anew.

References

Homero Aridjis, 2002—'Indian Is Beautiful', in Tom Hayden, ed, 2002—*The Zapatista Reader*. New York: Thunder's Mouth Press

John Arquilla, Graham Fuller, Melissa Fuller, and David Ronfeldt, 1998—*The Zapatista Social Netwar in Mexico*. Santa Monica: RAND Arroyo Center

Big Noise Tactical, 1998—*Zapatista*, at http://www.bignoisefilms.org/films/features/90-zapatista (Inactive April 2017)

Big Noise Tactical, 2000—*This Is What Democracy Looks Like*, at http://www.bignoisefilms.com/films/features/100-whatdemocracylookslike (Accessed April 2017)

Big Noise Tactical, 2003—*The Fourth World War*, at http://www.bignoisefilms.com/films/features/89-fourth-world-war (Inactive April 2017)

Ernst Bloch, 1986—*The Principle of Hope*, 3 volumes. Translators Neville Plaice, Stephen Plaice, and Paul Knight. Oxford: Basil Blackwell

Susan Buck-Morss, 2000—*Dreamworld and Catastrophe: The Passing of Mass Utopia in East and West*. Cambridge: MIT Press

Manuel Callahan, 2004a—'Zapatismo Beyond Chiapas', Chapter 16 in David Solnit, ed, 2004—*Globalize Liberation: How to Uproot the System and Build a Better World*. San Francisco: City Lights Books

Manuel Callahan, 2004b—'Zapatismo and Global Struggle: "A Revolution to Make a Revolution Possible"', in Eddie Yuen, Daniel Burton-Rose, and George Katsiaficas, eds, 2004—*Confronting Capitalism: Dispatches from a Global Movement*. Brooklyn: Soft Skull Press

George Collier and Elizabeth Lowery Quaratiello, 1999—*Basta! Land & The Zapatista Rebellion in Chiapas*. Oakland: Food First Books

Lee Cormie, 2017—'Re-Creating The World: Communities of Faith in the Struggles For Other Possible Worlds', in Jai Sen, ed, 2017a—*The Movements of Movements, Part 1: What Makes Us Move?*. Volume 4 in the *Challenging Empires* series. New Delhi: OpenWord, and Oakland, CA: PM Press

Richard Day, 2005—*Gramsci Is Dead: Anarchist Currents in the Newest Social Movements*. Toronto: Between the Lines

Olivier de Marcellus, 2001—'Peoples' Global Action: Dreaming Up an Old Ghost', Chapter 7 in Midnight Notes, eds, 2001—*Auroras of the Zapatistas: Local & Global Struggles of the Fourth World War*. Brooklyn: Autonomedia

EZLN (Ejército Zapatista de Liberación Nacional), 2001—'Second Declaration of La Realidad for Humanity and Against Neoliberalism', in Juana Ponce de León, ed, 2001—*Our Word Is Our Weapon* (Toronto: Seven Stories Press), at http://nadir.org/nadir/initiativ/agp/chiapas1996/en/dec2real.html (Accessed April 2017)

Andrew Flood, 2003—'Dreaming of a Reality Where the Past and the Future Meet the Present', in Notes from Nowhere, eds, 2003—*We Are Everywhere: The Irresistible Rise of Global Anti-Capitalism*. New York: Verso

Gabriel García Márquez and Roberto Pombo, 2004—'The Hourglass of the Zapatistas', in Tom Mertes, ed, 2004—*A Movement of Movements: Is Another World Really Possible?*. New York: Verso

Adolfo Gilly, 1998—'Chiapas and the Rebellion of the Enchanted World', in Daniel Nugent, ed, 1998—*Rural Revolt in Mexico: US Intervention and the Domain of Subaltern Politics*. Durham, NC: Duke University Press

Neil Harvey, 1998—*The Chiapas Rebellion: The Struggle for Land and Democracy*. Durham, NC: Duke University Press

John Holloway, 2002a—'Zapatismo and the Social Sciences', in *Capital & Class*, 78

John Holloway, 2002b—*Change the World Without Taking Power: The Meaning of Revolution Today*. London: Pluto Press

Fouad Kalouche and Eric Mielants, 2017—'Antisystemic Movements and Transformations of the World-System, 1968–1989', in Jai Sen, ed, 2017a—*The Movements of Movements, Part 1: What Makes Us Move?*. Volume 4 in the *Challenging Empires* series. New Delhi: OpenWord, and Oakland, CA: PM Press

Alex Khasbabish, 2006—'An Echo That Reechoes: Transnational Activism and the Resonance of Zapatismo', in *AmeriQuests*, vol 2 no 1, at http://ejournals.library.vanderbilt.edu/ameriquests/viewarticle.php?id=44 (Accessed April 2017)

Alex Khasnabish, 2007—'Insurgent Imaginations', in *Ephemera: Theory and Politics in Organization*, vol 7 no 4, pp 505–526, at http://www.ephemerajournal.org/sites/default/files/7-4khasnabish.pdf (Accessed April 2017)

Alex Khasnabish, 2008a—*Zapatismo Beyond Borders: New Imaginations of Political Possibility*. Toronto: University of Toronto Press

Alex Khasnabish, 2008b—'"A Tear in the Fabric of the Present": The Rhizomatic Resonance of Zapatismo and Radical Activism in the North of the Americas', in *Journal for the Study of Radicalism*, vol 2 no 2, pp 27–52

Paul Kingsnorth, 2003—*One No, Many Yeses: A Journey to the Heart of the Global Resistance Movement*. London: The Free Press

Naomi Klein, 2002b—'Rebellion in Chiapas', in Naomi Klein with Debra Ann Levy, ed, 2002—*Fences and Windows: Dispatches from the Front Lines of the Globalization Debate*. Toronto: Vintage Canada

Xochitl Leyva Solano, 2017—'Geopolitics of Knowledge and the Neo-Zapatista Social Movement Networks', in Jai Sen, ed, 2017a—*The Movements of Movements, Part 1: What Makes Us Move?*. Volume 4 in the *Challenging Empires* series. New Delhi: OpenWord and Oakland, CA: PM Press

Xochitl Leyva Solano and Christopher Gunderson, 2017—'The Tapestry of Neo-Zapatismo: Origins and Development', in Jai Sen, ed, 2017a—*The Movements of Movements, Part 1: What Makes Us Move?*. Volume 4 in the *Challenging Empires* series. New Delhi: OpenWord and Oakland, CA: PM Press

Staughton Lynd and Andrej Grubacic, 2008—*Wobblies & Zapatistas: Conversations on Anarchism, Marxism and Radical History*. Oakland: PM Press

Subcomandante Insurgente Marcos, 2002a [1994]—'Testimonies of the First Day', in Tom Hayden, ed, 2002—*The Zapatista Reader*. New York: Thunder's Mouth Press. Originally published in *La Jornada*, January 19 1994

Subcomandante Insurgente Marcos, 2002b—'The Fourth World War Has Begun', in Tom Hayden, ed, 2002—*The Zapatista Reader*. New York: Thunder's Mouth Press

Subcomandante Insurgente Marcos, 2004—'The Seven Loose Pieces of the Global Jigsaw Puzzle (Neoliberalism as a Puzzle)', in Žiga Vodovnik, ed, 2004—¡Ya Basta!: Ten Years of the Zapatista Uprising. Oakland: AK Press

Subcomandante Insurgente Marcos (for the Indigenous Revolutionary Clandestine Committee—General Command of the Zapatista Army for National

Liberation—EZLN), September 2008—'Zapatistas Call for Worldwide Festival of Dignified Rage', at http://interactivist.autonomedia.org/node/11604 (Accessed April 2017)

Shannan Mattiace, 1997—'Zapata Vive!: The EZLN, Indigenous Politics, and the Autonomy Movement in Mexico', in *Journal of Latin American Anthropology*, vol 3 no 1, pp 32–71

David McNally, 2017—'From the Mountains of Chiapas to the Streets of Seattle: This Is What Democracy Looks Like', in Jai Sen, ed, 2017a—*The Movements of Movements, Part 1: What Makes Us Move?*. Volume 4 in the *Challenging Empires* series. New Delhi: OpenWord, and Oakland, CA: PM Press

Roel Meijer, 2017—'Fighting for Another World: Yusuf al-'Uyairi's Conceptualisation of Praxis and Permanent Revolution', in Jai Sen, ed, 2017a—*The Movements of Movements, Part 1: What Makes Us Move?*. Volume 4 in the *Challenging Empires* series. New Delhi: OpenWord, and Oakland, CA: PM Press

Jean Meyer, 2002—'Once Again, the Noble Savage', in Tom Hayden, ed, 2002—*The Zapatista Reader*. New York: Thunder's Mouth Press

Carlos Monsiváis, 2002—'From the Subsoil to the Mask That Reveals: The Visible Indian', in Tom Hayden, ed, 2002—*The Zapatista Reader*. New York: Thunder's Mouth Press

Gloria Muñoz Ramírez, 2008—*The Fire & the Word: A History of the Zapatista Movement*. San Francisco: City Lights Books

Peter North and David Featherstone, 2017—'Localisation as radical praxis and the new politics of climate change', in Jai Sen, ed, 2017a—*The Movements of Movements, Part 1: What Makes Us Move?*. Volume 4 in the *Challenging Empires* series. New Delhi: OpenWord, and Oakland, CA: PM Press

Notes from Nowhere, eds, 2003—*We Are Everywhere: The Irresistible Rise of Global Anti-Capitalism*. New York: Verso

Andres Oppenheimer, 2002—'Guerrillas in the Mist', in Tom Hayden, ed, 2002—*The Zapatista Reader*. New York: Thunder's Mouth Press

Eric Selbin, 2003—'Zapata's White Horse and Che's Beret: Theses on the Future of Revolution', Chapter 7 in John Foran, ed, 2003—*The Future of Revolutions: Rethinking Radical Change in the Age of Globalization*. New York: Zed Books

Lynn Stephen, 2002—*Zapata Lives!: Histories and Cultural Politics in Southern Mexico*. Berkeley: University of California Press

James Toth, 2017—'Local Islam Gone Global: The Roots of Religious Militancy in Egypt and Its Transnational Transformation', in Jai Sen, ed, 2017a—*The Movements of Movements, Part 1: What Makes Us Move?*. Volume 4 in the *Challenging Empires* series. New Delhi: OpenWord, and Oakland, CA: PM Press

Virginia Vargas, 2017—'International Feminisms: New Syntheses, New Directions', in Jai Sen, ed, 2017a—*The Movements of Movements, Part 1: What Makes Us Move?*. Volume 4 in the *Challenging Empires* series. New Delhi: OpenWord and Oakland, CA: PM Press

John Womack, Jr, 1999b—*Rebellion in Chiapas*. New York: The New Press

Lesley J Wood, 2004—'Bridging the Chasms: The Case of Peoples' Global Action', Chapter 5 in Joe Bandy and Jackie Smith, eds, 2004—*Coalitions Across Borders: Transnational Protest and the Neoliberal Order*. Lanham, MD: Rowman and Littlefield Publishers

Notes

1. EZLN 2001, p 126.
2. According to the Zapatistas, the time we are living through now is that of "the Fourth World War". While the Third World War—more commonly known as the 'Cold War'—ended with the collapse of the Soviet Union and the ascendancy of neoliberal capitalism, the Fourth World War is "a new world war", a war of neoliberal capitalism against humanity; see Subcomandante Insurgente Marcos 2004, p 257.
3. Ed: Since the author wrote this essay from Canada, and some such "mass radicalised movements" have indeed taken place in the Global North during these past some years (2011–2013)—and including, significantly, in Canada, such as the students' movement in Québec, the Idle No More and Defenders of the Land movements among First Nations peoples, and others—I think I should point out here that this essay was finalised in 2009, ie before these movements burst onto the scene, and to take responsibility for this delay in publication.
4. Buck-Morss 2000, pp 11–12.
5. Bloch 1986, p 12.
6. See Khasnabish 2008a.
7. Selbin 2003, p 84.
8. Day 2005.
9. See Khasnabish 2008a; Khasnabish 2008b; Khasnabish 2007; and, Khasnabish 2006.
10. García Márquez and Pombo 2004, pp 4–5.
11. ibid, p 5.
12. Callahan 2004a, pp 218–219.
13. Marcos 2002a (1994).
14. This is the way most Zapatista communiqués are signed.
15. Subcomandante Insurgente Marcos 2004, p 77.
16. Ed: At one level, and although this book has no pretensions of being encyclopaedic in this 'coverage' of contemporary or recent movement, this collection itself gives some indication of the range and depth of what has been and is taking place in the world. But for surveys of recent movements, see the essays in this book by David McNally and Fouad Kalouche and Eric Mielants (McNally 2017, Kalouche and Mielants 2017), and also by Lee Cormie, Virginia Vargas, and Peter North and David Featherstone (Cormie 2017, Vargas 2017, and North and Featherstone 2017); and also for discussions of a very important 'other' world of contemporary movement—of political Islam—see the essays in this book by Roel Meijer and by James Toth (Meijer 2017, Toth 2017).
17. Ed: For complementary discussions, see also the essays in this book by Xochitl Leyva Solano, 'Geopolitics of Knowledge and the Neo-Zapatista Social Movement Networks' (Leyva Solano, 2017), and 'The Tapestry of Neo-Zapatismo: Origins and Development' by Xochitl Leyva Solano and Christopher Gunderson (Leyva Solano and Gunderson, 2017).
18. See Muñoz Ramírez 2008.
19. Womack, Jr 1999b, pp 18–19.
20. Stephen 2002.

21. FLN 1980, cited in Stephen 2002, p 152.
22. Collier and Quaratiello 1999, p 158.
23. Harvey 1998, p 165.
24. ibid, p 166.
25. ibid, p 165.
26. ibid, p 166.
27. ibid, p 166.
28. ibid, p 198.
29. Gilly 1998, p 303.
30. ibid, p 303.
31. See Arquilla, Fuller, Fuller, and Ronfeldt 1998.
32. Gilly 1998, p 309.
33. ibid, p 309.
34. Aridjis 2002; Gilly 1998; Mattiace 1997; Monsiváis 2002.
35. Rick Rowley interview, September 20 2004. Most of the cited interviews are available in my book *Zapatismo Beyond Borders* (Khasnabish 2008a)—but not all. They exist in their complete form only in unpublished transcripts.
36. See Meyer 2002, and Oppenheimer 2002.
37. See Marcos 2002b, and also Marcos, September 2008. Ed: The present and immediate past tenses used in this part of the essay only reflects the fact that it was finalised during the times that all this was taking place, and as the author explains in the early parts of the essay, the research on which it is based was in many ways a part of what was happening.
38. Kingsnorth 2003, p 7.
39. Callahan 2004b, pp 218–219.
40. Klein 2002b, p 219.
41. ibid, pp 220–221.
42. Notes from Nowhere 2003.
43. ibid, p 31.
44. The effects of Zapatismo's resonance have undoubtedly been felt transnationally, but this does not mean they have been evenly distributed or manifested in the same way everywhere. As someone located in the Global North, my own work has focused on the significance of Zapatismo for the radical imaginations of activists in this space, particularly because the horizon of radical politics in the North of the Americas has appeared so barren for so long. However, this is not to say that the Zapatista struggle has not been relevant in the Global South. Indeed, given the 'left turn' in Latin America in recent years, the Zapatistas have often been self-consciously positioned by other radical movements in Latin America (from the Landless Workers Movement in Brazil to the popular assemblies in Argentina to the *cocaleros*—coca growers—in Bolivia) as a movement of central importance within a larger fabric of renewed struggle. Perhaps due to the presence of other radicalised and popular actors on the Southern political landscape, the Zapatistas have functioned as a dynamic element of this fabric rather than an inspiration for it.
45. Notes from Nowhere 2003, p 34; Muñoz Ramírez 2008, p 144.
46. Kingsnorth 2003, p 37.

47. CUPW actually served as the regional convenor for PGA in North America from 1998–1999, a role taken over—although not very successfully—by the Montreal-based Anti-Capitalist Convergence (CLAC) after 1999.
48. Dave Bleakney interview, March 25 2004.
49. Friederike Habermann interview, April 2004.
50. Lynd and Grubacic 2008, pp 10–11.
51. EZLN 2001, p 125.
52. ibid, p 125.
53. Flood 2003, p 74.
54. Notes from Nowhere 2003, p 96.
55. Kingsnorth 2003, p 73.
56. de Marcellus 2001, p 105.
57. Peoples' Global Action, 'Brief History of PGA', at http://www.nadir.org/nadir/initiativ/agp/en/pgainfos/history.htm; Wood 2004.
58. Wood 2004.
59. ibid.
60. Big Noise Tactical, 1998.
61. Big Noise Tactical, 2000.
62. Big Noise Tactical, 2003.
63. Big Noise Tactical, 'About Us', at http://www.bignoisefilms.com/about.htm (Inactive April 2017).
64. Rick Rowley interview, September 20 2004.
65. Jacquie Soohen interview, September 20 2004.
66. Marcos 2002b.
67. Rick Rowley interview, September 20 2004.
68. Day 2005.

OpenWord

Afterword

Learning to Be Loyal to Each Other:
Conversations, Alliances, and Arguments
in the Movements of Movements
Laurence Cox

We must learn to be loyal, not to 'East' or 'West', but to each other.
—European Nuclear Disarmament Appeal, 1980[1]

An Overwhelming Task

I should start this Afterword with a confession. When Jai Sen as editor asked me to write an essay reviewing and responding to this book as a whole, I found the request hugely exciting—but also incredibly daunting, almost impossible to live up to. At an individual level, many of the authors are extraordinary human beings, and figures who carry an aura with them that goes beyond their own: In their lives and their words, they express the realities of the struggles of enormous numbers of people, in some cases across great spans of time, engaging with huge challenges. Collectively, too, this book is an unparalleled record of thought and action, an attempt to grasp something of the immediate backdrop to where our movements are now. It comes out of a long series of practices, among them the 'auroras of the Zapatistas', popular struggles in India, the Social Forum movement, the extraordinary summit protests, the attempts to remake states in Latin America and—not least—the work of Jai Sen, Peter Waterman, and their many collaborators, who have attempted to construct conversations between the experiences of these different movements in books like this, online, and in and around the Forums. It is a great privilege to read the resulting book, but there is almost a sense of vertigo in trying to grasp the struggles that lie behind the individual chapters, let alone in reading them collectively.[2]

In the end, the only basis I can find for my own responses and reflections lies in the way in which my own work has been shaped by some of these same experiences and practices, in more local and specific ways. Along with others, and after many years of involvement in a range of different movements, I became part of the process of networking between movements in Ireland from the late 1990s, including the 'Grassroots Gatherings' series of movement encounters from 2001 to the present[3] and the protest against the EU's 2004 enlargement summit,[4] all of which fed into a new wave of movement alliances. At the National University of Ireland Maynooth several of us set up and now run an MA for activists from different movements based on popular education methodology.[5] Internationally this practice of 'learning from each other's struggles' developed into the online journal *Interface*, a network of activist researchers supporting dialogue between movements and academia and across movements.[6] I have also been involved in a dialogue between Marxism as a theory from and for social movements and academic social movement research, which has found shape among other things in co-writing the book *We Make Our Own History*[7] with Alf Gunvald Nilsen, who works on social movements in the Global South, and attempting in our own way to grasp the 'movements of movements' theoretically and historically from an activist point of view. In all of this, I—and I think most of those I have worked with on these various projects—have been conscious of being shaped by, and participating in, this wider experience of people in movement, struggling for a better world: Too many, and too diverse, to ever really know closely even within a single country, let alone globally.

In some ways, perhaps, writing this wider experience, as *The Movements of Movements* attempts, is strictly speaking impossible—to engage with what Marx variously called "the movement as a whole" and "the real movement of society"; but precisely the impossibility of this task is what gives this book its strength. Rather than taking refuge within a particular political discourse, national or regional context, disciplinary theory, movement issue or theme, type of strategy or tactic, particular kind of organisation or institution, the book presents a challenge that can't be so easily dodged; one that comes from explicitly recognising each of these as partial, and asking what kinds of ways of speaking with and listening to each other can do most to deepen and broaden our understanding. Boaventura de Sousa Santos's phrase "an ecology of knowledges" is helpful here, with its clear implication that there is no perspective from which one can claim to see the whole—or put another way, that what we are reaching for is a way of speaking across worlds, but with all the humility and awareness of barely understanding and barely making ourselves understood even for specific purposes that comes from living in a world of seven thousand million of our own peers.

Talking about Movements

So what are we doing when we speak and write about movements? Some years ago I was involved in an abortive attempt to create a dictionary for European movements from within the networks around the movement think tanks of the Transnational Institute, Transform, and the Rosa Luxemburg Institute.[8] The challenge was—and remains—a real one: Even within what is often represented as a homogenous space, we do not mean the same thing by what we say.[9] Conversely, we often mean something comparable but spoken in different ways; in different countries and movements, activists often express broadly similar practices through different inherited languages. In the past, allegiances to powerful internationals—not only the Second, Third, and Fifth but also those of anarchism and radical nationalism, of liberalism, feminism and so on—obscured this fact through their construction of powerful centres.

Today it is perhaps less the relative power of Moscow—or for that matter US feminism—that is at stake, and more the way in which our movements have adapted to neoliberalism by constructing themselves as a series of niche markets: Just as afficionad@s of a particular kind of jazz, metal, or folk come to have a very skewed map of the world which essentially represents particular touring circuits and record labels, so too do activists. We are dependent on what for lack of a better word can be called export / import channels: The networks through which we come to hear particular versions of struggles elsewhere (on social media, as visiting speakers, in reports from movements abroad, in the one-line explanations we get of how this or that author is situated politically). What those of us outside India, or South Africa, or the US, think we know about the struggles within such huge countries is almost inevitably dependent on such arrangements.

Almost inevitably—but the kind of work represented in this volume has sought precisely to overcome these self-referential accounts and to open our ears to the limits of our knowledge about the rest of the world—and, by extension, our own countries and for that matter our own movements. In this sense we have to be multilingual: Operating for everyday purposes within our own mother tongues but shifting to other languages when we meet in different spaces, and so becoming conscious of the peculiarities of our own and how hard it can be to say what we want in some other form—while learning to doubt how well we are understanding each other.

Of course, in reality, none of us are born speaking activist theory: Even growing up in movement households it is something, like the vocabularies of love, which we have to learn to inhabit for ourselves and remake for our own purposes as we come to be agents in our own right. And like the language of love, it is inevitably metaphorical, perhaps particularly so when we think we are being most concrete. A party, to take that apparently concrete term, first meant literally 'a part', and was used—as late as the manifesto "of the communist party" in 1848[10]—to mean a faction or tendency (within a parliament and, later, a movement). It is also from our own movements that parties in the modern sense were formed, starting with the mass party (as in Germany's Social Democratic Party) and then the cadre party (as in the Bolsheviks). Of course those forms have themselves in turn been superseded by history: The rise of party-states in the state socialist and postcolonial worlds, of catch-all parties in the postwar Global North, of sectarian micro-parties, of parties as electoral alliances between micro-parties, of instant parties constructed online, and so on all mean that when we say 'party', we are really asking a question rather than pointing to a single, clearly-understood thing. This is not less true for 'union', 'NGO', 'movement', 'struggle', 'campaign', and all the rest of it—as we know when we try to make alliances with one another.

Some of the time—as in the first flush of love—it may not seem to matter so much what we mean if we can agree to agree that it means the same thing;

and many alliances which do not have to bear very much pressure can be constructed on this basis. Of course, it is only when we are actually trying to work together in the teeth of real pressure from outside that we come to see what we actually did mean and how far we have actually understood each other. What can we say, then, about the metaphors we use to grasp that strange experience of 'movement'?

At some level, I want to suggest, movement theory comes from movement practice and is developed as a tool to help us do concrete things. Sometimes movements exist in a 'state of nature', cut off from other movements and having to invent all their terms themselves, more or less consciously. More commonly, they repurpose and rework an older language that belonged to a previous movement in the same space. Or, as Alf and I suggest,[11] they "reclaim, reuse and recycle" a form of frozen or sedimented movement theory from some academic source which has preserved the ideas of a previous generation of activists.

But because we are starting from different social experiences, different local cultures, different processes of movement development, and different forms of intellectual socialisation, it is not strange that mutual incomprehensibility is a frequent experience. When we cannot rely on a mechanical similarity that comes from comparable sources, it is really only through alliance-building and long conversations that we can come to speak each other's languages, or develop a new, creolised, language that expresses our new and more complex reality: New and more complex because we now have to speak effectively to a wider range of realities and say something that works across these.

Not every movement language, it should be said, is subject to these pressures. Sectarianism is defined among other things precisely by being impervious to any real learning from its interlocutors: Its only concern is to fit a selective account of what they think within its own framework. But this is not different for academic languages which are only answerable to their own disciplines and where the determining power relationships do not include the movements themselves; and it is also true for the kind of celebrity writing which is mostly concerned with its reception in the centres of intellectual production which determine its saleability. Or—put more constructively—if we *do* owe allegiance to an organisation, to a discipline, or to publishing, we also owe it to the movements we are working with to ensure that they form a determining part of our conversations and not simply the raw materials we work on.

There is a good side to this, however: Language is a tool that we use to enable not only communication but also collaboration. It is in listening to each other and trying to communicate across difference that we come, sometimes, to forge effective alliances and overcome our own partial situations, in part: To engage more deeply with the other worlds that shape our movements and the other worlds they are trying to make.

Of course this does not always happen: Language can have many purposes. For example, the century-old distinction between agitation, organisation, and education[12] suggests that some ways of movement talking are more useful for talking to those who are *not* yet active (agitation). Those same languages—the language of outrage and a call to action—are only sometimes useful when directed at other activists. They can mean, or be understood as, a lack of respect—a failure to recognise that the other person is just as committed and engaged as we are, and an assertion of the central importance of *our* issue as against theirs. Though there are of course times when internal agitation is necessary to raise awareness of issues which are being ignored or excluded.

So too, an organising language can be used to express a macho, 'just do it' impatience with questions (themselves often the fruit of bitter experience) about the implications of fetishising action as against strategy; or it can be used to construct a nuanced relationship between two *different* ways of doing things, their different tempos and fields of action—which can, perhaps, enable a different way of working to arise in a new movement. An educational language too can represent a means whereby a certain kind of movement intellectual tries to bring everything into a zone where they are likely to be central—or it can be a very different kind of (collective, popular, self-) education where what is heard, and thought, learned, and done is of more importance than what is spoken directly.

Just as with love, where we may be aware that different cultures or different relationships have more or less of a language of praise and romance, a language of daily tasks and care, a language of articulated feelings, or a language of bodies and children, and that any of these can be (used as) a barrier to communication just as much as a tool for real connection and collaboration across time—so too with movements. How can we speak our different kinds of languages together in ways that help to make movements work, and that are more shaped to contributing to our shared spaces and practices than to asserting our own place within that space?

My experience has become that celebrating and/or demonising movements and organisations has little real value; or put another way, the spaces in which this is the primary activity are not spaces geared towards collaboration between movement participants. Rather, they are spaces of recruitment and opinion politics, of asserting our own value through ridiculing others or praising those who we feel reflect well on ourselves. But the world in which we award stars or red marks to other groups is not one in which we build links with them: Particularly, it might be said, when we do so on the basis of our allegiance elsewhere (to some superior version of Theory, whether academic or sectarian; an assertion of the primacy of our own Issue as against all others; or our ability to provoke particular kinds of reaction from an audience approached via commercial publishers or the opinion politics of the Internet and social media). There are words to describe the activity of turning other people's painful and difficult struggles into fodder for our own personal strategies, but they are not pleasant ones.

The Mexican scholar of Latin American history and politics Adolfo Gilly, reflecting on his reading of many different kinds of radical theory, talks about how the best approaches share "a concern with the preoccupations of the people, based on the impulse to understand their world and what motivates them".[13] This suggests a critical, and more constructive, means of talking *between* languages, which neither assumes the automatic and unquestioning validity of each language in its present form nor that one language can be 'right' and another 'wrong'. Gilly again:

> [parties in Latin America] often think they are the ones organizing and instructing the people on how to mobilize, but that's not the case—they were the best institutional form for securing particular ends, and the impulse comes from elsewhere, from long years of suffering, from an intolerable reality.[14]

This goes equally for movements, organisations, and intellectual traditions: They may not be the best form, and people can change as they assess this, more or less consciously.

So we can have a serious and honest discussion about the adequacy of a particular (intellectual, organisational, cultural) form to needs; and along with this a discussion of the selectivity of which needs are met, or not met, by particular approaches, with a view to developing the practice of movements—a critical dialogue of solidarity geared to finding ways of working together that enhance what we are all trying to do.

However, this also has to be earned. The trust and respect of our interlocutors has to be earned, not least through their seeing that we are trusting them, and being open about our own standpoints (in a way that the intellectual or political sneer excludes)—but also that we are respecting them fully. In particular, of course, we have to respect that they understand the everyday experience of their own world far better than we ever can, and that there is a relationship between that experience and the strategies and languages they are choosing to deal with it.

That does not mean that we necessarily agree with their interpretation of that experience, or their strategies: To my mind, respecting others as equals entails including our own perspectives in the conversation, and being open to discussion (or argument). But it does mean recognising (in a materialist way) that other people are not actually going to accept our assertions about what they should be doing on the basis of where we stand—nor, perhaps, should they: The real gain of our encounters is often simply a clearer understanding of where each other is situated and why they struggle in the way they do.

If at times we are able to suggest something sensible to others, or make an argument that strikes them with force, it is usually because we have listened to them—and to others like them—closely and are able to bring out the discontents they are not fully articulating, or that they are not managing to resolve through the forms they have chosen. In my experience the ability to do this is usually (perhaps not always) a result of being aware of the learning processes of *other* people who have already gone through a similar process: Familiarity with the struggles of those who became second-generation feminists, for example, can help us say something useful to some teenage girls (not all); or familiarity with working-class community education can help us say something useful to people who have previously accepted their place in the social and cultural order (or not found effective ways of resisting it). But these are skilled and cautious conversations, depending on decades rather than years of *listening* and *learning* and on a basis of honesty and equality.

In a similar vein, I want to say, university-based rants against the limitations of contemporary movements are easily recognised for what they are, as is the desire to elevate one's own cultural capital (the particular theoretical variant, or life experience, one is staking claim to). They may offend and hurt, but I suspect that this is often secondary, in that their form shows how little they are intended as dialogue: The movements mentioned in such rants are caricatures, punching bags against which our authors show off their cleverness and radicalism at the expense of people who are risking much in their attempts to bring about *any* change in the present situation. This does not mean that we should not criticise the ways in which reformists seek to shut down discussion of—for instance—repression, the limits of capitalism, ecological destruction, racism, settler societies, patriarchy, and so on. But if we are serious about wanting to change this, we have to do so either by honest engagement where we think something can be learned, or by bringing the missing subjects into the conversation and letting them speak for themselves. I have never seen a rant about police violence change the opinion of someone who believes the police version of events, for example; I have though seen direct encounters with real victims shake such belief to the core.

To my mind this is a core tenet of political responsibility: To think about what we are doing when we say something, and why we are doing it, to consider its intended effect on others, but also its actual effects, to think about how it is distributed and how it is understood; and to see our speech as an integral and conscious part of our practice and hold it up to the same standards.

This is the foundational proposition of the MA in Community Education, Equality and Social Activism at Maynooth. Grounded in a long experience of popular education struggles around class, gender, ethnicity, ecology, and anti-capitalism, the central learning point of the course comes from sharing an intense space over a long period with very different others who are also, unmistakably, one's peers as organisers, community activists, and radical educators (and I am referring equally here to participants, to the activist staff, and to the other activists we bring in, visit, or work with in the course of a year). In the space of a weekend, or even a week at a space like a social forum, we naturally gravitate to those who are like us and with whom we can have more or less fruitful conversations; but the most useful work takes place on the margins of the formal presentations and debates, in networking with those who are not quite like us.

Over a year spent with activists who scare us, upset us, argue with us, and in other ways bother our own sense of who we are, we have to come to take them more seriously. Not necessarily to agree with them—but to recognise that their experiences are as real and valid as ours, to understand what they actually mean when they say something, and to come to intuit something of why a particular response makes sense to them. As we say when we bring the group together at first, most do not need to learn how to connect with the activists who are most like them: The real challenge is in making the allies they actually need to win, those who do not automatically see the world, or respond to it, in the same way.

One great merit of this book, then, is precisely to keep drawing attention to the wider movements (plural) of movements—or (put more generally) the movement realities that lie outside our own immediate experience, network of allies, political niche, and so on. If at times the perspective that comes from attempting to integrate these very different perspectives and the struggles that lie behind them is a vertiginous one, still doing so strengthens the muscles that we need to use when engaging with the specific movement realities that we actually bump up against outside of our own existing practice. Without these muscles, or the orientation that makes us want to learn and listen, make allies, and develop shared projects, it is we who are condemned to remain in relative isolation, trapped within the limits of our own social and political order—who are unable to move.

Loyalty to Each Other: A Humanist Perspective

How then can we hold these two perspectives together? Jai Sen's remarkable Introduction attempts to draw our attention to the widest boundaries of movement, to go "beyond the fields we know".[15] I think there are at least three steps in his dance (but he may see more, or fewer). Rather than repeat his analysis, I will try to argue alongside him, perhaps accompanying him in the dance, but from my own perspective.

Firstly, Sen reminds us, we should set the movements we know in contrast with those we do not; or (as we put it in Interface or our MA) we need to learn from each other's struggles, even or particularly those we are not already connected with. Or, as social movements researchers might say, we need the comparative perspective that can help us to think about our movements *as* movements. Secondly, those movements come out of deeper social realities and injustices: They do not exist in and of themselves. E P Thompson's famous comment "no worker in history ever had surplus value taken out of his [sic] hide without finding a way of resisting"[16] points to this: Behind the movement are the people who move, and the things they move against. Alf Nilsen and I try to generalise this Marxist point: We need to understand how movements grow out of the material social relationships that shape people's lives, and to see the people and their lives.

Thirdly, movement is in some sense *what we do*, as full human beings—or rather as human beings who are attempting to become more fully ourselves in the act of movement. Our lives are diminished by the fact of living in a world marked by oppression, exploitation, and stigmatisation, whether we are among the victims, among the beneficiaries, or among the bystanders. In recognising and struggling against these structures, and in creating other kinds of relationships—of solidarity and communication, of resistance and creation—we become more fully human. In this sense, movements represent some of the best that the human spirit has to offer, in a world which prefers to offer degradation and violence, ignorance and obsession, isolation and despair.

I want though to enter a small point of disagreement, in relation to Sen's comments about "faith" (or rather, religion) and movements.[17] It is, of course, absolutely true that religion is an important aspect of many movements, either as a 'given' feature of the social world which is then drawn upon in movement (as, for example, the US Civil Rights Movement drew on the black churches of the South) or as a mode of movement organising (as, for example, in the use of conversion to Buddhism by Indian Dalits resisting caste).

But (temporarily putting on the rather different hats of a scholar of religion and an engaged religious practitioner), it seems to me that the key questions to be asked of *any* religious behaviour or way of talking are what needs it expresses and what people are doing with it. The same religion that can represent the self-defence of a minority in one place can be a central form of domination in another; or in a time and place where some people use religion as a means of asserting and organising ethnic power, others find it imprisoning (for example, in relation to gender). When we meet each other as potential allies in the social world, then, what is most important is to try and understand what *this* particular religious expression is actually expressing—which is not an easy question, as only a small number of adherents are typically in a position to say, lucidly, why and how it has become their preferred organising mode.

This is not only true of religious language and action. Marxism and the language of class became languages of oppression used by states covering substantial parts of the world for several decades during the twentieth century. Most of the world today is formed into nation-states, often built on the basis of anti-imperial or democratic movements which first expressed themselves in terms of ethnicity, nationhood, or race. In less direct forms, we have seen forms of feminism and, more recently, gay / lesbian (not yet, to my knowledge, bi / trans / queer) emancipation pressed into service to justify Western military interventions.[18]

Put another way, there is no safe place to stand within language or theory: It is in 'real human practice' that the actual meaning of particular words, organisations, and traditions in particular places becomes clear. When is a trade union a form of liberation, and when is it not? When is community activism a mode of the self-assertion of the poor, and when it is a form of clientelism? When is counterculture disruptive of central power relations, and when is it a new cultural niche? If we can ask these questions, we can also see that there is little point in making broad assertions of the form "X is ..."—and that we have rather to look at *what people are doing with it*. This, to my mind, is the fundamental importance of Marx's historical method. To return to religion, this is why Marxist historians have been able to write about religion variously as a mode used by elites to express their power, as a form of social control, as a mode of radical self-organisation, and as a quietist escape: It can be all of these, depending on circumstances.

To quote the European Nuclear Disarmament appeal of 1980, "We must learn to be loyal, not to 'East' or 'West', but to each other".[19] Activists wrote this in the context of a difficult, limited but nonetheless significant dialogue between Western European peace activists and Eastern European dissidents in the face of the threat of a 'limited nuclear war' between the USA and USSR, to be fought in Europe. The implication was of course not an uncritical acceptance of the other's views, but rather a ('materialist') recognition that the other spoke for a partial reality which was different from one's own and that it was through the encounter between the two that something could be changed.

The meaning here of "not to East or West" was of course the attempt to construct a dialogue between West Europeans who were radical in the context of their own states and opposed to Stalinism, and Eastern Europeans who were seeking, for example, a 'socialism with a human face' that would suit neither Moscow nor Washington. Today, we might seek other ways of being loyal to each other that do not involve ignoring who we are in our own realities, but ask more clearly on what basis we seek and offer solidarity across our different worlds, what it is we recognise when we are moved by each other's struggles to develop our own, and what kinds of loyalty we are hoping for.

Imagining Movement, Living Movement

The remainder of this Afterword responds, selectively, to the chapters in this book. Rather than simply summarise them, I have tried to pick out themes that—from my own idiosyncratic standpoint—may help either to make connections or to understand what we mean by the words we use to grasp what we and others are up to.

The opening 'Movementscapes' section gives a series of seven very different perspectives on how we might imagine the movements of movements—including, of course, very different senses of which movements are significant. In keeping with the perspective outlined above, I want to ask some questions of these perspectives, in terms of the practice they suggest or refer to, by way of developing a dialogue of critical solidarity which does not ask us to agree with the other but rather to find a common space for action.

What Democracy Looks Like

David McNally's chapter gives us a stirring overview of struggles against capitalist globalisation from the Zapatistas on.[20] He writes rightly that "oppressed people around the world regularly re-emerge as conscious makers of history", and shows us how "utilising mass strikes and uprisings, land occupations, popular assemblies, and direct democracy, [movements] are carving open the spaces of opposition to globalising capitalism. And yet ..."

His "And yet" though, is an interesting one: "[T]hey confront the dilemma of moving from a politics of resistance to a politics of liberation" ... "they only episodically venture toward the beginning of something entirely new" ... "Radical movements cannot change societies without such a vision" ... "[T]his search for a radically different society has to mean clarifying concepts of anti-capitalism". And here is where I start to have doubts: Historical doubts, and Marxist ones.

For if there is one thing the *Marxist* study of revolutions has shown, it is that, more often than not, the visions, concepts, and forms of organisation of and during revolutions have come out of the processes of mass mobilisation rather than preceding or producing them: Actual revolutionary movements are often filled with people who feel that they are challenging the king's bad advisors rather than the institution of monarchy, who challenge actually-existing religion in the name of true religion, who "anxiously conjure up the spirits of the past to their service", as Marx put it[21]—dressing up 1848 in the clothes of 1789, dressing up peasant revolutions in the Third World during the 1950s and 60s in the clothes of 1917 or of the Paris Commune of 1871, or for that matter, and in our times, dressing up resistance to capitalist globalisation in the clothes of an imagined but now defunct (communist) Party.

There have indeed been periods when The Party and The Programme have been effective tools. On the longer historical view, these were rather short periods, associated with the period of 'organised capitalism' in which the nation-state was a central economic actor and the central protagonist of modernisation, and in which the structured delivery of popular support to contending elites might be expected to deliver particular kinds of redistribution. There were also (we might now remember, looking back at the experience not just of actually-existing socialism but also that of independent post-colonial states) a series of disappointments, problems, and disjunctures between the visions, programmes, and organisation of such parties and the actual results; sufficiently so that we might wonder just how compelling the argument is, even in respect of that history.

But more broadly, I have come to have strong doubts about the general proposition that revolutions cannot be successful without a clear vision or a central organisation. I would say that it is only in a minority of cases that participants have had such visions or organisations going into revolutions; that neither vision or organisation is alone capable of *producing* revolutions; and that it would be more accurate to say that over time the *process* of revolution has led participants to reach their "hic Rhodus, hic salta" (a phrase—but also a play on words by Marx—in Latin, usually translated as "Rhodes is here, here is where you jump!", which spelt out means the point at which those taking part in the revolution suddenly had to make a leap into the unknown).[22] And when they do reach this stage (again following the classic Marxist historiography of revolutions), it is not through this external reaching for a vision or an organisation—but rather through the internal development of movements' own logic, what Alf and I have called "local rationalities".

For example, the Paris Commune *evolved* working-class democracy out of the structures of everyday life and in particular out of the self-organisation of small artisan workplaces and plebeian neighbourhoods into the democratic militias that formed the de facto basis of the National Guard, and the practical location for popular debate and action. This extraordinary, creative experience started from ideologies which had more to do with Blanquism and the heritage of previous radicalisms than with Marx (or Bakunin). The substance, it could be said, went beyond the form.

Something slightly more complex might be said of 1917: Although the military committee of the Petrograd Soviet, which carried out the October Revolution, came out of the process of council formation and radicalisation in a similar way, most Marxist commentators today would surely say that the organisation and programme of the Bolsheviks did *not* successfully translate into the state that Stalin built. And if we hold that there was any value in Leninism, we must surely also hold that it was *not* all that effective in making the kind of revolution that was intended.

My own feeling is that what today's movements need is not to look outside themselves for a vision of the future. There are more than enough such visions ('cookbooks for the future'), and most do not produce revolutions. Nor do they need to *import* a model of organising. If anything, they need to come to the point which Marx, in the *Eighteenth Brumaire*, describes thus: "There [in the liberal-heroic revolutions of the eighteenth century] the phrase went beyond the content—here [in the social revolutions] the content goes beyond the phrase". This is, of course, a *democratic* as well as a *social* perspective: It places the emphasis on the creative and reflective activity of ordinary people in their everyday struggles, and supports strategies that proceed from this and take it further, rather than to place the emphasis on the writers of visions and the organisers of parties.

I do not want, as the argument is sometimes put, to remove 'the conscious element' from the equation: I want to suggest that it is a question of seeing the 'conscious element' in everyday struggle, and attempting to find adequate forms for articulating this further, rather than identifying the 'conscious element' with a particular type of people engaged in a particular type of activity. I may be misreading McNally on this, but it seems to me that it is not in "the history of socialism" that we should be looking for our visions; rather, reading that history as activists can help us to see the non-linear relationship between the visions developed by movements in struggle and their actions, and the ways in which (to quote William Morris):

[People] fight and lose the battle, and the thing that they fought for comes about in spite of their defeat, and when it comes turns out not to be what they meant, and other [people] have to fight for what they meant under another name.[23]

This, I think, is a better way of reading how vision and organisation have worked— not only in relation to 1917, but also (for example) in relation to the welfare states now under massive assault in my own corner of Western Europe, the state social- isms now largely destroyed across the globe, the post-colonial states in so many parts of the world which have disappointed so many of the hopes that made them possible, or for that matter the uprisings of 1968 in Europe and North America, Mexico, and Japan. Something was gained in each case, but not what we thought or planned for; there were new battles to be fought; and the new organisational forms that were created turned out to have logics of their own.

Dialectics of Presence
In responding to McNally, then, I find myself echoing Drainville's comments in his essay in this book:

Where classical left internationalism was shaped by programmatic fights fought on behalf of abstract subjects, the 'new internationalism' drags actually-exist- ing human beings, in all their bounded plurality, into the terrain of the world economy.[24]

Of course, that plurality sometimes includes the *language* of the classical left, whether in post-colonial continuity with not-yet-resolved processes of struggling over the direction of national development, or in 'the second time as farce', as often happens in our universities. But Marxists, of all people, should not mistake the image of rationality for its substance. We need a sociology of knowledge (and not a morality play) that explains why, for example, the language of the classical left seems more attractive for many movements in Greece than for most in the

USA. And we also need to avoid the naïve assumption that if our comrades in India or Argentina use what seems to be the same language we use, or if our organisations have good relationships with one another, that this means we have a simple, transparent understanding of what, *in their own local contexts*, their language means.

Drainville's argument is, I think, a bottom-up one, or one that seeks to bring out bottom-up realities as against what he sees as the closure of categories like 'altermondialisme': "[T]ransnational praxis re-establishes the continuum of experience between global and local contexts of struggle, in a manner that may radicalise and socialise both". He also writes: "[W]e need to think from concepts of resistance drawn from what men and women acting against capitalist restructuring have already invented"—without losing the specificity of particular struggles but without losing touch with each other.

This is, I think, the spirit in which this book is couched, and it is one in which we stand to learn much from each other and, perhaps, win some real battles: It is precisely in the specificity of struggles that we are sufficiently grounded to do so—but at the same time, we need to be aware that if that is all we do, our gains will be incorporated into the wider system rather than contributing to create 'cracks' in capitalism.[25]

Social Imaginaries in the World-System

Kalouche and Mielants seem to be arguing, on grounds of definition, the opposite to McNally's case.[26] Where he sees movements as coming from below, but struggling to evolve visions and organisation, they write:

> We have not yet used the word 'movement' since it entails conscious and self-reflective teleology. ... Movements have rarely been expressions of the lower strata of the oppressed classes since they are usually intertwined with aesthetic ('bourgeois') values. Movements are motivated and directed, as conscious or self-reflective action, towards specific goals or aims that are provided through social imaginaries at particular social-historical intersections. It is *always* [my emphasis] through emerging social imaginary significations (in the name of something that becomes historically accessible to others within a social imaginary) that movements may undermine dominant economic, social, political, or cultural aspects of social-historical institutions.[27]

For these authors, then, movements are defined by the conscious element, and that conscious element is in a sense a prisoner of "social imaginaries". The periods 1968–1989 and up to the present, they tell us, "have been marked by the permeation of the world-system's multiple cultural systems by dominant capitalist social imaginaries". This feels circular to me, and perhaps a reflection of the different things we are looking at. There is no doubt that Kalouche and Mielants are talking about something real. Societies do indeed shape culture, and intellectuals of a certain ("aesthetic, 'bourgeois'") kind operate at the leading edge of that culture, in more or less interesting ways.[28] And there is indeed a sort of change which consists of the inner logic of that culture coming to operate in some sense against its current manifestations—within limits, of course. But is that all there is? Is this all that happens?

I want to think about two examples. One is the extraordinary impact of the Zapatistas—which I believe has been *because* they were not operating within the dominant social imaginary, but were speaking from a very different place, which resonated powerfully elsewhere because it was not simply a mild inflection, or avant-garde version, of neoliberal rhetoric. The other, older, experience is that of what was once called "the social movement",[29] the coming to self-consciousness and self-organisation of what slowly became spoken about as "the social question" or even more simply as "society": The vast masses of people who were not spoken for in the languages of eighteenth-century politics and culture, and the emergence of radically different ways of being, speaking, and acting that shook the world.

For Kalouche and Mielants however, this is far too simplistic: "[W]hile anti-systemic movements were actively looking to control the state, systemic forces were developing into polished and perfected ways of producing desires and needs and of shaping subjectivities. ... [S]ystemic forces were engaged—for a long period culminating in 1968 and beyond—in moving away from a centre (the state) to permeate all aspects of 'material life', thus dominating social imaginaries and inhabiting the 'cultural worlds' at the basis of a less stable 'interstate system'".

Well, there is something to this: This is one of the things that Foucault's disciples, and today's producers of commercial culture, seek to do. But it is perhaps mistaken on our part—politically as well as analytically—to assume that they are entirely successful in this. There is certainly both need and space for an engaged critique of these processes, just as we need a critique of the ways in which some kinds of movement elites transmit the cultural shape of the wider society in their organising practice. But if we are to have a real conversation, I think it has to allow for the world to be larger than this. Carpenters may look at trees and only see the tables that could be made from them; and cultural critics may look at the top-down processes through which elites seek to shape culture, seeing the need to point out the blindness of others and in so doing elevate their own trade to a position of centrality. But even within the frameworks of cultural studies, there is by now rather a long history of demonstrating the active nature of reception, including critical reception.[30] Returning to the discussion with Jai Sen above: Religions are mostly constructed by elites, and yet popular movements regularly appropriate them to say things which were not dreamed of by their founders or by the hierarchies they created. It is just as well that this is the case: If we were to push the top-down cultural critique to its limits, we would have to say that the only ways out are those provided by cultural critics (or radical theologians)—and we would also have to say that the historical record gives little ground for hope that their comments will change world-systems.

I would suggest something different: If we seek always and everywhere to find the effects of a dominant culture, we will find it, and we will confirm the importance of our own analysis, while being unable to do much with it, as the conclusion of Kalouche and Mielants's essay suggests. Conversely, if we recognise that people have needs—which are not simply produced by the system as Kalouche and Mielants suggest, but may even bang up against it (to take a mundane but powerful example, the need for water regularly bangs up against attempts to privatise and commodify this—and people consciously resist the demand to imagine themselves as consumers), we can see that, unevenly but persistently, people can and do find ways of organising around and expressing these needs; nor do they always cast these needs in the form of 'identity'.

These things are uneven, and contested. In Ireland at present, some individuals do accept the logic of consumerism—when it seems to suit them. For instance, the 43 per cent of the population who have officially paid their water charges at time of writing fits rather well with the proportion who believe that their interests are best met by the traditional centre-right parties. The rest, not so much. Of these, some of course are free riders, but most have a broader picture: Participants and opponents agree that the struggle is not just about water but about austerity. Of the vast numbers of people who are involved in directly resisting the installation of meters, in local assemblies, and in producing counter-publics and engaging in mass marches, many—but not all—link the struggle against austerity here in Ireland to the struggles in Greece or Spain; many—but not all—link the struggle against austerity to that against neoliberalism or capitalism; and many—but not all—link it to struggles against privatisation and the IMF in the Global South. These things are not given, but to be fought for. It is this process which the top-down definition of the situation fails to see, and fails to contribute to, in its concern to show how movements are 'cultural dupes', unconsciously playing out parts scripted for them elsewhere.

Storming Heaven

Tariq Ali's piece deserves reading in full.[31] There is, I think, an element of 'erano belli nostri tempi' —'our days were great ones'—that is well justified by his own experience and contribution at the time. I would read something else into it, though, when he says: "How can the lyrical sharpness of politics in 1968 be anything but alien to the spirit of this age that has followed? The radical politics and culture of 1968 do not cater to the needs of the current rulers any more than they did to the needs of the rulers of that time. The autonomy of the past has to be defended".

What recognising, and practising, that autonomy can do, I think, is give our present-day actions an urgency, and a scale of vision, that is easily lost. Ali was writing in 2008, and in Britain, which was perhaps not the most inspiring of times and places, and it would be easy to respond that there were other uprisings, even at the time, that he does not mention. But I think it is important to speak for what is fixed in our own emotions and social experience—if it can be done without dismissing others. We do need that bigger picture, somehow, to become real for us as part of our everyday experience, to infuse the mundane actions of any day's struggle with the bigger picture of what they connect to and what they can mean. I am walking around the corner of a dusty mountain track; but I am also, perhaps, storming heaven. This latter only exists in my understanding and in my relations with the others who are doing the same thing: It cannot be read off from seeing my feet move.

What the highpoints of movement such as 1968 offer us is the chance to see ourselves in this kind of relationship to others, around the world, rather than in relationship to how we progress our individual issue within a particular local setup, or the dominant structures of meaning production. Coming to be loyal to each other is, above all, this: Coming to let our reality be defined by each other's worlds, on the basis of whatever form of mutual recognition we can negotiate. It is, of course, easier to see ourselves as simply trying to change one corner of a given world, within familiar rules—or to engage in forms of identity competition with others. To take that larger position is to grow beyond, but remain rooted in, our own realities—allowing those realities to become plural.

Being Indigenous: One Foot Outside

Alfred and Corntassel, as Indigenous activists, present Indigenousness as "oppositional, place-based existence, along with the consciousness of being in struggle against the dispossessing and demeaning fact of colonisation by foreign peoples", and go on to write that "[Indigenous Peoples'] existence is in large part lived out as determined acts of survival against colonising states' efforts to eradicate them culturally, politically, and physically".[32] They present a situation at once of extreme weakness and of inherent resistance: "How can we resist further dispossession and disconnection when the effects of colonial assaults on our own existence are so pronounced and still so present in the lives of all Indigenous people?".

Not being Indigenous (but where I live in a postcolonial state, and have been increasingly studying both moments of anti-imperial solidarity and imperial collusion), I want to respond from the outside, in relation to three elements of Indigenous resistance which have had effects in my part of the world.

The first—on the part of a small fishing and farming community in the northwest of Ireland facing a Shell pipeline, and who have developed solidarity links to the Ogoni of the Niger Delta (who have their own history of battles with Shell)—is the extraordinary power of apparently weak groups when their existence is under threat. In recent years Canadian indigenous groups have been remarkably successful at defeating oil pipelines, a matter of major concern to the rest of the planet. In Ireland, where the pipeline has now been built by Shell after some 14 years of struggle, the costs have been such as to minimise the likelihood of fracking being successful. A central reason for this is that the threat of the pipeline is precisely the destruction of communities, families, place, and ways of life directly tied to the land and the sea. As a result, local resistance was able to be far more determined and uncompromising than many more traditional forms of movement precisely because of how much was at stake. As with Indigenous communities and struggles, this combination of community and place—which is a part of a wider tradition of rural ecological struggle in disadvantaged parts of Ireland—has an anti-systemic potential which movements that find it easier to 'negotiate' do not have; and such struggles can be strategic in powerful ways even when numbers are small and opposing power is apparently overwhelming.[33]

What this points to, secondly, is the extent to which Indigenous groups and others have one foot outside the apparently all-encompassing whole that is the capitalist (patriarchal, racialised, etc) world-system. Of course, as Alfred and Corntassel remind us, the system may go very deep indeed; it may be a painful work of recovery to get to the point where 'one foot' is a fair estimation of how much of one's weight can be rested outside of it. *But what is strategically crucial is that there is an outside*, and that the communities in struggle are aware of this. That outside lies in the existence (or recovery, or re-imagining) of other ways of being that consciously seek not to imitate the system but rather, to imagine, know, and build other ways. Indigenous groups play a crucial role in this for the rest of us, because they remind us that the system is not eternal: That it has a history (and hence an ending) and an outside (and hence a limit). There are other such limits, set by the depths and richness of human needs beyond advertising, electoral systems, managerialism, trade agreements, and all the rest of it. These are the grounds of resistance, of the creation of alternatives (or rediscovery of old ways), and of the independent and self-confident critique of what exists. For other movements therefore, Indigenous resistance is a powerful reminder to get on with resistance in our own contexts.

Thirdly, Alfred and Corntassel's rich and multidimensional image of what constitutes Indigenous identity—or, as they observe, what might be an aspiration in this direction—is a challenge to the rest of us and what are often our quite impoverished ways of envisioning the future. (I include in this the forms of nationalism and religious identity which we have experienced in the modern world and among which many post-colonial societies now operate). There is—we now know, after the failure of such cultural nationalisms to deliver emancipation—no liberating path to redefining 'the' way of life that could replace the system. And yet, freed from this notion of nationhood, it remains clear that "history, ceremony, language and land", together with relationships, community, plants, and animals—the full richness of the human experience—offer strength in our resistance and in our envisioning of other futures. Perhaps, here, what we non-Indigenous should be inspired to is not the attempt to appropriate elements of Indigenous culture but rather to engage with the implications of the irreducibility of Indigenousness as insisted on by so many Indigenous radicals.

There is no one way of life that we should all live; nor can we all read off from our ancestry (often mixed and mobile) what we should be individually. And yet, human beings create cultures (and languages, religions, relationships to the land, communities, etc) all the time; it is what we do as a species, and often very rapidly. Can we imagine a world of co-existing—even of mutually interpenetrating—worlds which contain 'a wealth of needs', and where we do not have to communicate with one another along the artificially impoverished terms of narrow economic exchange? If we seek a world of real freedom, can we do other than recognise that this will allow each to find, rediscover, or create our own places in different ways? And can we commit to the politics that will make this possible, starting with the politics and movements of surviving Indigenous populations?

Indigenous Feminism

Andrea Smith argues that movements' failure to challenge heteropatriarchy leads us all to internalise social hierarchy, and (in her context, the USA) to seek a "kinder, gentler" US; or for Indigenous movements to seek nation-states rather than a more open and inclusive form of sovereignty. It leads racial justice movements there to imitate "white, Christian America" in a homophobic emphasis on the "Black family" or "Native family". It enforces a split between our public, protesting selves and our private, gendered selves—creating inaccessible movements. And it leads to single-issue organising strategies that accept the wider structures of domination.[34]

In place of this, she argues for "revolution by 'trial and error'", in which we share "our struggles, our successes, and our failures", giving examples of the attempt to proliferate "making power" in Latin American Indigenous-led movements and Incite!'s exploration of how to construct "movements that engage our whole selves, and from which we get back as much as we give". Her work has been very productive in this respect: The book *The Revolution Will Not Be Funded*,[35] where she played a key role, has been an inspiration to many Irish activists, despite our very different political situations.[36]

Building on Smith's arguments, it seems to me that the only way we can challenge the system as a whole *is to see it as a whole*, even with our different starting-points and primary concerns. If we do not recognise, whatever language we use, that there is some kind of relationship between class societies, empire-building and colonisation, racialisation, patriarchy, heteronormativity, and so on, we can only construct partial movements. In this context, calls to recognise a specific issue as *the* strategic issue are not so much the point; in the real world, people mobilise in concerted and sustained ways around issues that they feel in their own lives (not necessarily in individualised ways), and the question is rather of how we can make connections between those movements rather than which is most important. Part of the challenge, particularly for those of us working with words and working in universities, is not to let this process of alliance-building be overridden either by the analytic effort of theorising and prioritising or by the systemic logics of competition: To say 'My issue is the most fundamental one' is simultaneously to accept a retreat back to the boundaries of those movements within which this claim is credible. That may still mean several hundred million people, but it is not enough, in a world of billions. We do not have to give up the place where we stand, personally, politically, or intellectually, in order to find ways of making alliances: We simply have to commit ourselves not to prioritise the logic of competition in places where it does not belong.

Neo-Zapatismo

Xochitl Leyva Solano's fascinating piece discusses the social movement networks of "alliances and convergences" around the EZLN at both local and global levels.[37] I share her positioning within "a long tradition that seeks to produce knowledge which is useful not only for academics but that, above all, supports the strengthening of the processes of transformation, liberation, and emancipation put into motion by the collectives, organisations, and movements of which I am an active part" and her commitment to think beyond a "totality that makes us believe that there is literally no way out".

Critiquing the RAND Corporation's theory of Zapatista "social netwar", and discussing the shifting discourses of the EZLN, she summarises her research on neo-Zapatista networks in Europe. While in Ireland the direct role of these networks was limited, their indirect role in the development of anti-capitalist networks of resistance completely bears out Leyva Solano's research, running from alliance-building in the later 1990s through to the development of an overt anti-capitalist movement in the early years of this century, with significant connections to parts of the anti-war movement and contemporary anti-austerity struggles. She writes that "knowledge is always situated" and hence "all knowledge is partial and contingent".

In Ireland, our understanding and involvement in movements was certainly combined in this way: The impact of the Zapatistas made it possible for us to conceive of a "proximal zone of development" which took existing movements further. (For some of us, this was also informed by the experience of 1968, the history of the workers' movement, and the experience of movement networks elsewhere.) In doing this we were part of a process whereby movements articulated themselves *beyond* the existing system and came to find allies in one another on the basis of a mutual recognition of commitments to different forms of popular democracy, bottom-up organising, grassroots networking, feminist practice, and community activism. These movements were both rooted in their specific realities and struggles and able to reach out beyond themselves: We needed both moments, and we needed, perhaps, the radical otherness of the Zapatistas, outside of the familiar, known, provincialism of day-to-day movement routines, to imagine both more deeply and understand better what we were doing, or trying to do, as we put one foot in front of the other. Xochitl Leyva Solano's essay is an eloquent and powerful reminder of this.

Making Our Own History: Critically Engaging with the Movements of Movements

This book's challenge to understanding the 'movements of movements' is a challenging task, and one which I have been grappling with for many years.[38] When Alf Nilsen and I wrote *We Make Our Own History: Marxism and Social Movements in the Twilight of Neoliberalism*,[39] our strategy was to attempt to understand the complexities of movements in a humanist, demystified way by focussing on movements as situated, developmental human practice. 'Situated' because who we are, and the material circumstances of our lives, are fundamental to how we act; 'developmental' because movements rise and fall, as well as becoming more or less radical, networked, transformative, human, and so on; and 'practice' because movements have to be *done* or *made,* in more or less skilled ways.

In relation to Section 2 of this book, but more generally the diversity of movements and of what kind of thing we mean when we say movement, *We Make Our Own History* explores the range of levels of collective agency that movements are capable of going through—not in order to come up with some fixed ranking, but rather to see what might become possible (rather than simply celebrating or condemning the current state of movements, which does not help) and what might be needed to fulfil the needs expressed in our movements and reach their most radical goals. We look at the local rationalities represented in how subaltern populations live their daily lives and attempt to meet their needs under given conditions; the militant particularisms that arise when these daily strategies come under attack from above; the campaigns into which such militant particularisms can coalesce in alliance with their peers; the wider social movement projects which bring together multiple campaigns around a vision of a different way of organising the world; and the organic crises which such challenges to the status quo can sometimes give rise to.

We also, and importantly, try to theorise the collective agency of the powerful, wealthy, and culturally privileged—"social movements from above"—in particular those which give rise to new ways of organising the world, such as neoliberalism. When we think of these *as* collective agency like our own (albeit collective agency which can draw on very different kinds of resources), it becomes possible to theorise power relationships in terms which are not totally removed from our own experience, with less theology and more practical understanding perhaps (a lesson learnt from Gramsci and resistance to fascism).

Using this broad framework, we try to think historically about the current wave of movements, in particular where we are in terms of the strength or weakness of the hegemonic alliance around neoliberalism and our differing capacities, in different locations, to bring it—the hegemonic alliance—(further) into crisis and to create possible alternatives. We might think of the current wave in terms of relationships across time: For example, continuities from earlier counter-hegemonic alliances that flowed into and became the global 'movement of movements' and forced changes of regime in Latin America; from there into the movement against US wars in the Middle East and a rising tide in the Arab world; and into indignad@s / anti-austerity / Occupy movements in the Global North—but it becomes possible to ask these questions practically rather than as a matter of definition: How, and why, do particular events, particular mobilisations connect to others or stand isolated?

One thing which becomes clear in our analysis—and which this volume also shows—is the relatively greater ease of making connections, politically and intellectually, between Western Europe, North America, Latin America, South Asia, and Indigenous struggles. There is a history to this particular set of connections, intersections, discussions, mobilities, and arguments, which simultaneously makes it easier for activists to feel that they understand one another and to organise together across distances. Of course this is a matter of degree: There are other networks of movements, and it is not that movements in the Arab world, or in Sub-Saharan Africa or East Asia (for example) are necessarily 'isolated'. Nor am I suggesting that all is homogenous and uncontentious within the "movement (singular) of movements".

Rather, and partly in contrast with Jai Sen's argument in his Introduction to this book,[40] I believe that the distinction between the totality of 'movements (plural) of movements' and the specific networks which at any given time constitute the 'movement of movements' is a real and useful one. That we know more about each other in certain contexts is part and parcel of our better connections within the movement (singular) of movements as it has been constructed between its participants thus far. Asserting this is not, then, a call to rest on our laurels, but rather a call on the one hand to deepen and broaden connections from what has already been achieved—and on the other hand to move away from celebrating the fact of isolation, which is valuable as academic rhetoric (or as social media headline) but not good news in political terms. Movements that seek to challenge deep-seated power relationships, and not just insert themselves within given local power structures, need to look for wider alliances. This is a crucial piece of movement learning which should not be forgotten in the celebration of the specific, or of struggles in 'unlikely' places: *Of course* people fight where they stand, and start from their own local rationalities; equally, most such struggles are defeated or subsumed, without broader solidarity. A 'forgotten' struggle has a problem, and needs allies.

Conversely, even a partial and limited set of alliances such as that represented by the movement of movements is a huge achievement, and nothing is gained by using its limitations to deny its existence or significance. If we do not see the most recent waves of movement historically—in relation to earlier movements, and earlier movement waves—we will neither understand them intellectually nor be able to take things further politically.[41] In this sense, there is much to be said for the book's strategy of closing its story around 2010: Because "the owl of Minerva only takes flight at dusk", or in other words, we know things differently when we have acted past them than when we are still trying to articulate them. Both modes of knowledge are crucial for human action, but their shapes are not the same.

Another way of putting this is to say that the structures whereby we know and work with one another are not fixed, but something to work on. It is always hard to assess how deep particular connections go, and one key question has to be whether a verbal acknowledgement of other movements represents significant internal realities within a particular movement, or just a sort of hobby for a handful of network-minded or internationally-minded people. This is where the importance of Jai Sen's, and Peter Waterman's, work comes, and why alliance-building processes—from the various Social Forum movements to People's Global Action, from the circuits of the various international lefts to issue-specific networks such as that against Shell—matter. The journal *Interface* represents a smaller contribution in the same direction: Deepening the 'ecology of knowledges' and enabling us to imagine ourselves and work together as part of a wider world—negotiating the balancing act between staying true to ourselves and our own specific, local struggles and standing in glorious isolation. Even the radical specificity of Indigenous activism entails networks across peoples and across continents, and this is no weakness.

I should also say a word here about "the twilight of neoliberalism". On the one hand this judgement comes from a recognition that *all* previous capitalist accumulation strategies have had a relatively short lifespan (only of several decades); and that precisely because they are based on complex alliances, there are good reasons why such things are hard to hold together past a certain point, and any serious strategy for defeating them therefore has to entail disaggregating such alliances and their structures of consent and coercion.

On the other hand, this recognition that the structures of the world-system are constructed alliances also means that we cannot expect to have a blueprint, like an elite-in-waiting which hopes to take over a once-colonial state structure relatively unchanged. If we are to be successful in challenging these structures, it can only be on the basis of being alive to this reality and of continuing, deepening, and extending the conversations between movements from below that can allow us to shape an alternative kind of alliance for a different (and more diverse) kind of world, and disaggregate hegemony.

Hence *neither* One Agreed Programme *nor* Fragmented Resistance for its own sake: The phrase 'a movement of movements' itself sketches out a programme of bringing together the various different tacit knowledges, hidden worlds, and forms of good sense that arise from our different partial perspectives to create a wider view of what is wrong with the world, how we are coping with that, what we are doing about it, what we might be able to do, together. Such a programme is a process, not a given: Among other things, it is itself a movement from whatever 'movement of movements' we have at present towards whatever 'movements of movements' we can connect with beyond our present starting points.

Struggles for Other Worlds

Many of the essays in Section 2 of this book have a powerful orientation to practice. Anand Teltumbde's essay on Dalit movements highlights both the weaknesses of much contemporary Dalit activism in its tendency to follow populist leadership which fails to speak to Dalit experience of the effects of capitalist globalisation—and the need for the Indian left to take caste seriously as a strategic political issue.[42] Jeff Corntassel's chapter, seeking a 'spiritual revolution' against colonial definitions of the self, highlights the weaknesses of Indigenous rights discourses in that they encourage a state-centred rather than community-centred framing of movement goals, and so reproduce the power structures that Indigenous demands should seek to transcend. He develops a complex argument for sustainable self-determination which focuses on Indigenous communities' own terrains of action.[43] Notably, he calls for social forum meetings which take place in Indigenous homelands to acknowledge this and follow the protocols of those cultures.

Xochitl Leyva Solano and Christopher Gunderson's extraordinary piece on the many threads which went into neo-Zapatismo defies easy summary, and explicitly disavows the attempt "to identify here what is of universal significance for counter-systemic movements".[44] What it does show, I feel, is the reality of powerful movements: That they are built out of complex and contested human practices, following many different trajectories (for example: traditions of Indigenous revolt, liberation theology, the guerrilla left) but not in any sense a simple reading-off of some Idea. Rather, it is situated human beings who come to take up particular ideas, traditions, organisations, and strategies for their own purposes, interpreting and developing them in their own ways, in conflict and alliance with others. Real, sustained movement is not a simple importing of a model or theory, placing an academic or political organisation as the key protagonist, but this process of patient work, dialogue, conflict, and learning. It does not reduce easily down to the printed page, but its effects reverberate through time.

Roma and Ashok Choudhary's powerful chapter on forest rights movements in India tells an interesting counterpart to the Chiapas story: The 250-year-long struggles of Adivasis, other deprived communities, and women in the forests, and their contemporary struggle to maintain an independent identity from Maoist movements.[45] Forest people's struggles have moved into a phase of creating alternative models to neoliberalism, within the perspective of democratic self-governance, popular control of natural resources, and against displacement. In this context, there has been a development of organic intellectual leadership as against the traditional party-linked or independent middle-class vanguards. This poses new challenges for linkage between different movements, and for a process which is developing in the teeth of state repression and pressure from Maoist organisations.

All these chapters restore the primary sense of *movement*, underlining 'development' and 'process' rather than the sense of a fixed 'thing'. Movements try to move: It is not easy, and they do not always succeed, or get it right (in their own terms). But if we do not have this vision—that ordinary people attempt, even under the toughest of circumstances, to shape and challenge their own circumstances—we fall back into a world populated only by leaders and theorists, organisations and ideas, in which everything falls from the sky and is only 'carried' by ordinary people.

Emilie Hayes's chapter on three waves of feminism in North America, I think, makes a related point: On the one hand she notes the many problems that arise from trying to tell even a selected and limited story when so many different, conflicting, and original experiences, people, and ideas are involved. On the other hand, some framework like that of waves—involving a sense of time and of tide, of the histories of mobilisation, and of interconnections and conflicts—is important for us to be able to think any movement *as* movement, as people whose struggles and ideas relate to one another and do not simply stand in isolation.[46] A history of individual feminist acts would necessarily be different to a history of 'the feminist movement'—which only exists in this interrelation. She explores, critically, the importance of open space and related approaches—in second-wave "structurelessness" or the present-day World March of Women—in providing "an opportunity for dissent, thus allowing for new movements with more specific aims to emerge".

In a companion essay, Virginia Vargas explores some of the developments of international feminisms from a Latin American starting point, particularly focussing on the feminist *Encuentros* from 1981–2005, the state-related feminisms associated in particular with UN conferences, and feminisms within the World Social Forum, notably the Feminist Dialogues process.[47] She writes of newer movement developments: "These struggles do not erase the differences among groups; on the contrary, what emerges is a multiplicity of meanings, as the social space of experience expands both locally and globally." She notes that the feminist presence in the WSF has helped in "making visible other dimensions of the political, bringing onto the stage new social and political actors, and incorporating new transformative dimensions, drawn from everyday life". Parallel to Hayes's arguments on open space, she argues that the openness of the Forum has been a strength rather than a weakness in this respect. Openness, of course, brings its own contradictions: In the 2007 Nairobi Forum "there was an exceptional presence of church groups from Africa and around the world, including a US-based pro-life organisation. Several of these groups organised an anti-abortion march inside the Forum. Later, in the closing ceremony, there was a verbal attack on a speaker who was a lesbian activist".

This issue goes directly to the heart of the difficulties I have with Lee Cormie's piece on "faith communities" in global justice movements.[48] The central problem—that the dominant form of religious organising in today's world is deeply conservative and closely tied up with patriarchal and statist power—is mentioned only as an aside ("One kind of religion—'fundamentalism': Christian, Hindu, Muslim [and market]—is frequently referred to, and condemned"). The rest of the chapter seems to consist of special pleading—both for activists to say nicer things about religion and to take religion more seriously. As a *critical* practicing Buddhist and a researcher on the anti-colonial dimensions of the Buddhist revival—whose outcomes have not always been happy ones—I think we can do better than that.

To take a close parallel: Marxists have learned over the years that when we declare our allegiances, other activists will criticise us and be wary of us. They are not wrong to do so, if we consider what 'Marxism' has often meant in world history. Furthermore, we have developed an ethics of *leaving* organisations whose politics we cannot defend. I am not sure however, why activists should ask any less of religious people, or if 'being religious' means that we are somehow inherently more sensitive to criticism or less ethically responsible for the organisations we belong to.

To me, this is what follows from a Marxist focus on human practice, which is a close attention not to the labels we hang on ourselves but to what we actually do and how we are with each other: I cannot expect a free pass from those who do not share my particular religious or theoretical affiliation, but rather to be evaluated and listened to in terms of what I do and the movements I am involved in. Cormie is right to say that many groups and communities organised on a religious basis do good work; of course—but they can (and should) then be engaged with on the basis of that work, and not for being 'a faith community'. One other thing which needs to be said is that just as Marxists have a responsibility to do what they can to give 'Marxism' a positive meaning in present-day practice, so too do the religious have a responsibility to clean up their own houses, insofar as they understand themselves as being part of a 'community'.

In Ireland, where theocratic power has devastated the lives of so many people, this is the minimum we can ask of those who want to organise under a religious banner—not to become the token 'good religious person' whose actions elsewhere are used to justify unchanged religious power structures, but rather to *do something* about those same power structures. Recalling Vargas's chapter, one would hope that progressive religious groups at the 2007 WSF challenged the homophobic and intolerant behaviour of their co-religionists, or at a minimum gave adequate warning to those who were not familiar with the particularities of these groups as to what to expect.

From a humanist perspective, then, or simply from that of someone who does not share a particular religious or political perspective, it is surely reasonable to return the focus to actual human practice and its meanings. Mahmoud Mohamed Taha, in François Houtart's short presentation, is valuable in this respect: "working towards a humanistic socialism and an opening for a multicultural state in his country, Sudan".[49] I would comment that along with the recognition that "Islamist movements have hardened, leaving little space for differing orientations", we should also acknowledge that Marxist movements' "rejection of Islam in all its forms" was a reasonable one for those who made it, and a choice that deserves at least as much respect as the actions of those who remained with a problematic religious power structure.[50] If arguments for and against religion are particularly sharp in those countries where religious power has been particularly damaging, I would suggest from an Irish perspective that we owe at least as much openness to those who have made the often difficult (in some countries even life-threatening) choice to leave, or convert.[51]

James Toth's chapter tells a fascinating story of the roots of Islamic militancy in southern Egypt and its ultimate links with al-Qa'ida.[52] It is arguably a story of human practice gone wrong, or (to return to Teltumbde) of a failure to make the right kinds of connections: In a situation of struggles against the injustices of underdevelopment and the failure of Nasserite left nationalism, a mode of explanation which blames degeneration not only on colonialism but "the adoption of French legal codes and the secularist abolition of the Caliphate, later nationalism and its elevation of leaders to godlike status, and, more recently, assaults by crusaderism, Zionism, communism, and others hostile to Islam" and the development among migrants of "religious associations that re-created and reinforced the intimacy of an imagined but bygone village community". As elsewhere, the combination of bottom-up development on religious lines and state repression created a space over time for a new kind of militancy (perhaps also, Toth suggests, a result of the dominance of moderates within the Muslim Brotherhood, leading to separate organisation).

Roel Meijer discusses the ideological basis of jihadi Salafism as a modern social movement, focussing on Yusuf al-'Uyairi, the founder of al-Qa'ida on the Arabian Peninsula.[53] In an interesting counterpoint to Cormie and Houtart, he ascribes to al-'Uyairi a "Leninist and Maoist logic of praxis, the eulogy of the revolutionary will and knowledge whose incontestable logic is based on the moral superiority of self-sacrifice, and as having a privileged access to truth during the struggle". On the basis of this chapter at least, it is hard to disagree that "'Uyairi's work is thoroughly modernist". On the other hand, I have to say that this presentation does not sound as alien or "dismaying to those living out other realities" as Meijer suggests. It sounds in some ways rather similar to the logics of many urban guerrilla organisations in the post-1968 West, for example, not least in its practical implications of a vanguardist elite focussed on military action, leading to a combination of increasing separation from popular struggles and an ever-greater need for spectacle to reinforce the problematic claim that the terrain of violence is the most important one, what Toth describes as "the major clash of the twenty-first century". In most countries which have experienced these conflicts, other Marxists and movement activists have criticised and faced down these kinds of positions, insisting on the need for real social change to be found-ed in mass participation and highlighting how the logic of spectacular violence ultimately served elite power.[54]

It is absolutely important, it might be said, to recognise the roots of injustice from which movements grow. Even movements which we despise nevertheless represent some real needs, which moreover will not be met following that path (recall the widespread nineteenth-century observation that "anti-semitism is the socialism of fools"). It is also important to understand the strategic thinking of particular organisations and traditions. But then it is also crucial to criticise it, and organise differently in ways which support the development of *organic* intellectual capacity and speak more adequately to the needs of those who, today, support destructive movements. There are many who would like to make 'jihad vs McWorld' into "the major clash of the twenty-first century";[55] but it is important to undermine that strategy on all sides—in other words, to find ways in our own worlds of organising which do not simply dismiss the needs of those who are des-perate but equally do not instrumentalise them. We need to be loyal, so to speak, 'not to East or West but to each other'; or rather, to refuse loyalty to those who would claim it in the name of religion or of the modern project alike. Religions and modernity alike are valuable only to the extent that they serve human needs and provide a real way forward.

As always, Peter Waterman's reflections—in this case on "labour's others", and more specifically the internationalisms of new worker movements outside of the traditional union form—are thought-provoking and wide-ranging, avoiding easy closure and instead encouraging reflection on the different possible ways of organising, and of conceptualising what is happening in this space.[56] At the risk of oversimplifying, it seems to me that what Waterman is doing, here and elsewhere, is to place the emphasis firmly on the *movement* rather than the *movement organisation*. What he is saying is that in a world where most people are in paid employment and many are organised in some way but where conventional union membership is in continued decline in its one-time strongholds while representing only a tiny fraction of workers in the Global South, we need to pay attention to the wider question of how particular forms of organising can be more or less adequate to the struggles of their participants, or intended participants, rather than to fetishise a particular organisational form as the only possible way forward.

Cho Hee-Yeon's account of the anti-globalisation movement in South Korea is a fascinating case in point.[57] Cho charts the "peculiar career" of Korean popular movements, showing how radical forces within the movements found resistance to neoliberalism and participation in the global anti-war movement a source of strength. In this context, there has been a shift from an older anti-imperialism to a contemporary anti-empire movement, which he defines as a "new global united front movement of differences". He writes "transnational global politics is not headed for extinction but, to the contrary, is emerging strongly. The anti-empire movement as a global united front movement is a key actor for waging and spreading such a global politics."

But what is politics? Emir Sader and Daniel Bensaïd both give determined, if to my mind unconvincing answers to this question, from somewhat different statist perspectives. Sader offers an interesting but selective overview of resistance to neoliberalism in Latin America, starting with the national-developmentalism of the 1940s on and moving through the guerrilla movements from the Cuban Revolution on, up to the realignment on neoliberal lines after 1990.[58] At this point, highlighting the resistance of movements to neoliberalism from 1994 onwards, Sader argues against "the dichotomy of 'state versus civil society'" in order to replace it with a different one between public and market spheres, in which "the autonomy of social movements" is placed in scare quotes as representative of movements that are "unable to move forward into challenging neoliberal hegemony". Such movements—in Sader's view—include not only Argentinian autonomists, as might be expected, but also the Zapatistas. In some ways, though, an analysis which fails to see the way in which the latter movement challenges neoliberal hegemony deconstructs itself—and more to the point, fails to offer any serious *materialist* analysis of why movements might find the politics of the traditional left problematic. (In this essay, it is only in relation to Bolivia—where this critique is treated as resolved by the creation of the MAS [the *Movimiento al Socialismo*, the 'Movement toward Socialism']—that we are even told what the problem was.)[59]

In saying this, I do not want to ignore the hugely significant experiment of 'leftist' governments in Latin America, which as Sader says might be called "post-neoliberal" (although in 2015, rather than when this essay was first written in 2008, we might want to say that the record is somewhat more mixed even in terms of resistance to neoliberalism). Rather, I want to suggest that politics is not only about these macro-struggles, and to focus purely on the goal of "challenging neoliberal hegemony" (important though that is!) is, often, to instrumentalise others and to reproduce logics of power which are themselves not only problematic but at times lethal.

Movements, as popular agents, have good reason to want to see more than simply distributive outcomes. Indeed this is surely one of the main Marxist lessons from the global movement wave of 1968: That a purely instrumental and distributive solution, however good, is not enough.[60] More specifically, of course, when the instrumental focus is entirely on the level of global capitalism, some other important arenas of power are missed. We might mention workplace power (by no means resolved by nationalisation); land ownership and reform; power and exploitation within the family; the situation of Indigenous populations; and the new national-extractivism in Latin America. Increasingly we are seeing movements which once supported radical governments in Latin America dissociate themselves, move into opposition, and face repression. But this was perhaps utterly predictable: Because, as Sader observes, Latin America has had left governments before, and these problems are not new. To write as though the difficulty is simply in the "venom" (his word) directed by the Zapatistas at López Obrador, however, and not to recognise the rather longer history of disappointment both by left governments and by election-oriented mobilisation, is to condemn the left, including the electoral left, to repeating the mistakes of the past.

Much the same kind of response might be made to Daniel Bensaïd's essay on the "return of strategy", although it should be said here that the "we" which is the subject of this piece is very explicitly the particular Trotskyist tradition to which he belonged.[61] I will limit myself to two observations. Firstly, while it is perfectly reasonable to criticise others for their weaknesses and failings, there is something odd about not applying the same standards to one's own politics. As he argues, *Rifondazione comunista* may have disappointed in Italy, for example, but can we really say that his *Ligue communiste révolutionnaire* did so well in France? Perhaps not, in that the LCR dissolved itself two years after this essay was written, into a rather different kind of party.[62]

Or—if we are to be so critical of the illusions, utopias, and defeats suffered by others—precisely what should we say of a list of "great revolutionary experiences of the twentieth century" which Bensaïd argues includes "The Russian Revolution, the Chinese Revolution, the German Revolution, the popular fronts, the Vietnamese war of liberation, May 1968, Portugal, and Chile"? We can't quite misquote Ken MacLeod—"They were all defeats"[63]—but it does rather have to be said that even those which were successes in their own terms now seem, at least, ambiguous.

What is sauce for the goose does have to be sauce for the gander: Would it be so hard to admit that it is not only Others who have less than a shining track record to show for themselves, but also us? Such experiences do not, perhaps, tell us What To Do in any simple sense; but they do (and here I agree with Bensaïd) tell us something about how people organise in certain circumstances: In other words, about movement realities.

And here, as with Sader, one might reasonably say that there is a difference, and a legitimate one, between the realities of popular movements in struggle and the goals of Trotskyists, or other state-centred lefts. That is no bad thing in itself; as I have argued above, it is important to find ways of articulating situated movement realities with each other, across issues and internationally. This is the difference between a 'campaign' and a 'social movement project', after all. But to treat movement realities as simply the raw material for party plans is something rather different. In *We Make Our Own History*, Alf and I write of party-centric Marxisms:

> [This] marks far more the impoverishment of this form of 'Marxism' and its inability to grapple with the question of popular agency. Marxism is *not* the position that in all times and all places the political party is the best way to organise (counterposed, presumably, to anarchism). Rather, we would argue that its defining feature in a much deeper sense is a commitment to structured popular agency, to representing 'the interests of the movement as a whole', and hence to strategies of alliance-building between movements, of identifying the most radical common potential, and of close attention to the interests underlying different tendencies within movements, not as a means of dismissal but as a means of understanding and preventing movement capture by elites ...
>
> [T]he Marxist emphasis has to be on the *movement*, not the party: a party is worthy of Marxist interest only to the extent that it is successful in placing the movement first. More broadly, the Marxist question should be one about how popular agency is currently structured—or the competing types of structure which movements adopt. Rather than fetishising a particular mode of organising either as universally valid (and hence defining a new Marxist 'tradition'), or as sweeping all before it because it is new, the useful question is one of the *relationships* between different types of popular organising in a given time and place, and how they reinforce one another or cancel each other out, not only in the struggle against capital and the state but also in the internal struggle to

articulate 'good sense' against 'common sense' and to become political subjects rather than objects.

There are reasons, perhaps, why forms of strategy which have ignored this have not produced what could be called emancipatory results.

The volume finishes with three chapters that, while arguing their case, are more open in tone. Peter North and David Featherstone's piece on trade local-isation and climate change allows space for left critiques of localisation while arguing that it need not be conservative or xenophobic and noting the scope for a combination of localism and internationalism, with particular reference to some practices of the Brazilian MST.[64]

Guillermo Delgado-P's chapter on Bolivia as "a social movements state" returns to some of the themes of Sader's and Bensaïd's pieces in a more dialectical way, showing the interrelationship between movements and state in a situation which is, after all, not new in world politics but constantly challenging for those involved in it.[65] While Bolivia offers no easy 'lessons' or 'models' to be transferred elsewhere, it provides a powerful basis for reflection on the complexities involved not only in what Alf and I call 'movement-become-state' but also in the ensuing tensions that are familiar from previous revolutions (democratic, nationalist, and socialist) when the state does not express movements fully or neatly. This happens not only because of the resistances from forces of the old regime and the international order, but also because of the different strategies pursued by the new, or newly-reformed, state itself, in turn leading to significant tensions with movements. To say this is not to reject political strategies articulated at the level of the state: It is to note that movements are important in their own right, and not simply as tools for achieving power, something which Delgado-P's chapter articulates clearly.

Finally, Alex Khasnabish explores the "resonance the Zapatista struggle achieved among activists transnationally".[66] He writes:

> [T]his encounter between Zapatismo and diverse communities of radical activ-ists has produced novel ways of imagining and enacting struggle toward a more dignified, democratic, just, and peaceful future. Beyond this, these experiences and this consciousness are beginning to materialise the possibility for the artic-ulation of a new political terrain and political practice rooted in a mutual recog-nition of dignity and humanity, an affirmation of diversity, and the reclamation of the capacity to build a world capable of holding many worlds precisely because we are the only subjects capable of bringing it into being.

Such radical imagination has always been one of the key elements of the encoun-ters that constitute the 'movement(s) of movements'—and previous generations of international encounters.

And Lastly: Learning and Listening

This book—along with its companion volume, *The Movements of Movements, Part 2: Rethinking Our Dance*[67]—documents the extraordinary capacities of human beings in struggle to transform social relationships, remake the world, and overturn what seemed fixed and unchangeable—in many different shapes and forms. In this context, we are compelled to encounter each other, for good or ill. In the space that lies between fundamentalist attacks or sectarian polemic on the one hand, and interfaith love-ins or the simple celebration of everything that exists on the other, there lies, perhaps, a space of learning. This learning, I have tried to argue, comes from listening not only to what the other says but also trying to understand what the other is saying *by the fact of their existence as social movement, as a collective subject*—even or especially when we disagree with what is said and done. Gramsci suggests at one point that to really defeat an opponent is to show that your position can account for and subsume theirs; even if it is easier simply to dismiss the existence of the other, it is certainly less productive politically in the long run.

Learning and listening are not simply political strategies: They are practical necessities in a world in which none of us can claim 360-degree vision or speak from all positions simultaneously. One of the most important political challenges of going beyond the centrality of the nation-state as the privileged locus of action is recognising and grasping the potential of the variety of actors and movements which need not just to act together, but to raise themselves to considerable heights of understanding and capacity for action. These are not impossible goals: This book, and the political and intellectual processes reflected in the work of its authors, are testimony to that.

In the Introduction, Sen writes eloquently about the challenges involved in attempting to select authors and "to make the book truly international, intercultural, and transcommunal, both in terms of the contributors as well as in terms of the essays included". Of course this cannot mean a simple numerical representativity: If this can be achieved in terms of gender it becomes far more challenging when it was sought in terms of ethnicity or geography, and would break down completely if it was attempted in relation to social class. Instead, the book approaches difference by seeking and highlighting key moments of otherness: Indigenous activists and Dalits, writers on Zapatismo and Islam, feminists and Marxists, above all authors from and working on the Global South (understood in structural rather than geographic terms). This is neither the comforting representation of the political platform nor the soothing homogeneity of the academic book.

The academic homes of so many of the authors (not all) are striking, nonetheless. In some ways this is a fact of our times, and one which Sen (and this series) is contributing to relativising: The proportion even of movement-oriented intellectual work which takes place within universities. Our challenge—for those of us in this situation—is always to ask how we can relate our work back to movements, and how to avoid 'institutional capture'. The construction of this book has the great merit of placing *movements*—and not a particular academic field or type of performance—in the centre: It is a book from and for movements and those interested in movement. The scholarship represented here bears witness to that (as does Sen's excellent editing): Too often in academic work the logics which have to be obeyed mean answering *upwards*—to promotion committees and commercial publishers, to anonymous referees and funding agencies. But when handled properly, the intellectual logics of movements are that much *sharper:* We are describing, analysing, and critiquing people putting themselves, even their lives, on the line; and our suggestions and proposals can have huge implications, for ourselves and others. The difference between the almost theological pursuit of academic respectability and the situation of putting our whole selves into what we write can be huge: There is a reason why it is movements which push new fields of study into universities and not the reverse.[68] The writing is ferociously sharp, but (in most cases) the opposite of inaccessible, at least for those who have sharpened their thinking in struggle. The movements write the author, and not the other way around.

The movements which write through the authors in this book represent an extraordinary combination of experiences *outside* the banal grind of everyday life and thought in neoliberalism. Put them side by side: The long histories of movements since 1968; waves of feminisms challenging the dull power of patriarchy; Indigenous struggles moving from the margins to the centres of political discourse in so many settler societies; Dalits and Adivasis overturning South Asian forms of oppression; the Zapatistas catalysing struggle around the world; the extraordinary Latin American cycle of movement experiments; Islamic politics and its new languages of organising; and the ongoing grumble of labour, still refusing to have surplus value taken out of its hide without fighting back.

All of these are woven together in this book in a process that goes beyond the existing circuits of the 'movement of movements', but is also shaped by those experiences. The result is like, and yet unlike, our existing movement realities: To some extent, perhaps, it is what we might hope to bring together not only on the page, but in struggle, together. That moment is within reach—not only of the imagination, but also of our organising languages and our networks. It still has to happen; or perhaps we still have to find ways of making it real in ways that speak back to the struggles we come from and help them develop. And yet the book is a real contribution to that process.

This particular challenge, but also the wider one of *listening to* and *learning from* each other, is a way of growing, as human beings. It is not in acquiring new words or expressing ourselves beautifully, still less in imitating what is often a very damaging education system, that we truly develop. It is in somehow extending our sense of self so as to include the voices and challenges of others, and in turn of the realities and struggles they speak from. This is why movement matters: It is how we change our world, *and* how we change ourselves. In the process, perhaps, we can become less loyal to this or that movement organisation or political tradition, and more loyal to each other. In so doing, we become more fully ourselves, in all our depth and complexity—and develop the alliances that we need to struggle for a better world.

References

Taiaiake Alfred and Jeff Corntassel, 2017—'Being Indigenous: Resurgences against Contemporary Colonialism', in Jai Sen, ed, 2017a—*The Movements of Movements, Part 1: What Makes Us Move?*. Volume 4 in the *Challenging Empires* series, New Delhi: OpenWord and Oakland, CA: PM Press

Tariq Ali, 2017—'Storming Heaven: Where Has the Rage Gone?', in Jai Sen, ed, 2017a—*The Movements of Movements, Part 1: What Makes Us Move?*. Volume 4 in the *Challenging Empires* series, New Delhi: OpenWord and Oakland, CA: PM Press

Benjamin R Barber, 1995—*Jihad vs McWorld: Terrorism's Challenge to Democracy*. New York: Ballantine Books

Daniel Bensaïd, 2017—'The Return of Strategy', in Jai Sen, ed, 2017a—*The Movements of Movements, Part 1: What Makes Us Move?*. Volume 4 in the *Challenging Empires* series. New Delhi: OpenWord and Oakland, CA: PM Press

Cho Hee-Yeon, 2017—'From Anti-Imperialist to Anti-Empire: The Crystallisation of the Anti-Globalisation Movement in South Korea', in Jai Sen, ed, 2017a—*The Movements of Movements, Part 1: What Makes Us Move?*. Volume 4 in the *Challenging Empires* series. New Delhi: OpenWord, and Oakland, CA: PM Press

Lee Cormie, 2017—'Re-Creating The World: Communities of Faith in the Struggles for Other Possible Worlds', in Jai Sen, ed, 2017a—*The Movements of Movements, Part 1: What Makes Us Move?*. Volume 4 in the *Challenging Empires* series. New Delhi: OpenWord, and Oakland, CA: PM Press

Jeff Corntassel, 2017—'Rethinking Self-Determination: Lessons from the Indigenous-Rights Discourse', in Jai Sen, ed, 2017a—*The Movements of Movements, Part 1: What Makes Us Move?*. Volume 4 in the *Challenging Empires* series. New Delhi: OpenWord and Oakland, CA: PM Press

Laurence Cox, 2010—'Another World Is Under Construction? Social Movement Responses to Inequality and Crisis', in *Irish Left Review*, at http://www.irishleftreview.org/2010/05/17/world-construction-social-movement-responses-inequality-crisis/ (Accessed April 2017)

Laurence Cox, 2011—'Gramsci in Mayo: A Marxist Perspective on Social Movements in Ireland'. Paper to Conference on 'New Agendas in Social Movement Studies', National University of Ireland Maynooth

Laurence Cox, 2013a—'*Eppur si muove*: Thinking 'The Social Movement' ['And yet, it does move!: Thinking 'The Social Movement'], in Colin Barker et al, eds, 2013—*Marxism and Social Movements*. Chicago: Haymarket

Laurence Cox, 2013b—*Buddhism and Ireland: From the Celts to the Counter Culture and Beyond*. Sheffield: Equinox

Laurence Cox, 2014a—'Movements Making Knowledge: A New Wave of Inspiration for Sociology?', in *Sociology*, vol 48 no 5, pp 954–971

Laurence Cox, 2014b—'Waves of protest and revolution: Elements of a Marxist analysis', at http://eprints.maynoothuniversity.ie/4867/ (Accessed April 2017)

Laurence Cox and Alf Nilsen, 2014—*We Make Our Own History: Marxism and Social Movements in the Twilight of Neoliberalism*. London: Pluto

Guillermo Delgado-P, 2017 —'Refounding Bolivia: Exploring the Possibility and Paradox of a Social Movements State', in Jai Sen, ed, 2017a—*The Movements of Movements, Part 1: What Makes Us Move?*. Volume 4 in the *Challenging Empires* series. New Delhi: OpenWord, and Oakland, CA: PM Press

André C Drainville, 2017—'Beyond *Altermondialisme*: Anti-Capitalist Dialectic of Presence', in Jai Sen, ed, 2017a—*The Movements of Movements, Part 1: What Makes Us Move?*. Volume 4 in the *Challenging Empires* series. New Delhi: OpenWord, and Oakland, CA: PM Press

Lord Dunsany, 1924—*The King of Elfland's Daughter*, at http://www.gutenberg.ca/ebooks/dunsany-kingofelflandsdaughter/dunsany-kingofelflandsdaughter-00-h.html (Accessed April 2017)

END (European Nuclear Disarmament), April 1980—'European Nuclear Disarmament Appeal', in E P Thompson and Dan Smith, eds, 1980—*Protest and Survive*. A Penguin Special, p 223–226

Cristina Flesher Fominaya, 2015—'Cultural Barriers to Activist Networking: Habitus (In)action in Three European Transnational Encounters', in *Antipode*, doi: 10.1111/anti.12166.

Agnes Gagyi, 2013—'The Shifting Meaning of Autonomy', in Cristina Flesher Fominaya and Laurence Cox, eds, 2013—*Understanding European Movements: New Social Movements, Global Justice Struggles, Anti-Austerity Protest*. (London: Routledge)

Todd Gitlin, 1980—*The Whole World is Watching: Mass Media in the Making and Unmaking of the New Left*. Berkeley: University of California Press

Stuart Hall, 1980—'Encoding/decoding', in Centre for Contemporary Cultural Studies, ed, 1980—*Culture, Media, Language: Working Papers in Cultural Studies, 1972–79.*, (London: Hutchinson), pp. 128–38

Patrick Hamon and Hervé Rotman, 1988—*Génération (vol 2): Les années de poudre* ['Generation (vol 2): The Gunpowder Years', in French]. Paris: Seuil

Emilie Hayes, 2017—'Open Space in Movement: Reading Three Waves of Feminism', in Jai Sen, ed, 2017a—*The Movements of Movements, Part 1: What Makes Us Move?*. Volume 4 in the *Challenging Empires* series. New Delhi: OpenWord and Oakland, CA: PM Press

Josephine Ho, 2017—'Is Global Governance Bad for East Asian Queers?', in Jai Sen, ed, 2017b—*The Movements of Movements, Part 2: Rethinking Our Dance*. Volume 5 in the *Challenging Empires* series. New Delhi: OpenWord, and Oakland, CA: PM Press

John Holloway, 2010—*Crack Capitalism*. London: Pluto

François Houtart, 2017—'Mahmoud Mohamed Taha, Islamic Witness in the Contemporary World', in Jai Sen, ed, 2017a—*The Movements of Movements, Part 1: What*

Makes Us Move?. Volume 4 in the *Challenging Empires* series. New Delhi: Open-Word, and Oakland, CA: PM Press

Incite!, 2009—*The Revolution Will Not Be Funded: Beyond the Non-Profit Industrial Complex*. Boston: South End Press

Fouad Kalouche and Eric Mielants, 2017—'Antisystemic Movements and Transformations of the World-System, 1968–1989', in Jai Sen, ed, 2017a—*The Movements of Movements, Part 1: What Makes Us Move?*. Volume 4 in the *Challenging Empires* series. New Delhi: OpenWord, and Oakland, CA: PM Press

Alex Khasnabish, 2017—'Forward Dreaming: Zapatismo and the Radical Imagination', in Jai Sen, ed, 2017a—*The Movements of Movements, Part 1: What Makes Us Move?*. Volume 4 in the *Challenging Empires* series. New Delhi: OpenWord, and Oakland, CA: PM Press

Xochitl Leyva Solano, 2017—'Geopolitics of Knowledge and the Neo-Zapatista Social Movement Networks', in Jai Sen, ed, 2017a—*The Movements of Movements, Part 1: What Makes Us Move?*. Volume 4 in the *Challenging Empires* series. New Delhi: OpenWord and Oakland, CA: PM Press

Xochitl Leyva Solano and Christopher Gunderson, 2017—'The Tapestry of Neo-Zapatismo: Origins and Development', in Jai Sen, ed, 2017a—*The Movements of Movements, Part 1: What Makes Us Move?*. Volume 4 in the *Challenging Empires* series. New Delhi: OpenWord and Oakland, CA: PM Press

Ken MacLeod, 1996—*The Stone Canal*. London: Random

Karl Marx and Frederick Engels, 1848—*Manifesto of the Communist Party*, at https://www.marxists.org/archive/marx/works/1848/communist-manifesto/ (Accessed April 2017)

Karl Marx, 1852—*The Eighteenth Brumaire of Louis Bonaparte*, at https://www.marxists.org/archive/marx/works/1852/18th-brumaire/ch01.htm (Accessed April 2017)

David McNally, 2017—'From the Mountains of Chiapas to the Streets of Seattle: This Is What Democracy Looks Like', in Jai Sen, ed, 2017a—*The Movements of Movements, Part 1: What Makes Us Move?*. Volume 4 in the *Challenging Empires* series. New Delhi: OpenWord, and Oakland, CA: PM Press

Roel Meijer, 2017—'Fighting for Another World: Yusuf al-'Uyairi's Conceptualisation of Praxis and Permanent Revolution', in Jai Sen, ed, 2017a—*The Movements of Movements, Part 1: What Makes Us Move?*. Volume 4 in the *Challenging Empires* series. New Delhi: OpenWord, and Oakland, CA: PM Press

William Morris, 1886—*A Dream of John Ball*, at https://www.marxists.org/archive/morris/works/1886/johnball/johnball.htm (Accessed April 2017)

Frances Mulhern, 2011—*Lives on the Left: A Group Portrait*. London: Verso.

Peter North and David Featherstone, 2017—'Localisation as Radical Praxis and the New Politics of Climate Change', in Jai Sen, ed, 2017a—*The Movements of Movements, Part 1: What Makes Us Move?*. Volume 4 in the *Challenging Empires* series. New Delhi: OpenWord, and Oakland, CA: PM Press

Roma and Ashok Choudhary, 2017—'Ecological Justice and Forest Right Movements in India: State and Militancy—New Challenges', in Jai Sen, ed, 2017a—*The Movements of Movements, Part 1: What Makes Us Move?*. Volume 4 in the *Challenging Empires* series. New Delhi: OpenWord, and Oakland, CA: PM Press

Emir Sader, 2017—'The Weakest Link? Neoliberalism in Latin America', in Jai Sen, ed, 2017a—*The Movements of Movements, Part 1: What Makes Us Move?*. Volume 4 in the *Challenging Empires* series. New Delhi: OpenWord, and Oakland, CA: PM Press

Jai Sen, 2017a—'The Movements of Movements: An Introduction and an Exploration'. Introduction to Jai Sen, ed, 2017a—*The Movements of Movements, Part 1: What Makes Us Move?*. Volume 4 in the *Challenging Empires* series New Delhi: OpenWord, and Oakland, CA: PM Press

Jai Sen, ed, 2017b—*The Movements of Movements, Part 2: Rethinking Our Dance.* Volume 5 in the *Challenging Empires* series. New Delhi: OpenWord, and Oakland, CA: PM Press

Andrea Smith, 2017—'Indigenous Feminism and the Heteropatriarchal State', in Jai Sen, ed, 2017a—*The Movements of Movements, Part 1: What Makes Us Move?*. Volume 4 in the *Challenging Empires* series. New Delhi: OpenWord and Oakland, CA: PM Press

Anand Teltumbde, 2017—'Dalits, Anti-Imperialism, and the Annihilation of Caste', in Jai Sen, ed, 2017a—*The Movements of Movements, Part 1: What Makes Us Move?*. Volume 4 in the *Challenging Empires* series. New Delhi: OpenWord and Oakland, CA: PM Press

E P Thompson, 1966—*The Making of the English Working Class.* London: Penguin

James Toth, 2017—'Local Islam Gone Global: The Roots of Religious Militancy in Egypt and Its Transnational Transformation', in Jai Sen, ed, 2017a—*The Movements of Movements, Part 1: What Makes Us Move?*. Volume 4 in the *Challenging Empires* series. New Delhi: OpenWord, and Oakland, CA: PM Press

Virginia Vargas, 2017—'International Feminisms: New Syntheses, New Directions', in Jai Sen, ed, 2017a—*The Movements of Movements, Part 1: What Makes Us Move?*. Volume 4 in the *Challenging Empires* series. New Delhi: OpenWord and Oakland, CA: PM Press

Hilary Wainwright, 1994—*Arguments for a New Left: Answering the Free Market Right.* Oxford: Blackwell

Peter Waterman, 2017—'The Networked Internationalism of Labour's Others', in Jai Sen, ed, 2017a—*The Movements of Movements, Part 1: What Makes Us Move?*. Volume 4 in the *Challenging Empires* series. New Delhi: OpenWord, and Oakland, CA: PM Press

Raymond Williams, 2006—*Politics of Modernism: Against the New Conformists.* London: Verso.

Notes

1. END (European Nuclear Disarmament), April 1980.
2. I wish to record my deepest thanks to Jai Sen for his kindness and patience in supporting me while writing this chapter, as well as for his immensely careful editing.
3. http://grassroots.pageabode.com/.
4. http://struggle.ws/eufortress/index.html.
5. http://ceesa-ma.blogspot.com.
6. *Interface: a journal for and about social movements*, at http://www.interfacejournal.net/ (Accessed April 2017).
7. Cox and Nilsen 2014.

8. I would like to take the opportunity here to apologise to all concerned for the fact that this project did not get further.

9. Flesher Fominaya 2015, Gagyi 2013.

10. Marx and Engels 1848.

11. Cox and Nilsen 2014, p 6.

12. This distinction was used in so many different movements from the late nineteenth and early twentieth century that it is not clear who first came up with it.

13. Mulhern 2011, p 170.

14. ibid, p 171.

15. Dunsany, 1924.

16. Thompson, 1966, p 115.

17. Sen 2017.

18. Ed: For a closely-argued related discussion, in this case of the suppression of civil society and free expression, see the essay by Josephine Ho in the companion book to this one (Ho 2017).

19. END (European Nuclear Disarmament), April 1980.

20. McNally 2017.

21. Marx 1852.

22. ibid.

23. Morris 1886.

24. Drainville 2017.

25. Holloway 2010.

26. Kalouche and Mielants 2017.

27. I am not sure how this mode of analysis is not vulnerable to their own critique of Castells and Touraine's definition of movements; in their own words, "such criteria could not elucidate the nature of movements but would rather 'construct' it".

28. Williams 2006.

29. Cox 2013a.

30. Hall 1980.

31. Ali 2017.

32. Alfred and Corntassel 2017.

33. Cox 2011.

34. Smith 2017.

35. Incite! 2009.

36. Cox 2010.

37. Leyva Solano 2017.

38. I like Jai Sen's distinction between the 'movement of movements' and the 'movement"s" of movements', but would say that both are important. We certainly have to attempt to grasp the full range of what movements are happening, globally, and use that to attempt to extend our own alliances. At the same time, the (relative) empirical reality of a movement of movements, in the sense of a relatively coherent network (to whose construction Sen among others has contributed hugely) should not be overlooked. As always in social movements, we have to keep one eye on who we are already talking to and working with, and one eye on who we might hope to include in those conversations—or be included by.

39. Cox and Nilsen 2014.

40. Sen 2017.
41. Cox 2014b.
42. Teltumbde 2017.
43. Corntassel 2017.
44. Leyva Solano and Gunderson 2017.
45. Roma and Choudhary 2017.
46. Hayes 2017.
47. Vargas 2017.
48. Cormie 2017. As a Buddhist and scholar of religions, I do not find the word 'faith', which is particularly linked to some forms of Christian rhetoric, usefully represents the huge diversity of the world's religious practices.
49. Houtart 2017.
50. As ex-Muslims have observed, there is something rather problematic about the proposition that it is fine for those born Christian to become secular or atheist, but not for those born Muslim.
51. Cox 2013b.
52. Toth 2017.
53. Meijer 2017.
54. See, for example, Gitlin 1980, or Hamon and Rotman 1988.
55. Barber 1995.
56. Waterman 2017.
57. Cho 2017.
58. Sader 2017.
59. Ed: For a discussion of the dynamics of the politics of MAS in Bolivia—up to 2009—see the essay by Guillermo Delgado-P in this book (Delgado-P 2017).
60. Wainwright 1994.
61. Bensaïd 2017.
62. Ed: Just for the record, and in relation to this point, Daniel Bensaïd wrote the original version of his essay in 2007, but the version published here was finalised with him two years later in June 2009, just six months before he died—and therefore, perhaps ironically, around the time that the author says the LCR was dissolving.
63. MacLeod 1996, p. 215
64. North and Featherstone 2017.
65. Delgado-P 2017.
66. Khasnabish 2017.
67. Sen, ed, 2017.
68. Cox 2014a.

Recommended Web Pages and Blogs

Barrikada Zapatista: http://barrikadazapatista.wordpress.com/

Centro de Documentación Sobre Zapatismo: http://www.cedoz.org/site/

Chiapas Media Project: http://www.chiapasmediaproject.org/

De Tod@s Para Tod@s: http://detodos-paratodos.blogspot.com/2009/03/concluye-el-
encuentro-de-mujeres-mama.html

Enlace Zapatista: http://enlacezapatista.ezln.org.mx/

Europa Zapatista: http://www.europazapatista.org/

Mujeres y la Sexta: http://mujeresylasextaorg.wordpress.com/

Nacimiento de los Caracoles y de las Juntas de Buen Gobierno Zapatistas: http://
www.nodo50.org/pchiapas/chiapas/documentos/caracol/caracol.htm

Podcast de la Hora Sexta: http://lahorasexta.podomatic.com/

Primer Coloquio Internacional: http://www.coloquiointernacionalandresaubry.org/

Primer Festival de la Digna Rabia: http://dignarabia.ezln.org.mx/

Radio Insurgente: http://www.radioinsurgente.org/

Radio Zapatista: http://www.radiozapatista.org/IIEncuentro.htm

Rebeldia: http://revistarebeldia.org/

Red Contra la Represión: http://contralarepresion.wordpress.com/2010/06/

Rincón Zapatista: http://rinconzapatistazac.blogspot.com/

**Sistema Educativo Rebelde Autonomó Zapatista de Liberación Nacional -Zona de
los Altos de Chiapas:** http://www.serazln-altos.org/index.html

Union Rebelde: http://union-rebelde.blogspot.com/

Zapateando: http://zapateando.wordpress.com/

Zezta Internazional: http://zeztainternazional.ezln.org.mx/

Notes on the Editor

Jai Sen is an architect by training and first practice, became an activist around the rights of the labouring poor in Kolkata, India, in the mid 1970s, and then moved on to becoming a student of the history and dynamics of movement and of the globalisation of movement in the 1990s. Involved in the organising process of the World Social Forum in India during its first year there, 2002, he has since then been intensively engaged with and taken part in the WSF and world movements through the organisation he is associated with, CACIM (Critical Action: Centre in Movement), including as author, editor, and co-editor of several books and articles on the WSF and as moderator of the listserv WSFDiscuss—now re-incarnated as WSMDiscuss (World Social Movement Discuss). While living in Kolkata from the mid 70s to the late 90s, he was with Unnayan, a social action group, Vice-President of the Chhinnamul Sramajibi Adhikar Samiti ('Organisation for the Rights of Uprooted Labouring People'), and Convenor of the NCHR (National Campaign for Housing Rights) in India; and he also represented Unnayan on the founding Board of the Habitat International Coalition during 1987–91. He is now based in New Delhi, India, and Ottawa, Canada, on unceded Algonquin territory. jai.sen@cacim.net

Notes on the Contributing and Co-Series Editor

The late **Peter Waterman** (1936–2017), after retirement from the Institute of Social Studies, The Hague, in 1998, published various monographs, (co-)edited compilations and numerous academic and political papers—the latter almost all to be found online—and self-published his autobiography (*From Coldwar Communism to the Global Emancipatory Movement: Itinerary of a Long-Distance Internationalist*, available at http://www.into-ebooks.com/download/498/). His work was published in English (UK, USA, Canada, India), Hindi, Italian, Portuguese, German, Spanish, Japanese, and Korean. He had papers posted on the Montevideo-based Choike portal and compilations on the Finland-based Into website, and a blog on UnionBook. He was currently associated with, amongst others, the Programa Democracia y Transformación Global (Lima), with two online journals, *Interface: a Journal for and about Social Movements*, the *Global Labour Journal*, and with the Indian Institute for Critical Action—Centre in Movement (CACIM) in New Delhi. Here he co-edited books on the World Social Forums. After retirement he had invitations for teaching, lectures, and seminars from universities and movement-oriented bodies in Peru, South Africa, Sweden, Finland, Hong Kong, Germany, South Korea, the US, Ireland, and the UK.

Notes on the Contributors

The contributors to this volume are as follows, *listed here alphabetically* by **first name:**

Alex Khasnabish is an Associate Professor in the Department of Sociology and Anthropology at Mount Saint Vincent University in Halifax, Nova Scotia, Canada. He is the author of *Zapatismo Beyond Borders: New Imaginations of Political Possibility* (University of Toronto Press, 2008) and *Zapatistas: Rebellion from the Grassroots to the Global* (Zed Books, 2010); co-editor, with Jeffrey Juris, and contributor to *Insurgent Encounters: Transnational Activism, Ethnography, and the Political* (Duke University Press, 2013); and co-author, with Max Haiven, of *The Radical Imagination* (Zed Books, forthcoming). He researches and writes about the radical imagination, radical social justice struggles, and engaged research. His recent work has been published in *Interface, Cultural Studies ⟷ Critical Methodologies, ephemera,* and *Affinities.* alex.khasnabish@msvu.ca

Dr **Anand Teltumbde** is well known as an activist in peoples' struggles and in the human rights movement, and as a theoretician of contemporary issues. Associated with CPDR and IPHRC, both noted human rights organisations in India, he has been a part of numerous fact-finding missions and human rights struggles. He has been a vocal opponent of neoliberal globalisation, against which he has written and spoken extensively over the last two decades. He was one of the organisers of the *Mumbai Resistance* in 2004. He has published over 15 books and numerous articles, which are available in most Indian languages. Among his recent books are: *Hindutva and Dalits: Perspectives for Understanding Communal Praxis* (2005), *Anti-Imperialism and Annihilation of Castes* (2005), and *Khairlanji: A Strange and Bitter Crop* (2008). tanandraj@gmail.com

André C Drainville is Professor of Transnational Sociology at Laval University in Québec City, Canada. He has published two academic books—*Contesting Globalisation: Space and Place in The World Economy* (2004) and *A History of World Order and Resistance: The making and unmaking of global subjects* (2012)—two novels (*Anxious Moments Before the Next Big Event* and *Les carnets jaunes de Valérien Francoeur* ('The Yellow Notebooks of Valérien Francoeur', in French), and more than two dozen scientific articles on matters of global power and counter-power, critical theory, and pedagogy. andre.drainville@soc.ulaval.ca

Andrea Smith, is a co-founder of *Incite! Women of Color Against Violence and the Boarding School Healing Project.* She is the author of *Native Americans and the Christian Right: The Gendered Politics of Unlikely Alliances* (Duke, 2008), and

Conquest: Sexual Violence and American Indian Genocide (South End Press, 2005). Through Incite!, she is the co-editor of *The Color of Violence* (South End Press, 2006) and of *The Revolution Will Not Be Funded* (South End Press, 2007). She also teaches at University of California–Riverside, in Media and Cultural Studies. mangosteen366@gmail.com

Ashok Choudhary is a veteran in the field of social development in India, working in unorganised sector labour movements and organising forest workers since the 1970s. In the 1980s he initiated a forest workers' cooperative among villagers living in the Shivalik forest ranges in Saharanpur in UP. In the 1990s he was a key member in the foundation and formation of the National Centre for Labour. He is the founding member of the National Forum of Forest People and Forest Workers in 1998, and since its transformation in June 2013 into the All India Union of Forest Working People (AIUFWP), its General Secretary. He has been with the Uttar Pradesh land rights network since 1997; Vice President of the New Trade Union Initiative (NTUI) since inception in 2001; and in 2007 participated in the formation of Sangharsh, a common platform for campaigns in India working on community rights over common resources. ashok.chowdhury@gmail.com

Christopher Gunderson, PhD (Sociology, Graduate Center of the City University of New York) is Assistant Professor of Sociology at Howard University in Washington, DC. His dissertation, 'The Provocative Cocktail: The Intellectual Origins of the Zapatista Uprising 1960–1994', was completed following a year of research in Mexico under the auspices of the Centro de Investigaciones e Estudios Superiores en Antropologia Social (CIESAS) in Chiapas. He previously spent two years in Chiapas working on the construction of a medical clinic in the Zapatista autonomous municipality of Libertad de los Pueblos Mayas and conducting human rights observation work in several Zapatista communities. christophergunderson01@gmail.com

The late **Daniel Bensaïd** (1946–2010) was a key participant in 'the movement of May 1968' in France when he was a student at the University of Nanterre, as an activist in the *Ligue Communiste Révolutionnaire* (LCR, 'Revolutionary Communist League'). He continued through his life to be a leading member of the LCR. He was born in Toulouse in 1946 and died on January 12 2010. An alumnus of the École normale supérieure de Saint-Cloud, he also taught philosophy at the University of Paris VIII. He was the author of thirty books and towards the end of his life, ran the magazine *Contretemps* (Editions Syllepse). A specialist on Marx, among his books are *Karl Marx—Les hiéroglyphes de la modernité* ['Karl Marx—The hieroglyphics of modernity'] (Textuel, 2001), *Marx l'intempestif: Grandeurs et misères d'une aventure critique (XIXè, XXè siècles)* ['The Ill-Timed Marx: The Highs and

Lows of a Critical Adventure (19th and 20th Centuries)', in French] (Fayard 1995), and *Le sourire du spectre* ['The Spectre's Smile', in French] (Michalon, 1999), and *Marx mode d'emploi* ['The Marx Manual', in French] (La Découverte, 2009).

David Featherstone is Senior Lecturer in Human Geography at the University of Glasgow. He is the author of *Resistance, Space and Political Identities: The Making of Counter-Global Networks* (Wiley-Blackwell, 2008) and *Solidarity: Hidden Histories and Geographies of Internationalism* (Zed Books, 2012). His key theoretical and political concerns are with how solidarities and geographies of connection between different place-based struggles can produce more equal and plural forms of globalisation and internationalism. He has been involved in various campaigns and political movements, including This Land is Ours and the successful mobilisations against Elsevier's links to the arms' trade. David.Featherstone@glasgow.ac.uk

David McNally is an activist and Professor of Political Science at York University in Toronto, Ontario, and past chair of the university's Department of Political Science. He is a member of the New Socialist Group, and author—among many other writings—of *Another World Is Possible: Globalisation and Anti-Capitalism* (Winnipeg: Arbeiter Ring Publishing, and London: Merlin Press, 2006), and of *Monsters of the Market: Zombies, Vampires, and Global Capitalism* (Chicago: Haymarket Books, 2012). dmcnally@yorku.ca

Emilie Hayes is a Community Developer at a community health centre in Ottawa, Canada. During her MA studies in Sociology at Carleton University, Canada, she focused on citizenship studies and education and was a student participant in the critical course Open Space and Dissent in Movement. Prior to returning to school to pursue graduate studies, Emilie worked at the University of Guelph in Canada coordinating programmes and services for students to explore their role as citizens. hayes.emilie@gmail.com

Emir Sader, a sociologist, is Professor of Public Policies at the University of Rio de Janeiro, Brazil. He was earlier Director of the Laboratory of Public Policies at the State University of Rio de Janeiro (UERJ), Executive Secretary of CLACSO, the Latin American Council of Social Sciences, and president of the Latin American Sociology Association. emirsader@uol.com.br

Eric Mielants is Associate Professor in Sociology in the College of Arts and Sciences at Fairfield University in the US and Research Associate of the Maison des Sciences de l'Homme in Paris. He has written articles and essays on racism, capitalism, social theory, and contemporary migration issues which have also been published in Dutch, French, Korean, Spanish, Turkish, and Japanese. He is the author of *The Origins of Capitalism and the Rise of the West* (Temple University Press, 2007) and co-edited *Caribbean Migration to Western Europe and the United States* (Temple University Press, 2009) and *Mass Migration in the World-System: Past, Present and Future* (Paradigm Press, 2010). emielants@fairfield.edu

Fouad Kalouche is Associate Professor of Philosophy at Albright College, in Reading, Pennsylvania, in the US. He is currently writing on theories of transformation and of political subjectivisation (relying on Nietzsche, Castoriadis, Foucault, and Deleuze). He has published articles and book chapters on the contemporary transformations of capitalism and on the modes of production of subjectivity, as well as on Ancient and Modern Philosophy. fkalouche@alb.edu

The late **François Houtart** was a Catholic priest, liberation theologian, and scholar of movements. The last position he held was as Professor at the Instituto de Altos Estudios Nacionales (National Institute of Higher Studies) in Quito, Ecuador. He was closely associated with the Fundación del Pueblo Indio del Ecuador (Foundation of the Indigenous Peoples of Ecuador) and Vice President of the World Forum for Alternatives. From earlier on, he was the founder of CETRI (Centre Tricontinental), a Belgian non-governmental organisation, and Special Representative of the President of the General Assembly of the UN in the Commission on the Reforms of the Financial and Monetary System, headed by Joseph Stiglitz. He was one of the initiators of the World Social Forum, and former chair of the International League for the Liberation of the Peoples and an expert for the Vatican Council II. As a sociologist, he wrote more than forty books, and founded the magazine *Alternatives Sud*.

Guillermo Delgado-P is a Lecturer of Latin American Ethnology and Field Studies Director in the Anthropology Department at the University of California Santa Cruz, in the US. For ten years (2001–2011) he served as Editor of the *Bolivian Research Review* [www.bolivianstudies.org], and is co-chair of The Indigenous Research Center of the Americas (IRCA) at the University of California, Davis, USA. He served as LASA Section Chair (2012–2013). He is co-editor, with John Brown Childs, of *Indigeneity: Collected Essays* (Santa Cruz, CA, 2012); a contributor to: *Selva Vida. De la Destrucción de la Amazonía al Paradigma de la Regeneración* ['The Living Forest: From the Destruction of the Amazon to a Paradigm of Regeneration', in Spanish] (IWGIA, Casa de las Américas, 2013); *Giros Culturales en la Marea Rosa de América Latina* ['Cultural Shifts in the Pink Tide of Latin America', in Spanish] (2012), and *Grabbing Back: Essays Against the Global Land Grab* (AK Press, 2014). guiller@ucsc.edu

Dr **Cho Hee-Yeon** is a long-time activist and today Professor at the NGO Graduate School and Director of the Democracy and Social Movements Institute (DaSMI), Sungkonghoe University, in Seoul, South Korea. In the mid-1990s, he was involved in organising the People's Solidarity for Participatory Democracy (PSPD). He has initiated a Master of Arts programme in Inter-Asia NGO Studies (MAINS) at Sungkonghoe University, co-sponsored by the Asia Regional Network for New Alternatives (ARENA), and is also a co-representative of the Korea Progressive Academy Council and the National Association of Professors for Democratic Society. He has written many books including *Social Movement and Organizations in South Korea, Democracy and Social Movements in South Korea, The State, Democracy and the Political Change in South Korea*, and *Park Chung-Hee and the Developmental Dictatorship*, and is an editorial member of the journal *Inter-Asia Cultural Studies: Movement*. chohy7@gmail.com

James Toth is an anthropologist who studies Egypt, the Arab world, and the wider Islamic community. He has written on grass-roots development, religious movements, women and agriculture, and the impact of globalization on the Middle East. He has taught at the American University of Cairo and at Northeastern University, and, since 2011, has worked at New York University in Abu Dhabi and the American University in Sharjah. He is the author of *Rural Labor Movements in Egypt and Their Impact on the State, 1961–1992* (University Press of Florida, 1999) and *Sayyid Qutb: The Life and Legacy of a Radical Islamic Intellectual* (Oxford University Press, 2013). jt112@nyu.edu

Jeff Corntassel (Cherokee Nation) is currently Associate Professor and Graduate Advisor in Indigenous Governance at the University of Victoria. Professor Corntassel's research and teaching interests include sustainable self-determination and Indigenous political mobilization/Indigenous nationhood movements. His research has been published in *Alternatives, American Indian Quarterly, Canadian Journal of Human Rights, Decolonization, Human Rights Quarterly, Nationalism and Ethnic Studies*, and *Social Science Journal*. His first book, entitled *Forced Federalism: Contemporary Challenges to Indigenous Nationhood* (University of Oklahoma Press, 2008), examined how Indigenous nations in the US have mobilised politically as they encounter new threats to their governance from state policymakers. His next book is a co-edited volume (with Professor Tom Holm) entitled *The Power of Peoplehood: Regenerating Indigenous Nations*, which brings together native scholars from Canada and the US to discuss contemporary strategies for revitalising Indigenous communities. ctassel@uvic.ca

Laurence Cox co-edits the open-access, activist/academic social movements journal *Interface* (http://interfacejournal.net) and co-directs the MA in

Community Education, Equality and Social Activism at the National University of Ireland Maynooth. He has been involved in many different movements and campaigns, in Ireland and internationally, over the past three decades, focussing particularly on building alliances between different movements and communities in pursuit of a more radical vision and practice. As a researcher and writer he has focussed particularly on the development of movements' own 'intellectual means of production', in collaboration with activists and popular educators inside and outside academia. He is co-author of *We Make Our Own History: Marxism and Social Movements in the Twilight of Neoliberalism* (Pluto, 2014) and co-editor of *Understanding European Movements: New Social Movements, Global Justice Struggles, Anti-Austerity Protest* (Routledge, 2013); *Marxism and Social Movements* (Brill / Haymarket, 2013); and *Silence Would Be Treason: Last Writings of Ken Saro-Wiwa* (Daraja, 2013). laurencecox.wordpress.com; laurence.cox@nuim.ie

Lee Cormie has a long association with progressive social movements in the Americas, including indigenous movements, and is a student of the debates about systemic injustices and alternatives ('another world is possible'), of the challenges of translation across movements, traditions, and contexts, and of the inescapability/desirability of epistemological diversity and pluralism in new ecologies of knowledges. Till recently, he taught at the Faculty of Theology at St Michael's College and at the Toronto School of Theology, in Toronto, Canada, where he focused on the new waves of liberation theologies and interdisciplinary studies. lee.cormie@utoronto.ca

Peter North is Reader in Alternative Economies in the Department of Geography and Planning at the University of Liverpool. He has a longstanding interest in social movements, utopias, and alternative economic experiments counterposed to neoliberal globalisation. He is the author of two books, as well as a number of book chapters and journal articles, on alternative currency movements as a challenge to globalisation; his book *Money and Liberation: The Micropolitics of Alternative Currency Movements* (2007) focuses on radical financial experiments in the UK, New Zealand, Hungary, and Argentina, in historical perspective. His current research and activism focuses on climate change and peak oil, and he is a founder member of Transition South Liverpool, working locally on climate change. p.j.north@liverpool.ac.uk

The late **Peter Waterman** (1936–2017), after retirement from the Institute of Social Studies, The Hague, in 1998, published various monographs, (co-)edited compilations and numerous academic and political papers—the latter almost all to be found online—and self-published his autobiography (*From Coldwar*

Communism to the Global Emancipatory Movement: Itinerary of a Long-Distance Internationalist, available at http://www.into-ebooks.com/download/498/). His work was published in English (UK, USA, Canada, India), Hindi, Italian, Portuguese, German, Spanish, Japanese, and Korean. He had papers posted on the Montevideo-based Choike portal and compilations on the Finland-based Into website, and a blog on UnionBook. He was currently associated with, amongst others, the Programa Democracia y Transformación Global (Lima), with two online journals, *Interface: a Journal for and about Social Movements*, the *Global Labour Journal*, and with the Indian Institute for Critical Action—Centre in Movement (CACIM) in New Delhi. Here he co-edited books on the World Social Forums. After retirement he had invitations for teaching, lectures, and seminars from universities and movement-oriented bodies in Peru, South Africa, Sweden, Finland, Hong Kong, Germany, South Korea, the US, Ireland, and the UK.

Roel Meijer is a researcher at the Department of the Middle East at Radboud University in Nijmegen, The Netherlands, and a member of Clingendael, a Dutch think tank in The Hague. He is the author of several papers on the radical Islamic movement, including 'Towards a Political Islam' (2009), and is the editor of *Global Salafism: Islam's New Religious Movement* (London: Hurst & Company, 2009). roel-meijer@planet.nl

Roma has been working as a social activist on the issue of forests, land, wages, and gender issues with Dalit, tribal, and minority sections for the last twenty years. Presently working in state of Uttar Pradesh, India, on issues of land, forests, tribals, and displacement, and on strengthening local initiatives and people's organisation and helping to form strong women's leadership, she was a founder member and later Organising Secretary of the National Forum of Forest People and Forest Workers (NFFPFW), which in June 2013 was transformed into the All India Union of Forest Working People (AIUFWP), where she is now the Deputy General Secretary. She is also a Secretary of the New Trade Union Initiative (NTUI); associated with the Uttar Pradesh Land Reform and Labour Rights Campaign Committee (UPLRCC); a Specialist nominated as people's organisations' representative on the State Level Monitoring Committee constituted under the Forest Rights Act in Uttar Pradesh; and a member of the Joint Review Committee constituted by the Ministry of Environment and Forests and the Ministry of Tribal Affairs in the Government of India to review the implementation of the Forest Rights Act in the country. romasnb@gmail.com

Shailja Patel is an internationally acclaimed Kenyan poet, writer, and public intellectual. Her first book, *Migritude*, published in Italy, Sweden, and the US, was #1

on Amazon's bestsellers in Asian Poetry, and was shortlisted for Italy's Camaiore Poetry Prize. Patel was African Guest Writer at Sweden's Nordic Africa Institute and poet-in-residence at the Tallberg Forum. She has appeared on the BBC World Service, NPR, and Al-Jazeera, and published by *Le Monde Diplomatique* and *The Africa Report*, among others. Her work has been translated into 16 languages. Honors include a Sundance Theatre Fellowship, a Creation Fund Award from the National Performance Network, the Fanny-Ann Eddy Poetry Award from IRN-Africa, the Voices of Our Nations Poetry Award, a Lambda Slam Championship, and the Outwrite Poetry Prize. Patel is a founding member of the civil society coalition Kenyans For Peace, Truth and Justice. The African Women's Development Fund named her one of Fifty Inspirational African Feminists for the 100th anniversary of International Women's Day. Poetry Africa honored her as Letters To Dennis Poet, continuing the legacy of renowned South African anti-apartheid activist Dennis Brutus. She represented Kenya at Poetry Parnassus, in the London Cultural Olympiad. shailja@shailja.com / www.shailja.com

Taiaiake Alfred is the Director of the Indigenous Governance Programme and holds the Indigenous Peoples Research Chair at the University of Victoria. He is Kanien'kehaka (Mohawk), and was born in August of 1964 at Tiohtiá:ke (Montreal) and raised in the community of Kahnawake. Taiaiake served as an infantryman in the US Marine Corps, and later earned a Bachelor's degree in history from Concordia University and an MA and PhD in government from Cornell University. He has long been involved in the public life of his own and other Indigenous nations. He is the author of three books, *Heeding the Voices of Our Ancestors: Kahnawake Mohawk Politics and the Rise of Native Nationalism* (1995) and *Peace, Power, Righteousness* (1999), both from Oxford University Press, and from Broadview Press, *Wasáse: Indigenous Pathways of Action and Freedom* (2005). He is a full Professor in the Faculty of Human and Social Development and holds adjunct status in the Department of Political Science. gta@uvic.ca

Tariq Ali is a British-Pakistani historian, novelist, filmmaker, political campaigner, and commentator. He is a member of the editorial committee of the *New Left Review* and *Sin Permiso*, and regularly contributes to *The Guardian*, *CounterPunch*, and the *London Review of Books*. He is the author of several books, including *Can Pakistan Survive? The Death of a State* (1991), *Clash of Fundamentalisms: Crusades, Jihads and Modernity* (2002), *Bush in Babylon* (2003), *Conversations with Edward Said* (2005), *Street Fighting Years: An Autobiography of the Sixties* (2005), *Pirates of the Caribbean: Axis of Hope* (2006), *A Banker for All Seasons* (2007), and *The Duel* (2008), and of the celebrated Islam Quintet (over 1998–2010). tariq.1.ali@googlemail.com

Virginia (Gina) Vargas is a veteran Peruvian feminist sociologist and founder of the Centro Flora Tristan in Peru. She is one of the 1,000 women nominated for the Nobel Peace Prize for the year 2006. She is associated with the Articulación Feminista Marcosur in Latin America, and the Programa Democracia y Transformación Global (Programme on Global Democracy and Transformation) in San Marcos University, Lima. She has taught at universities worldwide and currently teaches the Master of Sexuality and Public Policies course at San Marcos University in Lima, Peru, and is the author of *Feminismos en America Latina: Su aporte a la política y a la democracia* ('Feminisms in Latin America: Implications for Politics and Democracy', in Spanish) (Lima: Universidad Nacional Mayor de San Marcos and Centro Flora Tristán, 2008). She is a member of the WSF International Council. ginvargas@gmail.com

Dra. Xochitl Leyva Solano is researcher and professor at the Centre for Higher Research of Social Anthropology (CIESAS) located in Chiapas, Mexico, and an active member of the Universidad de la Tierra–Chiapas ('University of the Earth—Chiapas'). She is member of Neo-Zapatista and anti-systemic networks as well as those promoting decolonised activist research. Among her books are *Poder y Desarrollo Regional* ('Power and Regional Development', in Spanish) published in Mexico in 1993; *Lancandonia al filo del agua* ('Lacandonia at the edge of the water', in Spanish), co-authored with Gabriel Ascencio in 1996; *Encuentros Antropológicos: Power, Identity and Mobility in Mexican Society,* edited with Valentina Napolitano and published in London in 1998; and in 2008, *Gobernar en la diversidad: experiencias indígenas desde América Latina* ('Governing in Diversity: Indigenous experiences in Latin America', in Spanish), co-edited with Araceli Burguete and Shannon Speed in Mexico and *Human Rights in the Mayan Region*, co-edited with Shannon Speed and Pedro Pitarch and published by Duke University Press. xleyva@mac.com

Index

'Passim' (literally 'scattered') indicates intermittent discussion of a topic over a cluster of pages.

Anishnaabe, 214
'another world is possible' (slogan), 17, 99, 112, 150
anti-colonialist movements, 85
anti-immigrant and anti-immigration policies, 84, 86
anti-summit protests, 57, 107, 474, 475, 592. *See also* World Trade Organization protests
'anti-systemic' movements, 69–97
anti-sweatshop movement, 106, 107–8
anti-war movement. *See* peace movement
anti-woman violence, Islamist, 414n79
APPO. *See* Popular Assembly of the Peoples of Oaxaca (APPO)
Arab pan-nationalism, 82–83
Arab Socialist Union (ASU), 395, 396
Arendt, Hannah, 103, 104
Argentina, 156–57, 493–513 passim; PRT, 499, 520, 522
Arguing about War (Walzer), 382
Arquette, Mary, 211
Articulación Feminista Marcosur (AFM). *See* Feminist Articulation Marcosur (AFM)
Artous, Antoine, 522–23
Ascencio, Gabriel, 235, 236
Asia-Europe Meeting (ASEM), Seoul (2000), 474, 479
Australia, 84, 206, 207, 209
autarky, 539, 542–43
autonomous zones, 156
autonomy, Indigenous. *See* self-determination, Indigenous
'Awda, Salman al-, 420, 426–27, 430, 434
Ávila, Betania, 320
Ayiri, Yusuf al-. *See* Uyairi, Yusuf al-
Azzam, Abdalla, 401

Badiou, Alain, 124
Balibar, Étienne, 366n100
Banco del Sur, 506, 510, 513
Bandung Conference (1955), 489n15
Bangladesh, 126, 134
Banna, Hasan al-, 382, 386, 392, 410n31, 411n38
Barros, Marcelo, 342–43
Basayev, Hawa, 434
'Battle in Seattle' (1999). *See* World Trade Organization protests: Seattle

Baumgardner, Jennifer, 291, 301
Bayat, Asef, 412n47
Beauvoir, Simone de: *Second Sex*, 126
Bechtel Corporation, 60
Beck, Ulrico, 317
Benjamin, Brit, 365n71
Bensaïd, Daniel: 'Return of Strategy', 517–34, 633, 634–35
Bertrand Russell War Crimes Tribunal, 119, 121
Betto, Frei, 322
Bharatiya Janata Party, 83, 341
Big Noise Tactical, 592–96
bin Laden, Osama, 379, 400, 401, 402, 403, 404, 420, 421
Black Dwarf, 123, 124, 137
black Americans. *See* African Americans
Blair, Tony, 68n30
Bleakney, Dave, 587–88
Bloch, Ernst, 578
Bolivia, 48, 60–61, 236, 268, 495–513 passim, 577–75, 636
Bondgenoten. *See* FNV Bondgenoten
Bookchin, Murray, 543
Botswana, 202
Bové, José, 548
Brahmins and Brahminism, 187, 195, 197, 272
Brand, Dionne, 299
Brazil, 79, 493–500 passim, 504–13 passim, 517, 526. See also *Movimento Sem Terra* (MST)
Britain, 121–22; Deskaheh and, 204–5; in Egypt, 387; imperialism, 188; in India, 195–96, 197, 270, 288nn15–16, 546; Jewish Socialists' Group, 341–42; neo-Zapatistas, 171, 172; protests, 121, 535; in Sudan, 371; Treaty of Waitangi, 225n23
British Columbia Treaty Process, 135–36
Brundtland Commission, 212
Buck-Morss, Susan, 578
Buddhism, 369, 613
Buddhist Peace Fellowship (BPF), 340–41
Burgat, François, 409n28
Bush, George W., 59, 491n25, 546

Cabañas, Lucio, 245
Cajete, Gregory, 139–40
Callahan, Manuel, 581, 586

A Note on the *Challenging Empires* Series

The *Challenging Empires* series emerged in 2007 from a book produced in 2004 by the editor of the present work, Jai Sen, with Peter Waterman, Arturo Escobar, and Anita Anand. *World Social Forum: Challenging Empires* was an international anthology that critically examined the World Social Forum and the global debates around this emerging phenomenon and located the 2004 edition of the WSF that was held in Mumbai, India, within this larger world. With most chapters of the original English version available online, the book was also translated into German, Hindi, Japanese, and Spanish, and an updated second edition in English was published from Canada in 2008.

The success of this book prompted Jai Sen and the late Peter Waterman to outline a series of volumes—the *Challenging Empires* series—that would critically assess the history and impact of contemporary social movement, including the WSF.

The first subsequent volume in the new series was *World Social Forum: Critical Explorations*, published by OpenWord in 2012.

The two books in the major two-part volume entitled *The Movements of Movements* are the next items. Whereas *Critical Explorations* addressed the World Social Forum alone, these two volumes—*The Movements of Movements, Part 1: What Makes Us Move?*, and its companion volume *The Movements of Movements, Part 2: Rethinking Our Dance*—are about the larger world/s of world movement, and appear at a time when movements for social change and justice are increasingly visible throughout the world. Largely focussed on the period 2006–2010 but also reaching back to 1968 and earlier and forward right up to 2014–15, the books bring together some fifty essays on the epistemological landscape and praxis of world movement. With authors again—as in the earlier volumes in the series —of various ages, races, and persuasions from a wide range of movements, the books attempt to open and deepen conversations between and across movements, drawing readers into those conversations. These volumes (volumes 4 and 5 in the *Challenging Empires* series) go far beyond the WSF, looking at other more spontaneous, structured, and virtual movements.

We are co-publishing *The Movements of Movements* in two parts with an important new actor in international movement publishing, PM Press. The present volume, *Part 1*, lays out and discusses the landscape of contemporary movement and presents and juxtaposes a wide range of movements for change. *Part 2* will directly complement this volume, critically reflecting on movement praxis and on possible futures. Both volumes end with a major essay—appearing as an Afterword—critically locating the collections of essays in our emerging world.

OpenWord and the series editor welcome suggestions and criticism. Send this either to the series editor—see the 'Notes on the Editor' for details—or to OpenWord at www.openword.net.in.

Earlier titles in the *Challenging Empires* series:

World Social Forum: Challenging Empires. Edited by Jai Sen, Anita Anand, Arturo Escobar, and Peter Waterman. Viveka Foundation, New Delhi, India, 2004. (Abridged versions available at http://www.choike.org/nuevo_eng/informes/1557.html and at http://www.openspaceforum.net/twiki/tiki-index.php?page=WSFChallengingEmpires2004)

Volume 2 World Social Forum: Challenging Empires (Revised International Edition) Edited by Jai Sen and Peter Waterman. Black Rose Books, Montreal, Canada, 2009. http://blackrosebooks.net/products/view/WORLD+SOCIAL+FORUM/32439

Volume 3 World Social Forum: Critical Explorations. Edited by Jai Sen and Peter Waterman. OpenWord, New Delhi, India, 2012. http://www.openword.net.in/critical-explorations

OpenWord

OpenWord (http://openword.net.in), the publishing arm of the India Institute for Critical Action: Centre in Movement (www.cacim.net) was founded in 2007 to promote a spirit, culture, and practice of critical openness. It is an expression of the experiences of members and associates and of their attempts to promote critical sociopolitical and cultural action and movement and to contribute to a broader and more effective transformational social power.

OpenWord plans to publish in different fields, looking beyond the boundaries of political, economic, cultural, and academic dogma and privileging authors from the structurally marginalised, with a particular focus on, indigenous peoples, Dalits, and women.

OpenWord seeks to reach young people—students, activists, workers, thinkers, and artists. Commissioning and/or sourcing work from all walks of life and depths of experience, it aims to produce enjoyable publications that challenge us to think beyond accepted boundaries.

OpenWord practises and promotes a culture of open publishing. It critically engages with emerging practices, such as copyleft, open, and non-conventional models of content ownership. **OpenWord** will constantly push existing boundaries to more empowering principles of authorship, ownership, and dissemination of knowledge.

Based in India, **OpenWord** is exploring ways to build a transcultural, global Editorial Collective and to publish material from across the world. It will actively seek to be transnational, transcultural, and transcommunal, thereby contributing to a planetary awareness and consciousness. It will constantly seek both established and new thinking from all parts of the world.

http://www.openword.net.in
openword@openword.net.in
A division of CACIM
R-21 South Extension Part II—Ground floor
New Delhi 110 049
India
cacim@cacim.net

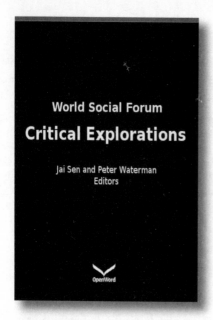

WORLD SOCIAL FORUM
Critical Explorations
Edited by Jai Sen and Peter Waterman

Volume 3 in the *Challenging Empires* series.

This volume brings together 36 essays from around the world—from authors young and old, women and men, black brown and white, and activists, scholars, and those in between, from the South and the North—that enable us all to critically explore and understand the important contemporary phenomenon called the World Social Forum; *and so to better know what kind of world we want to see and to build*. It is a sequel to the widely-acclaimed 2004 book titled *World Social Forum: Challenging Empires*.

Available internationally at http://www.into-ebooks.com/book/world_social_forum/ and in India at http://pothi.com/pothi/book/ebook-jai-sen-world-social-forum-critical-explorations

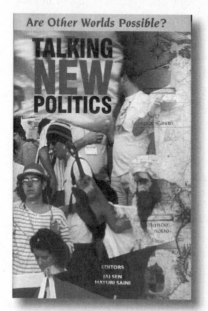

TALKING NEW POLITICS
Edited by Jai Sen and Mayuri Saini

Book 1 in the *Are Other Worlds Possible?* series. Zubaan Books http://www.openword.net.in

This book, the first in a series of three that explore the new ideas generated by the discussions that took place, comprises of chapters based on the presentations made by academics and activists during the seminars, as well as the discussions arising from the presentations. Can the World Social Forum help us to conceptualise and actualise a new politics? Can this new politics be free from violence—of all kinds? Can the experience and knowledge of great movements such as the movement for the environment, and the women's movements, contribute to the creation of a new politics? How can such a politics be sustained?

Publications from OpenWord, CACIM, and other associated publishers

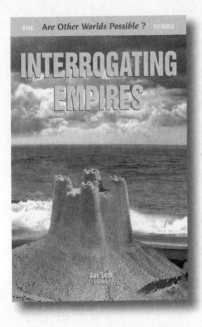

INTERROGATING EMPIRES
Edited by Jai Sen

Book 2 in the *Are Other Worlds Possible?* series. OpenWord and Daanish Books (2011); http://www.openword.net.in

This book is a close look at some of the empires that govern our lives and that we are constantly socialised to believe in and accept, by society, by family, by education, by the market and the media, and by the institutions we are all part of at one point or another in our lives: The empires of patriarchy, casteism, racism, nationalism, and religious communalism—and where each of these is quite aside from what is popularly referred to as "globalisation," even as they interlock with it.

IMAGINING ALTERNATIVES
Edited by Jai Sen

Book 3 in the *Are Other Worlds Possible?* series. OpenWord and Daanish Books (2012); http://www.openword.net.in

People in social and political movements—especially those involved with the World Social Forum—quite commonly say that "Another world is possible"; a world very different from the one we today know. But what do they mean by this? What "other world/s"? Do such worlds only exist in some people's imaginations? And even if they are real, how do we get into these other worlds? And anyway, are such other worlds necessarily more open and more just than the one we know?

This book, the third in the *Are Other World Possible?* book series and preferably read along with the other two (*Talking New Politics* and *Interrogating Empires*), critically explores three of the most important "other worlds" that human beings have so far tried building: Socialism, Cyberspace, and the University.

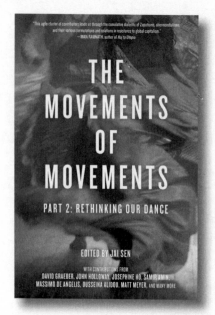

THE MOVEMENTS OF MOVEMENTS
Part 2: Rethinking Our Dance
Edited by Jai Sen
$29.95
ISBN: 978-1-62963-380-0

Our world today is not only a world in crisis but also a world in profound movement, with increasingly large numbers of people joining or forming movements: local, national, transnational, and global. The dazzling diversity of ideas and experiences recorded in this collection capture something of the fluidity within campaigns for a more equitable planet. This book, taking internationalism seriously without tired dogmas, provides a bracing window into some of the central ideas to have emerged from within grassroots struggles from 2006 to 2010. The essays here cross borders to look at the politics of caste, class, gender, religion, and indigeneity, and move from the local to the global.

Rethinking Our Dance, the second of two volumes, offers a wide range of essays from frontline activists in Afghanistan, Argentina, Brazil, Niger, and Taiwan, as well as from Europe and North America that address the question, "What do we need to do in order to bring about justice and peace?" *The Movements of Movements* aim to make the bewildering range of contemporary movements more meaningful to the observer and also to be a space where global movements speak to each other.

This book will be useful to all who work for egalitarian social change—be they in universities, parties, trade unions, social movements, or religious organisations.

Contributors: Kolya Abramsky, Ezequiel Adamovsky, Oussenia Alidou, Samir Amin, Chris Carlsson, John Brown Childs, Lee Cormie, Anila Daulatzai, Massimo De Angelis, The Free Association, David Graeber, Josephine Ho, John Holloway, François Houtart, Jeffrey Juris, Michael Löwy, Tomás Mac Sheoin, Matt Meyer, Muto Ichiyo, Rodrigo Nunes, Michal Osterweil, Shailja Patel, Geoffrey Pleyers, Stephanie Ross, and Nicola Yeates.

"Possible futures right now in the making become legible in how The Movements of Movements doesn't shy away from the complex and unsettling issues that shape our time while thinking through struggles for social and ecological justice in the wider contexts of their past and present."
—Emma Dowling, senior lecturer in sociology at Middlesex University, London

PM Press was founded at the end of 2007 by a small collection of folks with decades of publishing, media, and organizing experience. PM Press co-conspirators have published and distributed hundreds of books, pamphlets, CDs, and DVDs. Members of PM have founded enduring book fairs, spearheaded victorious tenant organizing campaigns, and worked closely with bookstores, academic conferences, and even rock bands to deliver political and challenging ideas to all walks of life. We're old enough to know what we're doing and young enough to know what's at stake.

We seek to create radical and stimulating fiction and non-fiction books, pamphlets, T-shirts, visual and audio materials to entertain, educate, and inspire you. We aim to distribute these through every available channel with every available technology—whether that means you are seeing anarchist classics at our bookfair stalls; reading our latest vegan cookbook at the café; downloading geeky fiction e-books; or digging new music and timely videos from our website.

PM Press is always on the lookout for talented and skilled volunteers, artists, activists, and writers to work with. If you have a great idea for a project or can contribute in some way, please get in touch.

PM Press
PO Box 23912
Oakland CA 94623
510-658-3906
www.pmpress.org

FRIENDS OF PM

These are indisputably momentous times—the financial system is melting down globally and the Empire is stumbling. Now more than ever there is a vital need for radical ideas.

In the many years since its founding—and on a mere shoestring—PM Press has risen to the formidable challenge of publishing and distributing knowledge and entertainment for the struggles ahead. With hundreds of releases to date, we have published an impressive and stimulating array of literature, art, music, politics, and culture. Using every available medium, we've succeeded in connecting those hungry for ideas and information to those putting them into practice.

Friends of PM allows you to directly help impact, amplify, and revitalize the discourse and actions of radical writers, filmmakers, and artists. It provides us with a stable foundation from which we can build upon our early successes and provides a much-needed subsidy for the materials that can't necessarily pay their own way. You can help make that happen—and receive every new title automatically delivered to your door once a month—by joining as a Friend of PM Press. And, we'll throw in a free T-shirt when you sign up.

Here are your options:
- $30 a month: Get all books and pamphlets plus 50% discount on all webstore purchases
- $40 a month: Get all PM Press releases (including CDs and DVDs) plus 50% discount on all webstore purchases
- $100 a month: Superstar—Everything plus PM merchandise, free downloads, and 50% discount on all webstore purchases

For those who can't afford $30 or more a month, we have Sustainer Rates at $15, $10, and $5. Sustainers get a free PM Press T-shirt and a 50% discount on all purchases from our website.

Your Visa or Mastercard will be billed once a month, until you tell us to stop. Or until our efforts succeed in bringing the revolution around. Or the financial meltdown of Capital makes plastic redundant. Whichever comes first.